ABC's of
RELATIONSHIP
SELLING
through Service

Fourth Canadian Edition

Charles M. Futrell
Texas A & M University

Mark Valvasori
Mohawk College

McGraw-Hill Ryerson

Toronto Montréal Boston Burr Ridge, IL Dubuque, IA Madison, WI New York
San Francisco St. Louis Bangkok Bogotá Caracas Kuala Lumpur Lisbon London
Madrid Mexico City Milan New Delhi Santiago Seoul Singapore Sydney Taipei

McGraw-Hill Ryerson

ABC's of Relationship Selling through Service
Fourth Canadian Edition

ISBN-13: 978-0-07-098493-6
ISBN-10: 0-07-098493-X

2 3 4 5 6 7 8 9 10 TCP 0

Printed and bound in Canada.

Care has been taken to trace ownership of copyright material contained in this text; however, the publisher will welcome any information that enables them to rectify any reference or credit for subsequent editions.

Vice-President and Editor-in-Chief: Joanna Cotton
Executive Sponsoring Editor: Leanna MacLean
Executive Marketing Manager: Joy Armitage Taylor
Developmental Editors: Rebecca Walker and Arlene Bautista
Editorial Associate: Stephanie Hess
Supervising Editor: Jessica Barnoski
Copy Editor: Karen Rolfe
Team Lead, Production: Jennifer Hall
Cover Design: Dave Murphy/Valid Design
Cover Image: Aleksandar Videnovic
Interior Design: Dave Murphy/Valid Design
Page Layout: Aptara®, Inc.
Printer: Transcontinental Printing Group

Library and Archives Canada Cataloguing in Publication

Futrell, Charles
   ABC's of relationship selling through service / Charles M. Futrell,
Mark Valvasori.—4th Canadian ed.

Early previous Canadian eds. published under title: ABC's of
relationship selling.

Includes bibliographical references and index.
ISBN 978-0-07-098493-6

   1. Selling—Textbooks. I. Valvasori, Mark II. Futrell, Charles. ABC's of
relationship selling. III. Title.

HF5438.25.F87 2009   658.85   C2008-907888-8

Charles M. Futrell is the federated professor of marketing at Texas A&M University (TAMU) in College Station, Texas. He has a B.B.A., M.B.A., and Ph.D. in marketing. Dr. Futrell is a former salesperson turned professor. Before beginning his academic career, he worked in sales and marketing capacities for eight years with the Colgate Company, the Upjohn Company, and Ayerst Laboratories.

Dr. Futrell serves as a frequent reviewer for several academic journals. He is on the editorial advisory board of the *Journal of Marketing Theory and Practice*. His research in personal selling, sales management, research methodology, and marketing management has appeared in numerous national and international journals, such as the *Journal of Marketing* and the *Journal of Marketing Research*. An article in the Summer 1991 issue of the *Journal of Personal Selling & Sales Management* ranked Dr. Futrell as one of the top three sales researchers in America. He was also recognized in *Marketing Education*, Summer 1997, as one of the top 100 best researchers in the marketing discipline.

Dr. Futrell served as the American Marketing Association's chair of the Sales and Sales Management Special Interest Group (SIG) for the 1996–97 academic year. He was the first person elected to this position. Dr. Futrell was elected Finance chair for the Sales SIG's 1998–99 term. In 2005, this AMA group presented him with its Lifetime Achievement Award for commitment to excellence and service in the area of sales. Mu Kappa Tau, the National Marketing Honor Society, recognized him for exceptional scholarly contributions to the sales profession in 2000. This is only the fourth time this recognition has been bestowed since its creation in 1988.

Dr. Futrell has written or cowritten eight successful books for the college and professional audience. Two of the most popular books are *Fundamentals of Selling: Customers for Life*, Sixth Edition, and *ABC's of Relationship Selling through Service*, Tenth Edition, both published by McGraw-Hill Ltd. These books are used in hundreds of U.S. and international schools. More than 300,000 students worldwide have benefited from his books.

In 1997 Dr. Futrell began using his Web site and group e-mails in his sales classes, which often have 100 students in each section. Students sign up for both a lecture period and lab time. In each semester's six labs, students are videotaped in activities such as making a joint sales call, panel interview, selling oneself on a job interview, product sales presentations, and various experiential exercises.

TAMU's College of Business Administration and Graduate School of Business is one of the largest business programs in the United States, with more than 6,000 full-time business majors. Approximately 50 percent of the marketing department's 800 majors are in Dr. Futrell's personal selling and/or sales management classes at various times. He has worked with close to 10,000 students in sales-related classes.

Dr. Futrell's books, research, and teaching are based on his extensive work with sales organizations of all types and sizes. This broad and rich background has resulted in his being invited to be a frequent speaker, researcher, and consultant to industry.

Mark Valvasori is a professor in the business management program at Mohawk College of Applied Arts and Technology in Hamilton, Ontario. He holds a degree in business administration with a major in marketing from Saint Francis Xavier University in Antigonish, Nova Scotia. Professor Valvasori began his business career with the T. Eaton Company of Canada and spent three years self-employed in franchise development and sales for a national outdoors-adventure game.

Professor Valvasori's academic career spans 24 years as an educator. In addition to being a full-time professor at Mohawk College, he has developed and facilitated many seminars, workshops, and training programs in the areas of Marketing, Sales, and Customer Service.

Professor Valvasori teaches his sales classes in the Xerox Sales and Marketing Lab at Mohawk College. Fashioned after one of Xerox's training facilities, the lab makes use of a simulated buyer's office environment, which is isolated from the main classroom. Using a one-way mirror and hidden filming and recording devices, students are able to perform role-plays in a non-threatening environment, have them recorded, then analyze their performances afterward.

When Professor Valvasori isn't teaching or writing, he is very active in his community, having coached a variety of sports from the elementary to university level.

PART 2

PREPARATION FOR RELATIONSHIP SELLING   59

CHAPTER 3

The Psychology of Selling: Why People Buy   60

PART 3

THE RELATIONSHIP SELLING PROCESS   147

CHAPTER 8

The Approach—Begin Your Presentation Strategically   210

CHAPTER 9

The Presentation—Elements of Effective Persuasion   237

CHAPTER 12

Follow-up—Maintain and Strengthen the Relationship   336

PART 4

KEYS TO A SUCCESSFUL SELLING CAREER   359

CHAPTER 13

Time, Territory, and Self-Management   360

CHAPTER 14

Retail, Business, Services, and Nonprofit Selling   383

Welcome to the Fourth Canadian Edition of *ABC's of Relationship Selling through Service!*

This is the second edition of this textbook that has included the word *Service* in its title. *Service* refers to making a contribution to the welfare of others. It involves looking after your customers. Why is this so important? Professional buyers today need the top-notch services of salespeople to keep their own companies successful. As you read through this book, it should become apparent that the provision of good service by professional salespeople serves to add value to the customer's experience. There is still some work to be done to correct the image of the sales professional. We can accomplish this by illustrating the wonderful things professional salespeople do. This edition emphasizes helping others through the use of empathy. This sales philosophy is based upon treating others respectfully, with a deep understanding of—and concern for—your customer's needs.

This, and previous editions of *ABC's of Relationship Selling through Service* was driven by the advice of sales experts and professional reviewers. Teaching professionals have contributed greatly to the foundation of this textbook. The authors have worked diligently to incorporate the suggestions of many sales educators. This has resulted in several changes to the book over the last few editions, including a change in chapter sequencing as well as many welcome topic additions. Believing, as many do, that ethical behaviour is becoming paramount in modern business practices, the topic of sales ethics appears frequently throughout the text. It has a prominent place in the chapter sequencing and students are provided with many opportunities to consider their own sales ethics through the many new ethical dilemmas presented throughout the text.

The structure of this book lends itself to the practical component of selling. In the text you will find practical selling tips and many opportunities to reflect on some of the many issues facing today's salespeople. One of the key additions of this edition is a chapter-ending exercise titled, "Playing the Role." In it, readers are asked to take on the role of a salesperson facing a tough sales situation, then role-play a solution.

You will also find an expanded discussion of technology available to salespeople to help them look after their customers more effectively and efficiently.

With the world changing as rapidly as it is, selling is becoming an increasingly more complex and challenging field. In light of this, readers will find many newly developed "Selling Tips" and "Selling Globally" pedagogical features. These provide readers with information on the "best practices" of successful salespeople.

It is one of the goals of this Fourth Canadian Edition to give students the up-to-date information they need to compete in today's fast-paced, competitive, demanding, and increasingly electronic marketplace. *ABC's of Relationship Selling through Service* is written by salespeople turned teachers. The authors have many years of experience applying the concepts discussed in this book. Over the years, selling has been taught to many thousands of college students, businesspeople, and industry sales personnel, developing and using the strategies, practices, and techniques presented in this textbook. Every day, time is spent interacting with professional salespeople and sharing insights with colleagues and students. This book is the result of these experiences.

The *ABC's* Approach

The *ABC's of Relationship Selling* was conceived as a method of providing ample materials that allow readers to construct their own sales presentations after studying the text. This allows the instructor the flexibility of focusing on the "how-to-sell" approach within the classroom. Covering the basic foundations for understanding the concepts and practices of selling in a practical, straightforward, and readable manner, it provides students with a guide to use in preparing sales presentations and role-playing exercises. Some of the additions in this edition take the *ABC's* another step further in terms of its hands-on, practical approach. The additional exercises allow students to think on their feet and apply sound reasoning skills to solve sales problems.

The Philosophy behind This Book

The title should help you understand the philosophy of this book. A student of sales should understand the fundamentals—the basics—of personal selling. *All of them*. We do not advocate one way of selling as the best route to success. There are many roads to reaching one's goals!

We *do* believe that a salesperson should have an assortment of selling skills and should be very knowledgeable, even an expert, in the field. Based on the situation, the salesperson determines the appropriate actions to take for a particular prospect or customer. No matter what the situation, however, the basic fundamentals of selling can be applied.

There is no place in our society for high-pressure, manipulative selling. The salesperson is a problem solver, a helper, a solution provider, a service provider, and an adviser to the customer.

If the customer has no need, the salesperson should accept that and move on to help another person or firm. If the customer has a need, however, the salesperson should and must go for the sale. All successful salespeople we know believe that once they determine the customer is going to buy someone's product—and that their product will satisfy that customer's needs—it is their job to muster all their energy, skill, and know-how to make that sale. That is what it's all about!

Basic Organization of the Book

We have worked hard to ensure this edition of *ABC's of Relationship Selling through Service* will provide students with the basic foundation for understanding all of the major components of selling. The chapters are divided into four parts:

■ *Selling as a Profession.* This first part in the book emphasizes the history, careers, rewards, and duties of the professional salesperson and illustrates the importance of the sales function to the organization's success. It also examines the social, ethical, and legal issues in selling.

■ *Preparation for Relationship Selling.* This section presents the nuts and bolts of effective communication and the important elements of buyer behaviour, and also presents the background information salespeople use to develop their sales presentations.

■ *The Relationship Selling Process.* At the heart of the book, this part covers the entire selling process from prospecting to follow-up. State-of-the-art selling strategies, practices, and techniques are presented in a "how-to" fashion.

■ *Keys to a Successful Selling Career.* The importance of the proper use and management of one's time and sales territory is given thorough coverage as well as an exploration of different types of sales jobs.

Text and Chapter Pedagogy

Many reality-based features are included in this Fourth Canadian Edition to stimulate learning. One major goal of this book is to offer better ways to convey sales knowledge to the reader. To do this, the text includes numerous special features:

Sales Success Stories. Each part opens with a success story of a Canadian college or university graduate who has gone on to succeed in professional selling. This will show readers that there is indeed light at the end of the tunnel.

Chapter Topics and Objectives. Each chapter begins with a clear statement of learning objectives and an outline of major chapter topics. These devices provide an overview of what is to come and can also be used by students to see whether they understand and have retained important points.

Sales Challenge/Solution. The text portion of each chapter begins with a real-life challenge that sales professionals face. The challenge pertains to the topic of the chapter and will heighten students' interest in chapter concepts. The challenge is resolved at the end of the chapter, where chapter concepts guiding the salesperson's actions are highlighted.

Making the Sale. These boxed items explore how salespeople, when faced with challenges, use innovative ideas to sell.

Selling Tips. These boxes offer the reader additional selling tips for use in developing their role-plays.

Sales Application Learning Exercises. (S.A.L.E.S.) At the end of appropriate chapters, this multi-part, sequential exercise guides students through the process of preparing an effective sales presentation.

Selling Globally. These boxed items take the idea of sales one step further and allow readers to see what happens or should happen when selling outside Canada.

Playing the Role. New to this edition, at the end of each chapter, students are presented with a real-life sales problem. They are then asked to assume a particular role and dramatize their solution to the problem.

Exhibits. Many aspects of selling tend to be confusing at first. "What should I do?" and "How should I do it?" are two questions frequently asked by students in developing their role-plays. To enhance students' awareness and understanding, many exhibits have been included throughout the book. These exhibits consolidate key points, indicate relationships, and illustrate selling techniques.

Chapter Summary and Sales Application Questions. Each chapter closes with a summary of key points. The sales application questions are a complementary learning tool that enables students to check their understanding of key issues, think beyond basic concepts, and determine areas that require further study. The summary and application questions help students discriminate between main and supporting points and provide mechanisms for self-teaching.

Key Terms for Selling/Glossary. Learning the selling vocabulary is essential to understanding today's sales world. This is facilitated in three ways. First, key concepts are boldfaced and completely defined where they first appear in the text. Second, each key term, followed by the page number where it was first introduced and defined, is listed at the end of each chapter. Third, a glossary summarizing all key terms and definitions appears at the end of the book for handy reference.

Ethical Dilemma. These challenging exercises provide students an opportunity to experience ethical dilemmas faced in the selling job. Students should review Chapter 2's definition and explanation of ethical behaviour before discussing the ethical dilemmas.

Further Exploring the Sales World. These projects ask students to go beyond the textbook and classroom to explore what's happening in the real world. Projects can be altered or adapted to the instructor's school location and learning objectives for the class.

Cases for Analysis. Each chapter ends with brief but substantive cases for student analysis and class discussion. These cases provide an opportunity for students to apply concepts to real events and to sharpen their diagnostic skills for sales problem solving.

What's New in This Edition?

In addition to updating several cases, boxed features, exercises, and problem material throughout the text, this Fourth Edition of *ABC's of Relationship Selling through Service* has introduced several new topic areas.

New to the fourth edition are the following areas:

- International Gift Giving (Chapter 2)
- Cell Phone Considerations and Instant Messaging (Chapter 5)
- Getting Motivated (Chapter 6)
- Managing Gatekeepers (Chapter 7)
- Tips for PowerPoint Presentations (Chapter 9)
- Negotiation Checklist (Chapter 10)
- Developing an Assertiveness Action Plan (Chapter 11)
- Creating an Effective Sales Environment (Chapter 13)
- The Retail Approach—A Developing Art (Chapter 14)

A new feature in the text, "Playing the Role," appears at the end of each chapter. This feature allows students to immerse themselves in the everyday decision-making that modern salespeople face and to role-play or dramatize their solutions.

Also new to this edition is an expanded coverage of the technologies available to modern salespeople with discussion of GPS, PDA, iPods, and other technologies.

This edition of the *ABC's* contains updated information from the Canadian Professional Sales Association (CPSA), including its Code of Ethics as well as up-to-date descriptions and salary information for different kinds of sales professionals in Canada. This organization is leading the way for Canadian salespeople, offering many benefits and educational opportunities for its members.

The Plan of This Textbook

Personal selling and the sales job involve much more than you might imagine. The plan of this textbook provides you with the *fundamentals* of what selling is all about. Some of the major topics you will study include:

- The role of the sales force in the firm's marketing efforts
- Why people and organizations buy what they do
- Verbal and nonverbal communications
- The importance of knowing your and your competition's products
- An in-depth discussion of the selling process
- Self, time, and sales territory management
- Retail, business, services, and nonprofit selling
- The external environment—social and legal issues in selling.

Salespeople are managers of the sales generated from their customers. There is much to know if you want to be a successful sales professional.

Teaching and Learning Supplements

ACT! Express Software, included with every copy of *ABC's of Relationship Selling through Service*, is a free demonstration version of *ACT! Express*, a tool that will help students effectively manage contacts and make the most of their interactions with prospects, customers, clients, vendors, and suppliers. Appendix B found on the Online Learning Centre, also leads students through a Personal Selling Experiential Exercise using the *ACT! Express* software.

Videos—featuring segments to accompany various topics in the textbook. Accompanying teaching notes are available from the Online Learning Centre.

 Online LearningCentre

Online Learning Centre—the textbook's Online Learning Centre includes role-plays, videos, a glossary, multiple-choice questions, true/false questions, and Internet exercises, as well as problem-solving exercises. Also included are key terms and topics.
Visit www.mcgrawhill.ca/olc/futrell.

Also featured on the Online Learning Centre are all the necessary instructor supplements, including

- Computerized Test Bank, which allows instructors to select and edit test items and add their own questions. Various versions of each test can be custom printed.
- Test Bank in Rich Text Format
- Microsoft PowerPoint Presentations and a PowerPoint Presentations Guide
- The *Instructor's Manual*, which is loaded with ideas on teaching the course, chapter outlines, and answers.

i-Learning
ADVANTAGE
McGraw-Hill Ryerson

Your Integrated Learning Sales Specialist is a McGraw-Hill Ryerson representative who has the experience, product knowledge, training, and support to help you assess and integrate products, technology, and services into your course for optimum teaching and learning performance. Whether it's how to use our test bank software, helping your students improve their grades, or how to put your entire course online, your *i*Learning Sales Specialist is there to help. Contact your local *i*Learning Sales Specialist today to learn how to maximize all McGraw-Hill Ryerson resources!

McGraw-Hill Ryerson offers a unique *i*Services package designed for Canadian faculty. Our mission is to equip providers of higher education with superior tools and resources required for excellence in teaching. For additional information, visit www.mcgrawhill.ca/highereducation/iservices.

Content Cartridges are also available for course management systems, such as WebCT and Blackboard. These platforms provide instructors with user-friendly, flexible teaching tools. Ask your *i*Learning Sales Specialist for details.

Primis Online

Through McGraw-Hill Ryerson's custom publishing division, *Primis*, instructors are able to select cases to accompany *ABC's of Relationship Selling through Service* in a number of ways. Create your own case set, or browse the selection of cases that correspond to the chapter material. Contact your McGraw-Hill Ryerson *i*Learning Sales Specialist for more information.

CourseSmart

CourseSmart—CourseSmart brings together thousands of textbooks across hundreds of courses in an eTextbook format providing unique benefits to students and faculty. By purchasing an eTextbook, students can save up to 50 percent off the cost of a print textbook, reduce their impact on the environment, and gain access to powerful Web tools for learning including full text search, notes and highlighting, and e-mail tools for sharing notes between classmates. For faculty, CourseSmart provides instant access to review and compare textbooks and course materials in their discipline area without the time, cost, and environmental impact of mailing print exam copies. For further details contact your *i*Learning Sales Specialist or go to www.coursesmart.com.

Acknowledgements

I would like to recognize the many people who contributed in some way, to the content, philosophy, and underlying foundation of this textbook.

The professionals at McGraw-Hill Ryerson were a pleasure to work with. Their encouragement, advice, and friendly e-mails kept this project on task. The number of people needed to bring a textbook to print still amazes me and readers seldom see this. My development editors, Rebecca Walker and Arlene May Bautista, provided just the right amount of nudging to keep me on track.

As always, I feel it's important to acknowledge those who have helped shape my selling philosophy. Often people want to talk with me about selling or buying. Discussions always seems to revolve around great sales practices or shady sales schemes. I enjoy these conversations as they inevitably lead me to write about and teach the "best practices" and the pitfalls for salespeople to avoid. So many thanks to all those sales professionals and acquaintences who were so willing to share their experiences with me. They really do help shape the way I think about and teach selling.

To my colleagues in the marketing department at Mohawk College who are all expert salespeople and buyers in their own way: Bill Lucas, Pat Kolodziejski, Janice Shearer, Deborah Weston, and Rick Deverson, thank you for your support and willingness to share your many stories and expertise about salespeople and sales, which helped immensely in the development of this textbook.

As always, a special thank-you must go to the thousands of students I've taught in my 22 years at Mohawk College who were always willing to share their sales stories. Many of these students have gone on to great careers in sales and it is very rewarding to see you succeed. This edition of *ABC's* is dedicated to my students; past, present and future—for they are the ones who provide me with the motivation to write.

To my family, Bernice, Mark Jr., Gillian, and Lauren. Thank you for your patience. I'll be finished soon.

Once again, I must thank the many reviewers who provided feedback on the development of this textbook. Your input and comments are highly valued and really do help in the Canadianization of this text. Your willingness to share your collective experience and your thoughtful suggestions have improved the book. I appreciate the diversity of your views, and know that the topical coverage in *ABC's* benefits from your comments, so a special thank-you to

Julie Brown, Conestoga College

William Clymer, Durham College

George Dracopoulos, Vanier College & McGill University

Keith Gruben, Centennial College

Athena Hurezeanu, Seneca College

Peter Jurczak, Humber College

Georgia Kandias, Seneca College

Deborah Lawton, Thompson Rivers University

Bill Lucas, Mohawk College

Harvey McPhaden, Ryerson University

Randal Singer, British Columbia Institute of Technology

Wendy Threader, Algonquin College

Maria Vincenten, Red River College

Padma Vipat, Douglas College

Keith Wallace, Kwantlen University

Mark Valvasori
Mohawk College

PART 1

A SALES SUCCESS STORY

Louis Gagnon graduated from the Business Administration program at St. Clair College in 1977. His sales career began at Canada Packers where he progressed quickly from sales rep to major account manager. He moved to Xerox Canada Ltd. in 1981. He progressed through numerous positions and is currently vice president of sales.

Louis was initially attracted to sales by the challenge and rewards that sales offered; results are clear for everyone to see. He was initially inspired by one of his college professors who stressed that satisfied customers stay with their sales reps for a very long time.

Louis particularly enjoys the satisfaction he feels when he's able to solve customers' problems with his products or services.

For aspiring salespeople, Louis states, "Keep one thing in mind. People buy off of people." When asked what makes a great salesperson, he has five recommendations:

1. Listen
2. Be organized
3. Use your resources
4. Show initiative
5. Sell every step of the way.

Louis adds, "I hear each and every day from a variety of people who say that 'selling is not for me,' and yet I wonder how they know when they have never tried. Salespeople come in all forms from extroverts to introverts and all points in between." You never know until you try.

SELLING AS A PROFESSION

This introductory part of *ABC's of Relationship Selling Through Service* is an overview of the sales profession, in which we will examine the sales job itself as well as different types of selling careers. This part includes

1

THE LIFE, TIMES, AND CAREER OF THE PROFESSIONAL SALESPERSON

MAIN TOPICS

What Is Selling?

Why Choose a Sales Career?

Is a Sales Career Right for You?

Success in Selling—What Does It Take?

Relationship Selling

Sales Jobs Are Different

What Does a Professional Salesperson Do?

Relationship Marketing

Building Relationships through the Sales Process

LEARNING OBJECTIVES

This chapter introduces you to the rewarding career of professional selling. After studying this chapter, you should be able to:

- Define and explain the term *selling*.
- Explain why everyone sells, even you.
- Discuss the reasons that people might choose a sales career.
- Identify the many different types of sales jobs and discuss their responsibilities.
- Define the characteristics that are needed for success in building relationships with customers.
- Discuss the rewards inherent in a sales career.
- List and explain the 10 steps in the sales process.

FACING A CAREER CHALLENGE

Chin Lee graduated from Conestoga College with a degree in computer technology. After graduation, Chin was hired by a major technology-oriented company in eastern Canada as a computer technician. After three years in this position, he decided that it was time for a change; he requested and was given a transfer to the sales department.

"My first love was computers. I went to school to become an expert in technology but this became a bit boring after a few years. When I moved to sales, I was very frightened at first as I didn't have a lot of practice dealing with people and their problems, but I soon learned that my technical knowledge allowed me to become very proficient at solving customer problems. The more I worked with people, the more I enjoyed it. It was exciting and very rewarding."

Chin never looked back. Before long, he had become one of the leading producers in the sales department. With that came many financial and personal rewards, as well as job offers from some of his client companies. However, Chin felt he had the perfect job and decided to stay put.

David Ogilvy, one of the fathers of modern advertising, said it best: "We sell or else." His implication was that nothing happens in business until someone sells something and an exchange takes place.

The efforts of salespeople have an impact on virtually every field of business. Selling is an honourable, challenging, and rewarding career.

Chapter 1 examines the reasons that people choose sales careers, and provides information about factors critical for success in sales.

WHAT IS SELLING?

Many people consider *selling* and *marketing* synonymous. However, selling is actually only one of many marketing components. In business, **personal selling** refers to the personal communication of information to persuade a prospective customer to buy something—a good, service, idea, or something else—that satisfies the individual's needs on a personal level, or on a business level when an individual is purchasing for a company.

This definition of selling involves one person communicating with an individual or a group to make a sale. The salesperson often works with prospects or customers to examine their needs, provide information, suggest a product to meet their needs, and provide after-sale service to ensure long-term satisfaction.

Everybody Sells!

If you think about it, everyone is involved with selling. Children develop communication skills early in life to get what they want. When you want something or want someone to do something, you use your natural selling skills. When you attempt to get a date, ask for a pay raise, urge your professor to raise your mark, provide cost-effective solutions to buyers, or deal with customer service representatives in large companies, you are using personal selling skills. Perhaps after completing this textbook, you will become more effective in each of the above situations. Your ability to communicate effectively is crucial to your success in life.

Sales courses are full of not only people who want to improve their professional selling skills for increased success in their business lives, but also individuals who want to enhance their personal communication skills. Learning how to communicate to others how your ideas or products can satisfy their needs will be invaluable throughout your life.

MAKING THE SALE
Virtual Presentations

Kristi Peters, a manufacturer's agent, represents Steam Technologies, a company specializing in steam-generating equipment used in many industrial applications. Kristi relishes the job, as it allows her to apply her knowledge and skills of engineering technology and marketing.

Kristi is adept at communicating the benefits of Steam Technologies to a variety of customers. At first, she found it a little difficult to overcome the stereotype of the sales professional. Many customers found it surprising that a female would be involved with a technical product, and calling on companies using the product for industrial applications was initially challenging. As Kristi states, "There is often some initial reluctance, but once they discover that I really know my stuff, we are able to build quite a good professional relationship."

One of Kristi's responsibilities is to locate potential users of her product line, contact them, and introduce her product's many uses. Because her prospects are often diverse in both their needs and geographic areas, she finds it difficult to travel to each one to make a customized presentation. During her time learning professional selling skills she had studied the benefits of digital photography and Web conferencing. She turned this idea into action by purchasing both a digital movie camera and digital SLR. When visiting her customers, she got permission to photograph and film the steam technologies in action.

Using this digital information and presentation software, Kristi has been able to edit it into an effective sales aid. Now, rather than travelling thousands of kilometres each year to meet customers and introduce her product, Kristi makes an effective presentation by telephoning prospects and having them log on to her Web site so she can communicate in real time while demonstrating her products on her prospect's monitor.

Kristi has saved thousands of hours in travel time without sacrificing the effectiveness of visual presentations. Now she uses her time to close the deal. Her productivity has increased sharply, and she has recently begun to make virtual group presentations using Web conferencing software. As she states, "Technology has come a long way and it is still moving ahead rapidly—by keeping up, I'm able to accomplish twice as much as I used to."

Although trained as professional purchasing agents or buyers, many of these professionals also see the value of learning effective sales skills. Some might believe that they are simply trying to learn the "tricks" of the trade to arm themselves for the onslaught of sales representatives. The truth of the matter is that most simply want to enhance their performance by gaining an understanding of the salesperson's perspective, which leads to more effective purchasing, negotiation, and selling.

The skills and knowledge gained from a selling course can be used by a student who plans to go into virtually any field, such as law, financial services, medicine, or journalism, or by those who start their own business.

In today's competitive environment, where good interpersonal skills are so valued, the lack of selling capability puts people at a disadvantage. So as you read this book and progress through the course, think about how you can use the material both personally and in business.

Exhibit 1–1 shows a simplified organizational chart for a marketing-oriented organization. Although research departments can study markets to determine their buying habits and needs, it is the sales force that acts as front-line representatives for companies. Part of the selling job entails learning about market needs, relaying that information to company strategists, and communicating to the market how the company's products can satisfy their needs. Although personal selling is only one part of the promotional element, which in turn is only one part of the marketing mix, today's companies understand the importance of using well-trained and effective salespeople—and the contribution that they make to the bottom line.

EXHIBIT 1–1

Where selling fits in.

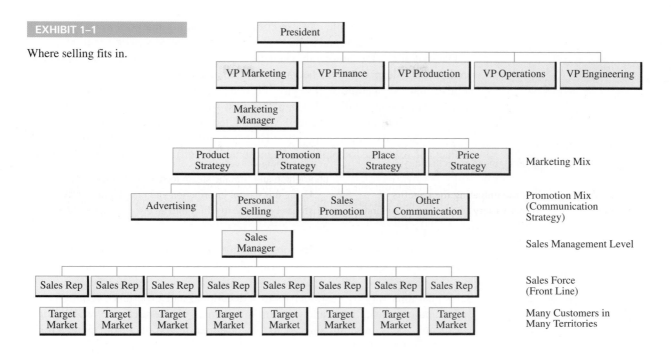

Five major reasons for choosing a sales career are (1) the wide variety of sales jobs available, (2) the freedom of being on your own, (3) the challenge of selling, (4) the opportunity for advancement in a company, and (5) the rewards of a sales career.

The Sales Force— Past, Present, and Future

Historically, due to the attitudes and philosophies of business owners, salespeople have developed a reputation for being fast talking, high pressure, and slick. Salespeople were expected to "hustle" business and "push" their products on people. It's no wonder that the sales profession has developed such a bad reputation.

As companies started to adopt a marketing philosophy, where consumers' needs are considered first and foremost, the sales job started to change. Because of increased competition, more sophisticated and knowledgeable consumers, and the expectation of consumers that their needs will be met, salespeople today have evolved into true professionals who are expected to have product expertise and to develop a long-term relationship with their customers. Salespeople today are becoming "business solution providers"—or, as some have suggested, "buying facilitators."

Modern salespeople must perform a thorough needs analysis of each potential buyer, then create value for their buyers by developing a relationship with them to identify and satisfy their changing needs on an ongoing basis.

Advances in technology have had a huge impact on the selling profession in recent years and will continue to do so. In particular, information technology provides both opportunities and threats to tomorrow's sales force.

After the events of September 11, 2001, and with rising fuel and transportation costs, many salespeople are reconsidering the need for travelling. Armed with wireless technology, salespeople can provide prospects and customers with increased service, in less time, from anywhere around the globe. Salespeople will travel less and use online audio and video conferencing more. They can use customer relationship management (CRM) software to keep in contact and track a variety of information about the purchase behaviour of customers.

In addition, salespeople can use computer telephony integration (CTI), which provides voice mail, fax, and e-mail, as well as remote access to information.

Does all of this technology threaten the existence of salespeople? Some observers predict that salespeople will become obsolete as e-commerce soars. However, we believe that salespeople will always be needed, although their role may change slightly; salespeople will evolve into "business success coaches." For example, prospective customers may have access via the Internet to information about your products and those of your competitors. However, they will still need your personal contact and expertise to help them diagnose their specific needs and to communicate the best solution to satisfy them.

From a demographic perspective, the sales force of the future increasingly will reflect Canada's diverse ethnic mix. For example, there are now many opportunities for women in professional selling, especially in industries where males have traditionally dominated.

There are many types of sales jobs available in Canada, falling into several categories; nevertheless, the same basic principles of selling will always apply.

Types of Sales Employment

Sales positions vary by customer focus, educational and experience requirements, duties and responsibilities, and position in a company's hierarchy. In retail selling, salespeople focus on selling directly to the consumer of a product from either a traditional retail store, or through door-to-door selling, home demonstrations, and so on. In most types of selling, salespeople are selling in a business-to-business setting. These positions can involve selling products to an intermediary for resale or further processing, or selling products to companies that will then use them to run their business.

You will note that as the type of sales job becomes more complex and better paying, the education requirements become higher. Many higher-paying sales positions today are filled by people who combine formal educational background with some product-related education.

Careers in Selling

The following sales positions are representative of the sales profession in Canada. Salary figures and brief job descriptions originate from Monster.ca, a leading online global careers network.

Sales clerks typically sell merchandise in a retail store, assisting customers with sales, returns, exchanges, and product knowledge. This type of sales job requires a high school diploma and up to two years of related experience. A sales clerk should possess knowledge of common practices and procedures relating to a particular product field. Sales clerks average $31,800 to $39,000 annually, depending on location, type of company, and experience.

Customer service representatives are responsible for processing orders, preparing correspondence, and ensuring customer satisfaction in a variety of businesses. A high school diploma and two to five years of related experience is typically required, along with a general understanding of the tasks necessary to achieve sales and customer service goals. In this position, salespeople have some latitude to attain their goals. Customer service reps (CSRs) average $31,000 to $45,000 annually.

Merchandisers are not your typical salesperson. They are often referred to as "support" salespeople and are responsible for setting up displays and providing product literature in a customer's premises. Merchandisers usually have good knowledge of the field in which they are working and often have a college diploma or associated degree. Merchandisers earn from $32,000 to $44,000 annually. Many merchandisers work flexible hours, including part time.

Order desk clerks are often referred to as inside sales reps in that they process and review orders received by mail, telephone, or online. This position requires a high school diploma and up to two years of related experience. Strict guidelines are followed and clerks should have a working knowledge of the products and procedures of their company. Annual salaries in this field average from $35,000 to $45,000.

Sales representatives are responsible for developing new business and interacting with existing customers to increase sales of an organization's products and/or services. Sales reps typically have at least a high school diploma and several years of experience in a particular field. Sales reps are more independent and are expected to use their own judgment and experience to plan and achieve sales goals. Sales reps average $55,000 to $81,000 annually.

Senior sales representatives have similar duties to a sales representative, the difference being that they are required to perform more complicated tasks and are often expected to lead and direct others. A great degree of latitude and creativity is expected here, and senior reps typically report to a manager. The higher complexity of the job allows them to earn from $72,000 to $110,000 per year.

Technical sales representatives can earn from $43,000 to $95,000 per year depending on their level of expertise and the nature of the products they deal with. These sales reps typically have at least a college diploma and possibly an undergraduate or graduate degree. Technical sales reps are typically responsible for increasing sales to accounts by interacting with customers and providing them with technical knowledge and solutions.

Key account representatives oversee the customer relationships within a designated territory. These reps identify key accounts and develop ongoing relationships with them to increase sales. This popular job requires a college diploma or university degree and, in most cases, several years of experience in the field. These reps require good judgment and creativity to help them establish and achieve goals. Key account reps earn from $67,000 to more than $100,000 annually.

Business solutions specialists collaborate with customers and use their education and experience to develop product enhancements or alterations necessary for a sale. These reps normally have extensive experience and must understand and perform a variety of tasks related to their field. They often must direct the work of others, and for these skills they earn from $58,000 to $78,000 annually.

Top sales executives can earn salaries from $160,000 to $243,000 per year. Reporting to top management, these sales executives plan and direct all aspects of an organization's sales policies, objectives, and initiatives. This position typically requires a bachelor's degree and several years experience.

Source: "Salary Centre," at www.monster.ca.

A continuum of sales jobs, comparing complexity and salary.

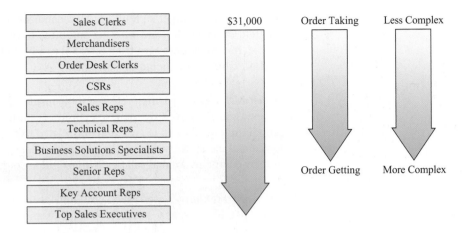

| Sales Clerks |
| Merchandisers |
| Order Desk Clerks |
| CSRs |
| Sales Reps |
| Technical Reps |
| Business Solutions Specialists |
| Senior Reps |
| Key Account Reps |
| Top Sales Executives |

$31,000 → (arrow down)

Order Taking → Order Getting

Less Complex → More Complex

Order Takers versus Order Getters

Order takers may ask what the customer wants or even wait for the customer to order. They do not have a sales strategy and do not use creative sales presentations. Order-takers seldom attempt to "close" a sale. Although they do perform many useful services, few truly *create* sales.

Order getters, on the other hand, are responsible for generating new business through many different means. Companies strive to employ the most effective order getters as these people drive the success of the company through creative sales strategies and effective sales presentations. Order getters face an infinitely more difficult task; therefore, they usually earn much more than the order taker.

Exhibit 1–2 shows a continuum of sales jobs and compares their complexity and salaries.

Freedom of Action: You're on Your Own

A second reason that people choose a sales career is the freedom it offers. A sales job provides possibly the greatest relative freedom of any career. Experienced employees in outside sales usually receive little direct supervision and may go for days, even weeks, without seeing their bosses. The term *outside sales* refers to selling activities external to the employer's premises. These contracts involve person-to-person contact between the sales representative and customer or prospective customer. By contrast, inside sales occur on the premises, as in retail selling or telemarketing.

Although duties and sales goals are explained by a boss, salespeople are expected to carry out their job duties and achieve goals with minimum guidance. They usually leave home to contact customers around the corner or around the world.

Job Challenge Is Always There

Working alone with the responsibility of a territory capable of generating thousands (sometimes millions) of dollars in revenue for a company is a personal challenge. Salespeople often deal with hundreds of different people and firms. It is much like operating your own business, without the burdens of true ownership.

Opportunities for Advancement Are Great

Successful salespeople have many opportunities to move into top management positions, and, in many instances, this advancement comes quickly. For example, General Mills and Quaker Oats may promote successful salespeople to managerial positions, such as district sales managers, after they have been with the company for only two years.

EXHIBIT 1–3

Selling services offers excellent career opportunities; banks, hotels, airlines, and travel agencies are industries that need professional salespeople.

A sales personnel **career path**, as shown in Exhibit 1–4, is the upward sequence of job movements during a sales career. Occasionally people without previous sales experience are promoted to sales management positions. However, usually a career in sales management begins with an entry-level sales position.

Most companies have two or three successive levels of sales positions, beginning at the junior or trainee level. Beginning as a salesperson allows a person to

- Learn about the attitudes and activities of the company's salespeople.
- Become familiar with customer attitudes toward the company, its products, and its salespeople.
- Gain first-hand knowledge of products and their applications, which is most important in technical sales.
- Become seasoned in the business world.

EXHIBIT 1–4

A sales personnel career path.

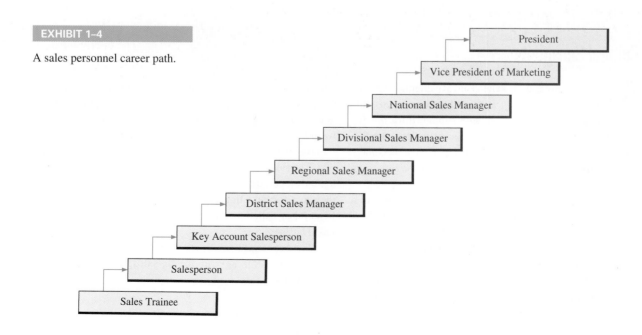

Sales managers frequently mention that this position represents their first major step toward the top; they are on the management team. Instead of being responsible for $1 million in sales as a salesperson, the manager is responsible for $10 million.

With success, many jobs throughout the sales force and in the corporate marketing department open up. These jobs can include sales training, sales analysis, advertising, and product management.

Two Career Paths   Don't let Exhibit 1–4 mislead you—many salespeople prefer selling to managing people. They want to take care of themselves rather than others. In some companies, a salesperson may even earn more money than the manager.

Many companies have recognized the value of keeping some salespeople in the field for their entire sales career. They do a good job, know their customers, and love what they are doing—so why promote them if they do not want to move up within the organization?

Rewards: The Sky's the Limit

As a salesperson, you can look forward to two types of rewards: **nonfinancial** and **financial**.

Nonfinancial Rewards

Sometimes called psychological income or intrinsic rewards, nonfinancial rewards are generated by the individual, not given by the company.

Successfully meeting the challenges of the job produces a feeling of self-worth: You realize that your job is important. Everyone wants to feel good about a job, and a selling career allows you to experience these good feelings and intrinsic rewards daily. Salespeople often report that the nonfinancial rewards of their jobs are just as important to them as the financial rewards.

For example, some companies offer their top performers foreign postings in exotic locations. In other companies, management attempts to motivate salespeople by

SELLING GLOBALLY

Cultural Sensitivity

Andrew Stevens and his sales team travelled to Japan to begin negotiations with a major Japanese electronics firm in hopes of becoming the sole supplier of a revolutionary new building technology recently developed in Canada. Mr. Stevens recognized that Japan could become a major market for this technology so these negotiations were critical.

Things started out well. The sales team was invited to a formal company reception with senior company executives and government officials in attendance. During a speech by one of the dignitaries, Mr. Stevens leaned over to his Japanese counterpart and made an offhand remark about the Japanese Royal Family. Several minutes later, his counterpart left the room momentarily. For the rest of the evening, it appeared that the hosts were distancing themselves from the Canadian sales team. Over the next few days, despite a congenial front, negotiations turned sour and Stevens's team wasn't able to gain a commitment for anything.

Over the next few weeks, Stevens met with more rejection. The sales team was getting nowhere. Finally, they gave up and returned to Canada. Something had happened and they just couldn't figure out what it was. Upon returning home, they called a post-mortem meeting to discuss their failed business trip.

What happened?

Can you offer any advice to salespeople who sell internationally?

providing recognition in the form of public advertising and internal promotion of top performers. How often in a company do you see the top administrators recognized? For the sales department, this is a common practice, whereby salespeople are given the recognition they deserve. After all, if it weren't for them, the company probably wouldn't be in operation.

Financial Rewards

Success also brings financial rewards. Both corporate and field sales managers typically receive higher salaries than others (such as production, advertising, product, or personnel managers) at the same organizational level. Besides salary, many firms offer their sales personnel other remuneration or perks. For example, recognizing the need for a certain level of customer entertainment, many companies offer club memberships for business use as well as personal memberships for health clubs. Group medical plans, including dental, extended health, disability, and life insurance, are common. Most companies now offer mobile phones for sales representatives, and many offer laptop computers for use from home. Other offerings can range from pension plans and stock purchases to personal financial planning and low-interest personal loans. Many companies embrace the concept of life-long learning and provide educational reimbursement programs for employees seeking to further their education.

Cash **incentives** include performance bonuses based on achievement of sale targets. Other bonuses based on overall company performance in sales or profitability are also common. All-expenses-paid vacations, gifts of electronic goods, and gift vouchers can be used as rewards for sales.

Although there is some variation by region, one of the enduring aspects of professional selling is some form of compensation for travel. Many companies provide company cars for use by their sales representatives. In the remaining companies, either a monthly allowance, a per-kilometre allowance, or a combination is provided.

Many people are attracted to selling because in a sales career, financial rewards are usually based solely on performance (see Exhibit 1–5).

EXHIBIT 1–5

The Canadian sales force is very diversified. There is room for everyone in a sales career.

EXHIBIT 1–6

Compensation ranges for inside, field, and management positions
Here's a sample of pay ranges, as detailed in the CPSA's *2007/2008 Sales Compensation and Benefits Report.*

Field Sales and Management Positions	
Sales and Marketing Directors	$81,800–170,600
Divisional or Regional Sales Directors	$82,800–171,600
Marketing and Sales Managers	$59,000–134,100
District Sales Managers	$51,600–94,900
Territory Sales Managers	$45,400–136,300
Technical Sales Representative—Senior	$55,600–127,200
Technical Sale Representative—Intermediate	$51,600–94,900
Technical Sales Representative—Junior	$32,100–81,500
Senior Sales Representative	$55,200–133,200
Intermediate Sales Representative	$42,500–76,000
Junior Sales Representative	$33,800–55,900
Key Account Representative	$63,500–118,000
Customer Service Representative	$33,800–62,200

You can use the Internet to compare sales jobs. Several Web sites listed at the end of this chapter have tools for researching sales salaries. The Web sites www.monster. ca and www.payscale.com have very useful tools that allow you to determine salary levels for various jobs requiring different levels of experience and education, and located in different areas of Canada.

IS A SALES CAREER RIGHT FOR YOU?

It may be too early in life to determine whether you really want to be a salesperson. The balance of this book will aid you in investigating sales as a career. Your search for any career begins with *you.* In considering a sales career, be honest and realistic. Ask yourself questions such as

- What are my past accomplishments?
- What are my future goals?
- Do I want the responsibility of a sales job?
- Do I mind travel? How much travel is acceptable?
- How much freedom do I want in the job?
- Do I have the personality characteristics for the job?
- Am I willing to transfer to another city? Another province?

Your answers to these questions can help you analyze the various types of sales jobs and establish criteria for evaluating job openings. Determine the industries, types of products or services, and specific companies in which you have an interest.

College placement offices, libraries, and business periodicals offer plenty of information on companies as well as sales positions in them. Conversations with friends and acquaintances who are involved in selling or have been in sales can give you realistic insight into what challenges, rewards, and disadvantages the sales vocation offers. To better prepare yourself to obtain a sales job, you must understand what companies look for in salespeople.

A Sales Manager's View of the Recruit

The following discussion of what sales managers consider when hiring a salesperson is based on a summary of a talk given by a sales manager to a sales class.

> We look for outstanding applicants who are mature and intelligent. They should be able to handle themselves well in the interview, demonstrating good interpersonal skills. They should have a well-thought-out career plan and be able to discuss it rationally. They should have a friendly, pleasing personality. A clean, neat appearance is a must. They should have a positive attitude, be willing to work hard, be ambitious, and demonstrate a good degree of interest in the employer's business field. They should have good grades and other personal, school, and business accomplishments. Finally, they should have clear goals and objectives in life. The more common characteristics on which applicants for our company are judged are (1) appearance, (2) self-expression, (3) maturity, (4) personality, (5) experience, (6) enthusiasm, and (7) interest in the job.

A sales job has not only high rewards but also many important responsibilities. Let us review the characteristics of a successful salesperson.

SUCCESS IN SELLING—WHAT DOES IT TAKE?

Throughout this book you will read comments from salespeople about their jobs. Over the years, we have asked thousands of salespeople the question "What makes a salesperson successful?" The nine most frequently mentioned characteristics are (1) love of their job, (2) willingness to work hard, (3) need to achieve success, (4) optimistic outlook, (5) knowledge of their job, (6) careful use of selling time, (7) ability to ask questions and listen to customers, (8) customer service, and (9) being physically and mentally prepared for life and the job. Some of these characteristics are described more fully below.

Love of Selling

The successful salesperson is an individual who loves selling, finds it exciting, and is strongly convinced that the product being sold offers something of great value.

Salespeople quoted throughout this book comment about how their enthusiasm for their work helps them to be successful. They possess an eagerness to do the job well, which causes them to work hard at selling.

MAKING THE SALE

Don't Quit

When things go wrong, as they sometimes will,
When the road you're trudging seems all uphill,
When the funds are low and the debts are high,
And you want to smile, but you have to sigh,
When care is pressing you down a bit—
Rest if you must, but don't you quit.
Life is queer with its twists and turns,
As every one of us sometimes learns,
And many a person turns about
When they might have won had they stuck it out.

Don't give up though the pace seems slow—
You may succeed with another blow.
Often the struggler has given up
When he might have captured the victor's cup;
And he learned too late
When the night came down,
How close he was to the golden crown.
Success is failure turned inside out—
So stick to the fight when you're hardest hit—
It's when things seem worst that you mustn't quit.

Author Unknown

Willingness to Work Hard

A positive attitude toward work works wonders! Successful people are often described as lucky. However, they spell luck W-O-R-K. The harder they work, the luckier they get.

Need to Achieve Success

Successful salespeople say that even though they enjoy it, selling requires long hours of hard work, day in and day out, to reach personal goals. A 10-to-12-hour workday is common—including many Saturdays and Sundays. It is their love of work and their need for success that motivate the top sellers. The need to achieve also involves persistence.

Have an Optimistic Outlook

Salespeople credit a positive attitude toward their companies, products, customers, themselves, and life as major reasons for their success. Successful salespeople are enthusiastic, confident, and consider themselves successful. Sure, salespeople have times when things do not go as they want, yet their positive attitude helps them through. They continually look for methods to improve their attitude.

Successful salespeople say that their greatest enemy is procrastination. They know that the early bird gets the worm. They are do-it-now people. They pick up the phone, mail a letter, or make a sales call today. In no other career is the need to think positively more important. Make sure you have a positive, enthusiastic attitude toward yourself, your work, and your customers. This involves

- Believing in yourself
- Thinking of yourself as a success
- Being positive in your outlook on life and the job.

Be Knowledgeable

Successful salespeople place great emphasis on being thoroughly knowledgeable in all aspects of their business. This helps them to project a professional image and build customer confidence.

Knowledge also includes awareness of the most up-to-date ideas concerning selling skills. Successful salespeople are expert at developing and presenting talks that sell their products. They constantly educate themselves on methods to better determine customers' needs and to effectively communicate the benefits of their products to satisfy those needs.

SELLING TIPS

The Canadian Professional Sales Association

The Canadian Professional Sales Association (**CPSA**) is a national association comprising more than 30,000 sales and marketing professionals located in communities of all sizes in every part of Canada.

The CPSA was founded in 1874; today, CPSA members represent the full spectrum of the sales profession, including senior managers, entrepreneurs, sales managers, and sales representatives.

Providing sales professionals with the tools and resources to succeed has remained CPSA's mandate. CPSA members enjoy special rates on travel and hotels, car leasing and rentals, insurance, and financial services. CPSA has an outstanding professional development program that includes an extensive library of sales and marketing materials, national seminar and conference sessions, and sales training courses. This program enhances CPSA's commitment to sales professionals across Canada.

Visit the CPSA Web site to learn more at www.cpsa.com.

EXHIBIT 1–7

Salespeople work hard to become experts on their products and those of their competitors. Only then can they effectively use selling skills to provide information that helps customers.

Salespeople read books and magazine articles on selling, and attend sales training courses to learn how to sell their products better. This knowledge is incorporated into sales presentations that are rehearsed until they sound like a natural conversation between seller and buyer.

Be Ruthless about Time

The most successful people are ruthless about guarding their time. In daily activities, they instinctively understand the powerful secret to success called the Pareto principle.

The Pareto principle is named after 19th-century economist Vilfredo Pareto, who found that in any human activity, the biggest results usually arise from a small number of factors. For example, studies have shown that most people spend 80 percent of their time on the least important 20 percent of their jobs, and only 20 percent doing the work that yields 80 percent of their bottom-line results.

Successful salespeople define the specific results that practically guarantee success. Then they ruthlessly arrange daily priorities to invest 80 percent of their time into the 20 percent of work with the greatest results payout. Since there is only so much time in the day for contacting customers, and there are so many demands on their time, successful salespeople value time and use it wisely by carefully planning their day's activities. Which customer will be called on, what product will be presented, and how to present it must be planned carefully.

Ask Questions and Then Listen to Uncover Customer Needs

Joe Gandolfo, who sold more than *$1 billion* of life insurance in a single year, has a sign on his office wall that reads, "God gave you two ears and one mouth, and He meant for you to do twice as much listening as talking."

Good salespeople are good listeners. They ask questions to uncover prospects' needs and then listen as prospects answer the questions and state their needs. Then they show how their products will fulfill these needs. The ability to identify and meet customer needs separates the successful salesperson from the average salesperson.

Empathy is the ability to put yourself in someone else's shoes. In subsequent chapters, you will learn the importance of determining customers' needs and

MAKING THE SALE
What Is Your Value?

Top-performing salespeople are always striving to be the best they can be. Each of us has control of our destiny. We will be what we want to be. Consider, for example, a plain bar of iron that is worth about $5. Made into a horseshoe, it's worth about $11; made into screwdrivers, it's worth about $15; made into needles, it's worth about $3,500. The same is true for another kind of material—YOU! Your value is determined by what you decide to make of yourself.

determining the many factors that can influence your prospects in their purchase decision making. Developing your empathy will allow you to feel what your prospect is feeling and be affected by what is affecting your prospect. Empathetic salespeople can be much more effective at satisfying customer needs and hence will become much more successful than those who don't care.

Serve Your Customer

The most important characteristic for establishing a lasting sales relationship with a customer is willingness to provide service. Customers must believe that you care about them and their welfare. Successful salespeople respect their customers, treat them fairly, like them, and develop a good working relationship with them that is like a partnership.

Be Physically and Mentally Prepared

With physical preparedness comes mental strength. Knowing that you are in shape, mentally and physically, to deal with today and tomorrow is important to your success.

Ten minutes of aerobic exercise per day will improve cardiovascular fitness if you can't wedge 30-to-60-minute exercise periods into your schedule three to five times per week.

What we choose to eat, drink, and smoke directly influences our physical and mental processes. Learn about the dietary and physical aspects of your body, and commit to sustaining your mental and physical fitness.

RELATIONSHIP SELLING

Salespeople are no longer adversaries who manipulate people for personal gain. They want to be consultants, partners, and problem solvers for customers. Their goal is to build a long-term relationship with clients through **relationship selling**. Salespeople seek to benefit their employer, themselves, and customers.

In recent years, the distinction between a salesperson and a professional has blurred because the salesperson of today is a pro. Many salespeople know more about their field and product than the buyer does. This expertise enables the seller to become the buyer's partner, a counsellor on how to solve problems. Today's salesperson provides information that helps customers make intelligent choices to achieve their short-and long-term objectives. Service and follow-up are then provided to ensure satisfaction with the purchase. This sequence builds *customer loyalty*—a relationship.

Exhibit 1–8 shows the four main elements in the customer relationship process used by salespeople to build relationships. They analyze customers' needs, recommend a solution and gain commitment for the purchase, implement the recommendation, and maintain and grow the relationship.

EXHIBIT 1–8

Main elements in the customer relationship process.

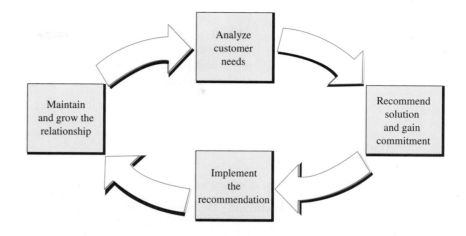

Analyze customer needs

Recommend solution and gain commitment

Implement the recommendation

Maintain and grow the relationship

SALES JOBS ARE DIFFERENT

As you can see, sales jobs are different from other jobs in several ways. Here are some major differences:

- Salespeople represent their companies to the outside world. Consequently, opinions of a company and its products are often formed from impressions left by the sales force. The public ordinarily does not judge a firm by its office or factory workers.

- Other employees usually work under close supervisory control, whereas the outside salesperson typically operates with little or no direct supervision. Moreover, to be successful, salespeople must often be creative, persistent, and show great initiative—all of which require a high degree of motivation.

- Salespeople probably need more tact, diplomacy, and social poise than other employees in an organization. Many sales jobs require the salesperson to display considerable emotional and social intelligence in dealing with buyers.

- Salespeople are among the few employees authorized to spend company funds. They spend this money for entertainment, transportation, and other business expenses.

MAKING THE SALE
What Is a Customer?

- Customers are the most important people in any business. Customers are not dependent on us. We are dependent on them.

- Customers are not an interruption of our work. They are the purpose of it.

- Customers do us a favour in doing business with us. We aren't doing customers a favour by waiting on them.

- Customers are part of our business—not outsiders. Customers are not just money in the cash register.

- Customers are human beings with feelings, and they deserve to be treated with respect.

- Customers are people who come to us with needs and wants. It is our job to fill them.

- Customers deserve the most courteous attention we can give them.

- Customers are the lifeblood of this and every business.

- Customers pay your salary. Without customers we would have to close our doors.

- Don't ever forget it!

■ Some sales jobs frequently require considerable travelling and time spent away from home and family. At times, salespeople deal with customers who seem determined not to buy the sellers' products. These challenges, coupled with the physical demands of long hours and travelling, require mental toughness and physical stamina rarely demanded in other types of jobs.

Selling is hard work! It requires intelligence, the desire to achieve, and the ability to overcome difficulties.

WHAT DOES A PROFESSIONAL SALESPERSON DO?

The salesperson's roles or activities can vary from company to company, depending on whether sales involve goods or services, the firm's market characteristics, and the location of customers. For example, a salesperson selling Avon products performs similar, but somewhat different, job activities from the industrial salesperson making sales calls for General Electric.

Most people believe that a salesperson only makes sales presentations, but there is much more to the job than person-to-person selling. The salesperson functions as a **territory manager**—planning, organizing, and executing activities that increase

EXHIBIT 1–9

A professional salesperson . . .

. . . helps meet the needs and solve the problems of the customer

. . . makes presentations to new and current customers

. . . sells to wholesalers and distributors

. . . handles customer complaints

sales and profits in a given territory. A sales territory comprises a group of customers assigned within a geographical area. Exhibit 1–9 indicates a few typical activities of a salesperson. As a salesperson is essentially a manager of a territory, he or she performs the following nine functions:

1. **Creates new customers:** To increase sales and replace customers that will be lost over time, many types of sales jobs require a salesperson to prospect. Prospecting is the lifeblood of sales because it identifies potential customers. Salespeople need the ability to *close*, or make the sale.

2. **Sells more to present customers:** Tomorrow's sales come from selling to new customers and selling to present customers again, and again, and again.

3. **Builds long-term relationships with customers:** Earning the opportunity to sell a present customer more product means the salesperson must have a positive, professional business relationship with people and organizations that trust the salesperson and the products purchased.

4. **Provides solutions to customers' problems:** Customers have needs that can be met and problems that can be solved by purchasing goods or services. Salespeople seek to uncover potential or existing needs or problems, and show how the use of their products or services can satisfy needs or solve problems.

5. **Provides service to customers:** Salespeople provide a wide range of services, including handling complaints, returning damaged merchandise, providing samples, suggesting business opportunities, and developing recommendations on how the customer can promote products purchased from the salesperson.

   If necessary, salespeople may occasionally work at the customer's business. For example, a salesperson selling fishing tackle may arrange an in-store demonstration of a manufacturer's products and offer to repair fishing reels as a service to the retailer's customers.

6. **Helps customers resell products to their customers:** A major part of many sales jobs is helping wholesalers and retailers resell the products that they have purchased. The salesperson helps wholesale customers sell products to retail customers and helps retail customers sell products to consumers.

   Consider a Quaker Oats salesperson selling a product to grocery wholesalers. Not only must the wholesaler be contacted but also grocery retailers must be called on, sales made, and orders written up and sent to the wholesaler. In turn, the wholesaler sells and delivers the products to the retailers. The Quaker Oats salesperson also develops promotional programs to help the retailer sell the firm's products. These programs involve supplying advertising materials, conducting store demonstrations, and setting up product displays.

7. **Helps customers use products after purchase:** The salesperson's job is not over after the sale is made. Often, customers must be shown how to obtain full benefit from the product. For example, after a customer buys an IBM computer system, technical specialists help the buyer learn how to operate the equipment.

8. **Builds goodwill with customers:** A selling job is people-oriented, entailing face-to-face contact with the customer. Many sales are based, to some extent, on friendship and trust. The salesperson needs to develop a personal, friendly, businesslike relationship with everyone who may influence a buying decision. This ongoing part of the salesperson's job requires integrity, high ethical standards, and a sincere interest in satisfying customers' needs.

What does a professional
salesperson do?

1. Creates new customers
2. Sells more to present customers
3. Builds long-term relationships with customers
4. Provides solutions to customers' problems
5. Provides service to customers
6. Helps customers resell products to their customers
7. Helps customers use products after purchase
8. Builds goodwill with customers
9. Provides company with market information.

9. **Provides company with market information:** Salespeople provide information to their companies on such topics as competitors' activities, customers' reactions to new products, complaints about products or policies, market opportunities, and their job activities. This information is so important for many companies that their salespeople are required to send in weekly or monthly reports on activities of the firm's competition in their territory. Salespeople are a vital part of their employers' information retrieval system.

Reflect Back   Review the nine functions shown in Exhibit 1–10 to see whether you could do any or all of them. Carefully think about the second and third functions. To be successful, a salesperson must close sales and build relationships with the same person or organization in order to sell more. To do both is challenging to any person. It requires salespersons to solve problems, provide service, help resell, teach how to use the product, build goodwill, and keep their employer up to date on customers' needs and feelings toward the product and service.

This book is about these nine functions and much more. When combined and properly implemented, these nine job activities produce increased sales for the organization and more rewards for the salesperson. See the Making the Sale box "A Typical Day for a Xerox Salesperson" for an example of how a salesperson integrates these activities.

RELATIONSHIP MARKETING   Organizations target new and present customers, to ensure that they'll have customers today and tomorrow.

Relationship marketing creates customer loyalty by paying continuous attention to important customers. Organizations use combinations of products, prices, distribution, promotions, and service to achieve this goal.

An organization using relationship marketing is not seeking a simple sale or transaction. It has targeted a major customer that it would like to sell to now and in the future. The company wants to demonstrate to the customer that it has the capabilities to serve the account's needs in a superior way, particularly if a committed relationship can be formed. The type of selling needed to establish a long-term collaborative relationship is complex. General Motors, for example, prefers suppliers that can sell and deliver a coordinated set of goods and services to many locations, quickly solve problems that arise in their different locations, and work closely with GM to improve products and processes.

MAKING THE SALE

A Typical Day for a Xerox Salesperson

You are responsible for sales coverage, time, and budget. Help is available and you'll have plenty of marketing and service support, but you're expected to work independently, without constant direction.

Your day is devoted primarily to customer contact. Potential customers may phone the branch and ask to see a Xerox representative. More likely, however, you will acquire customers by making appointments or by visiting businesses to meet the decision makers, discuss their needs, and offer solutions to their problems. As part of your position, you'll make product presentations, either at the Xerox branch office or at the customer's office. You will also spend a fair amount of time on the telephone following up leads, arranging appointments, and speaking with managers in a variety of businesses and organizations.

In working with customers, you'll need to solve a number of problems. What Xerox product best fits the customer's needs? How do Xerox products compare with the competition? Should the machine be purchased or leased? What's the total cash outlay—and per-copy cost—for the machine and its service? How should the product be financed? Where should the machine be placed for maximum efficiency? What training is needed for employees? How can Xerox products meet future office needs?

You'll also be engaged in a number of customer support activities, such as expediting product deliveries, checking credit, writing proposals, and training customer employees in the use of the product. You also might refer customers to other Xerox sales organizations and make joint calls with representatives from these organizations.

Each day will bring you new challenges to face and problems to solve. Your days will be busy and interesting.[1]

Most companies, unfortunately, are not set up to meet these requirements. Many organizations still sell customers and then forget them. More progressive organizations, though, develop a close relationship—even a partnership—with their customers.

Levels of Relationship Marketing

What type of relationships should an organization have with its customers? Is keeping a relationship worth the cost? To answer these questions, let's define the three general levels of selling relationships with customers:

- Transaction selling: customers are sold and not contacted again.
- Relationship selling: the seller contacts customers after the purchase to determine whether they are satisfied and have future needs.
- Partnering: the seller works continually to improve the customers' operations, sales, and profits.

Most organizations focus solely on the single transaction with each customer. When you go to McDonald's and buy a hamburger, that's it. You never hear from the company again unless you return for another purchase. The same thing happens when you go to a movie, rent a DVD, open a bank account, visit the grocery store, or have your clothes cleaned. Each example involves low-priced, low-profit products. Also involved are a large number of customers who are geographically dispersed, making it very difficult and quite costly to contact customers. The business is forced to use **transactional selling**.

Relationship marketing focuses on the transaction—making the sale—along with follow-up and service after the sale. The seller contacts the customer to ensure satisfaction with the purchase. The Cadillac Division of General Motors contacts each buyer of a new Cadillac to determine the customer's satisfaction with the car. If that person is not satisfied, General Motors works with the retailer selling the car to make sure the customer is happy.

Partnering is a phenomenon of the 1990s and the 21st century. Businesses' growing concerns over the competition not only in Canada but also internationally revitalized their need to work closely with important customers. The familiar **80/20 principle** states that 80 percent of sales often come from 20 percent of a company's customers. Organizations now realize the need to identify their most important customers and designate them for their partnering programs. The organization's best salespeople are assigned to sell and service these customers.

BUILDING RELATIONSHIPS THROUGH THE SALES PROCESS

Much of your course will revolve around the sales process. The **sales process** refers to a sequence of actions by the salesperson that leads toward the customer taking a desired action and ends with a follow-up to ensure purchase satisfaction. This desired action by a prospect is usually buying, which is the most important action. Such desired actions also can include advertising, displaying, or reducing the price of the product.

In the course of a normal workweek, many salespeople have to play the role of detective, researcher, listener, educator, entertainer, persuader, negotiator, and supporter. The many activities that make up a salesperson's day or week may appear haphazard to the casual observer, but they are actually part of a step-by-step process.

The sales process is a logical series of 10 steps that increase the chances of not only making a sale but also creating a customer. These steps are listed in Exhibit 1–11 and are discussed in detail in the following chapters.

Selling Is for Large and Small Organizations

Many textbook examples are from big business, typically because readers recognize the Ford Motor Company or McDonald's. Even though Canada's large organizations are easily recognizable and extremely important to our prosperity, it is easy to overestimate the importance of big business because of its greater visibility. Small businesses seem dwarfed by corporate giants. Yet small firms, even though less conspicuous, are a vital component of our economy.

Small business contributes significantly to our economy. The Canadian Federation of Independent Business represents approximately 100,000 small and medium-sized

---

EXHIBIT 1–11

Ten important steps in the customer relationship selling process.

1. *Prospecting.* Locating and qualifying prospects
2. *Preapproach.* Obtaining interview; determining sales call objective; developing customer profile, customer benefit program, and sales presentation strategies
3. *Approach.* Meeting prospect and beginning customized sales presentation
4. *Presentation.* Further uncovering needs; relating product benefits to needs using demonstration, dramatization, visuals, and evidence statements
5. *Trial close.* Asking prospects' opinions during and after presentation
6. *Objections.* Uncovering objections
7. *Meet objections.* Satisfactorily answering objections
8. *Trial close.* Asking prospect's opinion after overcoming each objection and immediately before the close
9. *Close.* Bringing prospect to the logical conclusion to buy
10. *Follow-up and service.* Serving customer after the sale.

enterprises (SMEs) across Canada. Recent statistics indicate that this sector is creating the majority of job growth in Canada. Fifty-eight percent of all Canadian employment is contributed by small and medium-sized businesses (companies with fewer than 500 employees). Further, 36 percent of Canadian employment is contributed by small business (fewer than 50 employees) and this sector has shown the most employment growth in our economy.

Small enterprises run the gamut from a corner news vender to a developer of optical fibres. Small-business owners sell gasoline, flowers, and coffee. They publish magazines, haul freight, teach languages, and program computers. They make wines, motion pictures, and high-fashion clothes. They build new homes and restore old ones. They repair plumbing, fix appliances, recycle metals, and sell used cars. They drive taxicabs, run cranes, and fly helicopters. They drill for oil, quarry sand and gravel, and mine exotic ores. They forge, cast, weld, photoengrave, electroplate, and anodize. They also invent antipollution devices, quality control mechanisms, energy-saving techniques, microelectronic systems—the list goes on.

Often, small-business entrepreneurs cannot compete head to head with giant firms. However, most large firms started small and then prospered by using many of the concepts, ideas, and practices discussed in this textbook. Due to this fact, we use many small-business examples.

SUMMARY OF MAJOR SELLING ISSUES

Personal selling is an old and honourable profession. It has helped improve much of the world's standard of living and provided benefits to individual buyers through the purchase of products. Millions of people have chosen a sales career because of the availability of sales jobs, the personal freedom sales provides, its challenge, the multitude of opportunities for success, and its nonfinancial and financial rewards.

A person can become a successful salesperson through company and personal training and by developing skills and abilities that benefit customers. Also important are a belief in the product or service being sold, working hard, wanting to succeed, and maintaining a positive outlook toward both selling and oneself. In addition, a

ETHICAL DILEMMA

I Probably Won't See Her Again Anyway

As you are making your presentation to Julie, you realize that her company is moving in a direction that will likely mean that she will be unlikely to buy your product in the future. Her company is moving to a different manufacturing method that will require her to buy smaller, more efficient machinery than what you currently offer. Your company is considering moving in that direction but no decision has been made yet.

Being that she is new in her position, you know that you could convince her to give you the order but you also know that she will have to replace your equipment prematurely to be consistent with her company's strategy. At this point, you doubt that you'll be calling on her much in the future so you are thinking. "Do I just get the order and get out—after all, I do have a family to feed," or do you just bow out and leave without the order?

How do you handle this situation based on what you've learned in this chapter?

successful salesperson should be knowledgeable, able to plan, and able to use selling time wisely. En route to success, salespeople develop a range of skills through study and practice, enhancing their ability to think strategically, relate to others, and understand the technical aspects of their business.

The remainder of this book expands on these topics to provide you with the background either to improve your present selling ability or to help you decide whether a sales career is right for you.

MEETING A CAREER CHALLENGE

In reviewing the example at the start of the chapter, let's compare your advice with Chin Lee's career decision.

Without any formal training in sales and after a very shaky start as a computer technician, Chin was given a transfer to the sales department.

After making the transfer, he said, "I quickly learned that training is essential for success—especially in sales. In retrospect, I wish I had had the opportunity to take a sales course as part of my computer technology studies."

Chin has become one of the top salespeople at his company. His advice: "If you don't have it, get training. Your confidence increases, and when it does, your performance improves. Moving into a sales career is the best move I have made. I highly recommend a career in sales."

PLAYING THE ROLE

Role A: Recently hired salesperson of Canadian Paper Supply, a mid-size paper supply company located in the middle of a major metropolitan city in Alberta. You are unhappy with your job. You are stressed out as you had expected that you would be making a lot more money after three months on the job so you are meeting with your sales manager. Aside from the money and stress, think of three other work-related factors that may be causing your unhappiness and stress. Be prepared to discuss these at your meeting.

Role B: Sales manager of the company in the situation above. You are preparing to meet with a disgruntled employee who was hired just three months ago. You understand that she has some concerns regarding her job. Be prepared to handle any concerns that she may have. Can you motivate her to improve her performance? Should you just ask for her resignation?

Prepare your role for an in-class dramatization of this meeting between salesperson and sales manager.

KEY TERMS FOR SELLING

80/20 principle, 22
career path, 9
CPSA, 14
empathy, 15
financial rewards, 10
incentive, 11
nonfinancial rewards, 10
order getters, 8

order takers, 8
partnering, 22
personal selling, 3
relationship marketing, 20
relationship selling, 16
sales process, 22
territory manager, 18
transactional selling, 21

SALES APPLICATION QUESTIONS

1. The term *salesperson* refers to many types of sales jobs. What are the major types of sales jobs available?
2. *a.* If you were the sales manager for a fast-growing mobile phone company and were asked by your boss to hire 15 new salespeople as soon as possible, what would you look for on applicants' resumés to help you develop a short list of those you would like to interview?
   b. What type of compensation and incentive plan would you offer new recruits?
3. People choose a particular career for many reasons. What are some reasons someone might give for choosing a sales career?
4. "A career in sales is a career in dishonesty and crookedness." Formulate a constructive argument against this position, citing information from the chapter.
5. Those new to a sales job often experience some feelings of anxiety and fear. What advice would you give to a sales rookie to help him or her develop a confident attitude?

SALES WORLD WIDE WEB EXERCISE

Find Out about a Career in Sales!

Looking for a job? Would you consider a sales job? Want to find out more about a sales career? Here are some examples of useful Web sites.

www.marskell.com

www.canada-careers.com

http://careerbeacon.com

www.careerbuilder.com

www.careers.org

www.pharmaceutical-sales.com

www.shsinc.com

www.monster.ca

www.hrsdc.gc.ca

www.cpsa.com

www.salesexcellence.com

working.canada.com

www.workopolis.com

In addition, look at your school's home page. Many schools refer you to career opportunities. Also go to the Web site of a specific company. Many companies have hyperlinks from their home page to their job openings.

FURTHER EXPLORING THE SALES WORLD

1. Interview one or more salespeople and write a brief report on what they like and dislike about their jobs, why they chose a sales career, what activities they perform, and what they believe it takes to succeed at selling their products.

2. Contact your school's placement office and report on what staff there believe firms recruiting people for sales positions look for in applicants.

3. Visit the Canadian Professional Sales Association Web site (http://cpsa.com). Describe the steps that one would need to take to become certified; that is, to receive the CSP designation.

SELLING EXPERIENTIAL EXERCISE

Are You a Global Traveller?

Our global environment requires that Canadian sales personnel learn to deal effectively with people in other countries. The assumption that foreign business leaders behave and negotiate in the same manner as Canadians is false. How well prepared are you to live with globalization? Consider the following items, writing the numbers reflecting your views on another sheet of paper.

Are you guilty of	Definitely No				Definitely Yes
1. Being impatient? Do you think "Time is money" or "Let's get straight to the point"?	1	2	3	4	5
2. Having a short attention span or bad listening habits, or being uncomfortable with silence?	1	2	3	4	5
3. Being somewhat argumentative, sometimes to the point of belligerence?	1	2	3	4	5
4. Being ignorant about the world beyond your borders?	1	2	3	4	5
5. Having a weakness in foreign languages?	1	2	3	4	5
6. Placing emphasis on short-term success?	1	2	3	4	5
7. Believing that advance preparations are less important than negotiations themselves?	1	2	3	4	5
8. Being legalistic and believing a deal is a deal, regardless of changing circumstances?	1	2	3	4	5
9. Having little interest in seminars on the subject of globalization, failing to browse through international topics in libraries or magazines, or not interacting with foreign students or employees?	1	2	3	4	5

Total Score _____

Total your score. If you scored less than 27, congratulations. You have the temperament and interest to do well in a global company. If you scored more than 27, it's time to consider a change. Regardless of your score, go back over each item and make a plan of action to correct deficiencies indicated by answers of 4 or 5 to any question.[2]

CASE 1–1

Is a Career in Sales Right for You?

Janice Jones graduated from a Canadian community college with a diploma in Marketing Management. At 22, she was an engaging person, an active community volunteer, and heavily involved in extracurricular activities at her college. She played on the varsity basketball team and served in a leadership capacity on her school's student government. While doing this, she maintained high enough grades to remain on the Dean's Honour list throughout her college career. Janice always loved selling. She excelled at it in any of her part-time retail jobs and loved meeting people. She was a true "people person." Janice's short-term goal upon graduation was to make a lot of money so she could settle down and be comfortable before she was 30 years old.

CASE 1–1

Ishmar Patel was a recruiter for the Canadian division of a major business machine manufacturer. The company expansion plans created a need for 10 new salespeople so Ishmar was on the recruiting trail at colleges and universities across Canada. When he arrived on campus, he was given a pile of resumés to review in hopes of finding a few candidates to whom he would offer an interview. After a day of reviewing there were a few that caught his eye but in particular, he liked the resumé of Janice Jones. To him, she seemed to have all of the qualities that often lead to success in sales, so he offered her an interview.

During the interview, Janice was outstanding. She presented herself well and was confident in her abilities. Ishmar informed Janice of the responsibilities of the job and the tremendous earnings potential. In fact, he informed her that some of the current salespeople were earning in excess of $200,000 per year. Janice's eyes lit up as she visualized herself being able to reach her short-term financial goals. Ishmar was so impressed by her interview that he offered her the job and, not known to shy away from challenges, Janice accepted.

Janice immediately purchased a new car and a new wardrobe as her new position would require her to have reliable transportation and always appear professional. She was proud of her new position but over the course of the first few months, she felt overwhelmed. She had a tough time getting appointments and was beginning to take the rejection personally. Her stress levels were increasing each week. She found that even after getting appointments with prospective buyers, only half were actually giving her the order.

If she kept up her current level of sales, she determined that she would earn approximately $60,000 in her first year of sales. She was disappointed with this. After hearing in the interview that many of her colleagues were earning six-figure salaries, she thought that she could easily reach these figures, if not exceed them. After all, she had always succeeded in anything she put her mind to.

Near the end of the third business quarter, Janice had a particularly poor week of sales. Combined with the fact that she had just received notice of a rent increase, she wondered if she was in the wrong line of work. Janice set up a meeting with her sales manager for the following Monday morning. She spent the weekend depressed about the meeting; she was contemplating quitting her job and moving on to something different. She hated thinking this way as she had always enjoyed selling and planned a career in it.

1. How should Janice's sales manager handle the meeting?
2. Should Janice consider switching careers? Why or why not?
3. What qualities did Janice have that would make her an attractive sales recruit?
4. Were Janice's expectations too high as she entered a sales career?
5. What can professors do to better prepare students for a sales career?

2

ETHICS FIRST . . . THEN CUSTOMER RELATIONSHIPS

LEARNING OBJECTIVES

This chapter is one of the most important in this text. Social, ethical, and legal issues for sales professionals are often personal and technical in nature, yet they are essential for understanding how to be an outstanding professional. After studying this chapter, you should be able to:

- Understand the principles set forth in the CPSA Code of Ethics.

- Describe management's social responsibilities.

- Understand how to demonstrate social responsibility.

- Explain what influences ethical behaviour.

- Describe management's role in addressing ethical responsibilities.

- Discuss ethical dealings among salespeople, employers, and customers.

IS ETHICAL BEHAVIOUR IMPORTANT?

In relationship selling, a great deal of value is placed on developing long-term relationships with customers. This leads to more sales, more profits, and satisfaction of stakeholder needs.

Salespeople and companies practising poor ethical behaviour will find it difficult to maintain long-term relationships with their customers. Today's customers expect and demand more from their suppliers. A salesperson's "shady" reputation will make it difficult to survive in today's business world.

Sales personnel constantly are involved with social, ethical, and legal issues. Actually, everyone is—including you. If you found a bag full of $100 bills lying on the side of the road, would you keep it? Would you ever say you were sick to get extra time off work? Would you use the company car to run a personal errand? Have you ever broken the speed limit? Have you ever gone home with one of your employer's pens in your pocket?

Newspapers, radio, and television frequently have news stories of individuals and organizations involved in both good and bad practices. This chapter addresses many of the important social, ethical, and legal issues in selling. It begins by discussing

SELLING TIPS

The Canadian Professional Sales Association's Code of Ethics*

The CPSA Sales Institute Code of Ethics is the set of principles and standards that a certified sales professional will strive to adhere to with customers, organizations, competitors, communities, and colleagues.

The Certified Sales Professional pledges and commits to uphold these standards in all activities.

I will:

1. Maintain honesty and integrity in all relationships with customers, prospective customers, and colleagues and continually work to earn their trust and respect.
2. Accurately represent my products or services to the best of my ability in a manner that places my customer or prospective customer and my company in a position that benefits both.
3. Respect and protect the proprietary and confidential information entrusted to me by my company and my customers and not engage in activities that may conflict with the best interest of my customers or my company.
4. Continually upgrade my knowledge of my products/services, skills and my industry.
5. Use the time and resources available to me only for legitimate business purposes. I will only participate in

activities that are ethical and legal, and when in doubt, I will seek counsel.
6. Respect my competitors and their products and services by representing them in a manner which is honest, truthful and based on accurate information that has been substantiated.
7. Endeavour to engage in business and selling practices which contribute to a positive relationship with the community.
8. Assist and counsel my fellow sales professionals where possible in the performance of their duties.
9. Abide by and encourage others to adhere to this Code of Ethics.

As a certified sales professional, I understand that the reputation and professionalism of all salespeople depends on me as well as others engaged in the sales profession, and I will adhere to these standards to strengthen the reputation and integrity for which we will strive. I understand that failure to consistently act according to this Code of Ethics may result in the loss of the privilege of using my professional sales designation.

*Reprinted with permission of the Canadian Professional Sales Association, 2008.

FACING A SALES CHALLENGE

As the sales manager of a printing company, you are about to invest in a car leasing program that involves 18 company cars for your sales staff. Together with your comptroller, you have examined several leasing programs. You have narrowed down your selection to two leasing companies that offer very similar terms. You are meeting with the president of Equilease, a company with which you have never done business before. You know from your own prospect files that one of your sales representatives has tried to call on the purchasing manager of Equilease before to get some of their printing business; however, he could not sell the account.

As you meet with the president for lunch, you gently steer the conversation in the direction of printing services. Since he is very knowledgeable about printing services and prices, you ask him about ballpark prices charged by his existing supplier. You believe you could provide his company with higher-quality service at a better price.

Since the president of Equilease is in a good mood, you think about setting up a win–win situation. You are considering making this offer: Let's make this a double win. I'll give you 100 percent of our leasing business if you'll consider giving us 50 percent of your printing business. Fair enough?

Is there an ethical conflict in this situation? Would it be ethical to propose such a deal? (Continued at end of chapter.)

management's social responsibilities. Then it examines ethical behaviour, then the ethical issues involved in dealing with salespeople, employers, and consumers. The chapter ends by presenting ways an organization can help its sales personnel follow ethical selling practices.

MANAGEMENT'S SOCIAL RESPONSIBILITIES

In one sense, the concept of corporate social responsibility is easy to understand; it means distinguishing right from wrong and doing right. It means being a good corporate citizen. **Social responsibility** is management's obligation to make choices and take actions that contribute to the welfare and interests of society as well as to those of the organization.

As straightforward as this definition seems, social responsibility can be a difficult concept to grasp, because different people have different opinions as to which actions improve society's welfare. To complicate matters, social responsibility covers a range of issues, many of which have ambiguous boundaries between right and wrong.

Organizational Stakeholders

To understand social responsibility, managers determine to whom they are responsible. Enlightened organizations view the internal and external environment as a variety of stakeholders.

A **stakeholder** is any individual or group within or outside the organization that has a stake in the organization's performance. Each stakeholder has a different interest in the organization.

Exhibit 2–1 illustrates eight important stakeholders. These are represented by the acronym **CCC GOMES**. The first *C* refers to customers and the last *S* refers to suppliers. Owners', creditors', and suppliers' interests are served by managerial efficiency—that is, the use of resources to achieve profits. Managers and salespeople expect work satisfaction, pay, and good supervision. Customers are concerned with decisions about the quality and availability of goods and services.

EXHIBIT 2–1

Major stakeholders in the
organization's performance.

Other important stakeholders are the government and the community. Most corporations exist under the proper charter and licences, and operate within the limits of the laws and regulations imposed by the government, including safety laws and environmental protection requirements. The community includes local government, the natural and physical environments, and the quality of life provided for residents. Socially responsible organizations pay attention to all stakeholders.

An Organization's Main Responsibilities

Once a company is aware of its stakeholders, it has four main types of responsibilities: (1) economic, (2) legal, (3) ethical, and (4) discretionary. See Exhibit 2–2.

Economic Responsibilities

The business institution is, above all, the basic economic unit of society. Its responsibility is to produce the goods and services that society wants and to maximize profits for its owners and shareholders.

EXHIBIT 2–2

An organization's main
responsibilities.

Often, corporations are said to operate solely to maximize profits. Certainly, profits are important to a firm, just as an academic average is important to a student. Profit provides the capital to stay in business, expand, and compensate for the risks of conducting business. There is a responsibility to make a profit to serve society. Imagine what would happen to our society if large corporations (e. g., McCain Foods, Southam Newspapers, Telus Mobility) did not make a profit and went out of business. Thousands of people and the Canadian economy would be affected.

Legal Responsibilities

All modern societies lay down ground rules, laws, and regulations that organizations are expected to follow. Legal requirements are imposed by municipal councils and provincial legislators, and define what society deems important with respect to appropriate corporate behaviour. Organizations are expected to fulfill their economic goals within the legal framework.

In North America, recent highly publicized examples of abuse of ethical sales practices include some U. S.–based life insurance companies "churning" in the mid-1990 s. Churning is the illegal creation of new life insurance policies paid with the proceeds of old policies but without the authorization of the customer.

Even the Pension and Institutional Investment unit (RT Capital Management Inc.) of one of Canada's largest banks, was accused of trading irregularities. The result was heavy fines; a letter of apology from John Cleghorn, CEO of the parent company, Royal Bank of Canada; and the loss of customers.

Ethical Responsibilities

Ethical responsibility includes behaviours that are not necessarily codified into law and may not serve the corporation's direct economic interests. To be ethical, organizational decision makers should act with equity, fairness, and impartiality; respect the rights of individuals; and provide different treatment of individuals only when relevant to the organization's goals and tasks. Unethical behaviour occurs when decisions enable an individual or company to gain at the expense of society.

Discretionary Responsibilities

Discretionary responsibility is purely voluntary and guided by a company's desire to make social contributions not mandated by economics, law, or ethics. Discretionary activities include generous philanthropic contributions that offer no monetary return to the company and are not expected. We know of companies that have needed to reduce the size of their sales forces because of difficult economic circumstances. Instead of firing people, they stopped hiring, offered early retirements, and let normal turnover decrease sales force size. In addition, in situations where there has been an acquisition of a company, contractual obligations have been placed on the buyer by the seller to give first right of refusal in hiring the selling company's staff, who might otherwise be forgotten in the acquisition process.

Discretionary responsibility is the highest criterion of social responsibility, because it goes beyond societal expectations to contribute to the community's welfare. For example, Baxter International, a manufacturer and marketer of medical products, is using its environmental knowledge to help its customers set up pollution-reduction and recycling programs. Baxter has even set up an alliance with Waste Management to better assist customers in handling environmental problems. Baxter also has studied its own products and packaging to find ways to reduce waste. By reducing the waste created by its products, Baxter reduces the environmental problems of its customers.[1]

How to Demonstrate Social Responsibility

A corporation can demonstrate social responsibility in numerous ways. Actions that can be taken by all organizations include

1. Taking corrective action before it is required

2. Working with affected constituents to resolve mutual problems

3. Working to establish industry-wide standards and self-regulation

4. Publicly admitting mistakes

5. Getting involved in appropriate social programs

6. Helping to correct environmental problems

7. Monitoring the changing social environment

8. Establishing and enforcing a corporate code of conduct

9. Taking needed public stands on social issues.

10. Striving to make profits on an ongoing basis.

Companies that do not maintain ethical standards face tangible costs. Throughout the 1990s, the insurance industry in North America experienced major public relations setbacks and regulatory-body scrutiny, including court convictions and fines, as a result of unethical practices. For example, Metropolitan Life's revenue from new business plummeted 52.5 percent when the company was the subject of negative publicity concerning deceptive sales practices and churning.[2]

Some corporations, however, are using their positions to benefit society. For example, Procter & Gamble has assisted community projects by supplying expertise in areas such as marketing and training.[3] Actions such as these help to improve a company's image in the community and demonstrate its responsibility to society.

WHAT INFLUENCES ETHICAL BEHAVIOUR?

Organizations are composed of individuals. These individuals' morals and ethical values help shape those of the organization. Critical to making decisions in an ethical manner is the individual integrity of the organization's managers, especially those in top management positions. Thus, two major influences on the ethical behaviour of sales personnel are employees and the organization itself.

The Individual's Role

Everyone, employees and managers alike, brings certain ethical values to a job. Personality, family upbringing, personal experiences, religious background, and the particular situation all guide people in making decisions. Individuals usually can be placed into one of the following levels of moral development:

- **Level One: Preconventional.** At the **preconventional moral development level**, an individual acts in her own best interest and thus follows rules to avoid punishment or receive rewards. This individual would break moral and legal laws.

- **Level Two: Conventional.** At the **conventional moral development level**, an individual conforms to the expectations of others, such as family, friends, employer, boss, and society, and upholds moral and legal laws.

■ **Level Three: Principled.** At the **principled moral development level**, an individual lives by an internal set of morals, values, and ethics. These are upheld regardless of punishments or majority opinion. The individual would disobey orders, laws, and consequences to follow what he believes is right.

The majority of sales personnel, as well as people in general, operate at the conventional level. However, a few individuals are at level one, and it is estimated that fewer than 20 percent of individuals reach level three.

With his book *The Seven Habits of Highly Effective People,* Stephen Covey increased the level of awareness of ethics in general, and in corporations in particular. His research indicated that many effective businesspeople and organizations are principle-centred and have the ability to imbue employees with the tools necessary to function effectively in an ethical fashion, despite a perceived overall decline in North American business ethics.[4]

The Organization's Role

If the vast majority of people in our society are at the preconventional or conventional levels, it seems that most employees in an organization would feel they must "go along to get along"; in other words, they go along to keep their jobs. At most, they follow only formal policies and procedures.

However, how will sales personnel handle ethical dilemmas? What if there are no policies and procedures pertaining to some sales practices and a person is directed to do something by a superior that appears unethical? It is no wonder that media reports frequently feature unethical business practices; following the hear-no-evil, see-no-evil, speak-no-evil philosophy can simply reinforce a preconventional or conventional organizational climate.

MANAGEMENT'S ETHICAL RESPONSIBILITIES

The concept of ethics, like social responsibility, is easy to understand. However, ethics is difficult to define in a precise way. In a general sense, **ethics** is the code of moral principles and values that governs the behaviours of a person or a group with respect to what is right or wrong. Ethics sets standards as to what is good or bad in conduct and decision making.[5]

Unethical sales practices aren't new. The words *caveat emptor* (buyer beware) appeared on buildings in ancient Rome. Today, however, it is the sensational cases and lawsuits that heighten the public's perception of dishonesty.

The Conference Board of Canada, within its Canadian Centre for Business in the Community, addresses the issue of business ethics and acts as a resource to Canadian industry in advancing ethics policies and practices as integral parts of a company's corporate culture.

In recent research findings, the following notable information surfaced:

1. Forty-eight percent of employees in one survey had engaged in one or more unethical or illegal acts in the past year.

2. An Angus Reid poll determined that 79 percent of consumers always try to buy from companies they believe to be good corporate citizens.

3. Twenty-six percent of investors believe that social responsibility is an extremely important part of their investment decisions.

Many companies and their sales personnel get into trouble by assuming that if it's not illegal, it must be ethical. Ethics are powerful forces for good that can regulate behaviours both inside and outside the sales force. As principles of ethics and social responsibility become more widely recognized, companies can use codes of ethics and their corporate cultures to govern behaviour, thereby eliminating the need for additional laws governing right and wrong and regaining the trust of the public.

What Is an Ethical Dilemma?

Because ethical standards are not codified, disagreements and dilemmas about "proper" behaviour often occur. An ethical dilemma arises in a situation when each alternative choice or behaviour has undesirable elements due to potentially negative ethical or personal consequences. In ethical dilemmas, right or wrong cannot be clearly identified. Consider the following examples:

- Your boss says he cannot give you a raise this year because of budget constraints, but because of your good work this past year, he will look the other way if your expense accounts come in a little high.
- You are stationed at the corporate headquarters in Toronto and have 14 salespeople in countries all over the world. A rep living in another country calls to get approval to pay a government official $10,000 to okay an equipment purchase of $5 million. Such payoffs are part of common business practice in that part of the world.
- Your good friend, an industrial engineer, tells you three of your competitors have submitted price bids on his company's proposed new construction project. He suggests a price you should submit and mentions certain construction specifications his boss is looking for on this job.

Now let's turn to the three main ethical areas most frequently faced by sales personnel. These involve

1. Salespeople

2. Employers

3. Customers.

The URL www.the-cma.org/?WCE=C=47|K=225849 takes you to the Code of Ethics of the Canadian Marketing Association. Refer to this page as you read the following material pertaining to different types of ethical situations. Also refer to the Canadian Professional Sales Association's Code of Ethics at the beginning of this chapter to help guide your decisions.

ETHICS IN DEALING WITH SALESPEOPLE

Sales managers have both social and ethical responsibilities to sales personnel. Salespeople are a valuable resource; they are recruited, carefully trained, and given important responsibility. They represent a large financial investment and must be treated in a professional manner. Yet, occasionally, a company may place managers or salespeople in positions that force them to choose among compromising their ethics, not doing what is required, or leaving the organization. The decision depends on the magnitude of the situation. At times, situations arise in which it is difficult to say whether a sales practice is ethical or unethical. Sales managers face five ethical considerations: (1) the level of sales pressure to place on a salesperson, (2) decisions concerning a salesperson's territory, (3) whether to be honest with the salesperson, (4) what to do with the ill salesperson, and (5) employee rights.

Level of Sales Pressure

What is an acceptable level of pressure to place on salespeople? Should managers establish performance goals that they know a salesperson has only a 50–50 chance of attaining? Should the manager acknowledge that goals were set too high? If circumstances change in the salesperson's territory—for example, a large customer goes out of business—should the manager lower sales goals?

These are questions all managers must consider. There are no right or wrong answers. Managers are responsible for group goals, so there is a natural tendency to pressure salespeople to reach the manager's goals. Some managers motivate their people to produce at high levels without applying pressure while others place tremendous pressure on salespeople to attain sales beyond quotas. However, managers should set realistic and obtainable goals. They must consider individual territory situations. If this is done fairly and sales are still down, then pressure may be applied.

Decisions Affecting Territory

Management makes decisions that affect sales territories and salespeople. For example, the company might increase the number of sales territories, which often necessitates splitting a single territory. A salesperson may have spent years building the territory to its current sales volume only to have customers taken away. If the salesperson has worked on commission, this would mean a decrease in earnings.

Consider a situation of reducing the number of sales territories. What procedures would you use? Several years ago, a large manufacturer of health and beauty aids (shaving cream, toothpaste, shampoo) reduced the number of territories to lower selling costs. So, for example, three territories became two. Here is how one of the salespeople described it:

> I made my plane reservation to fly to our annual national meeting. Beforehand, I was told to bring my records up to date and bring them to the regional office in Calgary. I drove from Edmonton to Calgary with my bags packed to go to the national meeting. I walked into the office with my records under my arm. My district and regional managers were there. They told me of the reorganization and said I was fired. They asked for my car keys. I called my wife, told her what happened, and then caught a bus back home. There

were five of us in the region that were called in that day. Oh, they gave us a good job recommendation—it's just the way we were treated. Some people had been with the company for five years or more. They didn't eliminate jobs by tenure but by where territories were located.

Companies must deal with individuals in a fair and straightforward manner. It would have been better for the managers of these salespeople to go to their home-towns and explain the changes personally. Instead, they treated the salespeople unprofessionally.

One decision affecting a territory is what to do with extra-large customers, some-times called *key accounts*. Are they taken away from the salesperson and made into house accounts? Here, responsibility for contacting the accounts rests with someone from the home office (house) or a key-account salesperson. The local salesperson may not get credit for sales to this customer even though the customer is in the salesperson's territory. A salesperson states the problem:

> I've been with the company 35 years. When I first began, I called on some people who had one grocery store. Today, they have 208. The buyer knows me. He buys all of my regular and special greeting cards. They do whatever I ask. I made $22,000 in commissions from their sales last year. Now, management wants to make it a house account.

Here, the salesperson loses money. It is difficult to treat the salesperson fairly in this situation. The company does not want to pay large commissions, and 90 percent of the 208 stores are located out of the salesperson's territory. The manager should carefully explain this to the salesperson. Instead of taking the full $22,000 away from the salesperson, the company could pay a one-time bonus as a reward for building up the account.

To Tell the Truth?

Should salespeople be told they are not promotable, that they are marginal performers, or that they are being transferred to the poorest territory in the company so that they will quit? Good judgment must prevail. Tell the truth. What happens when you fire a salesperson? If a fired employee has tried and has been honest, many sales managers will tell prospective employers that the person quit voluntarily rather than being fired. One manager put it this way: "I feel he can do a good job for another company. I don't want to hurt his future."

The Ill Salesperson

How much help do you give to an alcoholic, drug-addicted, or physically or mentally ill salesperson? Many companies require salespeople to seek professional help for substance abuse, and, if they improve, offer support and keep them in the field. Yet, there is only so far a company can go. The firm cannot have an salesperson under the influence of drugs or alcohol calling on customers. If the illness has a negative effect on business, the salesperson should be taken out of the territory.

These are difficult decisions, and many organizations are recognizing the extent to which many employees need career-saving help. Employee Assistance Programs (EAPs) or Employee Family Assistance Programs (EFAPs) have been commissioned to provide extraordinary help to employees. These organizations provide counselling and remedial support for employees. The organizations function autonomously and confidentially, with the support of the company's management, to help the organizations retain valuable employees who are experiencing short-term personal problems. Coupled with a sales manager who shows a sincere, personal interest in helping a salesperson in difficulty, these innovative programs greatly contribute to a person's chances of recovery.

Employee Rights

The sales manager must be up to date on ethical and legal considerations regarding employee rights and must develop strategies for the organization in addressing those rights. Here are several important questions that all managers should be able to answer:

- Under what conditions can an organization fire sales personnel without violating the law?
- What rights do and should sales personnel have regarding the privacy of their employment records and access to them?
- What can organizations do to prevent harassment of any type, and other forms of bias in the workplace?

Employee rights are rights desired by employees regarding their job security and the treatment administered by their employers while on the job, irrespective of whether those rights are currently protected by law or collective bargaining agreements of labour unions. Let's briefly examine two employee-rights questions.

Privacy

Canadians may be surprised to discover that we have no specific constitutional right to privacy. We do have some protection against unreasonable privacy invasions through the Canadian *Charter of Rights and Freedoms.* However, the *Charter* does not regulate the practices of private enterprise directly. This situation applies not only to what we would consider confidential information but also to a company's data.[6]

One area of privacy that has been the subject of scrutiny and legal action is the broad area of customer lists. A general rule has been established that an organization's private information is the property of the organization and cannot be used in another enterprise without permission of the originating company. This concept has been legally tested on a number of occasions in Canada, especially in instances where a customer list has been taken from one company to another by an exiting employee and used to compete against the former company. Although courts have been precise about

EXHIBIT 2–4

Canadian human rights legislation protects workers from discriminatory hiring practices.

the theft of "physical information," they have been reluctant to apply judicial restraints on information that could reasonably be accumulated in the normal course of performing a job and applied in another organization (even a competitive one). This issue not only relates to the broader issue of business ethics but also provides a hint of the complexity of the subject from the employee's perspective and that of management.

Discrimination in Employment

Canada's human rights legislation prohibits the denial of employment for a broad range of characteristics. These include but are not limited to

- Race or colour
- Religion
- Physical or mental disability
- Age
- Sex
- Marital status
- Family status
- Sexual orientation
- Language.

The definition of discrimination has been extended to encompass the topic of sexual harassment. Although the assumption is usually made that this is strictly an issue that arises from traditional superior/subordinate relationships, harassment could arise between a salesperson and a customer. What would you do if harassed by a customer? What would you do if you were the manager of the person who was being harassed? The intent of the legislation targeted at reducing harassment in the workplace is simple—a harassment-free workplace—however, as we will see, the complexity of the subject is a significant management challenge.

What exactly is harassment? The Human Rights Commission defines it in an unequivocal way: "Harassment is any unwanted physical or verbal conduct that offends or humiliates you. Such conduct can interfere with your abilities to do a job or obtain a service."[7]

The Commission goes on to identify the forms that harassment can take, namely "threats, intimidation, or verbal abuse; unwelcome remarks or jokes about subjects like your race, religion or age, displaying sexist, racist, or other offensive pictures or posters . . ."

An act can be deemed harassment not only in a superior/subordinate relationship: "the harasser could be the same or opposite sex, may be a supervisor, co-worker or someone providing you with a service such as a bank officer or a clerk in a government department."[8]

Employers are responsible for preventing racial and sexual discrimination and harassment within their companies and in their relationships with customers and suppliers. Organizations should recognize and value the diversity of Canada's workforce, and work to encourage all employees to respect others.

The attitude of any organization to these complex social issues begins at the top. Effective employee training can establish the required level of expectations for compliance within the organization. Specific training in the areas of objective performance appraisal and compensation policies will ensure a level of compliance. Going a step further, comprehensive inclusion and communication of all human rights and harassment legislation to company employees in company policy manuals, employee handbooks, and information sessions will indicate the company's level of commitment to the process and to its employees. Finally, monitoring and verifying compliance and taking appropriate immediate remedial action for noncompliance will complete the management process.

Is there a benefit for organizations that embrace these important concepts? Acknowledging and recognizing the necessity of employee rights in any organization will lead to

- A high-quality work environment
- More effective selection and recruitment of new hires; the company will be seen as a good place to work and will attract better-quality people
- Reduced risk of the significant financial penalties associated with noncompliance of the law, but more importantly, reduced risk of negative publicity that could have a negative long-term impact on business
- A match between employer and employee rights, expectations, and obligations.

Both organizations and employees benefit from anti-discrimination measures. Organizations benefit from reduced legal costs, since not observing employee rights is illegal, and their image as a good employer increases, resulting in enhanced organizational attractiveness. This makes it easier for the organization to recruit a pool of qualified applicants. And, although critics suggest that expanded employee rights, especially job security, may reduce management flexibility and profitability, expanded employee rights may be an impetus for better planning, resulting in increased profitability.

Increased profitability also may result from the benefits employees receive when their rights are observed: employees may experience feelings of being treated fairly and respectfully, increased self-esteem, and a heightened sense of job security. Employees who have job security may be more productive and committed to the organization than those who do not. As employees begin to see the guarantees of job security as a benefit, organizations also gain through reduced wage-increase demands and greater flexibility in job assignments.

SALESPEOPLE'S ETHICS IN DEALING WITH THEIR EMPLOYERS

Salespeople, as well as sales managers, may occasionally misuse company assets, moonlight, or cheat. Such unethical practices can affect co-workers and need to be prevented before they occur.[9]

Misusing Company Assets

Company assets most often misused are automobiles, expense accounts, samples, and damaged-merchandise credits. All can be used for personal gain, or as bribes and kickbacks to customers. For example, a credit for damaged merchandise can be given to a customer when there has been no damage, or valuable product samples can be given to a customer.

Moonlighting

Salespeople are not closely supervised and, consequently, they may be tempted to take a second job—perhaps on company time. Some salespeople attend university or college on company time. For example, a salesperson may enroll in an evening MBA program but take off in the early afternoon to prepare for class.

Cheating

A salesperson may not play fair in contests. If a contest starts in July, the salesperson may not turn in sales orders for the end of June and lump them with July sales.

This salesperson can easily download company data and take them with him to his next employer.

A salesperson might arrange, with or without the customer's permission, to ship merchandise that is not needed or wanted. The merchandise is held until payment is due and then returned to the company after the contest is over. The salesperson also may overload the customer to win the contest.

Affecting other Salespeople

Often, the unethical practices of one salesperson affect other salespeople within the company. Someone who cheats in winning a contest is taking money and prizes from other salespeople. A salesperson also may not split commissions with coworkers or may take customers from co-workers.

Technology Theft

A salesperson or sales manager may quit, or be fired, and take the organization's customer records to use for his or a future employer's benefit. (See Exhibit 2–5.) How is that possible? Well, it's getting easier to do these days because more and more companies provide their sales personnel with computers, software, and data on their customers.

ETHICS IN DEALING WITH CUSTOMERS

Many ethical questions can arise in the activities of professional salespeople. Companies should develop and implement business conduct guidelines to ensure that their sales personnel will avoid being implicated in an unethical or illegal activity.

This salesperson must be careful about the claims made in the sales presentation. If he says, "This equipment will increase production 2 percent," and it doesn't, the sales person and his company may find themselves in court.

Self-Regulation   For many years, companies that sold direct to consumers had a poor reputation. Salespeople were described as pushy, and in some cases used unethical sales practices. Concerned with their future relationships with customers, many professional associations across Canada, such as the Investment Dealers Association of Canada and the Direct Sellers Association, began to practise self-regulation; they created a set of guiding principles that members must abide by to retain their membership. Self-regulation provides salespeople with many professional opportunities as well as intangible benefits. These self-regulating associations allow for

- Professional credibility and increased profile
- Quality standards and accountability
- Increased public trust and confidence
- Ways and means (enforcement of guidelines to prevent unskilled practice or unprofessional conduct)
- Documented proof of membership and practice
- The ability for consumers to make more informed decisions
- Recognition of specialized expertise
- Disciplinary action by peers as opposed to people outside the organization.

A good example of a self-regulatory association is the Direct Sellers Association of Canada. On its Web site, the organization lists its basic principles as follows:

All active DSA members shall conform to the principles of fair competition as generally accepted in business, with particular regard to

- the terms of the offer and the methods and form of the contact with the consumer;
- the methods of presentation and demonstration of, and information about the product;
- the fulfillment of any obligation arising from the offer or any operation connected with it, including delivery.[10]

This Code reflects the pledge of all active DSA members to carry out their activities in conformity with the laws of Canada, its provinces and territories. This Code is a measure of self-regulation by the Direct Sellers Association. It is not a law, and its obligations may require a level of ethical behaviour which exceeds existing legal requirements. Non-observance does not create any civil responsibility. With termination of its membership in the DSA, a company is no longer bound by the Code, the provisions of which remain applicable to events or transactions occurring during the time a company was a member of the DSA.

All active DSA members believe that their business dealings should be carried out at a level well above the minimum required by law and that integrity and customer satisfaction are their two most valued objectives.

Active DSA members shall voluntarily assume responsibility toward their consumer with respect to fair sales methods and product value, and shall make every effort to ensure consumer satisfaction.

All active DSA members recognize their responsibility to fully inform salespersons as to the characteristics of the products offered to enable them to give the consumer all necessary information.

In addition, the association has established some guiding principles specifically with respect to its association with consumers:

One of the major goals of the Direct Sellers Association of Canada is to protect consumers from unscrupulous and unfair business dealings. The DSA's strict Codes of Ethics and

SELLING GLOBALLY
International Gift Giving

Management of West Coast Technologies, a Canadian company, was excited about their upcoming trip to Asia and Europe to drum up business for their new computer networking hardware. They were going in with a management directive to "spend what it takes" to get the job done. Jane Johnson, the sales manager responsible for leading the sales team, felt that it was imperative that they get off on the right foot with each prospect. She thought that bringing gifts for them would certainly accomplish this. She had heard that gift giving in many societies can make the difference in cultivating long-lasting relationships.

Jane went on a shopping spree. Her shopping list included an expensive bottle of fine Canadian whiskey, a beautifully carved stainless steel knife, and a very expensive bottle of Niagara ice wine.

With gifts in hand, Jane and her team headed to China. Their meetings were going well. The Chinese were quite receptive to the sales team and their products, and said they'd make a decision by the end of the week. Near the end of their meeting, Jane presented the stainless steel knife to Sun Hwang, head of the Chinese delegation. Mr. Hwang looked a little bewildered. The sales team never heard back from Mr. Hwang and couldn't understand why.

Off they went to Pakistan. They landed in Islamabad, the nation's capital and were met by Raj Singh, the president of Pakistan Network Systems, one of the country's largest companies. Mr. Singh hosted his guests for dinner at his home the night before their business meetings. It was a relaxed dinner; Jane got along extremely well with her host and they shared information about each other freely. She found that Raj was a very educated man, extremely friendly, and a devout Muslim. Jane was very impressed by him and thought that they would be doing business soon. Near the end of their meeting the following day, Jane presented Mr. Singh with the bottle of fine Canadian whiskey. Raj opened the gift and smiled politely. The sales team ended up leaving Pakistan without a firm commitment.

Their next stop was France, where they had meetings lined up with one of the country's leading communications companies. Again, they were greeted by their French prospects and invited to a formal dinner reception in the executive dining room at the company headquarters in Paris. As the Canadian sales team arrived at the dinner, Jane made a point of presenting the host with the high-quality ice wine that she had brought. The host, Mr. Losier, appeared a little perplexed but graciously accepted the gift. Mr. Losier then instructed the servers to make sure the ice wine was served at the head table, rather than the wine that had been selected. Losier and the sales team never really hit it off together and, not surprisingly, no deals were signed.

Back at their hotel, Jane and her team were bewildered as to why they were not getting any business. They didn't want to return home empty-handed. Gabe, one of the salespeople, remembered a contact that he had made with a government official in Turkey and fortunately, he was able to contact him and request that he try to line up some contacts in his country on very short notice. The Turkish contact hinted to Gabe that he would expect a "token of appreciation" for his efforts upon their arrival. Gabe passed this message on to Jane. She wondered what she should do. After careful consideration, Jane decided that none of the gift giving so far had any benefit at all, so she decided that there would be no gift giving in this situation.

The team landed in Turkey and were met by the government official, who escorted them to their hotel for the evening. He mentioned that he had set up some key meetings over the next few days and they could expect a call to finalize the details. Gabe found his conversations with his contact that evening a little awkward—something seemed a little odd. The sales team never got their call.

What went wrong with the sales trip?

What would you suggest to Jane Johnson for future sales trips?

What are the ethical considerations of gift giving?

Business Practices must be adhered to by member companies and this commitment must be renewed yearly.

Under the Code's provisions, consumers may rest assured that salespeople representing DSA member companies will:

- Tell you who they are, why they're approaching you and what products they're selling
- Explain how to return a product or cancel an order

MAKING THE SALE

Is This Man Really Dying to Make a Sale?

He made his sales pitch over the phone, and he was good: There existed a little-known but tantalizing investment opportunity, and if I got into it early I could make an awesome profit.

Then I said, "Sounds good to me. I will buy several million shares." There was a gasp from the other end of the line. "How many?" he said. "Several million," I said, in my coolest manner. By now he was panting. And I felt guilty. He was just trying to make a living.

On the other hand, he was trying to gouge me out of my net worth. So I offered him a deal. "I will go for it if you will sign a paper." "What kind of paper?" he asked. "I would like you to sign a piece of paper saying that if this investment fails, you will kill yourself. Or, if you can't fulfill your end of it, I can terminate you."

He sounded stunned. "You expect me to kill myself?" "It seems reasonable to me," I said. "You are asking me to risk the food on my family's table, the roof over their heads. So it seems to me that if this is a foolproof investment, the least you can do is put your life on the line."

The man actually stuttered. You don't hear many stutterers these days. He said, "You have to be kidding." I told him, in a most grave tone: "No, I am not kidding. It seems reasonable to me that if this is a good deal and if I can't lose money on it, and if you are so kind as to offer this opportunity to a total stranger rather than to your friends and loved ones, the least you can do is stake your life on it."

There was a long pause on the other end. Then he said, "That's the most ridiculous thing I've ever heard." Now my feelings were hurt. Here was a man trying to persuade me to put my blood, meaning the rewards of my labours, into an investment, and he was quibbling over a petty deal.

"You won't agree to kill yourself?" I asked. "That is ridiculous," he said. "So is your pitch," I said. He hung up. I knew he wasn't sincere. Odds are that he didn't ask his grandmother to put her dough into that stock. So my advice to any potential investors is this: Ask them if they will leap off a bridge if you lose money. If they refuse, it isn't a good deal."*

*Author unknown.

- Respect your privacy by calling at times that best suit your convenience and wishes
- Respect your right to end a sales call.

When you make a purchase, you can count on DSA member companies to provide you with

- Accurate and truthful information on the price, quality, performance, quantity and availability of their products or services
- A written receipt in clear language
- Their own name and address and the name and address of the company represented
- A complete description of any warranty or guarantee, limited or full.

You can count on DSA member companies to

- Make sure all testimonials and endorsements are truthful, current and authorized by the person or organization quoted
- Base any product claims on substantiated facts.[11]

Bribes   Occasionally, a salesperson might attempt to **bribe** a buyer.[12] Money, gifts, entertainment, and travel opportunities may be offered. At times, there is a thin line between good business and misusing a bribe or gift. A $10 gift to a $10,000 customer may be merely a gift, but how do we define a $4,000 ski trip for buyers and their spouses?

Many companies forbid their buyers to take gifts of any size from salespeople. However, bribery does exist. It is estimated that bribes and kickbacks account for approximately 50 percent of white-collar crimes committed annually in North America.

MAKING THE SALE

Conflict of Interest?

The real estate salesperson assured the young couple that she would work hard to find them the right house. "Consider me your scout," she said. "I'll find you the best house for the least money."

The couple was reassured, and on the way home they talked about their good fortune. They had a salesperson working for them. With prices so high, it was nice to think they had professional help on their side.

The family selling the house felt the same way. They carefully chose the real estate salesperson because, with house prices all over the place these days, they hoped a good salesperson might win them several thousand dollars more. They had another reason to choose carefully: At today's prices, the 6 percent sales commission is a lot of money. "If we have to pay it," they reasoned, "we're better off paying it to the best salesperson."

How can both parties expect the best deal? How can a salesperson promise the seller the most for the money and then make the same promise to the buyer?

In the same vein, how can a salesperson whose commission rises or falls with the price of the house being sold be expected to cut into her income? Isn't her total allegiance to the person paying her?

Critics complain that regulators haven't made greater efforts to clarify matters to protect both buyers and sellers. Two explanations are sometimes offered. First, this is more a human than a legal problem; even if warned, buyers will continue to assume that salespeople work solely for them, rather than for the seller, who pays the salesperson a commission.

Second, a good salesperson sometimes can come close to serving the desires of both parties. The point is arguable, but the justification offered is that the salesperson's compromises may be necessary to save a sale from falling through.

A somewhat similar situation exists in the stock market, where many small investors view their stockbroker as a confidant and adviser.

Buyers may ask for cash, merchandise, or travel payments in return for placing an order with the salesperson. Imagine that you are a salesperson working on a 5 percent commission. The buyer says, "I'm ready to place a $20,000 order for office supplies with you. However, another salesperson has offered to pay my expenses for a weekend in Las Vegas in exchange for my business. You know $500 tax-free is a lot of money." You quickly calculate that your commission is $1,000. You'd still make $500. Would it be hard to pass up that $500?

Many large organizations, such as the Northern Alberta Institute of Technology's (NAIT's) purchasing department, publish internal policies to the public. NAIT's policies are available on the Institute's Web site and describe guidelines within which the purchasing function conducts its business. Sellers to this organization are expected to abide by the policies. Although much of the information focuses on procedural issues for internal users of the purchasing department, there is an ethical overtone in many of the policies that reflects the fact that the Institute is publicly funded, and appropriate procedures must be followed to ensure impartiality and stewardship when making buying decisions.

Misrepresentation   Today, even casual misstatements by salespeople can put a company on the wrong side of the law. Most salespeople are unaware that they assume legal obligations—with accompanying risks and responsibilities—every time they approach a customer. Nevertheless, we all know that salespeople sometimes oversell. They exaggerate the capabilities of their products or services and sometimes make false statements just to close a sale.

Often, buyers depend heavily on the technical knowledge and professional integrity of salespeople. Yet sales managers and staff find it difficult to know just how far they can go with well-intentioned sales talk, personal opinion, and promises. They may not realize that, by using certain statements, they can embroil their companies in a lawsuit and ruin the business relationship they are trying to establish.

When a customer relies on a salesperson's statements, purchases the product or service, and then finds that it fails to perform as promised, the supplier can be sued for **misrepresentation** and **breach of warranty**.

You can avoid such mistakes, however, if you're aware of the law of misrepresentation and breaches of warranty relative to the selling function, and if you follow strategies that keep you and your company out of trouble. Salespeople must understand the difference between sales puffery (opinions) and statements of fact—and the legal ramifications of each. There are preventive steps to follow; salespeople must work closely with management to avoid time-consuming manufacturing and delivery delays, and costly legal fees.

What the Law Says

The majority of transactions in which a Canadian sales representative participates fall within the scope of the *Sale of Goods Act*. This law separates goods from property and deals with the effect of fraud, misrepresentation, mistake, or other invalidating causes.

Misrepresentation is a complex legal concept since there is a provision in law that distinguishes between innocent misrepresentation and fraudulent misrepresentation.

Innocent misrepresentation is a misstatement unknown as such by the party making it. In general, a party misled by such statements is not entitled to sue for damages but may be in a position to void a contract.

Fraudulent misrepresentation is a misstatement that was known as such by the party making the statement. If this misrepresentation induced the making of a contract, and the buyer determined that the contract was deficient as a result of the misstatement, the contract could be voided or damages sought.

In addition, a buyer has remedies in law for transactions that fall within the *Sale of Goods Act*. For example, buyers can reject the goods in a transaction for the following reasons:

1. When the seller has been in breach of a condition of a sales contract

2. Where there has been a breach of warranty by the seller; for example,

   ■ Nondelivery of goods
   ■ Delayed delivery of goods.

Unfortunately, Canadian law books on this subject are filled with cases where the seller overpromised and underdelivered, resulting in financial damages and damage to the selling company's reputation.

The following is an illustration of how Canadian law would likely apply according to the Sales *of Goods Act:*

An independent sales rep sold heavy industrial equipment. He went to a purchaser's construction site, observed his operations, then told the company president that his proposed equipment would "keep up with any other machine then being used," and that it would "work well in cooperation with the customer's other machines and equipment."

The customer informed the rep that he was not personally knowledgeable about the kind of equipment the rep was selling, and that he needed time to study the rep's report. Several weeks later, he bought the equipment based on the rep's recommendations.

After a few months, he sued the rep's company, claiming that the equipment didn't perform according to the representations in sales literature sent prior to the execution of the contract and to statements made by the rep at the time of sale. The equipment manufacturer defended itself by arguing that the statements made by the rep were nonactionable opinions made innocently by the rep, in good faith, with no intent to deceive the purchaser.

The court would likely favour the customer, because the rep's statements were "predictions" of how the equipment would perform, making them more than mere sales talk. The rep would likely be held responsible for knowing the capabilities of the equipment he was selling, and his assertions would be deemed statements of fact, not opinions. Furthermore, it would likely be found that it was unfair that a knowledgeable salesperson would take advantage of a naive purchaser.[13]

Staying Legal

You don't have to be a lawyer to stay legal. If you are involved in selling long-term, high-cost, sophisticated products and services on a contractual basis, it is likely that one of your primary responsibilities will be to have the sales contracts prepared before closing a deal. This will involve direct involvement with your company's attorneys, who will ensure that these contracts are not only legal but also able to pass the scrutiny of the buyer's legal experts.

The following suggestions provide guidance in avoiding legal disputes:

- Understand the difference between statements of fact and statements of praise made during a sales presentation. If your company has been in business for some time and has a record of serving customers, it may be difficult to separate the two. Honesty is the best policy. If your company has a level of experience and expertise in the industry in which it competes, an honest presentation of the features, advantages, and benefits of your product or service, combined with your professionalism, will keep you out of trouble.

- Be accurate when describing a product's capabilities. Don't make speculative claims, particularly with respect to predictions concerning what a product will do. Here is an opportunity to enhance your sales presentation with the use of objective criteria. These are data about your product, and tests or surveys performed and made available by an outside resource such as an independent market research company or a testing laboratory.

- If your product is a technical product or has a technical component associated with it, you need to know the latest specifications of the product. Although your company usually prepares the official information that is available to customers, it never hurts to review and question any information that you are not comfortable with and that you are asked to accept as true.

- Certain laws vary by province and by municipality. Get acquainted with local laws.

- Don't offer opinions. In the heavy-equipment business involving bulldozers, earth movers, and power shovels, questions regarding capacity and durability factors needed to perform certain types of jobs will already be answered by success stories from current customers. In a new application, it is not unusual for the seller and the potential customer to test out certain equipment for particular applications where no past data exist.

Price Discrimination

Price discrimination is covered by the *Competition Act* and exists when the following conditions can be proven:

- A discount, rebate, allowance, price concession, or other advantage was granted to one customer and not to another.
- The customers are competitors.
- The price discrimination occurred in respect of articles of similar quality and quantity.
- The act of discrimination was part of a practice of discrimination.

An interesting aspect of price discrimination in Canada is that the buyer is seen as liable along with the seller in price discrimination cases. The law was structured intentionally to restrain large-volume buyers from demanding discriminatory pricing.

Tied Selling or Tie-in Sales

A firm engages in **tied selling** when it makes the purchase of one or more goods or services conditional on the purchase of others. This can be accomplished either through making the tied selling an overt condition of purchase or through some form of inducement such as a price for the bundle of tied goods lower than the sum of the individual prices of the goods if purchased separately. The two most common types of tied sales are bundling and requirements tying. **Bundling** (or package tie-in) occurs when a product is sold only on the condition that some specified number of units of some other product are purchased from the same supplier (for example, in order to purchase a unit of B from a supplier, a consumer must also purchase two units of A from the same supplier); with a requirements tie, consumers must make all of their purchases of product A from a firm if they want to purchase product B from that firm.

The law, however, concedes that these requirements can be either anti-competitive or pro-competitive. Tying may be anti-competitive when it shuts out or forecloses on competitors that also supply the tied product(s). Foreclosure leads to a reduction in the choice of suppliers of the tied goods. If the level of foreclosure is such that consumers are adversely affected either through higher prices, less variety, or both, then antitrust intervention is warranted. However, tying can also be pro-competitive if it allows suppliers to take advantage of economies of scope in production, sale, and distribution, or if it reduces transactions costs. The fact that many products supplied in competitive markets are commonly tied together suggests that pro-competitive rationales for tying are pervasive. The Competition Bureau has recommended against an outright ban on tying in any market, unless it is clear that the only motivation for a tie is to foreclose on competition.

Examples of potentially pro-competitive instances of tied selling in financial markets involve the provision of various forms of credit, mortgages, or loans. At some stage in the process of providing a customer with these products, the financial institution must incur the cost of assessing the creditworthiness of the customer. Once an institution has incurred this cost for the provision of one product, it need not incur it again to provide the same customer with other credit-related products. By bundling a group of such products together, the institution provides these services at a lower cost to the customer than if each product had to be purchased separately.[14]

Exclusive Dealing

In **exclusive dealing**, a manufacturer or marketer prohibits channel members from carrying competitive products. Although this prohibition is not automatically illegal under the *Competition Act,* the usual legal test is whether competition is restricted.

Reciprocity   **Reciprocity** refers to buying a product or service from someone if that person or business agrees to buy from you. Once again, if this practice is seen to limit competition, legal action can be taken under the *Competition Act.*

Consumer Protection   The foregoing sections deal primarily with business-to-business situations and provide evidence of the complexities of selling today.

We also need to recognize that there is another level of the law that deals with the consumer. For example, in British Columbia, door-to-door selling requires a provincial licence. Although there are some exceptions (real estate salespeople, for example), anyone engaged in direct selling to consumers in their residence must be licensed.

In addition, extensive consumer protection is contained in the *British Columbia Consumer Protection Act.* Most provinces have enacted similar protective legislation. One protection in the legislation is the **cooling-off period**. In our example of door-to-door selling, if a consumer enters into a contract for goods or services valued at more than $50, the consumer has 10 days during which she has the right to cancel that contract without penalty.

Further discussion on consumer protection laws is beyond the scope of this textbook, but if you are interested in this subject, your local Better Business Bureau is an excellent resource.

MANAGING SALES ETHICS   Surveys to determine managers' views of business ethics have found the following:

- All managers feel they face ethical problems.
- Most managers feel they and their employers should be more ethical.
- Managers are more ethical with their friends than with people they do not know.
- Even though they want to be more ethical, some managers lower their ethical standards to meet job goals.
- Managers are aware of unethical practices in their industry and company ranging from price discrimination to hiring discrimination.
- Business ethics can be influenced by an employee's superior and company environment.

Organizations now recognize the importance of improving their social responsiveness and ethical climate. Managers must take active steps to ensure that the company stays on ethical ground. Management methods for helping organizations to be more responsive include (1) top management taking the lead, (2) carefully selecting leaders, (3) establishing and following a code of ethics, (4) creating ethical structures, (5) formally encouraging whistle blowing, (6) creating an ethical sales climate, and (7) establishing control systems.

Business Ethics   In the past many have considered business ethics an oxymoron. Today, however, business ethics is a management discipline.

The Centre for Ethics and Corporate Policy, founded more than 10 years ago, is headquartered in Toronto, and includes among its board of directors and membership Canada's largest and most respected companies. As further evidence of the impact of ethics on Canadian business, recent research indicates that 90 percent of college and university business programs have at least one course in ethics in their curricula.

ETHICAL DILEMMA
The Boss Made Me Do It

Your prospect insists that her company must have delivery of your product in four weeks to meet a national advertising rollout. The company has made a tremendous investment in its ad campaign. After extensive prodding by you and your managers, the production department cannot do any better than a six-week delivery. Your boss orders you to promise the customer delivery within four weeks. What is the most ethical action to take?

1. Tell your boss that you do not believe that it is right to lie to the customer. State that you will not pass the four-week lead time along but would be more than happy to tell the customer about the true six-week lead time. Tell your boss that you cannot support dishonesty within the company.

2. Do as your boss says and promise the four-week delivery time, even though you know there is no possibility of meeting the deadline.

3. Tell your boss to pass the information to the customer himself. That way, you do not have to actually lie to your customer.

4. Would you resign your position over this type of situation?

The field of ethics in general historically has been the focus of philosophers, academics, and social scientists. However, in today's highly complex, increasingly international marketplace, managers constantly face ethical dilemmas such as conflicts of interest, misuse of company resources, and human rights violations.

In ethics there are few absolutes in terms of right and wrong. More frequently, the ethical question is situational and lacking in precedent. Certain guidelines can provide a template for developing and maintaining ethical standards.

Create an Ethical Sales Climate

The single most important factor in improving the climate for ethical behaviour in a sales force is the action taken by top-level managers. Sales managers must help develop and support their codes of ethics. They should publicize the code and their opposition to unethical sales practices to their subordinate managers and their salespeople. A stronger level of ethical awareness can be achieved during sales meetings, training sessions, and when contacting customers while working with salespeople (job shadowing).[15]

Leader Selection Is Important

Since so few individuals are at the principled level of moral development, it is critical to choose managers carefully. Only people who have the highest level of integrity, standards, and values should assume leadership positions.

Senior Management

An organization's senior managers must develop ethical standards for their businesses and exhibit compliance to these standards. If leadership is shown at this level, the majority of employees will follow that lead (see Exhibit 2–7). Involvement in basic forms of ethical organizations such as the local Better Business Bureau or an industry or professional association with a code of ethics is a start. In terms of Canada's larger international companies, involvement in ethical industry associations, and with organizations such as the Centre for Ethics and Corporate Policy and the Conference Board of Canada, will ensure receipt of a flow of current information on ethics.

EXHIBIT 2–7

Top-level management sets the climate for ethical behaviour in the sales force.

Establish a Code of Ethics

A **code of ethics** is a formal statement of the company's values concerning ethics and social issues. It states those values or behaviours that are expected and those that are not tolerated. These values and behaviours must be backed by management action. Without top management support, there is little assurance that the code will be followed.

The two types of codes of ethics are principle-based statements and policy-based statements. Principle-based statements affect corporate culture, define fundamental values, and contain general language about company responsibilities, quality of products, and treatment of employees. General statements of principle are often called *corporate credos*. Examples of internationally recognized companies with corporate credos are Johnson & Johnson, Starbucks, and Levi Strauss. Canadian companies operating on a global basis and displaying a commitment to ethical standards include Nortel Networks, with its ethical commitment to "eCitizenship." In addition, TLC Laser Eye Centre provides statements of "Core Values" that guide the organization in a highly competitive market.

Policy-based statements generally outline the procedures to be used in specific ethical situations. These situations include marketing practice, conflicts of interest, observance of laws, proprietary information, political gifts, and equal opportunities. Examples of policy-based ethics can be found in international companies' policies such as Textron's (makers of Bell helicopters and Cessna aircraft) "Business Conduct Guidelines," Honeywell Inc.'s "Code of Ethics," supported further by a corporate ethics officer, and Motorola, whose "Code of Ethics" is enhanced by an ethics hotline, a communication line available for all stakeholders.

Create Ethical Structures

An **ethical committee** is a group of executives appointed to oversee company ethics. The committee provides rulings on questionable ethical issues and assumes responsibility for disciplining wrongdoers. This responsibility is essential if the organization is to directly influence employee behaviour. An **ethical ombudsman** is an official given the responsibility of being the corporate conscience who hears and investigates ethical complaints and informs top management of potential ethical issues. For example, some companies, such as the Royal Bank, have an office of the ombudsman who will "provide an impartial avenue for unresolved concerns and will recommend changes to improve customer and employee experiences."[16]

Encourage Whistle Blowing

Employee disclosure of illegal, immoral, or illegitimate practices on the employer's part is called **whistle blowing**. Companies can provide a mechanism for whistle blowing as a matter of policy. All employees who observe or become aware of criminal practices or unethical behaviour should be encouraged to report the incident to their superiors, to a higher level of management, or to an appropriate unit of the organization, such as an ethics committee. Formalized procedures for complaining can encourage honest employees to report questionable incidents. For example, a company could provide its employees with a toll-free number to report unethical activities to top management. This silent-witness program may encourage employees to report incidents because they do not have to confront personnel. This program is especially valuable if the employee's own manager is involved in unethical practices. However, with such programs, careful verification is necessary to guard against vindictive employees.

Establish Control Systems

Establish control systems. Employ methods to determine whether salespeople give bribes, falsify reports, or pad expenses. For example, check sales made from low bids to determine whether procedures have been followed correctly. Dismissal, demotion, suspension, reprimand, or withholding of sales commissions are be possible penalties for unethical sales practices.

SUMMARY OF MAJOR SELLING ISSUES

Ethics and social responsibility are hot topics. Ethical behaviour pertains to values of right and wrong, and ethical decisions and behaviour are typically guided by a value system. For an individual manager, the ability to make correct ethical choices will depend on both individual and organizational characteristics, including his own level of moral development and the corporate culture in which he works.

Corporate social responsibility concerns a company's values toward society. Organizations can be good corporate citizens by evaluating their social performance through four criteria: economic, legal, ethical, and discretionary.

Social responsibility in business means profitably serving employees and customers in an ethical and lawful manner. Extra costs can accrue because a firm takes socially responsible action, but this is a part of doing business in today's society, and it pays in the long run.

Salespeople and managers must be ethical in dealing with salespeople, employers, and customers. Ethical standards and guidelines for sales personnel must be developed, supported, and policed. In the future, ethical selling practices will be even more important to conducting business profitably. Techniques for improving social responsiveness include leadership, codes of ethics, ethical structures, whistle blowing, and establishing control systems. Finally, research suggests that socially responsible organizations perform as well as—and often better than—organizations that are not socially responsible.

MEETING A SALES CHALLENGE

In essence, the sales manager was seeking reciprocity. The contemplated deal is clearly unethical. In some cases, such a deal may even be unlawful. Companies that are aware of their legal and ethical responsibilities protect themselves and their employees from unnecessary exposure to illegal activity like this.

For example, IBM marketing representatives are urged to follow the specific steps set forth in IBM's "Business Conduct Guideline"—a policy-based code of ethics—which states, "You may not do business with a supplier of goods or services." Reasonable? *Yes.* Important? *Absolutely.*

Remember that your career and the future of your company depend on creating values that last. This objective depends on making decisions we can live with tomorrow, not on what we might get away with today.

PLAYING THE ROLE

Role A: Sales rep for Canadian Paper Supply. Your conscience is finally getting to you. You've been overcharging some of your loyal customers over the past few months to increase your commissions. In fact, you've even double-billed one customer, knowing that its accounts payable department is disorganized and would likely pay you twice. The guilt has caused you to become depressed and you've been drinking more heavily recently then hiding your hangovers with painkillers. Your overall performance has been slipping, so you arrange a meeting with your superiors to discuss your situation.

Role B: Sales manager and/or general manager of Canadian Paper Supply. A troubled employee is meeting with you to discuss some personal problems he has been experiencing and feels are affecting his job performance. After listening to his problems, what should you do? How do you handle employees in these situations? What are your options?

Prepare your role for an in-class dramatization of this situation.

KEY TERMS FOR SELLING

breach of warranty, 46
bribe, 44
bundling, 48
CCC GOMES, 30
code of ethics, 51
conventional moral development level, 33
cooling-off period, 49
discretionary responsibility, 32
employee rights, 38
ethical committee, 51
ethical ombudsman, 52

ethics, 34
exclusive dealing, 48
misrepresentation, 46
preconventional moral developmental level, 33
price discrimination, 48
principled moral development level, 34
reciprocity, 49
social responsibility, 30
stakeholder, 30
tied selling, 48
whistle blowing, 52

SALES APPLICATION QUESTIONS

1. Which of the following situations represent socially responsible actions by firms?
   a. Creating recreation facilities for sales personnel
   b. Paying for university courses associated with an MBA program
   c. Allowing sales personnel to buy company products at a discount

2. How should sales managers promote and enforce ethical practices? Describe some ethical situations that sales managers may face in dealing with salespeople.

3. Imagine that you are being encouraged to inflate your expense account. Do you think your choice would be most affected by your individual moral development or by the cultural values of the company for which you worked? Explain.

4. Have you ever experienced an ethical dilemma? Evaluate the dilemma with respect to its impact on other people.

5. Do you think a code of ethics combined with an ethics committee would be more effective than leadership alone for implementing ethical behaviour? Discuss.

6. Discuss the difference between sales "exaggeration" and "misrepresentation." How can you avoid mistakes that could prove costly to the firm?

7. Some companies consider customers and employees to be more important stakeholders than shareholders are. Is it appropriate for management to define some stakeholders as more important than others? Should all stakeholders be considered equal?

SALES WORLD WIDE WEB EXERCISE

Corporate Ethics Research

If you had to guess which corporations in North America deserve to be called the best corporate citizens, which companies would you choose? To make this job easier, *Business Ethics Magazine* conducts an annual survey that ranks the top 100 corporations on ethical measures pertaining to treatment of stakeholders including customers and employees. Go to the Web site for *Business Ethics Magazine,* www.business-ethics.com, and review the leaders in this unique survey. Research these companies by going to their Web sites, and determine each organization's commitment to ethical business practices and social responsibility.

FURTHER EXPLORING THE SALES WORLD

1. Contact your local Better Business Bureau and prepare a report on local laws regulating the activities of salespeople.

2. The *Journal of Public Policy & Marketing* has a "Legal Developments in Marketing" section. Report on several legal cases in this section that are related to a firm's personal selling activities.

3. Talk to a sales manager about the social, ethical, and legal issues involved in the job. Does the manager's firm have
   a. A code of ethics?
   b. An ethics committee?
   c. An ethical ombudsman?
   d. Procedures for whistle blowing? Get copies of any Internet, magazine, or newspaper articles relating to topics discussed in this chapter. Report your findings.

4. Visit the *Competition Act* Web site at http://laws.justice.gc.ca/en/C-34/. Describe at least two marketing practices that some unethical salespeople could be tempted by. What are the implications for salespeople of using these practices?

SELLING EXPERIENTIAL EXERCISE

Ethical Work Climates

On a separate sheet of paper, answer the following questions by writing down the number that best describes an organization for which you have worked:

	Disagree				Agree
1. Whatever is best for everyone in the company is the major consideration here.	1	2	3	4	5
2. Our major concern is always what is best for the other person.					
3. People are expected to comply with the law and professional standards over and above other considerations.					
4. In this company, the first consideration is whether a decision violates any law.					
5. It is very important to follow company rules and procedures here.					
6. People in this company strictly obey company policies.					
7. In this company, people are mostly out for themselves.					
8. People are expected to do anything to further the company's interests, regardless of the consequences.					
9. In this company, people are guided by their own personal ethics.					
10. Each person in this company decides for himself or herself what is right and wrong.					

Total Score _____

Total your score. These questions measure the dimensions of an organization's ethical climate. Questions 1 and 2 measure caring for people, questions 3 and 4 measure lawfulness, questions 5 and 6 measure rules adherence, questions 7 and 8 measure emphasis on financial and company performance, and questions 9 and 10 measure individual independence. Questions 7 and 8 are reverse scored. (That is, if you answered "five," your actual score to write down is "one"; a "four" is really a "two," etc.) A total score above 40 indicates a very positive ethical climate. A score from 30 to 40 indicates an above-average ethical climate. A score from 20 to 30 indicates a below-average ethical climate, and a score below 20 indicates a very poor ethical climate.

Go back over the questions and think about changes that you could have made to improve the ethical climate in the organization. Discuss with other students what you could do as a manager to improve ethics in future companies you work for.[17]

CASE 2–1
Fancy Frozen Foods*

Last Friday, Bill Wilkerson of Fancy Frozen Foods (FFF) was confronted with a situation that he has not resolved successfully. Grady Bryan, a purchasing agent for Smith Supermarket Chain, Inc., made it apparent to Bill that if he wanted to retain the company's business in frozen food sales, special action would be necessary. In a telephone conversation, Grady suddenly got onto the subject of his new fishing boat and how

*This case is adapted from a case prepared by Bill A. Wilkerson, a salesperson, as a basis for classroom discussion and not to illustrate either effective or ineffective handling of an administrative position. Company names have been changed.

CASE 2–1

much better it would perform with an 80-horsepower, inboard-outboard Evinrude motor. Bill and Grady have been fairly friendly, having done business together for the past four years. However, a conversation of this kind seemed out of the ordinary to Bill, especially during a long-distance call for which he was paying. What got Bill's attention was Grady's subtle mention of a competitor, Specialty Frozen Foods, whose territorial sales representative had stopped in to price some outboard motors after lunch with Grady. This alerted Bill to the complicated situation he faced. He realized it would take some thought to enable his company to retain Smith's exclusive business.

Fancy Frozen Foods

Fancy Frozen Foods (FFF) operates in Manitoba and Saskatchewan, with Brandon and Regina the two largest markets. FFF carries a complete line of frozen foods that it manufactures and wholesales, enabling them to undercut most wholesalers' prices. The company currently employs 20 salespeople. Their territories are divided according to geographic size, keeping salespeople's travel time to a minimum. Salespeople are paid a set salary of $12,000 yearly and commission of 3 percent for everything above a designated quota. Quotas differ by territory. They are set according to the relative potential of each market.

The company has no formal written policy regarding gift giving and entertainment. However, in the past, the president emphasized that customers may not receive gifts worth more than $25. In addition to this, FFF owns a ranch in Saskatchewan. The company invites each of its customers for a three-day vacation, involving hunting and other outdoor activities.

Smith Supermarket Chain

Smith has 15 supermarkets in Saskatchewan and 13 outlets in Manitoba. All of these accounts are currently serviced exclusively by FFF. Grady Bryan, in one of his various duties as warehouse ordering agent in the Brandon area for Smith, selects sellers of frozen foods. The 13 store managers call in their weekly frozen food orders to Grady, who then compiles the orders and calls in the order to Bill Wilkerson of FFF. This type of system is used to obtain lower prices than if each individual outlet made an order. The order is sent to the central warehouse, where it is broken down for individual outlets and scheduled for delivery in an efficient fashion.

What to Do?

Bill is confronted with a situation that he has never faced. He has, in the past, given Grady modest gifts in line with the president's wishes, and occasionally taken Grady to lunch. The company-sponsored hunting trips are another form of entertainment. However, none of these things, at least to Bill, indicated that Bill would succumb to a suggested bribe of this proportion. The crux of the matter is not that Bill's previous practices have indicated he would comply with this request but that Bill's competition has shown a blatant willingness to employ unethical tactics to gain Smith's frozen food sales. The question is, should Bill take the chance of losing the 13 accounts by not offering the bribe, or should he succumb to the bribe and avoid the risk?

Questions

1. What is the main problem presented in this case?
2. What must Bill do?

CASE 2–2
Sports Shirts, Inc.

"I'm glad you came in, Marge. I've been wanting to talk to you." Anne Jackson, sales manager for the Atlantic region of Sports Shirts, Inc., greeted one of her salespeople, Marge Phillips, as she entered the office. The company marketed a line of sports clothing consisting primarily of three styles of running suits.

"What about?" asked Marge.

"You know, since you've been with us, I've always considered you one of our top salespeople. You always meet quotas. You always find new accounts. But I've got a problem that we need to discuss. I got a letter from one of your customers. He claims he couldn't sell the goods you sold him even if he tried all year. And he's also claiming that our running suits aren't worth a dime—that they fall apart soon after the customer buys them. He included some sales data that seemed to point to the fact that he always has a large quantity of our merchandise left at the end of the season. Now, normally, I would just pass this off as a store's sour grapes because of declining sales, but this isn't the first time this has happened. I've received several such letters recently. What do you think the problem might be?"

"I don't see that we really have a problem. I do get complaints about the quality of the merchandise, but that's not my problem. Besides, I just concentrate on the profit-potential figures for the retailers, and quality seems a secondary consideration in that context. You give me a quota, and I meet it. What am I supposed to do, refuse to sell them as much as they will take? It's not my fault if they overbuy! I guess I'm just a top-notch salesperson."

The facts certainly indicate that Marge was a good salesperson. Some of her co-workers had said that she could sell snow to the Inuit. They call her "Load 'em down Marge." In three years with the company, she has already worked her way up to being the top salesperson in the company. Her sales figures are shown in Exhibit A.

The running suits Marge sells are made from one of the several combinations of materials and labour that resulted in suits of different durability. Cost and durability data are summarized in Exhibit B. The company chose the second alternative of the three listed.

There were many complaints about the quality of the running suits that the firm marketed. Seams came apart after only a few washings, consumers complained. "We sell good running suits, but you can't expect them to last forever," was management's reply.

EXHIBIT A

Sales Data

Year	Quota (000)	Sales (000)	New Accounts
1	$400	$450	20
2	440	460	23
	V	V	V

EXHIBIT B

Relative Cost of Merchandise

		Cost	
Year	Material	Labour	Rating*
A	$1.28	$2.00	5
B	1.45	3.00	10
C	1.95	4.00	20

*The durability rating was basically a measure of the number of washings garments could go through and still look good.

CASE 2–2

The manager had other concerns about Marge. However, she was doing such an excellent selling job and was making the company so much money that the manager did not want a confrontation. In fact, sales for the entire region had increased 17 percent this year. Much of the increase was due to Marge's influence on other salespeople, who applied many of her selling techniques. There were rumours that Marge was considering buying into a partnership and becoming a manufacturer's agent specializing in high-fashion clothing. Sales would certainly be affected if Marge left the company. In fact, Anne was concerned that Marge would hire away the firm's better salespeople.

Anne remembered when Marge was hired. She had always wanted to sell in the clothing industry, but no one would give her the opportunity. So, on graduation from college, Marge went to work for a large department store chain. In two years, she moved from manager of the women's clothing department in one of the smaller stores to head buyer of women's wear for the entire chain. Marge said she wanted more out of life than a $25,000-a-year job could give. So Anne hired her on a straight commission of 10 percent on sales up to quota and 15 percent on all sales after quota. This year Marge would earn $98,000, with a sales increase of more than 40 percent.

Anne did not believe Marge had worked fewer than 12 hours a day since she began. She plowed back much of her earnings into customer goodwill and it appeared to have helped her sales. Gifts and entertainment were a large overhead expense item for her. The only expense the company paid was an amount up to 1 percent of a salesperson's actual sales, and this had to go for entertaining. Marge said she spent more than $15,000 on her customers in addition to the $4,600 the firm paid.

During the recent year-end performance appraisal session, Anne was surprised when Marge accepted her next year's $1 million sales quota so calmly. Marge said it would be no problem. In fact, she estimated that her sales would increase to between $1.5 and $2 million. When asked why, Marge said a friend of hers was now buyer for the retail chain for which she once worked. The buyer had worked for Marge until Marge quit to begin working at Sports Shirts. Marge recalled discovering that her friend was receiving kickbacks of more than $5,000 in cash, merchandise, and vacation trips. Marge said nothing to the chain's management, mainly because she was doing the same thing, which her friend did not know. So Marge was sure she could sell this buyer her entire line of running suits. Further, last year Marge began requiring many of her customers to buy all of the styles and sizes she sold in order to receive the best-selling models.

However, Marge did ask for an additional 1 percent in entertainment expenses. Last summer, she gave a party with a live band and professional dancers for buyers. Marge felt this greatly increased sales and wanted to continue the practice. However, it was quite expensive.

Corporate management had begun to ask about Marge's management capabilities. They felt that if she could train salespeople as well as she sold, she would make a great sales manager.

Questions

1. How would you describe Marge Phillips's success?
2. Is she a good salesperson? Do her sales results justify her methods of selling?
3. What should Anne do?

PART 2

PREPARATION FOR RELATIONSHIP SELLING

This part of the book address the basic sales knowledge needed by salespeople. Being knowledgeable about buyer behaviour, communication skills, products, prices, distribution, promotion, and competition are essential to sales success. Included in this part are

3

THE PSYCHOLOGY OF SELLING: WHY PEOPLE BUY

LEARNING OBJECTIVES

People and organizations typically buy the benefits of a product. This chapter explores how and why both organizations and individuals buy. It emphasizes the need for salespeople to understand their prospects and communicate how their propositions will benefit those prospects. After studying this chapter, you should be able to:

- Explain the role of needs analysis in selling.

- Understand the differences between consumer and organizational buying behaviour.

- Understand how to adapt to different types of business buyers.

- Recognize the importance of determining the factors that influence buyer behaviour.

- Understand the role of the buying centre in B2B buying.

- Understand how buyers' personality and social style contribute to their buying behaviour.

- Understand how buyers move through a decision-making process when buying.

- Identify the factors that influence buying decisions.

- Understand and explain the different types of business-to-business buying decisions.

- Show why buying is a choice decision.

FACING A CAREER CHALLENGE

Seven years ago John Salley graduated with a computer science degree. One year later, he earned his MBA with an A average. John was on every campus recruiter's list as an outstanding applicant. He had the brains, personality, looks, and motivation of a winner. IBM convinced him to take a sales job.

John was at the top of his class in the IBM sales-training program. However, his results during his first two years in sales were just average. He could not understand why, because his knowledge of the products was outstanding. John could discuss in great depth the most technical aspects of his products. John loved sales but felt things had to change.

If you were in John's position, what would you do? (Continued at end of chapter.)

Like many people, John Salley has done everything it takes to be successful in sales, yet for some reason never reached his maximum potential. To be successful, salespeople need to be knowledgeable, even expert, on everything we discuss in this part of the book, "Preparation for Relationship Selling."

Chapter 3 examines why and how an individual buys. We discuss the influences on a purchase and connect them to the various steps in the customer's buying process. This chapter presents selling techniques that will aid you later in developing your sales presentation. These techniques also can help John Salley in his efforts to improve his sales performance. He needs to know why people buy.

WHY PEOPLE BUY—THE BLACK-BOX APPROACH

The question of why people buy has interested salespeople for many years.

Prospective buyers are usually exposed to various sales presentations. The prospect internalizes or considers this information before deciding whether to purchase. This process of internalization is referred to as a **black box** because we cannot see into the buyer's mind—meaning that the salesperson can apply the stimuli (a sales presentation) and observe the behaviour of the prospect, but cannot witness the prospect's decision-making process.

The classic model of buyer behaviour shown in Exhibit 3–1 is called a **stimulus–response model**. A stimulus (sales presentation) is applied, resulting in a response (sale or no sale). This model assumes that prospects respond in some predictable

EXHIBIT 3–1

Black-box theory of buyer behaviour.

Sales Presentation	Influences on Buyer Behaviour	Sale/No Sale
Stimulus	**Social Factors** – Roles – Family Influence – Reference Groups – Culture – Subculture **Psychological Factors** – Motivation – Learning – Attitudes – Personality – Values **Personal Factors** – Income – Gender – Age – Situation	**Response**

manner to the sales presentation. Unfortunately, it does not tell us why they buy or do not buy the product. This information is concealed in each prospect's black box.

The exhibit shows the difficulty in attempting to determine how prospects will respond to a particular sales presentation. Many factors inside the black box can and will have an impact on the prospect's decision making. Empathy is the key—salespeople who can put themselves in their prospects' shoes have a much better chance of getting the response they want because they will be better able to provide the correct stimuli.

Salespeople seek to understand as much as they can about the mental processes that yield the prospects' responses. We do know that

- People buy for both practical (rational) and psychological (emotional) reasons.
- Salespeople can use specific methods to help determine the prospects' thoughts during sales presentations.
- Buyers consider certain factors in making purchase decisions.

This chapter introduces these three critical topics and the importance of understanding each in terms of its affect on people's behaviour.

PSYCHOLOGICAL INFLUENCES ON BUYING

Since personal selling requires understanding human behaviour, each salesperson must determine a prospective customer's motivations, perceptions, learning, attitudes, and personality. Furthermore, the salesperson should know how each type of behaviour might influence a customer's purchase decision.

Motivation to Buy Must Be Present

Human beings are motivated by needs and wants, which build up internally, creating a desire to buy products or services (e.g., a new computer or transportation to another city). Because people buy things to satisfy needs and wants, it is important to differentiate between the two.

Needs are the basic requirements of human life—food and water, shelter, clothing, security, interaction with others, and self-fulfillment. We are all born with needs that must—to a greater or lesser degree—be satisfied throughout our lives. Needs are at the "must have" level.

Wants are not required to sustain life. They are discretionary items on the "would like to have" level—gourmet meals and fine wine, a spacious home in a prestigious neighbourhood, designer fashions, and so on. We are not born with wants—we learn them. Our knowledge, experiences, culture, and personality all influence what we want.

Given that we live in a developed country where basic needs are often easily met, wants are more powerful motivators than needs. As consumers, satisfying wants becomes essential to achieving and sustaining the lifestyle we desire. For example, people need transportation, but some want a Porsche while others prefer a Ford Mustang.

This example illustrates that both practical or rational reasons (the need for transportation) and emotional or psychological reasons (the desire for the prestige of owning a Porsche) influence buying behaviour. One buyer might have only rational, logical reasons for buying, while another might have only emotional reasons for purchasing. Yet another buyer may have a blend of both rational and emotional reasons for buying a product. A salesperson must determine a prospect's reasons in order to tailor the presentation for maximum impact.

EXHIBIT 3–2

Customers are motivated to buy by both practical and emotional needs.

Keep in mind that, although people buy to satisfy their own personal needs and wants, sometimes they buy to satisfy the needs and wants of others. If you are selling footwear to a retail shoe store chain, for example, the buyer's decision may be based on a need to impress his superiors with profitability, or to meet the warehouse manager's demand for a better delivery schedule, or to please store managers with attractive packaging. Meeting the needs of the buyer may also involve satisfying the needs of those whom the buyer represents.

Awareness of Needs: Some Buyers Are Unsure

Buyers are not always fully aware of their needs. For example, a homeowner might want to fix a cracked driveway that also has lumps and potholes but may not realize that aging drain tiles running beneath the driveway are clogged or have collapsed and need to be replaced before the driveway is resurfaced.

It is important that both buyer and salesperson have a clear understanding of why a purchase is being made and what results the customer hopes to achieve by buying. A high level of need awareness enables the salesperson to focus on the most appropriate product for the buyer's situation, and helps the buyer to make the best purchase decisions.

Let's say you are ill and pay a visit to your doctor. "What's the trouble?" she asks. "I feel terrible," you reply. "Okay, take this for a week, then come and see me," she says while hastily writing a prescription on a small pad of paper. Astonished, you accept the piece of paper from your doctor and leave the office. The visit lasted 30 seconds. What is wrong with this picture? The doctor does not know enough about your discomfort. She cannot possibly recommend effective treatment without having more information about your problem. How confident would you be about swallowing the medication prescribed? Not very! This same principle is true in selling.

Sometimes buyers with limited needs awareness think they know what product they should buy. This can prove risky because the product they purchase may not satisfy their needs. For example, a prospect might begin by saying, "I'd like to buy a new car, and I want a Cadillac sedan loaded with accessories." During a brief needs analysis by the salesperson, however, the buyer divulges, "I take my family camping on weekends during the spring, summer, and fall." In this case, buying the Cadillac sedan may be a mistake because a station wagon or sport utility vehicle would better fit the buyer's situation.

Economic Needs: The Best Value for the Money

An **economic need** is the buyer's need to purchase the most satisfying product for the money. Economic needs include price, quality (performance, dependability, durability), convenience of buying, and service.

Many salespeople mistakenly assume that people base their buying decisions solely on price. This is not always correct. A higher product price relative to competing goods often can be offset by such factors as service, quality, better performance, friendliness of the salesperson, or convenience of purchase.

SOCIAL INFLUENCES ON BUYING

Canadian salespeople and those who do business in Canada face a unique challenge due to our country's cultural diversity of the Canadian population. Ethnic groups often retain their traditions and behaviours, making selling domestically in Canada similar to selling globally in terms of understanding the different ways that different groups behave in their buying behaviour.

This adds more hidden mental processes to the black box. Each culture has its own way of doing business, and the wise salesperson will prepare for this. The Selling Globally box featured on page 65, "Are You Ready for Your International Sales Trip?" may have applications within our own country.

Reference Groups

A college student decides that she needs a new sweater to wear to a party the following weekend. While in the dressing room at a clothing store, the student holds a sweater up to the mirror and asks herself, "What will my friends think if I wear this to the party?" It is arguable that this would be the most important consideration in purchasing the sweater and that most purchase decisions are made with some consideration of other people's reactions.

A reference group is any group that directly or indirectly affects one's behaviour. In the case of the sweater above, the student was wondering about reassurance from her friends. In other situations, reassurance might come from one's family, co-workers, celebrities, or social groups. This phenomenon applies to business situations as well. Although purchasing agents and other decision makers are more rational in their decision making, they often still seek personal reassurance from their coworkers, supervisors, and others, which may affect their decision about what to buy and possibly even from whom. Again, empathy is important—if salespeople can determine which reference group a buyer is influenced by, they can include that in the sales presentation.

Roles

A father tells the salesperson in an electronics store that he's looking for a new family computer. Should the salesperson proceed to a detailed presentation as to why this father should buy one particular computer over another? What role is the father playing in this family purchase? Is he the *buyer*? Is he the *user*? Who will act as an *influencer* in the decision, and who ultimately will be the *decider*? These roles are played out in many buying situations. The salesperson would use a different sales presentation or at least different sales appeals for each different role; while the buyer might be most interested in price, the user would probably be most interested in the features of the product.

This doesn't apply to only consumer goods. In business-to-business selling, where purchasing decisions are far more rational, many people in the buying organization may become involved in the buying decision. This is commonly known as a "multiple buying influence." Although the purchase of a new stapler may be a relatively simple decision, imagine selling a mainframe computer to a large company. Many roles would be involved. The purchasing department would be responsible for negotiations and writing the cheque. The information technologists would heavily influence the decision, as would the service technicians. The top executives of the company might have to get involved due to the high expense involved. Even a receptionist may play a part in that he or she would have some control over the flow of information into and out of the buying office.

An adept salesperson would have a keen understanding of how buying decisions are made and who is involved in them. Once the process is understood, a presentation could be tailored to satisfy the needs of each of the participants.

Learning   When consumers are deciding which product to purchase, one of their first sources of information is their own memory. By thinking back, they will remember any good or bad experiences to apply to their purchase decision. Buyers are recalling a "learned" experience.

If you have ever purchased something that you were dissatisfied with and ultimately couldn't get any satisfaction from, you probably believe that buying the same product again likely will result in the same dissatisfaction. Similarly, if you were very satisfied with a product and its performance, you probably believe that purchasing it again likely will have the same outcome.

Satisfaction is the difference between what one expects from a situation and what is delivered. If you have unreasonable expectations of a product's performance, its actual performance likely will disappoint you. Conversely, if salespeople can deliver more than prospects expect, the resulting satisfaction level will encourage customers to repeat their behaviour to ensure satisfaction.

It is not necessary to know everything about the prospect; however, the salesperson must gather enough of the right information about the buyer's needs to offer appropriate solutions. The salesperson must also determine the buyer's need priorities. For example, it is rarely possible to obtain high quality and low price at the same time, so the salesperson must learn which is of greater importance to the prospect.

SELLING GLOBALLY

Are You Ready for Your International Sales Trip?

1. Read about the geography, history, and politics of the country or region you are visiting.
   (Check out *The World Factbook* Web site: www.cia.gov/library/publications/the-world-factbook)

2. Gain an understanding of the ethnic and social makeup of your destination.

3. Are you familiar with the country or region's religious and cultural nuances?

4. Have you familiarized yourself with any recent news and developments?

5. Can you access local interpreters or guides who can help you get around?

6. Are the business ethics of the country consistent with your own standards? If not, how will you handle it?

7. Are you familiar with local currencies?

8. Will you be able to provide for your dietary needs?

9. Familiarize yourself with local transportation methods, schedules, and costs.

10. Develop an appreciation for cultural diversity.

11. Research, research, research.

You're no longer in Canada—be ready for it.

When a salesperson increases needs awareness in the minds of herself and the buyer, she demonstrates professionalism, smoothes the buyer's decision-making process, reduces the chance of facing overwhelming objections, and increases the likelihood of long-term customer satisfaction. Just like the doctor, a salesperson must diagnose the situation before prescribing a solution.

YOUR BUYER'S PERCEPTION

Why would two people have the same need but buy different products? Likewise, why might the same individual at different times view your product in diverse ways? The answers to both questions involve how the person perceives your product.

Perception is the process by which a person selects, organizes, and interprets information. The buyer receives the salesperson's product information through the senses: sight, hearing, touch, taste, and smell. These senses act as filtering devices that information must pass through before it can be used.

Each of the three perception components plays a part in determining buyers' responses to you and your sales presentation. Buyers often receive large amounts of information in a short period, and they typically perceive and use only a small amount of it. Some information is ignored or quickly forgotten because of the difficulty of retaining large amounts of information. This process is known as **selective exposure** because only a portion of the information an individual is exposed to is selected to be organized, interpreted, and allowed into awareness.

Why does some information reach a buyer's consciousness while other information does not? First, the salesperson may not present the information in a manner that ensures proper reception. For example, too much information may be given at one time. This causes confusion, and the buyer tunes out. In some cases, information may be haphazardly presented, which causes the buyer to receive it in an unorganized manner.

A sales presentation that appeals to the buyer's five senses helps penetrate perceptual barriers. It also enhances understanding and reception of the information as you present it. Selling techniques such as asking questions, using visual aids, and demonstrating a product can force buyers to participate in the presentation. This feedback helps determine whether they understand your information. See Exhibit 3–3.

EXHIBIT 3–3

The questions asked by this salesperson help him understand the buyer's perceptions, attitudes, and beliefs.

MAKING THE SALE

Find the Fs

Count the number of Fs in the sentence below. How many did you find the first time you read the sentence?

> FEATURE FILMS ARE
> THE RESULT OF YEARS
> OF SCIENTIFIC STUDY
> COMBINED WITH THE
> EXPERIENCE OF YEARS

We often miss what may be right under our noses, such as buying signals. How many Fs are there? There are six, but three are part of the word *of,* which has a different sound. You would be surprised at the number of people who miss the answer.

Second, buyers tend to allow information to reach consciousness if it relates to needs they recognize and want to fulfill. If, for example, someone gives you reasons for purchasing life insurance, and you do not perceive a need for it, there is a good chance that your mind will allow little of this information to be perceived. However, if you need life insurance, you will listen carefully to the salesperson. If you are uncertain about something, you will ask questions to increase your understanding.

A buyer's perceptual process also may result in **selective distortion** or the altering of information. It frequently occurs when information is received that is inconsistent with a person's beliefs and attitudes. When buyers listen to a sales presentation on a product that they perceive as being of low quality, they may mentally alter the information to coincide with present beliefs and attitudes, thereby reinforcing their perceptions. Should buyers believe that the product is of high quality, even when it is not, they may change any negative information about the product into positive information. This distortion can substantially affect a salesperson's efforts.

Selective retention can also influence perception. Here, buyers may remember only information that supports their attitudes and beliefs, and forget what does not. After a salesperson leaves, buyers may forget the product's advantages stressed by the salesperson because they are not consistent with the buyer's beliefs and attitudes.

These perceptions help explain why a buyer may or may not buy. The buyer's perceptional process acts as a filter by determining what part of the sales message is heard, how it is interpreted, and what product information is retained. Therefore, two different sales messages given by two different salespeople, even though they concern similar products, can be received differently. A buyer can tune out one sales presentation, tune in the other presentation, and purchase the perceived product.

While you cannot control a buyer's perceptions, often you can influence and change them. To be successful, you must understand that perceptual barriers can arise during your presentation. Learn to recognize when they occur and how to overcome them.

Example of a Buyer's Misperceptions

Assume, as an example, that a woman is shopping for a ceiling fan for her home. The three main features of the product she is interested in are price, quality, and style. While shopping around, she has seen two brands, the Hunter and the Economy brand. The information she has received on these two brands has caused her to conclude that all ceiling fans are basically alike. Each brand seems to offer the same features and advantages. Because of this attitude, she has formed the belief that she should purchase a low-price fan, in this case, the Economy ceiling fan. Cost is the key factor influencing this purchase decision.

She decides to stop at one more store, which sells Casablanca fans. She asks the salesperson to see some lower-priced fans. These fans turn out to be more expensive than either the Hunter or Economy models. Noting their prices, she says to the salesperson, "That's not what I had in mind." She walks away as the salesperson says, "Thanks for coming by."

What should the salesperson have done? When the customer walked into the store, the salesperson knew her general need was for a ceiling fan. However, the customer had wrongly assumed that all brands are alike. It was the salesperson's job to first ask fact-finding questions of the customer such as: "Where will you use the fan?" "What colour do you have in mind?" "Is there a particular style you are interested in?" "What features are you looking for?" and "What price range would you like to see?" These questions allow the salesperson to determine the customer's specific needs and her attitudes and beliefs about ceiling fans.

Learning the answers to these questions enables the salesperson to explain the benefits of the Casablanca fan as compared to the Hunter and Economy brands. The salesperson can show that fans have different features, advantages, and benefits, and why there are price differences among the three fans. The buyer can then make a decision as to which ceiling fan best suits her specific needs. Knowledge of a buyer's learned attitudes and beliefs can make sales; with this information, a salesperson can alter the buyer's perceptions or reinforce them when presenting the benefits of the product.

ATTITUDES AND BELIEFS

A person's **attitudes** are learned predispositions toward something. These feelings can be favourable or unfavourable. If a person is neutral toward the product or has no knowledge of the product, no attitude exists. A buyer's attitude is shaped by past and present experience.

Creating a positive attitude is important, but it alone does not result in your making the sale. To sell to someone, you also must convert a buyer's belief into a positive attitude. A **belief** is a state of mind in which trust or confidence is placed in something or someone. The buyer must believe your product will fulfill a need or solve a problem. A favourable attitude toward one product rather than another comes from a belief that one product is better.

Also, a buyer must believe that you are the best person from whom to buy. If you are not trusted as the best source, people will not buy from you. Assume, for example, that someone decides to buy a 19-inch, portable Sony colour television. Three Sony dealers are in the trading area and each dealer sells at approximately the same price. The purchaser likely will buy from the salesperson believed to be best, even though there is no reason not to trust the other dealers.

If buyers' perceptions create favourable attitudes that lead them to believe your product is best for them and that they should buy from you, you make sales. Often, however, people may not know you or your product. Your job is to provide information about your product that allows buyers to form positive attitudes and beliefs. Should buyers' perceptions, attitudes, and beliefs be negative, distorted, or incorrect, you must change them. As a salesperson, you spend much time creating or changing people's learned attitudes and beliefs about your product. *This is the most difficult challenge a salesperson faces.*

**CONSIDER
THE BUYER'S
PERSONALITY**

People's personalities also can affect their buying behaviour by influencing the types of products that fulfill their particular needs. **Personality** can be viewed as the individual's distinguishing character traits, attitudes, or habits. While it is difficult to know exactly how personality affects buying behaviour, it is generally believed that personality influences a person's perceptions, attitudes, and beliefs, and his or her buying behaviour.

Self-Concept

One of the best ways to examine personality is to consider a buyer's **self-concept**, the view of the self. According to self-concept theory, buyers possess four images:

1. The **real self**—people as they actually are
2. The **self-image**—how people see themselves
3. The **ideal self**—what people would like to be
4. The **looking-glass self**—how people think others regard them.

As a salesperson, attempt to understand the buyer's self-concept, since it may be the key to understanding the buyer's attitudes and beliefs. For example, if a man is apparently unsatisfied with his self-image, he might be sold through appeals to his ideal self-image. You might compliment him by saying, "Mr. Buyer, it is obvious that the people in your community think highly of you. They know you as an ideal family man and good provider for your family [looking-glass self]. Your purchase of this life insurance policy will provide your family with the security you want [ideal self]." This appeal is targeted at the looking-glass self and the ideal self. Success in sales is often closely linked to the salesperson's knowledge of the buyer's self-concept rather than the buyer's ideal self.

**FACE-TO-FACE
WITH YOUR
BUSINESS BUYER**

As you have read, the black box approach to buyer behaviour has a great degree of relevance when selling to consumers because their decisions are often based on satisfying their own personal needs. There is also some application of these theories to business buyers—they are human and still seek personal satisfaction on many levels.

EXHIBIT 3–4

Discuss benefits to fulfill people's needs and to increase sales.

Industrial salespeople work closely with customers to design products and systems that fit their needs.

Consumer goods salespeople show customers how to increase sales by setting up strategic merchandise displays.

At the very least, you have become more sensitive to the idea that people are quite different and are certainly affected by many different types of influences.

Personality Typing

Carl Gustav Jung (1875–1961), with Sigmund Freud, laid the basis for modern psychiatry. Jung divided human awareness into four functions: (1) thinking, (2) intuiting, (3) feeling, and (4) sensing.* He argued that most people are most comfortable behaving in one of these four groups. Each group, or personality type, has certain characteristics formed by past experiences.

Exhibit 3–5 shows guidelines you can use to identify someone's personality style. You can determine styles by identifying the key trait, focusing on time orientation, identifying the environment, and analyzing what people say. Imagine that four of your buyers say the following things to you:

a. "I'm not interested in all those details. What's the bottom line?"
b. "How did you arrive at your projected sales figure?"
c. "I don't think you see how this purchase fits in with our whole operation here."
d. "I'm not sure how our people will react to this."

How would you classify their personality styles?[†]

Adapt Your Presentation to the Buyer's Style

The major challenge is to adapt your personal style to best relate to the people you deal with. For example, if you think about the customer you best relate to, the one whom you find it easiest to call on, the odds are that her primary personality style is similar to yours. The person hardest for you to call on usually has a primary style that differs from yours.

Increase your skill at recognizing the style of the people you deal with. Once you recognize the basic style of a buyer, for example, you can modify your presentation to the buyer's style to achieve the best results. Let's examine a suggested tailored selling method based on the prospect's personality-type preferences.

The Thinker Style

This person places high value on logic, ideas, and systematic inquiry. Completely preplan your presentation with ample facts and supporting data, and be precise. Present your material in an orderly and logical manner. When closing the sale be sure to say, "Think it over, Joe, and I'll get back to you tomorrow," whenever the order does not close on the spot.

The Intuitor Style

This person places high value on ideas, innovation, concepts, theory, and long-range thinking. The main point is to tie your presentation into the buyer's big picture. Strive to build the buyer's concepts and objectives into your presentation whenever possible. In presenting your material, be sure you have ample time.

In closing the sale, stress time limitations on acting. A good suggestion is to say, "I know you have a lot to do—I'll go to Sam to get the nitty-gritty handled and get this off the ground."

---

*Numerous methods of personality typing exist. We use Jung's classification because of his scientific reputation.

[†]Answers: (a) Senser, (b) Thinker, (c) Intuitor, and (d) Feeler.

EXHIBIT 3–5

Guidelines to identifying personality style.

Guideline	Thinker	Intuitor	Feeler	Senser
How to describe this person	A direct, detail-oriented person. Likes to deal in sequence on her time. Very precise, sometimes seen as a nitpicker. Fact oriented.	A knowledgeable, future-oriented person. An innovator who likes to abstract principles from a mass of material. Active in community affairs by assisting in policymaking, program development, etc.	People oriented. Very sensitive to people's needs. An emotional person rooted in the past. Enjoys contact with people. Able to read people very well.	Action-oriented person. Deals with the world through the senses. Very decisive and has a high energy level.
The person's strengths	Effective communicator, deliberative, prudent, weighs alternatives, stabilizing, objective, rational, analytical, asks questions for more facts.	Original, imaginative, creative, broad-gauged, charismatic, idealist, intellectual, tenacious, ideological, conceptual, involved.	Spontaneous, persuasive, empathetic, grasps traditional values, probing, introspective, draws out feelings of others, loyal, actions based on what has worked in the past.	Pragmatic, assertive, directional, results oriented, technically skilful, objective—bases opinions on what he actually sees, perfectionist, decisive, direct and down to earth, action oriented.
The person's drawbacks	Verbose, indecisive, overcautious, overanalyzes, unemotional, nondynamic, controlled and controlling, overserious, rigid, nitpicking.	Unrealistic, fantasy-bound, scattered, devious, out of touch, dogmatic, impractical, poor listener.	Impulsive, manipulative, overpersonalizes, sentimental, postponing, guilt-ridden, stirs up conflict, subjective.	Impatient, doesn't see long term, status seeking, self-involved, acts first then thinks, lacks trust in others, nitpicking, impulsive, does not delegate to others.
Time orientation	Past, present, future.	Future.	Past.	Present.
Environment				
Desk	Usually neat.	Reference books, theory books, etc.	Personal plaques and mementos, family pictures.	Chaos.
Room	Usually has a calculator and computer runs, etc.	Abstract art, bookcases, trend charts, etc.	Decorated warmly with pictures of scenes or people. Antiques.	Usually a mess with piles of papers, etc. Action pictures or pictures of the manufacturing plant or products on the wall.
Dress	Neat and conservative.	Trendy or rumpled.	Current styles or informal.	No jacket; loose tie or functional work clothes.

The Feeler Style

This person places high value on being people-oriented and sensitive to people's needs. The main point to include in your presentation is the impact on people that your idea will have. The feeler likes to make small talk with you, so engage in conversation and wait for this person's cue to begin your presentation. The buyer will usually ask, "What's on your mind today?" or something similar. Use emotional terms and words, such as, "We're *excited* about this!"

In your presentation, start with something carried over from your last call or contact. Keep the presentation on a personal note. Whenever possible, get the buyer away from the office (lunch, coffee, etc.) on an informal basis; this is how this person prefers to do business. Force the close by saying something such as, "OK, Kamal, if there are no objections, let's set it up for the next week." Even if the buyer says no, you are not dead. The key with a feeler is to push the decision.

The Senser Style

This person places high value on *action*. The key point with a senser is to be brief and to the point. Graphs, models, and samples help as the senser can visualize your presentation. With a senser, verbal communication is more effective than written communication.

In presenting, start with conclusions and results and have supporting data to use when needed. Suggest an action plan—"Let's move *now*"; the buyer has to believe you know what to do.

In closing, give one best way. Have options, but do not present them unless you have to. An effective senser close is, "I know you're busy; let's set this up right *now.*"

Watch for Clues   Exhibit 3–6 shows two buyers' environments. Look at the environment guidelines listed in Exhibit 3–5 to identify each buyer's personality style.

The neatness of the desk and dress of the buyer on the left indicate he may be a thinker, whereas the buyer on the right appears to be a senser. The salesperson should alter the presentation to fit each person's style. However, determining a buyer's personality style is not always as easy as the example shown in Exhibit 3–6.

Determining Style
Can Be Difficult   Each of the four styles is present, to some degree, in all of us. However, one primary style is usually dominant, and another complementary style is used as a backup. The primary style employed by an individual often remains the same in both normal and stress situations, while the secondary style is likely to vary.

Some individuals do not have a primary or secondary style, but have a personal style comprising all four types. Dealing with this individual requires strong rapport (discussed later in the text) to isolate the prospect's strong personal likes and dislikes.

EXHIBIT 3–6

Environment provides clues to the buyer's style. What are the personality styles of the buyers who sit at these desks?

SOCIAL STYLE THEORY

Successful sales professionals should have a firm grasp of the negotiating process and a good understanding of people. Accomplished sales professionals know not only their own personal negotiating style but also their buyer's preferred style—and they use this knowledge to build a stronger relationship that will help them accomplish their goals.

Many sales professionals don't pay enough attention to the effects of behavioural styles on a negotiation. Many use the same approach in every negotiation and are surprised when they do not get consistently good results. But everyone is different and every negotiation is different. Salespeople who understand these differences and vary their approach to negotiations have a higher likelihood of successfully negotiating. Successful sales professionals tailor their approach to the behavioural style and needs of their buyers—it's a matter of empathy.

Being able to identify a buyer's preferred style and adapt your own style accordingly can be incredibly helpful in building long-term relationships. With this in mind, let's examine the characteristics that will help you identify your buyer's preferred style, and consider some tips to building relationships that lead to win–win outcomes.

Amiables

These are one of the easiest buyers to get an appointment with, yet one of the most difficult buyers to close. Buyers who use the Amiable style have a strong need to feel recognized and valued in the negotiating partnership. They place a great emphasis on relationships; therefore, they tend to focus more on feelings and less on facts. They will often begin a negotiation with social conversation that is unrelated to the negotiation. They are trusting, friendly, optimistic, and generally committed to outcomes that benefit both parties.

To build rapport with your Amiable buyer, show genuine respect and care for the prospect and his or her problems. Be sincere, and don't discount personal feelings. Remain positive and solution-oriented. Do not argue or engage in any "head to head" confrontation, which will most likely cause the Amiable to shy away and end the negotiation. Negotiate in a manner that builds trust, and understand that for your Amiable buyer negotiation is more than just business—it is personal. Never say to an Amiable, "Don't take it personally." Use testimonials, stories, and analogies. If you can help your prospect solve a problem he or she has with others, you will have a higher likelihood of success.

Drivers

Drivers and Amiables are often noted to be at opposite ends of the behavioural style continuum. While Amiables are focused on the relationship, Drivers are results-oriented and focused primarily on the bottom line. Drivers have a strong concern for positive outcomes and can be ruthless. They tend to be impatient, have little need for detailed information, and want to close the negotiation quickly. Drivers are self-confident, assertive, and can be aggressive. While both the Amiable and the Driver have a need to achieve a positive outcome, for the Driver, winning is all-important.

Be prepared with a Driver. Know your bottom line. Keep your interactions focused on business. This will help you remain confident, focused, and concise. Remember: "You can tell a Driver, but you can't tell them much, so don't try." Instead, ask questions that allow Drivers to discover solutions and suggest acceptable alternatives. Understand that when negotiating with a Driver, however ruthless your counterpart becomes, from the Driver's perspective it's not personal, just business.

Analyticals

Analyticals appear cautious and reserved. True Analyticals methodically explore all options, leaving no stone unturned in their quest for a fair and economical outcome. Analyticals have a strong need for facts, figures, and details, and won't move forward until they carefully analyze all available data. They tend to process information slowly and may be somewhat withdrawn or unemotional during the negotiation. They are organized, systematic, and approach the negotiation pragmatically, one step at a time.

To build rapport and gain respect from the Analytical, be prepared. Ensure that your research is complete and accurate. Keep your discussions factual and business related. Be honest and ethical, and demonstrate ways in which outcomes will be advantageous in terms of money, time, or resources conserved. When you present information regarding your product or service to an analytical buyer, always present both the pros and cons. Finally, be patient and respect the Analytical's need to process information methodically.

Expressives

These people care most about perceptions. Status and approval are important to Expressives. How they perceive things and how other people perceive them take precedence. They are mostly impulsive, colourful, egocentric, undisciplined, and spontaneous.

Actors, teachers, musicians, artists, art lovers, graphic designers, directors, and comedians often fall into the Expressive category. As an example, these people are often the ones who buy mostly for the sake of prestige of ownership, or to boost their standing in their organization or peer group. They may intentionally flaunt their purchases so that people will notice them.

Ultimately, your presentation or negotiation should show the prospect exactly how your product will make them look good.

How Do You Know?

Now that you have a general understanding of the different styles buyers use when negotiating, you may be wondering how to identify *your* buyer's specific style. There are four main ways: (1) research, (2) general observation, (3) listening, and (4) asking questions.

Use Your Head!

To learn about your buyer's personality before even meeting, do some research. Speak with other people who may know this prospect; read company literature. It is not always possible, but do your best to be prepared before you meet him or her for the first time.

Use Your Eyes!

You will get clues about your buyer's style through general observation. When you walk into your buyer's office, look around. The types of things that are displayed on the walls or desk can provide insight into what your buyer feels is important. Are family pictures or company photos displayed, indicating that relationships are important? If so, you may be negotiating with an Amiable. Are the walls covered with plaques and certificates noting achievements and displaying a pride in accomplishment? This may indicate that your buyer is a Driver. Is the office neat and organized, or are stacks of files and papers lying around? The neater and more organized the office is, the greater the likelihood that you are negotiating with an Analytical. It is important to note that you cannot determine your buyer's style by observation alone, but you can certainly gain some initial insights.

Use Your Ears!

Another important tool to help identify your buyer's style is listening. For example, an executive visits a custom tailor for a consultation for some additions to her wardrobe.

If she's an Analytical, during the meeting she will be preoccupied mostly with the details of the manufacturing process. Knowing precisely what type of material is used, how strong the stitching is, and whether the clothes are hand sewn or machine manufactured will all be of enormous interest.

On the other hand, a Driver will want to know how long the clothes will take, and how much it will cost.

The Amiable is mostly concerned with any disruption to her routine that might occur, her happiness with the new look, and her ability to please family, friends, or boss with an improved appearance.

The Expressive will be mostly interested with how good her new clothes will look, how the clothes change her appearance, and how attractive the clothes will make her to other people. She can't wait to wear them.

Use Your Mouth!

A third way to determine your buyer's behavioural style is by asking questions and listening carefully to the responses. For example, to determine if your buyer is a Driver or an Analytical, you could ask, "We have a 50-page document that supports our position. Would you like me to review the complete document with you, or would you like to see the two-page summary?" An Analytical will almost always want to review the entire document, while a Driver will usually want to see the two-page summary.

Other good questions to help you determine your buyer's style might be, "How are you doing today?" or "How was your weekend?" In response, Amiables will typically give some personal information. In fact, Amiables will often provide far more information than Drivers or Analyticals want to know! Drivers may respond with, "Fine," and quickly switch the topic to the business at hand.

Applying Your Knowledge of Behavioural Science

The ability to identify, understand, and respect your buyer's negotiating styles—and adapt your style accordingly—can help you build productive relationships that lead to win–win outcomes. Remembering one of the most important characteristics for sales people to have—*empathy*—will serve you well in every negotiation.

DIFFICULT CUSTOMERS

The personality theories discussed so far have been developed through research and shed some very good insights into the minds of buyers. However, over the years many salespeople have reported several variations of these theories and have developed suggestions for dealing with these people.

Angry People

Angry types may be power strugglers looking for a way to get the edge. They may also be intimidators—people who use anger to throw others off-guard. These two types are usually rewarded for their behaviour by people who want to avoid confrontations with them. You probably can't deflate their anger, but you can stop taking it personally. Remember that angry people generally have self-esteem issues that underlie their hostility.

Complainers

Complainers will never be happy with any solution. Try to turn the complaint around by asking, "If this solution won't work, what would?" Before you know it, complainers may be solving their own problems.

Know-It-Alls

These people like it when someone makes them feel important by asking questions that acknowledge their experience and qualifications. You might say, "You've been in this business a long time. Tell me how the business has changed over the years. What's the greatest challenge you face now?" That way, you can get lots of valuable information while making them feel appreciated. You'll also be able to offer an intelligent solution that makes sense to them.

Silent Types

These shy and reserved customers don't like to open up to strangers. Use some common ground to break the ice. Ask these customers open-ended questions, then be quiet and let them do the talking. You could also say "If we had to present this to others in your company, what would you suggest we do?" When they're actively involved, they'll open up more.

Indecisive Prospects

When customers are undecided, take a direct approach. Do some research so you can say, "I've been thinking about your concerns and doing some homework. What if we went this way as our next step?" Many times, these customers need someone to hold their hand during the process and make the decision for them. You can also share customer testimonials—when they see that other people have put their trust in you, they will, too.

Greedy Customers

These are people who try to take advantage of your business relationship by demanding that you cut your prices or add more services without increasing price. Try saying something like, "We will, as always, give you a fair price and the service we've promised. But we have a business just like you do and for us to remain in business, we have to stay within this price range. I'm sure you can understand." Stand your ground and remind them how your product or service adds value to their company. If they still don't see the value you offer, perhaps it's time to end the relationship.

What's the best advice for dealing with tough customers? Empathy. Be sure to listen to their concerns without interruption. Don't argue with them or get angry or frustrated. Get as much information as you can to understand each customer as an individual, and then adjust your selling techniques to each situation accordingly. It's the only way to turn tough customers into your best customers.

VIEWING BUYERS AS DECISION MAKERS

Earlier in this chapter we explored why people buy. Now we examine *how* they buy. Buyers, whether private consumers or industrial purchasing agents, are constantly exposed to information about various products. What steps do people go through in making a purchase decision?

Typically, buying involves the five basic steps shown in Exhibit 3–7. Buyers recognize a need, collect information provided by the salesperson, evaluate that information, decide to buy, and after the purchase determine whether they are satisfied with the purchase. This sequence reveals that several events occur before and after the purchase, all of which should be considered by the salesperson.

During this five-step sequence, the prospective customer makes several decisions leading up to—and after—the decision to buy. The purchase decision step is just one

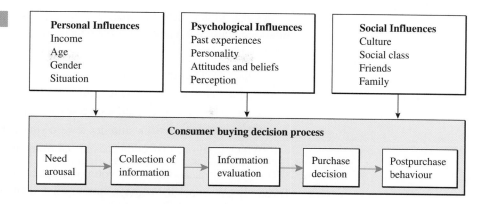

EXHIBIT 3–7

Personal, psychological, and social forces influence consumers' buying behaviour.

of these decisions—the "I will buy" decision. As discussed earlier, a salesperson uses trial closes to encourage buyers to make the series of minor decisions leading up to the purchase decision step. A close is used to prompt the buyer to make the "I will buy" decision.

As shown in Exhibit 3–7, numerous forces influence a consumer's buying behaviour. Rich people or older people, for example, often view purchases differently than lower-income or younger consumers. Psychological factors such as past experience with a salesperson—good or bad—certainly influence buying decisions. We all have had a friend or family member cause us to buy one product rather than another. Thus, whether we realize it or not, numerous factors influence why someone buys something.

Need Arousal

Remember from the first part of this chapter that buyers may experience a need, or the need can be triggered by the salesperson: this is called **need arousal**. It could be psychological, social, or economic; it could be a need for safety, self-actualization, or ego fulfillment. You must determine a person's needs to know what product information to provide. This information should relate the product's benefits to the person's needs.

Collection of Information

If buyers know which product satisfies a need, they buy quickly. The salesperson may need only to approach them; they already want to buy the product.

However, when buyers are faced with limited or extensive problem solving, they may want to **collect information** about the product. They might visit several retail stores and contact several potential suppliers. They may talk with a number of salespeople about a product's price, advantage, size, and warranty before making a decision.

Information Evaluation

A person's product **information evaluation** determines what will be purchased. After mentally processing all the information about products that will satisfy a need—and this may or may not include your product—a buyer matches this information with needs, attitudes, and beliefs. Only then will a **purchase decision** be made.

This evaluation process includes rating preferences on factors such as price, quality, and brand reputation. Attitudes on different products are based on either psychological or rational reasons.

At this stage, a salesperson can be effective. Providing information that matches product features, advantages, and benefits with a buyer's needs, attitudes, and beliefs increases the chances of a favourable product evaluation. So the salesperson is responsible for uncovering the person's needs, attitudes, and beliefs early in the discussion to match the product with the person's needs.

One way to get such information is to determine not only needs, beliefs, and attitudes but also the type of information a person needs before making the purchase decision. Here are some questions to which you have to find the answers:

- Which product attributes are important in this decision—price, quality, service?
- Of these attributes, which are most important?
- What are the prospect's attitudes toward your products?
- What are the prospect's attitudes toward your competitor's products?
- Which level of satisfaction is expected from buying the product?

This type of questioning tells you not only about the customer's needs but also involves the customer in the presentation and will convey the idea that you are truly interested in his needs. This attitude toward you is enough to create positive attitudes about your product.

Armed with this knowledge about the customer, the salesperson is in a better position to provide the information necessary for decision making and also to help the customer evaluate information in favour of your product. The information should be provided simply, clearly, and straightforwardly. It should seek to correct any negative information or impression about your product. Matching information with a customer's needs may enable you to

- Alter the person's beliefs about your product (e.g., by convincing the customer that your product is priced higher than the competition's because it is a quality product).
- Alter the person's beliefs about your competitor's products.
- Change the amount of importance a person attaches to a particular product attribute (e.g., by having the customer consider quality and service rather than price alone).
- Show unnoticed attributes of your product.
- Change the search for the ideal product into a more realistic pursuit, such as by substituting a $200,000 home for a $400,000 home, or showing a very tall prospect a mid-size car rather than a compact.

A company has no better promotional device than having its sales force help prospects and customers evaluate products on the market—and not merely its own products. The two-way communication between buyer and seller is exceptionally effective in providing the information needed to make the sale on the one hand, and to evaluate the product on the other. In many respects, salespeople are teachers (professors, if you will) who provide helpful information.

Purchase Decision

Is the sale made once the prospect states an intention to buy? No. Do not consider the sale final until the contract is signed or until you have the buyer's money, because there is still a chance for a change of mind. Even after a customer has selected a product, purchase intentions can be changed by these four basic factors:

1. The attitude of significant others, such as a relative, spouse, friend, or boss. Consideration should be given to both the intensity of another person's attitude and the level of motivation the buyer has to comply with or to resist this other person's attitude.
2. The perceived risk of buying the product—will the seller give a return on the money?

EXHIBIT 3–8

Other people can influence the prospect's decision to purchase.

This pharmaceutical rep must service and meet the needs of technicians, physicians, and buyers in hospitals that use his company's products.

This salesperson should sell to both people in the discussion. Otherwise, one person could talk the other out of buying the product.

3. Uncontrollable circumstances, such as not being able to finance the purchase of a house or to pass the physical examination for a life insurance policy.

4. The salesperson's actions after the decision has been reached—sometimes it is unwise to continue to talk about a product after this point; something could change the customer's mind.

Postpurchase   The decision process does *not* end with the purchase—not for the buyer at least! A product, once purchased, yields satisfaction and dissatisfaction. **Purchase satisfaction** comes from receiving benefits expected, or greater than expected, from a product.

The buyer can experience **cognitive dissonance** after the product's purchase. Dissonance causes tension over whether the right decision was made in buying the product. Some people refer to this as *buyer's remorse.* Dissonance increases with the importance of the decision and the difficulty of choosing between products. If dissonance occurs, buyers may get rid of a product by returning it or by selling it to someone else. Alternatively, they may seek assurance from the salesperson or friends that the product is a good one and that they made the correct purchase decision (positively reinforcing their beliefs).

You can help the buyer to be satisfied with the product and lower the level of dissonance in several ways. First, if necessary, show the buyer how to use the product properly. Second, be realistic in claims made for the product. Exaggerated claims may create dissatisfaction. Third, continually reinforce buyers' decisions by reminding them how well the product actually performs and fulfills their needs. Remember, in some situations buyers can return the product to the seller after purchase; this cancels your sale and hurts your chances of making future sales to this customer. Fourth, follow up after the sale to determine whether a problem exists. If so, help correct it. This follow-up is a great way to increase the likelihood of repeat business.

In summary, seek to sell a product that satisfies the buyer's needs. In doing so, remember that the sale is made only when the purchase is complete, and that you should continue to reinforce the buyer's attitudes about the product at all times, even after the sale.

CLASSIFYING BUYING SITUATIONS

Some people may appear to make up their minds quickly and easily either to buy or not to buy. The speed and ease of deciding which product to buy typically depend on the buying situation. People have more difficulty selecting, organizing, and interpreting information when purchasing an automobile rather than a litre of milk. Also, their attitudes and beliefs toward the automobile may not be well formed.

Although a few people have the type of personality (and resources) that allow them to quickly purchase an expensive product like an automobile, this is unusual. When purchasing some types of products, most people carefully compare competing brands and talk to salespeople. As information is collected, attitudes and beliefs are formed toward each product. People must decide which product has the most desirable features, advantages, and benefits. When considering several brands, people may seek information on each one. The more information collected, the greater the difficulty they may have in deciding which product to buy.

The purchase decision is viewed as a problem-solving activity falling into one of three classifications shown in Exhibit 3–9. These situations are routine decision making, limited decision making, and extensive decision making.

Routine Decisions

Many products are purchased repeatedly. People give little thought or time to the routine purchase; they fully realize the product's benefits. These are called low-involvement goods. Milk, cold drinks, and many grocery items often are purchased through **routine decision making**.

For a customer making a routine purchase decision, reinforce that this is a correct buying decision. It is important to have the product in stock. If you do not have it, the customer may go to another supplier.

For someone not currently using your product, the challenge is to change this person's product loyalty or normal buying habits. The features, advantages, and benefits of your product should be directly compared to the buyer's preferred brand.

Limited Decisions

When buyers are unfamiliar with a particular product brand, they seek more information when making a purchase decision. In this case, there is **limited decision making**—a moderate level of buyer involvement in the decision. The general qualities of goods in the product class are known to the buyer; however, buyers are not familiar with each brand's features, advantages, and benefits. For example, they may perceive that Xerox, 3M, and Canon copiers are the same in performance.

EXHIBIT 3–9

The three classes of buying situations.

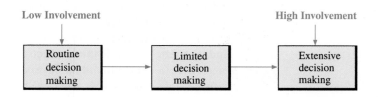

These buyers have more involvement in buying decisions in terms of shopping time, money, and potential dissatisfaction with the purchase than in the routine purchase decision. They seek information to aid them in making the correct decision. Develop a sales presentation to provide buyers with the necessary knowledge to make brand comparisons and to increase their confidence that the purchase of your product is the correct decision. Occasionally, the purchase of some products requires prospective buyers to go one step further and apply extensive decision making.

Extensive Decisions

Buyers seeking to purchase products such as insurance, a home, or an automobile are highly involved in making the buying decision. They may be unfamiliar with a specific brand or type of product, and have difficulty making the purchase decision. This kind of purchase requires more of an investment in time and money than the limited decision. This situation demands **extensive decision-making** and problem-solving activities.

In making extensive decisions, buyers believe that much more is at stake relative to other buying decisions. They may become frustrated during the decision-making process, especially if a large amount of information is available. They may become confused—not knowing what product features they are interested in because of unfamiliarity with the products. Buying an automobile or a life insurance policy, for example, entails potentially confusing purchase decisions.

Determine all possible reasons for the buyer's interest in a product. Then, in a simple, straightforward manner, present only enough information to allow the buyer to make a decision. At this time, product comparisons can be made, if necessary. You also can help the buyer evaluate alternative products.

In summary, your job is to *provide buyers with product knowledge that allows them to develop positive beliefs that your products fulfill their needs.* Determining the type of decision process a buyer is engaged in is critical to you as a salesperson.

BUSINESS-TO-BUSINESS BUYING SITUATIONS

Similar to the buying situations above, organizations of all types are faced with different types of buying situations. In each situation, buying organizations will likely use a different practice or method of ensuring that their needs are satisfied. These changes in buying methods are of great concern to salespeople—understanding how organizational purchases are made will increase the chances of entering into relationships with them.

Typically, when organizations have a need to be fulfilled, their purchase will fall into one of three recognized buying situations.

1. Straight rebuy—In this situation, products are typically purchased on a routine basis by an organization without much investigation. An office secretary ordering office supplies from Grand & Toy over the Internet would be an example of a straight-rebuy situation.

2. Modified rebuy—With many products, changing technology and competition will cause organizations to go beyond a regular reorder and do a thorough investigation of competitors to find the best value. This would likely occur with the purchase of desktop computers, fax machines, and small equipment.

3. New task or new buy—When an organization is purchasing a product for the first time or the purchase is a significant one, it is often referred to as a new-buy situation. A major piece of machinery or a long-term supply contract are good examples of this type of buying situation.

EXHIBIT 3–10

Other people can influence the prospect's decision to purchase.

This rep must service and meet the needs of the many people that use his company's products.

This salesperson should sell to both people in the discussion. Otherwise, one person could talk the other out of buying the product.

The situations having the biggest impact on sales professionals are the modified-rebuy and new-buy situations because of the more extensive involvement levels by the buying organizations. The more elaborate the purchase, the more involved the companies get in the purchase process.

Exhibit 3–11 shows the implications of the three different buying situations. As shown, the newer the task, the more involved companies will get. Typically, with large purchases there is a multiple buying influence or the establishment of a buying centre. This means that there are many people involved in the purchase, each of whom has a different stake in it. The following roles are typically played within a buying centre:

- Users: those who ultimately will be using the product
- Gatekeepers: those responsible for controlling the flow of information
- Influencers: depending on the product, a variety of company personnel who have some interest in the buying outcome
- Deciders: those who ultimately decide on the provider—could be executives, board of directors, etc.
- Buyers: often the purchasing agent or finance department.

When a salesperson is preparing a proposal for an organization, he or she must take into account the complexity of the purchase and should ask him- or herself these questions about the buying centre:

- Which members take part in the buying process?
- What is each member's relative influence on the decision?
- What criteria are important to members in the evaluation process?

EXHIBIT 3–11

Characteristics of buying situations.

	Straight Rebuy	Modified Rebuy	New Task
Involvement level	Low	Medium	High
People involved	Few	More	Many
Selling implications	Some	More	Many

ETHICAL DILEMMA

Do the Right Thing—Creating a Need?

Samantha was leery about door-to-door selling but saw some tremendous income potential when she joined the Good Health Filter Company (GHFC). She thought, "With all the hullabaloo about air pollution and its contribution to ill health, these filters should be a cinch to sell." GHFC manufactured furnace air filters and claimed that they would reduce indoor air pollution by 90%. The company chose to distribute its products directly to homeowners so salespeople could deliver a standardized sales presentation.

During her training, Samantha was given a sales kit that included sales literature and an actual filter that was loaded with contaminants that no homeowner would like to see in their home. The demonstration filter had been exposed to conditions that would not be found in most normal homes and was left in place longer than the recommended replacement interval. The idea was that people would see the filter and perceive it as being effective at improving their health. When combined with the "scary" sales literature, it would be tough for people to say no. In reality, the filter was less effective than most of the air filters that could be purchased at any home improvement store.

Samantha couldn't miss. Each time she made a presentation, she emphasized how the home's occupants would enjoy healthier air. At twice the cost of regular air filters, she was making some healthy commissions.

1. Is she doing anything wrong?

2. Is she creating a need that in reality may not really be present?

3. Are "scare tactics" a legitimate selling technique?

SATISFIED CUSTOMERS ARE EASIER TO SELL

It is easier to sell a customer than a stranger—especially a satisfied customer! That's why building a relationship—keeping in touch after the sale—is so important to a salesperson's success. Sales representative Sally Fields says

> It took me five tough years to build up my customer base. Now selling is easy and fun. But the first months were terrible. Calling only on strangers got old, but I hung in there. I was going to succeed—no matter how hard I had to work.

EXHIBIT 3–12

Businessman on cell phone in airport.

A businessman talks on his cell phone and types on his laptop in an airport terminal.

The more strangers I sold, the more friends (customers) I had. It is easy to sell a friend. So in the mornings I contacted possible new customers and in the afternoons I visited customers to make sure they were happy with their purchases and sell them more office supplies. Today, 80 percent of my monthly sales comes from [repeat] customers. I still make cold calls to keep sharp. By next year my goal is to have 95 percent sales come from [repeat] customers. To do that I must do all I can to make sure customers are happy and find new customers. The relationships I build today will take care of my tomorrow!

Fields owes her success to doing everything she can to ensure her customers are happy with their purchases and her organization's service. Her yearly income is now more than $100,000. She has built her business through hard work, selling, and service. We'll discuss follow-up and service again later in the book.

SUMMARY OF MAJOR SELLING ISSUES

As a salesperson, be knowledgeable about factors that influence your buyer's purchase decision. You can obtain this knowledge, which increases your self-confidence and the buyer's confidence in you, through training and practice.

The salesperson should understand the characteristics of the target market (consumer or industrial) and how these characteristics relate to the buyer's behaviour to better serve and sell to customers.

Psychological factors include the buyer's motives, perceptions, learning, attitudes, beliefs, and personality—all of which influence the individual's needs. To determine these buying needs, you can ask questions, observe prospects, listen to them, and talk to their associates about their needs. Established relationships strongly influence buying decisions, making satisfied customers easier to sell to than new prospects.

The individual goes through various steps or stages in the three buying situations of routine decision making, limited decision making, and extensive decision making. Find out who is involved in the buying decision and the main factors that influence the decision, including various psychological and practical buying influences.

Realize that not all prospects will buy your products, at least not all of the time, due to the many factors influencing their buying decisions. You need to uncover buyers' needs, solve buyers' problems, and provide the knowledge that allows them to develop personal attitudes toward the product. These attitudes result in positive beliefs that your products will fulfill their needs. Uncovering prospects' needs is often difficult, since they may be reluctant to tell you their true needs or may not really know what and why they want to buy. People usually buy to satisfy a need, fulfill a desire, and obtain a value.

MEETING A SALES CHALLENGE

John Salley took the advice of Joe Gandolfo, who has reportedly sold more life insurance than any other person in the world. Joe's philosophy is that "selling is 98 percent understanding human beings and 2 percent product knowledge." Do not let that statement mislead you. Joe is extremely knowledgeable about insurance, tax shelters, and pension plans. In fact, he spends several hours a day studying recent changes on pensions and taxation. "But," Joe says, "I still maintain that it's not product knowledge but understanding of human beings that makes a salesperson effective."

John had his sales region's training director work with him two days a week for a month. John's sales presentations were analyzed and found to concentrate almost entirely on the technical features and advantages of the products. The training director contacted six of John's customers. Each said they often did not understand him because he was too technical. John immediately began emphasizing benefits and discussing features and advantages in nontechnical terms. Slowly his sales began to improve. Today, John Salley is a true believer in the phrase, "It's not what you say, but how you say it."

PLAYING THE ROLE

The situation: You are the salesperson for Canadian Paper Supply and you have four appointments scheduled for today. Each prospect represents a relatively large order of your paper products. You expect that you will be dealing with four different types of social styles so you must be prepared for each one.

Role A: The salesperson. Be prepared to recognize and deal properly with each style of buyer.

Role B: An Amiable buyer. Be prepared to present yourself as this type of buyer.

Role C: An Expressive buyer. Be prepared to present yourself as this type of buyer.

Role D: An Analytical buyer. Be prepared to present yourself as this type of buyer.

Role E: A Driver buyer. Be prepared to present yourself as this type of buyer.

Prepare your role for an in-class dramatization of a sales meeting. Note: It would be ideal if the salesperson did not have prior knowledge of the prospect. It is up to each salesperson to recognize which type of personality he or she is dealing with.

KEY TERMS FOR SELLING

attitudes, 68
belief, 68
black box, 61
cognitive dissonance, 79
collect information, 77
economic need, 64
extensive decision making, 81
ideal self, 69
information evaluation, 77
learning, 65
limited decision making, 80
looking-glass self, 69
need arousal, 77
needs, 62

perception, 66
personality, 69
personality typing, 70
purchase decision, 77
purchase satisfaction, 79
real self, 69
routine decision making, 80
selective distortion, 67
selective exposure, 66
selective retention, 67
self-concept, 69
self-image, 69
stimulus–response model, 61
wants, 62

SALES APPLICATION QUESTIONS

1. What three types of buying situations may the buyer be in when contacted by a salesperson? Briefly describe each type.
2. What are the psychological factors that may influence the prospect's buying decision?
3. Although you do not have to be a psychologist or understand exactly how the buyer's mind works, you do need to uncover the buyer's motives.
   a. Why?
   b. What techniques can be used to uncover the buyer's motives?
4. Try to remember a significant purchase that you've made recently. How did you proceed through the decision-making process? What were the major factors that influenced yjour decision?
5. It is obvious that people in the consumer market are subject to many influences in their decision-making process. Does the same hold true for professional purchasing agents who purchase for their companies?
6. For each of the different types of social styles, highlight two techniques that a salesperson could use to help them "get along."

SALES WORLD WIDE WEB EXERCISES

What Is Your Personality?

Communication skills help customers do a better job of relating product benefits to customer needs, which increases the salesperson's productivity. An essential part of having good communication skills is to better understand your own personality.

To better understand yourself, first complete the selling experiential exercise at the end of this chapter. It is entitled "What's Your Style—Senser, Intuitor, Thinker, Feeler?" This exercise uses an adaptation of the Myers–Briggs Temperament Indicator. The Keirsey Temperament Sorter URL below has you complete a more comprehensive Myers–Briggs type indicator.

To further your understanding of the real you, go to these sites and complete several of the personality exercises you feel are important for salespeople:

www.2h.com, IQ, Personality, and Entrepreneurial Tests

www.keirsey.com/cgi-bin/keirsey/newkts.cgi, the Keirsey Temperament Sorter

www.humanmetrics.com/cgi-win/JTypes2.asp

www.yahoo.com, type in *emotional intelligence*

www.ntlf.com/search.epl, type in *emotional intelligence*

www.sric-bi.com/VALS/

Write a short report summarizing what the personality tests uncovered about you. Do you believe the tests accurately assessed your personality and the real you?

FURTHER EXPLORING THE SALES WORLD

1. Keep a diary of your purchases for two weeks. Select five or more of the products you purchased during that period and write a short report on why you purchased each product and what you believe are the features, advantages, and benefits of each product.

2. Shop for a product costing more than $100. Report on your experience. Find out whether the salesperson is on a commission-pay plan. Do you think it affected the way in which he or she treated you?

STUDENT APPLICATION LEARNING EXERCISES (SALES)

Part 1

At the end of appropriate chapters, beginning with Chapter 3, you will find Student Application Learning Exercises (SALES). SALES are meant to help you construct the various segments of your sales presentation by building on one another.

1. State the product that you plan to sell.

2. Briefly describe the individual or organization to which you will sell.

3. From this chapter, identify and list the factors that are most likely to influence the purchase of your product. Pay particular attention to your buyers' needs.

4. Identify the information that you will have to uncover before you start planning your sales presentation.

SELLING EXPERIENTIAL EXERCISE

What's Your Style—Senser, Intuitor, Thinker, Feeler?

Complete the Problem-Solving Diagnostic Questionnaire (Exhibit A), then check the scoring key that appears in Exhibit B.[1] There are no right or wrong answers; just read each item carefully, then respond with your answer.

According to Jung, gathering information and evaluating information are separate activities. People gather information either by *sensation* or *intuition* but not by both simultaneously. People using *sensation* would rather work with known facts and hard data, and prefer routine and order in gathering information. People using *intuition* would rather look for possibilities than work with facts and prefer solving new problems and using abstract concepts.

EXHIBIT A

Questionnaire to determine your style.

Indicate your responses to the following questionnaire on a separate sheet of paper. There are no right or wrong responses to any of these items.

Part I. Write down the number and letter of the response that comes closest to how you usually feel or act.

1. I am more careful about
   a. People's feelings.
   b. Their rights.
2. I usually get on better with
   a. Imaginative people.
   b. Realistic people.
3. It is a higher compliment to be called
   a. A person of real feeling.
   b. A consistently reasonable person.
4. In doing something with many people, it appeals more to me
   a. To do it in the accepted way.
   b. To invent a way of my own.
5. I get more annoyed at
   a. Fancy theories.
   b. People who do not like theories.
6. It is higher praise to call someone
   a. A person of vision.
   b. A person of common sense.
7. I more often let
   a. My heart rule my head.
   b. My head rule my heart.
8. I think it is a worse fault
   a. To show too much warmth.
   b. To be unsympathetic.
9. If I were a teacher, I would rather teach
   a. Courses involving theory.
   b. Fact courses.

Part II. Write down the letters of the words in the following pairs that appeal to you more.

10.	a. compassion	b.	foresight
11.	a. justice	b.	mercy
12.	a. production	b.	design
13.	a. gentle	b.	firm
14.	a. uncritical	b.	critical
15.	a. literal	b.	figurative
16.	a. imaginative	b.	matter-of-fact

EXHIBIT B

Scoring key to determine your style.

The following scales indicate the psychological functions related to each item. Use the point value columns to arrive at your score for each function. For example, if you answered *a* to the first question, your *1a* response in the feeling column is worth zero points when you add up the point value column. Instructions for classifying your scores follow the scales.

Sensation	Point Value	Intuition	Point Value	Thinking	Point Value	Feeling	Point Value
2 *b*__	1	2 *a* ___	2	1 *b* ___	1	1 *a* ___	0
4 *a*__	1	4 *b* ___	1	3 *b* ___	2	3 *a* ___	1
5 *a*__	1	5 *b* ___	1	7 *b* ___	1	7 *a* ___	1
6 *b*__	1	6 *a* ___	0	8 *a* ___	0	8 *b* ___	1
9 *b*__	2	9 *a* ___	2	10 *b* ___	2	10 *a* ___	1
12 *a*__	1	12 *b* ___	0	11 *a* ___	2	11 *b* ___	1
15 *a*__	1	15 *b* ___	1	13 *b* ___	1	13 *a* ___	1
16 *b*__	2	16 *a* ___	0	14 *b* ___	0	14 *a* ___	1
Maximum point value:	(10)		(7)		(9)		(7)

Classifying total scores:

■ Write *intuition* if your intuition score is equal to or greater than your sensation score.

■ Write *sensation* if your sensation score is greater than your intuition score.

■ Write *feeling* if your feeling score is greater than your thinking score.

■ Write *thinking* if your thinking score is greater than your feeling score.

People evaluate information by making judgments about the information gathered. People evaluate information by *thinking* or *feeling*. These represent the extremes in orientation. *Thinking* individuals base their judgments on impersonal analysis, using reason and logic rather than personal values or emotional aspects of the situation. *Feeling* individuals base their judgments more on personal feelings, such as harmony, and tend to make decisions that result in approval from others.

According to Jung, only one of the four functions—sensation, intuition, thinking, or feeling—is dominant in an individual. However, the dominant function is usually backed up by one of the functions from the other set of paired opposites. Exhibit C shows the four problem-solving styles that result from these match-ups.[2]

Questions

1. Look back at your scores. What is your personal problem-solving style? Read the action tendencies. Do they fit?

2. Studies show that the sensation–thinking (ST) combination characterizes many managers in Western industrialized societies. Do you think the ST style is the best fit for most jobs in today's society?

3. Also look back at Exhibit 3–5, guidelines to identifying personality style. Compare yourself and others you know to the guidelines. Is there a match between you and the individual style? What about your roommate, spouse, parents, or siblings?

4. How can you use this information to improve your communication ability?

EXHIBIT C	Personal Style	Action Tendencies
The four styles and their tendencies.	Sensation-thinking	■ Emphasizes details, facts, certainty ■ Is a decisive, applied thinker ■ Focuses on short-term, realistic goals ■ Develops rules and regulations for judging performance
	Intuitive-thinker	■ Shows concern for current, real-life human problems ■ Is a creative, progressive, perceptive thinker ■ Emphasizes detailed facts about people rather than tasks ■ Focuses on structuring organizations for the benefit of people
	Sensation-feeling	■ Prefers dealing with theoretical or technical problems ■ Is pragmatic, analytical, methodical, and conscientious ■ Focuses on possibilities using interpersonal analysis ■ Is able to consider a number of options and problems simultaneously
	Intuitive-feeling	■ Avoids specifics ■ Is charismatic, participative, people oriented, and helpful ■ Focuses on general views, broad themes, and feelings ■ Decentralizes decision making, develops few rules and regulations

CASE 3-1
Top-Line MP3 Players

As a salesperson for Top-Line MP3 players, you have been asked to research customers' attitudes and beliefs toward your brand of MP3 players. With this information, you will determine whether your company has the correct product line and suggest selling points for the company's salespeople when discussing MP3 players with customers who come into the retail stores.

You decide to hold an open house on a Sunday in one of your typical stores located in an upper-income neighbourhood, and advertise your special prices. During the open house you ask everyone to be seated, thank them for coming, and ask them to discuss their attitudes toward your company's MP3 players.

Some people believe that MP3 players should be shopped for without considering brands; once a brand is selected, they go to the stores that carry the particular brand and buy from the store with the best price. Most people collect information on MP3s from personal sources (such as friends), commercial sources (such as advertising, salespeople, and product literature), and public sources (such as *Consumer Reports*). Sixty percent had narrowed their choice to MP3 players from Samsung, Sanyo, and Top-Line, and they seem to look for three things: price, quality, and style.

Questions

1. Given this information on why people buy MP3 players, what should salespeople be instructed to do when a customer enters their store?

2. If you were a salesperson representing Top-Line MP3 players and calling on purchasing agents from different retail chains, briefly describe what you might do if faced with the following type of buyer personalities:
   a. Driver
   b. Amiable
   c. Expressive
   d. Analytical

Luca Alexander sold a full line of high-end office furniture for SOFM. He called on all types of businesses to show his product line of finely crafted office goods. While he had a tremendous knowledge of his product line, he was having great difficulty relating to some of his prospects. He made four presentations last week that he thought he would close but somehow he left each without securing the sale. This is his account of each case:

Monday: Arrived at Friendly Jim's Glass Repair Company at 8:00 A.M. Friendly Jim himself greeted me at the door with a warm handshake and invited me to join him for breakfast. We sat down and Jim started discussing his wonderful weekend of golfing. Having already eaten breakfast and knowing I had a busy day ahead of me, I asked Jim if we could just get down to business and I started talking about our product. I stayed for an hour and haven't heard anything from him since.

Tuesday: Arrived at Gentleman James Electronics on Tuesday morning; I was about 10 minutes late due to heavy traffic and a little dishevelled due to the poor weather. I asked James if he would like to discuss the product over a coffee in the staff lounge. He didn't seem too sociable and seemed to want to rush the whole meeting, thus I felt a little uncomfortable during my presentation. I did most of the talking and told him how much his staff would appreciate him for purchasing this new high-end office furniture. He didn't buy.

Wednesday: Arrived at Top Notch Solutions, a technical consulting firm that wanted to furnish its new office high-rise. I met with Sally Smith—who was impeccably dressed—in her office, which was kept as tidy as any office I had ever seen. It was a bit overwhelming and I had forgotten some of my presentation materials in my office so I tried to improvise. I couldn't remember exact figures so often had to ballpark some of my estimates to her. I had really hoped to get this contract but haven't heard anything yet.

Thursday: Met with Sam Chang of Acme Importing at a downtown restaurant for breakfast. While waiting for him, I noticed him pull up in his brand new Jaguar convertible and park it right in front of the restaurant. I couldn't help but notice the expensive jewellery he was wearing—in fact, it appeared like he was showing it off. I spoke with him about the high-quality manufacturing process of our office furniture line and, for some reason, he seemed a little disinterested.

Questions

1. Can you see any possible causes for Luca's failure in these situations?
2. How might you have handled each situation differently?

4

COMMUNICATION FOR SUCCESSFUL SELLING: HOW TO BUILD RELATIONSHIPS

MAIN TOPICS

Communication: It Takes Two

Nonverbal Communication: Watch for It

Barriers to Communication

Master Persuasive Communication to Maintain Control

Communication Style

Netiquette for Sales Professionals

Listening: The Key to Unlocking Buyers' Needs

LEARNING OBJECTIVES

The ability to communicate effectively, both verbally and nonverbally, is crucial to sales success. This chapter introduces this important sales skill. After studying this chapter, you should be able to:

- Discuss the salesperson's communication process.
- Discuss and demonstrate the importance of using nonverbal communication when selling.
- Define and recognize different types of nonverbal signals.
- Discuss how appearance and handshaking can enhance communication.
- Recognize potential barriers to communication.
- Recognize the importance of empathy and listening to communication.
- Discuss the different types of communication styles that people use.
- Discuss and demonstrate the essentials of professional e-mail netiquette.
- Discuss the steps that lead to better listening.

Amos Skaggs, purchasing agent, stands as a salesperson enters his office. "Hi, Mr. Skaggs," the salesperson says, offering his hand. Skaggs returns a limp, one-second handshake and sits down behind his desk. He begins to open his afternoon mail, almost as though no one else were in the room.

The salesperson sits down and begins his canned sales talk by saying, "Mr. Skaggs, I'm here to show you how your company can lower manufacturing costs by 10 percent."

Skaggs lays his mail down on his desk, leans back in his chair, crosses his arms, and with a growl says, "I'm glad to hear that. You know something, young fellow; pretty soon it won't cost us anything to manufacture our products."

"Why is that?" the salesman mumbles, looking at the floor.

"Well, you are the ninth person I've seen today who has offered to save us 10 percent on our costs."

Skaggs stands up, leans over the table, and says slowly, "I believe I've heard enough sales pitches for one day."

The initially enthusiastic salesperson now apologetically says, "If this is not a good time for you, sir, I can come back at a later date."

The problem facing this salesperson is common. The buyer has been seeing salespeople all day. Basically, they say the same thing: "Buy from me and I'll save you money." What message has Skaggs sent to the salesperson? If you were the salesperson, what might you do now? Continued at end of chapter.

While many factors are crucial to sales success, the ability to communicate effectively is critical. This chapter describes several factors influencing communication, along with barriers to effective communication. Also examined is the often ignored—though always critical—topic of nonverbal communication. The balance of this chapter provides techniques to improve sales communication.

COMMUNICATION: IT TAKES TWO

Communication, in a sales context, is the act of transmitting verbal and nonverbal information and understanding between seller and buyer. This definition presents communication as an exchange of messages with some type of response expected between seller and buyer.

Communication during the sales presentation takes many forms. Research has found that face-to-face communication is composed of *verbal, vocal,* and nonverbal communication messages. One researcher found the total impact of communicated messages as 7 percent verbal, 38 percent tone of voice, and 55 percent nonverbal expressions.[1] That means that uninformed salespeople ignore a major part of the communication process that occurs during buyer–seller interaction. How the sales message is given can be as important to making the sale as what is said. Nonverbal communications are critical in communication between buyer and seller, and an awareness of nonverbal communication is a valuable tool in successfully making a sale.

Vocal communication includes such factors as voice quality, pitch, inflection, and pauses.

Salesperson–Buyer Communication Process Requires Feedback

Exhibit 4–1 shows a basic communication model of the salesperson–buyer communication process. Communication occurs when a sender transmits a message through some type of medium to a receiver who responds to that message. The eight major communication elements are defined as follows:

SELLING TIPS

Say What You Mean

At least six messages are involved in the communication process:

1. What you mean to say
2. What you really say
3. What the other person hears
4. What the other person thinks is heard
5. What the other person says about what you said
6. What you think the other person said about what you said.

It gets complicated, doesn't it? Sue and I were holding hands looking at a gorgeous moon together. As we shared the moment, I was feeling romantic. If we followed the six messages, that incident would have looked something like this:

1. What you mean to say   ("The moon puts me in a romantic mood.")
2. What you really say   ("Isn't that a brilliant moon?")
3. What the other person hears   ("The moon is bright.")
4. What the other person thinks is heard   ("Yes, its bright enough for a walk.")
5. What the other person says about what you said   ("Yes, it's bright enough to hit a golf ball by.")
6. What you think the other person said about what you said   ("I don't feel romantic.")

We can miss each other's meanings altogether by the time the six messages are completed, without realizing what has happened. Because all of us are constantly in the process of encoding and decoding messages, we need to learn to ask questions, or restate the point for clarification of meaning. Our goal is to say what we mean straightforwardly so listeners do not have to decode—and perhaps misconstrue—our meaning.

- **Source:** The source of communication (also called the communicator); in our case, it's the salesperson.
- **Encoding process:** The conversion by the salesperson of ideas and concepts into the language and materials used in the sales presentation.
- **Message:** The information conveyed in the sales presentation.
- **Medium:** The form of communication used in the sales presentation and discussion; most frequently words, visual materials, and body language.
- **Decoding process:** Receipt and translation (interpretation) of the information by the receiver (prospective buyer).
- **Receiver:** The person the communication is intended for; in our case, it's the prospect or buyer.
- **Feedback:** Reaction to the communication as transmitted to the sender. This reaction may be verbal, nonverbal, or both.
- **Noise:** Factors that distort communication between buyer and seller. Noise includes barriers to communication, which we discuss later.

EXHIBIT 4–1

The basic communication model has eight elements.

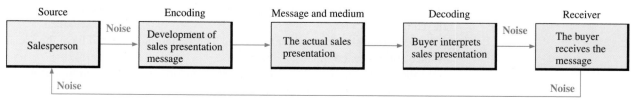

A salesperson should develop a sales presentation (encoding) so that the buyer has maximum understanding of the message (decoding). Clear verbal discussion, use of visual aids such as pictures or diagrams, and development of models or samples of the product are several ways a salesperson might communicate a sales message.

One-way communication occurs when the salesperson talks and the buyer only listens. The salesperson needs a response or feedback from the buyer to know whether the buyer understands the message. Once feedback or interaction and understanding between buyer and seller exists, two-way communication has been established.

Two-way communication is essential to make the sale; the buyer must understand your message to make a buying decision. Two-way communication gives the salesperson the ability to present a product's benefits, instantly receive buyer reactions, and answer questions. Buyers usually react both verbally and non-verbally to sales presentations.

NONVERBAL COMMUNICATION: WATCH FOR IT

Recognition and analysis of nonverbal communication in sales transactions is relatively new. However, the presence and use of nonverbal communication has been acknowledged for years.

People communicate nonverbally in several ways. Four major **nonverbal communication** channels are the physical space between buyer and seller, appearance, handshake, and body language.

Physical Space

The concept of **territorial space** refers to the preferred distance that humans keep between themselves in certain situations.

Salespeople should be careful not to violate territorial space; to do so may set off the customer's defence mechanisms and create a barrier to communications. Most North Americans have four main types of distances to consider—intimate (up to 0.5 metres), personal (0.5 metres to 1.5 metres), social (1.5 metres to 3.5 metres), and public (greater than 3.5 metres).

Intimate space of up to a half metre, or about arm's length, is the most sensitive zone, since it is reserved for close friends and loved ones. To enter intimate space in the buyer–seller relationship, for some prospects, could be socially unacceptable—possibly offensive.

During the presentation, a salesperson should carefully listen and look for signs that the buyer feels uncomfortable, perhaps that the salesperson is too close. A buyer may deduce from such closeness that the salesperson is attempting to dominate or overpower, resulting in buyer resistance. If such uneasiness is detected, the salesperson should move back to reassure the customer.

Personal space is the closest zone a stranger or business acquaintance is normally allowed to enter. Even in this zone, a prospect may be uncomfortable. Barriers, such as a desk, often reduce the threat implied when someone enters this zone.

Social space is the area normally used for a sales presentation. Again, the buyer often uses a desk to maintain a distance of 1.5 metres or more between buyer and seller. A salesperson standing while facing a seated prospect may seem too dominating to the buyer. Thus, the salesperson should normally stay seated to convey a relaxed manner.

A salesperson should consider beginning a presentation in the middle of the social distance zone, 2 to 2.5 metres.

Public space can be used by a salesperson making a presentation to a group of people. It is similar to the distance between teacher and student in a classroom.

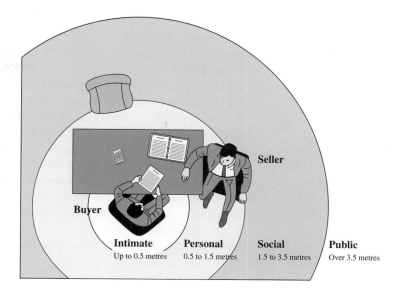

EXHIBIT 4–2

Office arrangements and
territorial space.

People are at ease and thus easy to communicate with at this distance, since they do not feel threatened.

Space Threats   Territoriality causes people to feel that they should defend their space or territory against **space threats**. The salesperson who pulls up a chair too close, takes over all or part of the prospect's desk, leans on or over the desk, or touches the objects on the desk runs the risk of invading a prospect's territory. Be careful not to create defensive barriers.

Space Invasion   The prospect who allows you to enter personal and intimate space is saying, "Come on into my space; let's be friends." In this case you can use space to your advantage.

In most offices, the salesperson sits directly across the desk from the prospect; this defensive barrier allows the prospect to control much of the conversation and remain safe from **space invasion**. Often, seating is prearranged, and some prospects might consider it a space threat if you moved your chair when calling for the first time.

However, if you have a choice between a chair across the desk or beside the desk, take the latter seat, as shown in Exhibit 4–2. Sitting beside the prospect lowers the desk communication barrier. If you are friends with the buyer, move your chair to the side of the desk. This helps create a friendly, cooperative environment between you and the buyer.

Appearance

Other common methods of nonverbal communication are signals conveyed by a person's physical appearance and handshake. Once territorial space has been established, general appearance is the next medium of nonverbal communication conveyed to a customer by a salesperson. Appearance not only conveys information such as age, sex, height, weight, and physical characteristics, but also provides clues to personality.

Style Hair Carefully

According to many image and communication consultants, a person's hairstyle is one of the first things people notice. It is often the basis of our image, and can communicate how we think of ourselves and our stage in life. Hairstyles can take many forms, from classic looks to trend-setting new styles. Your style should depend on your personal characteristics and possibly the industry in which you are working.

Many experts suggest that Canadian business style is mainly about being neat, appropriate, and non-distracting. Correct hairstyles enhance a person's personality, face, and dress. For example, long hair, traditionally frowned upon for salespeople, is acceptable when it is appropriate for your profession, complementary to your face and personality, and not distracting.

Some companies frown upon facial hair for men; if yours is open to it, consider keeping yours closely groomed, with a moustache not extending below the upper lip (thereby allowing the mouth to be seen clearly). Sideburns depend on the hairstyle, but for the business look they shouldn't extend below the middle of the ear. Of course, in some trendier industries males can get away with longer, less traditional hairstyles. Also, note that eyebrows shouldn't be so bushy as to create a distraction.

Regardless of personal preference, successful salespeople often practise "mirroring," whereby they consciously try to appear similar to their prospects and/or meet their expectations in order to open the lines of communication more easily.

Look the Part—Dress as a Professional

You get only one chance to make a first impression, and your appearance plays a large role. Always look professional. Although "business casual" dress is sweeping the business world, people who rely on face-to-face contact with clients must adhere to different rules. Mirroring, as mentioned above is a good strategy.

Following are a few basic guidelines that will help you project professionalism through your appearance. These will not apply to every situation; appearance standards vary between industries so it is best to rely on a company dress code—or, at the very least, your own common sense. Perhaps observing senior people in your own company would be a wise strategy until you learn the industry norm.

General Appearance Tips

- It is always better to be a little overdressed than underdressed.
- Always have neatly combed and styled hair. Stick to traditional hair colours. Long, flyaway hair might distract customers; tie it back if you can.
- Shoes should always be clean and polished.
- Don't apply cologne or perfume before going to meet a customer. Strong scents can be offensive, and some people can have allergic reactions.
- Earrings have traditionally been for women only. No other piercings should be visible in most cases.
- Tattoos are still frowned upon by some, so highly visible ones should be avoided.
- Always wear neatly pressed clothes.
- Always keep your vehicle clean in case you have to provide transportation.
- Avoid smoking in front of a customer.
- Be comfortable with yourself but conscious of your image.

To look sharp, be sharp, and feel sharp, the correct clothes, grooming, attitude, and physical conditioning are required. This applies to your career, to interviewing, and to your life.

Choose a suit that means business.

Natural fibres, a good fit, and current styles are important.

Physical conditioning produces the stamina and positive mental attitude necessary to be a success.

First impressions are crucial. Remember that you are representing your organization—and your customer's perception of that organization begins with you.

Special Tips for Men

- Suits: Traditional colours are blue, grey, and black; avoid brown, green, and bright colours. Solids or light patterns (pinstripe, tweed, light plaid, herringbone) are best. Recommended fabrics are wool or silk. Wool blends are good for year-round wear.

- Shirts: White or light, solid colours are best. Recommended fabric is a cotton blend (not 100 percent cotton, which is difficult to keep pressed). Choose a button-down collar if you're not wearing a tie. Wear an undershirt if possible.

- Ties: Medium width, knotted tightly, length to belt buckle. Correct tie pin placement is at the fourth button down.

- If you attend a casual-dress affair, wear something considered "business casual"; for example, an Oxford or polo shirt with a sweater and dress slacks. Dark colours are more powerful. Avoid sweatshirts, T-shirts, tight polo shirts, blue jeans, and sneakers.

Special Tips for Women

■ Suits are best, either with skirt or pants, as they add credibility.

■ The best colours are navy, charcoal, medium to dark blue, tan, red, and white. Avoid pink. Stick with soft patterns or solids. White blouses are best.

■ The best materials for a suit are wool, wool blend, linen, or synthetic. Stick with classic styles and avoid trends.

■ Long, wool coats are best in winter. Good colours are camel, navy, charcoal, or black.

■ If you attend a casual-dress affair, wear something considered "business casual"; for example, a nice blouse or shirt with a sweater and dress pants. Black is a good colour here. Avoid short skirts.

Even when you are away from work, be conscious of how you look; carry the professional image everywhere you go.

Handshake   There are three parts to the handshake:

1. How you extend your hand.
2. How you apply pressure.
3. The length of engagement.

Although handshakes have nothing to do with a person's character, sometimes people on the receiving end will base their perception of you on based on the quality of your handshake (see Exhibit 4–4).

1. How you extend your hand. When you extend your hand, you have three choices.

   a. Palm down may be a power play. If you feel strong and are trying to exude confidence then you automatically will offer your hand palm down. This forces the other person to offer palm up, and he or she may feel subservient. This is not a great relationship builder.

   b. Palm vertical ("Let's work together"). This may be the best way to offer a handshake. It sends the signal of cooperation: "I want to work with you." This technique is excellent to establish a trusting relationship.

   c. Palm up ("I am fully at your service"). Salespeople often offer a handshake palm up. This is a subtle way of indicating that you're there to please. While this may appear to be a good technique, the desired outcome should be that you are partners—with neither party dominating the other.

Extend your hand slowly; suddenly extending your hand may startle your prospect and appear unnatural. It is best to maintain eye contact during the handshake, which will send a message of confidence to the prospect.

2. How you apply pressure. In the Western world, people sometimes form their opinion of someone based on the strength of their grip. Therefore, it is important for salespeople to ensure that they engage in a handshake properly. Ideally, offer a palm-vertical hand and ensure that your hand is fully engaged with the other person. Letting someone get hold of your fingers may inadvertently send the signal that you are weak and lack confidence. With full engagement, it is difficult for either party to fully "control" the handshake. Aim for making contact between the base of your prospect's thumb and the base of yours.

Remember that the handshake is often a cultural issue. In other parts of the world, to apply pressure is regarded as impolite. If a North American woman with a good

EXHIBIT 4–4

People on the receiving end may base their entire perception of you on the quality of your handshake.

firm hand grip goes to the Far East, she should be warned that taking a man's hand and giving it a firm press signals to him that the woman has a sexual interest.

3. The length of engagement. This aspect of handshaking also has many implications. If you ask people how long a good handshake should last, they often say three or four seconds. Try it—this is a long handshake and could send unwanted signals. In Canada, a professional handshake should be two to three shakes. Any longer, and you may appear to be making a power play. Any shorter, and you may appear uninterested. Note, though, that in some cultures—South America, for example—a short engagement is regarded as rude. You should pump about a dozen times, and hold for much longer!

Other Tips

- Watch for sweaty palms, which occur due to nervousness or stress. Often, an individual's stress level is measured by the temperature of the fingertips: the more stressed he or she is, the colder the fingertips, and the body reacts with sweating palms. Learn from this—when you shake hands with a customer whose hand feels warm to the touch, he or she is probably more relaxed than you are. Conversely, if the hand feels cold and clammy, he or she is probably more stressed and nervous than you. If you have habitually sweaty palms, try to relax so you can enter the handshake stage with confidence.
- Make eye contact. When shaking hands, you are attempting to establish a warm and caring relationship with your prospect. Making eye contact will prove your sincerity and get the relationship off to a good start.

See Exhibit 4–5 for some other cultural nuances regarding the handshake.

EXHIBIT 4–5

Five tips for international handshaking.

1. International protocol dictates that you shake hands with everyone in a room—omissions are noticed and are considered a rejection.

2. Women should initiate handshakes and shake hands with other women and men. Not extending her hand to a European male will cause a North American businesswoman to lose credibility.

3. Western and Eastern Europeans reshake hands whenever they're apart for even a short period of time (e.g., lunch).

4. French and Japanese businesspeople shake hands with one firm gesture. In Japan, the handshake may be combined with a slight bow, which should be returned.

5. In Arab countries, handshakes are a bit limp and last longer than typical North American handshakes. Latin Americans also tend to use a lighter, lingering handshake. In all cases, don't pull your hand away too soon; such a gesture will be interpreted as a rejection.

Body Language

From birth, people learn to communicate their needs, likes, and dislikes through nonverbal means. The salesperson can learn much from a prospect's raised eyebrow, smile, touch, scowl, or reluctance to make eye contact during a sales presentation. The prospect can communicate with you without uttering a word. An ability to interpret these signals is an invaluable tool to the successful sales professional, The salesperson's skilful use and control of physical actions, gestures, and overall body position also are helpful.

Acceptance signals indicate that your buyer is favourably inclined toward you and your presentation. These signals give you the green light to proceed. While this may not end in a sale, at the least the prospect is saying, "I am willing to listen." Common acceptance signals include

- *Body angle:* Leaning forward or upright at attention.
- *Face:* Smiling, pleasant expression, relaxed, eyes examining visual aids, direct eye contact, positive voice tones.
- *Hands:* Relaxed and generally open, perhaps performing business calculations on paper, holding on as you attempt to withdraw a product sample or sales materials, firm handshake.
- *Arms:* Relaxed and generally open.
- *Legs:* Crossed and pointed toward you or uncrossed.

Salespeople frequently rely only on facial expressions as indicators of acceptance. This practice may be misleading since buyers may consciously control their facial

EXHIBIT 4–6

Which of the five communication modes can a salesperson look for with these customers?

expressions. Scan each of the five key body areas to verify your interpretation of facial signals. A buyer who increases eye contact, maintains a relaxed position, and exhibits positive facial expressions gives excellent acceptance signals.

Acceptance signals indicate that buyers perceive that your product might meet their needs. You have obtained their attention and interest. You are free to continue with your planned sales presentation.

Caution signals should alert you that buyers are either neutral to or skeptical about what you say. Caution signals are indicated by

- *Body angle:* Leaning away from you.
- *Face:* Puzzled, little or no expression, averted eyes or little eye contact, neutral or questioning voice tone, saying little, and then only asking a few questions.
- *Arms:* Crossed, tense.
- *Hands:* Moving, fidgeting with something, clasped, weak handshake.
- *Legs:* Moving, crossed away from you.

It is important to recognize and adjust to caution signals. First, they indicate blocked communication. Buyers' perceptions, attitudes, and beliefs regarding your presentation may cause them to be skeptical, judgmental, or uninterested in your product. They may not recognize that they need your product or that it can benefit them. Even though you may have their attention, they show little interest in or desire for your product.

Second, if caution signals are not handled properly, they may evolve into disagreement signals, which cause a communication breakdown and make a sale difficult. Proper handling of caution signals requires that you

- Adjust to the situation by slowing down or departing from your planned presentation.
- Use open-ended questions to encourage your buyers to talk and express their attitudes and beliefs: "Have you ever needed to measure the efficiency of your workers?" or "What do you think about this benefit?" are examples of open-ended questions.
- Carefully listen to what buyers say, and respond directly.
- Project acceptance signals. Be positive, enthusiastic, and smile. Remember, you are glad to be there to help buyers satisfy their needs. Refrain from projecting caution signals even if a buyer does so. If you project a positive image in this situation, there is greater probability that you will change the situation and make the sale.

Disagreement signals tell you to stop the planned presentation immediately and quickly adjust to the situation. Disagreements, or red-light signals, indicate that you are dealing with a person who is becoming uninterested in your product. Anger or hostility may develop if you continue the presentation. Your continuation can cause a buyer to feel an unacceptable level of sales pressure resulting in a complete communication breakdown. Disagreement signals may be indicated by

- *Body angle:* Retracted shoulders, leaning away from you, moving the entire body back from you, or wanting to move away.
- *Face:* Tense, showing anger, wrinkled face and brow, little eye contact, negative voice tones, or suddenly silent.
- *Arms:* Tense, crossed over chest.

EXHIBIT 4–7

What nonverbal signals are these buyers giving you?

 1. When you mention your price, this purchasing agent tilts her head back, raises her hands, and assumes a rigid body posture. What nonverbal signals is she communicating, and how would you move on with the sale?

 2. As you explain your sales features, this buyer looks away, clasps his hands, and crosses his legs away from you. What nonverbal signals is he communicating, and how would you move on with the sale?

 3. As you explain the quality of your product, this company president opens his arms and leans toward you. What nonverbal signals is he communicating, and how would you move on with the sale?

Answers

1. Your buyer is sending red signals. That means you are facing nearly insurmountable barriers. You've got to stop what you are doing, express understanding, and redirect your approach.

2. This buyer is sending yellow signals that warn you to exercise caution. Your own words and gestures must be aimed at relaxing the buyer or the prospect may soon communicate red signals.

3. This buyer is sending green signals that say everything is "go." With no obstacles to your selling strategy, simply move to the close.

- *Hands:* Motions of rejection or disapproval, tense and clenched, weak handshake.
- *Legs:* Crossed and away from you.

Handle disagreement signals by trying the following four techniques. First, stop your planned presentation. There is no use in continuing until you have changed disagreement signals into caution or acceptance signals. Second, temporarily reduce or eliminate any pressure on the person to buy or to participate in the conversation. Let the buyer relax as you slowly move back to your presentation. Third, let your buyer know you are aware that something upsetting has occurred. Show that you are there to help, not to sell at any cost. Finally, use direct questions to determine a buyer's attitudes and beliefs, such as, "What do you think of . . . ?" or "Have I said something you do not agree with?"

Remember to pay attention to nonverbal communication:

- Recognize nonverbal signals.
- Be able to interpret them correctly.
- Be prepared to alter a selling strategy by slowing, changing, or stopping a planned presentation.
- Respond nonverbally and verbally to a buyer's nonverbal signals.

BARRIERS TO COMMUNICATION

Salespeople often lose sales by failing to recognize communication barriers between buyer and seller. Communication breaks down in the sales situation for eight main reasons.

1. *Differences in perception:* If the buyer and seller do not share a common understanding of information contained in the presentation, communication breaks down. The closer a buyer's and seller's perceptions, attitudes, and beliefs, the stronger communication will be between them. Cultural differences are easily misperceived by buyers and sellers. See, for example, the Selling Globally box.

2. *Buyer does not recognize a need for product:* Communication barriers exist if the salesperson is unable to convince the buyer of a need or that the salesperson represents the best supplier to buy from.

3. *Selling pressure:* There is a fine line between what is acceptable sales pressure or enthusiasm and what the buyer perceives as a high-pressure sales technique. A pushy, arrogant selling style can quickly cause the prospect to erect a communication barrier.

4. *Information overload:* You may present the buyer with an excess of information. This overload may cause confusion or perhaps offend, and the buyer will stop listening. The engineer making a presentation to a buyer who is not an engineer may concentrate on the technical aspects of a product, but the buyer may want only a small amount of information.

5. *Disorganized sales presentation:* Sales presentations that seem unorganized to the buyer tend to cause frustration or anger. Buyers commonly expect you to understand their needs or problems, and to customize your sales presentation to their individual situation. If you fail to do this, communication can fall apart.

6. *Distractions:* When a buyer receives a telephone call or someone walks into the office, distractions occur. A buyer's thoughts may become sidetracked, and it may be difficult to regain attention and interest.

SELLING GLOBALLY

Cross-Cultural Communication

Earlier in the text, we discussed the necessity of being sensitive to cultural diversity. Consider these guidelines to enhance your cross-cultural communication effectiveness.

1. For those whose native language is not English, use simple, concise, and clear language.

2. Be perfectly clear while avoiding exaggerations.

3. Be careful to avoid slang and figures of speech. They may mean nothing at all to the listener or cause confusion.

4. Avoid sales "puffery" ("This is the best product in the world . . ."). This could be interpreted literally and create problems down the road.

5. Use caution when using humour. It can be useful in building rapport but may inadvertently offend someone.

6. Avoid even minor profanity. What may be acceptable in our culture can turn out to be highly offensive in other cultures so don't use it.

7. Be aware of cultural body language; in some cultures, if you were to give the buyer two thumbs up, he or she may throw you out of the office.

8. Watch the tone of your voice. Although some cultures see a loud, expressive tone as a sign of your excitement and enthusiasm, others may see it as rude and forceful.

SELLING TIPS

Don't Complicate Things

How can you simplify the following statements?

1. A mass of concentrated earthly material perennially rotating on its axis will not accumulate an accretion of bryophytic vegetation.

2. Individuals who are perforce constrained to be domiciled in vitreous structures of patent frangibility should on no account employ petrous formations as projectiles.

3. A superabundance of talent skilled in the preparation of gastronomic concoctions will impair the quality of a certain potable solution made by immersing a gallinaceous bird in embullient Adams ale.

Answers

1. A rolling stone gathers no moss.

2. People who live in glass houses shouldn't throw stones.

3. Too many cooks spoil the broth.

7. *Poor listening:* At times, the buyer may not listen to you. This result often occurs if you do all or most of the talking, not allowing the buyer to participate in the conversation.

8. *Not adapting to buyer's style:* Salespeople who preferred talking to showing should keep in mind that clients may instead prefer to see the product. It is critical for salespeople to use different communication styles for different clients, as discussed in Chapter 3. Most successful salespeople have learned to match their customers' communication styles.

MASTER PERSUASIVE COMMUNICATION TO MAINTAIN CONTROL

Salespeople want to be good communicators to persuade people to purchase their products. **Persuasion** means the ability to change a person's belief, position, or course of action.

Chapters 6 to 12, on the selling process, go into greater detail on specific persuasion techniques. For now, let's review several factors that help to develop persuasive communication skills.

Feedback Guides Your Presentation

Learn how to generate feedback to determine whether your listener has received your intended message. Feedback refers to a recognizable response from the buyer. A shake of the head, a frown, or an effort to say something are all signals to the salesperson. If the salesperson fails to notice or respond to these signals, no feedback can occur, which means faulty or incomplete communication.

Often, feedback must be sought openly because the prospect does not always give it voluntarily. By interjecting questions into the presentation that require the customer to give a particular response, you can stimulate feedback. Questioning, sometimes called **probing**, allows the salesperson to determine the buyer's attitude toward the sales presentation.

A large communications firm included this type of feedback in its training sessions. The company's sales trainers suggested to their trainees that they use specific questions in their presentations. Some of the questions were

- Do you think you are paying too much for telecommunications services?
- Are you happy with the service you have now?
- Are you happy with the system that your present supplier has installed for your company?

These questions were intended to draw negative responses from the customers concerning the relationship with their present supplier. The questions provided the company's sales representatives with a method of determining how the prospect felt about the competitor. The responses allowed the salespeople to discuss the specific features, advantages, and benefits of their products relative to the competition. Future chapters will fully discuss the appropriate questioning techniques for your presentation.

Empathy Puts You in Your Customer's Shoes

Empathy is the ability to identify and understand another person's feelings, ideas, and situation. As a salesperson, you need to be interested in what the buyer is saying—not just in giving a sales presentation. Many of the barriers to communication mentioned earlier can be overcome when you place yourself in the buyer's shoes. Empathy is saying to a prospect, "I'm here to help you," or asking, "Tell me your problems and needs so I can help *you*." Empathy is also evidenced by a salesperson's display of sincerity and interest in the buyer's situation.

Empathy means acknowledging at times that a prospect may not need your product. Take, for example, the Scott Paper Company salesperson who finds that the customer still has 90 percent of the paper towels purchased three months ago. There is no reason to sell this customer more paper towels. It is time to help the customer sell the paper towels now on hand by suggesting displays, price reductions, and formats for newspaper advertisements. It is always wise to adopt your customer's point of view in order to meet the customer's needs best.

Keep It Simple

The new salesperson was sitting with his boss in a customer's office waiting for the buyer. As they heard the buyer come into the office, the sales manager said, "Remember, a **KISS** for him." No, he was not saying to give the buyer a kiss but to use the old selling philosophy of **k**eep **i**t **s**imple, **s**alesperson.

An overly complex, technical presentation should be avoided when it is unnecessary. Use words and materials that are understood easily by the buyer. The skilled salesperson can make a prospect feel comfortable with a new product or complex technology through the subtle use of nontechnical information and a respectful attitude.

Creating Mutual Trust Develops Friendship

Salespeople who develop a mutual, trusting relationship with their customers cannot help being successful. This type of relationship eventually results in high credibility for the salesperson and even friendship. The buyer appreciates being sold products that perform to expectations and were worth their price, and that the salesperson did everything promised. Building mutual trust is important to effective long-run communication.

COMMUNICATION STYLE

Our communicating skill determines how successfully we interact with others, whether one-on-one or in a large group. Imagine three people placed in a buying group are listening to your sales presentation.

The visual person says, "I can't see how your product will meet our needs. Just show me what you see as the outcome."

The kinesthetic person may respond, "He has touched on all the heavy issues. Why can't you grasp his meaning?"

The auditory person then says, "It doesn't sound like either of you knows what you're talking about." They've each explained their ideas in their own language and can't understand why the others don't get it. Salespeople must be sensitive to the learning or sensory systems of their prospects to maximize their communication effectiveness.

Visual learners like to see things. Providing a simple graph outlining the performance results of your product versus the competition would be far more useful than simply saying, "Ours is better."

Kinesthetic learners prefer to touch and do things. Bringing in a product sample and allowing them to handle it and use it would be a very effective way of proving your product's benefits.

Auditory learners like to listen. A simple verbal presentation will communicate your message.

When making presentations, it is imperative that you make an effort to determine the learning style(s) of the person or people you are presenting to by observing and listening carefully. Be prepared to communicate using a variety of communication tools. Visuals, demonstrations, prospect involvement, and clear, concise language will ensure that you meet the needs of all buyers in a group.

NETIQUETTE FOR SALES PROFESSIONALS

When salespeople communicate by letter, they typically follow certain rules of etiquette, including guidelines for formatting the letter and addressing the recipient. When communicating by e-mail, you need to follow a similar set of rules, often referred to as "netiquette." **Netiquette** can enhance the effectiveness of your e-mail communication—just as not following it can result in very poor customer perception and relationships.

When you compose an e-mail message, you control three elements of that communication:

1. *The subject line*, which describes the content of the message.

2. *The message body*, which is the text that makes up the main part of the message.

3. *The signature*, which is the equivalent of a business card that tells the reader who you are, what you do, and where to find you.

The Subject Line

- Should accurately convey what the message is about
- Should be no more than four to six words
- Should not "shout" by using all capital letters
- Should not seem too aggressive or obviously sales oriented
- Should be worded so the message is not perceived as spam.

The Message Body

- Should convey information effectively and concisely
- Should not take too much of the recipient's time or technical resources due to excessive length or file size
- Should be sent in plain text, which is most universal (HTML formatting may result in the recipient's not being able to read the message)
- Should not include information that would be better communicated using a different medium, such as a phone call or a link to a Web page
- Should not offend the reader
- Should address all the points or answer all the questions in the original message, if it is a reply.

The Signature

- Should be included in every message
- Should contain all the information the reader needs about you: your name, title, company name, company URL, mailing address, and telephone and fax numbers
- Should be complete and up to date.

Sales Netiquette—A Brief Checklist

1. When sending a first-time e-mail, state where you obtained the recipient's e-mail address.
2. Put something meaningful in the subject box.
3. Ensure your name appears professionally in the "from" box.
4. Do not send unsolicited attachments; wait for permission.
5. Use an e-mail letterhead for highly formal correspondence.
6. Create a professional-looking signature for consistency.
7. Use correct grammar and spelling.
8. Don't be the first to use first names. Use formal salutations (Mrs. Smith or Mr. Jones) until your correspondent does otherwise.
9. Stay formal with international e-mailing until your correspondent indicates otherwise.
10. Be concise!
11. Don't use smileys or emoticons.
12. Don't send junk or include business clients on your "joke" list.
13. Don't send unaddressed mass e-mails (spam).
14. If replying to a message, include in your reply just the section you're replying to, not the entire original.
15. Remember to use empathy; consider how you would feel if you received the e-mail.

LISTENING: THE KEY TO UNLOCKING BUYERS' NEEDS

Hearing refers to being able to detect sounds. **Listening** means deriving meaning from sounds that are heard. Not everything you hear is worth your undivided attention; however, listening is a communication skill critical to success.

Salespeople often believe that their job is to talk rather than to listen. Nevertheless, if they talk *and* listen, their persuasive powers increase. Since people can listen (about 400 words per minute) roughly twice as fast as the average rate of speech, it is understandable that a person's mind may wander while listening to a salesperson's presentation or that the salesperson may tune out a prospect. To keep the buyer listening, ask questions, get the buyer involved in the conversation, and use visual aids. If you ask a question, carefully listen to the answer.

Listen to Words, Feelings, and Thoughts

When someone speaks, he or she is expressing thoughts and feelings. However, most of us listen to only the words.

Listen *behind* the words for the emotional content of the message, which is conveyed in the nuances of voice and body language. Some people, such as sensers (discussed in Chapter 3), give you little emotional information. That's all right, because

MAKING THE SALE

Do You Have Any of These Listening Habits?

No one is perfect. We all have some bad listening habits that we get away with when we talk to our family and friends. In a business context, however, leave these bad habits behind and practise active listening. To gain insight into your listening habits, read through this list of common irritating listening habits and be honest with yourself; notice what you are guilty of and use this awareness to begin eliminating them.

1. You do all the talking.
2. You interrupt when people talk.
3. You never look at the person talking or indicate that you are listening.
4. You start to argue before the other person has a chance to finish.
5. Everything that is said reminds you of an experience you've had, and you feel obligated to digress with a story.
6. You finish sentences for people if they pause too long.
7. You wait impatiently for people to finish so that you can interject something.
8. You work too hard at maintaining eye contact and make people uncomfortable.
9. You look as if you are appraising the person talking to you, looking him or her up and down.
10. You overdo the feedback you give—too many nods of your head and "uh-huhs."

you deal with them in a factual, business-only style. Feelers, on the other hand, reveal their emotions, and in turn, they appreciate your acknowledgement of their feelings. It is appropriate to discuss their feelings and treat them more as friends than as strictly business associates.

You can hear the emotions behind the words in several ways. First, look for changes in eye contact. After establishing a comfortable and natural level of eye contact, any sudden deviations from the norm tip you off to emotional content in the message. People tend to look away from you when they talk about something embarrassing. When this happens, make a quick mental note of what it pertained to and treat that subject delicately. Also, give a person the courtesy of looking away momentarily yourself—as if you are saying, "I respect your privacy."

Listen *between* the words for what is not said. Some people reveal more by what they don't say. A salesperson was talking to the president of a large paper mill. "I simply asked him what kind of training he had for his salespeople. He went into a long discourse on all the seminars, training films, videotapes, and cassettes they had from the parent company, suppliers, industry associations, and in-house programs. I sat, listened, and took notes. At the end of his speech I said to him, 'I noticed you didn't mention anything about time management for salespeople.' He raised his voice and emphatically said, 'You know, just this morning I was talking to a guy and I told him we have to have some time-management training for our salespeople.'"

The lesson here is to get the prospect talking—so you can listen actively. Take notes, look for clues to emotions, and don't interrupt or start thinking about your next question. See Exhibit 4–8.

The Three Levels of Listening   Whenever people listen, they are at one of three basic levels of listening. Each requires various degrees of concentration by the listener. As you move from the first to the third level, the potential for understanding and clear communication increases.

Marginal Listening   Marginal listening, the first and lowest level, involves the least concentration, and typically listeners are easily distracted by their thoughts.

EXHIBIT 4–8

Active listening is important to your sales success. Concentrate, take notes, look for clues, and don't interrupt!

During periods of marginal listening, a listener exhibits blank stares, nervous mannerisms, and gestures that annoy the speaker and cause communication barriers. The salesperson hears the message, but it doesn't sink in. There is enormous room for misunderstanding when a salesperson is not concentrating on what is said. Moreover, the prospect cannot help but feel the lack of attention, which may be insulting and diminish trust. It may be funny when family members continually patronize each other with, "Yes, dear," regardless of what is said. In real life, however, it is not funny:

Prospect: What I need, really, is a way to reduce the time lost due to equipment breakdowns.

Salesperson: Yeah, OK. Let's see, uh, the third feature of our product is the convenient sizes you can get.

Salespeople of all experience levels may be guilty of marginal listening. Beginners who lack confidence and experience may concentrate so intensely on what they are supposed to say next that they stop listening. Old pros, by contrast, have heard it all before. They have their presentations memorized and want the prospect to hurry and finish talking so the important business can continue. These traditional salespeople forget that the truly important information lies in what the prospect says.

Evaluative listening   Evaluative listening, the second level of listening, requires more concentration and attention to the speaker's words. At this level, the listener actively tries to hear what the prospect says but isn't making an effort to understand the intent. Instead of accepting and trying to understand a prospect's message, the evaluative listener categorizes the statement and concentrates on preparing a response.

The evaluative listening phenomenon is a result of the tremendous speed at which a human can listen and think. It is no surprise that evaluative listening is the level of listening used most of the time. Unfortunately, it is a difficult habit to break, but it can be done with practice.

Prospect: What I need, really, is a way to reduce the time lost due to equipment breakdown.

Salesperson (defensively): We have tested our machines in the field, and they don't break down often.

Use your eyes to get "the rest of the story." Pay attention to the prospect's body language and non-verbal facial and body movements to get the full meaning of what they are saying.

In this example, the salesperson reacted to one aspect of the prospect's statement. Had the salesperson withheld judgment until the end of the statement, he could have responded more objectively and informatively.

In evaluative listening, it is easy to be distracted by emotion-laden words. At that point, you aren't listening to the prospect. Instead, you are obsessed with the offensive word and wondering what to do about it. This practice is a waste of time for both you and the prospect. It increases personal and relationship tension and throws your communication off course. To avoid the problems of marginal and evaluative listening, practise active listening.

Active Listening   Active listening is the third and most effective level of listening. The active listener refrains from evaluating the message and tries to see the other person's point of view. Attention is on not only the words spoken but also the thoughts, feelings, and meaning conveyed. Listening in this way means the listener puts herself into someone else's shoes. It requires the listener to give the other person verbal and non-verbal feedback.

Prospect: What I need is a way to reduce the time lost due to equipment breakdowns.

Salesperson: Could you tell me what kind of breakdowns you have experienced?

In this example, the salesperson spoke directly to the prospect's concerns—not around them. Her desire to make a presentation was deferred so she could accomplish a more important task—effectively communicating with the prospect.

Active listening is a skill that takes practice in the beginning, but after a while, becomes second nature. The logic behind active listening is based on courtesy and concentration.

Active listening is sometimes difficult to do, especially for the novice salesperson. The novice may continue to talk about a particular situation or problem. However,

SELLING TIPS

Nine Steps to Becoming a Better Listener

- Stop talking, to show the prospect that you want to listen.

- Watch carefully for nonverbal signals, and be sure to project positive nonverbal signals. Simple head nods and lively facial expressions can encourage your prospect to continue to provide you with information.

- Learn to "listen ahead." Trying to anticipate where a discussion is heading during a dialogue allows you to determine the conclusion in advance of your required response, which allows you to relax and improve information absorption.

- Learn to periodically validate communicated information. By mentally and even verbally validating the accuracy and completeness of information points made by the prospect, especially during pauses, you can allow yourself to absorb more information more easily, especially information forthcoming in the continued dialogue.

- Utilize active listening techniques. By periodically mentally summarizing and restating the major points communicated by the prospect, you add tremendous clarity to the information exchanged thus far.

- Strive to understand versus judging. Working to consciously understand what the prospect is saying versus the natural tendency of judging will allow you to absorb what is actually said more than any other listening development technique.

- Use your eyes to get "the rest of the story." By paying attention to the prospect's body language and nonverbal facial and body movements or hand gestures you can see what the whole body, not just the mouth, is trying to tell you.

- Mentally prepare common responses. By mentally developing and rehearsing in advance of a sales call how you are going to respond to, for example, common sales prospect purchase objections, you can then listen more effectively. A comprehensive mental inventory of common responses will also give you more confidence in any selling situation.

- Ask questions to clarify meaning. This will allow you to remove any ambiguity and will lead to the best possible solution to the prospect's problem.

the salesperson must *learn to listen*. It is a key to sales success. People like and appreciate a listener, as this poem says so well:

> His thoughts were slow,
> His words were few,
> And never made to glisten,
> But he was a joy
> Wherever he went.
> You should have heard him listen.
>
> —*Author Unknown*

Your Attitude Makes the Difference

While a variety of methods and techniques exist in selling, truly effective sales persuasion is based on the salesperson's attitude toward the sales job and customers. **Enthusiasm** is a condition in which an individual is filled with excitement about solving the customer's problems.

The highly successful salesperson goes all out to help customers. Strive to make the buyer feel important, and show that you are there solely as a problem solver. Do this by expressing sincere interest such as asking questions instead of talking at the buyer.

Salespeople who have established **credibility** with their customers through continued empathy, willingness to listen to specific needs, and continual enthusiasm toward their work and customers' business can make claims that their customers treat

EXHIBIT 4–10

Computers help you to remember.

Computers are great tools for recording what was discussed in the sales call.

as absolute truth in some cases. Combining enthusiasm with evidence statements greatly improves a salesperson's persuasion.

Evidence Statements Make You Believable   Using highly credible sources can improve the persuasiveness of the sales presentation message. **Evidence statements** substantiate claims made by the salesperson. For example, pharmaceutical companies often quote research studies done by outstanding physicians at prestigious medical schools to validate claims of product benefits. These statements add high credibility to a sales message.

Evidence statements are sometimes called **proof statements**. While the difference may be subtle, the use of supporting statements as evidence recognizes that it is

ETHICAL DILEMMA
High Pressure or Good Selling?

Nico was a large man. He was a star football player at university and measured six and a half feet tall and 280 pounds. He worked out regularly to retain his muscular stature. He had chiselled facial features and a shaved head. Nico had tremendous self-confidence, almost to the point of being arrogant. He always dressed impeccably but he could come across as an extremely intimidating person.

Nico worked as a salesperson for a major manufacturer of photocopiers. He was a fierce competitor and worked hard to close every sale. During some presentations, if things weren't going well, Nico would often change his communication style. He found that if he sat more upright, sometimes even leaning over the prospect's desk and raising the volume of his voice slightly, prospects sometimes became more cooperative.

What seems to be happening here?

Is this behaviour ethical?

Can you suggest a better way of dealing with these situations?

ultimately the customer who will determine whether the information you have provided is proof enough to accept that information. Remember, what is proof for sales representatives may not have the same relevance to customers.

Salespeople sometimes quote acknowledged experts in a field on the use of products. Demonstrating that other customers or respected individuals use the products encourages customer belief in the validity of information presented in a sales presentation. People place greater confidence in a trustworthy, objective source (particularly one not associated with the salesperson's firm) and are therefore more receptive to what is said by the salesperson.

SUMMARY OF MAJOR SELLING ISSUES

Communication is a transmission of verbal and nonverbal information and understanding between salesperson and prospect. The communication process comprises a sender (encoder) who transmits a specific message to a receiver (decoder) who responds to that message. The effectiveness of this communication process can be hampered by noise that distorts the message as it travels. A sender can judge the effectiveness of a message and media choice by monitoring the feedback from the receiver.

Barriers to constructive communication result from the perceptional differences between the sender and receiver, cultural differences, outside distractions, or how sales information is conveyed. Regardless of their source, barriers must be recognized and either overcome or eliminated if communication is to succeed.

Nonverbal communication has emerged within the past 10 or 15 years as a critical component of the overall communication process. Recognition of nonverbal communication is essential for sales success in today's business environment. Awareness of the prospect's territorial space, a firm and confident handshake, and accurate interpretation of body language are critical to a salesperson's success.

Overall persuasive power is enhanced through development of several key characteristics. The salesperson who creates a relationship based on mutual trust with a customer by displaying empathy (desire to understand the customer's situation and environment), a willing ear (more listening, less talking), and a positive attitude of enthusiastic pursuit of lasting solutions for the customer's needs and problems increases the likelihood of making the sale.

MEETING A SALES CHALLENGE

In this imaginary sales call, buyer and seller communicated both verbal and nonverbal messages. Here, nonverbal messages conveyed both parties' attitudes better than the actual verbal exchange. The salesperson's negative reactions served to increase Amos Skaggs's hostile attitude. He could sense that the salesperson did not understand his problem and was there only to sell him something—not to solve his problem. This impression caused a rapid breakdown in communication. The end result, as in this case, is usually no sale.

The salesperson may have reacted correctly to Skaggs. Since Skaggs is in a bad mood, coming back another day may be best. If the salesperson cannot come another day, then the salesperson needs to stop the planned presentation and let the buyer know he understands. He should show that he is there to help. But most of all, he must project a positive attitude and not be frightened by Skaggs.

PLAYING THE ROLE

The Situations: 1. B is meeting with A to make a presentation about his/her paper products. B hopes to land A's account, which will result in a tremendous increase in sales volume.

2. Same situation as above except that C is making the sales call.

Role A: Purchasing Agent for Halton Print Works. Being a talkative type, after your initial greeting, you want to tell the salesperson all the details of the wonderful weekend that you've had.

Role B: Salesperson for Canadian Paper Supply. As an impatient type, you are to play the role of a poor listener. Read about all the poor listening habits in this chapter and dramatize them during your conversation with your prospect.

Role C: Salesperson for Canadian Paper Supply. You are a patient person. Read about the habits of effective (active) listeners and listen properly to the same story about the wonderful weekend your prospect had.

Prepare your roles for an in-class dramatization of both good and bad listening techniques.

KEY TERMS FOR SELLING

acceptance signals, 100
caution signals, 101
communication, 92
credibility, 111
decoding process, 93
disagreement
   signals, 101
empathy, 105
encoding process, 93
enthusiasm, 111
evidence statements, 112

feedback, 93
hearing, 107
intimate space, 94
KISS principle, 105
listening, 107
medium, 93
message, 93
netiquette, 106
noise, 93
nonverbal
   communication, 94

personal space, 94
persuasion, 104
probing, 104
proof statements, 112
public space, 94
receiver, 93
social space, 94
source, 93
space invasion, 95
space threats, 95
territorial space, 94

SALES APPLICATION QUESTIONS

1. Draw the salesperson–buyer communication process. Describe each step in the process. Why is a two-way communication important in this process?
2. This chapter outlined several forms of nonverbal communication.
   a. Give an example of a salesperson making a good first impression through the proper use of an introductory handshake.
   b. What signals should the salesperson look for in a buyer's body language? Give several examples of these signals.
3. A salesperson may spend hours developing a sales presentation and yet the buyer does not buy. One reason for losing a sale is that the salesperson and the buyer do not communicate. What barriers to communication may be present between seller and buyer during a sales presentation?
4. When two people are talking, each wants the listener to understand. What can a salesperson do to help ensure that the buyer is listening?
5. You arrive at the industrial purchasing agent's office on time. This is your first meeting. After you have waited five minutes, the agent's secretary says, "She will see you." After the initial greeting, the purchasing agent asks you to sit down. For each of these three situations determine
   a. What nonverbal signals is she communicating?
   b. How would you respond nonverbally?
   c. What would you say to her?
      i. She sits up straight in her chair behind her desk. She clasps her hands together and with little expression on her face says, "What can I do for you?"

     ii. She sits down behind her desk. She moves slightly backward in her chair, crosses her arms, and while looking around the room says, "What can I do for you?"

     iii. She sits down behind her desk. She moves slightly forward in her chair. She seems hurried, yet she is relaxed toward your presence. Her arms are uncrossed. She looks you squarely in the eye, and with a pleasant look on her face says, "What can I do for you?"

6. In each of the following selling situations

    a. What nonverbal signals is the buyer communicating?

    b. How would you respond nonverbally?

    c. What would you say?

     i. The buyer seems happy to see you. Because you have been calling on him for several years, the two of you have become business friends. In the middle of your presentation, you notice the buyer slowly lean back in his chair. As you continue to talk, a puzzled look comes over his face.

     ii. As you begin the main part of your presentation, the buyer reaches for the telephone and says, "Keep going; I need to tell my secretary something."

     iii. As a salesperson with only six months' experience, you are somewhat nervous about calling on an important buyer who has been a purchasing agent for almost 20 years. Three minutes after you have begun your presentation, he rapidly raises his arms straight up into the air and slowly clasps his hands behind his head. He leans so far back in his chair that you think he is going to fall backward on the floor. At the same time, he crosses his legs away from you and slowly closes his eyes. You keep on talking. Slowly the buyer opens his eyes, uncrosses his legs, and sits up in his chair. He leans forward, placing his elbows on the desk top, propping his head up with his hands. He seems relaxed as he says, "Let me see what you have here." He reaches his hand out for you to give him the presentation materials you have developed.

     iv. At the end of your presentation, the buyer leans forward, his arms open, and he smiles as he says, "You really don't expect me to buy that piece of junk, do you?"

SALES WORLD WIDE WEB EXERCISE

Dress to Get a Job!

This chapter discusses verbal and nonverbal communication. One of the key nonverbal communication tools is your dress.

Review each of the following Web sites. Note that continual review of sites such as these will keep you abreast of appropriate dress codes for job interviews and when you join the workforce.

    www.managementhelp.org/career/dress.htm

    www.ask.com, type in "How to dress for success"

    www.symsdress.com

FURTHER EXPLORING THE SALES WORLD

Using questions is an effective method for a salesperson to obtain feedback from a buyer. For the next two days, try using questions in your conversations with other people, and report on your results. These questions should reflect an interest in the person you are talking to as well as the topic being discussed. Using the words *you* and *your* should increase feedback and create an atmosphere of trust.

For example, questions such as "What do you mean?" "What do you think?" "How does that sound?" can be used in your conversation to encourage listeners to participate and to help determine how they feel about the topic of conversation.

Asking people's opinions also can result in a positive response, since they may feel flattered that you care about their opinion. Questions can help you guide the direction of topics discussed in conversation. Try to determine people's reactions to your questions and report your findings in class.

STUDENT APPLICATION LEARNING EXERCISES (SALES)
Part 2

SALES are meant to help you construct the various segments of your sales presentation. SALES build on one another so that as you complete each exercise, you are constructing more of your sales presentation.

In Part 1, you identified the information that you would need to help you tailor your sales presentation.

1. Summarize the needs that you plan to satisfy with your product proposal.

2. Review the discussion in this chapter on the importance of nonverbal communication. Develop a checklist to help you prepare your presentation. Be sure to include things such as dress, grooming, the handshake, body language, and so on.

3. Review the listening techniques discussed in this chapter and list ways in which you can enhance your listening effectiveness with your prospect.

SELLING EXPERIENTIAL EXERCISE

Listening Self-Inventory

Instructions: Read the following questions and write *yes* or *no* for each statement on a separate sheet of paper. Mark each answer as truthfully as you can in light of your behaviour in the last few meetings or gatherings you attended.

	Yes	No
1. I frequently attempt to listen to several conversations at the same time.	____	____
2. I like people to give me only the facts and then let me make my own interpretation.	____	____
3. I sometimes pretend to pay attention to people.	____	____
4. I consider myself a good judge of nonverbal communications.	____	____
5. I usually know what another person is going to say before he or she says it.	____	____
6. I usually end conversations that don't interest me by diverting my attention from the speaker.	____	____
7. I frequently nod or frown to let the speaker know how I feel about what he or she is saying.	____	____
8. I usually respond immediately when someone has finished talking.	____	____
9. I evaluate what is being said while it is being said.	____	____
10. I usually formulate a response while the other person is still talking.	____	____
11. The speaker's delivery style frequently keeps me from listening to content.	____	____
12. I usually ask for people's points of view.	____	____
13. I make a concerted effort to understand other people's points of view.	____	____
14. I frequently hear what I expect to hear rather than what is said.	____	____
15. Most people believe that I have understood their points of view when we disagree.	____	____

According to communication theory, the correct answers are as follows: No for questions 1, 2, 3, 5, 6, 7, 8, 9, 10, 11, 14; and Yes for questions 4, 12, 13, 15. If you missed only one or two questions, you strongly approve of your own listening habits, and you are on the right track to becoming an effective listener in your role as a salesperson. If you missed three or four questions, you have uncovered some doubts about your listening effectiveness, and your knowledge of how to listen has some gaps. If you missed five or more questions, you probably are not satisfied with the way you listen, and your friends and co-workers may feel you are not a good listener either. Work on improving your active listening skills.[2]

CASE 4-1
Skaggs Manufacturing

John Alvez arrived promptly for his 10 A.M. meeting with Martha Gillespie, the buyer for Skaggs Manufacturing. At 10:15, when she hadn't arrived, John asked her secretary if she was out of the office for the morning. The secretary smiled and said, "She'll probably be a few minutes late." John resented this delay and was convinced that Martha had forgotten the appointment.

Finally, at 10:20, Martha entered her office, walked over to John, said hello, and promptly excused herself to talk to the secretary about a tennis game scheduled for that afternoon. Ten minutes later, Martha led John into her office. At the same time, a competing salesperson entered the office for a 10:30 appointment. With the door open, Martha asked John, "What's new today?" As John began to talk, Martha began reading letters on her desk and signing them. Shortly after that, the telephone began to ring, whereupon Martha talked to her husband for 10 minutes.

As she hung up, Martha looked at John and suddenly realized his frustration. She promptly buzzed her secretary and said, "Hold all calls." She got up and shut the door. John again began his presentation when Martha leaned backward in her chair, pulled her golf shoes out of a desk drawer, and began to brush them.

About that time, the secretary entered the office and said, "Martha, your 10:30 appointment is about to leave. What should I tell him?" "Tell him to wait; I need to see him." Then she said, "John, I wish we had more time. Look, I think I have enough of your product to last until your next visit. I'll see you then. Thanks for coming by."

John quickly rose to his feet, did not shake hands, said "OK," and left.

Questions

1. What nonverbal cues did the salesperson, John Alvez, experience when contacting Martha Gillespie?
2. If you were John Alvez, how would you have handled the situation?

CASE 4-2
Western Office Supply

Judy Picard sells cellular telephones for Western Office Supply in Winnipeg. Today she is calling on Bill Taylor, purchasing agent for a large manufacturing firm. Two weeks earlier, she had made her first sales call to Western, and had left a demonstrator for the company executives to try out. The previous evening, Bill had called Judy and asked her to come in so he could give her an order. After their initial hellos, the conversation continued:

Bill: Judy, thanks for coming by today. Our executives really like your equipment. Here is an order for four phones. When can you deliver them?

Judy: Is tomorrow too soon?

CASE 4–2

Bill: That is perfect. Leave them with Mei, my secretary. [*Bill says over the intercom*] Mei, Judy will deliver the phones tomorrow. Mei, I want you to go ahead and take them to Sally, Anita, and Salisha. Women sure understand the use of modern equipment.

Judy: Bill, thanks for your help.

Bill: Forget it Judy, I wish I could have helped more. Your cellular phones can reduce the telephone tag we play with each other and customers. Customers are leaving us because they can't reach our salespeople when they are out on the road contacting customers.

Judy: You're right; many of my customers use them for that very reason.

Bill: I know, but some executives still feel they don't want them. They don't want their phone to ring when they're in with a customer. Plus, the cancer scare has them worried. I wish the men in our company felt the same way the women do about using these things.

Questions

Analyze and describe the conversation between Judy Picard and Bill Taylor. What should Judy do now?

5

SALES KNOWLEDGE: CUSTOMERS, PRODUCTS, TECHNOLOGIES

MAIN TOPICS

Sources of Sales Knowledge

Knowledge Builds Relationships

Know Your Customers

Know Your Company

Know Your Product

Know Your Resellers

A FABulous Approach to Buyer Need Satisfaction

Position Your Product with a Unique Selling Proposition

Advertising Aids Salespeople

Sales Promotion Generates Sales

Pricing Your Product

Know Your Competition, Industry, and Economy

Personal Computers and Selling

Knowledge of Technology Enhances Sales and Customer Service

The Internet and the World Wide Web

LEARNING OBJECTIVES

Successful salespeople are knowledgeable individuals. Many salespeople are experts in their field. After studying this chapter, you should be able to:

- Explain the importance of knowledge to sales professionals.

- Discuss the general areas of knowledge needed for increased sales success.

- Understand the importance of features, advantages, and benefits.

- Develop a FAB worksheet.

- Develop and use a unique selling proposition.

- Explain the purpose of planogram software for many types of salespeople.

- Explain the main technologies used by salespeople.

- Determine different sources of sales knowledge.

FACING A SALES CHALLENGE

You are proud of the products you sell and tell everyone they are the Cadillac of the industry, the best on the market, light years ahead of the competition. Of course you have worked for the company for only two weeks. But the sales training course you took last week clearly convinced you that your products are much better than any others. During one presentation on a new detergent for washing machines, you concentrated on discussing the quality of the product: how well it cleans, its environmental safety, how much users like its pleasant scent. The grocery store buyer said, "I couldn't care less about the quality of your products."

Why did the buyer respond in a negative way? What is the buyer interested in?[1]

Salespeople need to know many things. It's important to discuss features, advantages, and benefits (FABs)—but which FABs interest the buyer? a retailer, wholesaler, manufacturer, or consumer? Each is likely interested in similar, but different, FABs.

This chapter examines the basic body of knowledge essential for a salesperson's success. Knowing about products and customers is only part of it. The professional salesperson must also know about his company's policies; procedures; marketing efforts; distribution channel; competitors; the industry; and the economy. Of course, the salesperson must also keep current with computers, software applications, and other technologies as new advances occur.

SOURCES OF SALES KNOWLEDGE

Knowledge for selling is obtained in two ways: First, most companies provide some formal sales training through preliminary training programs and sales meetings. Second, the salesperson learns by being on the job.

Employers provide **sales training** that includes information on job-related culture, skills, knowledge, and attitudes to to increase sales volume, salesperson productivity, and profitability.

Successful companies thoroughly train new salespeople and maintain ongoing training programs for their experienced sales personnel.

However, as in many professional careers, selling is a skill truly developed only through *experience*. Some sales managers hire only experienced people to fill even entry-level selling positions. Indeed, some corporations do not allow people to fill marketing staff positions unless they have had field sales experience with the company or a major competitor.

SELLING TIPS

Salespeople need strength in the following four areas of selling:

1. *Product knowledge:* Know how to communicate both the technical and emotional components of your products.

2. *Sales techniques:* Understand the process. From prospecting onward, salespeople must stay up to date on best practices, and industry developments in terms of technology and technique.

3. *Procedural knowledge:* Know how to write up sales reports and contracts, the processes of arranging for service calls and returned goods, and of your company's policies and procedures.

4. *Customer service skills:* Know how to thank a customer, service his or her account, and invite him or her back. Stay current in exceptional customer service practices.

Sales experience improves a salesperson's abilities by showing how buyers perceive a product or product line; revealing unrecognized or undervalued product benefits or shortcomings; voicing a multitude of unanticipated protests and objections; displaying numerous moods and attitudes over a short period; and generally providing a challenge that makes selling a skill that is never mastered—only improved.

No author or sales trainer can simulate the variety of situations that a salesperson confronts over the span of a career. We can provide only general guidelines as a framework for action; actual selling experience alone gives a person direct feedback on how to function in a specific selling situation.

KNOWLEDGE BUILDS RELATIONSHIPS

Salespeople's selling knowledge will increase the salesperson's self-confidence and build the buyer's confidence in the salesperson, as well as build relationships.

Knowledge Increases Confidence of Salespeople and Buyers

Salespeople who call on, for example, computer systems engineers, university professors, or aerospace experts may be at a disadvantage. In some cases, they have less education and experience than prospects in their fields of expertise.

Imagine making a sales call on a distinguished heart surgeon. Can you educate her in the use of your company's synthetic heart valves? Not really, but you can offer help in supplying product information from your firm's medical department. This personal service, your product knowledge, and her specific needs will make the sale. Knowledge about your company, its market, and your buyer enables you to build your self-confidence, which results in increased sales.

Furthermore, prospects want to do business with salespeople who know their business and the products they sell. When a prospect has confidence in the salesperson's expertise, a sales presentation becomes more acceptable and believable.

Strive to be an expert on all aspects of your product, which will allow you to answer questions confidently and field objections raised by prospects. Often, within minutes buyers can tell whether salespeople know what they are talking about. They ask questions and quickly form an impression of the salesperson; a relationship begins. Typically, the more knowledge you have, the higher your sales.

KNOW YOUR CUSTOMERS

How can you match your product's benefits with a buyer's needs if you don't know your customers? If you are selling to someone you've never seen before—such as in a retail store—you have to ask about the buyer's needs. Business-to-business selling also requires asking numerous questions, sometimes spending weeks with a customer before a sale. Refer to Chapter 3 for details about conducting customer needs analysis.

KNOW YOUR COMPANY

Knowledge of your firm helps you project an expert image to the prospect. The type and extent of company knowledge to be used depends on the company, its product lines, and the industry. (See Exhibit 5–1.) In general, consumer-goods

EXHIBIT 5–1

What would you need to know for selling . . .

. . . computers to consumers?

. . . electrical equipment to an engineer?

salespeople require little information about the technical nature of their products; however, selling high-technology products (computers, rocket-engine components, complex machinery, etc.) to highly knowledgeable industrial buyers requires extensive knowledge.

General Company Information

All salespeople need to know the background and present operating policies of their companies to do their job effectively. Information on company growth, policies, procedures, production, and service facilities is often used in sales presentations.

Company Growth and Accomplishment

Knowledge of your firm's development since its origin provides you with promotional material and builds confidence in your company. An IBM office products salesperson might say to a buyer:

> In 1952, IBM placed its first commercial electronic computer on the market. That year, our sales were $342 million. Currently, our sales are projected to be over $80 billion. IBM has reached these high sales figures because our advanced, technological office equipment and information processors are the best available at any price. This IBM "Star Trek I" system I am showing you is the most advanced piece of equipment on the market today. It is five years ahead of any other computer!

Policies and Procedures

To give good service, be ready to tell a customer about policies: how an order is processed; how long it takes for orders to be filled; your firm's returned-goods policy; how to open a new account; and what to do in the event of a shipping error. When you handle these situations quickly and fairly, your buyer gains confidence in you and your firm.

SELLING GLOBALLY
Technology—Curse or Saviour

Another business trip? Bernie Dougall hated the thought of travelling to Asia for another sales meeting with his colleagues from around the globe but a problem had arisen with one of his company's Eastern European customers. Senior management for his international hardware company preferred that sales managers meet in person to discuss important issues, so Bernie felt obliged to attend. However, Bernie had recently read about technologies that could render such meetings obsolete, so he investigated further.

In his conversation with Lauren Mathews, his company's communications consultant, he learned the following:

Personal meetings won't become obsolete because most people still prefer to meet face to face—bad news for Bernie. However, new technologies such as VoIP, WiFi, and interactive videoconferencing will certainly change the way people meet and exchange information. These technologies won't reduce the number of meetings; but, in fact, by encouraging "virtual" meetings, they could facilitate even more global management meetings or brainstorming sessions. The good news is that many of these meetings will require no travel.

Now Bernie was listening. The technology for effective virtual meetings is already here. A high-quality video capability over the Net allows for higher-resolution video feeds from several users. Participants can simply pass a Webcam-equipped laptop around the room so they can see their counterparts around the world (and be seen) while they're speaking. Now Lauren really had Bernie's attention. He made a note to speak to his managers about this.

Bernie told Lauren about the meetings he had recently attended and complained that many were interrupted by people receiving mobile phone calls, text messages, or e-mails on their BlackBerrys or PDAs. It was a tough audience, he complained. Lauren agreed and pointed out that this phenomenon put pressure on speakers to keep the audience's attention.

She explained that good speakers use wireless connectivity to conduct more effective meetings by forcing involvement and participation. Some bring their wireless PCs to the podium and invite real-time questions.

Other technologies revolutionizing meetings and conferences include the following:

- **Social networking:** Self-serve registration kiosks can help you determine who is attending which sessions, which will help you arrange to "run into" them.

- **Audience response:** This technology lets speakers survey the audience. It is rarely used but the potential is great. The electronic key pads can be used to build consensus and set agendas. The technology is getting cheaper, more reliable, and easier to use.

- **Blogs:** Conference organizers are starting to generate online diaries in which participants write about the day's activities. Following these blogs will help you keep track of what's going on at the conference, and perhaps revise session selections and identify new prospects.

- **Digital pens:** Rather than leave meetings with pages of notes you can barely read, you can buy a digital pen that converts your handwritten notes into Word documents, making them much more accessible.

- **Infinite audiences:** Not able to attend? Technology allows you to buy "live" access to meetings, through videoconferencing software.

At the conclusion of his conversation with Lauren, Bernie pondered these technologies and wondered how they could be implemented into his sales job. He definitely saw less travel in his future.

Production Facilities

Many companies require their new salespeople to tour their production facilities to give them a first-hand look at the company's operations. This is a good opportunity to gain product knowledge. For example, a carpet company salesperson can say, "When I was visiting our production plant, I viewed each step of the carpet-production process. The research and development department allowed us to watch comparison tests between our carpets and competitors' carpets. Our carpets did everything but fly—and they are working on that!"

Service Facilities

Many companies, such as Intel and Ikon Office Solutions, have both service facilities and service representatives to help customers. Being able to say, "We can have a service representative there the same day you call our service centre," strengthens a sales presentation, especially if service is important for the customer (as it is in the computer and office copier industries).

KNOW YOUR PRODUCT

Knowledge about your company's product and your competitors' is a major component of sales knowledge. Become an expert on your company's products. Understand how they are produced and their level of quality. Product knowledge may include such technical details as

- Performance data
- Physical size and characteristics
- How the product operates
- Specific features, advantages, and benefits of the product
- How well the product is selling in the marketplace.

Many companies have their new salespeople work in the manufacturing plant (e. g., on the assembly line) or in the warehouse (filling orders and receiving stock). This hands-on experience may cost the salesperson sweat and sore muscles for a couple of weeks or months, but the payoff is a world of product knowledge and help in future selling that could not be earned any other way. Often, new salespeople in the oil and gas industry roughneck and drive trucks during the first few months on the job. At Finning International, one of the largest Caterpillar dealers in the world, new salespeople work in sales administration positions for six months, learning the features, advantages, and benefits of all the pieces of heavy equipment before dealing directly with customers.

Much is learned at periodic company sales meetings. At sales meetings, a consumer-goods manufacturer may concentrate on developing sales presentations for the products to receive special emphasis during the company sales period. Company advertising programs, price discounts, and promotional allowances for these products are discussed. Although little time may be spent on the technical aspects of consumer products, much time is devoted to discussing the marketing mix for these products (product type, promotion, distribution, and price).

A complete understanding of your product is not enough in itself to fully satisfy the needs of prospects; understanding how your product relates to the prospect's needs is critical.

KNOW YOUR RESELLERS

It is essential to understand the channel of distribution used by your company to move its products to the final consumer. Knowledge of each channel member (also called reseller or intermediary) is vital. Wholesalers and retailers often stock thousands of products, and each may have hundreds of salespeople calling on its buyers. Know as much about each channel member as possible. Some important information you will need includes

- The likes and dislikes of each channel member's customers
- Product lines and the assortment each one carries

- When each member sees salespeople
- Distribution, promotion, and pricing policies
- What quantity of which product each channel member has purchased in the past.

While most channel members will have similar policies concerning salespeople, keep abreast of the differences.

A FABULOUS APPROACH TO BUYER NEED SATISFACTION

Successful salespeople use a powerful technique called **benefit selling**; the salesperson relates a product's benefits to the customer's needs, using the product's features and advantages as support. This technique is often referred to as the **FAB selling technique** (**f**eature, **a**dvantage, and **b**enefit):*

- A product **feature** is any tangible or intangible characteristic of a product.
- A product **advantage** is the performance characteristic of a product that describes how it can be used or will help the buyer.
- A product **benefit** is a favourable result the buyer receives from the product because of a particular advantage that has the ability to satisfy the buyer's need.

The Product's Features: So What?

Products have features (tangible or intangible characteristics) such as the following:

Size	Terms	Packaging
Colour	Quantity	Flavour
Taste	Price	Service
Quality	Shape	Uses
Delivery	Ingredients	Technology.

Descriptions of a product's features answer the question, What is it? When used alone in the sales presentation, features have little persuasive power.

The Product's Advantages: Prove It!

Once a product feature is presented to the customer, the salesperson usually begins to discuss the advantages provided by that product's characteristics. The chances of making a sale are increased by describing the product's advantages, how a product can be used, or how it will help the buyer. Examples of product advantages (performance characteristics) follow:

- It is the fastest-selling soap on the market.
- You can store more information and retrieve it more rapidly with our computer.
- This machine will copy on both sides of the page instead of only one.

How does the prospective customer know that your claims for a product are true? Imagine that a prospect is thinking, "Prove it!" Be prepared to substantiate any claims you make.

Although your chances of making a sale increase when you discuss both the features and the advantages of your product, you must learn how to stress product benefits in your presentation that are important to the prospect. Once you have mastered this selling technique, your sales will increase.

---

*Some companies train their salespeople using only features and benefits; they see an advantage and benefit as identical. However, most companies use FAB.

The Product's Benefits: What's in It for Me?

People are interested in what results they will receive by buying and using the product or service. Emphasizing benefits appeals to the customer's personal motives by answering the question, What's in it for me? In your presentation, stress how the prospect will benefit from the purchase rather than stressing the features and advantages of your product, as shown in Exhibit 5–2.

To illustrate the idea of buying benefits instead of only features or advantages, consider four items: (1) a diamond ring, (2) digital photo frame, (3) STP motor oil, and (4) movie tickets. Do people buy these products or services for their features or advantages? No; people buy the product's benefits, such as

- A diamond ring—an image of success, an investment, or to please a loved one
- A digital photo frame—memories of places, friends, or family
- STP motor oil—engine protection, car investment, or peace of mind
- Movie tickets—entertainment, escape from reality, or relaxation.

As you can see, people buy benefits—not features or advantages. These benefits can be both practical, such as an investment, and psychological, such as an image of success. The salesperson needs to discuss benefits to answer the prospect's question, What's in it for me?

> Vacuum cleaner salesperson to householder: "This vacuum cleaner's high-speed motor (feature) works twice as fast (advantage) with less effort (advantage), which saves you 15 to 30 minutes in cleaning time (benefit) and the aches and pains of pushing a heavy machine (benefit).

Notice that the benefit specifically states the favourable results of buying the vacuum cleaner, which answers the buyer's question, What's in it for *me?* You can see the benefits are specific statements and not generalizations. Instead of saying, "This vacuum cleaner will save you time," say, "You will save 15 to 30 minutes."

Notice that a benefit can result in a further benefit to the prospect. For example, "By saving cleaning time (a benefit), you reduce the aches and pains of pushing a

---

EXHIBIT 5–2

Discuss benefits to fulfill people's needs and to increase sales.

Industrial salespeople work closely with customers to design products and systems that fit their needs.

Consumer goods salespeople can show customers how to increase sales by setting up strategic merchandise displays.

heavier machine (a benefit of a benefit) because the high-speed motor (advantage) pulls it (advantage)." Examples of general product benefits include

- Greater profit
- Time savings
- Increased sales
- Cost reductions
- More customers drawn into retail store
- Elimination of out-of-stock merchandise.

Order Can Be Important

Some salespeople prefer to state the benefit and then state that the feature or advantage makes the benefit possible, such as, "The *king-size* (feature) Tide will bring you *additional profits* (benefits) because it is the *fastest-selling size* (advantage)." In this example, the advantage supports the statement of benefits.

Although stating the benefit first is preferable, you can discuss the FAB in any particular order:

> Air conditioning salesperson to customer: "This air conditioner has a high energy-efficiency rating (feature) that will save you 10 percent on your energy costs (benefit) because it uses less electricity (advantage)."

> Sporting goods salesperson to customer: "With this ball, you'll get an extra 5 to 10 metres on your drives (advantage) helping to reduce your score (benefit) because of its new solid core (feature)."

> Salesperson to buyer of grocery store health and beauty aids: "Our economy size (feature) sells the best of all brands (advantage) in stores like yours. You can increase store traffic 10 to 20 percent (benefit) and build your sales volume by at least 5 percent (benefit) by advertising and reducing its normal price (feature) in next Wednesday's ad."

New salespeople should practise using feature, advantage, and benefit phrases in their sales conversation:

> The . . . (feature) . . . means you . . . (advantage) . . . with the real benefit to you being . . . (benefit). . . .

This FAB sequence allows you to easily remember to state the product's benefit in a natural, conversational manner. For example, "The *new solid-core centre of the Gunshot Golf Ball* means you *will have an extra 5 to 10 metres on your drives,* with the real benefit to you being *a lower score*." Substitute any features, advantages, and benefits among a variety of transition phrases to develop FAB sequences. Several sequences can be used one after another to emphasize your product's benefits.

Try it. Read the golf ball FAB sequence aloud. Then do it again, using your own phrasing. Create several variations of transition language that you feel comfortable using.

Matching FABs to Buyer Needs

Exhibit 5–3 illustrates the concept that buyers have important needs as well as relatively unimportant buying needs.

EXHIBIT 5–3

Match buyer's needs to product's benefits and emphasize them in the sales presentation.

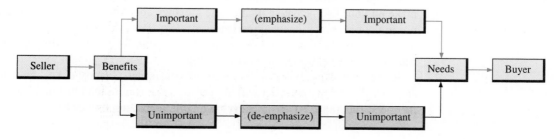

When presenting FABs, emphasize product benefits that satisfy important buyer needs. De-emphasize benefits that would satisfy unimportant needs. Suppose your product had benefits involving service, delivery, time savings, and cost reductions. Let us also suppose that, during needs analysis, you discover that delivery is not important to the buyer. In this case, concentrate on discussing service, time savings, and cost reductions.

This selling strategy is important; low-performance salespeople often discuss benefits of little or no interest to the prospect.

The Three Realms—Selling the Whole Package

Buyers are not interested in only products or services. **Three realms** of selling actually make up the complete package a customer gets when she buys. As a skilled salesperson, you must sell

- Yourself
- Your company
- Your products and services.

You may be selling the greatest products at the lowest prices, made by the most respected company around, but the prospect will not buy from you if she does not believe you and trust your word. Buyers want to deal with salespeople who are reliable, honest, and knowledgeable and who will be there for them should they need help. You are also part of the sales package. Sell yourself as part of the value the buyer will receive by buying from you.

POSITION YOUR PRODUCT WITH A UNIQUE SELLING PROPOSITION

A unique selling proposition (USP) clearly answers the question, "Why should I buy from you?" Let's face it—in most selling situations it is this question going through a prospect's mind, so you should answer it clearly.

If you have competition, you should develop at least one USP and possibly several. The more you have, the easier it is to position your product in your prospect's mind.

Developing a USP

To develop a successful USP, ask yourself several questions about your product or business:

1. What attributes set your product or business apart from direct competitors? You will not necessarily use all of these, but more questions will help you decide what to focus on.
2. Which of these attributes are most important to your prospects?
3. Which of these attributes are truly unique and would be difficult for your competition to imitate?
4. Which of these attributes are most easily communicated and demonstrated to your prospects?

Using Your USP

Once you have carefully thought out the key attributes of your product or service that make up your USP, create a memorable message about these important attributes to use in your presentations and marketing strategy. For example, guaranteed next-day delivery could become a unique selling proposition for you providing that (1) it's true, and (2) none of your competitors offer it.

Remember, though, that seldom are two customers exactly alike—so using the same USP for every prospect will not get the same result. You must understand your prospect's buying motives and develop a USP to best suit him or her.

ADVERTISING AIDS SALESPEOPLE

Personal selling, advertising, publicity, and sales promotion are the main factors of a firm's promotional effort. Companies sometimes coordinate these promotional tools in a promotional campaign. A sales force may be asked by the corporate marketing manager to concentrate on selling Product A for April and May. Product A is simultaneously promoted on television and in magazines, and direct-mail samples or coupons for Product A are sent to consumers.

Keeping abreast of your company's advertising and sales promotion activities is critical. By incorporating these data into your sales presentation, you can provide customers with a world of information that they probably know little about—and that information can secure the sale. Knowing your company's advertising budget, schedule, and messages can be a terrific aid in your sales presentation. When asked, "Can you guarantee that this product will sell in my store?" you can explain the advertising support that the product will be given by your company.

SALES PROMOTION GENERATES SALES

Sales promotion involves activities or materials other than personal selling, advertising, and publicity used to create sales. Sales promotion can be divided into consumer and trade sales promotion. **Consumer sales promotion** includes samples, coupons, contests, and demonstrations to consumers. **Trade sales promotion** encourages resellers to purchase and aggressively sell a manufacturer's products by offering incentives such as sales contests, displays, special purchase prices, and free merchandise (for example, buy 10 cases of a product and get one case free).

These promotions, along with things like point-of-purchase (POP) displays, can be very useful sales tools for an enterprising salesperson. Sales promotion offers may prove to the retailer or wholesaler that the selling firm will assist actively in creating consumer demand. This, in turn, improves the salesperson's probability of making the sale.

Shelf Positioning Is Important to Your Success

Another important sales stimulator is the shelf positioning of products. **Shelf positioning** refers to the physical placement of the product within the retailer's store. **Shelf facings** are the number of individual products placed beside each other on the shelf. Determine where a store's customers can easily find and examine your company's products, and place products in that space or position them with as many shelf facings as the store allows. See Exhibit 5–4.

Planogram Software

Recognizing the importance of shelf positioning and point of purchase displays, companies such as Shelf Logic, PlanoGraphics, and Spaceman have developed *planogram software* to help sales reps, buyers, and merchandisers make the best use of selling space.

A planogram is a blueprint of where products should be placed on display shelves. The software usually stores the width, depth, and height of each product and its SKU, along with an electronically stored visual of the product. The software user can then automatically create a planogram by dragging and dropping products on different shelves while estimating stock turnover and optimal restocking times. Shelf designs can be done in colour, which helps retailers determine how the colours will work together.

The software can further automate the process of calculating the product layout range of the entire category before the layout is produced. This allows the

Sales reps know that good shelf positioning and shelf facings boost sales.

category manager or buyer to determine space allocation of different products while considering sales and margins, and keeping in line with the company's marketing objectives.

For further information, check out the following Web sites, some of which show the software in action:

www.shelflogic.com
www.planographics.com/planmac.html
www.acnielsenspaceman.com/spcmnsum.asp

Premiums

The premium has come a long way from being just a trinket in a Cracker Jack box; today, it is a major marketing tool. Canadian businesses spend millions of dollars on consumer and trade premiums and incentives because premiums create sales.

A **premium** is an article of merchandise offered as an incentive for the user to take some action. The premium may act as an incentive to buy, to sample the product, to come into the retail store, or to request further information. Premiums include contests, consumer premiums, and dealer premiums.

PRICING YOUR PRODUCT

Salespeople must know the selling price of each of their products along with any discounts that may be offered to the customer. Often, management will determine that certain price discounts may be given under certain circumstances to buyers. Detailed knowledge of these discounts can become part of a sales presentation and a price negotiation.

Salespeople should have a thorough understanding of the arithmetic in **markup** and discount structures for different types of product. This will allow them to explain pricing mechanisms and profitability for their customers.

At the end of this text is a further discussion of the various pricing issues salespeople must be able to explain to buyers. Appendix A, "Sales Arithmetic and Pricing," has information useful for developing a sales presentation for the class project role-play.

KNOW YOUR COMPETITION, INDUSTRY, AND ECONOMY

Today's successful salespeople understand their competitors' products, policies, and practices as well as their own. It is common for a buyer to ask a salesperson, "How does your product compare to the one I'm currently using?" If unable to confidently answer such a question, a salesperson will lose ground in selling. (See Exhibit 5–5.)

One way to obtain information on competitors is through advertisements. From a competitor's advertising, Joe Mitchell, a salesperson representing a small business machines firm, developed a chart for comparing the sales points of his machines against the competition. Joe does not name the competitive equipment on the chart. Instead, he calls them Machine A, Machine B, and Machine C. When he finds a claimed benefit in one of the other machines that his product does not have, he works to find a better benefit to balance it.

> Maybe the chart isn't always useful, but it certainly has prepared me to face a customer. I know just what other machines have—and what they do not have—that my prospect might be interested in. I know the principal sales arguments used in selling these machines and the benefits I must bring up to offset and surpass competition. Many times a prospect will mention an advertisement of another company and ask about some statement or other. Because I've studied those ads and taken the time to find out what's behind the claims, I can give an honest answer and I can demonstrate how my machine has the same feature or quality and then offer additional benefits. Of course, I never run down a competitor's product. I just try to run ahead of it.

An industrial-goods salesperson and an industrial buyer work for different companies but are in the same industry. The industrial buyer often seeks information from salespeople on the industry itself, and how economic trends might influence the industry as well as both of their companies. Thus, the salesperson should be well

EXHIBIT 5–5

What does this automotive salesperson need to know about her products and competition?

informed about the industry and the economy. This information is available in the company records, television, radio, the **Internet**, newspapers such as the *National Post* and *The Globe and Mail,* industrial and trade periodicals, and magazines such as *Canadian Business.*

Another key source of information for salespeople and marketing managers is research provided by companies such as ACNielsen, a marketing information company.

Sales reps often use ACNielsen's analysis to augment their sales presentations and show their clients that their recommendations are based on solid research.

PERSONAL COMPUTERS AND SELLING

For most college and university graduates these days, computers and other sales technologies are not at all intimidating. However, the nontechnical person may be apprehensive about being able to use a computer and its software properly. However, computer manufacturers, software suppliers, and company training programs quickly and effectively train people and provide easy-to-use computer software. The top 10 uses of personal computers by salespeople are shown in Exhibit 5–6.

If you have little computer knowledge, start learning! Take a beginning computer course through a local college or university's continuing education program. It is never too late.

KNOWLEDGE OF TECHNOLOGY ENHANCES SALES AND CUSTOMER SERVICE

Sales force technology and automation come in a variety of sizes and applications. In addition to desktop and laptop computers, PDAs such as the Palm products made by 3Com and BlackBerries made by Research in Motion are used by salespeople to improve their productivity and connectivity. The salesperson's appointment schedule, to-do list, and contacts are always close at hand in a pocket, purse, or briefcase, and the data—including **e-mail**—can be transferred easily and quickly between the hand-held device and a laptop or desktop computer.

Technology helps salespeople increase their productivity effectiveness and allows them to gather and access information more efficiently. You can use computer technology to improve communication with the home office, others on your sales force, and customers. Salespeople also use technology to create better strategies for targeting and tracking clients. Sales force automation breaks down into three broad areas of functionality covering (1) personal productivity, (2) communications, and (3) order processing and customer service.

EXHIBIT 5–6

Top 10 PC applications.

PC applications are focused on the customer. Here are the top 10 uses of PCs by salespeople in order of use:

1.	Customer/prospect profile	6.	Sales presentation
2.	Lead tracking	7.	Time/territory management
3.	Call reports	8.	Order entry
4.	Sales forecasts	9.	Travel and expense reports
5.	Sales data analysis	10.	Checking inventory/shipping status.

* Material reprinted with permission of ACNeilson.

EXHIBIT 5–7

The PC has numerous
applications.

This salesperson uses his PC to analyze customer data while developing his sales presentation.

Personal Productivity

Many software programs can help a salesperson increase **personal productivity** through more efficient data storage and retrieval, better time management, and enhanced presentations. Let's discuss five of the most popular.

Contact Management

Contact management is a listing of all the customer contacts that a salesperson makes in the course of conducting business. This file is like an electronic Rolodex and should include such information as the contact's name, title, company, address, phone number, fax number, and e-mail address. It also may include additional information such as the contact's particular industry, date of last order, name of administrative assistant, birthday, children, and so on.

A sales force automation system allows you to easily retrieve this information in a variety of formats. You can sort contacts according to any one of the pieces of information you are tracking. For instance, you may be going to Halifax and want a list of contacts in that area who have made a purchase in the past six months. Another example of sorted information that you may require is a list of customers by postal code for mailing labels, or perhaps a list of your clients with birthdays in October.

A handheld computing device eliminates the weight and bulkiness of a paper-based time management system.

Calendar Management

For salespeople, improvement of time management directly increases productivity.

When a salesperson schedules appointments, telephone calls, or to-do lists on an electronic calendar, the system automatically checks for conflicts, eliminating the need for rescheduling. An electronic calendar can assign a relative priority to each item. It also can create an electronic link between a scheduled event and a particular contact or account so that the appointment or call information is accessible as both part of the salesperson's calendar and part of the contact or account history. This makes the information contained in the calendar much more useful, since it can be viewed from different perspectives.

For the sales manager, electronic **calendar management** automatically consolidates information concerning the whereabouts of the entire sales force. Information is automatically generated when salespeople schedule their appointments, whether from in the office or in the field.

Automated Sales Plans, Tactics, and Ticklers

Sales strategies often fall into a sequence of events that can be identified and plotted. A traditional example involves a thank-you letter sent immediately after an initial sales call and a follow-up telephone call three days later. In the real world, it may be difficult for busy salespeople to track all the details. As a result, important follow-up items sometimes get overlooked. If this happens, a salesperson's diligent prospecting efforts may be wasted and valuable prospects squandered.

MAKING THE SALE

The Computer as a Sales Assistant

It's 7:30 A.M., and you're getting ready to leave your hotel room. You turn to your computer and say, "System on."

"Good morning," the machine responds. "Are you ready to review your appointment calendar?"

"Sure. First, summarize e-mail traffic. I didn't have a chance to scan last night because I got in so late."

"You have received 37 messages in the past 24 hours. Twenty are low priority and have been filed in your home machine for review when your trip is over. Ten are medium priority and are stored in my memory for review at your convenience today. I suggest you scan the seven high-priority messages before you begin the day's activities."

"First, let's go over my day's schedule. I remember I had six appointments. Are they still on?"

"One was cancelled. During the newswire scan you requested, I picked up serious traffic problems that should be resolved by late afternoon, so I contacted the electronic agents of two of your appointments and rescheduled. They have confirmed the new times. I interfaced with your car's mapping system yesterday, and the preferred routes are available in my memory."

"Any hot points I should remember?"

"Two of your appointments have had birthdays within the past two weeks. Winston of United Products sent a letter of complaint about a delayed shipment four months ago. My records state the issue was resolved to UP's satisfaction. A special promotion we began last week for American International appears to already have had a positive impact."

"Good. Let's go over the trends and analysis for each meeting. Sound off. I'll remember better if I just read the text."

A sales force automation system begins working as soon as the initial meeting is entered into the system. A few simple commands tell it to remind you to send a thank-you letter and schedule a follow-up phone call. The system also can notify the sales manager if these things are not done.

Another sales situation might call for a regular follow-up every year or two after the sale, depending on the *itch cycle* associated with your product. It is particularly easy for this type of follow-up call to be neglected. The problem becomes more likely if the salesperson who made the original sale leaves the company or is promoted. When that happens, the customer often falls through the cracks. Automated sales tactics and ticklers prevent this from happening.

Geographic Information Systems

A **geographic information system** allows salespeople to view and manipulate customer and prospect information on an electronic map. Customer information can be accessed directly from contact-management data and sorted accordingly, allowing you to plan sales calls geographically and use your time most efficiently. Customer buying patterns that otherwise might not be apparent may be revealed.

Computer-based Presentations

The computer can be a powerful presentation tool, allowing salepeople to create dramatic and interactive **computer-based presentations** at relatively low cost. Once created, they can be customized for a particular customer or prospect or to take advantage of a particular sales opportunity.

USB **flash drives** (memory sticks), DVDs, and CD-ROMs can eliminate having to carry around heavy and cumbersome catalogues and other information. Information can be found accurately and quickly by searching.

MAKING THE SALE

The Salesperson's Business Card—Telephone, Fax, Pager, E-mail, and the Web

Today's business cards often show multiple phone numbers and addresses: fax, mobile, and pager numbers, as well as e-mail and Web addresses.

Brent Harvey was an inside corporate sales representative with Seagate Software in Vancouver. He had his direct phone line prominently displayed on his business card. Customers and prospects had the choice of reaching him quickly or using Seagate's automated answering and directory system, which was reached via the company's main number, also listed on his card.

The company's fax number and Web site address was also listed on Harvey's card, along with his e-mail address; however, his mobile phone and pager numbers were not. "I don't want everyone to page me, so I only give my pager number to top customers," said Harvey. "I only use my cell phone when travelling."

Harvey used a Casio handheld computer as a portable means of keeping track of appointments, to-do lists, and e-mail correspondence while away from his desk. He was able to connect the device to his desktop or laptop as needed and connect a modem card and a phone line to his handheld when travelling to send and receive e-mails.

As an inside sales rep, Harvey found it particularly important to remain connected electronically. "E-mail is critical to my business," he said. "Three applications I have open all the time are e-mail, contact manager, and Web browser. I rarely use fax now because it is too expensive and time consuming."

Salespeople can use their laptops to present the presentation or hook up to an LCD projector, an electronic whiteboard, or large LCD panel display. These technologies provide vivid detail to prospects and are excellent when presenting to groups.

Using wireless technology, salespeople can go online from practically any location and connect with their home office (for instant updates on inventory levels) or with Web sites to find current information for their prospects.

iPods Improve Sales

iPods and MP3 players allow salespeople to show data and videos to prospects, as well as train themselves on product knowledge and selling skills. Imagine a salesperson preparing to call on a major customer;—the iPod's sound and video clip features enable the seller to review such things as objection handling and closing techniques, as well as a video sales presentation role-play of the product being presented to the buyer—while sitting in the customer's waiting room. What a great way to get mentally prepared.

Communications   Today's most popular sales force automation systems involve **word processing**, e-mail, and fax technology.

Word Processing

Written communication plays a large part in the lives of most salespeople. Particularly important is the need for written communication with customers. A thank-you letter mailed immediately after an initial sales call often can make the difference between a favourable impression and one that is not as favourable. Sometimes it can make or break a sale. In spite of its potential impact, this simple task frequently is overlooked because the salesperson lacks an easy way to get it done; there always seem to be other, more pressing things to do. A word processing system can shorten the time it takes to accomplish this task to no more than a minute or two.

EXHIBIT 5–9

Technology is enabling salespeople to do a better job selling and servicing their customers.

Videoconferencing is excellent for presentations and training.

Mobile technology is essential for customer relationship management.

E-Mail

E-mail has become the norm for many of today's business communications and is therefore necessary for effective, inexpensive business communication. For instance, when you are trying to contact a customer who is temporarily out of town, e-mail may be your best bet. If you truly want to be close to your customers, e-mail can have a tremendous impact, whether you rarely leave the office or are based in the field.

Fax Capabilities and Support

Laptops equipped with fax modems provide the ability to prepare and fax a document—from your car, perhaps—without having to print a hard copy. You can receive documents in the same manner. Fax modems represent a convenient, inexpensive way to handle much of a salesperson's written communication from the road.

Order Processing and Customer Service

The process of obtaining, generating, and completing an order by a manual system may take a number of days or even weeks to complete and confirm. Automated systems shorten the sales-and-delivery cycle tremendously. While in your customer's office, you can check the inventory status of merchandise on the sales order, receive approval for your client's credit status, and begin the shipping process immediately. Salespeople's automated order entries directly update the company computer without having to be re-entered back at the home office.

A True Mobile Office

Notice the accessibility of the the **GPS**, mobile phone, and PDA. Other than the GPS, these gadgets should be avoided while driving—for safety's sake.

Salespeople's Mobile Offices

Some salespeople have installed small offices in their vehicles, such as minivans. For salespeople who need to be constantly in touch with their clients, minivans are a perfect solution for working through dead time. A vehicle can be equipped with a fully functional desk, swivel chair, light, computer, printer, fax machine, mobile phone and satellite. phone. From their **mobile offices**, salespeople can stay in constant touch with their customers.

GPS and PDA

A well-equipped salesperson will have several gadgets to enhance selling effectiveness. Salespeople often travel extensively—both by land and air and it is imperative that they manage their time well and stay in communication. A modern sales rep may employ three simple technologies to accomplish this.

1. Global Positioning Systems (GPS)—Forget getting lost while on the road. A GPS is a radio navigation system that uses satellite technology to pinpoint locations to within a metre. Sales reps can use an in-vehicle GPS to determine their exact whereabouts and the direction in which they are heading. By entering a postal code, business name, or street address using a touch screen display, a sales rep can be guided both audibly and by visual street maps to his or her desired destination. Imagine the time savings and reduction in stress.

2. Personal Digital Assistant (**PDA**)—You're never far from the information you need when you use a PDA. Essentially handheld computers, they have become much more versatile over the years. PDAs can be used for calculations, clock and calendar, accessing the Internet, sending and receiving e-mails, video recording, word processing, storing addresses, making and editing spreadsheets, scanning bar codes, listening to music, playing computer games, recording survey responses, and even global positioning. Newer PDAs also have both colour screens and audio capabilities, enabling them to be used as mobile phones (smartphones), Web browsers, or portable media players. Many PDAs can access the Internet, intranets or extranets via Wi-Fi, or Wireless Wide-Area Networks (WWANs) with many of them employing touch screen technology.[2]

3. Mobile Phones—The mobile phone is a device used for mobile communication that uses a network of specialized base stations known as cell sites. More than just a phone, current mobile phones offer other services such as text messaging, e-mail, access to the Internet, and the ability to send and receive photos and video. When selecting a mobile phone, salespeople must consider the features that will enhance their ability to do their job. One consideration is whether a GSM or CDMA phone should be used. While there are many technical considerations to take into account, one major factor is where you will be selling. Due to the inherent technology, GSM phones are used by salespeople who travel the world as GSM phones have much better global coverage than CDMA.[3]

Mobile Phone Considerations

Millions of people subscribe to wireless service in Canada; it has become an essential tool in sales. Although mobile phones bring significant convenience, such as checking your e-mail and **surfing the Internet** from your phone, mobile phone etiquette should be practised to avoid interrupting or ruining sales calls and meetings.

1. The person you are with is the most important person to talk to. Whether you are with a customer, potential buyer, or supervisor, program your ringer to vibrate or turn your phone off. You may even decide to let your voicemail take the call and return the call at a more convenient time. This applies to pagers also.

2. Use text messaging to simplify your life. If you are expecting important information from a colleague but need to be in a public area, ask her to text you instead.

3. Turn off your phone during meetings, sales calls, and presentations. Talking on the phone during any of these can be disruptive and violates basic courtesy. Just the ring tone of your phone is enough to interrupt a speaker, so if you are expecting an important call, switch to silent mode and use text messaging.

4. Don't engage in **cell yell**. Yelling on a mobile phone can be offensive to anyone around you. There is no need to speak louder on your mobile phone than you would on any other phone.

THE INTERNET AND THE WORLD WIDE WEB

The Internet provides salespeople with access to research, data, people, and vast amounts of information. It is a great sales tool—if you know how to fully use it.

Instant Messaging

Instant messaging (IM) offers real-time communication and easy collaboration, which makes it similar to genuine conversation. Unlike e-mail, IM shows the parties if and when a peer is available. Most systems allow a user to set an "online" or "away" message so peers are notified when the user is available, busy, or away from the computer. However, because they are not forced to reply immediately to incoming messages, some people consider communication via instant messaging to be less intrusive than communication via phone. Some systems allow the sending of messages to people not currently logged on (*offline messages*), thus removing much of the difference between instant messaging and email.[4]

Instant messaging allows instantaneous communication between a number of parties. This is similar to teleconferencing but lacks the non-verbal component of communication unless the parties are using a Webcam.[5]

Video Calling

While mobile phones and instant messaging may be excellent for quick and easy communication, they lack the non-verbal behaviour we learned about in Chapter 4. **Video calling**, to some extent, meets this challenge.

The World Wide Web

The Internet and the World Wide Web are often thought of as the same thing; however, they are not. The Internet refers to the physical infrastructure of the interconnected global computer network—just imagine a giant mass of cables and computers. The **World Wide Web** (also known as the Web or W3) is a part of the Internet that houses Web sites that provide text, graphics, video, and audio information on millions of topics. Individuals, companies, government agencies, schools, and many other types of organizations develop Web sites to promote ideas, products, or organizations.

Web sites can provide valuable information to salespeople.

Every screenful of information (commonly called a **Web page**) usually has a number of pointers to other pages of information on the Web. (See Exhibit 5–10.) These pointers, or **links**, are what give the Web its name; all the links together form a web of information that spans the globe.

At appropriate places throughout this textbook, you will find Web exercises related to sales. The "Globe" icon points to the sales Web exercises, which we encourage you to try.

As a salesperson, you need to know how to use all sales technology, including the Web. Here are a few sites to visit:

- www.theweathernetwork.com: Find the weather forecast for anywhere in the world.
- www.mapquest.ca: Get driving directions to anywhere.
- www.canada411.ca: Locate phone numbers for people and businesses. (Try finding yourself.)

SUMMARY OF MAJOR SELLING ISSUES

Company knowledge includes information on a firm's history, development policies, procedures, products, distribution, promotion, and pricing. A salesperson also must know the competition, the industry, and the economy. This knowledge can build self-confidence.

Wholesalers and retailers stock thousands of products, which often makes it difficult to support any one manufacturer's products the way the manufacturer wants. To aid channel members in selling products, manufacturers offer assistance in advertising, sales promotion aids, and pricing allowances. In addition, many manufacturers spend millions of dollars to compel consumers and industrial buyers to purchase from channel members and the manufacturer.

National, retail, trade, industrial, and direct-mail advertising create demand for products and are powerful selling tools for the salesperson during sales presentations. Sales promotion activities and materials are another potential selling tool for the salesperson to use when selling to consumer and industrial buyers. Samples, coupons,

ETHICAL DILEMMA
Using Blogs in Sales

Alex Serpino worked as a manufacturer's agent representing three different food producers in a large Western Canadian market. He prided himself on keeping abreast of everything going on in his industry so he could relay that information to his customers. Having recently upgraded his computer literacy, Alex was introduced to the world of blogging. He thought this would be a wonderful tool for him to share his industry knowledge and educate readers about the food business. This was working well when Alex came up with a new idea. He thought that if he carefully discussed some of the shortcomings of his competitors in his blogs, it might attract more customers to him.

Is this something Alex should consider? After all, it could improve his business.

contests, premiums, demonstrations, and displays are effective sales promotion techniques employed to help sell merchandise.

The salesperson should be able to discuss price, discounts, and credit policies confidently with customers. Customers want to know the salesperson's list and net price, and whether there are any transportation charges. Discounts (quantity, cash, trade, or consumer) represent important buying incentives for the buyer. The buyer also wants to know the terms of payment. The salesperson needs to understand company credit policies to open new accounts, see that customers pay on time, and collect overdue bills. See Appendix A at the end of the book for additional discussions on pricing.

Finally, success in sales requires knowledge of the many technologies used to sell and service customers. Computers, word processing, e-mail, faxes, pagers, mobile phones, the Internet, and the World Wide Web have quickly become part of the professional's sales kit.

MEETING A SALES CHALLENGE

To be successful, salespeople need to be knowledgeable. However, being an expert on the product is only part of what it takes to be a top performer. You also need to know how to use good communication and selling skills.

We now know that empathy is a critical skill for relationship building and effective selling.

It's all about benefits. Sure, this seller wants to sell her customers a good product, but the reseller is possibly more interested in whether she can sell the product once she buys it, and how much money she will make. Resellers are "bottom-line" oriented; because they want to know what's in it for them, they concentrate on discussing return on investment. If you empathized with her, you would have realized this and probably changed your presentation to make these very valid points.

PLAYING THE ROLE

The Situation: Two salespeople are debating the issue of modern technology and its use in selling. Assume the role of one of them and prepare arguments to support their position. Now, informally debate the issue using your supporting arguments.

Role A: "Old-World Sales Rep." Your feelings are that technology is taking the personal touch out of selling and is turning off too many customers.

Role B: "Modern Sales Rep." You feel that technology has too many benefits **not** to be used by the professional salesperson.

KEY TERMS FOR SELLING

advantage, 125
benefit, 125
benefit selling, 125
blogs, 123
calendar management, 134
cell yell, 139
computer-based presentations, 135
consumer sales promotion, 129
contact management, 133
e-mail, 132
FAB selling technique, 125
feature, 125
flash drive, 135
geographic information system, 135
GPS, 137
instant messaging, 139
Internet, 132

links, 140
markup, 130
mobile offices, 138
PDA, 138
personal productivity, 133
premium, 130
sales training, 120
shelf facings, 129
shelf positioning, 129
social networking, 123
surfing the Internet, 138
three realms, 128
trade sales promotion, 129
video calling, 139
Web page, 140
word processing, 136
World Wide Web, 139

SALES APPLICATION QUESTIONS

1. A salesperson's knowledge needs to extend into many areas such as knowledge about the company; product; upcoming advertising and promotional campaigns; company price, discount, and credit policies; the competition; the industry; and the economy. These are all vital for sales success. For each of these categories, explain how a salesperson's knowledge can lay the groundwork for successful selling.

2. How do salespeople generally acquire their sales knowledge?

3. Explain how a salesperson's knowledge can be converted into selling points used in the sales presentation. Give two examples.

4. A salesperson must have a good understanding of the competition, customers, and everything connected with the company. Why should a salesperson take time to be up to date on facts about the economy and the industry?

5. What is the difference between a product's shelf positioning and its shelf facings? How can a salesperson maximize both shelf positioning and shelf facings? Why is this important?

6. Companies use numerous premiums in their efforts to market products. Why? What types of premiums do they use? How can a salesperson use a premium offer in a sales presentation to a wholesaler or a retailer?

7. What are the major types of advertising that a manufacturer might use to promote its products? How can a salesperson use information about the company's advertising in a sales presentation?

8. Before firms such as McCain and Schneider's introduce a new consumer product nationally, they frequently place the product in a test market to see how it will sell. How can a salesperson use test information in a sales presentation?

9. What is cooperative advertising? Explain the steps involved.

10. Why do companies advertise?

11. Consumer sales promotion and trade sales promotion try to increase sales to consumers and resellers, respectively. Several promotional techniques follow; classify each item as a consumer or trade promotional technique and give an example for each one. Can any of the promotions be used for both consumers and the trade?

   a. Coupons on or inside packages

   b. Free installation (premium)

c. Displays
d. Sales contests
e. Drawings for gifts
f. Demonstrations
g. Samples.

**SALES WORLD
WIDE WEB
EXERCISE**

**Business
Intelligence: Can
the Web Help?**

A few clicks of the mouse can provide an avalanche of free—but priceless—information about competitors. Useful Web sites include

www.scip.org

www.fuld.com

www.hoovers.com

www.canoe.ca

www.newsbot.msnbc.msn.com

www.individual.com

news.excite.com

www.sedar.com

Research one or more companies you have an interest in working for or that you know or have worked for in the past.

**FURTHER
EXPLORING THE
SALES WORLD**

Choose one of the following products:

■ GPS

■ iPod

■ Mobile phone

Now let's practise **uncovering relevant benefits**. Start by considering the product's attributes:

■ **Features**. What does the product offer? "This application handles multiple users concurrently."

■ **Advantages**. What do the features do? "This application provides essential information in real time."

■ **Benefits**. What do the features mean? "This information will allow your managers to keep their fingers on the company's financial pulse at all times."

■ **Needs**. What do the features satisfy? "This feature will provide cost savings, control, and efficiency."

1. Develop a FAB worksheet for your selected product as you would present it to a fellow student working in a retail store.

2. Develop a FAB worksheet for your selected product as you would present it to a purchasing agent for an electronics store if you are representing a manufacturer.

STUDENT
APPLICATION
LEARNING
EXERCISES
(SALES)

Part 3

SALES are meant to help you construct the various segments of your sales presentation. SALES build on one another so that as you complete each exercise you are constructing more of your sales presentation.

A. Develop a Feature/Advantage/Benefit worksheet for the product that you have selected to sell.

After reviewing parts 1 and 2 of this SALES exercise in Chapters 3 and 4, for each FAB package that you list, identify the prospect need that you are attempting to satisfy.

Sample Worksheet for Photocopier Prospect

Need	Feature	Advantage	Benefit
Increased productivity	High-speed processing	Will produce 100 copies per minute	Less time wasted at photocopier—higher productivity
Improve company's image	High-resolution, full-colour capability	Produces crisp, high-quality colour photocopies	Customers who look at your copied material will be impressed by its high quality

B. Review the section of the chapter dealing with developing a unique selling proposition (USP). Based on this information and the highlights of your FAB worksheet, develop an appropriate USP for your presentation.

**SELLING
EXPERIENTIAL
EXERCISE**

**How Is Your Sales
Self-Confidence?**

You may think you have a good attitude for sales, but if you do not have the confidence to meet customers and prospects you do not know, all is lost. This exercise can help measure your self-confidence. Read each statement and then, on a separate sheet of paper, write the number you believe best describes you.

	High				Low
I can convert strangers into friends quickly and easily.	5	4	3	2	1
I can attract and hold the attention of others even when I do not know them.	5	4	3	2	1
I love new situations.	5	4	3	2	1
I'm intrigued with the psychology of meeting and building a good relationship with someone I do not know.	5	4	3	2	1
I would enjoy making a sales presentation to a group of executives.	5	4	3	2	1
When dressed for the occasion, I have great confidence in myself.	5	4	3	2	1
I do not mind using the telephone to make appointments with strangers.	5	4	3	2	1
Others do not intimidate me.	5	4	3	2	1
I enjoy solving problems.	5	4	3	2	1
Most of the time, I feel secure.	5	4	3	2	1

Total Score _____

Total the numbers to get your score. If you scored more than 40, you are self-confident enough to consider selling as a profession. If you rated yourself between 25 and 40, you need more experience in dealing with people. A score of less than 25 may indicate that you need to build your sales self-confidence.[6]

CASE 5–1
Technophobia

Denise Haller had a wonderful personality. She was always known as a warm and caring individual who would go out of her way to help people in need. She was a great listener and terrific conversationalist, which explains why she was liked by so many people. Denise excelled in her studies, especially in general arts courses; her only struggle came when she decided to take some computer courses. She didn't enjoy learning about computers. In fact, Denise shied away from most new technologies; she preferred doing things the "old-fashioned way," using more personal face-to-face communication.

Upon graduation from college, Denise thought she could parlay her personal skills into a successful sales career. She had what it took; a great personality, excellent communication skills, and a desire to help people solve their problems. These traits came through during her interviews and she was offered several sales jobs after only one week of job interviews. The position she accepted was with a growing company in Southern Ontario that specialized in providing advertising novelties to different-sized companies. She thought the fast pace and opportunity to meet many new people would be an exciting one that she would enjoy.

She spent the first couple of weeks flipping through catalogues to familiarize herself with her product offerings. When she felt she knew her product lines well enough, she set out to develop some sales leads. She sat down at her desk, flipped through the Yellow Pages, and started dialling. Her personality alone allowed her to make several appointments for the following week so she was gearing up to start selling.

She showed up to her first meeting on Monday with catalogues in hand and started showing her products. Toward the end of her 30-minute appointment, the buyer gave her a small order. The second appointment was a little different. She met with a group of four buyers but had only one set of catalogues so it was difficult to deal with all four at once. She didn't make out as well in this meeting.

She knew she had a meeting after lunch to a group of three buyers so she stopped for a coffee and to plan her next meeting. At this meeting, she decided to introduce just one catalogue at a time and to discuss products individually. She found that the buyers seemed to be getting a little bored after 20 minutes of this. They did mention that they might be interested in ordering 5,000 frisbees with their company logo on them and inquired if she had the inventory to handle this. She didn't know offhand and promised to get back to them in the morning; hence, she ended up without a firm commitment from them. She was getting a little discouraged at this point but needed to get ready for the last appointment of the day, her fourth. This one held promise, she thought, so she did her best to get her excitement level up. As she entered the office and introduced herself to the secretary, she was informed by the secretary that the meeting had been cancelled and that she had been trying to get hold of her all day, leaving messages on her office answering machine. Denise left feeling dejected.

CASE 5–1

Questions

1. What do you think was wrong with Denise's selling style?
2. Can you recommend any changes that she should consider?
3. In terms of sales knowledge, can you suggest any areas that Denise needs to develop?
4. What types of technology would be useful for Denise to adopt? Explain how she might make use of them.

PART 3

THE RELATIONSHIP SELLING PROCESS

The selling skills used by successful salespeople are discussed in this part of the book. Selling skills involve prospecting, planning, presenting, handling objections, closing, follow-up, and servicing after the sale. Included in this part are

6

PROSPECTING—THE LIFEBLOOD OF SELLING

MAIN TOPICS

The Sales Process Has 10 Steps

Steps Before the Sales Presentation

Prospecting—The Lifeblood of Selling

Prospecting Guidelines

How to Qualify a Prospect

Referrals

The Referral Cycle

LEARNING OBJECTIVES

In this chapter, we examine the first step in the sales process—prospecting. After studying this chapter, you should be able to:

- Define and describe the 10 steps in the sales process.

- Explain why prospecting can be considered the "lifeblood of selling."

- Defend the importance of prospecting.

- Describe the various methods of prospecting.

- Demonstrate how to properly qualify a prospect.

- Describe the importance of referrals to a salesperson's success.

- Explain the concept of the "sales funnel."

FACING A SALES CHALLENGE

Larry Gasslein, John Alexander, and Mitali Das had just sat down for their weekly sales meeting when Larry said, "Selling Apple's new Power Mac in our market will not be easy for us. The city only has 200,000 people; the region has 275,000. Yet there are 20 or more companies selling personal computers in the area. The Source, IBM, Future Shop, and the others are tough competitors. I'm not sure where to begin."

"Larry, our best prospects—and the ones to begin seeing this afternoon—are our present customers. These are the ones currently using our Apple PCs, as well as customers who buy our equipment and office supplies," said John. "These people know us and already have accounts set up."

"That's OK for you," replied Mitali, "however, many of my present customers already have PCs. So, I'm not sure I can count on selling many to them. I'm going to have to explore new territories, knock on doors, and dial-for-dollars to even come up with leads."

Larry broke in with, "Let's go after the IBM customers. IBM has the biggest market share in our area. We need to hit them head-on."

"No way," replied John, "we could get creamed if we got into a war by attacking IBM or any of our other competitors."

"But with all of our advertising," Larry continued, "the company's service, and our fair price on a state-of-the-art Power Mac, we can regain our market share."

"Hold it, hold it," Mitali said. "Let's start over and develop a plan that will allow us to uncover as many prospects as quickly as we can. After all, we need to push this new product and get the competitive edge before the competition knows what hit 'em."

If you were one of these salespeople, how would you respond? What would be your sales plan?

EXHIBIT 6–1

The selling process has 10 important steps.

10 Follow-up
9 Close
8 Trial close
7 Meet objections
6 Determine objections
5 Trial close
4 Presentation
3 Approach
2 Preapproach
1 Prospecting

The first two parts of this book give much of the background a salesperson needs for making an actual presentation. However, you can be the most knowledgeable person on topics such as buyer behaviour, competitors, and product information, yet still have difficulty being a successful salesperson unless you are thoroughly prepared for each part of the sales call. Part III of this book examines the various elements of the sales process and sales presentation. We begin by reviewing the sales process. Then we discuss methods of prospecting that may help Larry, John, and Mitali plan their sales program.

THE SALES PROCESS HAS 10 STEPS

As discussed in Chapter 1, the sales process refers to a sequence of actions by the salesperson that leads toward the customer taking a desired action and ends with a follow-up to ensure purchase satisfaction. Although many factors may influence how a salesperson makes a presentation in a particular situation, a logical sequence of steps can greatly increase the chances of a sale. These 10 steps are listed in Exhibit 6–1. Step 1 is discussed in this chapter, and the others are discussed in greater detail in upcoming chapters. Steps 3 through 9 compose the sales presentation itself. Before a sales presentation can be attempted, several important preparatory activities should be carried out.

STEPS BEFORE THE SALES PRESENTATION

As indicated in Exhibit 6–2, successful salespeople prospect; this involves obtaining an appointment with the prospect and planning the sales interview before meeting with the prospect. Like a successful lawyer, the salesperson does a great amount of

Before the sales presentation.

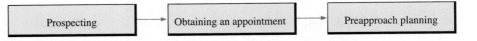

background work before meeting the judge—the prospect. A general rule states that a good sales process involves 20 percent presentation, 40 percent preparation, and 40 percent follow-up, especially when selling large accounts. At Xerox, the national account manager will spend up to 18 months preparing a detailed description of a potential national account. This report, which can easily end up being 50 pages, is basically a business plan for selling the prospect. Thus preparation time for this sales call would be greater than the 40 percent general rule.[1]

PROSPECTING— THE LIFEBLOOD OF SELLING

Let's face it. If salespeople didn't prospect, they would likely have no one to sell to, make very little money, and be of little use to their employer. It is necessary to actively prospect for two reasons:

Why Prospect?

1. To develop new customers and increase sales.
2. To replace customers lost each year.

Salespeople who work on commission are able to increase their sales and therefore their paycheques by actively soliciting new business.

Exhibit 6–3 illustrates the importance of prospecting. Look closely at the many reasons that customers may be lost each year.

Not All Prospects Are Created Equal

Prospecting is the first step in the selling process. Salespeople are usually able to obtain **leads**, which are simply the names of individuals who may have a need for the salesperson's product. For some types of salespeople, effective prospecting is the key to their livelihood as salespeople; for others, leads are simply provided for them to

The ferris wheel concept.

Sources of Leads
- Cold canvassing
- Endless chain referral
- Orphaned customers
- Sales lead clubs
- Prospect lists
- Trade shows
- Direct response advertising
- Web sites
- Educational seminars
- Non-competing salespeople
- Lists and directories
- Centre of influence

On   Off

Loss of Customers
- Deaths
- Poor service
- Bankruptcies
- Mergers
- Relocations
- Poor economic conditions
- No longer a need for product
- Competition takes over
- New purchasing agents
- Technology change
- No more demand

This diagram illustrates the **"ferris wheel" concept** of prospecting. Notice that there are as many opportunities for prospects to get off the ferris wheel as there are for getting on. If salespeople do not work diligently to keep the wheel full, there will be few customers left after a while.

follow up on. To be a true **prospect**, a lead must first be qualified. Qualifying a lead means that a salesperson must first determine if a person or organization has the potential to buy the good or service for sale. To become a **qualified prospect**, the following must be determined:

1. Does the prospect have the **M**oney to buy?
2. Does the prospect have the **A**uthority to buy?
3. Does the prospect have the **D**esire to buy?

A simple way to remember the qualifying process is to use the acronym "**MAD**." The salesperson must first determine that the prospect will be able to proceed with the purchase. One of the main objectives of qualifying a lead is to save time. There is no point preparing and planning a major presentation to a prospect who has no money or doesn't have the authority to make a decision.

To understand prospecting, remember old westerns. After equipping him- or herself with the knowledge and resources needed, a gold prospector stakes out a claim (establishes a sales territory) on a piece of land where the likelihood of finding gold (customers) is high. The process may involve scraping the bed of a stream with a pan to lift out silt (leads). By sifting the silt (leads) the prospector is eliminating the debris (unqualified) and hopefully is left with real gold (qualified prospects) that she can cash in.

HOW TO QUALIFY A PROSPECT

To save time and effort, all leads should be subjected to the qualification process. Necessary information can be obtained using several means:

- Asking the referral for information
- Researching the company prospectus and other materials
- Keeping your industry knowledge up to date (perhaps you have read about a pending expansion of a local company)
- Speaking with non-competing salespeople.

The most effective way of qualifying prospects is by simply asking them. This can be done during the pre-approach stage or, as a last resort, during the approach stage. The following are some simple questions that may be asked.

Money	Authority	Desire
How much were you budgeting for this type of purchase? Are you prepared to spend this budget?	Is anyone else going to be in on the decision or are you the main decision maker?	How urgently do you need this product?
What kind of price range were you considering?	Is this product for you or are you buying for someone else?	Are you replacing an older product?
Were you thinking of paying cash for this or financing it?	Who is (are) the main decision maker(s) for this purchase?	Is your current product not satisfying you anymore?

As you can see, if the lead cannot be not qualified, you may waste a great deal of time pursuing leads that will not or cannot become customers. Don't not make assumptions about MAD; ask.

Motive, Means, and Opportunity: Another Way of Looking at Qualifying

As discussed, a primary reason for proper qualification is to allocate your resources (time) efficiently. Ultimately, salespeople need to find out *why* someone would buy something in the first place, and *how* could they buy it if they wanted to.

Motives

In Chapter 3, we discussed why people buy. In terms of qualifying, a salesperson needs to have an understanding of the prospect's business, its goals and objectives, and its performance relative to these goals. If there is a discrepancy between where the business is or is heading and where it should be, then a solution is needed. This is where salespeople often come in, asking qualifying questions:

- Why does this discrepancy create a problem?
- Why did it occur?
- Why haven't you acted before?
- What would happen if we solved this problem?
- Why invest in this problem rather than other investments?
- Are there any risks in solving this problem?
- Can someone else in the company solve this problem?
- Is it really important that you do something about it?

The answers to these questions will reveal many different types of buying motives, both corporate and personal.

Means

Once the motive is established, you need to qualify for means, or ability to buy. Qualifying questions include

- Can you afford my proposed solution?
- How will you justify the purchase?
- Will it ultimately be approved? How?
- How will you pay for it or finance it?
- Is there a third party involved (lender, etc.)?
- Who will ultimately give approval?
- Are all resources in place to utilize my solution?
- Will you get good value and will you provide us with referrals?

Opportunity

Once the motive and means are identified, it is up to you to provide the opportunity to buy. If the motives and means are present, it is certainly worth your effort to get the solution implemented. However, if the prospect's means and motives are not entirely present then you will have to weigh your efforts carefully. Perhaps you could consider ending your efforts here to avoid wasting time.

Salespeople may be tempted to leave the tough questions like, "How will the purchase be financed" until the end of the sales process; however, these details should be handled as early as possible because tension and the perception of risk will increase toward the end of the sales cycle.

Where to Find Prospects

Prospecting requires both creativity and diligence on the part of the salesperson. Sources of prospects can be many and varied or few and similar, depending on the service or good sold. Naturally, people selling different services and goods might not

MAKING THE SALE

Shift Prospecting Into a Higher Gear

Many salespeople feel the pressure to manage their own lead generation and increase sales levels. It is often a case of having to regroup and rethink current prospecting practices. This is not always an easy task for salespeople so they may need to shift into the next gear. It doesn't have to cause a radical departure from current prospecting methods—it may be merely a case of rethinking how these methods could be made more efficient. Ask these questions:

1. Are you concentrating on leads with the best potential?

2. Are you being empathetic and looking at your prospects through their eyes with an understanding of their critical needs and issues?

3. Have you defined your ideal customer—those consistent with your current best customers, thus creating a better close ratio?

4. Have you researched the buying cycles (How and when they purchase products. Is there a buying centre? What time(s) of the year do they evaluate and/or buy?) of your prospects, hence improving the timing of your call?

5. Are you calling on the right people—those decision makers whose approval will improve your odds?

6. Have you created a strong business proposition so that prospects in higher levels of an organization will give you the time of day?

use the same sources for prospects. A salesperson of oil-field pipe supplies would make extensive use of various industry directories in a search for names of drilling companies. A life insurance salesperson would use personal acquaintances and present customers as sources of prospects. A pharmaceutical salesperson would scan the local newspaper looking for announcements of new physicians and hospital, medical office, and clinical laboratory openings. A sales representative for a company such as General Mills or Quaker Oats would watch for announcements of the construction of new grocery stores and shopping centres.

Planning a Prospecting Strategy

Frequently, salespeople, especially new ones, have difficulty prospecting. Meeting strangers and asking them to buy something can be uncomfortable. To be successful, prospecting requires a strategy. Like most skills, prospecting can be constantly improved by a dedicated salesperson. Some salespeople charge themselves with finding X number of prospects per week. Indeed, in many companies the sales force is asked to allocate a portion of each working day to finding and contacting new prospects. A successful salesperson continually evaluates prospecting methods, comparing results to find a prospecting strategy that will result in the most effective contact rate.[2]

Prospecting Methods

The methods by which a salesperson obtains prospects may vary. Several of the more popular prospecting methods are shown in Exhibit 6–3.

Make a list of what your ideal prospect would be. Ask yourself the following questions:

- Who are my ideal prospects?
- Which economic bracket do they usually fall into?
- What kinds of organizations do they belong to?
- What characteristics do most of my existing customers share?
- Are they married, single, widowed, or divorced?
- Do they have children?
- Do they have particular political leanings?

■ Do they have similar occupations, education, hobbies, illnesses, transportation needs, or family concerns?

And the key question:

■ Where am I most likely to find the greatest number of people who fit my prospect profile?

Lists and Directories

There are several sources of lists and directories that are fruitful for salespeople selling in Canada. Some are free; however, many charge for their services.

Scott's Directories

www.scottsdirectories.com

Scott's provides access to the accurate business contact information. Updated monthly, an annual online account allows users

■ Freedom to download the Scott's Directories' data
■ Unlimited searching using multiple search criteria—minimum of 25, depending on database
■ Unlimited viewing and printing
■ Insert your own notes, contact names, titles, and other details
■ Unlimited mailing labels via 12 Avery templates—no formatting required.

The screen below is a sample from Scott's Directories. As you can see, users can click on one of several search modes. For example, a sales rep selling group insurance to companies employing over 50 people could click under Demographic, Number of Employees, then enter search criteria that will result in a list of companies meeting these criteria.

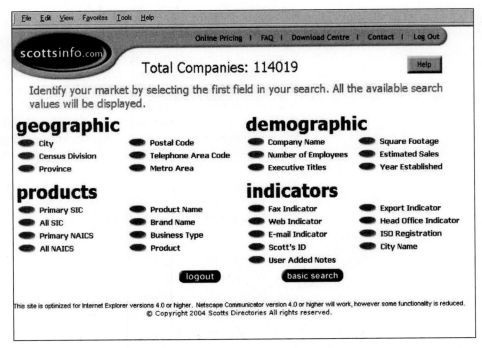

For each company selected, users are provided with information similar to this:

Company:	Steelcase Canada Limited	**Scott's ID:**	18476871
Address:	1 Steelcase Rd. W.	**# of Employees:**	700
	Markham, ON	**Sales:**	G-$75–100 Million
	L3R 0T3	**Square Footage:**	725000
	Telephone: 905-475-6333	**Year Established:**	1954

Web Site:	www.steelcase.com
Census Division:	York Regional Municipality
Executives:	Mr Matthew Ross—Controller
	Mr Darryl McCarthy—IT Mgr
	Mr Gene Lai—VP—Ops
	Mr Gale Moutrey—Dir—Mktg
	Mrs Kelly Jarvis—Dir—HR
	Mr Stav Kontis—Pub Rel Mgr

NAICS Code(s):	337214 - Office Furniture (except Wood) Manufacturing Primary
	339950 - Sign Manufacturing Secondary
	339940 - Office Supplies (except Paper) Manufacturing Secondary
	337215 - Showcase, Partition, Shelving and Locker Manufacturing Secondary
	337214 - Office Furniture (except Wood) Manufacturing Secondary
	337213 - Wood Office Furniture, including Custom Architectural Woodwork, Manufacturing Secondary
	333920 - Material Handling Equipment Manufacturing Secondary
	321999 - All Other Miscellaneous Wood Product Manufacturing Secondary
SIC Code(s):	2521 - Wood Office Furniture Primary
	3993 - Signs and Advertising Specialties Secondary
	2541 - Wood Office and Store Fixtures, Partitions, Shelving, and Lockers Secondary
	2499 - Wood Products, Not Elsewhere Classified Secondary
	3952 - Lead Pencils, Crayons, and Artists' Materials Secondary
	3537 - Industrial Trucks, Tractors, Trailers, and Stackers Secondary
	2542 - Office and Store Fixtures, Partitions, Shelving, and Lockers, Except Wood Secondary
	2522 - Office Furniture, Except Wood Secondary
Product(s):	Seating: office, Furniture: office, Furniture kits, Furniture: computer, Work stations, Work stations: computer, Storage units, Desks: computer, Shelving, Tables, Partitions: office, Carts, Easels, Boards: white, Pedestals, Panels: display, Boards: graphic visual
Business Type:	Manufacturer
Brand Name(s):	BALUSTRADA, PAYBACK, REQUEST, REPLY, FIRSTFILE, MIGRATIONS, ARCHIPELAGO, ENEA, PARADEL, MAXSTACKER, FOYER, DITTO, DECK, COMPANY, BERKELEY, RAF SYSTEM, GARLAND, DEJA, COLLABORATION

ISO(s):	9001, 14000
Legal Name:	Steelcase Canada Limited
Parent Company:	Steelcase Inc.
	Grand Rapids, MI

© 2006 BIG Directories LP.

As you can see, this information could prove invaluable to many types of salespeople. The database is available to businesses in print, CD, or online formats. The illustration below shows other examples of online directories. Other possible information sources include Industry Canada, at http://www.ic.gc.ca and Canada Business Directory www.canadianbusinessdirectory.ca.

This site could prove useful to salespeople as it allows searching of people and businesses by geographic area with links to company Web sites. Using this one tool, a salesperson could find the name of a particular type of business in a particular geographic area along with the company's phone number and link to its Web site, research the company, and then get specific directions and a map to that company's location. (411.ca)

Develop Lists of Prospects

List Number One Go to the library or use the Internet and look up the North American Industry Classification System (NAICS) code number for your ideal prospects' businesses (every type of business has a specific NAICS code). Related industries have similar numbers; scan the directory to locate the numbers that fit your prospects' profile. The results should provide you with an excellent prospect list.

List Number Two What kinds of publications do your ideal prospects likely read? Find out whether these publications sell lists of subscribers. If a publication's readership matches your prospect profile well enough, this list should be well worth the cost.

List Number Three Search out list brokers. These are firms that sell lists of businesses that can form the start of a prospect database. These firms offer a variety of criteria that allow you to define the types of businesses you want to create a quality prospect list.

Dun & Bradstreet Canada offer a service called Dun's Market Identifier (DMI), which provides up to 18 elements of information on prospects.

If you've been selling for a while, you've surely built up a backlog of inactive accounts. Weed out the names who, for whatever reason, will never buy. The rest are solid prospects. Call them again, and find out why they're not buying from you anymore. What would it take to change that? They may have stopped ordering your type of product altogether, or they may have gone with a competitor because of a special one-time offer, or there may have been a management change and therefore a change in buying patterns. You have to determine why the customer stopped buying from you. After you do that, re-establishing contact and turning that prospect into a customer again is standard sales procedure.

Endless-Chain Referral

Cold-calling is tough! Contacting strangers day after day is challenging even for the most motivated individuals. Yet many new salespeople have to begin their sales careers by cold-calling to get customers. Once someone is sold, the salesperson has two possibilities for future sales.

First, satisfied customers are likely to buy again from the salesperson. That is why it is so important to build a relationship with your customer. Second, the customer often refers the salesperson to someone she knows. This process is known as the **endless-chain referral method** of prospecting, and it is a very effective method for finding customers. *Repeat sales* and *customer referrals* are the two best sources of future sales, with repeat sales from customers being better. A **referral** is a person or organization recommended to you by someone who feels that this person or organization could benefit from you or your product.

Don't ask current customers, "Do you know anyone else who could use my product?" Rarely are clients eager to judge whether colleagues are prepared to make a purchase. Instead, ask whether your customer knows any other individuals or organizations who might be interested in finding out about your product.

If you sense hesitation from customers to give out referrals, it's probably because they are afraid that their associates may not want to be pestered. Say, "Let me tell you what I'm going to do with any names you give me. I will make one phone call to each party, indicate that you were nice enough to give me their names, and give them a brief outline of what we do.

"If they express an interest, we will get together, and I will give them the same professional service I've given you. If, on the other hand, they express no interest, I will thank them for their time and never call them again." This approach puts your customers at ease and moves solid, new prospects onto your lead list.

Don't forget that your prospects may be friends, neighbours, or relatives—anyone and everyone you know or come into contact with. They may know people who are looking for your product and the great service you provide your customers.

Orphaned Customers

Salespeople often leave their employers to take other jobs; when they do, their customers are **orphaned customers**. A salesperson should quickly contact such customers to begin developing relationships. Orphans can become a lead-generating gold mine.

Sales Lead Clubs

Organize a group of salespeople in related but non-competitive fields to meet twice a month to share leads and prospecting tips. To get started, write a formal mission statement, charge dues to ensure commitment, and grant membership to only one salesperson from each specific field. Next, set up administrative procedures and duties to keep the club on track and committed to its stated mission.

Finally, establish guidelines for what constitutes a good lead, and track prospect information and effectiveness. Group the leads by effectiveness so members can better

SELLING GLOBALLY
Prospecting in Hong Kong?

Try to make appointments as far in advance as possible—even months before.

Be punctual—it shows respect. Plan your travel times well due to the often-heavy traffic conditions. A sincere and humble apology is necessary if you're late.

Generally there is a six-day workweek. Business hours are usually 9:00 A.M. to 5:00 P.M.; however, on Saturdays, offices may be open during the morning hours.

Business trips are best scheduled during the late fall or from March to June to avoid vacation and celebration times. Chinese New Year is a major holiday period so avoid this time.

Watch what you wear. Dark-coloured business suits for men and subdued colours for women are best. Avoid wearing blue or white at social events; these colours are associated with death and mourning.

understand which leads can help other members. You may even have every member who closes a lead contribute to a kitty. Each month the winner is the member who provided the most closed leads.

Many North American cities have organizations called "executive associations" (the Ottawa Executives Association, for example) formed by local businesses to foster the success of members through sales leads and networking. There are 100 such organizations throughout North America, including 13 in Canada, with additional links to Great Britain, South Africa, and Switzerland.

Become an Expert—Get Published

Although you may give away your services as a writer for nothing, the benefits make your efforts well worth the time. Submit articles about your field or industry to journals, trade magazines, and newspapers. Fill your submissions with information that people can genuinely use, then edit and proofread carefully. Next, have a colleague look it over and provide feedback. Instead of payment, ask the publication to include your address and telephone number at the end of the article and print a little blurb about your expertise, which you may provide.

By convincing an editor that you're an expert in your field, you become one. Once prospects think of you as an expert, you'll be the one they contact when they're ready to buy. In addition, prospects who call you for advice can come to depend on you and your product. Thus, you attract prospects without having to go out prospecting.

Public Exhibitions and Demonstrations

Exhibitions and demonstrations frequently take place at trade shows and other types of special interest gatherings (see Exhibit 6–4). Often, related firms sponsor a booth at such shows and staff it with one salesperson.[3] As people walk up to the booth to examine the products, a salesperson has only a few minutes to qualify

EXHIBIT 6–4

Trade shows draw a crowd.

leads and get names and addresses to contact them later at their homes or offices for demonstrations. Although salesperson–buyer contact is usually brief, this type of gathering gives a salesperson extensive contact with a large number of potential buyers over a brief time. Remember, however, that success at trade shows stems from preparation. Here are several things to do:

- Set up an interesting display to get people's attention. A popcorn machine, juggler, or expensive giveaway are good ideas.
- Write your message so that it fits on the back of a business card.
- Practise communicating two or three key points that get your message across succinctly. Get it down pat, but don't memorize your sales pitch, or it may sound canned.
- Make a list of the major buyers at the show you want to pursue for contacts.
- Set up your display to maximize visibility based on the flow of traffic.
- Be assertive in approaching passers-by. Instead of the common "Hello" or "How are you?" try "Do you use [product or service] in your operations?" or "Have you seen [product or service]? If I can show you how to be more profitable, would you be interested?" Next offer them a sample to handle but not to keep. Don't let them take the item and move on without talking to you.
- Use lead cards to write down prospect information for efficient and effective post-show follow-up.
- Be prepared for rejection. Some buyers will ignore you. Don't take it personally. Be brief but professional. Your time is too valuable to waste on non-prospects.

Centre of Influence

Prospecting via the **centre-of-influence method** involves finding and cultivating people in a community or territory who are willing to cooperate in helping to find prospects. They typically have a particular position that includes some form of influence over other people, as well as information that allows the salesperson to identify good prospects. For example, a person who graduates from a university and begins work for a local real estate firm might contact professors and administrators at his alma mater to obtain the names of teachers who have taken jobs at other universities and are moving out of town. He wants to help them sell their homes.

Clergy, salespeople who are selling non-competing products, officers of community organizations such as the chamber of commerce, and members of organizations such as the Lions Club or a country club are other individuals who may function as a centre of influence. Be sure to show your appreciation for this person's assistance. Keeping such influential people informed of the outcome of your contact with the prospect helps to secure future aid.

Direct Mail

In cases where there are a large number of prospects for a product, **direct-mail prospecting** is sometimes an effective way to contact individuals and businesses. Direct-mail advertisements have the advantage of contacting large numbers of people, who may be spread across an extended geographical area, at a relatively low cost compared to using salespeople. People who request more information from the company subsequently are contacted by a salesperson.

Telephone and Telemarketing

Use of **telephone prospecting** to contact a large number of prospects across a vast area is far less costly than use of a canvassing sales force, though usually more costly than mailouts.[4]

The person-to-person contact provided by the telephone allows for interaction between the lead and the caller—enabling a lead to be quickly qualified or rejected.

One example of telephone prospecting is the aluminum siding salesperson who telephones a lead and asks two questions that quickly determine whether that person is a prospect.

Telephone Salesperson: Sir, how old is your home?

Lead: One year old.

Telephone Salesperson: Is your home brick or wood?

Lead: Brick.

Telephone Salesperson: Since you do not need siding, would you recommend we contact any of your neighbours or friends who can use high-quality siding at a competitive price? [Endless-chain technique]

Telemarketing involves telecommunication technology and trained personnel to conduct planned, measurable marketing activities directed at targeted groups of consumers.

The internal process of a telemarketing centre is shown in Exhibit 6–5. Many firms initiate telemarketing ventures by featuring a toll-free phone number or coupon in an advertisement. When the coupon response or a telephone call comes into the centre, a trained specialist handles it. This person may take an order (in the case of a telephone call) or transfer the person to a telephone selling (or *teleselling*) unit. The specialist may provide information or service. The specialist also can determine whether the customer has sufficient potential to warrant a face-to-face sales call. The duties of a telemarketing specialist are based on the type of product being sold and to whom it is sold.

From thousands of such contacts with the public, a firm can develop a valuable database that produces many informational reports. Many companies use telemarketing centres in this way.

EXHIBIT 6–5

The processing system within a telemarketing centre.

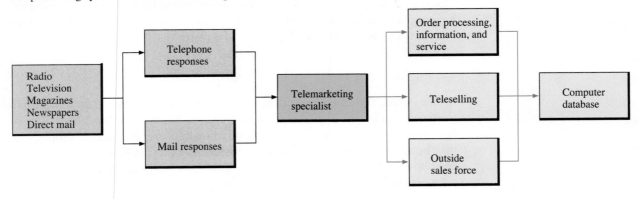

Observation

A salesperson often can find prospects by constantly watching what is happening in his or her sales area—the **observation method**. Office furniture, computer, and copier salespeople look for new business construction in their territories. New families are excellent leads for real estate and insurance salespeople. Always keep your eyes and ears open for information about people who need your product.

Networking

For many salespeople, prospecting never ends. They are always on the lookout for customers. Everyone they meet may be a prospect or that person may provide a name that could lead to a sale. The term given to making and using contacts is **networking**.

Of the many ways to find new prospects, networking can be the most reliable and effective. People want to do business with, and refer business to, people they know, like, and trust. Relationship building is critical today.

Building a network is important, but cultivating that network brings sales. Your goal is to cultivate your network to carve a niche for yourself so that when one of those contacts, or someone he knows, needs your type of product or service, you are the *only* possible resource to come to mind.

Here are several tips for cultivating your network to dramatically increase your referral business:

1. Focus on meeting the centre-of-influence people discussed above. These people have established good reputations and have many valuable contacts. You can find key people in your industry at trade association meetings, trade shows, or any business-related social event.

2. Ninety-nine percent of your first conversation with a networking prospect should be about her business. People want to talk about their business, not yours.

3. Ask open-ended, feel-good questions like, "What do you enjoy most about your industry?"

4. Be sure to ask, "How would I know whether someone I'm speaking with would be a good prospect for you?" If you're on the lookout to find this person new business, he will be more inclined to do the same for you.

5. Get a networking prospect's business card. It's the easiest way to follow up with your new contact.

6. Send a handwritten thank-you note that day: "It was nice meeting you this morning. If I can ever refer business your way, I certainly will."

7. When you read newspapers and magazines, keep the people in your network in mind. If you find an article one of your contacts could use or would enjoy, send it.

8. Stay on your contacts' minds by sending them something every month; notepads with your name and picture are perfect. They will keep these pads on their desks and be constantly reminded of you and your product or service.

9. Send leads. The best way to get business and referrals is to give business and referrals.

10. Send a handwritten thank-you note whenever you receive a lead, regardless of whether it results in a sale.

When meeting people, tell them what you sell. Ask what they do. Exchange business cards and periodically contact them. Eventually, you will build a network of people talking to each other, sharing ideas, and exchanging information. You can also use

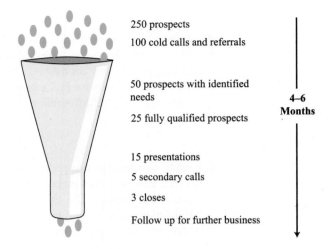

EXHIBIT 6–6

The sales funnel. Note that the funnel can take up to 6 months to clear itself. If salespeople don't work diligently to keep it full then dry spells will certainly ensue.

250 prospects

100 cold calls and referrals

50 prospects with identified needs

25 fully qualified prospects

15 presentations

5 secondary calls

3 closes

Follow up for further business

4–6 Months

several of the previously discussed methods of prospecting to build your network, such as the endless-chain or centre-of-influence methods.

Prospecting Guidelines

Although prospecting will vary depending on the product or good, generalizations can be made. Use three criteria to develop the best prospecting method:

1. *Customize* a prospecting method to fit the specific needs of your individual firm. Do not copy another company's method; however, it's all right to adapt someone's method.
2. Concentrate on *high-potential* customers first.
3. Always call back on prospects who did not buy. If you have a new product, do not restrict yourself to present customers only. A business may not have purchased your present products because they did not fit the business's present needs; your new product may be exactly what they need.

Keep knocking on your prospects' and customers' doors to help them solve problems through the purchase of your product. Only in this way can you maximize your long-term sales and income. See Exhibit 6–6 for an illustration of the "sales funnel" approach to thinking about prospecting.

REFERRALS

Many salespeople are reluctant to ask for referrals. Yet referrals create business and sales.

Objections

Some clients may not want to give referrals for the following reasons:

- Clients are afraid of upsetting friends and relatives.
- Clients do not want friends to think they're being talked about.
- Clients may believe in the product but not in the salesperson.
- Clients fear the salesperson may not be around in the future.
- Clients do not feel they can benefit from giving the salesperson referrals.

It is absolutely essential to address these objections when asking for referrals. By doing so, you will obtain more referrals, get more appointments, and make more sales.

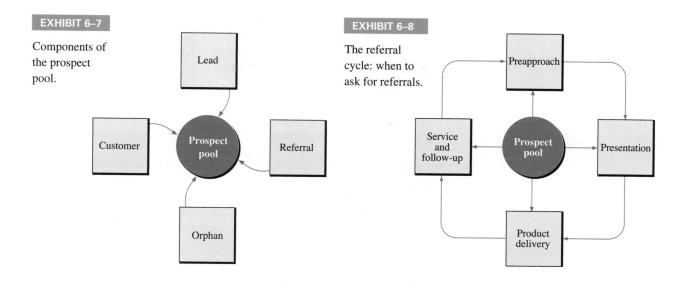

EXHIBIT 6–7

Components of the prospect pool.

EXHIBIT 6–8

The referral cycle: when to ask for referrals.

As shown in Exhibit 6–7, a prospect pool is usually created from the four sources discussed above: leads, referrals, orphaned customers, and current customers.[5]

Most salespeople do not like to cold call. Their goal is to have a prospect pool of customers, referrals, and, when available, orphans. The secret to reaching this goal is the referral cycle.

THE REFERRAL CYCLE

Obtaining referrals is a continuous process; salespeople should always be looking for the right opportunity to find a referral. The **referral cycle** provides guidelines for a salesperson to ask for referrals in four situations commonly experienced by salespeople, as shown in Exhibit 6–8.

You can begin the referral cycle in the presentation, product delivery, preapproach, or service phase. However, wherever you are in the referral cycle, you can begin at that point. Perfect your techniques so that you will be working to get referrals at

SELLING TIPS

Get Motivated. Break out of that Slump.

Salespeople often find themselves in a bit of a prospecting slump, which adversely affects morale. What can you do?

1. Don't become paralyzed by panic! If you feel desperate, you may resort to desperate measures that may become counterproductive.

2. Focus on what you're trying to accomplish and stay positive.

3. Don't give up. Keep your sense of humour.

4. Get back to basics. Think of the things that have worked well for you and reconnect to them.

5. Work a little harder. Commit to a few days of more effort. Good things happen to those who work hard.

6. Ask for help. Ask a colleague or sales manager to review some of your tactics with you.

7. Avoid negative events and people. To stay on top of your game, don't let external events or people drag you down.

8. Change your pace. Try a different environment. Sometimes change can lift your mood.

every phase of the cycle simultaneously. Direct any contact with the prospect toward presenting yourself and your product in such a way as to overcome any objections you could face later when asking for referrals and, of course, when making a sale.

Salespeople must sell the product and sell the prospect on providing referrals. This is referred to as the **parallel referral sale**. Equal emphasis must be given to both the product sale and the referral sale.

When to Ask

The Preapproach

Take great care during the preapproach phase of the referral cycle. Whether the initial contact is face to face or via telephone, the effectiveness of your approach will determine whether you are given the opportunity to make a sales presentation.

Many prospects will hang up the phone as soon as they suspect an attempt is being made to sell them something. If, in the first several seconds, you fail to overcome their initial feelings of discomfort and intrusion, your chances of developing a relationship are slim.

Mentioning that a firm or business acquaintance of theirs recommended that you call helps alleviate some of their initial anxiety. This is one reason that working on referrals is so effective. Certainly, people are willing to listen a bit longer if they know a person they trust has initiated this personal contact. Here's an example:

> Hello, is this John? . . . Hi, John, my name is Kim Lee from Merrill Lynch. George and Barbara Smith are clients of mine. I met with them last week and helped them set up their retirement program. They were really pleased with both my products and service. *And since I work primarily through referrals,* they were kind enough to mention that you might be interested in learning about the value I have to offer.
>
> I'd like to set up a time to stop by your home or office and share some ideas that you may find of great benefit. *It's not really important to me that we do business;* all I ask is if you appreciate the time we share together, if you feel that you benefit from the time we spend together, and, most importantly, if you respect my integrity, *you would be willing to pass my name on to a friend or business associate who may also benefit from my services,* just as George and Barbara did. Is that fair enough?

We have begun the process of selling the prospect—and we hope customer—on giving us one or more referrals. We are telling John that it is not important for us to make a sale. We are asking if he feels it is reasonable, if and only if he is happy with us, that he pass our name on just as his friends did. It is easy for John to answer yes. We have presented our offer in a non-threatening manner that was endorsed by his friends George and Barbara.

To say "it's not really important to me that we do business" is very unusual. People are not accustomed to hearing a salesperson say that it is not important to make a sale.

The Presentation

Depending on your particular industry, the situation in which you present your product for sale may be called by a variety of names: meeting, appointment, interview, or presentation. Throughout this book we refer to it as the presentation.

During the presentation you have the greatest opportunity to influence your prospect. Remember that your prospect will scrutinize everything you say and do.

The presentation phase of the referral cycle actually begins when you sit down with your prospect for the purpose of making a sales presentation. As comfortably as possible, you should make a conscious effort to mention the referring person. This may be a remark as simple as: "George told me that you like to golf. Did you get a chance to get out this week?" or "Barbara mentioned that you like to garden. Did the last frost we had affect your plants at all?"

This initial contact plants the seed for the beginning of the parallel referral sale. During the next 10 or 15 minutes, there should be no discussion about the product or service being offered. This time is best used to build rapport and help break down any barriers between the prospect and his or her perception of you as a salesperson. To accelerate this process, you should mention the referring person as often as possible. The walls of resistance have fallen when you begin to feel comfortable with your prospects. If you do not feel comfortable with your prospects, they certainly will not feel comfortable with you.

Once you establish rapport, take a moment to explain to your prospects what will occur during the time you will be together. Then, when appropriate, mention the referrals. Here are two examples:

> John and Nonnie, if you're happy with my service, I hope you will be willing to pass my name on to other people who would appreciate the same honesty and integrity I have extended to you. I don't do this because I'm a good person; I do it because it makes good business sense. If I take care of you, you'll take care of me. And my livelihood depends on getting referrals.
>
> My success and the success of my business are totally dependent on getting quality referrals from my clients. I realize that you will introduce me to your friends, family, and business associates only if the quality and integrity of the service I provide surpasses that to which you've grown accustomed.

Product Delivery

Almost every selling profession has some type of product delivery phase, although the phase is more obvious with some products than others. For example, in the life insurance industry it involves the agent physically handing the policy to the client. In real estate, it is the day the sale closes on the home or property. With computers, it is the day that the system is installed and usable. Whatever your product, identify the precise moment that your product becomes of value to your customer, and at this point the product delivery phase begins. Here's an example of how to ask for a referral at this point:

> I'm sure by now, John, you realize that I work strictly through referrals. I am constantly striving to bring my clients even greater service by improving my business. I have a very important question for you and would appreciate your giving this some thought. Is there any one thing that you would like to see me change or improve that would increase the likelihood of my getting referrals from you in the future?

Service and Follow-up

Customer service is the performance of any helpful or professional work or activity for a customer. The service and follow-up phase of the referral cycle provides you with ongoing opportunities to maintain contact with your clients. Whenever you have contact with your clients, it may be possible to get more referrals. High-quality service creates a professional and caring image that clients are more eager to share with their friends, family, and business associates; high-quantity service helps keep you and your product fresh in the minds of clients.

For many salespeople, the product delivery phase represents the end of the relationship with their clients. First, the nature of the business may not require any additional service. Second, although there may be a need for continued service, salespeople are so preoccupied with prospecting or selling that they cannot devote adequate time to providing good service. Third, salespeople may not realize that providing quality customer service will result in more business. Here is an example of what might be said during a typical annual follow-up:

> Hello, John. This is Kim Lee. As I promised when we first did business, this is my "official" once-a-year call to let you know that I am thinking about you. Do you have any questions? Is there anything I can do for you? . . . I also want to make sure you and Nonnie have received your birthday cards and quarterly newsletters. What do you think of my newsletters? . . . Terrific. I'll let you go now. Don't forget, you've got my number if you need any help. Please keep me in mind when talking to your friends and business associates. As you know, John, I depend on quality clients like you and Nonnie to keep me in business. One of the reasons I work so hard to help my customers is because of the people you refer to me. Your referrals are really appreciated. (Pause) John, is there anyone you or Nonnie feel I should help? (Pause) Thank you very much! I look forward to seeing you soon. Goodbye.

Don't Mistreat the Referral

One final thought on referrals—don't mistreat them! The salesperson who mistreats a referral can lose both the referring customer and the prospect.

Once you have sold the referral, and gotten more referrals, ask the *new* customer to contact the *referring* customer on her experience with you. Now you have two customers giving you referrals. This interaction can create the endless chain of referrals, helping to quickly fill your prospect pool with only customers and referrals.

Tracking Referrals

Keeping track of referrals is just as important as staying in contact with customers. Whether you use index cards or a computerized contact system, it's important to keep detailed records on all information you collect on the prospect/customer. (See the review of computerized customer contact programs in Chapter 5 and the discussion of the customer profile in Chapter 7.)

SUMMARY OF MAJOR SELLING ISSUES

The sales process involves a series of actions beginning with prospecting for customers. In the first step, the salesperson must find prospects to contact.

Prospecting involves locating and qualifying the individuals or businesses that have the potential to buy a product. A person or business that might become a prospect is a *lead*. This question can determine whether someone is qualified: Does the prospect have the money, ability and desire for my product or service?

Several of the more popular prospecting methods are cold calling and endless-chain methods, public exhibitions and demonstrations, locating centres of influence,

ETHICAL DILEMMA

You are a salesperson of mutual funds and other financial services. The person who manages your personal and business finances is also your best friend and a Chartered Accountant. Over lunch one day, you are discussing your decreasing sales levels and your accountant friend mentions that as a key centre of influence, he could provide you with the names of some key people who he knows have money to invest. In exchange for these names, he mentions that he expects you to pay him 25% percent of your commissions resulting from the leads he provides.

What do you tell him?

Is it ethical of him to make this request?

What should you consider here?

direct mailouts, and observation prospecting. To obtain a continuous supply of prospects, the salesperson should develop a prospecting method suitable for their particular situation.

Once a lead has been located and qualified as a prospect, the salesperson can make start the referral cycle, with the goal of increasing referrals.

MEETING A SALES CHALLENGE

The proposed prospecting systems were fairly well analyzed by Larry Gasslein, John Alexander, and Mitali Das. Old customers are easy to see, and they know the company. However, just because a firm buys one thing from a company does not mean that it will buy another. (Companies often are fooled by their corporate egos into thinking that their existing customers will buy just about anything they make.)

Going after IBM seems to scare John for some reason. However, what will IBM do it wouldn't do competitively anyway? Larry, John, and Mitali's company has competition on all sides from many firms. If their company has a good cost story to tell, then they should go after the big users to whom the cost savings will be significant.

In short, all the ideas have virtues and none should be excluded from consideration. New blood is needed. You can't stay in business by just relying on one set of customers. So much depends, however, on the particular territory. Some territories may have few old customers or few IBM stores. The salesperson must adapt to the characteristics of the territory.

PLAYING THE ROLE

The situation: As a new sales rep (one of four) selling advertising for a local radio station, you have been cold calling on businesses for two weeks, trying to drum up some business. You've been pretty successful but six prospects just weren't ready to commit. You've been working hard so you book off a Monday to enjoy a long weekend. On that Monday, three of these prospects phone in and ask for you. Because you're not there, the prospects get clarification on some issues from your colleagues, each of whom spends about 20 minutes with a prospect. Over the phone, each prospect commits to some advertising time. Because your colleagues spent time with these people and wrote up the order, they felt entitled to the commission.

Role A: You—Feel entitled to the commission

Role B: A Sales Colleague—Feels entitled to the commission

Role C: A Sales Colleague—Feels entitled to the commission

Role D: A Sales Colleague—Feels entitled to the commission. Prepare an argument as to why you should get credit for the sales. Your colleagues feel entitled to the commission as they had to spend time with the customers; they will defend their choice to take the credit. Play out these roles in an attempt to resolve the situation.

SALES APPLICATION QUESTIONS

1. What is the difference between a lead and a prospect? What should you do to qualify a potential customer?

2. This chapter defined prospecting as the lifeblood of selling.
   a. Where do salespeople find prospects?
   b. List and briefly explain the prospecting methods discussed in this chapter. Can you think of other ways to find prospects?

3. Assume that you have started a business to manufacture and market a simple inventory management system selling for between $5,000 and $10,000. Your primary customers are small retailers. How would you uncover leads and convert them into prospects without personally contacting them?

4. Assume that you had determined that John Firestone, vice president of Pierce Chemicals, was a prospect for your paper and metal containers. You call Mr. Firestone to see whether he can see you this week. When his secretary answers the telephone, you say, "May I speak to Mr. Firestone, please?" and she says, "What is it you wish to talk to him about?" How would you answer her question? What would you say if you were told, "I'm sorry, but Mr. Firestone is too busy to talk with you?"

5. You are a new salesperson. Next week, your regional sales manager will be in town to check your progress in searching for new clients for your line of industrial chemicals. You have learned that Big Industries, Inc., a high-technology company, needs a supplier of your product. Also, a friend has told you about 12 local manufacturing firms that could use your product. The sales potential of each of these firms is about one-tenth of Big Industries. Knowing that your sales manager expects results, explain how you will qualify each lead (assuming the 12 smaller firms are similar).

6. a. Assume you are a salesperson for the manufacturer of each of the following products:
   - Photocopiers
   - LCD projection system
   - Energy-saving fluorescent lightbulbs.

   Develop a prospect list of 10 organizations in your area that would qualify as potential customers.
   b. Describe how you would make contact with each organization.
   c. Assume that you have made contact, and discuss how you would qualify your prospect.

SALES WORLD WIDE WEB EXERCISES

Getting Connected

Assume that you have just joined an organization with a very well established sales department and have been given a new territory. Your sales manager has indicated that it is your responsibility to ensure that the office and your customers always have access to you, even when you are on the road. Use the following URLs to assess the type of technology that you might choose to meet your boss's communication requirements. The first exercise will provide you with some knowledge of the hardware available to you. Next, seek out a service provider that meets your needs, such as Rogers, or your local phone service provider such as Manitoba Telecom Services (MTS), SaskTel, Telus, Aliant, or Bell Canada.

www.wirelessadvisor.com

www.nokia.ca

www.motorola.com

www.blackberry.com

FURTHER EXPLORING THE SALES WORLD

Contact several salespeople in your community and ask them to discuss their prospecting system and the steps they use in planning their sales calls. Write a short paper on your results and be prepared to discuss it in class.

SELLING EXPERIENTIAL EXERCISE

Your Attitude toward Selling

To measure your attitude toward selling, complete this exercise. A 5 indicates strong agreement; a 1 strong disagreement.

		Disagree				Agree
1.	There is nothing demeaning about selling a good or service to a prospect.	1	2	3	4	5
2.	I would be proud to tell friends selling is my career.	1	2	3	4	5
3.	I can approach customers, regardless of age, appearance, or behaviour, with a positive attitude.	1	2	3	4	5
4.	On bad days—when nothing goes right—I can still be positive.	1	2	3	4	5
5.	I am enthusiastic about selling.	1	2	3	4	5
6.	Having customers turn me down does not cause me to be negative.	1	2	3	4	5
7.	The idea of selling challenges me.	1	2	3	4	5
8.	I consider selling to be a profession.	1	2	3	4	5
9.	Approaching strangers (customers) is interesting and usually enjoyable.	1	2	3	4	5
10.	I can always find something good in a customer.	1	2	3	4	5

Total Score _____

Total your score. If you scored more than 40, you have an excellent attitude toward selling as a profession. If you rated yourself between 25 and 40, you appear to have serious reservations. A rating under 25 indicates that another type of job is probably best for you.

CASE 6–1
Canadian Equipment Corporation

You work for the Canadian Equipment Corporation selling office equipment. You enter the reception room of a small manufacturing company. You hand the receptionist your business card and ask to see the purchasing agent. "What is this in reference to?" the secretary asks, as two other salespeople approach.

Questions

Which of the following alternatives would you use and why?

a. Give a quick explanation of your equipment, ask whether the secretary has heard of your company or used your equipment, and again ask to see the purchasing agent.

b. Say, "I would like to discuss our office equipment."

c. Say, "I sell office equipment designed to save your company money and provide greater efficiency. Companies like yours really like our products. Could you help me get in to see your purchasing agent?"

d. Give a complete presentation and demonstration.

CASE 6–2
Montreal Satellites

As a salesperson for Montreal Satellites, you sell television satellite dishes for homes and businesses. After installing a satellite in Jeff Sager's home, you ask him for a referral. Jeff suggests you contact Tom Butler, his brother-in-law.

Mr. Butler is a well-known architect who designs and constructs unique residential homes. Your objective is to sell Mr. Butler a satellite for his office and home in hopes he will install them in the homes he builds. Certainly, he is a centre of influence and a good word from him to his customers could result in numerous sales. Thus, another objective is to obtain referrals from Mr. Butler.

Questions

1. After eight attempts, you now have Mr. Butler on the telephone. What do you say in order to get an appointment and set the stage for getting referrals?

2. You get the appointment and are now in Mr. Butler's office trying to get him to buy a satellite for his home and office. Sometime during the presentation you will ask for a referral. What will you say?

3. Mr. Butler buys a satellite for his home but not his office. You install the satellite yourself and then spend 15 minutes showing Mr. and Mrs. Butler and their two teenagers how to use it. Before you leave, how do you ask for a referral?

4. Three months after the installation you are talking to Mr. Butler. How do you ask for a referral?

7

THE PREAPPROACH—PLANNING YOUR SALES CALL AND PRESENTATION

MAIN TOPICS

LEARNING OBJECTIVES

Preparing to meet your prospect is the second step in the selling process. The importance of proper preparation cannot be overstated. After studying this chapter, you should be able to:

- Explain the importance of sales call planning.

- Establish effective sales call objectives.

- Develop a customer benefit plan.

- Describe the prospect's mental steps in his or her decision making.

- Explain the different types of sales presentation methods and determine the best one to use.

- Better understand the importance of securing appointments.

- Develop an appointment-getting strategy.

- Develop an effective negotiation plan.

FACING A SALES CHALLENGE

After being hired, trained, and given a sales territory, you have been assigned by your boss to work with three of your company's salespeople. You immediately notice they are not doing what you've been trained to do. They walk into an office, introduce themselves, and ask whether the customer needs anything today. Prospects rarely buy, and customers tell them what they need. This doesn't seem like selling to you. It's order taking, and that type of job is not for you.

The problem is—how do you get someone to listen to you? How do you know what they think of your product? How do you know when they're ready to buy? Next Monday, you call on your first customer. What will you do?

Your job as a salesperson is to find prospects who need your product and convince them your product will satisfy their need. Now that you've completed your hard work in finding these prospects, let's not waste it. It is vitally important that you prepare properly to make contact with this prospect. This chapter introduces you to the importance of planning each sales call. It often takes hours to plan a sales presentation and only minutes to make; however, without proper preparation, your sales will suffer.

STRATEGIC CUSTOMER SALES PLANNING

EXHIBIT 7–1

The preapproach involves planning the sales presentation.

10
Follow-up

9
Close

8
Trial close

7
Meet objections

6
Determine objections

5
Trial close

4
Presentation

3
Approach

**2
Preapproach**

1
Prospecting

Once the prospect has been located, or the salesperson determines which customer to call on, the salesperson is ready to plan the sales call. Planning is often referred to as the **preapproach** (see Exhibit 7–1).

High-performing salespeople tend to be strategic problem solvers for their customers. **Strategic** refers to the customer's most important programs, goals, and problems. Top salespeople who are effective strategic problem solvers have the skills and knowledge to

- Uncover and understand the customer's *strategic needs* by gaining an in-depth knowledge of the customer's organization
- Develop solutions that demonstrate a *creative* approach to addressing the customer's strategic needs in the most efficient and effective manner possible
- Arrive at a *mutually beneficial agreement*.

These key terms—strategic needs, creative solutions, and mutually beneficial agreements—are critical to strategic problem solving. Properly achieved by the salesperson, they create a **strategic customer relationship**—a formal relationship that involves joint pursuit of mutual goals. Strategic goals for a customer typically include reducing costs or increasing productivity, sales, and profits. The strategic goals for a sales organization comprise increasing sales and profits.

Strategic Needs

The salesperson who understands the full range of the customer's needs is in a much better position to provide a product solution that helps the customer progress more efficiently and effectively toward achieving her organization's strategic goals. "The top salespeople have an in-depth understanding of our needs," said one business purchasing agent. "They can match up their products with these needs to help us reach our goals."

Creative Solutions

For each customer, a salesperson is often faced with a unique set of problems to solve. As a result, each customer requires a unique solution. The salesperson needs to use creative problem solving to identify the specific solution that meets each customer's needs. Instead of one product, the salesperson often must create the solution from a mix of goods and services. Usually, the solution represents one of two options:

1. A customized version or application of a product or service that efficiently addresses the customer's specific strategic needs.
2. A mix of goods and services—including, if appropriate, competitors' products and services—that offers the best possible solution in light of the customer's strategic needs.

The better a salesperson is at creatively marshalling all available resources to address a customer's strategic need, the stronger the customer relationship becomes. Today's salespeople need to be **creative problem solvers** who develop and combine nontraditional alternatives to meet the customer's specific needs.

Mutually Beneficial Agreements

To achieve a mutually beneficial agreement, salespeople and customers must work together to develop a common understanding of the issues and challenges at hand. Information about an organization's business strategies and needs is often highly confidential. But more and more customers, in the interest of developing solutions to help achieve their strategic goals, are willing to let salespeople cross the threshold of confidentiality.

The Customer Relationship Model

The customer relationship model shown in Exhibit 7–2 brings together the main elements of consultative selling. It shows that when salespeople meet the customer's strategic needs through creative solutions, both customer and seller reach their goals, cementing a long-term relationship. Strategic customer sales planning is extremely important to the success of today's salespeople.

For obvious reasons of time and cost, salespersons usually phone to make sales appointments. Though seemingly a simple task, obtaining an appointment over the telephone is frequently difficult. Business executives generally are busy and their time is scarce. However, the following practices can help in successfully making an appointment over the telephone:

- Plan and write down what you will say. This helps you organize and concisely present your message.
- Clearly identify yourself and your company.
- State the purpose of your call and briefly outline how the prospect may benefit from the interview.
- Prepare a brief sales message, stressing product benefits over features. Present only enough information to stimulate interest.
- Do not take no for an answer. Be persistent even if there is a negative reaction to the call.
- Ask for an interview so that you can further explain product benefits.
- Phrase your appointment request as a question. Your prospect should be given a choice, such as: "Would nine or one o'clock Tuesday be better for you?"

Successful use of the telephone in appointment scheduling requires an organized, clear message that captures interest quickly. Before you dial a prospect's number,

Consultative selling—customer relationship model.

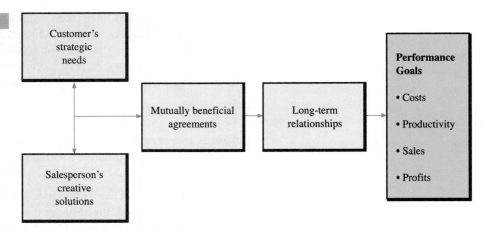

mentally or physically sketch out exactly what you plan to say. While on the telephone get to the point quickly (since you may have only a minute), disclosing just enough information to stimulate the prospect's interest. For example:

> Mr. West, this is Sally Irwin of On-Line Computer Company calling you from Toronto. Businesspeople such as yourself are saving the costs of rental or purchase of computer systems, while receiving the same benefits they get from the computer they currently have. May I explain how they are doing this on Tuesday at nine o'clock in the morning or would one o'clock in the afternoon be preferable?

PLANNING THE SALES CALL

Planning the sales call is crucial. See Exhibit 7–3. Although there are numerous reasons for planning the sales call, the most frequently mentioned are building confidence, developing an atmosphere of goodwill between the buyer and seller, creating professionalism, and generally increasing sales.

Planning is the key to success.

The sales team rehearses an upcoming sales call.

EXHIBIT 7–4

Steps in the preapproach: planning the sales call.

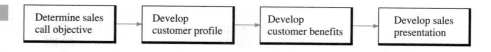

| Determine sales call objective | → | Develop customer profile | → | Develop customer benefits | → | Develop sales presentation |

Builds Self-Confidence

Most people are nervous when giving a speech before a large group of people. Nevertheless, this nervousness can be greatly reduced and self-confidence increased by planning what to say and practising. The same is true in making a sales presentation.

Develops an Atmosphere of Goodwill

The salesperson who understands a customer's needs and is prepared to discuss how a product will benefit the prospect is appreciated and respected by the buyer. This goodwill gradually aids in building the buyer's confidence, leading to a belief that the salesperson can be trusted to fulfill obligations.

Creates Professionalism

Good business relationships are built on your knowledge of your company, industry, and customers' needs. Show prospects that you are calling on them to help solve their problems or satisfy their needs.

Increases Sales

Like other beneficial pre–sales call activities, planning is most effective (and time efficient) when done logically and methodically.

Exhibit 7–4 depicts the four steps considered in **sales planning**. These steps are (1) determining the sales call objective; (2) developing or reviewing the customer profile; (3) developing a customer benefit plan; and (4) developing the individual sales presentation based on the previous three steps.

DETERMINING SALES CALL OBJECTIVES

Is it possible to make a sales call without having a **sales call objective** in mind? Why can't salespeople just go in and see what develops? They can; in fact, a survey call is a legitimate sales technique. However, if all the calls that salespeople make are survey calls, they should be working exclusively for the market research department.

The Precall Objective

Selling is not a very complex process; it's just difficult to do consistently. That's why, whether you regard it as an art or a science, the discipline of selling starts with setting a precall objective.

Remember that, by definition, a sales call must move systematically toward a sale. Often, we're not talking about elaborate planning; sometimes it takes only a few seconds before a call. But on every occasion, it's vital for the sales representative to answer one simple question: "If this call is successful, what will result?"

Focus and Flexibility

Writing down your precall objective increases the focus of your efforts. Salespeople who are just visiting customers to see what develops are merely well-paid tourists. Professional sales representatives move their customers toward a predetermined goal of a sale.

Obviously, if the precall objective turns out to be inappropriate as the sales call develops, it's easy to switch tactics.

Making the Objective Specific

When asked the purpose of a call, some salespeople say enthusiastically, "It's to get an order. Let's go!" Of course, everyone's in favour of getting orders, but that's more likely to happen if salespeople stop and ask themselves questions such as, What need of this prospect can I serve? Which product or service is best for this account? How large an order should I go for? Set a **SMART** call objective that is

Specific—"to get an order" is *not* specific.

Measurable—quantifiable.

Achievable—not too difficult to fulfill.

Relevant—has importance to you (e.g., making your quota).

Time bounded—at this call or before the end of the financial year.

It's amazing how often even veteran salespeople skip the precall objective step in favour of just seizing whatever opportunities present themselves. As a professional, it's your responsibility to head off this kind of behaviour. Commit to having an objective for every call, and after every call check your results against that objective.

It's not reasonable to expect a full commitment to buy your entire proposition during the first call; be realistic. Different products have different types and lengths of buying or selling cycles. Know the typical cycle in your industry, so you can set and prioritize realistic objectives for each of your sales calls.

A Sampling of Sales Call Objectives

- Establish rapport with your prospect.
- Find out your prospect's specific problems or needs.
- Determine the decision-making process in your prospect's company.
- Determine if you are in fact dealing with the decision maker.
- Find out if your prospect can afford your product.
- Supply your prospect with information about your product or service.
- Meet new people in the buying organization who may be involved in the purchase decision.
- Determine if any needs have changed since your previous visit.
- Provide references to your prospect.
- Determine who the competition is.
- Determine important purchasing criteria.
- Determine the stage of the buying process the prospect is in.
- Introduce your solution to key decision makers.
- Demonstrate the return on investment (ROI) for your proposition.
- Provide details of satisfied customers.
- Secure a commitment to purchase.
- Leave samples of product.
- Arrange for a follow-up visit to go over other details.
- Provide contact information for follow-up.

These objectives can be met during preliminary calls to your prospect and provide an excellent opportunity to build rapport and gain trust as opposed to rushing in and trying to sell your entire inventory during your first call.

Meeting these objectives will enable you to understand your prospect's situation as thoroughly as possible before you take up his or her time. Your prospects expect you to know something about their business.

Think through the sales call from your prospect's perspective. What does she want to hear? You've uncovered her key buying motives, so determine how you can satisfy them.

SELLING GLOBALLY
Don't Smell Rotten in Denmark!

Making appointments is not handled the same way in all countries. For example, there are some things that you'll have to be mindful of in Denmark.

Be punctual. It is very important here. You must be exactly on time for any business meetings and social meetings.

It is customary in Denmark, as in most European and South American countries, to write out the date in day, month, year, succession. February 3, 2009, is written 03.02.09. You wouldn't want to arrive at your meeting a month early or late.

Summer is not a good time for doing business in most Scandinavian countries; in Denmark, most companies don't like to do business during July and August and often have extended shutdowns so employees can take their weeks of paid vacation.

Companies often operate on a five-day schedule, with offices open from 8:00 A.M. to 5:30 P.M.

Moving Toward Your Objective

Even if a salesperson isn't making a formal presentation, the call should be planned. Although sometimes the sales call has a limited objective, guiding the customer in the direction of that preplanned outcome is what experienced salespeople do on most sales calls. They do it with such simple questions as

- If we can meet the spec, can you set up a trial?
- How soon will the vice president be available to make a decision?
- Can you schedule a demonstration before the end of the month?

GETTING THE APPOINTMENT

The practice of making an appointment before calling on a prospect can save hours in wasted time. When an appointment is made, a buyer knows you are coming. People are normally in a more receptive mood when they expect someone than when an unfamiliar salesperson pops in. Appointment making is often associated with a serious, professional image and shows respect for a prospect and his or her schedule.

From the salesperson's point of view, an appointment provides a time set aside for the buyer to listen to a sales presentation. This is important, since adequate time to explain a proposition improves the chance of making the sale. In addition, a list of appointments aids a salesperson in allocating each day's selling time. Appointments can be arranged by telephone or by contacting the prospect's office personally.

The Telephone—A Useful Sales Tool

Be prepared. A well-planned telephone call can be a very effective way to secure appointments with prospects and save a great deal of time. Don't be fooled into thinking that you can just wing it. Using the telephone requires a plan:

1. **Establish Your Objective(s).** Ultimately, your objective is just to get the appointment—so don't get into a long sales spiel over the phone, as this isn't the best communication tool. A secondary objective may be to arrange to have some material sent to the prospect with a later follow-up. Do your research before you call.

2. **Prepare an Opening Statement.** You have about 15 seconds to grab and hold your prospect's attention and establish that first impression:

- Ask for your prospect by name and then greet your prospect by name.
- Introduce yourself and your organization right away in a confident manner.
- Get the prospect's attention—set yourself apart from the competition. Remember, you are not simply a telemarketer, but a sales professional who is ready, able, and willing to help.

3. **Briefly outline your message.** This is the heart of your script. Describe your product or service, pointing out relevant benefits. Prospects want benefits that will heighten their desire to hear more. Speak their language and use industry jargon—assuming your prospect knows it. Be prepared to discuss success stories of companies using your product.

4. **Ask for what you want.** Remember, your objective is not to make a sale. What you want is to get your foot in the door—so ask for an appointment. Establish a time constraint in your request. Rather than, "Whenever you have a free moment . . ." try "I'd like to meet with you before next Friday, what's a good time?" Specify how much time you'll require based on your objective. "I'd like to meet for 15 to 20 minutes. . . ."

5. **Prepare for possible objections.** If a prospect is reluctant to meet with you, be prepared with some key reasons that he should—remember, prospects like benefits.

6. **Once the meeting has been confirmed, inquire briefly about some of the prospect's key buying motives to help you prepare for your meeting.** Use your judgment to see if your prospect seems open to this type of question. If she hesitates, lay off.

7. **Confirm all contact information.** Ensure you have the prospect's correct name, title, and address, and that she has yours as well. Repeat your contact information slowly so the prospect can write it down. Repeat the appointment time and place slowly so that she has a chance to enter it in her calendar.

8. **Thank the prospect for her time!**

9. **Provide a reminder.** It is often a good idea to call a day ahead and confirm the appointment with the prospect's secretary in case something has come up and she won't be there to see you. Making these calls can be an effective use of downtime.

Sample Call

Remember to smile while you're speaking. It makes a big difference! Here's a sample prospecting call.

Buyer: "Hello, Gillian Johnson speaking."
Seller: "Hello, Ms. Johnson, my name is Sally Seller and I'm with the Specialty Applications Centre with the Acme Computer Company—thank you for taking my call."
Buyer: "No problem, what can I do for you?"
Seller: "We specialize in the design and development of office automation software for companies such as yours that has been proven to reduce office overhead and increase productivity greatly. We have successfully implemented our product in many local businesses and all have found it to be of great benefit."
Buyer: "That sounds interesting, please tell me more."

MAKING THE SALE

Getting an Appointment Is Not Always Easy

The owner of an oil-field supply house in Leduc, Alberta, was Jack Cooper's toughest customer. He was always on the run, and Jack had trouble just getting to see him, much less getting him to listen to a sales presentation. Jack would have liked to take him to lunch so he could talk to him, but the owner never had time. Every day the owner called a local hamburger stand and had a hamburger sent to his office so he wouldn't have to waste time sitting down to eat.

Jack wanted to get the owner interested in a power crimp machine that would enable him to make his own hose assemblies. By making them himself, the owner could save about 45 percent of his assembly costs—and Jack would make a nice commission.

The morning Jack was going to make his next call, his wife was making sandwiches for their children to take to school. Jack had a sudden inspiration. He asked his wife to make two deluxe bag lunches for him to take with him.

Jack arrived at the supply house just before lunchtime. "I know you're too busy to go out for lunch," he told the owner, "so I brought it with me. I thought you might like something different for a change."

The owner was delighted. He even took time to sit down and talk while they ate. After lunch, Jack left with an order for the crimper—plus a standing order for hose and fittings to go with it!

Seller: "Well, Ms. Johnson, I'd love to show you some samples and give you a demonstration of this product. I'd like to arrange a meeting with you sometime before the end of next week for 15 to 20 minutes to go over our product."
Buyer: "To be honest, Sally, I really don't think we'd have a need for this type of product."
Seller: "Ms. Johnson, if you would allow me 15 minutes, I will show you how your company can experience the same kind of cost savings that many other companies in your line of business have."
Buyer: "Well OK. Sally, why don't we meet next Monday at 10:30 A.M. in my office."
Seller: "That sounds wonderful, I will see you then—that's next Monday at 10:30, in your office on the 10th floor at 125 Main Street West, is that correct?"
Buyer: "Yes, that's correct."
Seller: "Great! I'll give you my contact information as well—it's Sally Seller, and my number is 1-2-3-4-5-6-7."
Buyer: "That sounds great—see you then."
Seller: "Just two quick questions before we go—approximately how many office staff work in your company, and how many floors are they spread over?"
Buyer: "We have about 75 workers and they occupy three floors of this building."
Seller: "That's great and will allow me to put cost figures together for you. Thank you for your time and I'll see you next Monday morning."
Buyer: "OK—see you then."

Many business executives are constantly bombarded with an unending procession of interorganizational memos, correspondence, reports, forms, and *salespeople.* To use their time optimally, many executives establish policies to aid in determining whom to see, what to read, and so on. They maintain **gatekeepers** (secretaries or receptionists) to filter all correspondence, telephone messages, and people seeking entry to the executive suite. Successful navigation of this filtration system requires a professional salesperson who (1) is determined to see the executive and believes it can be done; (2) develops friends within the firm (many times

SELLING TIPS

Managing Gatekeepers

Gatekeepers are plentiful in today's business world. They control the flow of information into and out of corporate offices, which can make them a significant hurdle for many salespeople.

Good technique and manners go a long way. Treating gatekeepers as "lowly" assistants would be a big mistake. They have been assigned this job by their bosses to prevent unnecessary distractions. All calls will be screened unless the buyer is very familiar with the calling salesperson. If you are unfamiliar, then it's up to you to prove that you deserve to speak to the buyer, or get an e-mail address or voice mail etc.

The gatekeeper has been assigned to evaluate your call. If you pass the test, you're in. So how you speak and what you say to the gatekeeper counts.

1. Begin with a friendly, yet professional introduction. Be clear and concise. Try to address the gatekeeper by name. Ask if the gatekeeper can give you a few moments; if not, then ask for a more convenient time to call.

2. To capture attention, ensure that what you have to offer is a large reward with little risk. Your proposition should be captivating enough so that the gatekeeper will feel obliged to give you an appointment. "Our product has been proven to save companies like yours 25 percent of their operating costs."

3. Engage gatekeepers. They hold the power in this situation. The more time they invest in you, the more attention they will pay, and therefore will feel more responsibility. They want to do what's best for their boss and their company—so speak in those terms.

4. Listen carefully to any follow-up instructions that you may receive. It would be unfortunate if you secured an appointment then showed up on the wrong day with the wrong material in hand.

5. Try to get gatekeepers on your side both before and after the call. They may become your working partners in dealings with the company. Their experience will help you tremendously in your future dealings with this company.

including the gatekeepers); and (3) optimizes time by calling only on individuals who make or participate in the purchase decision.

Believe in Yourself

As a salesperson, believe that you can obtain interviews because you have a good offer for prospects. Develop confidence by knowing your products and by knowing prospects—their business and needs. Speak and carry yourself as though you expect to get in to see the prospect. Instead of saying, "May I see Ms. Vickery?" you say, while handing the secretary your card, "Could you please tell Ms. Vickery that Ray Baker from XYZ Corporation is here?"

Develop Friends in the Prospect's Firm

Successful salespeople know that people within the prospect's firm often indirectly help to arrange interviews and influence buyers to purchase a product. A successful car fleet salesperson states

> To do business with the boss, you must sell yourself to everyone on his staff. I sincerely like people—so it came naturally to me. I treat secretaries and chauffeurs as equals and friends. Ditto for switchboard operators and maids. I regularly send small gifts to them all. An outstanding investment.
>
> The little people are great allies. They can't buy the product. But they can kill the sale. Who needs influential enemies? The champ doesn't want anyone standing behind him throwing rocks. In many cases, all you do is treat people decently—an act that sets you apart from 70 percent of your competitors.

Respect, trust, and friendship are three key elements in any salesperson's success. Timing is also important.

ETHICAL DILEMMA
What Would You Do to Get the Appointment?

Dennis worked as an insurance and financial service salesperson. One of his markets was small to medium-sized businesses for group insurance and benefit plans. In a competitive field with many salespeople, he often found it difficult to get by the gatekeepers. The response often seemed to be, "Oh no, another insurance rep".

He started to resort to the following technique.

Gatekeeper: "Good morning, XYZ Company, how can I help you?"

Dennis: "Good morning, I would like to speak with [name of purchasing agent].

Gatekeeper: "What is the purpose of your call, please?"

Dennis: "It's a personal call."

What do you think? Would this work and solve the problem of getting by the gatekeeper?

Call at the Right Time on the Right Person

Both gatekeepers and busy executives appreciate salespeople who do not waste their time. Use past sales call records or call the prospect's receptionist to determine when the prospect prefers to receive visitors. Direct questions, such as asking the receptionist, "Does Mr. Smith purchase your firm's office supplies?" or "Whom should I see concerning the purchase of office supplies?" can help determine whom to see.

Do Not Waste Time Waiting

Once you have asked the receptionist if the prospect can see you today, you should (1) determine how long you will have to wait and whether you can afford to wait that length of time; (2) be productive while waiting by reviewing how you will make the sales presentation to the prospect; and (3) once an acceptable amount of waiting time has passed, tell the receptionist, "I have another appointment and must leave in a moment." When politely approached, the receptionist will usually attempt to get you in. If still unable to enter the office, you can ask for an appointment as follows: "Will you please see whether I can get an appointment for 10 on Tuesday?" Even if that time is unavailable, your comment implies the expectation of another interview time. If you establish a positive relationship with a prospect and with gatekeepers, waiting time normally decreases.

SELLING TIPS
Customer Call Reluctance—Your Worst Enemy

According to a study by Behavioral Sciences Research Press, the problem of call reluctance in sales is widespread and costly. Among the findings of the Dallas research and sales training firm:

■ The call-reluctant salesperson loses more than 15 new accounts per month to competitors.

■ Call-reluctant stockbrokers acquire 48 fewer new accounts per year than brokers who have learned to manage their fear.

■ In some cases, the call-reluctant salesperson loses $10,800 per month in gross sales.

■ In others, call reluctance costs the salesperson $10,000 in lost commissions per year.[1]

CALL RELUCTANCE

All salespeople experience call reluctance (see Exhibit 7–5) periodically; however, an estimated 40 percent of salespeople suffer a career-threatening bout of **call reluctance** (not wanting to contact a prospect or customer) at some point. In its milder forms, call reluctance keeps countless salespeople from achieving their potential. Research indicates that 80 percent of all first-year salespeople who don't make the grade fail because of insufficient prospecting.[2]

Countermeasures are numerous and depend on the type of call reluctance. But the initial step is always the same: "You must admit you have call reluctance and that your call reluctance is keeping you from earning what you're worth." For many salespeople, owning up to call reluctance is the most difficult part of combating it.

EXHIBIT 7–5

The 12 faces of call reluctance.

Think you might suffer from call reluctance? See if you fit one of the 12 classic types identified by researchers George Dudley and Shannon Goodson. They're listed in order from most common to least common.

1. **Yielder**
   Fears intruding on others or being pushy

2. **Overpreparer**
   Overanalyzes, underacts

3. **Emotionally unemancipated**
   Fears loss of family approval, resists mixing business and family

4. **Separationist**
   Fears loss of friends, resists prospecting among personal friends

5. **Hyper-pro**
   Obsessed with image, fears being humiliated

6. **Role rejector**
   Ashamed to be in sales

7. **Socially self-conscious**
   Fears intruding on others or being pushy, intimidated by upmarket customers

8. **Doomsayer**
   Worries, won't take risks

9. **Telephobic**
   Fears using the telephone for prospecting or selling

10. **Stage fright**
    Fears group presentations

11. **Referral aversions**
    Fears disturbing existing business or client relationships

12. **Oppositional reflex**
    Rebuffs attempts to be coached

How to Conquer the Fear

- First and foremost, you must admit to having call reluctance. Acknowledgment is a major step toward recovery, but it's not an easy move. Denial is the most frequent companion of call reluctance, and the problem is sometimes hard to identify. Salespeople "typically know something is wrong, but they may not know what it is," says behavioural scientist and call reluctance expert George Dudley. "Many who do know they are experiencing sales call reluctance don't feel secure admitting it to management, because many sales organizations still tend to feature cultlike, unrealistic emphasis on maintaining a positive attitude," Dudley explains.

- Second, determine your call reluctance type and adopt appropriate countermeasures. The numerous prescriptions often involve clearly and specifically identifying your fears or negative thoughts. Then you can tackle them head-on, one at a time. In a sense, curbing call reluctance is like breaking a bad habit. Some salespeople find token reward systems helpful; others use relaxation techniques. In one countermeasure known as thought zapping, you place a rubber band around your wrist. When a negative thought intrudes, you snap the rubber band sharply and immediately conjure up a positive mental image of yourself—recalling, for example, a time when you did well in a similar situation.

- Third, follow up, keep plugging, make calls. Taming call reluctance is work, and for many salespeople it takes continual effort. "Don't confuse a change in your outlook with a change in the number of contacts you initiate with prospective buyers," Dudley warns. If you're call reluctant, take heart in the knowledge that your problem actually may be a sign of commitment to selling. "Salespeople who are not motivated or goal-focused can never be considered call reluctant," says Dudley. Salespeople with authentic call reluctance care very much about meeting prospecting goals. "You simply cannot be reluctant to get something you don't want in the first place."

DEVELOPING A CUSTOMER PROFILE

A customer profile sheet, such as the one shown in Exhibit 7–6, can be a guide for determining the appropriate strategy to use in contacting each customer. Collect and review as much relevant information as possible regarding the firm, the buyer, and the individuals who influence the buying decision—before making a sales call—to properly develop a customized presentation. Also consider the material in Chapter 3 concerning why the buyer purchases. A **customer profile** should tell you such things as

- Who makes the buying decisions in the organization—an individual or committee?
- What is the buyer's background? The background of the buyer's company? The buyer's expectations of you?
- What are the desired business terms and needs of the account, such as delivery, credit, technical service?
- Which of your competitors successfully do business with the account? Why?
- What are the purchasing policies and practices of the account? For example, does the customer buy special-price-offer promotions, or see salespeople on only Tuesday and Thursday?
- What is the history of the account (for example, past purchases of your products, inventory turnover, profit per shelf metre, your brand's volume sales growth, payment practices, and attitude toward resale prices)?

EXHIBIT 7–6

Information used in a profile and for planning.

Customer Profile and Planning Sheet

1. Name:_____
   Address:_____
2. Type of business:_____
   Name of buyer:_____
3. People who influence buying decision or aid in
   using or selling our product:_____
4. Buying hours and best time to see buyer:_____
5. Receptionist's name:_____
6. Buyer's profile:_____
7. Buyer's personality style:_____
8. Sales call objectives:_____
9. Customer's important buying needs:_____
10. Sales presentation:_____
    a. Sales approach:_____
    b. Features, advantages, benefits:_____
    c. Method of demonstrating FAB:_____
    d. How to relate benefits to customer's needs:_____
    e. Trial close to use:_____
    f. Anticipated objections:_____
    g. Trial close to use:_____
    h. How to close this customer:_____
    i. Hard or soft close:_____
11. Sales made—product use/promotional plan agreed on:___
    _____
12. Post–sales call comments (reason did/did not buy; what to do on next call;
    follow-up promised):_____

Determine this information from a review of records on the company or through personal contact with the company.

Customer Relationship Management (CRM)

Gathering the information in Exhibit 7–6 to create a basic customer list may seem daunting. However, it can be simplified by contact management software, which allows professional salespeople to collect and manage large amounts of customer data.

Contact management software is a database system designed specifically to handle all aspects of contact management. It is designed primarily for sales professionals.

These programs will organize appointments, mail-outs, phone calls, and follow-ups for an almost unlimited number of contacts. You can search client information using predefined search patterns or by the criteria you define. You can download sales data and company records, providing virtual real-time sales status and eliminating a lengthy paper sales report. In short, these programs provide a valuable tool for helping professional salespeople organize, communicate with, and track their customers.

A number of excellent products are on the market:

- Maximizer, www.maximizer.com
- Act!, www.act.com
- FrontRange, www.frontrange.com
- Super Pro, www.superprosoftware.com

Visit these Web sites to get a list of product features, and to even download and explore a trial version. Included in this book is a copy of ACT!Express. Appendix B online will provide you with an experiential exercise in the mechanics of this top-selling contact management software.

DEVELOPING A CUSTOMER BENEFIT PLAN

Beginning with your sales call objectives and what you know about your prospect, you are ready to develop a **customer benefit plan**. The customer benefit plan contains the nucleus of the information used in your sales presentation; thus it should be developed carefully. Creating a customer benefit plan can be approached as a four-step process.

Step 1

Select the features, advantages, and benefits of your product to present to your prospect. (See Chapter 5.) Point out the needs it fulfills or the problems it solves. This clarifies why your product should be purchased.

Step 2

Develop your marketing plan. When selling to wholesalers or retailers, include how, once they buy, they will sell your product to their customers (for example, how a retailer should promote the product through displays, advertising, proper shelf space and positioning, and pricing). For an end-user of the product, such as the company that buys your manufacturing equipment, computer, or photocopier, develop a program showing how your product is most effectively used or coordinated with existing equipment.

EXHIBIT 7–7

Examples of topics contained in the marketing plan segment of your sales presentation.

Resellers	End Users

1. Advertising
  ■ Geographical
    —National
    —Regional
    —Local
    —Co-op
  ■ Type
    —Television
    —Radio
    —Direct-mail
    —Internet
2. Sales promotion
  ■ Contests
  ■ Coupons
  ■ Demonstrations
  ■ Samples
  ■ Sweepstakes
  ■ POP displays
3. Sales force
  ■ Working with their salespeople
4. Trade shows
	1. Availability
	2. Delivery
	3. Guarantee
	4. Installation
	  ■ Who does it?
	  ■ When?
	  ■ How?
	5. Maintenance/service
	6. Training on use
	7. Warranty

Exhibit 7–7 lists other topics often discussed in the marketing plan segment of a sales presentation. (Many of these topics were discussed in Chapter 5.)

Step 3

Develop your business proposition, which includes items such as price, percentage markup, margin, forecast profit per square metre of shelf space, return on investment, and payment plan. Value analysis (determining the best product for the money) is an example of a business proposition for an industrial product. Other topics discussed in the business proposition segment of a sales presentation are shown in Exhibit 7–8.

EXHIBIT 7–8

Examples of topics contained in the business proposition segment of your sales presentation.

Resellers	End Users

1. List price
2. Shipping costs
3. Discounts
  ■ Cash
  ■ Consumer
  ■ Quantity
  ■ Trade
  ■ Financing
    —Payment plans
    —Interest rate
4. Markup and margin
5. Profit
	1. List price
	2. Shipping costs
	3. Discounts
	  ■ Cash
	  ■ Quantity
	4. Financing
	  ■ Payment plans
	  ■ Interest rates
	5. ROI
	6. Value analysis

Step 4

Develop a suggested purchase order based on a customer benefit plan. A proper presentation of your customer needs analysis and your product's ability to fulfill these needs, along with a satisfactory business proposition and marketing plan, allows you to justify to the prospect what product and how much to purchase. This suggestion may include, depending on your product, such things as what to buy, how much to buy, what assortment to buy, and when to ship the product to the customer.

Develop visual aids to effectively communicate the information developed in these four steps. The visuals should be presented in the order you discuss them. Your next step is to plan all aspects of the sales presentation.

DEVELOPING A SALES PRESENTATION

The most challenging, rewarding, and enjoyable aspect of the buyer–seller interaction is the **sales presentation**. An effective sales presentation completely and clearly explains all aspects of a salesperson's proposition as it relates to a buyer's needs. Surprisingly, attaining this objective is not as easy as you might think. Few successful salespeople will claim that they had little trouble developing a good presentation or mastering the art of giving the sales presentation. How then can you, as a novice, develop a sales presentation that will improve your chances of making the sale?

You must select a sales presentation method according to your prior knowledge of the customer, your sales call objective, and your customer benefit plan. After you select a method, you are ready to develop your sales presentation. The particular sales presentation method that you select will make an excellent framework on which to build your specific presentation.

Planning the sales presentation involves developing Steps 3 to 9 of the sales presentation described earlier in Exhibit 7–1: the approach, presentation, and trial close method to determine objections; ways to overcome objections; additional trial closes; and the close of the sales presentation. Each step is discussed in the following chapters.

New salespeople often ask their sales trainers to be more specific about how to construct the sales presentation. In addition to the 10 steps in the selling process shown in Exhibit 7–1, they ask, "What's involved in the presentation itself?" Exhibit 7–9 summarizes the major phases within the sales presentation. Before briefly discussing them, let's review a few things.

Based on the homework you have done on the prospect or customer, create the opening (approach) of the presentation. This step is discussed in Chapter 8. Then prepare your FABs, marketing plan, and business proposition. They were discussed earlier in this chapter and in previous chapters. Based on what you believe the customer should buy, prepare a suggested purchase order and choose a closing method that feels natural for you to use when asking for the business. Should you make the sale or not make the sale, it is important to know how to exit the buyer's office. Closing the sale and the exit are discussed in Chapter 11.

Use visual aids and demonstrations to help create an informative and persuasive sales presentation. As mentioned earlier, the *last step* in planning your sales call is the development and rehearsal of the sales presentation.

In developing the sales presentation, think of leading the prospect through the five steps or phases that salespeople believe constitute a purchase decision. These phases are referred to as the **prospect's mental steps**.

THE PROSPECT'S MENTAL STEPS

When making a sales presentation, quickly obtain the prospect's full attention, develop interest in your product, create a desire to fulfill a need, establish the prospect's conviction that the product fills a need, and, finally, promote action by having the

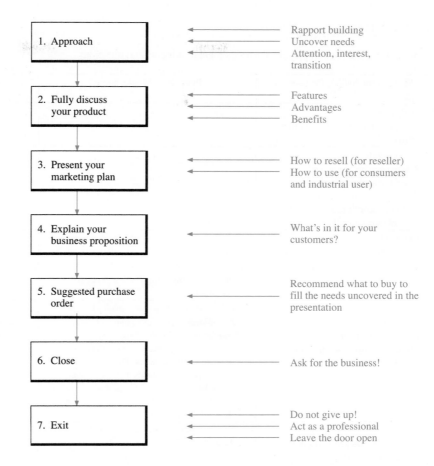

EXHIBIT 7–9

Major phases in your presentation: a sequence of events to complete in developing a sales presentation.

1. Approach — Rapport building / Uncover needs / Attention, interest, transition

2. Fully discuss your product — Features / Advantages / Benefits

3. Present your marketing plan — How to resell (for reseller) / How to use (for consumers and industrial user)

4. Explain your business proposition — What's in it for your customers?

5. Suggested purchase order — Recommend what to buy to fill the needs uncovered in the presentation

6. Close — Ask for the business!

7. Exit — Do not give up! / Act as a professional / Leave the door open

prospect purchase the product. (See Exhibit 7–10.) See Exhibit 7–11 for a summary of the prospect's thoughts and actions throughout the selling process.

Attention   From the moment you begin to talk, you have to quickly capture and maintain the prospect's **attention**. This may be difficult at times because of distractions, pressing demands on the prospect's time, or lack of interest, so carefully plan what to say and how to say it. Since attention-getters have only a temporary effect, be ready to quickly move to Step 2, sustaining the prospect's interest.

Interest   Before meeting with prospects, determine their important buying motives. These can be used to capture **interest**. If you cannot do this prior to your presentation you may have to determine them at the beginning of your presentation by asking questions. Prospects move into the interest stage if they listen to and enter into a discussion with you. Quickly strive to link your product's benefits to the prospect's needs. If this link is completed, prospects usually express a desire for the product.

Desire   Using the FAB formula (Chapter 5), strive to bring prospects from lukewarm interest to a **desire** for your product. Desire is created when prospects express a wish or want for a product like yours.

EXHIBIT 7–10

The prospect's five mental steps in buying.

Attention → Interest → Desire → Conviction → Purchase

EXHIBIT 7–11

The selling process and examples of prospect's mental thoughts and questions.

Steps in the Selling Process	Prospect's Mental Steps	Prospect's Potential Verbal and Mental Questions
1. Prospecting Salesperson locates and qualifies prospects.		
2. Preapproach Salesperson obtain interview, determines sales call objective, develops customer profile, customer benefit program, and sales presentation strategies.		
3. Approach Salesperson meets prospect, and begins customized sales presentation.	*Attention* due to arousal of potential need or problem. *Interest* due to recognized need or problem and the desire to fulfill the need or solve the problem.	Should I see a salesperson? Should I continue to listen, interact, devote much time to a salesperson? What's in it for me?
4. Presentation Salesperson further uncovers needs, relates product benefits to needs using demonstration, dramatization, visuals, and evidence statements.	*Interest* in information that provides knowledge and influences perceptions and attitude. *Desire* begins to develop based on information evaluation of product features, advantages, and benefits. This desire is due to forming positive attitudes that the product may fulfill the need or solve the problem. Positive attitudes are brought about by knowledge obtained from presentation.	Is the salesperson prepared? Are my needs understood? Is the seller interested in my needs? Should I continue to listen and interact? So what? (to statements about features) Prove it! (to statements about advantages) Are the benefits of this product the best to fulfill my needs?
5. Trial Close Salesperson asks prospect's opinion during and after presentation.	*Desire* continues based on information evaluation.	
6. Objections Salesperson uncovers objections.	*Desire* continues based on information evaluation.	Do I understand the salesperson's marketing plan and business proposition? I need more information to make a decision. Can you meet my conditions?
7. Meet Objections Salesperson satisfactorily answers objections.	*Desire* begins to be transformed into belief. *Conviction* established due to belief the product and salesperson can solve needs or problems better than competitive products. Appears ready to buy.	Let me see the reaction when I give the salesperson a hard time. I have a minor/major objection to what you are saying. Is something nonverbal being communicated? Did I get a reasonable answer to my objection?
8. Trial Close Salesperson asks prospects opinion after overcoming each objection and immediately before the close.	*Conviction* becomes stronger.	Can I believe and trust this person? Should I reveal my real concerns?
9. Close Salesperson brings prospect to the logical conclusion to buy.	*Action* (purchase) occurs based on positive beliefs that the product will fulfill needs or solve problems.	I am asked to make a buying decision now. If I buy and I am dissatisfied, what can I do? Will I receive after-the-sale service as promised? What are my expectations toward this purchase? Why don't you ask me to buy? Ask one more time and I'll buy.
10. Follow-up Salesperson provides customer service after the sale.	*Satisfaction or Dissatisfaction.*	Did the product meet my expectations? Am I experiencing dissonance? How is the service associated with this product? Should I buy again from this salesperson?

To better determine whether the product should be purchased, prospects may have questions for you and may present objections to your product. Plan how you will anticipate prospects' objections and provide information to maintain their desire.

Conviction   Although prospects may desire a product, they still have to be convinced that your product is best for their needs and that you are the best supplier of the product. In the **conviction** step, strive to create a strong *belief* that the product is best suited to the prospect's specific needs. Conviction is established when no doubts remain about purchasing the product from you.

Purchase or Action   Once the prospect is convinced, plan the most appropriate method of asking the prospect to buy or act. If each of the preceding steps has been implemented correctly, closing the sale—asking the prospect to **purchase** or take some **action**—is the easiest step in the sales presentation.

SALES PRESENTATION METHODS—SELECT ONE CAREFULLY   Salespeople work with customers in different ways. As discussed in Chapter 1, salespeople may be involved in transactional, relationship, or partnering selling. Thus, salespeople face a variety of situations, such as

- **Salesperson to buyer:** A salesperson discusses issues with a prospect or customer in person or over the phone.
- **Salesperson to buyer group:** A salesperson gets to know as many members of the buyer group as possible.
- **Sales team to buyer group:** A company sales team works closely with the members of the customer's buying group.
- **Conference selling:** The salesperson brings company resource people to discuss a major problem or opportunity.
- **Seminar selling:** A company team conducts an educational seminar for the customer company about new developments.

The type of presentation selected will depend on which of these categories your customer is in.

The sales presentation involves a persuasive vocal and visual explanation of a business proposition. Of the many ways of making a presentation, four methods are presented here to highlight the alternatives available to help sell your products.

As shown in Exhibit 7–12, the four sales presentation methods are memorized, formula, interactive need-satisfaction, and problem–solution selling methods.[3] The basic difference among the four methods is the percentage of the conversation controlled by the salesperson. In the more structured memorized and formula-selling techniques, the salesperson normally has a monopoly on the conversation, while the less-structured methods allow for greater buyer–seller interaction; both parties participate equally in the conversation. Transactional selling generally is more structured, whereas partnering requires a more customized presentation, with relationship selling typically somewhere in between. See Exhibit 7–12.

EXHIBIT 7–12

The structure of sales presentations.

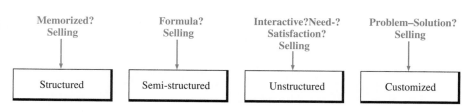

The Memorized Sales Presentation

The **memorized presentation** is based on either of two assumptions: that a prospect's needs can be stimulated by direct exposure to the product via the sales presentation, or that these needs have already been stimulated because the prospect has made the effort to seek out the product. In either case, the salesperson's role is to develop this initial stimulus into an affirmative response to an eventual purchase request.

The salesperson does 80 to 90 percent of the talking during a memorized sales presentation, only occasionally allowing the prospect to respond to predetermined questions, as shown in Exhibit 7–13. Notably, the salesperson does not attempt to determine the prospect's needs during the interview but gives the same canned sales talk to all prospects. Since no attempt is made at this point to learn what goes on in the consumer's mind, the salesperson concentrates on discussing the product and its benefits, concluding the pitch with a purchase request. The seller hopes that a convincing presentation of product benefits will cause the prospect to buy.

National Cash Register Co. (now AT&T Global Information Solutions) pioneered the use of canned sales presentations. During the 1920s, an analysis of the sales approaches of some of its top salespeople revealed to NCR that they were saying the same things. The firm prepared a series of standardized sales presentations based on the findings of its sales approach analysis, ultimately requiring its sales force to memorize these approaches for use during sales calls. The method worked quite well for NCR and was later adopted by other firms. Canned sales presentations are still used today, mainly in telemarketing and door-to-door selling.

Actually, parts of any presentation may be canned, yet linked with freeform conversation. Over time, most salespeople develop proven selling sentences, phrases, and sequences in which to discuss information. They tend to use these in all presentations.

Despite its impersonal aura, the canned or memorized sales presentation has distinct advantages, as seen in Exhibit 7–14.[4]

- It ensures that the salesperson gives a well-planned presentation and that the same information is discussed by all the company's salespeople.
- It both aids and lends confidence to the inexperienced salesperson.
- It is effective when selling time is short, as in door-to-door or telephone selling.
- It is effective when the product is nontechnical—such as books, cooking utensils, and cosmetics.

EXHIBIT 7–13

Participation time by customer and salesperson during a memorized sales presentation.

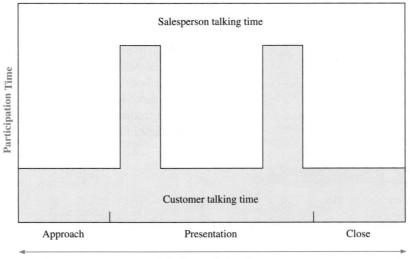

EXHIBIT 7–14

Dyno Electric Cart memorized presentation.

Situation: You call on a purchasing manager to elicit an order for some electric carts (like golf carts) to be used at a plant for transportation around the buildings and grounds. The major benefit to emphasize in your presentation is that the carts save time; you incorporate this concept in your approach. For this product, you use the memorized stimulus–response presentation.

Salesperson: Hello, Mr. Pride, my name is Karen Nordstrom, and I'd like to talk with you about how to save your company executives' time. By the way, thanks for taking the time to talk with me.

Buyer: What's on your mind?

Salesperson: As a busy executive, you know time is a valuable commodity. Nearly everyone would like to have a few extra minutes each day and that is the business I'm in, selling time. While I can't actually sell you time, I do have a product that is the next best thing . . . a Dyno Electric Cart—a real time-saver for your executives.

Buyer: Yeah, well, everyone would like to have extra time. However, I don't think we need any golf carts. [First objection.]

Salesperson: Dyno Electric Cart is more than a golf cart. It is an electric car designed for use in industrial plants. It has been engineered to give comfortable, rapid transportation in warehouses, and plants, and across open areas.

Buyer: They probably cost too much for us to use. [Positive buying signal phrased as an objection.]

Salesperson: First of all, they cost only $2,200 each. With a five-year normal life, that is only $400 per year plus a few cents in electricity and a few dollars for maintenance. Under normal use and care, these carts require only about $100 of service in their five-year life. Thus, for about $50 a month, you can save key people a lot of time. [Creative pricing—show photographs of carts in use.]

Buyer: It would be nice to save time, but I don't think management would go for the idea. [Third objection, but still showing interest.]

Salesperson: This is exactly why I am here. Your executives will appreciate what you have done for them. You will look good in their eyes if you give them an opportunity to look at a product that will save time and energy. Saving time is only part of our story. Dyno Carts also save energy and thus keep you sharper toward the end of the day. Would you want a demonstration today or Tuesday? [Alternative close.]

Buyer: How long would your demonstration take? [Positive buying signal.]

Salesperson: I need only one hour. When would it be convenient for me to bring the cart in for your executives to try out?

Buyer: There really isn't any good time. [Objection.]

Salesperson: That's true. Therefore, the sooner we get to show you a Dyno Cart, the sooner your management group can see its benefits. How about next Tuesday? I could be here at 8:00 and we could go over this item just before your weekly management group meeting. I know you usually have a meeting Tuesdays at 9:00 because I tried to call on you a few weeks ago and your secretary told me you were in the weekly management meeting. [Close of the sale.]

Buyer: Well, we could do it then.

Salesperson: Fine, I'll be here. Your executives will really be happy! [Positive reinforcement.]

As may be apparent, the memorized method has several major drawbacks:

- It presents features, advantages, and benefits that may not be important to the buyer.
- It allows for little prospect participation.

- It is impractical to use when selling technical products that require prospect input and discussion.

- It proceeds quickly through the sales presentation to the close, requiring the salesperson to close or ask for the order several times, which may be interpreted by the prospect as high-pressure selling.

In telling of his early selling experiences, salesperson John Anderson remembers that he was once so intent on presenting his memorized presentation that halfway through it the prospect yelled, "Enough, John, I've been waiting for you to see me. I'm ready to buy. I know all about your products." Anderson was so intent on giving his canned presentation, and listening to himself talk, that he did not recognize the prospect's buying signals.

For some selling situations, a highly structured presentation can be used successfully. Examine this method's advantages and disadvantages to determine whether this presentation is appropriate for your prospects and products.

Some situations may seem partially appropriate for the memorized approach but require a more personal touch. Such circumstances warrant the examination of formula selling.

The Formula Presentation

The **formula sales presentation**, often referred to as the *persuasive selling presentation,* is like the memorized method: it is based on the assumption that similar prospects in similar situations can be approached with similar presentations. However, for the formula method to apply, the salesperson must first know something about the prospective buyer. The salesperson follows a less structured, general outline in making a presentation, allowing more flexibility and less direction.

The salesperson generally controls the conversation during the sales talk, especially at the beginning. Exhibit 7–15 illustrates how a salesperson should take charge during a formula selling situation.[5] For example, the salesperson might make a sales opener (approach); discuss the product's features, advantages, and benefits; and then start to solicit comments from the buyer using trial closes, answering questions, and handling objections. At the end of the participation curve, the salesperson regains control over the discussion and moves in to close the sale.

The formula selling approach obtains its name from the salesperson using the attention, interest, desire, and action (AIDA) procedure of developing and giving the

EXHIBIT 7–15

Participation time by a customer and salesperson during a formula sales presentation.

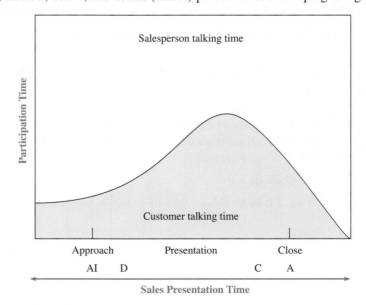

sales presentation. We add conviction (C) to the procedure because the prospect may want or desire the product, yet not be convinced this is the best product or the best salesperson from whom to buy.

Straight rebuy and modified rebuy situations, especially with consumer goods, lend themselves to this method. Many prospects or customers buy because they are familiar with the salesperson's company. The question is, How can a salesperson for Quaker Oats, Revlon, Gillette, Procter & Gamble, or any other well-known manufacturer develop a presentation that convinces a customer to purchase promotional quantities of a product, participate in a local advertising campaign, or stock a new, untried product?

The consumer products division of Smith Kline Beecham has developed a sequence, or formula, for its salespeople to follow. They refer to it as the *10-step productive retail sales call*. The Beecham salesperson sells products such as Cling Free Sheets, Aqua-Fresh toothpaste, Aqua Velva, and Sucrets. The 10 steps and their major components are shown in Exhibit 7–16.

EXHIBIT 7–16		

The 10-step productive retail sales call.

Step No.		Action
1. Plan the call		■ Review the situation.
		■ Analyze problems and appointments.
		■ Set objectives.
		■ Plan the presentation.
		■ Check your sales materials.
2. Review plans		■ Before you leave your car to enter the store, review your plans, sales call objectives, suggested order forms, and so on.
3. Greet personnel		■ Give a friendly greeting to store personnel.
		■ Alert the store manager for sales action.
4. Check store conditions		■ Note appearance of stock on shelf.
		■ Check distribution and pricing.
		■ Note out-of-stocks.
		■ Perform a quick fix by straightening shelf stock.
		■ Report competitive activity.
		■ Check back room (storeroom):
		—Locate product to correct out-of-stocks.
		—Use reserve stock for special display.
		■ Update sales plan if needed.
5. Approach		■ Keep it short.
6. Presentation		■ Make it logical, clear, interesting.
		■ Tailor it to dealer's style.
		■ Present it from dealer's point of view.
		■ Use sales tools.
7. Close		■ Present a suggested order (ask for the order).
		■ Offer a choice.
		■ Answer questions and handle objections.
		■ Get a real order.
8. Merchandising		■ Build displays.
		■ Dress up the shelves.
9. Record and report		■ Complete them immediately after the call.
10. Analyze the call		■ Review the call to spot strong and weak points. How could the sales call have been improved? How can the next call be improved?

A formula approach sales presentation.

Formula Steps	Buyer–Seller Roles	Sales Presentation
Summarize the situation for *attention* and *interest*.	**Salesperson:**	Ms. Hansen, you've said before that the shortage of shelf space prevents you from stocking our family-size Tide—though you admit you may be losing some sales as a result. If we could determine *how much* volume you're missing, I think you'd be willing to *make* space for it, wouldn't you? [Trial close.]
State your marketing plan for *interest*.	**Buyer:**	Yes, but I don't see how that can be done.
	Salesperson:	Well, I'd like to suggest a test—a weekend display of all four sizes of Tide.
	Buyer:	What do you mean?
Explain your marketing plan for *interest* and *desire*.	**Salesperson:**	My thought was to run all sizes at regular shelf price *without* any ad support. This would give us a pure test. Six cases of each size should let us compare sales of the various sizes and see what you're missing by regularly stocking only the smaller sizes. I think the additional sales and profits you'll get on the family size will convince you to start stocking regularly. [Reinforce key benefits.] What do you think? [Trial close.]
Buyer appears to be in *conviction* stage.	**Buyer:**	Well, maybe. [Positive reaction to trial close.]
Suggest an easy next step or *action*.	**Salesperson:**	May I enter the six cases of family-size Tide in the order book now? [Close.]

Formula selling is effective for calling on customers who currently buy and for prospects about whose operations the salesperson has learned a great deal. In such situations, formula selling offers significant advantages:

- It ensures that all information is presented logically.
- It allows for a reasonable amount of buyer–seller interaction.
- It allows for smooth handling of anticipated questions and objections.

When executed in a smooth, conversational manner, the formula method of selling has no major flaws, as long as the salesperson has correctly identified the prospect's needs and wants. The Procter & Gamble formula sales presentation in Exhibit 7–17 can be given to any retailer who is not selling all available sizes of Tide (or of any other product). In this situation, a formula approach is used when calling on a customer the salesperson has sold to previously. If the salesperson did not know a customer's needs and used this Tide presentation, customer objections likely would arise early in the presentation—as they also sometimes do with the memorized sales presentation method. The formula technique is not adaptable to a number of complex selling situations; these require different sales presentations.

Chapter 4 defined and discussed **needs analysis**, which forms the basis for the interactive need-satisfaction presentation.

The Interactive Need-Satisfaction Presentation

The **interactive need-satisfaction presentation** is different from the memorized and the formalized approach; it is designed as a flexible, free-flowing, and interactive sales presentation. It is the most challenging and creative form of selling, requiring quick thinking and confidence on the part of the salesperson.

EXHIBIT 7–18

The interactive need–satisfaction approach encourages a problem-solving teamwork approach.

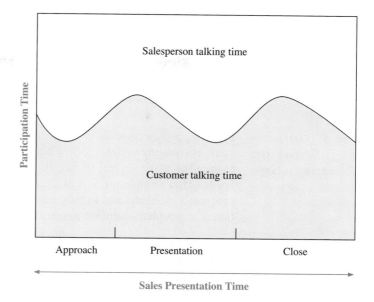

As Exhibit 7–18 and Exhibit 7–19 illustrate, the key to this strategy is equal participation by the salesperson and prospect. This is a partnership approach in which the buyer and seller are encouraged to solve the buyer's problem(s) together.

Often, the salesperson will begin this presentation with a probing question, "What are you looking for in a new robotics system for your company?" After this, there is

EXHIBIT 7–19

An interactive need–satisfaction presentation.

Salesperson: Mr. Friend, you really have a large manufacturing facility here. How large is it?

Buyer: We have approximately 20 hectares under one roof.

Salesperson: It certainly seems like a long walk from the executive offices to the plant area.

Buyer: It's approximately one kilometre.

Salesperson: How do your executives get down there?

Buyer: They usually just hitch a ride with one of the machine operators.

Salesperson: Do you see any problems with that?

Buyer: Well, actually I do. For one, it slows down my machine operators and second, it's downright dangerous sometimes.

Salesperson: Have you ever given any thought to how this problem might be solved?

Buyer: Aside from moving sidewalks, I don't know what we can do.

Salesperson: Well, besides the concerns you've shown, there would be many other benefits in solving this in-plant transportation problem. Let's find a quieter place to sit down. I think that *we* can come up with several possible solutions.

(From here, the salesperson can move into more questions that would expose more problems and then discuss products that would solve these problems, creating a team effort.)

a continuous interchange of information between the two parties. The salesperson probes for needs, then provides solutions for these needs. As problems arise, problems are solved. The constant interaction in this type of presentation results in the prospect's needs being solved by both parties, which will leave both satisfied. This teamwork approach is effective not only in completing sales, but also in establishing long-term buyer–seller relationships.

The Problem–Solution Presentation

In selling highly complex or technical products such as insurance, industrial equipment, accounting systems, office equipment, and computers, salespeople often are required to make several sales calls to develop a detailed analysis of a prospect's needs. After completing this analysis, the salesperson arrives at a solution to the prospect's problems and usually uses both a written analysis and an oral presentation. The **problem–solution presentation** usually consists of six steps:

1. Convincing the prospect to allow the salesperson to conduct the analysis.
2. Making the actual analysis.
3. Agreeing on the problems and determining that the buyer wants to solve them.
4. Preparing the proposal for a solution to the prospect's needs.
5. Preparing the sales presentation based on the analysis and proposal.
6. Making the sales presentation.

The problem-solution presentation is a flexible, customized approach involving an in-depth study of a prospect's needs, and requires a well-planned presentation. Often, the need-satisfaction and problem-solution presentations are used when it is necessary to present the proposal to a group of individuals.

THE GROUP PRESENTATION

At times you will meet with more than one decision maker for a group presentation.[6] Many group presentation elements are similar to other types of presentations. However, the group presentation, depending on size, may be less flexible than a one-on-one meeting. The larger the group, the more structured your presentation to avoid everyone jumping in with feedback and ideas simultaneously. As the salesperson in charge, you can structure the presentation to provide a question-and-answer period at the end of or during the presentation. Ideally, you have spoken with most or all of the decision makers involved during the analysis phase to determine their needs. The points you discuss will address thoughts they have expressed regarding the problems at hand. In the initial part of the presentation, you should accomplish the following:

Give a Proper Introduction

State your name and company, and explain in a clear, concise sentence the premise of your proposal. For example, your statement might sound like this: "Good morning. I'm Jeff Baxter from International Hospitality Consultants. I'm here to share my findings, based on research of your company and discussions with Mary Farley, that suggest my company can help increase your convention bookings by 15 to 30 percent."

Establish Credibility

Give a brief history of your company that includes the reason the business was started, the company philosophy, its development, and its success rate. Mention a few companies that you have worked with, especially if they are big names. This reassures the client by letting the group know who you are and the extent of your experience and credibility.

Provide an Account List

Have copies of an account list available for everyone in attendance. It would be monotonous to list each company that you've worked with. Instead, hand out copies either in advance or while you talk. This list shows the various sizes, locations, and types of companies you've helped in the past.

State Your Competitive Advantages

Succinctly tell the group where your company stands relative to the competition. Don't get into a detailed analysis of comparative strengths and weaknesses; make it clear that you can do better than the competition.

Give Quality Assurances and Qualifications

Get the group on your side by stating guarantees at the beginning. This shows pride in your product. If your company has an impressive money-back guarantee or an extended warranty, mention it. Also, give your company's qualifications and credentials. For example, "We are certified by Environment Canada to treat or move toxic waste," or "I have copies of the test reports from an independent lab."

Cater to the Group's Behavioural Style

Every group comprises individuals with personal styles. However, a group also exhibits an overall or dominant style; that is, it has a decision-making mode that characterizes one of the four behavioural styles. (See Chapter 3.) If you can quickly determine the group style, you will hold the listeners' attention and give them what they want more effectively. Some people are more impatient than others. If you don't address their needs, you will lose their attention.

Get the Group Involved in the Presentation

After establishing the credibility of your company, involve the group in the presentation; go around the room asking for everyone's input into the decision-making criteria for making the purchase. Preface this with, "I spoke to Marius, Isabel, and Sue and learned their views on what your company would like to see changed in this area. In my research, I discovered it would also benefit you to have X, Y, and Z improved. I'd like to hear all your thoughts on this matter." Ask each person to add to the list of benefits and the decision-making criteria. To help shape your presentation, take notes, perhaps on a flip chart, of what everyone says.

The Proposal

When you prepare for a group, write a **proposal** document that ranges from one page to an entire notebook with data, specifications, reports, and solutions to each individual's specific problems. The proposal document is a reference source that tells your customer what she bought if she said yes and what she didn't buy if the answer was no. This document addresses everything you and your prospect discussed in the analysis phase: problems, success criteria, decision-making criteria, and how your product or service answers each. At the end, include relevant documents and copies of testimonial letters from satisfied customers.

During your presentation, do not read from the document. It is not the presentation; it is strictly a resource to give to your prospect after a decision is made. When making your presentation, do not expect to cover every point in the proposal unless you are brief. Your presentation will focus on the issues that relate to the customer's specific need gap; tangential information should be provided only in the document. Remember that proposal documents don't sell products; people sell products. The document is no substitute for a first-rate presentation.

Avoid Prices

Don't include prices in the proposal document. First, some people will go directly to the prices without reading through the document. Second, prices tend to prejudice non–decision makers—who should not be concerned with prices. If the decision maker asks why the prices are missing, tell him, "I thought you would prefer the flexibility of showing the document to other people without their knowing prices. It's a matter of confidentiality." The third reason is politics. Imagine a board of directors that has not had a raise in two years looking at a document that proposes a $2 million computer for the company.

Make it clear that you would be more than happy to talk about prices with the appropriate people, the decision makers. It is important to present prices in the proper perspective and context.

When you share the proposal document, address each problem and give specific information about your solutions. Make sure you discuss features, advantages, and benefits—and get feedback from the group. Ask trial closes such as:

- ■ "Can you see any other advantages to this?"
- ■ "How do you feel about that? Do you think that would solve the problem?"

Summarize Benefits   At the end, summarize your proposal by giving a benefits summary: "Here is what you will get if you accept my proposal." Talk about how the benefits will address their specific problems.

Before your presentation, find out from your primary contact in the company whether the group will make a decision while you are there or whether they will discuss it and inform you later. You also should know whether they are responsible for the financial aspects of the purchase. If so, you will have to talk about the costs and the benefits they will receive in relation to the costs. If they will not be concerned with prices, don't discuss them.

When you have completed the benefits summary, solicit impressions from the group. Ask whether they agree that the solution you proposed would solve their problem or meet their needs. Without asking for it, get a feeling for the

---

MAKING THE SALE
Characteristics for Successful Negotiation

The following 10 personal characteristics necessary for successful negotiation can help you determine the potential you already possess and also identify areas where improvement is needed. On a separate piece of paper, write the number that best reflects where you fall on the scale. The higher the number the more the characteristic describes you. When you have finished, total the numbers.

1. I am sensitive to the needs of others.   1 2 3 4 5 6 7 8 9 10

2. I will compromise to solve problems when necessary.   1 2 3 4 5 6 7 8 9 10

3. I am committed to a win–win philosophy.   1 2 3 4 5 6 7 8 9 10

4. I have a high tolerance for conflict.   1 2 3 4 5 6 7 8 9 10

5. I am willing to research and analyze issues fully.   1 2 3 4 5 6 7 8 9 10

6. Patience is one of my strong points.   1 2 3 4 5 6 7 8 9 10

7. My tolerance for stress is high.   1 2 3 4 5 6 7 8 9 10

8. I am a good listener.   1 2 3 4 5 6 7 8 9 10

9. Personal attack and ridicule do not unduly bother me.   1 2 3 4 5 6 7 8 9 10

10. I can identify bottom-line issues quickly.   1 2 3 4 5 6 7 8 9 10

If you scored 80 or more, you have characteristics of a good negotiator. You recognize what negotiating requires and seem willing to apply yourself accordingly. If you scored between 60 and 79, you should do well as a negotiator but have some characteristics that need further development. If you scored less than 60, go over the items again to identify key areas on which to concentrate as you negotiate. Repeat this evaluation again after you have had practice negotiating.[7]

disposition of the group. If you are working with one person, it is easier to ask for an impression.

At the end of your summary, ask if there are any questions. At this point, you are close to the end of your allotted time. When someone asks a question that is answered in your proposal document, refer him to the appropriate section of the document and assure him that a complete answer is provided.

NEGOTIATING SO EVERYBODY WINS

No matter what type of presentation method you use, or whether you talk to one person or a group of people, be prepared to negotiate. Many salespeople negotiate during the confirming phase of the sale

Style of negotiating include cooperative, competitive, attitudinal, organizational, and personal. Inexperienced negotiators often operate in the competitive mode because they mistakenly think the shrewd businessperson is one who wins at the other's expense. With a win–lose attitude in mind, they "don't show all their cards" and use other strategies to gain the upper hand. Often this is done at the expense of the business relationship.

If you see prospects as adversaries rather than business partners, you will have short-term, adversarial relationships. The tension, mistrust, and buyer's remorse created are not worth the small gains earned from this negotiating style. There is a better way.

Professional salespeople negotiate in a way that achieves satisfaction for both parties. They rely on trust, openness, credibility, integrity, and fairness. Their attitude is not, "How can I get what I want out of this person?" It's "There are many options to explore that will make both of us happy. If two people want to do business, the details will not stand in the way." It is important *not* to negotiate the details before your customer has made a commitment to your solution.

Phases of Negotiation

If your product or service requires negotiating on a regular basis, set the stage for negotiation early in the sales process. You can do several things to prepare for negotiation from the beginning.

Planning

After completing a competition analysis, you know how your company compares to the competition for price, service, quality, reputation, and so on. This knowledge is important at negotiation time. You may be able to offer things the competition cannot, so point out these comparisons to your prospect when the time is right.

Before you make a proposal to a client, search your company's sales records to find any reports of previous sales to your prospect or similar businesses. If these records documented the successes and failures of negotiating, you will learn from other salespeople's experience. For this reason, in your call reports include details of what transpired during every negotiation. The knowledge gained from these records is not a strategy per se but an insight into the priorities of this market segment. For example, certain businesses may value service more than price, or they may care more about help in training and implementation than about a discount.

During your preparation, review the various bargaining chips available to you. Some of the questions to answer are

- What extra services can I offer?
- How flexible is the price or the payment plan?
- Are deposits and cancellation fees negotiable?

- Is there optional equipment I can include at no cost?
- Can my company provide free or discounted training?
- What items in the negotiation will be non-negotiable for me?
- How can I compensate for these items?

Meeting

When you meet a prospect, you start building the relationship by proving you are credible, trustworthy, and the type of person your prospect likes to do business with. If you are all of these things, you will eliminate tension and ease the negotiation process.

As proof of this concept, imagine selling your car to a friend. Now imagine selling it to a stranger. Who would be easier to negotiate with? The friend, of course. For both of you, the top priority is the relationship; the secondary priority is the car deal.

Studying

When you study a prospect's business, look at the big picture. As mentioned earlier in the book, don't focus on features of your products; look for benefits you can provide. Look beyond a prospect's demands for reasons. You can ask, "What are you trying to accomplish by asking for this?" After you are told, you may be able to say, "We can accomplish that another way. Consider this alternative . . ." The more options for providing benefits, the more flexible the negotiation.

During this phase, you must find out what other companies' products or services your prospect is considering. This information gives insight into what he or she is looking for and willing to pay. If you are selling a half-million-dollar CAT scanner and your prospect is also considering a three-quarter-million-dollar CAT scanner, you know your product is not priced too high. If, however, your prospect is looking at a lot of lower-priced units, it may be an uphill struggle to get the prospect to spend what you're asking. Knowing who your competitors are will help you assess bargaining strengths and weaknesses.

There are three levels of desire: *must have, should have,* and *would be nice to have.* Be clear about these levels and how they create limits for negotiations. Obviously, *must haves* are much less flexible than *would be nice to haves.*

SELLING TIPS

Negotiating

- When you give up something, try to gain something in return. When you give something for nothing, there is a tendency for people to want more. Therefore, balance what you give and receive. For example, "Ill lower the price if you pay in full within 30 days," or "I'll give you 10 percent off, so we will charge for additional services such as training."
- Look for items other than price to negotiate. For example, offer better terms, payment plans, return policies, and delivery schedules, lower deposits or cancellation fees, or implementation and training programs. Often these items

are provided for less than your company would lose if you lowered the price.

- Do not attack your prospect's demand; look for the motive behind it. Never tell a prospect his demand is ridiculous or unreasonable. Remain calm and ask for the reason behind the desire.
- Do not defend your position; ask for feedback and advice from the prospect. If you meet resistance to an offer, don't be defensive. Say something like, "This is my thinking. What would you do if you were in my position?"

Proposing

Proposing is another phase that indirectly affects subsequent negotiations. Every step in the sales process build toward what may come later. During your presentation, tie features and advantages to benefits, and emphasize unique benefits. In this way, your product or service and company are positioned above the rest. Position yourself as well. Don't be afraid to let your prospect know she is getting you and everything you have promised to do after the sale.

The successful resolution of a negotiation starts with a commitment to do business together. It is then necessary for both parties to maintain common interests and resolve any conflicts cooperatively. The key to selling and negotiating is to always seek a win–win solution in which both buyer and seller are happy.[8]

WHAT IS THE BEST PRESENTATION METHOD?

Each of these sales presentation methods is effective when properly matched with the situation. For example, the memorized method can be used when time is short and the product is simple. Formula selling is effective in repeat purchases or when you know or have already determined the needs of the prospect.

The need-satisfaction method is most appropriate when information needs to be gathered from the prospect, as is often the case in selling industrial products. The problem–solution presentation is excellent for selling high-cost technical products or services, and especially for sales involving several sales calls and a business proposition. To help improve sales, you should understand and be able to use each method based on the particular situation.

Before developing the presentation, know which presentation method you will use. Then, plan what you will do when talking with your prospect.

SUMMARY OF MAJOR SELLING ISSUES

Most salespeople agree that careful planning of the sales call is essential to success in selling. Planning helps build confidence, develops an atmosphere of goodwill, creates professionalism, and increases sales. By having a plan, salespeople can decide what they want to accomplish, then later measure their accomplishments.

Sales call planning includes three basic elements. First, establish a call objective that is specific, measurable, and beneficial to the customer. Second, research your customer and develop a detailed profile so you can properly customize your presentation. Third, develop your customer benefit plan, which gives your prospects specific reasons that they should buy your product.

To improve your chances of making a sale, you must master the art of giving a good sales presentation. An effective presentation will work toward solving the customer's problems. The sales presentation method selected should be based on prior knowledge of the customer, your sales call objective, and your customer benefit plan.

Sales presentation methods differ depending on what percentage of the conversation is controlled by the salesperson. In the memorized presentation, or stimulus–response method, the salesperson does 80 to 90 percent of the talking, with each customer receiving the same sales pitch. Although this method ensures a well-planned presentation and is good for certain non-technical products, it is also somewhat inflexible, allowing little prospect participation. The formula presentation, a persuasive selling presentation, is similar to the first method, but it takes the prospect into account by answering questions and handling objections.

The most challenging and creative form of selling uses the interactive needs-satisfaction presentation. This flexible method begins by raising questions about what the customer specifically needs. After you are aware of the customer's needs, you can then show how your products fit these needs.

When selling highly complex or technical products like computers or insurance, a problem–solution presentation is appropriate. This method involves making a detailed analysis of the buyer's specific needs and problems and designing a proposal and presentation to fit these needs. This customized method often uses a selling team to present the specialized information to the buyer.

In comparing the four presentation methods, no one method is best. Each must be tailored to meet the particular characteristics of a specific selling situation or environment.

MEETING A SALES CHALLENGE

The purpose of your sales presentation is to provide information so the prospect can make a rational, informed buying decision. You provide this information using your FABs, marketing plan, and business proposal.

The information you provide allows the buyer to develop positive personal *beliefs* toward your product. The beliefs result in *desire* (or *need*) for the type of product you sell. Your job is to convert that need into a want and into the *attitude* that your product is the best product to fulfill a certain need. Furthermore, you must convince the buyer not only that your product is the best but also that you are the best source. When this occurs, your prospect has moved into the *conviction* stage of the mental buying process.

When a real need is established, the buyer will want to fulfill that need, and there is a high probability that she will choose your product. Whether to buy is a "choice decision," and you provide the necessary information so that the customer chooses to buy from you.

When you are prepared, the prospect or customer recognizes it. This recognition gives you a better chance of giving and completing your presentations, without being cut off and therefore, increases your sales, because the more presentations you give, the more people you sell. Veteran salespeople have a tendency not to prepare; many get lazy and fall into a bad habit of "winging it." Top sales professionals rarely are unprepared. Do you want to be an order taker or an order getter? Your success is entirely up to you!

PLAYING THE ROLE

Manage the Gatekeeper

The situation: You are a salesperson and wants an appointment with the head purchasing manager of your college. You sell a new software program that you know would improve the productivity of the administrators of your college.

Role A: The salesperson—prepare to make a call to your college to get an appointment with the purchasing agent.

Role B: The gatekeeper—prepare to screen the call; your boss is a busy person. You should eventually let the salesperson speak to the purchasing agent.

Role C: The purchasing agent—You speak to salespeople all the time; does this one deserve an appointment?

Dramatize this situation in class, having prepared your roles.

KEY TERMS FOR SELLING

action, 189
attention, 187
call reluctance, 182
competitive advantage, 197
conviction, 189
creative problem solvers, 173
customer benefit plan, 184
customer profile, 183
desire, 187
formula sales presentation, 192
gatekeeper, 179
interactive need-satisfaction
   presentation, 194
interest, 187

memorized presentation, 190
needs analysis, 194
preapproach, 172
problem–solution presentation, 196
proposal, 197
prospect's mental steps, 186
purchase, 189
sales call objective, 175
sales planning, 175
sales presentation, 186
SMART, 176
strategic, 172
strategic customer relationship, 172

SALES APPLICATION QUESTIONS

1. What are the elements to consider when planning a sales call? Explain each one.
2. An important part of planning a sales call is the development of a customer benefit plan. What are the major components of the customer benefit plan? What is the difference in developing a customer benefit plan for a Procter & Gamble salesperson selling consumer products versus an industrial salesperson selling products for a company such as IBM?
3. Outline and discuss the sequence of events in developing a sales presentation.
4. Define the term *selling process*. List the major steps in the selling process on the left side of a page of paper. Beside each step of the selling process, write the corresponding mental step that a prospect should experience.
5. Think of a product sold through one of your local supermarkets. Assume you were recently hired by the product's manufacturer to contact the store's buyer to purchase a promotional quantity of your product and to arrange for display and advertising. What information do you need for planning the sales call, and what features, advantages, and benefits would be appropriate in your sales presentation?
6. What are the four sales presentation methods discussed in this chapter? Briefly explain each method; include any similarities and differences in your answer.
7. Some people concentrate on the needs-fulfillment phase of the sales presentation. Are they correct in their approach? Why or why not?
8. Assume that a salesperson already knows the customer's needs. Instead of developing the customer's needs as part of the sales presentation, he goes directly to the close. What are your feelings about this type of sales presentation?
9. *a.* Identify the four stages of negotiation as they appear in the chapter.
   b. Within each stage, describe what you could do to enhance the effectiveness of the negotiation process.

SALES WORLD WIDE WEB EXERCISES

The most challenging, rewarding, and enjoyable aspect of the sales job is the sales presentation. An effective presentation completely and clearly explains all aspects of a salesperson's proposition as it relates to a buyer's needs. To learn more about

1. Can You Improve Your Presentation?

effective presentations, use your favourite search engine(s) and some or all of the following URLs:

Presentation Resources

www.smartbiz.com/sbs/cats/sales.htm

www.lib.washington.edu/business/guides/pre.html

Presentations and Technology

www.microsoft.com/office/rtc/livemeeting

www.knowledgesystems.com

www.presentations.com

Call Centres and Telemarketing

www.nucomm.net

www.commweb.com

Public Speaking

www.nsaspeaker.org

2. Researching Prospects

The more information you have about a potential customer, the better. If your prospect is a large, internationally recognized organization, you can retrieve information from many sources, including

The Globe and Mail Report on Business: www.globeandmail.com/business

The Financial Post: www.nationalpost.com/financialpost

Business Week: www.businessweek.com

Forbes: www.forbes.com

Fortune: www.fortune.com

Fast Company: www.fastcompany.com

The business section of your local newspaper also can be a valuable resource for local companies.

For detailed information on organizations in Canada and the United States, two sites are worth investigating:

- www.sedar.com This is Canada's electronic securities documentation filing system. The database is massive and contains current and historical annual reports for Canadian companies that are registered on any of Canada's stock exchanges.

- www.edgar-online.com This is a similar site, but is based in the United States. It uses the Securities and Exchange Commission database, provides recent activities within the SEC, and provides current and historical annual report information.

FURTHER EXPLORING THE SALES WORLD

1. Ask a buyer for a business in your community about what salespeople should do when calling on a buyer. Find out whether the salespeople that this buyer sees are prepared for each sales call. Ask why or why not something was purchased. Do salespeople use the FAB method as discussed in Chapter 5? Does the buyer think privately, "So what?" "Prove it!" and "What's in it for me?" Finally, ask what superiors expect of a buyer in the buyer's dealings with salespeople.

2. Assume that you are a salesperson selling a consumer item such as a wristwatch. Without any preparation, make a sales presentation to a friend. If possible, record your sales presentation. Analyze the recording and determine the approximate

conversation time of your prospect. On the basis of your analysis, which of the four sales presentation methods discussed in Chapter 7 did you use? How early in the sales presentation did your prospect begin to give you objections?

STUDENT APPLICATION LEARNING EXERCISES (SALES) Part 4

Having considered a product or service that you intend to present, develop a potential script that you may use to secure an appointment with your intended target buyer. Review "The Telephone—A Useful Sales Tool" in this chapter to help guide you in your preparation.

SELLING EXPERIENTIAL EXERCISE

Plan Your Appearance—It Projects Your Image!

The most successful people in customer contact jobs claim that being sharp mentally means communicating a positive self-image. Like an actor, interacting with others requires you to be on stage at all times. Creating a good first impression is essential. Also important is understanding the direct connection between your attitude and your self-confidence. The better your self-image when you encounter customers, clients, or guests, the more positive you are.

On a separate sheet of paper, rate yourself on each of the following grooming areas. If you write 5, you are saying that improvement is not necessary. If you write a 1, or 2, you need considerable improvement. Be honest.[9]

	Excellent	Good	Fair	Weak	Poor
■ Hairstyle, hair grooming (appropriate length and cleanliness)	5	4	3	2	1
■ Personal cleanliness habits (body)	5	4	3	2	1
■ Clothing and jewellery (appropriate to the situation)	5	4	3	2	1
■ Neatness (shoes shined, clothes clean, well pressed, etc.)	5	4	3	2	1
■ General grooming: Does your appearance reflect professionalism on the job?	5	4	3	2	1

When it comes to appearance on the job, I rate myself:

☐ Excellent   ☐ Good   ☐ Need improvement

SELLING EXPERIENTIAL EXERCISE

Is Selling for You?

You have learned much about selling so far in this course. Let's find out how much, and at the same time better understand your attitude toward selling. Three of the following 10 statements are false. Can you find them? (Cover the answers!)

1. Dealing with customers is less exciting than the work involved in most other jobs.
2. Selling brings out the best in your personality.
3. Salespeople are made, not born; if you don't plan and work hard, you'll never be exceptional at selling.
4. Attitude is more important in selling positions than in most other jobs.
5. Those good at selling often can improve their income quickly.
6. Learning to sell now will help you succeed in any job in the future.
7. In your first sales job, what you learn can be more important than what you earn.
8. Selling is less demanding than other jobs.
9. You have little freedom in most selling positions.
10. A smile uses fewer muscles than a frown.[10]

False statements: 1, 8, and 9.

CASE 7–1

Ms. Hansen's Mental Steps in Buying Your Product

Picture yourself as a Procter & Gamble salesperson who plans to call on Ms. Hansen, a buyer for your largest independent grocery store. Your sales call objective is to convince Ms. Hansen that she should buy the family-size Tide detergent. The store now carries the three smaller sizes. You believe your marketing plan will help convince her that she is losing sales and profits by not stocking Tide's family size.

You enter the grocery store, check your present merchandise, and quickly develop a suggested order. As Ms. Hansen walks down the aisle toward you, she appears to be in her normal grumpy mood. After your initial greeting and handshake, your conversation continues:

Salesperson: Your sales are really up! I've checked your stock in the warehouse and on the shelf. This is what it looks like you need. [You discuss sales of each of your products and their various sizes, suggesting a quantity she should purchase based on her past sales and present inventory.]

Buyer: OK, that looks good. Go ahead and ship it.

Salesperson: Thank you. Say, Ms. Hansen, you've said before that the shortage of shelf space prevents you from stocking our family-size Tide—though you admit you may be losing some sales as a result. If we could determine how much volume you're missing, I think you'd be willing to make space for it, wouldn't you?

Buyer: Yes, but I don't see how that can be done.

Salesperson: Well, I'd like to suggest a test—a weekend display of all four sizes of Tide.

Buyer: What do you mean?

Salesperson: My thought was to run all sizes at regular shelf price without any ad support. This would give us a pure test. Six cases of each size should let us compare sales of the various sizes and see what you're missing by regularly stocking only the smaller sizes. I think the additional sales and profits you'll get on the family size will convince you to start stocking it regularly. What do you think?

Buyer: Well, maybe.

Questions

1. Examine each item you mentioned to Ms. Hansen, stating what part of the customer benefit plan each of your comments addresses.
2. What are the features, advantages, and benefits in your sales presentation?
3. Examine each of Ms. Hansen's replies, stating the mental buying step she is in at that particular time during your sales presentation.
4. At the end of the conversation, Ms. Hansen said, "Well, maybe." Which of the following should you do now?
   a. Continue to explain your features, advantages, and benefits.
   b. Ask a trial close question.
   c. Ask for the order.
   d. Back off and try again on the next sales call.
   e. Wait for Ms. Hansen to say, "OK, ship it."

CASE 7–2
Machinery Lubricants, Inc.

Rami Semchuk sells industrial lubricants for machinery to manufacturing plants. Tomorrow, Rami plans to call on the purchasing agent for Acme Manufacturing Company.

For the past two years, Rami has been selling Hydraulic Oil 65 in drums to Acme. Rami's sales call objective is to persuade Acme to switch from purchasing oil in drums to a bulk oil system. Last year, Acme bought approximately 364 drums or 20,000 litres at a cost of $1.39 a litre or $27,800. A deposit of $20 was made for each drum. Traditionally, many drums are lost, and one to two litres of oil may be left in each drum when returned by customers. This is a loss to Acme.

Rami wants to sell Acme two 3,000 litre storage tanks at a cost of $1,700. He has arranged with Pump Supply Company to install the tanks for $1,095. Thus, the total cost of the system will be $2,795. This system reduces the cost of the oil from $1.39 to $1.25 per litre, which will allow it to pay for itself over time. Other advantages include having fewer orders to process each year, a reduction in storage space, and less handling of the oil by workers.

Questions

If you were Rami, how would you plan the sales call?

CASE 7–3
Cascade Soap

Syed Alam sells soap products to grocery wholesalers and large retail grocery chains. The following presentation occurred during a call he made on Bill Reese, the soap buyer for a grocery store.

Syed: Bill, you have stated several times that the types of promotions or brands that really interest you are ones that carry the best profit. Is that right?

Customer: Yes, it is. I'm under pressure to increase my profit per square metre in my department.

Syed: Bill, I recommend that you begin carrying the king-size box of Cascade. Let's review the benefits and economics of this proposal. King-size Cascade would cost you 86.8¢ a box. The average resale in this market is 99¢. That means that you would make 12.2¢ every time you sell a box of king-size Cascade. Based on my estimated volume for your store of $40,000 per week, you would sell approximately two cases of king-size Cascade per week. That is $19.80 in new sales and $2.44 in new profits per week for your store. As you can see, the addition of Cascade 10 to your automatic dishwashing detergent department will increase your sales and, even more importantly, increase your profits—and this is what you said you wanted to do, right?

Customer: Yes, I am interested in increasing profits.

Syed: Do you want me to give this information to the head stock clerk so that she can make arrangements to put king-size Cascade on the shelf? Or would you like me to put it on the shelf on my next call?

Questions

1. What sales presentation method is Syed using?
2. Evaluate Syed's handling of this situation.

CASE 7–4

A Retail Sales Presentation

A customer is looking at a display of Cross gold pens and pencils.

Customer: I'm looking for a graduation gift for my brother, but I'm not necessarily looking for a pen and pencil set.

Salesperson: Is your brother graduating from college or high school?

Customer: He is graduating from college this spring.

Salesperson: I can show you quite a few items that would be appropriate gifts. Let's start by taking a look at this elegant Cross pen and pencil set. Don't they look impressive?

Customer: They look too expensive. Besides, a pen and pencil set doesn't seem like an appropriate gift for a college graduate.

Salesperson: You're right, a Cross pen and pencil set *does* look expensive. Just imagine how impressed your brother will be when he opens your gift package and finds these beautiful writing instruments. Even though Cross pen and pencil sets look expensive, they are actually quite reasonably priced, considering the total value you are getting.

Customer: How much does this set cost?

Salesperson: You can buy a Cross pen and pencil set for anywhere from $15 to $300. The one I am showing you is gold-plated and costs only $28. For this modest amount you can purchase a gift for your brother that will be attractive and useful, will last a lifetime, and will show him that you truly think he is deserving of the very best. Don't you think that is what a graduation gift should be?

Customer: You make it sound pretty good, but frankly I hadn't intended to spend that much money.

Salesperson: Naturally, I can show you something else. However, before I do that, pick up this Cross pen and write your name on this pad of paper. Notice that in addition to good looks, Cross pens offer good writing. Cross is acclaimed as one of the best ballpoint pens on the market. It is nicely balanced, has a point that allows the ink to flow onto the paper smoothly, and rides over the paper with ease.

Customer: You're right; the pen writes really well.

Salesperson: Each time your brother writes with this pen, he will remember that you gave him this fine writing instrument for graduation. In addition, Cross offers prestige. Many customers tell us that Cross is one of the few pens they have used that is so outstanding that people often comment on it by brand name. Your brother will enjoy having others notice that the pen he uses is high in quality.

Customer: You're right. I do tend to notice when someone is using a Cross pen.

Salesperson: You can't go wrong with a Cross pen and pencil set for a gift. Shall I wrap it for you?

Customer: It's a hard decision.

Salesperson: Your brother will be very happy with this gift.

Customer: Okay. Go ahead and wrap it for me.

CASE 7–4

Salesperson: Fine. Would you like me to wrap up another set for you to give yourself?

Customer: No, one is enough. Maybe someone will buy one for me someday.

Questions

1. Describe the selling techniques being used by the retail salesperson.
2. Evaluate the salesperson's handling of this situation.

CASE 7–5
Negotiating with a Friend

Barney spotted a high-quality used car on a dealer's lot over the weekend. He would have bought it immediately if he had had more cash. The dealer will give him only $1,200 on a trade-in for his current automobile. The car Barney wants is really great, and chances are good it will be sold shortly. Barney has planned carefully and decided he can swing the deal if he can sell his present vehicle to a private party for around $2,000. This would give him $1,500 for a down payment and $500 for accessories he wants to add. The car is in good condition except for a couple of minor dents in the fender. The snow tires for his current car won't fit the new one but can probably be sold; that will help. Barney can remove the new stereo system he installed last month and place it in the new car.

Billie, one of Barney's coworkers, heard that Barney wants to sell his car and plans to talk to him about it. Her daughter is graduating from college in three months and will need a car to drive to work. Billie can afford only about $1,800 including any repairs that might be required, and she needs to reserve enough money for snow tires. Her daughter has seen the car and thinks it's sporty, especially with the stereo. Billie checked the blue book price for the model of Barney's car, and she knows the average wholesale price is $1,200 and the average retail price is $1,950.

Questions

1. What are Barney's objectives?
2. What are Billie's objectives?
3. What are likely to be the points of conflict?
4. What power does Barney have?
5. What power does Billie have?
6. How important is time to Barney?
7. How important is time to Billie?
8. What are some possible points of compromise?

8

THE APPROACH—BEGIN YOUR PRESENTATION STRATEGICALLY

MAIN TOPICS

The Right to Approach

The Approach—Opening the Sales Presentation

Technology in the Approach

Using Questions Results in Sales Success

Is the Prospect Still Not Listening?

Needs Analysis—A Key to Success

Be Flexible in Your Approach

LEARNING OBJECTIVES

You have selected your prospect, planned the sales call, and determined the appropriate presentation method. Now, you must determine how to begin the sales presentation. This step in the selling process is called the approach. After studying this chapter, you should be able to:

- Explain the importance of using a strategic approach and provide examples of approaches.

- Develop an approach strategy that will effectively make a good first impression.

- Develop an effective rapport.

- Identify and discuss the importance of different types of questioning.

- Explain the importance of effective needs analysis.

- Demonstrate your understanding of multiple-question approaches such as SPIN.

FACING A SALES CHALLENGE

You are making a cold call on the office manager of a local company. You assume that one of the manager's responsibilities involves ordering office supplies. Based on your experience with other companies, you suspect the volume of orders would be small but steady throughout the year.

As a salesperson for University Office Supplies, you especially want to sell your new equipment for mailing out invoices, along with the forms and other products associated with the service. Since this is a small company, you decide to go in cold, relying on your questioning ability to uncover potential problems and make the prospect aware of them.

You are now face to face with the manager. You have introduced yourself, and after some small talk you feel it is time to begin your presentation. Many salespeople face this situation several times each day. What would you do? What type of presentation would you use? How would you begin the presentation? (Continued at end of chapter.)

Have you ever been told, "You get only one opportunity to make a good first impression"? If the first minute of talking with a prospect creates a bad impression, it can take hours to overcome it—if you ever do. Many times, salespeople get only one chance to sell a prospect.

The approach—or beginning—of your presentation is essential to the prospect's allowing you to discuss your product any further. If done incorrectly, the prospect may stop you from telling your sales story.

This chapter introduces you to the *dos* and *don'ts* of beginning your sales presentation. Many salespeople are nervous about contacting prospects, so let's begin our discussion of the approach by seeing why you have the right to talk with a prospect (see Exhibit 8–1).

THE RIGHT TO APPROACH

You have the right (or duty) to present your product if you can show that it will definitely benefit the prospect. In essence, you have to prove *you* are worthy of the prospect's time and serious attention. You may earn the right to this attention in a number of ways:

- By exhibiting specific product or business knowledge
- By expressing a sincere desire to solve a buyer's problem and satisfy a need
- By stating or implying that your product will save money or increase the firm's profit margin
- By displaying an "at your service" attitude.

Prospects want to know how you and your product will benefit *them* and *the company* they represent. Your sales approach should initially establish, and then concentrate on, your product's key benefits for each prospect.

This strategy is especially important during the approach stage of a presentation because it aids in securing the prospect's interest in you and your product. At this point, you want this unspoken reaction from the prospect: "Well, I'd better hear this salesperson out. I may hear something that will be of use to me." Now that you have justified your right to sell to a prospect, determine how to present your product.

THE APPROACH— OPENING THE SALES PRESENTATION

Jorge Chavez spent days qualifying the prospect, arranging for an appointment, and planning every aspect of the sales presentation. In the first 60 seconds of the sales presentation, he realized his chance of selling was excellent. He quickly determined the prospect's needs and evoked attention and interest in his product because of the technique he used to begin the sales presentation.

A buyer's reactions to the salesperson in the early minutes of the sales presentation are critical to a successful sale. This short period is so important that it is treated as an individual step in selling (see Exhibit 8–1), and is referred to as the approach. Part of any approach is the prospect's first impression of you (see Exhibit 8–2).

Your Attitude during the Approach

It is common for a salesperson to experience tension in when contacting a prospect. Often this stress is brought on when the salesperson has preconceived ideas that things may go wrong during the sale. Prospects may be viewed as having negative characteristics that make the sales call difficult.

All salespeople experience some degree of stress at times. Yet successful salespeople often have learned a relaxation and concentration technique called **creative imagery**, which allows them to cope with stress. The salesperson envisions the worst that can happen. Then he or she prepares how to react to it and even accept it if necessary. The best that can happen is also envisioned, as seen in Exhibit 8–3. Then contingency plans are prepared in case the planned sales talk must be abandoned.

Salespeople should ask themselves, "What are the chances that things will go wrong?" Usually, the answer involves a low probability, particularly when careful planning has taken place before the sales call. A greater than 99 percent probability that things will go as planned should dim the fears of the most worry-prone salespeople.

The First Impression You Make Is Critical to Success

When you meet your prospect, initial impressions are based on appearance. If you make a good impression, your prospect is more likely to listen to you; if not, you may face communication barriers that are difficult to overcome.

The first impression is centred on the image projected by your (1) appearance and (2) attitude. Here are some suggestions for making a favourable first impression:

- Wear business clothes that are suitable and fairly conservative.
- Be neat in dress and grooming.
- Refrain from smoking, chewing gum, or drinking when in your prospect's office.
- Stand tall to project confidence.
- Leave all unnecessary materials (overcoat, umbrella, or newspaper) outside the office.
- Remain standing until the prospect offers a chair.
- Be enthusiastic and positive toward the interview.
- Smile, always smile! (Be sincere with your smile; it help you stay enthusiastic and positive toward your prospect.)
- Do not apologize for taking the prospect's time.
- Do not imply that you were just passing by and that the sales call was not planned.
- Maintain eye contact with the prospect.
- If the prospect offers to shake hands, do so with a firm, positive grip while maintaining eye contact.
- If possible, before the interview, learn how to pronounce your prospect's name correctly, and use it throughout the interview. Should the prospect introduce you to other people, remember their names by using the five ways to remember names shown in Exhibit 8–4.

During the approach stage of the presentation, the salesperson must project and maintain a positive, confident, and enthusiastic attitude no matter the prospect's mood when first encountered by the salesperson.

EXHIBIT 8–1

The third step in the sales process is the first step in the sales presentation.

10
Follow-up

9
Close

8
Trial close

7
Meet objections

6
Determine objections

5
Trial close

4
Presentation

**3
Approach**

2
Preapproach

1
Prospecting

EXHIBIT 8–2

Making sure your attitude is positive.

Tiny brain

Small ears make hearing difficult

Mouth programmed to say "No" and "Price too high"

Small heart

Leather windbags for lungs

Cold fish hands

Big stomach to hold free meals

Dizziness

Fear of memory lapse and brain disconnecting from mouth

Dryness in mouth

Adam's apple that won't work

Rapid heartbeat

Upset stomach

Sweating palms

Trembling hands

Weakness in knees

EXHIBIT 8–3

Creative imagery is a great way to relax while psyching yourself up before seeing your prospect.

Picture worst and best that can happen, plus success.

EXHIBIT 8–4

Five ways to remember a prospect's name.

1. Be sure to hear the person's name and use it: "It's good to meet you, Mr. Firestone."
2. Spell it out in your mind or, if it is an unusual name, ask the person to spell the name.
3. Relate the name to something you are familiar with, such as relating the name Firestone to Firestone automobile tires.
4. Use the name in the conversation.
5. Repeat the name at the end of the conversation, such as "Goodbye, Mr. Firestone."

Approach Techniques and Objectives

Approach techniques are grouped into three general categories: (1) opening with a statement; (2) opening with a demonstration; and (3) opening with a question or questions.

Your choice of approach technique depends on which of the four sales presentation methods you have selected based on your situation and sales presentation plan (see Exhibit 8–5). Using questions in a sales approach is feasible with any of the four presentation methods, whereas statements and demonstrations typically are reserved for either the memorized or formula sales presentation methods. Because of their customer-oriented nature, the need-satisfaction and problem-solution sales presentation methods always involve questions at the outset. This chapter reviews each of the approach techniques with examples of their uses and benefits.

Both the statement and demonstration approach techniques have three basic objectives:

1. To capture the *attention* of the prospect.
2. To stimulate the prospect's *interest*.
3. To provide a *transition* into the sales presentation.

Imagine the prospect silently asking three questions: (1) "Should I see this person?" (2) "Should I listen, talk with, and devote more time to this person?" and (3) "What's in it for me?" The answers to these questions help determine the outcome of the sale. If you choose to use either of these two approaches, create a statement or demonstration approach that causes the prospect to say yes to each of these three questions.

SELLING TIPS

Group Presentation Checklist

✓ Voice—how you say it is as important as what you say.

✓ Body language—give the right message.

✓ Appearance—dress appropriately.

✓ Progress logically—remember your objectives.

✓ Practise—to improve your skills.

✓ Details—who and how many will attend, their titles.

✓ Handouts—prepare enough handouts for everyone.

✓ No script—makes the presentation awkward.

✓ Prepare note cards—if necessary, and number them.

✓ Include visual aids—and have a backup plan.

✓ Devise a pleasant and professional greeting—identify yourself and your organization.

✓ Introduce your objectives—an idea of what you plan to present.

✓ Summarize key selling points

✓ Encourage interaction—but maintain control.

✓ Stay within a planned time limit—finishing early is better than late.

EXHIBIT 8–5

The approach techniques for each of the four sales presentation methods.

Sales Presentation Method	Approach Technique		
	Statement	Demonstration	Questions
Memorized (canned)	✓	✓	✓
Formula (persuasive selling)	✓	✓	✓
Interactive need-satisfaction			✓
Problem solving			✓

Rapport—The Relationship Builder

The approach technique will vary depending on the type of sales call. In a retail environment, for example, a friendly greeting and an offer to help the customer find what she's looking for is short and to the point but nonetheless important for establishing that initial positive relationship and creating a positive sales environment.

In more complex selling situations, especially in business-to-business selling, the initial rapport building will set the pattern for the remainder of the call. It this situation the knowledge of buyer personality types discussed in Chapter 3 will be important in determining the type of approach to use.

Rapport building can range from small talk to more formal discussions. In the case of business-to-business sales where your call is on the purchasing agent for the company, you will want to ensure that your approach is professional at all times. Your prospect planning can be helpful in providing you with information from which you can create some positive and powerful introductory comments. For example, in doing your customer and prospect research, you scan the business pages of your local newspaper and notice that your customer or prospect company has just won a prestigious business award. There is no better way to start a selling situation than with a congratulatory comment regarding an award recently won. It also indicates that you keep abreast of your customers' or prospects' businesses.

We recommend that rapport building be based on safe, relevant topics. Topics of politics, sex, and irrelevant small talk such as the weather are best replaced with a lead-in that is relevant to the business.

The second part of the approach is the planned, formal selling technique used as the introduction to your presentation. This aspect of the approach will also vary with the situation and can be either a simple statement, a demonstration, or a series of questions. For example, if you are planning a needs-based (questions) selling approach where a formal needs analysis (see Chapter 3) is required, you will want to bridge your rapport building smoothly to the next phase. If you create a rapport that is based on relevancy to the prospect company, the transition to the needs analysis is simplified. In many cases, a simple transition comment such as, "Well, it appears that the prospects for your company are very positive, Mr. Hughes. I'm certainly hoping that my company can contribute to that bright future. However, before we determine how my company can help, do you mind if I ask some specific questions about your business to ensure that I can provide the products [or services] you need?"

The Situational Approach

The situation you face determines which approach technique you use to begin your sales presentation. The situation is dictated by a number of variables that only you can identify. Some of the more common situational variables are

- The type of *product* you are selling
- Whether this is a *repeat call* on the same person

EXHIBIT 8–6

The approach leads quickly into
the sales presentation.

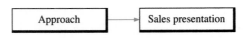

- Your degree of knowledge about the *customer's needs*
- The *time* you have for making the sales presentation
- Whether the customer is *aware of a problem.*

The sales approach can be a frightening, lonely experience. It can easily lead to ego-bruising rejection. Your challenge is to move the prospect from an often cold, indifferent, or sometimes even hostile frame of mind to an aroused excitement about the product. By quickly obtaining the prospect's attention and interest, you can make a smooth transition into the presentation that greatly improves the probability of making the sale (see Exhibit 8–6).

In addition to creating attention, stimulating interest, and providing for transition, using questions in your approach has the following objectives:

1. To *uncover* the needs or problems *important* to the prospect.
2. To determine whether the prospect wants to *fulfill* those needs or *solve* those problems.
3. To have the prospect *tell you* about these needs or problems and about the intention to do something about them.

Since people buy to fulfill needs or solve problems, the use of questions in your approach is preferable to statements or demonstrations. Questions allow you to uncover needs, whereas statements and demonstrations are used when you assume knowledge of the prospect's needs. However, any of the three approach techniques can be used by the salesperson in the appropriate situation. Exhibit 8–7 shows the three basic approach techniques and examples of each technique you will study.

Opening with Statements

Opening statements are effective if properly planned, especially if the salesperson has uncovered the prospect's needs before entering the office. Four statement approaches frequently used are (1) the introductory approach, (2) the complimentary approach, (3) the referral approach, and (4) the premium approach.

The **introductory approach** is the most common and the least powerful because it does little to capture the prospect's attention and interest. It opens with the salesperson's name and business: "Hello, Ms. Aronovitch, my name is John Gladstone, representing the Pierce Chemical Company."

The introductory approach is needed when meeting a prospect for the first time. In most cases, though, the introductory approach should be used in conjunction with another approach. This additional approach could be the complimentary approach.

EXHIBIT 8–7

Approach techniques for opening
the presentation.

Statements	Demonstrations	Questions
■ Introductory	■ Product	■ Customer benefit
■ Complimentary		■ Curiosity
■ Referral		■ Opinion
■ Premium		■ Shock
		■ Multiple question (SPIN)

Everyone likes a compliment. If the **complimentary approach** is sincere (and it *must* be sincere), is an effective beginning to a sales interview:

- Ms. Rosenburg, you certainly have a thriving restaurant business. I have enjoyed many lunches here. While doing so, I have thought of several products that could make your business even better and make things easier for you and your employees.

- Mr. Ahermaa, I was just visiting with your boss who commented that you were doing a good job in keeping your company's printing costs down. I have a couple of ideas that may help you to further reduce your costs!

Sometimes a suitable compliment is not in order or cannot be generated. Another way to get the buyer's attention is to mention a mutual acquaintance as a reference.

The use of another person's name, the **referral approach**, is effective if the prospect respects that person; it is important to remember, however, that the referral approach can have a negative effect if the prospect does not like the person:

- Ms. Kessler, my name is Carlos Ramirez, with the Restaurant Supply Corporation. When I spoke to your brother last week, he asked me to give you a chance to see Restaurant Supply's line of paper products for your restaurant.

- Hello, Mr. Gillespie. Linda Crawford with the Ramada Inn suggested that I contact you concerning our new Xerox copier.

One salesperson tells of asking the customer to tape-record a brief introduction to a friend. When calling on the friend, the salesperson placed the recorder on the desk and said, "Amos McDonald has a message for you, Ms. James . . . let's listen."

Few people can obtain a reference for every prospect they intend to contact (this may be especially true for a beginning salesperson). Even if you don't know all the right people, you can still get on track by offering the buyer something for nothing—a premium.

A **premium approach** is effective because everyone likes to receive something free. When appropriate, use free samples and novelty items in a premium approach.

- Early in the morning of her first day on a new campus, one textbook salesperson makes a practice of leaving a dozen doughnuts in the faculty lounge with her card stapled to the box. She claims that prospects actually come looking for her!

- "Mr. Jones, here is a beautiful desk calendar with your name engraved on it. Each month I will place a new calendar in the holder that, by the way, will feature one of our products. This month's calendar, for example, features our lubricating oil."

- "Ms. Fitzpatrick, this high-quality pen is yours, free, for just giving me five minutes of your time."

- "Ms. Flores [handing her the product to examine], I want to leave samples for you, your cosmetic representative, and your best customers, of Revlon's newest addition to our perfume line."

Creative use of premiums is an effective sales approach. Demonstrations also leave a favourable impression with a prospect.

Demonstration Openings

Openings using demonstrations are effective because they require the prospect to participate in the interview. The product approach is often used by itself or in combination with statements and questions.

In the **product approach**, the salesperson places the product on the counter or hands it to the customer, saying nothing. The salesperson waits for the prospect to begin the conversation. The product approach is useful if the product is new, unique, colourful, or an existing product that has changed noticeably.

If, for example, Pepsi-Cola completely changed the shape of its bottle and label, the salesperson would simply hand the new product to the retail buyer and wait for a reaction. In marketing a new pocket calculator for college students, the Texas Instruments salesperson might simply lay the product on the buyer's desk and wait.

Opening with Questions

Questions are the most common openers because they allow the salesperson to better determine the prospect's needs and require the prospect to participate in the sales interview. The salesperson should use only questions that experience and preplanning have proven receive a positive reaction from the buyer, since a negative reaction is hard to overcome.

Like opening statements, opening questions can be prepared to suit a number of selling situations. In the following sections, several basic questioning approaches are introduced. This listing is by no means exhaustive but introduces you to a selection of questioning frameworks. With experience, salespeople develop a knack for determining what question to ask which prospect.

Customer Benefit Approach

During this approach, the salesperson asks a question that implies the product will benefit the prospect. If it is their initial meeting, the salesperson can include both his and the company's name:

- Hi. I'm Cy Szakos of ABC Shipping and Storage Company! Mr. McDaniel, would you be interested in a new storage and shipping container that will reduce your transfer costs by 10 to 20 percent?
- Would you be interested in saving 20 percent on the purchase of our IBM computers?
- Ms. Frisini, did you know that several thousand companies—like yours— have saved 10 to 20 percent of their manufacturing cost as described in the *BusinessWeek* article? [Continue, not waiting for a response.] They did it by installing our computerized assembly system! Is that of interest to you?

Your **customer benefit approach** statement should be carefully constructed to anticipate the buyer's response. However, always be prepared for the unexpected, as when the salesperson said, "This office machine will pay for itself in no time at all." "Fine," the buyer said; "As soon as it does, send it to us."

A customer benefit approach can also be implemented through the use of a direct statement of product benefits. The three customer benefit questions shown earlier can be converted into benefit statements:

- Mr. McDaniel, I want to talk with you about our new storage and shipping container, which will reduce your costs by 10 to 20 percent.
- I'm here to show you how to save 20 percent on the purchase of our IBM computers.
- Ms. Frisini, several thousand companies—like yours—have saved 10 to 20 percent on their manufacturing cost by installing our computerized assembly system! I'd like 15 minutes of your time to show how we can reduce your manufacturing costs.

Benefit statements are useful in situations where you know the prospect's or customer's critical needs and have a short time to make your presentation. However, to ensure a positive atmosphere, statements can be followed by a short question—"Is that of interest to you?"—to verify that the benefits are important to the buyer. Even if you know of the buyer's interest, a positive response—"Yes"—to your question is a commitment: the buyer will listen to your presentation because of the possible benefits offered by your product.

Furthermore, you can use the buyer's response to this question as a reference point throughout your presentation. A continuation of an earlier example illustrates the use of a reference point:

- Mr. McDaniel, earlier you mentioned an interest in reducing your shipping costs. The [now mention your product's feature] enables you to [now discuss your product's advantages]. And the benefit to you is reduced shipping costs.

Sometimes, salespeople prepare an approach that temporarily baffles a prospect. One common method of baffling entails the exploration of human curiosity.

Curiosity Approach

In the **curiosity approach, t**he salesperson asks a question or does something to make the prospect curious about the product or service. See Exhibit 8–8. For example, a salesperson for McGraw-Hill Ryerson, the company that publishes this text, might use the curiosity approach by saying

- Do you know why professors such as yourself have made this textbook [as she hands the book to the prospect] the top seller in the market?

A salesperson in manufacturing might ask

- Do you know why a recent *BusinessWeek* article described our new computerized assembly system as revolutionary? [The salesperson briefly displays the *BusinessWeek* issue, then puts it away before the customer can request to look at the article. Interrupting a sales presentation by urging a prospect to review an article would lose the prospect's attention for the rest of the interview.]

EXHIBIT 8–8

The curiosity approach.

"Mr. Chan, do you know, why 300 banks use our customer information system?"

One manufacturer's salesperson sent a fax to a customer saying, "Tomorrow is the big day for you and your company." When the salesperson arrived for the interview, the prospect could not wait to find out what the salesperson's message meant.

In calling on a buyer who liked to smoke cigars, a salesperson set a cigar box on the buyer's desk. After some chatting, the buyer said, "What's in the box?" The salesperson handed the box to the buyer and said, "Open it." Inside was a product he wanted to sell. After he bought, the salesperson gave the buyer the cigars. Selling can be fun, especially if the salesperson enjoys being creative.

Opinion Approach

People are usually flattered when asked their opinion on a subject. Most prospects are happy to discuss their needs if asked correctly. Here are some examples:

- I'm new at this business, so I wonder if you could help me? My company says our Model 100 copier is the best on the market for the money. What do you think?
- Mr. Jackson, I've been trying to sell you for months on using our products. What is your honest opinion about our line of electric motors?

The **opinion approach** is especially good for the new salesperson because it shows that you value the buyer's opinion. Opinion questioning also shows that you will not challenge a potential buyer's expertise by spouting a memorized pitch.

Shock Approach

As its title implies, the **shock approach** uses a question designed to make the prospect think seriously about a subject related to the salesperson's product. For example,

- Did you know that you have a 20 percent chance of having a heart attack this year? (Life insurance)
- Did you know that home burglary has increased this year by 15 percent over last year, according to the local police? (Alarm system)
- Shoplifting costs store owners millions of dollars each year! Did you know that there is a good chance you have a shoplifter in your store right now? (Store cameras and mirrors)

This type of question is often used in transactional-type selling and must be used carefully, since some prospects may feel you are merely trying to pressure them into a purchase by making alarming remarks.

An Approach Checklist   We know that first impressions will often make or break the success of a sales presentation; therefore, preparation for the approach is essential.

1. Ensure you're meeting the right person (the "qualified" kind).
2. Confirm your appointment (as mentioned during the preapproach).
3. Familiarize yourself with the structure of your prospect's company.
4. Prepare your sales aids and visuals and have a back-up plan. Many salespeople find it useful to have an electronic presentation stored in their e-mail account or their company's Web site so they can access it if there are technical difficulties.
5. Ensure that you have directions and maps and anticipate traffic and drive times.
6. Arrive 10–20 minutes early in most situations to allow time for setup.
7. Organize all materials, and know exactly where they are so you can easily retrieve them. Customized materials are a nice touch.

8. Prepare a list of questions that you may need to ask to uncover problems.

9. Don't fret! Anticipate success and a positive experience.

10. Relax and enjoy it. Don't be too aggressive, and pay attention to your audience's reactions.

Proper planning and attention to detail will not go unnoticed by your prospects. Many salespeople have lost sales due to a lack of planning and preparation.

TECHNOLOGY IN THE APPROACH   A salesperson can quickly capture a prospect's attention and interest by using technology. Technology can be a wonderful way to creatively and professionally begin a sales presentation. Sounds, visuals, and touch cause the prospect's mind to instantly focus on the salesperson's words and actions.

SELLING GLOBALLY

Appreciating Our Multicultural Country

In Canada, people from many different cultural backgrounds present a tremendous opportunity for salespeople to increase their sales.

Salespeople should work to develop a diverse customer base. Salespeople who educate themselves on the differences in buying behaviour may see their investment pay off handsomely.

The general manager for a large construction company once had to make last-minute design changes to certain gambling rooms in a new casino because a potential high-stakes gambler, visiting the construction site, complained that the "energy" in the room was not just right. This is just one of many ways in which different cultures may vary in the way they do business.

Some Tips:

1. Remember that not all cultures are comfortable being greeted in the same way. You might assume that everyone wants to be met with a firm handshake; however, a handshake can actually be offensive to some people.

2. Don't assume that you know how prospects want to be greeted. Let them determine the most comfortable greeting by hesitating before extending your hand and seeing what they do first. Most men in Canada, regardless of cultural background, will offer a handshake and may even nod as they do so. Simply do the same.

3. Use caution between the genders. In some Middle Eastern and Asian cultures, women are very uncomfortable, if not forbidden, to touch an opposite-gender person other than their spouse.

4. Be sensitive to the fact that some culture are used to hugging and even kissing people on one or both cheeks. If this happens, take it as a sign that they are comfortable with you and return the gesture. Men from the Middle East often shake hands with a slight nod and then exchange kisses on both cheeks. Traditional Muslim men may shake hands and then touch the right palm of their hand to their heart as a sign of friendship. Men from this part of the world usually do not shake hands with women. They often do not introduce women who accompany them nor is it expected that you shake hands with women. This may appear very awkward—but it's business. The rule of thumb in international greeting then is: do your research and never assume anything!

5. Personal space varies among cultures. In Canada, we are used to shaking hands and then standing about a metre apart. However, Japanese people may bow or shake hands and then take a step back. This may seem awkward to a Canadian trying to communicate from a greater distance. Don't step forward to bridge the gap as will be a violation of their personal space. Some cultures prefer a smaller distance. These include people from the Middle East who may hug you and stay at that distance. Don't step back.

6. Some cultures avoid lots of direct eye contact. Don't be alarmed by this; it may be a sign of respect. On the other hand, certain cultures believe that "the eyes are the window to the soul," and hence will maintain complete eye contact. This can be just as uncomfortable for westerners. Be prepared for it.

However, salespeople should never rely on technology alone in case the technology does not perform at that given moment. As well, some buyers are still somewhat hesitant when it comes to technological advances.

USING QUESTIONS RESULTS IN SALES SUCCESS

Asking questions, sometimes called **probes**, is an excellent technique for (1) obtaining information from the prospect, (2) developing two-way communication, and (3) increasing prospect participation.

When using questions in selling, you need to know or anticipate the answer you want. Once you know the answer you want, you can develop the question. This procedure can be used to not only request information you do not have but also confirm information you already know.

Only questions that help make the sale should be asked, so use questions sparingly and wisely.

You can use four basic categories of questions at any point during the presentation: (1) direct, (2) open-ended, (3) rephrasing, and (4) redirect questions.

The Direct Question

The **direct question** or **closed-ended question** is answered in very few words. A simple yes or no answers most direct questions. They are especially useful in moving a customer toward a specific topic. Examples the salesperson might use are: "Mr. Berger, are you interested in saving 20 percent on your manufacturing costs?" or, "Reducing manufacturing costs is important, isn't it?" You can anticipate a yes response to these questions.

Never phrase the direct question as a direct negative–no question. A *direct negative–no question* is any question that can be answered in a manner that cuts you off completely. The retail salesperson says, "May I help you?" and the reply usually is, "No, I'm just looking." You are completely cut off.

Other types of direct questions ask "What kind?" or "How many?" The questions also ask for a limited, short answer from the prospect. The implication and need-payoff questions used in SPIN (discussed later in this chapter) are examples of direct questions used for the approach.

However, the answer to a direct question does not really tell you much, because little feedback is provided. You may need more information to determine the buyer's needs and problems, especially if you could not determine them before the sales call.

The Open-ended Question

To open up two-way communication, the salesperson can use an **open-ended question** by beginning the question with one of six words: Who, what, where, when, how, or why. Examples include

- Who will use this product?
- What features are you looking for in a product like this?
- Where will you use this product?
- When will you need the product?
- How often will you use the product?
- Why do you need or want to buy this type of product?

One-word questions such as "Oh?" or "Really?" can also be useful in some situations. One-word questions should be said so that the customer is prompted to continue talking. Try it—it works.

To practise using the open-ended questioning technique, ask a friend a question— any question—beginning with one of these six words, or use a one-word question,

MAKING THE SALE
Be Patient!

In selling, the person who asks the questions controls the situation. The information obtained from asking questions is necessary to determine the prospect's likes, dislikes, and areas to avoid. This valuable information also informs the salesperson whether the customer is ready to buy or whether the salesperson should continue selling.

Some salespeople are good at asking questions, but they tend to be impatient and don't offer the buyer an opportunity to answer. Remember—it doesn't matter how long it takes for a buyer's response. Be patient!

and see what answer you get. Chances are, the response will consist of several sentences. In a selling situation, this type of response allows the salesperson to better determine the prospect's needs.

The Rephrasing Question

The third type of question is the **rephrasing question**. At times, the prospect's meaning is not clearly stated. In this situation, if appropriate, the salesperson might say:

- "Are you saying that price is most important to you?" [sincerely, not too aggressively]
- "Then what you are saying is, if I can improve the delivery time, you would be interested in buying?"

This form of restatement allows you to clarify meaning and determine the prospect's needs. If the prospect answers yes to the second question, you would find a way to improve delivery. If the answer is no, you know delivery time is not an important buying motive; continue to probe for the real problem.

The Redirect Question

The fourth type of question is the **redirect question**. It is used to redirect the prospect to selling points that both parties agree on. There are always areas of agreement between buyer and seller even if the prospect is opposed to purchasing the product. The redirect question is an excellent alternative or backup opener. The following example clarifies the concept of redirective questioning.

Imagine you walk into a prospect's office, introduce yourself, and get this response, "I'm sorry, but there is no use in talking. We are satisfied with our present suppliers. Thanks for coming by." Respond by replacing your planned opener with a redirecting question. You might say:

- "Can we agree that having a supplier who can reduce your costs is an asset to your company?"
- "You would agree that manufacturers must use the most cost-efficient equipment to stay competitive these days, wouldn't you?"
- "Wouldn't you agree that you continually need to find new ways to increase your company's sales?"

Using a redirect question moves the conversation from a negative position to a positive or neutral one while re-establishing communication. The ability to redirect a seemingly terminated conversation using a question may impress the prospect simply by showing that you are not a run-of-the-mill order taker but a professional salesperson who sincerely believes in the benefits of your product.

Three Rules for Using Questions

The first rule is to use only questions that can easily be answered by the prospect. Avoid asking questions that are complicated or those that a prospect may not be able to answer. Salespeople are working to build a positive rapport at this stage of the process, so putting prospects on the defensive, or intimidating them, may prove harmful to this budding relationship.

The second rule is to pause after a question to allow the prospect time to respond. Waiting for an answer to a well-planned question is sometimes an excruciating process—seconds may seem like minutes. A salesperson must allow the prospect time to consider the question, and hope for a response. Failing to allow a prospect enough time defeats the major purpose of questioning, which is to establish two-way communication between the prospect and the salesperson.

The third rule is to listen. Many salespeople are so intent on talking that they forget to listen to what the prospect says (or disregard nonverbal signals). Salespeople need to listen consciously to prospects so they can ask intelligent, meaningful questions to determine their prospects' needs and how to solve them. Prospects appreciate a good listener and view a willingness to listen as an indication that the salesperson is truly interested in their situation.

IS THE PROSPECT STILL NOT LISTENING?

What happens when, using your best opening approach, you realize that the prospect is not listening? What about prospects who open mail, who fold their arms while looking at the wall or beyond you into the hallway, who make telephone calls in your presence, or who may even doze off?

This is the time to use one of your alternative openers. The prospect must be forced to participate in the talk by using either the question or demonstration approach. By handing the person something, showing something, or asking a question, attention can be briefly recaptured, no matter how indifferent a prospect is to your presence.

If you can overcome such preoccupation or indifference, the probability of your making a sale will greatly improve. This is why the approach is so important to the success of a sales call.

Never become flustered or confused when a communication problem arises during your approach. As mentioned earlier, the salesperson who can deftly capture another person's imagination earns the right to a prospect's full attention and interest.

NEEDS ANALYSIS—A KEY TO SUCCESS

During the first few minutes of the approach stage, salespeople will attempt to set the stage for the interview by establishing a rapport, getting the prospect's attention, and arousing his or her desire to listen to the presentation. Before getting into the presentation, it is very useful for salespeople to perform a needs analysis.

Learning the buyer's needs and wants and determining which are the most important is a key part of effective selling. It is accomplished through research, skillful questioning, listening, and observation. In business-to-business selling, research begins during prospecting (Chapter 6) and expands during the preapproach stage (Chapter 7), before you communicate with the buyer. Questioning, listening, and observing are particularly important once you are in contact with the buyer.

Needs analysis enables you as the salesperson to diagnose the buyer's situation before prescribing a product or service solution. Ideally, complete your analysis of buyer needs before starting to provide product information. Sometimes, however, buyers want you to start talking about your product right away because they are impatient or unaware of the value of exploring needs. Avoid the temptation to skip needs analysis altogether. At the very least, convince the prospect that it is worthwhile to spend a few minutes exploring key needs.

It is helpful to prevent potential buyer resistance to needs analysis. You can do this by sharing with the prospect your reasons for conducting needs analysis and then obtaining his or her agreement to participate before you begin asking needs analysis questions.

Needs Questions Should Focus on Results

What should a salesperson ask about during needs analysis? While the purpose is to discover important needs and wants, a question such as, "Do you need my product?" is likely to draw a negative response. Instead, needs analysis questions should focus on what *results* the buyer is seeking—what he or she desires to be different from the present.

Let's say a man walks into a hardware store and says to a salesperson, "I need a drill." How should the salesperson respond? A poor salesperson might point to the aisle and say, "Over there, in aisle three." Another might lead the man to the display of drills and begin describing the various makes and models available. Both of these employees would be making the mistake of omitting needs analysis.

A third salesperson might pose several questions such as, "What size of motor do you want?" and "Do you want the metal casing or the plastic?" and "Do you need one with a reverse gear?" This salesperson deserves credit for attempting to conduct needs analysis; however, the questions should be results focused, not product focused. Better questions would be, "What do you intend to use the drill for?" and "What type of holes do you need?" and "How many holes are you planning to drill?" and "What material will you be drilling through?" These types of questions delve into the results sought by the buyer and provide valuable information for the salesperson.

Although buyers have more product knowledge today than at any time in the past, the salesperson has the most product knowledge and is in the best position to help the buyer make decisions that will yield a satisfied customer in the long term.

Structure Needs Analysis Using Multiple-Question Approaches

Needs analysis is best done by using open-ended questions. One strategy is to begin by asking general questions and gradually move to more specific questions. For example, a photocopier salesperson might begin with, "How much do you expect your company will grow over the next two years?" and conclude with, "What would be the best timing for your staff to receive training on new equipment?"

Another method of organizing needs analysis questions is called **SPIN**. It involves using a series of four types of questions in a specific sequence.[1] SPIN stands for **s**ituation, **p**roblem, **i**mplication, and **n**eed payoff. Let's look at each step in the sequence.

In Step 1, the salesperson uses one or more questions to find out about the prospect's current general situation. These probes need to be related to the salesperson's product or service. For example, an electric cart salesperson might ask a prospect, "How large are your manufacturing plant facilities?"

The salesperson then moves to Step 2 by asking about specific problems, dissatisfactions, or difficulties perceived by the prospect relative to the current situation. Problem questions can raise the level of needs awareness. For example, "How often do your executives complain about having to do so much walking around the plant?" The goal is to have the prospect realize that she does, in fact, have a problem.

For Step 3, the salesperson explores the implications of the problems for the prospect. Implication questions reveal the true dimensions of the problems, and how they affect the prospect or the organization. An example used by the electric cart salesperson might be "What impact is the time and energy of this walking around the plant having on the efficiency of your executives?"

Determine the current Situation.

"How long has this problem been going on with your current product?"

"How many of your employees use this product each day?"

"Are you planning any expansion in the next couple of years?"

"Do you own the product or do you lease it?"

"Is your current product causing any other problems?"

Ask Problem questions.

"Have you had an increase in the number of service calls on this product recently?"

"Do your office workers find the downtime annoying?"

"Does extensive downtime have an impact on your bottom line?"

Ask about the Implications.

"What do your office workers do when this product is not functioning?"

"How much time do you think gets wasted each month waiting for a service call?"

"Are your customers being affected by this product's deficiencies?"

Ask about the Need payoff.

"If I could show you how our new product would reduce or eliminate service calls, would you be interested?"

"Would a one-hour response time by our service department make your office workers happier and more productive?"

"Would the increase in speed that this product would give you improve the customer service level that you could provide your clientele?"

In Step 4, the salesperson poses need–payoff questions that determine how motivated the prospect is to solve the problems. Need–payoff questions reveal what needs the prospect perceives as important. For example, the electric cart salesperson may ask, "How important is reducing your executives' travel time getting around the plant?"

Although the SPIN sequence is designed to move the conversation logically from one step to the next, situation, problem, and implication questions do not have to be asked strictly in order. You will generally begin with a situation question and follow with a problem question. However, you could ask a situation question, a problem question, and another situation question, for example. As well, you can ask more than one of each type. The need–payoff question is always last.

You enjoy selling but often find it difficult to get the ball rolling during sales interviews. You try to get the prospects' attention but they never seem to get turned on to your product. You know your product is good—in fact, previous customers have saved an average of 10 percent in their fuel costs while using it. One of your previous customers purchased your product at the same time as buying a new fleet of smaller, fuel-efficient vehicles, which resulted in that company using 50 percent less fuel in the following year.

With this information, you try a different approach to capture the attention of your next prospect. Read this dialogue:

Seller: "Mr. Buyer, the reason I'm here today is to introduce to you our fuel-saving device, which has been found to save 50 percent of fuel costs in some delivery fleets. Does this sound like it may be useful in your company?"

Buyer: "Fifty percent? That sounds fantastic—let me clear my desk here—I'd love to hear more."

Finally, you have a prospect who is truly interested in what you have to say. It worked!

Have you done the right thing?

What other techniques might you consider using?

Needs Analysis by E-Mail

Most salespeople conduct needs analysis while meeting face to face with the prospect or talking with him or her on the telephone. It is also possible to uncover needs and wants by sending the prospect a questionnaire by e-mail. This may be more appropriate than a face-to-face interview because of factors such as the distance between the salesperson and prospect, scheduling challenges, or the need for the prospect to consult with others to answer the questions. The questionnaire developed by Robert J. Watson, president of Robert Watson Photography, formerly known as Bear Photography Ltd., in Regina, is used in person or sent by e-mail depending on the situation (see Exhibit 8–9).

This questionnaire is quite extensive; however, an effective e-mail may simply ask the prospect, prior to the meeting, to identify two or three major buying criteria or motives. This information will certainly help in the presentation phase.

BE FLEXIBLE IN YOUR APPROACH

Picture yourself as a salesperson getting ready to come face to face with an important prospect, Ellen Myerson. You have planned exactly what you are to say in the sales presentation, but how can you be sure Myerson will listen to your sales presentation? You realize she is busy and may be indifferent to your being in the office; she probably is preoccupied with her own business-related situation, and several of your competitors already may have seen her today.

You have planned to open your presentation with a statement about how successful your laptop computer has been in helping office workers save time and eliminate errors in their keyboarding. When you enter the office, Myerson comments on how efficient her office workers are and how they produce error-free work. From her remarks, you quickly determine that your planned statement approach is inappropriate. What do you do now?

You might begin by remarking how lucky she is to have such conscientious office workers, and then proceed into the SPIN question approach, first asking questions to determine general problems that she may have, and then using further questions to uncover specific problem areas she might like to solve. Once you have determined specific problems, you can ascertain whether they are important enough for her to want to solve them in the near future. If so, you can make a statement that summarizes how your product's benefits will solve her critical needs, and test for a positive response. A positive response allows you to conditionally move into the sales presentation.

SUMMARY OF MAJOR SELLING ISSUES

As the first step in your sales presentation, the approach is a critical factor. To ensure your prospects' attention and interest during a memorized or formula mode of presentation, you may want to use a statement or demonstration approach. In more technically oriented situations where you and the prospects must agree on needs and problems, a questioning approach (SPIN, for instance) is in order. Generally, in developing your approach, imagine your prospects asking themselves, "Do I have time to listen to, talk with, or devote to this person? What's in it for me?"

Words alone will not ensure that you are heard. The first impression that you make on a prospect can negate your otherwise positive and sincere opening. To ensure a favourable impression in most selling situations, dress conservatively, be well groomed, and be truly glad to meet the prospect.

Your approach statement should be customized for each prospect. You can choose to open with a statement, question, or demonstration by using any one of the techniques.

EXHIBIT 8–9

A needs analysis questionnaire such as this one developed by Robert J. Watson, president of Bear Photography Ltd. in Regina can assist the salesperson during a face-to-face meeting. It can also be sent to the prospect by fax or e-mail.

Information about You and Your Wedding Plans

Date and Time of Wedding _____

Date and Time of Rehearsal _____

Bride's Name, Address, and Phone No. _____

Groom's Name, Address, and Phone No. _____

Following Wedding, Couple Will Reside At _____

Location of Wedding _____

Officiating Clergy and Phone Number _____

Bride's Parents _____

Groom's Parents _____

Honeymoon? Duration _____

Bride Will Be Dressing at _____

Time of Pictures at Bride's House _____

Bride's Attendants _____

Groom's Attendants _____

Ring bearer/Flower Girl _____

Total Number in Wedding Party _____

Location for Formal Pictures and Alternate Site _____

Reception to Be Held Where, What Time _____

Will There Be a Receiving Line? _____

Approx. Time of Cake Cutting, Garter, and Bouquet _____

How Did Bride and Groom Meet? _____

Any Special Hobbies or Shared Interests? _____

Any Special Picture Ideas? _____

Any Pictures Required of Special People? (List Below) _____

PHOTOGRAPH POSES
(Check Appropriate Boxes)

BRIDE'S HOUSE
- ☐ misc. getting ready shots
- ☐ bride and maid of honour
- ☐ bride pins flower on mother
- ☐ bride alone formal
- ☐ bride's headpiece with maid of honour
- ☐ bride and bridesmaids
- ☐ bride pins boutonniere on father
- ☐ bride puts on garter

CHURCH
- ☐ groom with best man
- ☐ bride and father out of car
- ☐ grandparents being seated
- ☐ bride's mother being seated
- ☐ bridesmaids walking down aisle
- ☐ bride and father walking down aisle
- ☐ wedding party from rear
- ☐ groom and attendants
- ☐ bride and father enter church
- ☐ groom's mother being seated
- ☐ flower girl and ring bearer in aisle
- ☐ maid of honour walking down aisle
- ☐ bride and groom kissing at altar
- ☐ wedding party from choir loft (if one)

CEREMONY
- ☐ bride and groom at altar
- ☐ communion (if applicable)
- ☐ bride and groom kiss
- ☐ bride and groom face congregation
- ☐ bride and groom exit church
- ☐ ring exchange
- ☐ unity candle ceremony (if applicable)
- ☐ signing register
- ☐ bride and groom coming down aisle

FORMALS
- ☐ bride and her family
- ☐ bride and groom with parents
- ☐ bride with women
- ☐ groom with men
- ☐ bride portraits
- ☐ ring shot
- ☐ groom and his family
- ☐ bridal party
- ☐ bride with men
- ☐ groom with women
- ☐ bride and groom portraits
- ☐ groom portraits

RECEPTION
- ☐ bride and groom enter hall
- ☐ head table
- ☐ bride and groom dance
- ☐ cake cutting
- ☐ groom removes garter
- ☐ receiving line
- ☐ speeches and toasts
- ☐ bride and groom dance with parents
- ☐ bride throwing bouquet
- ☐ groom throws garter

NOTES:

_____

_____

_____

_____

_____

_____

_____

_____

_____

_____

_____

_____

_____

_____

_____

_____

_____

_____

MEETING A SALES CHALLENGE

Questions are important tools for salespeople. They help uncover needs and problems, obtain valuable selling information, and qualify the prospect's interest and buying authority. So it pays to ask good ones.

Since you may need to first develop an analysis of the company operation, begin with questions that are direct, well aimed, and, most importantly, force the prospect to talk about a specific problem. Questions that cannot be answered *yes* or *no* provide the most information. A multiple-question approach, such as SPIN, would be appropriate for this situation.

Several alternative approaches should be ready in case you need to alter your plans for a specific situation.

Carefully phrased questions are useful at any point in a sales presentation. Questions should display a sincere interest in prospects and their situations. Skillfully handled questions employed in a sales approach can wrest a prospect's attention from distractions and centre it on you and your presentation. Questions are generally used to determine prospects' wants and needs, thereby increasing prospect participation in the sales presentation. Four basic types of questions discussed in this chapter are direct, open-ended, rephrasing, and redirect questions.

In using questions, ask the type of questions to which you can anticipate the answer. Also, remember to allow prospects time to completely answer the question. Listen carefully to their answers as a guide to how well you are progressing toward selling to them. Should you determine that your prospect is not listening, regain his or her attention. Techniques such as offering something or asking questions can refocus the prospect's attention.

PLAYING THE ROLE

The situation: You are a salesperson for a hockey stick manufacturer. Your company has just developed a revolutionary new hockey stick that is lighter. Its flexibility allows for better stickhandling and a harder shot. You have an appointment with the general manager of a professional hockey team and want them to purchase your sticks for the organization.

Role A: Sales Rep 1—Prepare an effective curiosity approach

Role B: Sales Rep 2—Prepare an effective shock approach

Role C: Sales Rep 3—Prepare an effective benefit approach

Role D: Sales Rep 4—Prepare an effective complimentary approach

Role E: General Manager for the pro hockey team)

Each rep should dramatize a prepared approach to the general manager. Observers can judge and defend which is the most effective.

SALES APPLICATION QUESTIONS

1. Explain the reasons for using questions when making a sales presentation. Discuss the rules for questioning that should be followed by the salesperson.
2. What are three general categories of the approach? Give an example of each.
3. In each of the following instances, determine whether a direct, open-ended, rephrasing, or redirect question is being used. Discuss the benefits of each of the four types of questions.
   a. "Now let's see whether I have this right; you are looking for a high-quality product and price is no object?"
   b. "What type of clothes are you looking for?"
   c. "Are you interested in Model 101 or Model 921?"
   d. "Well, I can appreciate your beliefs, but you would agree that price is not the only thing to consider when buying a copier, wouldn't you?"
   e. "When would you like to have your new Xerox 9000 installed?"
   f. "Are you saying that *where* you go for vacation is more important than the cost of getting there?"
   g. "You would agree that saving time is important to a busy executive like you, wouldn't you?"
4. Which of the following approaches do you think is the best? Why? Can you make suggestions as to how each could be improved?
   a. "Ms. Silva, in the past, you've made it a practice to reduce the facings on heavy-duty household detergents in the winter months because of slower movement."
   b. "Mr. Galdanzo, you'll recall that last time I was in, you expressed concern over the fact that your store labour was running higher than the industry average of 8 percent of sales."
   c. "Hi! I'm Jeanette Smith of Procter & Gamble, and I'd like to talk to you about Cheer. How's it selling?"
5. Assume you are a salesperson for POS Systems Corporation and you want to sell Mr. Malik, the owner/manager of a large independent supermarket, your computerized customer checkout system. You have just met Mr. Malik inside the front door of the supermarket. After your initial introduction, the conversation continues:

   Salesperson: Mr. Malik, your customers are really backed up at your cash registers, aren't they?

   Buyer: Yeah, it's a real problem.

   Salesperson: Do your cashiers ever make mistakes when they are in a rush?

   Buyer: They sure do!

   Salesperson: Have you ever thought about shortening checkout time while reducing cashier errors?

   Buyer: Yes, but those methods are too expensive!

   Salesperson: Does your supermarket generate more than $1 million in sales each month?

   Buyer: Yes, why?

   Salesperson: Would you be interested in discussing a method of decreasing customer checkout time 50 percent and greatly lessening the number of errors made by your cashiers, if I can show you that the costs of solving your problems will be more than offset by your savings?

    a. Using the framework of the SPIN approach technique, determine whether each of the above questions asked by the salesperson is a **s**ituation, **p**roblem, **i**mplication, or **n**eed–payoff question.

    b. If Mr. Malik says yes to your last question, what should you do next?

    c. If Mr. Malik says no to your last question, what should you do next?

6. As a salesperson for Gatti's Electric Company, Cliff Defee is interested in selling John Bonham more of his portable electric generators. John is a construction supervisor for a firm specializing in constructing large buildings such as shopping centres, office buildings, and manufacturing plants. He currently uses three of Cliff's newest models. Cliff just learned that John will be building a new manufacturing plant. As Cliff examines the specifications for the new plant, he believes John will require several additional generators. Two types of approaches Cliff might make are depicted in the following situations:

Situation A:

    Salesperson: I see you got the Jonesville job.

    Buyer: Sure did.

    Salesperson: Are the specs OK?

    Buyer: Yes.

    Salesperson: Will you need more machines?

    Buyer: Yes, but not yours!

Situation B:

    Salesperson: I understand you have three of our electric sets.

    Buyer: Yes, I do.

    Salesperson: I'm sure you'll need additional units on your next job.

    Buyer: You're right, I will.

    Salesperson: Well, I've gone over your plant specifications and put together the products you will need.

    Buyer: What I don't *need* are any of your lousy generators.

    Salesperson: Well, that's impossible. It's a brand-new design.

    Buyer: Sorry, I've got to go.

    a. Briefly describe both approaches in situations A and B. In both situations, Cliff is in a tough spot. What should he do now?

    b. What type of approach could Cliff have made that would have allowed him to uncover John's dissatisfaction? Would the approach you are suggesting also be appropriate if John were satisfied with the generators?

7. This is a cold call on the warehouse manager for Coats Western Wear, a retailer with four stores. You know most of the manager's work consists of deliveries from the warehouse to the four stores. Based on your experience, you suspect that the volume of shipments to the warehouse fluctuates; certain seasons of the year are extremely busy.

    As a salesperson for Hercules Shelving, you want to sell the manager your heavy-duty-gauge steel shelving for use in the warehouse. Since this is a relatively small sale, you decide to go in cold, relying only on your questioning ability to uncover potential problems and make the prospect aware of them.

You are now face to face with the warehouse manager. You have introduced yourself and after some small talk it is time to begin your approach. Which of the following questions would be best? Rank each from what you think would be best to worst.

a. "Have you had any recent storage problems?"
b. "How do you take care of your extra storage needs during busy seasons?"
c. "Can you tell me a little about your storage problems?"

SALES WORLD WIDE WEB EXERCISES

Can the World Wide Web Help Build Relationships?

The ultimate outcome of relationship selling is the building of a partnership between the seller and the buyer. More and more companies are using the Web to stay in touch with customers.

Look for documents, such as annual reports, that describe a company's sales, profits, markets, and customers. Check to see whether the company is collecting information from you, such as by having you complete a questionnaire. Then write a report to your boss discussing your findings. Include your suggestions on how an organization can use the Web to build long-term relationships with its customers and attract new customers.

FURTHER EXPLORING THE SALES WORLD

1. Television advertisements are developed to capture your attention and interest to sell a product or service quickly. Examine at least five commercials and report on the method each used to get your attention, stimulate your interest, and move you from this attention–interest phase into discussing the product. Determine whether the first few seconds of the commercial related to the product's features, advantages, or benefits, and if so, how? Using a tape recorder may help you.
2. Assume that you have a 30-minute job interview next week with a representative of a company you are really interested in. How would you prepare for the interview, and what could you do during the first few minutes of the interview to get the recruiter interested in hiring you? Can you see any differences between this interview situation and the environment of a salesperson making a sales call?

STUDENT APPLICATION LEARNING EXERCISES (SALES)

Part 5

For this part of your SALE, first select the method that you will use for your presentation (see Chapter 7). Next, write down the name of the approach technique you will use for this presentation method (Chapter 8).

Presentation method:

Approach technique:

Prepare statements that you will actually use in your approach, including what the buyer would likely say. Relate your approach to the FABs developed earlier in your FAB worksheet.

Seller:

Buyer:

Imagine that you have finished your approach. Write out the buyer–seller dialogue for two SELL Sequences. A SELL Sequence is an acronym: **S**how feature, **E**xplain advantage, **L**ead into benefit and **L**et customer talk. Create responses that your buyer will likely use to reply to each of the SELL sequences.

SEQUENCE 1
Seller:

Buyer:

SEQUENCE 2
Seller:

Buyer:

With a partner, role-play your approach and SELL sequences to see whether you are satisfied. If available, use a tape recorder to listen to your speed, voice inflections, phrases, and any other unwanted mannerisms such as slang, or repeating the words "uh," "okay," "like," or "I see." If you have access to a video camera, videotape your role-play to look for any physical mannerisms that could affect the quality of your approach such as a prolonged handshake, poor posture, loss of eye contact, or fidgeting. Upon completion, ask your partner if you and your approach strategy would have impressed her.

CASE 8–1
The Thompson Company

Before making a cold call on the Thompson Company, you did some research on the account. Barbara Thompson is both president and chief purchasing officer. In this dual capacity, she often is so rushed that she is impatient with salespeople. She is known for her habit of quickly turning down a salesperson and ending the discussion by turning and walking away. In looking over Thompson's operation, you notice that the inefficient metal shelving she uses in her warehouse is starting to collapse. Warehouse employees have attempted to remedy the situation by building wooden shelves and reinforcing the weakened metal shelves with lumber. They also have begun stacking boxes on the floor, requiring much more space.

You recognize the importance of getting off to a fast start with Thompson. You must capture her attention and interest quickly or she may not talk with you.

Questions

Which of the following attention-getters would you choose:

1. Ms. Thompson, I'd like to show you how Hercules shelving can save you both time and money.

2. Ms. Thompson, can you spare a few minutes of your time to talk about new shelving for your warehouse?

3. Ms. Thompson, how would you like to double your storage space?

CASE 8–2
The Copy Corporation

Assume you are contacting the purchasing agent for office supplies of a large chain of retail department stores. After hearing that the company is opening 10 new stores, you determine that it will need a copier for each store. Three months earlier, you had sold this purchasing agent a lease agreement on two large machines. The buyer wanted to try your machines in the company's new stores. If they liked them, you would get the account. Unknown to you, one of the machines is now causing the purchasing agent to experience pressure from a store manager to replace it immediately. As you walk into the purchasing agent's office, you say:

Salesperson: I understand you are opening 10 new stores in the next six months.

Buyer: I don't know who told you!

Salesperson: If you'll let me know when you want a copier at each store, I'll arrange for it to be there.

Buyer: Look, I don't want any more of your lousy copiers! When the leases expire, I want you here to pick them up, or I'll throw them out in the street. I've got a meeting now. I want to see you in three months.

Questions

1. Describe this situation, commenting on what the salesperson did correctly and incorrectly.
2. Develop another approach the salesperson could use to uncover the problems experienced by the purchasing agent.

CASE 8–3
Electronic Office Security Corporation

Ann Saroyan is a salesperson for the Electronic Office Security Corporation. She sells industrial security systems that detect intruders and activate an alarm. When Ann first began selling, she used to make brief opening remarks to her prospects and then move quickly into her presentation. Although this resulted in selling many of her security systems, she felt there must be a better method.

Ann began to analyze the reasons that prospects would not buy. Her conclusion was that even after her presentation, prospects still did not believe they needed a security alarm system. She decided to develop a multiple-question approach that would allow her to determine the prospect's attitude toward a need for a security system. If the prospect does not initially feel a need for her product, she wants her approach to help convince the prospect of a need for a security system.

Ann developed and carefully rehearsed her new sales presentation. Her first sales call using her multiple-question approach was with a large accounting firm. She asked the receptionist whom she should see and was referred to Joe Bell. After she waited 20 minutes, Bell asked her to come into his office. The conversation went like this:

1. **Salesperson:** This is a beautiful old building, Mr. Bell. Have you been here long?
   Buyer: About 10 years. Before we moved here, we were in one of those ugly glass and concrete towers. Now, you wanted to talk to me about office security.

2. **Salesperson:** Yes, Mr. Bell. Tell me, do you have a burglar alarm system at present?
   Buyer: No, we don't. We've never had a break-in here.

CASE 8–3

3. **Salesperson:** I see. Could you tell me what's the most valuable item in your building?
   Buyer: Probably the computer.

4. **Salesperson:** And is it fairly small?
   Buyer: Yes, it's not much bigger than a typewriter.

5. **Salesperson:** Would it be difficult to run your business without it—if it were stolen for example?
   Buyer: Oh, yes, that would be quite awkward.

6. **Salesperson:** Could you tell me a bit more about the problem you would face without your computer?
   Buyer: It would be inconvenient in the short term for our accounts and records people, but I suppose we could manage until our insurance gave us a replacement.

7. **Salesperson:** But without a computer, wouldn't your billing to customers suffer?
   Buyer: Not if we got the replacement quickly.

8. **Salesperson:** You said the computer itself is insured. Do you happen to know if the software—the programs, your customer files—is also insured?
   Buyer: I don't believe so; our insurance covers the equipment only.

9. **Salesperson:** And do you keep backup records somewhere else—in the bank, for example?
   Buyer: No, we don't.

10. **Salesperson:** Mr. Bell, in my experience, software isn't left behind after a theft. Wouldn't it be a serious problem to you if that software were taken?
    Buyer: Yes, you're right, I suppose. Redevelopment would certainly cost a lot. The original programs were expensive.

11. **Salesperson:** And even worse, because software development can take a long time, wouldn't that hold up your billings to customers?
    Buyer: We could always do that manually.

12. **Salesperson:** What effect would that have on your processing costs?
    Buyer: I see your point. It would certainly be expensive to run a manual system, as well as inconvenient.

13. **Salesperson:** And if you lost your software, wouldn't it also make it harder to process customer orders?
    Buyer: Yes. I don't have much contact with that part of the business, but without order processing and stock control I'm sure we would grind to a halt in a matter of days.

14. **Salesperson:** Are there any other items in the building that would be hard to replace if stolen?
    Buyer: Some of the furnishings. I would hate to lose this antique clock, for example. In fact, most of our furnishings would be very hard to replace in the same style.

15. **Salesperson:** So, if you lost them, wouldn't it hurt the character of your office?
    Buyer: Yes, it would be damaging. We've built a gracious, civilized image here, and without it we would be like dozens of other people in our business—the glass and concrete image.

CASE 8–3

16. **Salesperson:** This may sound like an odd question, but how many doors do you have at ground level?
    Buyer: Let me see . . . uh . . . six.

17. **Salesperson:** And ground-level windows?
    Buyer: About 10 or a dozen.

18. **Salesperson:** So there are 16 or 18 points where a thief could break in, compared with 1 or 2 points in the average glass and concrete office. Doesn't that concern you?
    Buyer: Put that way, it does. I suppose we're not very secure.

Questions

1. Did the dialogue between buyer and seller seem natural to you?
2. Did the salesperson use too many questions in her approach?
3. Analyze each of the salesperson's questions and state whether it is a situation, problem, implication, or need–payoff type of question.
4. Analyze each of the buyer's responses to the salesperson's questions and state what type of need the salesperson's question uncovered. Was it an implied or minor need response, or was it an explicit or important need response? Why?
5. How would you improve on this salesperson's approach?
6. After the buyer's last statement, which of the following would you do?
   a. Move into the presentation.
   b. Ask a problem question.
   c. Ask a need–payoff question.
   d. Ask for an appointment to fully discuss your system.

9

THE PRESENTATION—ELEMENTS OF EFFECTIVE PERSUASION

MAIN TOPICS

LEARNING OBJECTIVES

The fourth step in the selling process is the presentation. Here, you discuss with the buyer the product's features, advantages, and benefits; your marketing plan; and the business proposition. After studying this chapter, you should be able to:

- Discuss the purpose and essential steps of the sales presentation.

- Give examples of the six sales presentation mix elements.

- Understand the importance of the trial close.

- Describe difficulties that may arise during the sales presentation and explain how to handle them.

- State how to handle discussion of the competition.

- Explain how to properly assess the prospect's personality to determine the design of the sales presentation.

- Explain how cross-selling benefits a salesperson.

FACING
A SALES
CHALLENGE

You are a business electronics salesperson for Dynamic Electronics. You have been talking to a retailer about the features, advantages, and benefits of your new line of laptops with enhanced Wi-Fi technology. You have just told your customer that because of your new technology, there will be no "dead zones" within 100 kilometres of any urban area. Your customer then says, "That sounds wonderful, but I just don't know. I've had too many customers complaining about losing their Internet signal while on the road."

What do you do in this situation? You recognize that the customer has some doubts about whether your claims are accurate. How do you prove your new technology? What if the customer will not take your word for it? (Continued at end of chapter.)

The presentation part of the selling process is a persuasive vocal and visual explanation of a proposition. In developing your presentation, consider the elements you will use to provide the information a buyer needs to make a buying decision. At any time a customer may mention a concern, as in "Facing a Sales Challenge" above, a proper response is needed to make the sale.

This chapter discusses the elements of the presentation—the fourth step in the sales process (see Exhibit 9–1). We begin by examining the purpose and essential steps in the presentation. Next, we review and expand on the presentation techniques used by salespeople and how to handle the customer in the sales challenge. The chapter ends by discussing the importance of the proper use of trial closes and difficulties that may arise in the presentation, along with the need to customize your presentation for each individual situation and buyer.

THE PURPOSE OF THE PRESENTATION

The main goal of your presentation is to sell your product to your customer. However, we know that a prospective buyer considers many things before making a decision about what product to buy. As we have seen, the approach or first few minutes of the interview should be focused to determine the prospect's need, capture attention and interest, and allow for a smooth transition into the presentation.

The presentation provides knowledge via the features, advantages, and benefits of your product; marketing plan; and business proposal. This *knowledge* allows the buyer to develop positive personal beliefs toward your product. The *beliefs* result in *desire* (or *need*) for the type of product you sell. Your job, as a salesperson, is to convert that need into a want and into the *attitude* that your product is the best product to fulfill a certain need. Furthermore, you must convince the buyer that not only is your product the best but also that you are the best source from which to buy. When this occurs, your prospect has moved into the *conviction* stage of the mental buying process.

This sequence results in your making a sale, as shown in Exhibit 9–2. Whether to buy or not is a choice decision, and you have provided the necessary information so that the customer chooses to buy from you.

Assume, for example, that you are a salesperson for Dell and you want to sell 10 of your new personal computers costing $2,000 each to a company. The prospect's company uses your competitor's products, which cost $1,500 each. How should you conceptualize the prospect's thought processes regarding whether to buy or not buy from you (as shown in Exhibit 9–1) to develop your presentation?

The presentation is the heart of the sale. An effective approach allows a smooth transition into discussing your product's features, advantages, and benefits.

10
Follow-up

9
Close

8
Trial close

7
Meet objections

6
Determine objections

5
Trial close

**4
Presentation**
■ Participation
■ Asking questions
■ Evidence visualization
■ Persuasive communication
■ Demonstration
■ Dramatization

3
Approach

2
Preapproach

1
Prospecting

Begin by realizing that the prospect has certain attitudes toward the present personal computers. Next, appreciate that your prospect's job performance is judged by her management of certain responsibilities. Thus, improving the performance of company employees is important. However, the prospect knows nothing about you, your product, or your product's benefits. The prospect may feel that Dell products are good, high-quality, expensive products—or she may not.

Develop a SPIN approach to determine the buyer's attitudes toward personal computers in general and your personal computer specifically. Once you have addressed each of the four SPIN questions (see Chapter 8), and you feel more information about your product is needed, begin the presentation.

Present the product information that allows the buyer to develop a positive attitude toward your product. Next, possibly using a value-analysis proposal, show how your product can increase efficiency, reduce costs, and pay for itself in one year, using a return-on-investment (ROI) technique. A positive reaction from your prospect indicates that the desire stage of the mental buying process has been reached. There is a need for some brand of personal computer.

Now, show why your Dell personal computer is the best solution to the buyer's need and show that you will provide service after the sale. A positive response on these two items indicates that the prospect believes your product is best and that the conviction stage has been reached. The prospect wants to buy the Dell personal computer.

Up to this point, you have discussed your product's features, advantages, and benefits; your marketing plan; and your business proposition. You have *not* asked the prospect to buy. Rather, you have developed a presentation to lead the prospect through four of the five mental buying steps: the attention, interest, desire, and conviction steps. It may take you five minutes, two hours, or several weeks of repeat calls to move the prospect into the conviction stage.

You must move the prospect into the conviction stage before a sale is made. So hold off asking the prospect to buy until the conviction stage; doing otherwise usually results in objections, failure to listen to your whole story, and fewer sales. The sales presentation has seven major steps. Each step is taken in order to logically and sequentially move the prospect into the conviction stage of the buying process.

When a person buys something, they are actually buying a mental picture of the future in which your product helps to fulfill some expectation. The buyer has mentally conceived certain needs. Your presentation must create mental images that move your prospect into the conviction stage.

The five purposes of the presentation.

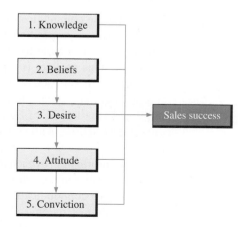

Three essential steps within the presentation.

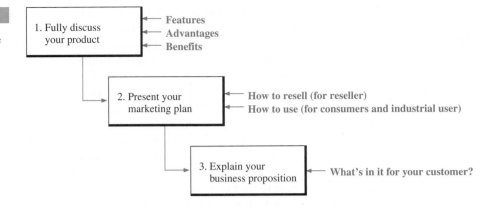

THREE ESSENTIAL STEPS WITHIN THE PRESENTATION

No matter which of the four sales presentation methods is used, your presentation must follow these three essential steps, also shown in Exhibit 9–3. The three steps are discussed in Chapter 7 under "Developing a Customer Benefit Plan."

Step 1

Fully discuss the *features, advantages,* and *benefits* of your product. Tell the whole story.

Step 2

Present your marketing plan. For wholesalers and retailers, this is your suggestion on how they should *resell* the product. For end users, it is your suggestion on how they can *use* the product.

Step 3

Explain your business proposition. This step relates the *value* of your product to its *cost.* It should be discussed last, since you always want to present your product's benefits and marketing plan relative to your product's price.

Remember Your FABs!

It is extremely important to emphasize benefits throughout the presentation. Using the SELL sequence communication technique when discussing the product, marketing plan, and business proposition greatly improves your chances of making the sale.

Exhibit 9–4 is a table used in a training program for a large restaurant supply distributor. This product is a pancake mix sold to hotels and food retail chains. Notice the FABs for each of the three essential steps within the presentation. Even for a product like pancake mix, salespeople must use benefits to paint a picture in the mind of the buyers of how this product will fulfill their needs. This is what **consultative selling** is all about—relating the product's benefits to the customer's needs.

Ideally, information in each of the steps shown in Exhibit 9–3 should be presented to create a picture in the prospect's mind of the benefits of the purchase. To do this, use persuasive communication and participation techniques, evidence statements, visual aids, dramatization, and demonstrations as you move through each of the three steps during the presentation.

Salespeople use these FABs in their presentations.

Features, Advantages, and Benefits of Bix Buckwheat Pancake Mix

Features	Advantages	Benefits
Product		
1. Traditional "farmhouse" recipe, with freshest ingredients; fortified with vitamins A, B, C, and D; no preservatives	1. Great tasting, fluffy, and light; highly nutritious	1. Provides an appealing item; expands breakfast menu; increases breakfast business
2. User needs only to add water, stir, and cook	2. Quick and easy to prepare	2. Requires minimal kitchen time and labour
Marketing Plan		
3. Just-in-time delivery	3. No need to store large quantities	3. Requires minimal inventory space; keeps inventory costs low
4. Local distribution centre	4. Additional orders can be filled quickly	4. Prevents out-of-stock situations
5. An experienced sales representative to serve account	5. Knowledge and background in food-service industry	5. Provides assistance for meeting changing needs and solving business problems
Business Proposition		
6. Quantity discounts	6. Reduces costs	6. Increases your profits
7. Extended payment plans	7. Reduces interest costs	7. Increases your profits

THE SALES PRESENTATION MIX

Salespeople sell different products in different ways, but all salespeople use six classes of presentation elements to some degree in their presentations to provide meaningful information to the customer. These elements are called the *presentation mix.*

The **sales presentation mix** refers to the elements the salesperson assembles to sell to prospects and customers. Although all elements should be part of the presentation, it is up to the individual to determine how much each element is emphasized. This determination is primarily based on the sales call objective, customer profile, and customer benefit plan. Let's examine each of the six elements, as shown in Exhibit 9–5.

Persuasive Communication

To be a successful salesperson, do you need to be a smooth talker? No, but you do need to consider and use factors that aid the clear communication of your messages. In Chapter 4, we discussed seven factors that help you be a better communicator:

1. Using questions.
2. Being empathetic.
3. Keeping the message simple.
4. Creating mutual trust.
5. Listening.[1]
6. Having a positive attitude and enthusiasm.
7. Being believable.

The Trial Close and SELL Sequence

In today's sales world prospects do not buy for a variety of reasons. Lack of trust, failure of the prospect to understand what's in it for him or her, and difficulty in seeing the pros and cons of buying are just a few. Because of this, it is imperative that

EXHIBIT 9–5

The salesperson's presentation
mix.

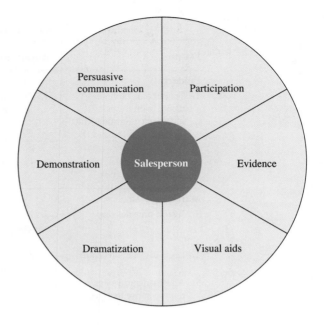

salespeople have a test they can use during a presentation to determine if they're on track or not.

The trial close is that very test. It can help you test your prospect's reactions at any time during the sales presentation (refer to Exhibit 9–1). It can help you understand how your prospect is thinking and feeling about your product or service. From this information, you can adjust your presentation to enhance your chances of making the sale. The trial close is often underutilized in selling, as salespeople are anxious about putting too much pressure on the prospect.

A trial close can be defined as any attempt to start closing the sale before completion of the sales presentation. It is just a test. It will help determine just how close the prospect is to buying. During a trial close, salespeople are really just asking for an opinion as opposed to a specific decision. There is little risk of a final "no" during a trial close, so salespeople shouldn't feel uncomfortable using them.

Salespeople often experience objections when trying to close a sale because the prospect wasn't encouraged to express her feelings or opinions about the product during the presentation. Simply asking things like, "What do you think so far?" or, "Can you see how this might improve your bottom line?" can help you elicit comments that can draw out your prospect's feelings.

So when should you attempt a trial close? When the prospect gives you a signal that she is interested in your product. This is known as a buying signal. Buying signals can take the form of questions, actions, comments, or expressions. For example, if the prospect straightens up and looks alert after you've just presented a FAB package, use a trial close. If the prospect has an inquisitive look on her face when you show her a return-on-investment visual, use a trial close. If the prospect's eyes light up when you show her a picture of your proposed solution, use a trial close. You get the picture.

Trial close early and often. Remember, you are just asking for an opinion, not the order. You have little to lose and much to gain. You will gain insight into how to proceed with your presentation. When a trial close is used in conjunction with a FAB or major selling point, this forms a SELL sequence (discussed in Chapter 11). The

SELL sequence is good way of determining a buyer's interest and is an effective form of persuasive communication.

Additional persuasive factors to consider in the presentation are logical reasoning, persuasive suggestions, a sense of fun, personalized relationships, trust, empathy, body language, a controlled presentation, diplomacy, and using words as selling tools.

Logical Reasoning

The application of logic through reasoning is an effective persuasive technique that appeals to prospects' common sense by requiring them to think about the proposition and to compare alternative solutions to problems. This is especially true when selling complicated proposals involving comparative cost data, when price versus benefits must be judged, and when the product is a radically new concept.

Logical reasoning involves a presentation constructed around three parts: a major premise, a minor premise, and a conclusion. Here is an example:

1. *Major premise:* All manufacturers want to reduce costs and increase efficiency.
2. *Minor premise:* My equipment will reduce your costs and increase your efficiency.
3. *Conclusion:* Therefore, you should buy my equipment.

If presented exactly in this straightforward manner, the logical formula may be too blunt; the prospect may raise defences. However, you can develop the framework or presentation outline to determine whether the prospect is interested in reducing costs and increasing manufacturing efficiency. If so, then present a value analysis that shows the benefits of your product over alternatives. Information such as performance data, costs, service, and delivery information can be presented in a persuasive manner using various elements of the presentation mix.

Persuasion through Suggestion

Suggestion, like logical reasoning, is used effectively to persuade prospects. The skilled use of suggestions can arouse attention, interest, desire, conviction, and action. Types of suggestions that may be considered for the presentation follow.

1. **Suggestive propositions** imply that the prospect should act now, such as, "Shouldn't you go ahead and buy now before the price goes up next month?" Prospects often like to postpone their buying decisions, so the suggestive approach can help overcome this problem.
2. **Prestige suggestions** ask the prospect to visualize using products that famous people, companies, or individuals the prospect trusts use, such as, "The National Professional Engineers Association has endorsed our equipment. That's why several hundred Fortune 500 manufacturers are using our products. This elite group of manufacturers finds the equipment helps increase their profits, sales, and market share. Is this of interest to you?"
3. **Autosuggestion** attempts to have prospects imagine themselves using the product. Television advertisements frequently use this form of suggestion. The salesperson visualizes the product, saying, "Just imagine how this equipment will look and operate in your store. Your employees will perform much better and they will thank you."
4. The **direct suggestion** is used widely by professional salespeople in all industries because it does not "tell" but suggests buying, which does not offend the buyer.

SELLING TIPS

Using Trial Closes

The trial close is an important part of the sales presentation. It asks for the buyer's feedback about what you have just said (e.g., FAB) or shown (e.g., testimonial letter). The trial close does not ask the prospect to commit or to buy. Here are some examples:

- How does our delivery schedule sound to you?
- What do you think of our money-back guarantee?
- Can you see how our moulded chair will enhance your employees' comfort level?
- Do these independent test results address your concerns about quality?

- How do you like our 24-hour technical support hotline?
- What is your impression of the capacity of our new pump?
- On a scale of 1 to 10, how do you feel our product will fit your needs?
- Are these the types of features you had in mind?
- Do you think your employees would see the benefits of this system?

As you can see, we've never directly asked the prospect to buy—we're just measuring their level of interest.

Such a suggestion might state: "Based on our survey of your needs, I suggest you purchase . . ." or "Let's consider this: We ship you three train carloads of Whirlpool washers and dryers in the following colours and models . . ."

5. The **indirect suggestion** is used for some prospects when it is best to be indirect in suggesting a recommended course of action. Indirect suggestions help instill in prospects' minds factors such as doubt about a competitor's products or desire for your product. The indirect suggestion makes it seem as if it is their idea: "Should you buy 50 or 75 dozen 350-mL cans of Revlon hairspray for your promotion?" or "Have you talked with anyone who has used that product?"

6. The **countersuggestion** evokes an opposite response from the prospect: "Do you really want such a high-quality product?" Often, the buyer will begin expanding on why a high-quality product is needed. This suggestion is an especially effective technique to include in the presentation if you have already determined that the prospect wants a high-quality product.

Make the Presentation Fun

Selling is fun, not a battle between the prospect and salesperson, so loosen up and enjoy the presentation. This is easy to do once you believe in yourself and what you are selling—so sound like it! Have the right mental attitude and you will be successful.

Personalize Your Relationship

One of the authors of this text worked for a large national consumer products manufacturer. The sales manager trained all sales reps to personalize their presentation. He would say, "You are enthusiastic; you believe in yourself, your products, your company; you give a very good presentation. To improve, however, you need to personalize your relationship with each of your customers. In some manner, let them know during your presentation that you have their best interests at heart." He would always say, "Show 'em that you love 'em."

The sales reps came up with the short phrase, "You have me." Once this phrase was incorporated into retailer presentations at the appropriate time, they saw a significant increase in total sales and sales-to-customer call ratio by saying something like: "You are not only buying my products but me as well. You have me on call 24 hours a day to help you in any way I can."

Yes, it sounds corny, but it helped show customers that the company and the sales rep cared for them. This helped build trust. You might choose a different way, but be sure to demonstrate that you look out for their interests.

Build Trust

Two of the best and easiest ways to build your persuasive powers with prospects are *being honest* and *doing what you say you will do*. This builds trust, which increases sales. Most professional buyers have long memories that can be used to your advantage if you follow through after the sale as you said you would when presenting the proposal.

Honesty is always the best policy, and it is an effective way to build trust. The salesperson should never claim more than the product can accomplish. If the product does not live up to expectations, apologize, return the product for credit, or trade for another product. This action is important in obtaining repeat sales. It builds trust; the next time the prospect is reluctant to buy, you say, "Haven't I always taken care of you? Trust me, this product is what you need. I guarantee it!"[2]

Be Empathetic

Many salespeople who have the task of dealing with purchasing agents at companies across Canada will tell you that regional differences exist in personalities and in buying styles. According to Marty Legein of Cetec, who has done extensive selling in all areas of Canada, "I have to use a different approach to my sales presentations depending on which region I am in." For example, it appears that buyers in the Maritimes are often laid back and friendly. With this type of buyer, relationship building is critical—once a positive rapport is established, these buyers will likely respond well to the need satisfaction presentation strategy.

In Quebec, it is important to acknowledge and recognize the province's distinct cultural differences, since, often, relationships are built around this principle. Ignoring this fact may isolate a salesperson, which would make any sales presentation very difficult.

In Ontario, which is often fast-paced, competitive, and impersonal, salespeople are often competing with many other salespeople for a company's business. Buyers don't always have the time for relationship building and are very interested in salespeople "getting to the point." Salespeople in these situations therefore should be well prepared to give the facts and figures and outline quickly the major FABs for a particular buyer. A formula strategy often works well in these situations.

The West is similar to the East—relationship selling is very important. Although buyers are still very knowledgeable, an element of trust must be established if salespeople are to be effective here.

Of course, Canada's cultural mosaic is much too diverse to stereotype everyone within a given region. However, knowledge of each region of Canada in terms of economic situation, cultural and ethnic diversity, and any regional difficulties may prove helpful in homing in on your prospect's needs.

Be Aware of Your Body Language

Just as you watch for buying signals from a prospect, the prospect watches your facial expressions and **body language**. Your nonverbal communication must project a positive image to the prospect, one that shows you know what you are taking about and understand the buyer's needs. Your customer will think, "I can trust this person."

The best nonverbal selling technique is the smile. As a sales manager once said, "It's often not what you say but how you say it, and you can say almost anything to anyone if you do it with a smile. So, practise your facial expressions and smile—always smile."

Control the Presentation

In making the presentation, direct the conversation to lead the prospect through the presentation and proposal. The salesperson often has to maintain control and know what to do if the prospect takes control of the conversation. For example, what do you do if the prospect likes to talk about hobbies, attacks your company or products for poor service or credit mix-ups, or is a kidder and likes to poke fun at your products?

When this happens, stay with a planned presentation if possible. If there is a complaint, address this first. If the prospect likes to talk about other things, do so briefly. When the prospect's attention and interest are hard to maintain, questions or some manner of eliciting participation in the presentation are the two best methods to re-channel the conversation.

Be sure to control the visual aids and any materials you use in the presentation. New salespeople often make the mistake of handing prospects their catalogue, price list, or brochures showing several products. When buyers are looking through these items, they are probably not listening. So, keep your product materials and discuss the information you want to present while prospects look at and listen to you.

Be a Diplomat

All salespeople face situations where the prospects believe they are right or know it all, and the salesperson has different opinions. For example, the salesperson previously may have sold the prospect's company a machine that always breaks down due to its operator, not the equipment—yet the salesperson's company is blamed. What should you do?

You have to be a diplomat when tempers rise. Retreat may be the best option; otherwise, you risk destroying the relationship. If you challenge the prospect, you could win the battle only to lose the war. This is a decision that the salesperson must make based on individual situations.

Simile, Metaphor, and Analogy

Words are selling tools. Similes, metaphors, analogies, pauses, silence, and changes in the rate of speaking, tone, and pitch are effective methods of gaining prospects' attention and capturing their interest in a proposal.

A **simile** is a direct comparison statement using the words *like* or *as:* A poorly manicured lawn is *like* a bad haircut. Our Sylvania Safe line bulbs are *like* a car's shatterproof windshield. Our diet drinks are *like* a chocolate milkshake. The carton folds *as flat as* a pancake for storage.

A **metaphor** is an *implied* comparison that uses a contrasting word or phrase to evoke a vivid image: Our power mowers *sculpt* your lawn. Our cabin cruiser *plows* the waves smoothly. The computer's *memory* stores your data. The components *telescope* into a five-centimetre-thick disk.

The **analogy** compares two different situations that have something in common, such as, "Our sun screen for your home will stop the sun's heat and glare before it hits your window. It's like having a shade tree in front of your window without blocking the view." Remember to speak the prospect's language by using familiar terminology and buzzwords in a conversational tone.

Participation Is Essential to Success

The second major part of the presentation involves techniques for motivating the prospect to participate in the presentation. Four ways to induce participation are

1. Questions
2. Product use
3. Visuals
4. Demonstrations.

We have already discussed the use of questions and will discuss the use of visuals and demonstrations later, so let's briefly consider having prospects use the product:

- If you sell stereos, let them see, hear, and touch them!
- If you sell food, let them see, smell, and taste it!
- If you sell clothes, let them touch and wear them!

By letting prospects use the product, you appeal to their senses: sight, hearing, touch, smell, and taste. Develop your presentation to appeal to the senses, since people often buy because of emotional needs, and the senses are key to developing emotional appeals.

Evidence Statements Build Believability

Salespeople must prove that they will do what they promise, such as helping to make product displays when the merchandise arrives. Usually, "prove it" means providing conclusive evidence to a prospect during a presentation that the product's benefits and the salesperson's proposal are legitimate.

Because salespeople often have a reputation for exaggeration, at times prospects are skeptical of the salesperson's claims. By incorporating **evidence statements** into the presentation, the salesperson can increase the prospect's confidence and trust that product claims are accurate. Several useful evidence techniques are the customer's past sales figures, the guarantee, testimonials, company evidence results, and independent research results.

Past Sales Help Predict the Future

Customers' past sales evidence statements are frequently used by salespersons when contacting present customers. Customers keep records of their past purchases from each of their suppliers; the salesperson can use these to suggest what quantities of each product to purchase. For example, the Colgate salesperson checks a customer's present inventory of all products carried, determines the number of products sold in a month, subtracts inventory from forecast sales, and suggests the customer purchase that amount. It is difficult for buyers to refuse when presentations are based on their sales records. If they are offered a price discount and promotional allowances, they might purchase three to ten times the normal amount (a promotional purchase).

SELLING TIPS
Storytelling

Many successful salespeople tell stories—true stories.[3] To use stories successfully, salespeople must combine them with presentations that are interesting, memorable, and persuasive. How? Combine stories with sales objectives. Include narratives, colourful comparisons, metaphors, and similes to help customers understand, believe, and remember what you say—to actually feel your message.

Storytelling in the sales world teaches or persuades your customers because there is a point to the stories that is relevant to the sale. To tell good stories, create a story inventory. First, make a list of all the tough questions, objections, and comments you've heard from customers. Then compile another list of customers who had similar concerns but overcame them, bought your good or service, and are happy they did. During follow-up, get customers to describe their business now and after their purchase and the lessons they learned from their experience. Match this list to your list of tough questions and objections.

Suppose a prospect asks why your product or service costs more than others on the market. Instead of launching into a general spiel about your product, create a story:

1. Think of a customer who had the same objection but decided to buy your product and is now a very happy and satisfied client.

2. Tell your prospect about this customer's world before making the purchase.

3. Recall the specific event or problem that motivated that customer to seek a solution.

4. Describe the customer's situation now with your product or service.

5. Explain the lesson the customer learned from this experience with your company.

6. Transfer this lesson to the prospect you're currently talking with.

A story can be long or short, but it must blend logic and emotion to make customers want to buy from you:

1. Know what you're telling. The storyteller must clearly understand the objectives illustrated by the story.

2. Reach out. Tell stories that have emotional components that customers can relate to.

3. Weave facts, figures, or other information into your stories to add to your customer's knowledge about the business at hand.

4. Use personal experience. Your stories should have some sort of connection to you personally to have the greatest impact.

Assume, for example, that a food store normally carries 10 dozen of the king-size Colgate toothpaste in inventory with 3 dozen on the shelf, and sells approximately 20 dozen a month. The salesperson produces the buyer's past sales record and says, "You should buy 7 to 10 dozen king-size Colgate toothpaste." If offering promotional allowances, the salesperson might say:

> The Colgate king-size is your most profitable and best-selling item. You normally sell 20 dozen Colgate king-size each month with a 30 percent gross profit. With our 15 percent price reduction this month only, and our advertising allowances, I suggest, based on your normal sales, that you buy 80 to 100 dozen, reduce the price 15 percent, display it, and advertise the discount in your newspaper specials. This sale will attract people to your store, increase store sales, and make your normal profit.

The salesperson stops talking to see the buyer's reaction. A suggested order plus an alternative on the quantity to purchase have been proposed. Does the quantity seem high? It may be high, just right, or low, but it is the buyer's decision. The salesperson is saying that, given your past sales and with my customer benefit plan, I believe you can sell X number of units.

Be realistic about your suggested increase in order size. Your honesty builds credibility with the buyer.

The Colgate salesperson might suggest purchases not only of toothpaste but also of all Colgate products. That same sales call could involve multiple presentations of several products that have promotional allowances plus the recommended purchase of 10 or more items based on present inventories and the previous month's sales.

The Guarantee

The guarantee is a powerful evidence technique. It assures prospects that if they are dissatisfied with their purchase, the salesperson or the company will stand behind a product. The manufacturer has certain product warranties that the retail salesperson can use in a presentation.

Furthermore, the consumer goods salesperson selling to retailers might say, "I'll guarantee this product will sell for you. If not, we can return what you do not sell." The industrial salesperson may explain the equipment's warranties, service policies, and state, "This is the best equipment for your situation that you can buy. If you are not 100 percent satisfied after you have used it for three months, I will return it for you."

Testimonials

Testimonials in the presentation as evidence of the product's features, advantages, and benefits are an excellent way to build trust and confidence. Today, manufacturers effectively advertise their consumer products using testimonials, and professional buyers are impressed by testimonials from prominent people, experts, and satisfied customers about a product's features, advantages, and benefits.

Company Evidence Results

Companies routinely furnish data concerning their products. Consumer goods salespeople can use sales data such as test market information and current sales data. Industrial salespeople use performance data and facts based on company research, as proof of their product's performance.

A consumer goods manufacturer gave its salespeople test market sales information to use in their presentations on a new product being introduced nationally. Using this information, a salesperson might say:

> Our new product will sell as soon as you put it on your shelf. The product was a success in our Eastern test market. It had 9.8 percent market share only nine months after the start of advertising. Laboratory tests proved our formula superior to that of the leading competition in our consumer product tests. There was a high repurchase rate of 50 percent after sampling. This means increased sales and profits for you.

Independent Research Results

Evidence furnished by reputable sources outside the company usually has more credibility than company-generated data. Pharmaceutical salespeople frequently tell physicians about medical research findings on their products published in leading medical journals by medical research authorities.

A sales representative for a large pharmaceutical company explains a typical day:

> I see as many physicians as possible and initiate a discussion with them about one of our products that will have importance to them in medicine. I point out advantages that our drugs have in various provinces by using third-party documentation published in current

EXHIBIT 9–6

Evidence statements help to prove what you say.

Feature	Advantage	Benefit	Evidence
■ New consumer product	Will be big seller	Excellent profits	Test-market results
■ High energy-efficiency rating	Uses less electricity	Saves 10 percent on energy costs	*Consumer Reports* magazine
■ Electronic mail software	Gets information to sales force instantly	Reduces mailing and telephone costs	Testimonials
■ Buy 100 cases	Reduces out-of-stocks	Increases sales, profits, customer satisfaction	Customer's past sales or personal guarantee

medical journals and texts. The information has much more meaning to a physician who knows that it is not I or my company that has shown our drug to have an advantage but rather a group of researchers who have conducted a scientific study. All of the material that we give to the physicians has been approved for our use by the government.

Publications such as *Straight Goods Online* and *Consumer Reports,* newspaper stories, and government publications may contain information the salesperson can use in the presentation. For an evidence statement referring to independent research results to be most effective, it should contain (1) a restatement of the benefit before proving it, (2) the evidence source and relevant facts or figures about the product, and (3) expansion of the benefit. Consider the following example of a salesperson's evidence statement:

I'm sure that you want a radio that's going to sell and be profitable for you (benefit restatement). Figures in *Consumer Reports* magazine indicate that the Sony XL-100 radios, although the newest on the market, are the third largest in sales (source and facts). Therefore, when you handle the Sony XL line, you'll find that radio sales and profits will increase, and more customers will come into your store (benefit expansion).

Evidence statements must be incorporated into the presentation. They provide a logical answer to the buyer's challenge of "prove it!"

Exhibit 9–6 shows four examples of using evidence to support what is said about FABs—features, advantages, and benefits. Evidence statements are a great way to help prove that what you have said is true. Often, evidence statements are presented through visual aids.

VISUAL AIDS HELP TELL THE STORY

In giving a sales presentation, as a salesperson you do two things: You *show* and *tell* the prospect about a proposal. You *tell* using persuasive communications, participation techniques, and evidence statements. You *show* by using visual aids.

People retain approximately 10 percent of what they hear but 50 percent of what they see. Consequently, you have five times the chance of making a lasting impression with an illustrated sales presentation rather than with words alone.

Visuals are most effective when you believe in them and have woven them into your sales presentation message. Use them to

■ Increase retention

■ Reinforce the message

■ Reduce misunderstanding

- Create a unique and lasting impression
- Show the buyer that you are a professional.

The visual presentation (showing) incorporates the three remaining elements of the presentation mix: visual aids, dramatization, and demonstration. Some overlap exists among the three; for example, a demonstration uses visuals and has some dramatics. Let's examine each element to consider how it can be used in a sales presentation.

Visuals, or visual aids, are devices that chiefly appeal to the prospect's vision with the intent of producing mental images of the product's features, advantages, and benefits. Many companies routinely supply salespeople with visuals for their products. Some common visuals are

- The product
- Charts and graphics illustrating product features and advantages such as performance and sales data
- Photographs and videos of the product and its uses
- Models or mock-ups of products, especially for large, bulky products
- Equipment such as videos, slides, PowerPoint presentations, and computers
- Sales manuals and product catalogue
- Order forms
- Letters of testimony
- A copy of the guarantee
- Flip-boards and posters
- Sample advertisements.

Most visual aids are carried in the salesperson's bag. See Exhibit 9–7. The sales bag should be checked before each sales call to ensure that all visuals necessary for the presentation are organized in a manner that allows the salesperson to easily access needed visuals. Only new, top-quality, professionally developed visuals should be used. Tattered, torn, or smudged visuals should be routinely discarded. The best visual aid is the actual product.

DRAMATIZATION IMPROVES YOUR CHANCES

Dramatics refers to talking or presenting the product in a striking, showy, or extravagant manner. Thus, sales expertise can involve **dramatization** or a theatrical presentation of products. However, dramatics should be incorporated into the presentation only when you are almost certain that the dramatics will work effectively. This point was not considered by the salesperson who set a buyer's trash can on fire. When the salesperson had difficulty extinguishing the fire with a new fire extinguisher, the buyer ran out of the room because of the extensive smoke. However, if implemented correctly, dramatics are effective. One of the best methods of developing ideas for the dramatization of a product is to watch television commercials.

- "We challenged the competition . . . and they ran!" says the Heinz tomato ketchup advertisement. Two national brands of ketchup and Heinz ketchup are poured into paper coffee filters held up by tea strainers. The competition's ketchup begins to drip and then runs through the filter. The Heinz ketchup does not drip or run, which indicates the high quality of Heinz ketchup relative to the competition.
- Bounty paper towel advertisements show coffee spilled and how quickly the product absorbs the coffee relative to the competitive paper towel.

EXHIBIT 9–7

Visual aids are an important part of this salesperson's presentation.

1. She reviews the call plan before seeing the buyer.

2. Products and visual aids are placed in her sales bag.

3. Some visual aids are furnished by her company.

4. She uses personally developed sales aids customized to her buyer.

■ The STP motor-oil additive advertisement shows a person dipping one screwdriver into STP motor-oil additive and another screwdriver into a plain motor oil. The person can hold with two fingers the end of the screwdriver covered with plain motor oil. The screwdriver covered with STP motor-oil additive slips out of the fingers—indicating that STP provides better lubrication for an automobile engine.

DEMONSTRATIONS PROVE IT

One of the best ways to convince a prospect that a product is needed is to show the merits of the product through a **demonstration**. If a picture is worth a thousand words, then a demonstration is worth a thousand pictures. Therefore, it is best to show the product, if possible, and have the prospect use it. If this is not feasible, then pictures, models, or videos are the best alternatives. Whatever the salesperson is attempting to sell, the prospect should be able to see.

The dynamic demonstration appeals to human senses by telling, showing, and creating buyer–seller interaction. See Exhibit 9–8.

Demonstrations are part of the dramatization and fun of your presentation. Do not underestimate their ability to make sales for you, no matter how simple they may

EXHIBIT 9–8

Virtual reality demonstration.

This prospect experiences what virtual reality is all about. A demonstration is worth a thousand pictures in helping make a sale.

appear. For example, a glass company once designed a shatterproof glass. This product was not standard equipment in automobiles then, as it is now. They had their salespeople going around the country trying to sell shatterproof glass. One of the salespeople completely outsold the rest of the sales force. When they had their convention, they said, "Joe, how come you sell so much glass?" He replied, "Well, what I've been doing is taking little chunks of glass, and a ball-peen hammer along with me on my sales calls. I take the little chunk of glass, and I hit it with the hammer. This demonstration shows that it's shatterproof. It splinters but doesn't shatter and fall all over the ground. This has helped me sell a lot of glass."

So, the next year they equipped every salesperson with a ball-peen hammer and little chunks of glass. But an interesting thing happened. Joe still far outsold the rest of the sales force. So, when the convention occurred the next year, they asked, "Joe, how is it you're selling so much? You told us what you did last year. What are you doing differently?" He replied, "Well, this year, I gave the glass *and* the hammer to the customer to let *him* hit it." You see, the first year he had dramatization in his demonstration. The second year, Joe had dramatization and participation in his demonstration. Again, it's often not what you say but how you say it that makes the sale.

A Demonstration Checklist

There are seven points to remember as you prepare your demonstration (see Exhibit 9–9). Ask yourself whether the demonstration is really needed and appropriate for your prospects. Every sale does not need a demonstration, nor will all products lend themselves to a demonstration.

If the demonstration is appropriate, what should the demonstration accomplish? Be sure you have properly planned and organized the demonstration; rehearse it so the demonstration flows smoothly and appears natural. Take your time in talking and going through your demonstration; make it look easy. Remember, if you, the expert, cannot operate a machine, for example, imagine how difficult it will be for the prospect.

Seven points to remember about demonstrations.

☑ Is the demonstration *needed* and *appropriate?*

☑ Have I developed a specific demonstration *objective?*

☑ Have I properly *planned* and *organized* the demonstration?

☑ Have I rehearsed to the point that the demonstration *flows smoothly* and appears to be *natural?*

☑ What is the probability that the demonstration will go as *planned?*

☑ What is the probability that the demonstration will *backfire?*

☑ Does my demonstration present my product in an *ethical* and *professional* manner?

The only way to ensure a smooth demonstration is to practise. Be prepared in case something goes wrong. An example is a former student who was demonstrating his new Kodak slide projector. Two bulbs in a row burned out as he demonstrated the product to a buyer for a large discount chain. He anticipated what could go wrong and always carried extra parts in his sales bag. When the first bulb went out, he talked of how easy it was to change bulbs, and when the second one blew, he said, "I want to show you that again," with a smile. He always carried two spare bulbs, but now he carries three.

Finally, make sure your demonstration presents the product in an ethical and professional manner. You do not want to misrepresent the product or proposal.

Use Participation in Your Demonstration

By having the prospect participate in the demonstration, you obtain his or her attention and direct it where you want it. Participation also helps the prospect visualize owning and operating the product. The successful demonstration aids in reducing buying uncertainties and resistance to purchase.

The salesperson has the prospect do four things in a successful demonstration.

1. Let the prospect do something simple.
2. Let the prospect work an important feature.
3. Let the prospect do something routine or frequently repeated.
4. Have the prospect answer questions throughout the demonstration.

First, ask the prospect to do something simple with a low probability of foul-ups. Second, in planning the demonstration, select the main features that you will stress in the interview, and allow the prospect to participate on the feature that relates most to an important buying motive. Again, keep it simple.

A third way to have a successful demonstration is by having the prospect do something with the product that is done frequently. Finally, receive feedback from the prospect throughout the demonstration by asking questions or pausing in your conversation. This is extremely important, since it will

- Determine the prospect's attitude toward the product
- Allow you to progress in the demonstration or wait and answer any questions or address any objections
- Aid in moving the prospect into the positive yes mood
- Set the stage for closing the sale.

Little agreements lead to the big agreement. Phrase questions in a positive manner such as "That is really easy to operate, isn't it?" instead of, "This isn't hard to operate, is it?" Although they ask the same thing, the response to the first question is positive instead of negative. The best questions force the prospect to place the product in use mentally, such as the question phrased, "Do you feel this feature could increase your employees' production?" This "yes" answer commits the buyer to the idea that the feature will increase employee production. Remember, it is often not what you say but how you say it.

Guidelines for Using Visual Aids, Dramatics, and Demonstrations

Although visual aids, dramatics, and demonstrations are important, their proper use is critical to be effective. When using them, consider

- Rehearsing by practising in front of a mirror, or filming yourself selling to a friend. Once you are ready to make the presentation, try it out on less important prospects. This practice allows you time to refine the presentation before contacting more important accounts.

- Customizing them to the sales call objective (the prospect's customer profile; the customer benefit plan), concentrating on the prospect's important buying motives, and using appropriate multiple appeals to sight, touch, hearing, smell, and taste. See Exhibit 9–10.

- Making them *simple* and *clear*.

- Being sure you control the demonstration by not letting the prospect divert you from selling. It can be disastrous to have the prospect not listen or pass up major selling points you wanted to present.

- Making them *true to life*.

- Encouraging *prospect participation*.

- Incorporating *trial closes* (questions) after showing or demonstrating a major feature, advantage, or benefit to determine whether it is believed and important to the prospect.

EXHIBIT 9–10

Which buyer senses are being appealed to by the seller?

TECHNOLOGY CAN HELP

Technology can provide excellent methods of presenting information to the buyer in a visually attractive and dramatic manner. Today, multimedia computers present video clips, play sound bites, show beautifully illustrated graphics, and can be connected to projection equipment for great presentations. Computer software can quickly crunch data—providing instant answers to buyers' questions. Salespeople selling products such as service, real estate, and industrial equipment can quickly show buyers a product's cost when considering different instalment payment schedules at various interest rates. Here are several examples of high-tech presentations.

- Xerox employs multimedia sales demonstrations with sophisticated graphics and animation to explain the features, advantages, and benefits of its printers and fax machines. It's a lot easier and more economical to hand a prospective customer a disk than it is to wheel in a large piece of equipment for a demonstration.

- Dun & Bradstreet developed a multimedia program that helps salespeople qualify leads by prompting prospective customers through a series of questions, with each consecutive question based on the person's previous response. Prospects work their way through the self-guided program and then fax or mail their responses, allowing sales reps to qualify prospects quickly and tailor their follow-ups to specific needs. Dun & Bradstreet used this type of interactive multimedia disk for direct marketing to Fortune 1000 companies.

- It can be difficult, for example, to illustrate a complex project without losing a customer's attention due to jargon and diagrams. But when sales reps from a large construction company used a computer-based, 3-D interactive multimedia presentation to win a multimillion-dollar hospital renovation contract, it was as easy as graphically lifting the roof off the hospital and taking the administrators on a step-by-step tour. It showed the client that the company knew the job as well as or better than competitors.

Overhead transparencies, 35-mm slides, and black-and-white handouts are being replaced by dynamic software packages such as PowerPoint, interactive multimedia programs, LCD or plasma colour screens, and multimedia projectors that bring computer images to life. Remember, it's often not what you say but how you say it that makes the sale.[4]

THE IDEAL PRESENTATION

In the ideal presentation, your approach technique quickly captures your prospect's interest and immediately finds signals that the prospect has a need for your product and is ready to listen. The ideal prospect is friendly, polite, relaxed, will not allow anyone to interrupt you, asks questions, and participates in your demonstration as planned. This allows you to move through the presentation skilfully.

The ideal customer cheerfully and positively answers each of your questions, allowing you to anticipate the correct moment to ask for the order. You are completely relaxed and sure of yourself when you come to the close. The customer says yes, and enthusiastically thanks you for your valuable time. Several weeks later, you receive a copy of the letter your customer wrote to your company's president glowing with praise for your professionalism and sincere concern for the customer.

MAKING THE SALE

Top Tips for Effective PowerPoint Presentations

There's nothing worse than a poor PowerPoint presentation. We've all seen them with too much animation, too much information, and gimmicky sound effects. The main objective of a PowerPoint presentation is to provide the information you feel will be necessary for your prospect(s) to leave with a clear idea and a favourable impression.

Tips:

- Use an Introduction Slide at the beginning to introduce your purpose and planned agenda. Use a welcoming slide if people will be sitting and waiting for things to begin.

- Limit each slide to 4–5 bullet points. Do not write out full sentences—just summarize your points.

- Don't fill the slide with pictures or animation, which will distract from your message.

- Don't overuse colour; limit to just a few.

- Watch your timing. Try to finish a little earlier than expected.

- Pictures are good if they are of high quality. Avoid clip art. Make the pictures relevant to your presentation.

- Adding your prospect's logo to your slide is a nice touch and personalizes your presentation.

- Use consistent backgrounds, particularly a custom background pertaining to your company.

- Proofread your slides. There's nothing worse than having an audience looking at a spelling or grammatical error for an extended amount of time.

- Summarize. Conclude your presentation with a summary slide of the key points you have made.

- Always have a backup plan. Technical difficulties may prevent you from using your equipment—so be ready.

CROSS-SELLING

I was at the hardware store the other day buying some taps for my kitchen sink. After selling me the taps, the clerk asked some questions, "Do you have enough propane at home to get the job done? How about lead-free solder? Have you considered some silicone caulking to prevent water from getting under your new taps?" These were all things I hadn't thought of and I ended up spending an extra $25 on materials, which perturbed me at first and I was a little upset with the sales clerk. It wasn't until I got home and finished the job that I realized that I in fact needed all these things and the clerk did me a huge favour in suggesting them. It probably saved me two or three trips back to the store and several hours of aggravation simply by an alert clerk doing some cross-selling.

Cross-selling or **add-on selling** is an excellent way to increase the value of a sale by not only selling more products but also providing the customer with better service. Cross-selling involves suggesting extra or complementary products or services to a customer in addition to the main product he is purchasing. It is often useful, where applicable, to develop a script to take advantage of cross-selling opportunities. Developing a script for an add-on product or service can act as a bridge from the closed order to additional product or service selling.

Before attempting to use your cross-selling script, have the original order in hand. In other words, make sure you have achieved your primary objective first. Get the customer's commitment, get all the order details, and only then attempt the cross-sell.

For example,

Thank you, Ms. Kim, for the photocopier order. By the way, did you know that we offer first-time purchasers like yourself a 50 percent discount on copy paper ordered with the copier? It will not only save you money but also eliminate the need of finding another supplier for paper—and our paper is specially formulated to take advantage of the many features of our machines. Would you like me to add a six-month supply of paper to the order?

The cross-sell should relate directly to the purchase, and the item should be relatively low cost in comparison to the original order (so that a major purchase decision is not necessary). A guideline is that the cross-sell should not exceed the purchase amount by more than 25 percent. From a scripting point of view, the item is a related item and therefore needs little or no description. Secondly, by adding the words "by the way" there is a casualness to the add-on that reduces the "hard sell" feeling that sometimes accompanies an add-on sale. The benefits are clearly expressed and, when done properly, most customers will see this as receiving extra value, not being pushed into an order.

Prepare well before creating your cross-sell script. Examine the type of prospect to whom you will be selling. How knowledgeable is he? Will he see the add-on as an extra value, or something requiring a little more thought? Will he require additional information to make the purchase decision?

Answers to these questions will dictate the type of add on(s) that you may choose. For example, if your preparation had revealed that your prospect had been having a nightmare with the previous photocopier in terms of too much downtime, expensive repairs, paper jamming, and so on, your cross-sell script could include add-ons like an extended warranty agreement and your specially formulated paper. These add-ons appeal directly to the prospect's buying motives and hence will be perceived as excellent value added.

Make cross-selling a habit. Be brief, to the point, and casual. It can have a tremendous impact on your sales figures and customer satisfaction levels. The following list provides some tips to help you cross-sell and up-sell:

1. **Close first and cross-sell later.** Do not attempt to up-sell or cross-sell until you have closed the first order. In our rush to up-sell we sometimes forget that the customer has an order to place. Selling additional items too early in the call might turn the customer off. You could lose the original sale.

2. **Follow the 25 percent rule.** The value of an add-on sale should not increase the overall order by more than 25 percent. Despite the fact that people are motivated to buy, too much up-selling may cause the customer to reconsider the entire purchase.

3. **Provide value.** On occasion, there will be an urge to use cross-selling and up-selling to move unwanted inventory. Never do this unless there is an inherent benefit to your customer. Don't saddle your prospect with unneeded merchandise just for your own benefit.

4. **Make sure it's related.** Limit your choice of add-on items to those that clearly relate to the original purchase. If a customer is buying machinery for her plant, don't try to sell her cleaning supplies for the washrooms just because you have some excess inventory of it.

5. **Plan ahead.** Cross-selling should be part of your sales plan. Appropriate up-sell products should be highlighted next to each major product in your sales notes.

6. **Be prepared.** Ensure that you are knowledgeable of the products or services that you are up-selling. Rehearse the skills necessary to get the customer to say yes. Know how to demonstrate how a particular add-on applies to and benefits the customer.

7. **Reap the rewards.** Your cross-selling efforts will be directly dependent on how motivated you are. Cross-selling and up-selling take additional time and effort. If you are not motivated, chances are the program will not succeed. Commit to the program and you are certain to increase your sales—and your compensation.

BE PREPARED FOR PRESENTATION DIFFICULTIES

Yes, a few sales presentations go incredibly smoothly; most, though, have one or more hurdles. Although all the difficulties you might face cannot be discussed here, the three main problems encountered during sales presentations are handling an interruption, discussing your competition, and making the presentation in a less-than-ideal situation.

How to Handle Interruptions

It is common for interruptions to occur during the presentation. The secretary comes into the office or the telephone rings, distracting the prospect. What should you do?

First, determine whether the discussion that interrupted your presentation is personal or confidential. If so, by gesture or voice you can offer to leave the room—this is always appreciated by the prospect. Second, while waiting, regroup your thoughts and mentally review how to return to the presentation. Once the discussion is over, you can

1. Wait quietly and patiently until you have regained the prospect's attention completely.
2. Briefly restate the selling points that had interested the prospect; for example, "We were discussing your needs for a product such as ours and you seemed especially interested in knowing about our service, delivery, and installation. Is that right?"
3. Do something to increase the prospect's participation, such as showing the product, using other visuals, or asking questions. Closely watch to determine whether you have regained the prospect's interest.
4. If interest is regained, move deeper into the presentation.

Should You Discuss the Competition?

Competition is something all salespeople must contend with every day. If you sell a product, you must compete with others selling comparable products. How should you handle competition? Basically, remember three considerations: (1) do not refer to a competitor unless absolutely necessary; (2) acknowledge your competitor only briefly; and (3) make a detailed comparison of your product and the competition's product.

SELLING GLOBALLY

Making a Deal in Mexico

Typically, Mexicans prefer doing business with people they know, so developing sincere relationships is critical.

In business culture, the relationship is probably more important than your competence, knowledge, or experience. In Mexico the family plays a dominant role and often extends into the business, with many companies being family owned.

The business culture in Mexico has a slower pace and warmer, friendlier atmosphere. Don't expect quick results; the relationship must be nurtured. Mexicans like to become involved in finding a solution, so partnership selling can be very useful.

Use visuals in your presentations. They should be of high quality but should not be used as a substitute for a strong relationship. You can expect a longer than normal negotiation and it will appear a little less formal—more like haggling.

Mexican businesspeople are often well informed about who they are doing business with, so be prepared. It helps if you are the one with the authority to act and not just a liaison for your company.

Any literature and correspondence is considered important so should be of high quality. Always handle documents with formality and respect so as not to offend anyone.

When the decision is made, it is important that it is summarized in a written agreement.

Do Not Refer to Competition

Reduce any surprises the buyer may present by properly planning for the sales call. In developing your customer profile, try to learn which competing products are used and your prospect's attitude toward your products and competitors' products. Based on your findings, the presentation can be developed without specifically referring to competition.

Acknowledge Competition and Drop It

Many salespeople believe their competition should not be discussed unless the prospect discusses it. Then, acknowledge competition briefly and return to your product. "Yes, I am familiar with that product's features. In fact, the last three of my customers were using that product and have switched over to ours. May I tell you why?"

Here, you do not knock competition, but acknowledge it and in a positive manner move the prospect's attention back to your products. If the prospect continues to discuss a competing product, you should determine the prospect's attitude toward it. You might ask, "What do you think about the IBM 6000 computer system?" The answer will help you mentally determine how you can prove that your product offers the prospect more benefits than your competitor's product.

Make a Detailed Comparison

At times, it is appropriate to make a detailed comparison of your product to a competing one, especially for industrial products. If products are similar, emphasize your company's service, guarantees, and what you do personally for customers.

If your product has features that are lacking in a competitor's product, refer to these advantages. "Our product is the only one on the market with this feature! Is this important to you?" Ask the question and wait for the response. A yes answer takes you one step closer to the sale.

Often the prospect can use both your product and a competitor's product. For example, a pharmaceutical salesperson is selling an antibiotic that functions like penicillin and kills bacteria resistant to penicillin. However, it costs 20 times more than penicillin. This salesperson would say, "Yes, Dr. Jones, penicillin is the drug of choice for _____ disease. But, do you have patients for whom penicillin is ineffective?" "Yes, I do," says the doctor. "Then, for those patients, I want you to consider my product because . . ."

Be Professional No matter how you discuss competition with your prospect, always act professionally. If you discuss competition, talk only about information that you know is accurate, and be straightforward and honest—not belittling and discourteous.

Your prospect may like both your products and the competitor's products. A loyalty to the competitor may have been built over the years; by knocking competition, you may insult and alienate your prospect. However, the advantages and disadvantages of a competitive product can be demonstrated acceptably if done professionally. One salesperson relates this story:

> Several customers I called on were loyal to my competitors; however, just as many were loyal to my company. I will always remember the president of a chain of retail stores who flew 500 kilometres to be at one of our salespeople's retirement dinners. In his talk, he

ETHICAL DILEMMA
Overstatement vs. Understatement

You are in the competitive field of selling high-capacity photocopiers. One of your prospects is looking for copiers that will reliably run up to 5,000 copies per day without being overloaded. After doing an analysis of the prospect's paper purchases over the last year, you extrapolate that 90 percent of her copiers ran at only 60 percent (3,000 copies per day) capacity over the last year. Your dilemma is this. Should you propose your medium-duty copier, which was designed for 3,500 copies per day, knowing that this will handle her needs most of the time based on the usage history? This will allow you to come in with a price about 15 percent below your competitors and will allow you to get this lucrative deal. After all, it is highly unlikely that a problem will ever arise.

What do you do?

noted how 30 years ago, when he opened his first store, this salesperson extended him company credit and made him a personal loan that helped him get started.

It would be difficult for a competing salesperson to sell to this loyal customer. When contacting customers, especially ones buying competitive products, it is important to uncover why they use competitive products before discussing competition in the presentation.

Making the Presentation in a Less-Than-Ideal Situation

The ideal presentation happens in a quiet room with only the salesperson, the prospect, and no interruptions. However, at times the salesperson may meet the prospect somewhere other than a private office and need to make the presentation under less than ideal conditions.

For short presentations, a stand-up situation may be adequate; however, when making a longer presentation, you may want to ask the prospect, "Could we go back to your office?" or make another appointment.

SUMMARY OF MAJOR SELLING ISSUES

The sales presentation is a persuasive vocal and visual explanation of a proposition. Although there are numerous methods for making a sales presentation, the four common ones are the memorized, formula, interactive need-satisfaction, and problem-solution selling methods. Each method is effective if used for the proper situation.

In developing your presentation, consider the elements of the sales presentation mix that you will use for each prospect. The proper use of persuasive communication techniques, methods to develop prospect participation, evidence statements, visual aids, dramatization, and demonstrations increases your chance of illustrating how your products will satisfy your prospect's needs.

It is often not what we say but how we say it that results in the sale. Persuasive communication techniques (questioning, listening, logical reasoning, suggestion, and the use of trial closes) help to uncover needs, to communicate effectively, and to pull the prospect into the conversation.

Evidence statements are especially useful in showing your prospect that what you say is true and that you can be trusted. When challenged, prove it by incorporating facts on a customer's past sales in your presentation, by guaranteeing the product will work or sell, or offering testimonials and company and independent research results.

To both show and tell, visuals must be properly designed to illustrate features, advantages, and benefits of your products through graphics, dramatization, and demonstration. This pairing allows you to capture the prospect's attention and interest; to create two-way communication and participation; to express your proposition in a clearer, more complete manner; and to make more sales. Careful attention to development and rehearsal of the presentation is needed to ensure it occurs smoothly and naturally.

Always prepare for the unexpected, such as a demonstration that falls apart, interruptions, the prospect's questions about the competition, or the necessity to make your presentation in a less than ideal place, such as the aisle of a retail store or in the warehouse.

The presentation part of the overall sales presentation is the heart of the sale. It is where you develop the desire, conviction, and action. By giving an effective presentation, you have fewer objections to your proposition, which makes for an easier sale close.

If you want to be a real professional in selling, acquire or create materials that convey your message and convince others to believe it. If you try to sell without using the components of the sales presentation mix, you are losing sales because of not what you say but how you say it. Exhibits, facts, statistics, examples, analogies, testimonials, and samples should be part of your repertoire. Without them, you are not equipped to do a professional job of selling.

MEETING A SALES CHALLENGE

The laptop's ability to resist dead spots is important to the customer who needs proof your technology will result in fewer dead spots. In this situation, the evidence statement should be authoritative, using independent research results if possible. Here is an example of an effective evidence statement:

"Mr. Jones, a laptop with our new WiFi technology will experience fewer dead zones than any of our competitors." (Restatement of the benefit.) "A recent study conducted by *Modern Computer Magazine* reported that our technology was 98% reliable. The next best was only 89% reliable." (Evidence of the benefit.) "And since our laptops are made utilizing this new technology, you'll seldom hear any complaints about these computers experiencing dead zones" (An expansion of the benefit.) "Is this WiFi technology feature something that your customers will appreciate?" (Trial close.)

PLAYING THE ROLE

Choose one of the following products:

Office chairs, photocopiers, HDTV, iPhone, GPS

Now, as a salesperson for this product, develop two examples of simile, metaphor, and analogy that could be used in a presentation of that product. Be prepared to dramatize these to a prospect (classmate). Observers can listen carefully to determine if the examples had a positive effect. That is, would the prospect find the product more attractive after hearing these techniques used? Have the observers comment on whether the statements sounded phony or realistic.

KEY TERMS FOR SELLING

add-on selling, 257
analogy, 247
autosuggestion, 243
body language, 246
consultative selling, 240
countersuggestion, 244
cross-selling, 257
demonstration, 252
direct suggestion, 243
dramatization, 251

evidence statements, 247
indirect suggestion, 244
logical reasoning, 243
metaphor, 247
prestige suggestions, 243
sales presentation mix, 241
simile, 246
suggestive propositions, 243
testimonials, 263
visuals, 250

SALES APPLICATION QUESTIONS

1. You plan to give a demonstration of a new fork-lift truck that has a hybrid engine to the purchasing agent of a company with a storage facility that covers 50 hectares. Which of the following is the best technique for your demonstration? Why?
   a. Let your prospect drive the fork lift.
   b. You drive the fork lift and ask the prospect to ride along so that you can discuss the truck's benefits.
   c. Leave a demonstrator and return a week later to see how many the prospect will buy.

2. When contracting a purchasing agent for your hybrid fork-lift truck, you plan to use your 10-page visual presenter to guide the prospect through your benefit story. This selling aid is a binder containing photographs of your truck in action along with its various colour options, a guarantee, and a testimonial. Should you:
   a. Hand over the binder? Why?
   b. Hold on to it? Why?

3. Assume you are halfway through your presentation when your prospect has to answer the telephone. The call lasts five minutes. What should you do?

4. Discuss the various elements of the sales presentation mix and indicate why you need to use visuals during your presentation.

5. In your evidence statement of the benefit, cite your evidence source, in addition to relevant facts or figures about your product. Which of the following is a correct evidence of a benefit?
   a. Well, an article in last month's *Appliance Report* stated that the Williams blender is more durable than the other top 10 brands.
   b. You'll get 10 percent more use from the Hanig razor.
   c. *Marathon* is the most widely read magazine among persons with incomes over $25,000 per year.
   d. Figures in *Marathon* magazine indicate that your sales will increase if you stock Majestic housewares in your store.

6. Examine the following conversation:

Customer: What you say is important, all right, but how do I know that these chairs will take wear and tear the way you say they will?

Salesperson: The durability of a chair is an important factor to consider. That's why all Crest chairs have reinforced plastic webbing seats. *Furniture Dealer's Weekly* states that the plastic webbing used in Crest chairs is 32 percent more effective in preventing sagging chair seats than fabric webbing. This means that your chairs will last longer and take the wear and tear that your customers are concerned about.

Look at each sentence in this conversation and state whether it is

    a. An expansion of the benefit.

    b. A restatement of the benefit.

    c. An evidence statement.

7. After a two-hour drive to see an important new prospect, you stop at a local coffee shop for a bite to eat. As you look over your presentation charts, you spill coffee on a half dozen of them. You don't have substitute presentation charts with you. What should you do?

    a. Phone the prospect and say that you'd like to make another appointment. Say that something came up.

    b. Keep the appointment. At the start of your presentation, tell the prospect about the coffee spill and apologize for it.

    c. Go ahead with your presentation, but don't make excuses. The coffee stains are barely noticeable if you're not on the lookout for them.

SALES WORLD WIDE WEB EXERCISE

High-Tech Presentations!

Search the following URLs to find information to help you create a presentation enhanced by technology:

Sales & Marketing Management Magazine

www.salesandmarketing.com

Selling Power Magazine

www.sellingpower.com

Videoconferencing

http://its.psu.edu/videoconf/

Use search engines to find Web sites on sales or presentation technology. Salespeople are using more multimedia presentations to convey their message. See what you can find out about methods, equipment, and the effectiveness of using multimedia in a sales presentation.

FURTHER EXPLORING THE SALES WORLD

1. What is one thing in this world on which you are an expert? Yourself! Develop a presentation on yourself for a sales job with a company of your choice. Relate this assignment to each of the 10 steps of the selling process.

2. Visit several retail stores in your community such as an appliance, bicycle, or sporting goods store and report on the demonstration techniques, if any, that were used in selling a product. Suggest ways that you would have presented the product.

3. Report on one television advertisement that used each of the following: an evidence statement, a demonstration, unusual visual aids, and a dramatization.

4. In your library are magazines where companies advertise their products to retail and wholesaler customers, along with information about current price discounts. Find at least three advertisements containing current price discounts offered by manufacturers to wholesalers or retailers. How might you use this information in a sales presentation?

STUDENT APPLICATION LEARNING EXERCISES (SALES)

Part 6

An important part of consultative selling is the use of questions to uncover the customer's needs. You have planned some of your questions in constructing your SELL sequences. SELL sequences should be contained in your discussion of the product, marketing plan, and business proposition.

Every important sales presentation should contain most—if not all—of the presentation mix ingredients shown in Exhibit 9–5 on page 242. To make SALE 6:

1. Construct and write out one SELL sequence. After your trial close, the buyer questions what you have just said. The buyer sounds unsure whether what you are saying is true. Create an evidence statement that shows your claim is true. See page 247.

   SELL sequence:

   Buyer's skeptical remark:

   Evidence statement:

2. Create one analogy, simile, and metaphor to use in your role-play. See page 246.

   Simile:

   Metaphor:

   Analogy:

3. Describe a demonstration you could do of one of your product's benefits. If possible, add dramatization. Remember, simply showing the product is not a demonstration.

4. Describe three visual aids you could use in your presentation. Flip-charts and notebooks are easy to develop, or you can place your visuals in a folder and pull one at a time out as you discuss it.

   Visual 1:

   Visual 2:

   Visual 3:

CASE 9–1
Dyno Electric Cart Company

You plan a call-back to Conway Pride and the president of his company to sell them several of your electric carts. (Refer to Exhibit 7–14 on page 191.) The company's manufacturing plant covers some 100 hectares and you have sold up to 10 carts to many companies smaller than this one. Since Pride allows you to meet with his company's president and maybe other executives, you know that he is interested in your carts.

You are determined to make a spellbinding presentation of your product's benefits using visual aids and a cart demonstration. Mr. Pride raised several objections during your last presentation that may be restated by other executives. Your challenge is to develop a dramatic, convincing presentation.

CASE 9–1

Questions

1. You plan to give a cart demonstration to show how effective it is in travelling around the plant. Which of the following is the best technique for the demonstration?

   a. Get Pride and the president involved by letting them drive the cart.

   b. You drive, letting them ride so they will listen more carefully to you.

   c. Leave a demonstrator and check back the next week to see how many they will buy.

2. You also plan to use a 10-page visual presenter to guide them through your benefit story. This selling aid is in a binder and contains photographs of your cart in action, along with its various colour options, guarantee, and testimonials. Should you:

   a. Get Pride to participate by letting him hold it?

   b. Handle it yourself, allowing him to watch and listen while you turn the pages and tell your story?

CASE 9–2

Major Oil, Inc.*

Tim Christensen sells industrial lubricants to manufacturing plants. The lubricants are used for the plants' machinery. He is calling on Petar Balogh, a purchasing agent for Acme Manufacturing Company. Petar currently buys Tim's Hydraulic Oil 65 in drums. Tim's sales call objective is to persuade Petar to switch from purchasing his oil in drums to a bulk oil system. The secretary has just admitted him to Petar's office.

Salesperson: Hello, Petar.

Customer: Well, if it isn't Tim Christensen, my lube oil salesperson! How is everything over at Major Oil these days?

Salesperson: Fine! We're adding to our warehouse, so we won't be quite as crowded. Say, I know you like to fly. I was just reading in a magazine about the old Piper Tri-Pacer.

Customer: Yeah! I do enjoy flying and fooling with old airplanes. I just got back this weekend from a fly-in over at Hamilton.

Salesperson: You don't say! What type of planes did they have?

Customer: They had a bunch of homebuilts. You know, many pilots spend from 5 to 15 years just building their own planes.

Salesperson: Would you like to build your own plane someday?

Customer: Yes, I would. But you know, this job takes so much time—and with my schedule here and some travel, I don't know if I'll ever get time to start on a plane, much less finish one.

Salesperson: Well, I don't know that I can save you that much time, but I can save the people in the plant time and reduce your cost of Hydraulic Oil 65. Also, I may even save your office some time and expense by not having to place so many orders.

*Case developed by George Wynn, professor of marketing, James Madison University, © 1998.

CASE 9–2

You know, we talked a couple of weeks ago about the possibility of Acme buying Hydraulic Oil 65 in bulk and thus reducing the cost per litre by buying larger quantities each time you order. In addition, you will save tying your money up in the $20 drum deposit or even losing the deposit by losing or damaging the empty drum.

Customer: Sounds like this is going to cost us some money.

Salesperson: Well, we might have to spend a little money to save a larger amount, plus make it easier and quicker in the plant. Do you know exactly what you are paying for Hydraulic Oil 65 now?

Customer: I think it's about $1.40 a litre.

Salesperson: That's close. Your delivery cost is $1.39 per litre, not counting drum deposit. You used approximately 20,000 litres of Hydraulic Oil 65 last year at a total cost of $27,800.

Customer: Between what I pay at the gas station and what we pay here, I see why Major Oil is getting bigger and richer all the time. How much money can you save us?

Salesperson: Well, we try to get by and make ends meet. However, I can save your company more than $2,800 per year on oil costs alone.

Customer: That sounds awful big. How are you going to do that?

Salesperson: I am going to show you how you can purchase oil in bulk, save 14¢ per litre on each litre you buy [14¢ times 20,000 litres equals $2,800], and eliminate handling those drums and having your money tied up in deposits. Last year, you purchased about 364 drums—and I'll bet you did not return all the drums to us.

Customer: I know we damaged some drums, and I imagine we furnished some trash barrels for our employees. I wonder how much of a total deposit we pay?

Salesperson: The total deposit on those drums was $7,280. Are you and your company totally satisfied with the performance of Hydraulic Oil 65?

Customer: It seems so. I have heard nothing to the contrary; and our bearing supplier, Timken, says that the oil is doing a first-class job. You know, this savings sounds good in theory, but will it really work? Besides, where will we put a big bulk system?

Salesperson: Petar, I've already thoroughly checked into what the total equipment and installation will cost. Here's a picture of the installation we made over at the Foundry and Machine Shop. We put the installation above ground to save the expense of digging holes for the tanks. The cover shown here in the picture protects the pump and motor from the weather, and the pipe into the shop goes underground. There's a control switch for the pump motor mounted inside the building next to the nozzle outlet. It looks good, doesn't it?

Customer: It certainly does, Tim, but what about the cost?

Salesperson: We can get two new 3,000-litre tanks delivered here for a cost of $1,700 from our tank supplier. This is about $120 less than what you could buy them for. Our quantity purchases of tanks give us a little better price—and we'll be glad to pass these savings on to you. I have checked with Pump Supply Company, and they have in stock the pump and motor with flexible coupling and built-in pump relief valve, just what we need for handling this oil. The cost is $475. The control

CASE 9–2

switch, pipe, pipe fittings, inside hose, and nozzle come to $120, and the person who does our installation work has given me a commitment to do all the installation work for $500, including furnishing the blocks to make the tank supports.

This totals $2,795, so let's round off to $2,800. And at a savings of 14¢ per litre, based on your present usage of 20,000 litres per year, this would be paid off in about 12 months, during which time you'd pay $1.25 per litre for your oil rather than the $1.39 you now pay. How does that sound to you, Petar?

Customer: That sounds pretty good to me, Tim. Didn't you have an article about this in a recent issue of your company magazine?

Salesperson: We sure did. It was in the March issue. Here it is, right here. The situation was a little different, but the basic idea is the same. Our company has used this idea to considerable advantage and over the past three years I have set up six installations of this type. Do you have any questions regarding the plan I've outlined?

Customer: Just one thing—you know we're short on space behind the warehouse. Have you thought about where we might locate an installation of this type?

Salesperson: Yes, I have, Petar. Recall one of our earlier conversations where you told me about your plans to clean up that old scrap pile near the corner of the warehouse? That would be an ideal location. We could then locate the control switch, filling hose, and nozzle right on the inside at the end of the assembly line so the units could have their initial oil fill just before they come off the assembly line. How would that fit into your plans?

Customer: That's a good idea, Tim. That way we can get that junk pile cleaned up, replace it with a decent looking installation, and then make our initial oil fill the last step in our assembly procedure.

Salesperson: Do you have any other questions, Petar?

Customer: No, I believe I've got the whole picture now.

Salesperson: Good. Now, to sum up our thinking, Petar, the total cost of installation will be about $3,000. Immediately on completion of the installation, and when you receive your first transport truckload shipment of Hydraulic Oil 65, instead of being billed at $1.39 per litre, as you are now paying for barrel deliveries, you will be billed $1.25 per litre. I'll work with Bill Smith, the plant superintendent, and I'll handle all the outside contacts so that we can make the installation with little turmoil.

Customer: That sounds good to me. When can we start the installation?

Salesperson: Tomorrow. I'll bring a contract for you to have your people sign. It should take about three to four weeks after the contract is signed.

Customer: Good. What do I need to do right now?

Salesperson: If you'll arrange to clean the junk out of the corner, then we'll be ready. I'll order the equipment and have it moving so that we can be ready in about four weeks. What would be the best time to see you tomorrow?

Customer: Any time will be okay with me, Tim.

Salesperson: Swell, Petar. Thanks for your help. I know you will be pleased with this new installation and also save money. See you tomorrow.

CASE 9–2

Questions

1. Evaluate Tim's sales presentation. Include in your answer comments on his approach, presentation, use of trial closes, handling of objections, and his close.

2. How would you develop visual materials to illustrate Tim's sales presentation, including the arithmetic?

3. Now that Tim has sold to Petar, what should Tim do next?

10

OBJECTIONS—ADDRESS YOUR PROSPECT'S CONCERNS

MAIN TOPICS	LEARNING OBJECTIVES
Welcome Objections!	When you learn how to skilfully handle your prospect's questions, resistance, and objections, you are a professional. After studying this chapter, you should be able to:
What Are Objections?	
When Do Prospects Object?	
Objections and the Sales Process	

Welcome Objections!

What Are Objections?

When Do Prospects Object?

Objections and the Sales Process

Five Major Categories of Objections

Responding to Objections

Points to Consider About Handling Objections

Dealing with Difficult Customers

Negotiating a Win–Win Outcome

When you learn how to skilfully handle your prospect's questions, resistance, and objections, you are a professional. After studying this chapter, you should be able to:

- Explain why you should welcome a prospect's objections.

- Describe what to do when objections arise.

- Discuss the basic points to consider in meeting a prospect's objections.

- Explain five major categories of objections.

- Present, illustrate, and use the four-step process for meeting prospect objections.

- Describe what to do after the four steps.

- Understand and use specific objection-handling techniques.

- Understand how to deal with difficult customers.

- Explain the process of negotiating with a win–win outcome.

FACING A SALES CHALLENGE

As you drive up into the parking lot of a top distributor of your home building supplies, you recall how only two years ago the company purchased the largest opening order you ever sold. Last year, their sales doubled, and this year you hope to sell them more than $100,000 worth.

As you wait, the receptionist informs you that since your last visit, your buyer, Mary Smalley, was fired and another buyer, Nonnie Young, was transferred to her position. Mary and you had become good friends over the past two years, and you hate to see her go.

As you enter the new buyer's office, Young asks you to have a seat and then says: "I've got some bad news for you. I'm considering switching suppliers. Your prices are too high."

What would you do in this situation? Salespeople commonly face challenges; in most presentations, they experience objections. How does a professional salesperson handle a difficult situation? (Continued at end of chapter.)

This chapter examines **objections**. It discusses how to meet objections, techniques to use in overcoming objections, and how to proceed after addressing an objection. Professionals welcome objections!

WELCOME OBJECTIONS!

When a prospect first gives an objection, *smile,* because that's when you start earning your salary. You want to receive personal satisfaction from your job and at the same time increase your salary—right? Well, both occur when you accept objections as a challenge that, handled correctly, benefit both your prospect and you. The more effectively you meet customers' needs and solve their problems, the more successful you will be in sales. If you *fear* objections, you will *fumble* your response, which often causes *failure.*

Remember, although people want to buy, they do not want to be exploited. Buyers who cannot see how your offering will fulfill their needs ask questions and raise objections. If you cannot effectively answer the questions or meet the objections, you will not make the sale. It is *your* fault, not the buyer's fault, that the sale was not made if you sincerely believe your offering fulfills a need, but the prospect still will not buy. The salesperson who can overcome objections when they are raised and smoothly return to a presentation will succeed.

WHAT ARE OBJECTIONS?

Interestingly, prospects who present objections often are easily sold on your product. They are interested enough to object; they want to know what you have to offer.

Opposition or resistance to information or to the salesperson's request is labelled a **sales objection**. Sales objections must be welcomed because they show the prospect's interest and help determine what stage the prospect has reached in the buying cycle—attention, interest, desire, conviction, or readiness to close.

WHEN DO PROSPECTS OBJECT?

The prospect may object at any time during your sales call—from introduction to close. Imagine walking into a retail store, carrying a sales bag, and the buyer yells out, "Oh no, not another salesperson. I don't even want to see you, let alone buy from you!" What do you say?

When one of us was faced with this situation, he said, "I understand. I'm not here to sell you anything, only to check your stock, help stock your shelves, and return any old or damaged merchandise for a refund." As he turned to walk away, the buyer said, "Come on back here; I want to talk to you."

If he had simply said "Okay," he would not have made that sale. He knew that he could benefit that customer, and his response and attitude showed it. The point is always to be ready to handle a prospect's objections, whether at the approach, during the presentation, after a trial close, after you have already met a previous objection, or during the close.

OBJECTIONS AND THE SALES PROCESS

Objections can occur at any time. Often, however, the prospect allows you to make a presentation, often asking questions along the way. Inexperienced salespeople traditionally finish their presentation and wait for the prospect's response.

Experienced, successful salespeople have learned to use the system shown in Exhibit 10–1. After the presentation, they use a trial close to determine the prospect's attitude toward the product and assess whether it is time to close.

Remember, the *trial close* asks for the prospect's opinion about what was said in the presentation. Typically, the trial close causes the prospect to ask questions or state objections. The salesperson should be prepared to respond in one of four ways:

1. If there is a positive response to the trial close immediately after the presentation, move to the close as shown in Exhibit 10–1, moving from Step 5 to Step 9.

2. If an objection is raised, understand or clarify it, respond to it, and attempt another trial close to see whether you have met the objection. If you have, then move to the close.

3. After meeting one objection, be prepared to determine whether there are other objections. You may have to move from Step 8 back to Step 6.

4. If, after responding to the objection and attempting a trial close, you have not overcome the objection, return to your presentation (Step 4) and further discuss the product relative to the objection.

To handle an objection effectively, a salesperson must be able to recognize the type, or category, of objection being raised by the buyer.

FIVE MAJOR CATEGORIES OF OBJECTIONS

Most objections that salespeople encounter are placed into the five categories shown in Exhibit 10–2. Each category represents a different area of concern or disagreement. When the buyer raises an objection, the salesperson must be able to mentally identify its category. Only then can she respond appropriately to the objection and address the buyer's true reason for resistance.

The Stalling Objection

When your prospect says, "I'll think it over," or "I'll be ready to buy on your next visit," you must determine whether the statement is the truth or whether it is a smokescreen designed to get rid of you. The **stalling objection** is a common tactic.

What you discovered in developing your customer profile and customer benefit plan can aid you in determining how to handle this type of objection. Suppose that before seeing a certain retail customer, you checked the supply of your merchandise in both the store's stockroom and on the retail shelf and this occurs:

Buyer: I have enough merchandise for now. Thanks for coming by.

Salesperson: Ms. Marcher, you have 50 cases in the warehouse and on display. You sell 50 cases each month, right?

When objections occur, quickly determine what to do.

10
Follow-up

9
Close

8
Trial close

7
Meet objections

6
Determine objections

5
Trial close

4
Presentation

3
Approach

2
Preapproach

1
Prospecting

You have legitimately questioned the wisdom of stalling. This buyer either has to order more merchandise from you or tell you why she is allowing her product supply to dwindle. An easily handled stall is illustrated in Exhibit 10–3. When the prospect says, "I'm too busy to see you now," you might ask, "When would be a good time to come back today?"

One of the toughest stalls to overcome arises in selling a new consumer product. Retail buyers are reluctant to stock consumer goods that customers have not yet asked for, even new goods produced by large, established consumer product manufacturers.

Another common stall is the alibi that your prospect must have approval from someone else, such as a boss, buying committee, purchasing agent, or home office. Since the buyer's attitude toward purchasing your product influences the firm's buying decision, it is important to determine the buyer's attitude toward your product.

When the buyer stalls by saying, "I will have to get approval from my boss," you can counter by saying, "If you had the authority, you would go ahead with the purchase, wouldn't you?" If the answer is yes, chances are that the buyer will positively influence the firm's buying decision. If not, you must uncover the real objections. Otherwise, you will not make the sale.

An additional response to the "I've got to think it over" stall is, "What are some of the issues you have to think about?" Or you may focus directly on the prospect's stall by saying, "Would you share with me some things that hold you back?"

Sometimes, the prospect will not answer the question. Instead, the response is, "Oh, I just need to get an opinion." You can follow up with a multiple-choice question such as, "Will you explore whether this is a good purchase in comparison to a competitor's product or do you wonder about the financing?" This helps display an attitude of genuine caring.

As with any response to an objection, communicate a positive attitude. Do not become demanding, defensive, or hostile. Otherwise, your nonverbal expressions may signal a defensive attitude—reinforcing the prospect's defences.

Your goal in dealing with a stall is to help prospects realistically examine reasons for and against buying now. If you are absolutely sure it is not in their best interest to buy now, tell them so. They will respect you for it. You will feel good about yourself. The next time you see these customers, they will be more trusting and open with you.

However, the main thing to remember is not to be satisfied with a false objection or a stall. Tactfully pursue the issue until you have unearthed the buyer's true feelings about your product. If this does not work (1) present the benefits of using your product now; (2) if there is a special price deal, mention it; and (3) if there is a penalty for delay, mention it. Bring out any or all of your main selling benefits and keep on selling!

The No-Need Objection

The prospect says, "Sounds good. I really like what you had to say, and I know you have a good product, but I'm not interested now. Our present product (or supply or merchandise) works well. We will stay with it." Standing up to conclude the interview, the prospect says, "Thanks very much for coming by." This type of objection can disarm an unwary salesperson.

Five major categories of objections.

| 1. Stalling objections | 2. No-need objections | 3. Money objections | 4. Product objections | 5. Source objections |

Imagine walking up to your prospect, who says, "I'm too busy to see you now." What would you say?

The **no-need objection** is used widely because it politely gets rid of the salesperson. Some salespeople actually encourage it by making a poor sales presentation. They allow prospects to sit and listen to a sales pitch without motivating them to participate by showing true concern and asking questions. Therefore, when the presentation is over, prospects can say quickly, "Sounds good, but . . ." In essence, they say no, making it difficult for the salesperson to continue the call. Although not always a valid objection, the no-need response strongly implies the end of a sales call.

The no-need objection is especially tricky because it also may include a stall. If your presentation was a solo performance or a monologue, your prospect might be indifferent to you and your product, having tuned out halfway through the second act. Aside from departing with a "Thanks for your time," you might resurrect your presentation by asking questions.

The Money Objection

The **money objection** encompasses several forms of economic concerns: I have no money; I don't have that much money; it costs too much; or your price is too high. These objections are simple for the buyer to say, especially in a recessionary economy.

Often, prospects want to know the product's price before the presentation, and they will not want you to explain how the product's benefits outweigh its costs. Price is a real consideration and must be discussed, but it is risky to discuss product price until it can be compared to product benefits. If you successfully postpone the price discussion, you must eventually return to it because your prospect seldom forgets it. Some prospects are so preoccupied with price that they give minimal attention to your presentation until the topic re-emerges. Other prospects falsely present price as their main objection to your product, which conceals the true objection.

By observing nonverbal signals, asking questions, listening, and positively responding to the price question when it arises, you can easily handle price-oriented objections.

Many salespeople think that offering the lowest price gives them a greater chance of sales success. Generally, this is not the case. Once you realize this, you can become even more successful. You might even state that your product is not the least expensive one available because of its benefits and advantages and the satisfaction it provides. Once you convey this concept to your buyer, price becomes a secondary factor that usually can be handled successfully.

Do not be afraid of price as an objection; be ready for it and welcome it. Quote the price and keep on selling. It is usually the inexperienced salesperson who makes

SELLING TIPS
Stalling Objections

A. I have to think this over.

   1. Let's think about it now while it is fresh in your mind. What are some of the items you need to know more about?

   2. I understand that you want more time to think. I would be interested in hearing your thoughts about the reasons for and the reasons against buying now.

   3. You and I have been thinking this over since the time we first met. You know that this is a terrific opportunity, you like the product, and you know it will save you money. Right? [If prospect says yes:] Let's go ahead now!

B. I'm too busy.

   1. I appreciate how busy you are. When could we visit for just a few minutes? [Stop or add a benefit for seeing you.]

C. I'm too busy. Talk to _____ first.

   1. Does he/she have the authority to approve the purchase? [If prospect says yes:] Thank you. I'll tell him/her you sent me. [If prospect says no:] Well, then why should I talk with him/her?

   2. We almost never deal with purchasing managers. This is an executive-level decision. I need to talk with you.

D. I plan to wait until [future time].

   1. Why?

   2. Some of my best customers said that. Once they bought, they were sorry they waited.

   3. You promise me you will buy this fall? [If prospect says yes, then:]

      a. OK, let's finalize the order today and I'll have it ready to arrive October 1.

      b. Great! Should I call you in September or October so we can set it up?

   4. What if I could arrange for it to be shipped to you now but you didn't have to pay for it until the fall?

---

this often minor objection into a major one. If the price objection becomes major, prospects can become excited and overreact to your price. The end result is the loss of the sale. If prospects overreact, slow down the conversation; let them talk it out and slowly present product benefits as related to cost.

One way to view the money objection concerns the price/value formula.

The Price/Value Formula

The price objection is a bargaining tool for a savvy buyer who wants to ensure the best, absolutely lowest price. But, often there is more to it than shrewd bargaining.

If the buyer is merely testing to be sure the best possible price is on the table, it's a strong buying signal. But perhaps the prospect sincerely believes the price is too high.

Let's define why one buyer might already be convinced the product is a good deal—fair price—but is just testing to make sure it's the best price, while another buyer may sincerely believe the asking price is more than the goods are worth.

Remember that cost is what concerns the buyer, not just the price. Cost is arrived at in the buyer's mind by considering what is received compared to the money paid. In other words, price divided by value equals cost:

$$\frac{\text{Price}}{\text{Value}} = \text{Cost}$$

In this price/value formula, the value is what the prospects see the product doing for them and/or their company. *Value* is the total package of benefits you have built for the prospect. Value is the solution you provide to the buyer's problems.

SELLING TIPS

No-Need Objections

A. I'm not interested.
  1. May I ask why?
  2. You are not interested now or forever?
  3. I wouldn't be interested if I were you, either. However, I know you'll be interested when you hear about. . . . It is very exciting! [If prospect still says no:] When would be a better time to talk?
  4. Some of my best customers first said that until they discovered . . . [state benefits].
  5. You are not interested? Then who should I talk to who would be interested in . . . [state benefits].

B. The . . . we have is still good.
  1. Good compared to what?
  2. I understand how you feel. Many of my customers said that before they switched over. However, they saw that this product would. . . . [discuss benefits of present product or service versus what you are selling].

  3. That's exactly why you should buy—to get a good trade now.
  4. What stops you from buying?

C. We are satisfied with what we have now.
  1. Satisfied in what way?
  2. What do you like most about what you have right now? [then compare to your product].
  3. I know how you feel. Often we're satisfied with something because we have no chance (or don't have the time) to compare it with something better. I've studied what you are using and would like a few minutes to compare products and show you how to. . . . [state benefits].
  4. Many of our customers were happy with what they had before they saw our product. There are three reasons they switched. . . . [state three product benefits].

The price will not change. The company sets that price at headquarters. The company has arrived at the price—based on costs, competition, and other salient factors. It is a fair price, and it's not going to change. So, the only thing to change is the prospect's perception of the value. For example, assume the buyer viewed the cost as follows:

$$\frac{\text{Price } 100}{\text{Value } 90} = \text{Cost } 1.11$$

The price is too high. You have to solve the prospect's problem with the product by translating product benefits into what it will do for the buyer. You have to build up the value:

$$\frac{\text{Price } 100}{\text{Value } 110} = \text{Cost } 0.90$$

Now that is more like it. The cost went down because the value went up.

The price/value formula is not the answer to "Your price is too high." It is only a description of the buyer's thinking process and an explanation of why the so-called price objection is heard so often. It tells us what we must do to answer the price objection.

Remember, at one extreme, the buyer may be sold on the product and simply testing to see if there is an extra discount. At the other extreme, the buyer may not see any benefit in the product or service but see only the price. When this is the case, "it costs too much" is a legitimate objection to be overcome by translating features into advantages into benefits for the buyer.

EXHIBIT 10–4

Imagine that this customer says, "I like your proposal but we are happy with our present supplier." What would you say?

The Product Objection

All salespeople encounter **product objections** that relate directly to the product. Not everyone likes the best-selling product on the market. At times, most buyers have fears over risks associated with buying a product—they are afraid that the product will not do what the salesperson says it will do, or that the product is not worth either the time and energy required to use it or the actual cost.

You also sell against competition. The prospect either already uses a competitive product, has used one, would like to use one, has heard of one, or knows people who have used one. Your reaction to a product must use a positive tone. The use of a guarantee, testimonial, independent research results, and demonstrations helps counter the product objection.

The Source Objection

The **source objection** is the last major category of objections typically faced by salespeople. Source objections relate to loyalty to a present supplier or salesperson. Also, the prospect may not like you or your company.

Prospects often discuss their like for a present supplier or salesperson. They may tell you that they do not like your company. Seldom, however, will someone directly say, "I don't want to do business with you."

Usually, handling a source objection requires calling on the prospect routinely over a period. It takes time to break this resistance barrier. Get to know the prospect and the prospect's needs. Show your true interest. Do not try to get all the business at once—go for a trial run, a small order. It is important to learn exactly what bothers the prospect.

Hidden Objections

Recognizing the type, or category, of objection can be a challenge for a salesperson, because the buyer often hides her true source of resistance. Prospects who ask trivial, unimportant questions or conceal their feelings under silence have **hidden objections**. They do not discuss their true objections to a product because they may feel that those objections are not your business, they are afraid objections will offend you, or they feel your sales call is not worthy of full attention.

SELLING TIPS

Money Objections

A. Your price is too high.
1. Compared to what?
2. How much did you think it would cost?
3. We can lower the price right now, but we need to decide what options to cut from our proposal. Is that what you really want to do?
4. Our price is higher than the competition's. However, we have the best value (now explain).
5. How high is too high?
6. If it were cheaper, would you want it?

B. I can't afford it.
1. Why?
2. If I could show you a way to afford this purchase, would you be interested?
3. I sincerely believe that you cannot afford *not* to buy this. The benefits far outweigh the price. Right?
4. You cannot afford to be without it! The cost of not having it is greater than the cost of having it. Think of all the business you can lose, the productivity you can lose, that lost income from not having the latest, best, and most reliable technology. You'll love it! You'll wonder how you've done without it! Let's discuss how you can afford it—OK?
5. Do you mean you can't afford it now or forever?

C. Give me a 10 percent discount and I'll give you an order today.
1. I always quote my best price.
2. If you give me an order for 10, 1 can give you a 10 percent discount. Would you like to order 10?
3. [Prospect's name], we build your product up to a certain quality and service standard—not down to a certain price. We could produce a lower-priced item, but our experience shows it isn't worth it. This is a proven product that gives 100 percent satisfaction—not 90 percent.

C. You've got to do better than that.
1. Why?
2. What do you mean by *better*?
3. Do you mean a longer service warranty? A lower price? Extended delivery? Tell me exactly what you want.

Such prospects may have a good conversation with you without revealing their true feelings. You have to ask questions and carefully listen to know the questions to ask that reveal their real objections to your product. Learning how to determine what questions to ask a prospect and how to ask them are skills developed by conscious effort over time. Your ability to ask probing questions improves with each sales call if you work on developing this ability.

Smoke Out Hidden Objections

With prospects who are unwilling to discuss their objections or who may not know why they are reluctant to buy, be prepared to smoke out objections by asking questions. Do what you can to reveal the objections. Consider the following questions:

- What would it take to convince you?
- What causes you to say that?
- Let's consider this, suppose my product would [do what prospect wants] . . . then you would want to consider it, wouldn't you?
- Tell me, what's really on your mind?

Uncovering hidden objections is not always easy. Observe the prospect's tone of voice, facial expressions, and physical movements. Pay close attention to what the

SELLING TIPS

Product Objections

A. Your competitor's product is better.

   1. You're kidding! [Act surprised.]

   2. Better in what way? [Have customer list features liked in the other product; then show how your product has the same or better features.]

   3. I'm interested in hearing your unbiased opinion of the two products.

   4. You've had a chance to look at their product. What did you see that impressed you?

   5. Are you referring to quality, service, features, or the product's value after five years of use?

B. The machine we have is still good.

   1. I understand how you feel. Many of my customers said that before they switched over. However, they found that the reason a new model makes an old model obsolete is not that the old one is bad but that the new one is so much more efficient and productive. Would you like to take a look at what these businesses found?

   2. That's exactly why you should trade now. Since your machine is still good, you still have a high trade-in value. When it breaks down, your trade-in value will go down, too. It's less expensive to trade in a workable machine than to wait for it to fail.

C. I'll buy a used one.

   1. When you buy a used product, you take a high risk. You buy something that someone else has used and probably abused. Do you want to pay for other people's mistakes?

   2. You may save a few dollars on your monthly payments, but you'll have to pay much more in extra service, more repairs, and downtime. Which price would you rather pay?

   3. Many of our customers thought about a used product before they decided to buy a new one. Let me show you why they decided that new equipment is the best buy. The cost comparisons will make it clear.

   4. I understand you want to save money. I like to save money. But, you have to draw the line somewhere. Buying a used product in this field is like shopping for a headache. Perhaps you should consider the smaller model for starters. At least you won't have any worries about its reliability!

D. I don't want to take risks.

   1. You feel it's too risky? We rarely hear that. What do you mean by risky?

   2. "Risky" compared to what?

   3. What could we do to make you feel more secure?

   4. [Prospect's name], it may be more risky for you not to buy. What is the price you may pay for low productivity in your plant?

prospect is saying. You may have to read between the lines occasionally to find the buyer's true objections. All these factors will help you discover whether objections are real or simply an excuse to cover a hidden objection.

Prospects may not know consciously what their real objections are. Sometimes they claim that the price of a product is too high. In reality, they may be reluctant to spend money on anything. If you attempt to show that your price is competitive, the real objection remains unanswered and no sale results. Remember, you cannot convince anyone to buy until you understand what a prospect needs to be convinced of.

RESPONDING TO OBJECTIONS   When a prospect raises an objection—or the salesperson uncovers one—the first thing the salesperson must do is silently decide whether to handle it right then or postpone it until later.

SELLING TIPS

Source Objections

A. I'm sorry; we won't buy from you.

1. Why not?

2. You must have a reason for feeling that way. May I ask what it is?

3. Are you not going to buy from us now or forever?

4. What could we do to win your business in the future?

5. Is there anyone else in your company who might be interested in buying our cost-saving products? Who?

6. I respect the fact you aren't buying from us this one time. However, I suspect that as you hear more about our fantastic products in the news and from customers, you will buy something from us in the future. Do you mind if I stop by periodically to update you on our new products?

7. Would you like to work with someone else in our company?

8. Is there anything about me that prevents you from doing business with our company?

B. I want to work with a more established company. We've done business with . . . for five years. Why should I change?

1. I understand how safe you feel about a relationship that goes back five years. And yet, I saw your eyes light up when you looked at our products. I can see that you're giving serious consideration to diversity. Just out of curiosity, could we compare the pros and cons of the two choices? Let's take a piece of paper and list the reasons for and against buying from us. The first reason against us is that we haven't worked with you for the past five years. What are some reasons for giving us a chance to prove ourselves?

2. I can only say good things about my competitor, and if I were you, I would go with him or her—unless, of course, you want a better product at a better price.

Handle Objections as They Arise

Usually, it is best to meet objections as they arise; postponement may cause a negative reaction, such as

- The prospect may stop listening until you address the objection.
- The prospect may believe you are trying to hide something.
- It may appear that you are not interested in the prospect's opinion.

Postponing Objections Is Sometimes Necessary

Often, the prospect may skip ahead of you in the sales presentation by asking questions that you address later in the presentation (see Exhibit 10–5). If you judge that the objection will be handled to your prospect's satisfaction by your customary method, and that the prospect is willing to wait until later in the presentation, you politely **postpone the objection**.

Prospect: Your price is too high.

Salesperson: In just a minute, I'll show you why this product is reasonably priced, based on the savings you will receive compared to what you currently do. Do you mind if I come back to price in a moment?

or

Salesperson: Well, it may seem like a lot of money. But let's consider the final price when we know the model you need, OK?

or

Salesperson: There are several ways we can handle your costs. If it's all right, let's discuss them in just a minute. [Pause. If there is no response, continue.] First, I want to show you . . .

Suppose you show your prospect your business proposition, and the prospect asks, "How much does this software cost?" What would you say?

or

Salesperson: I'm glad you brought that up [or, I was hoping you would want to know that] because we want to carefully examine the cost in just a minute. Is it okay with you if we discuss [a product benefit] first?

Four Steps to Effective Objection Handling

Many professional salespeople respond very effectively to buyer objections by following a four-step sequence. They use the same four steps regardless of which of the five categories of objections is raised. The sequence works especially well if the buyer is hiding the true concern or source of resistance. The four steps are (1) acknowledge the buyer's viewpoint, (2) identify the problem and clarify the concern, (3) meet the objection, and (4) trial close (see Exhibit 10–6). Let's examine each of the four steps more closely.

Step 1—Acknowledge the Buyer's Viewpoint

First, the salesperson communicates a recognition that the buyer is concerned and has an objection. The purpose is to let the buyer know that you have noted the point of contention and are not ignoring the buyer. Acknowledging does not mean understanding, and it definitely does not mean agreement.

Skilled salespeople use phrases such as "I hear what you are saying" or "I see that you are concerned" or "I'm glad you brought that up" to acknowledge what the buyer has said without agreeing and without fully understanding the message. The salesperson should always perform the acknowledging step by making a statement, not by asking a question.

Follow this four-step procedure when an objection is raised by a prospect.

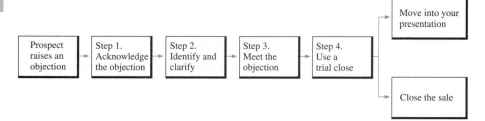

Step 2—Identify the Problem and Clarify the Concern

Next, the salesperson gains an understanding of the buyer's source of resistance. At this stage the salesperson learns what the objection is really all about and why the buyer is objecting. It is during this step that the salesperson uncovers the true category of objection if the buyer has been unclear or has kept it hidden.

Identifying the problem and clarifying the concern is an information-gathering step that can be performed by asking questions, or rephrasing, or both. It is similar to conducting needs analysis, except that the focus is narrowed to the issue at the heart of the objection. There is no limit as to how many questions or how much rephrasing should be used; the salesperson must achieve enough understanding to effectively meet and overcome the objection.

Intelligent questioning impresses a prospect in several ways. Technical questions show a prospect that a salesperson knows the business. Questions relating to a prospect's particular business show that a salesperson is concerned more with the prospect's needs than with just making a sale. Finally, people who ask **intelligent questions**, whether they know much about the product, the prospect's business, or life in general, often receive admiration. Buyers are impressed with the sales professional who knows what to ask and when to ask it. Examples of questions follow.

Prospect: This house is not as nice as the one someone else showed us yesterday.

Salesperson: Would you tell me why?

or

Prospect: This product does not have the [feature].

Salesperson: How much of a problem is that for you?

[This example is an excellent questioning technique to determine whether the objection is a smoke screen, a major or minor objection, or a practical or psychological objection.]

or

Prospect: I don't like your price.

Salesperson: Tell me, what bothers you about the price?

Notice that the questions in these examples are all open-ended. These types of questions are particularly effective when the buyer's objection is unclear, vague, or hidden. They encourage the buyer to talk and lead to better understanding for the salesperson.

When the buyer is more detailed and clear about the objection, you can **rephrase the objection** to confirm your understanding. Here is an example:

Buyer: I don't know—your price is higher than your competitors'.

Salesperson: I can appreciate that. You want to know what particular benefits my product has that make it worth its slightly higher price. [Or, What you're saying is that you want to get the best product for your money.] Is that correct?

Buyer: Yes, that's right.

Many salespeople leap on an objection before the other person has a chance to finish. The prospect barely says five words—and already the salesperson is hammering away. "I have to prove he is mistaken, or he won't take the product," is a panicky reaction to the first hint of any objection.

The prospect not only feels irritated at being interrupted, but also feels pushed and uneasy. Your prospect will ask, "Why's he jumping on that so fast and so hard? I smell a rat.[1]

Step 3—Meet the Objection

Once you fully understand the objection, you are ready to meet the objection.

If the buyer has requested information, provide it as clearly as possible. Most likely, you will need to be persuasive to overcome the objection; therefore, use appropriate FABs that address the specific concern raised by the buyer.

During this step evidence plays a particularly important role. Providing the prospect with support material such as a testimonial letter from a satisfied customer, or doing a demonstration for the buyer, will help you meet and overcome the objection.

As shown in Exhibit 10–7, your prospect has raised an objection that you have acknowledged, clarified, and answered; now what? Proceed to Step 4—use a trial close.

Step 4—Use a Trial Close

After meeting an objection at any time during the interview, you need to know whether you have overcome the objection. If you have not overcome it, your prospect may raise it again. Whether it resurfaces or not, if your prospect believes that an objection was important, failure to handle it—or your mishandling of it—will cost you the sale. Ideally, all objections raised should be met before closing the sale. So, after responding to the objection, use a trial close type of question simply to determine whether you have overcome the objection or not. Ask questions such as

- That clarifies this point entirely, don't you agree?
- That's the answer you're looking for, isn't it?
- With that question out of the way, we can go ahead—don't you think?

EXHIBIT 10–7

Imagine you are this pharmaceutical salesperson and you just answered this medical doctor's objections. What should you do now?

■ Do you agree with me that we've covered the question you raised, and given you a way to handle it?

■ Now that's settled entirely, isn't it?

■ That solves your problem, doesn't it?

Once you have confirmed overcoming an objection, immediately go to the next SELL sequence, or attempt to close the sale. Which of these actions you take depends on when in the sales process the objection surfaces. If it is early in the process, you will need to move back into your presentation. If your presentation is virtually completed, however, you will need to close the sale.

Move Back into Your Presentation

When you have answered and overcome an objection, make a smooth transition back into your presentation. Let the prospect know you are returning to your presentation with a phrase such as, "As we were discussing earlier…" Now, you can continue the presentation.

Move to Close Your Sale

If you have finished your presentation when the prospect raises an objection, and the prospect's response to your trial close indicates that you overcame the objection, your next move is to close the sale. If the objection was raised during your close, then it is time to close again.

As you move on to the close, you might summarize benefits discussed previously with a phrase such as, "Well, as we have discussed, you really like . . ." Then, again ask the prospect for the order. Chapter 11 gives you other ideas on how to ask for the order.

If You Cannot Overcome the Objection

If you cannot overcome an objection or close a sale because of an objection, be prepared to return to your presentation and concentrate on new or previously discussed FABs of your product. If you determine that the objection raised by your prospect is a major one that cannot be overcome, admit it, and show how your product's benefits outweigh this disadvantage.

Even if you are 100 percent sure that you cannot overcome the objection and that the prospect will not buy, go ahead and close. *Always ask for the order.* Never be afraid to ask your prospect to buy. The buyer says no to the product—not you. Someone else may walk into the prospect's office after you with a product similar to yours. Your competitor also may be unable to overcome this person's objection, but she may get the sale nonetheless just by asking for it!

POINTS TO CONSIDER ABOUT HANDLING OBJECTIONS

No matter what type of objections are raised by the prospect, there are certain basic points to keep in mind about handling objections.

■ Plan for objections.

■ Anticipate and forestall.

■ Understand objections.

■ Be positive.

■ Don't be afraid to pass up an objection.

■ Send it back with the boomerang method.

■ Use direct denial tactfully.

■ Try an indirect denial.

■ Use the compensation method.

■ Let a third party answer.

Plan for Objections

Plan for objections that might be raised by your presentation. Consider not only the reasons that prospects should buy but also why they should *not* buy. Structure your presentation to minimize the disadvantages of your product. Generally, do not discuss disadvantages unless prospects raise them in the conversation.

After each sales call, review the prospect's objections. Divide them into major and minor objections. Then develop ways to overcome them. Your planning for and rehearsal of overcoming objections allow you to respond in a natural and positive manner.

Anticipate and Forestall

Forestalling the objection means the salesperson discusses an objection before it is raised by the prospect. It often is better to forestall or discuss objections before they arise. The sales presentation can be developed to address anticipated objections directly.

For example, take an exterior house paint manufacturer's salesperson who learns that an unethical competitor is telling retail dealers that his paint starts to chip and peel after six months. Realizing the predicament, this salesperson develops a presentation that states, "Three independent testing laboratories have shown that this paint will not chip or peel for eight years after application." By using an evidence statement, the salesperson has forestalled or answered the objection before it is raised. This technique also can prevent a negative mood from entering the buyer–seller dialogue.

Although we have suggested that you not discuss disadvantages unless the prospect does, there are times when you can anticipate that a prospect will dwell on perceived weaknesses in your product. To defuse the potential for these kinds of objections, you can consider discussing disadvantages before the prospect does. Many products have flaws, and they sometimes surface as you try to make a sale. If you know of an objection that arises consistently, discuss it. If you acknowledge it first, you don't have to defend it.

For example, if you are showing real estate property, and en route to the location you say, "You know, before we get out there, I just want to mention a couple of things. You're going to notice that it needs a little paint in a few places, and I noticed a couple of shingles on the roof the other day that you may have to replace." When you arrive, your customer may take a look and say, "Well, those shingles aren't so bad and we're going to paint it anyway." Yet, if you reach the house without a prior warning of small defects, those items are often what a customer first notices.

Another way of using an anticipated objection is to brag about it and turn it into a sales benefit. A salesperson might say, "I want to mention something important before we go any further. Our price is a high one because our new computerized electronics provide technology found in no other equipment. It will improve your operation and eliminate the costly repairs you are now experiencing. In just a minute, I want to fully discuss your investment. Let's first discuss the improvements we can provide. Take a look at this."

This practice takes the sting out of the price objection because you have discussed it. It is difficult for a buyer to come back and say, "It's too high," because you have mentioned that already. So, there are times when you can anticipate objections and use them advantageously.

Understand Objections

When customers object, they do one of several things, as shown in Exhibit 10–8. They are either requesting more information, setting a condition, or giving a genuine objection.

EXHIBIT 10–8

What does a prospect mean by
an objection?

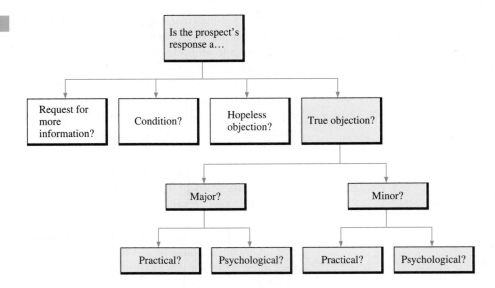

Request for Information

Many times, prospects appear to make objections when they are requesting more
information, which is why it is important to listen. If prospects request more information, chances are that they are in the conviction stage. You have created a desire;
they want the product, but they are not convinced that you have the best product or
you are the best supplier. If you feel this may be the case, supply the requested information indirectly.

Setting a Condition

At times, prospects may raise an objection that turns into a **condition of the sale**.
They are saying, "If you can meet my request, I'll buy," or "Under certain conditions,
I will buy from you."

   If you sense that the objection is a condition, quickly determine whether you can
help the prospect meet it. If you cannot, close the interview politely. Take the following real estate example:

   Prospect: It's a nice apartment, but the price is too high. I can't afford a $1,000 a
   month payment. [You do not know if this is an objection or a condition.]

   Salesperson: I know what you mean [acknowledging the prospect's viewpoint].
   If you don't mind my asking, what is your monthly salary?

   Prospect: My take-home pay is $1,400 a month.

   In this case, the prospect has set a condition on the purchase that cannot be met
by the salesperson realistically; it is not an objection. Continuing the exchange by
bargaining would waste time and possibly anger the prospect. Now that the prospect's income is known, the salesperson can show an apartment in the prospect's
price range.

Negotiation Can Overcome a Condition Often, conditions stated by the prospect
are overcome through negotiation between buyer and seller. **Negotiation** refers to
discussing how various elements of value might be changed or exchanged to reach

an agreement mutually satisfactory to both buyer and seller. Prospects may say things like, "I'll buy your equipment if you can deliver it in one month instead of three," or "If you'll reduce your price by 10 percent, I'll buy."

If you determine that this type of statement is a condition rather than an objection, through negotiation you may make the sale with further discussion and an eventual exchange of value between you and the buyer. In the example above, you might ask the manufacturing plant if equipment can be shipped to the prospect in two months instead of three. This arrangement may be acceptable to the prospect. You may have a present customer who has that piece of equipment but is not using it. You might arrange for the prospect to lease it from your customer for three months.

Suppose the prospect sets a price condition by saying, "I will buy your product only if you reduce your price by 10 percent." In this case, determine whether your company will reduce the price if the buyer will purchase a larger quantity or commit to buying over an agreed period (e.g., a two-, five-, or ten-year contract). An agreement such as this will yield the pricing sought by the customer, in return for more sales for your company.

There are two broad categories of objections. A hopeless objection is one that cannot be solved or answered. Examples of hopeless objections are "I already have one"; "I'm bankrupt"; and "I'd like to buy your life insurance, but the doctor only gives me 30 days to live." Hopeless objections cannot be overcome.

If your prospect does not buy, and no condition exists or the objection is not hopeless, it is your fault if you did not make the sale because you could not provide information to show how your offering would suit the buyer's needs.

The second category is the true objection; there are two types: major and minor.

SELLING GLOBALLY

Negotiating with the Chinese

Although Chinese business practices are gradually changing to accommodate Western ones, there is still a great deal of culture and history influencing them. The key to negotiation with the Chinese is to understand their deeply rooted values and customs.

In Canada, we may expect aggressiveness and assertiveness in a negotiation. Chinese place great value on things like respect, trust, and loyalty. This realization could provide the key to successful negotiations.

- **Patience.** Unlike Canadians and North Americans in general, Chinese businesses often require a "courting" process. It's unlikely things will get done during a single meeting. You need to adjust your sales call objectives. In China, you must establish a *guanxi* or relationship. These relationships should be between both companies and individuals.

- **Socialize.** Be prepared to spend some social time with your Chinese partners. What better way to build *guanxi*

than to eat, drink, and be merry? Interacting informally like this allows partners to really get to know each other.

- **Stay calm.** The Chinese place great value on harmony. Emotional outbursts and anger will surely upset your relationship. Work toward a mutually beneficial deal so that both you and your partner will look good to your respective bosses.

- **Develop contacts.** Using intermediaries is commonplace in China. A referral from a good source is an easy way to kick-start a business relationship. If the source is trusted by you and your potential partner, *guanxi* is almost guaranteed.

- **Watch the legal details.** Sticking a written contract in your partner's face may show a lack of trust that may undo much of the *guanxi*. Some contracts are not only unenforceable in China but also their very presence may sour a relationship enough to cause an end to your relationship.

EXHIBIT 10–9

Practical versus Psychological
Objections.

Practical	Psychological
■ Price	■ Resistance to spending money
■ Product is not needed	■ Resistance to domination
■ Prospect has an overstock of your or your competitor's products	■ Predetermined beliefs
■ Delivery schedules	■ Negative image of salespeople
	■ Dislikes making a buying decision

Major or Minor Objections

Once you determine that the prospect has raised a true objection, determine its importance. If it is of little or no importance, quickly address it and return to your presentation. Do not provide a long response or turn a minor objection into a major discussion item. The minor objection is often a defence mechanism of little importance to the prospect. Concentrate on objections directly related to the prospect's important buying motives.

Practical or Psychological Objection

Objections, minor or major, can be **practical** (overt) or **psychological** (hidden) in nature. Exhibit 10–9 gives some examples. A real objection is tangible, such as a high price. If this is a real objection, and the prospect says so, you can show that your product is of high quality and worth the price, or you might suggest removing some optional features and reducing the price. As long as the prospect states the real objection to purchasing the product clearly, you should be able to answer the objection.

However, prospects do not always clearly state their objections. Rather, they often give some excuse why they are not ready to make a purchase, which conceals real objections. Usually, the prospect cannot purchase the product until hidden objections are rectified. You must uncover a prospect's hidden objections and eliminate them.

Be Positive

When responding to an objection, use positive body language such as a smile. Strive to respond in a manner that keeps your prospect friendly and in a positive mood. Do not take the objection personally. Never treat the objection with hostility. Take the objection in stride by responding respectfully and showing sincere interest in your prospect's opinion.

At times, the prospect may raise objections based on incorrect information. Politely deny false objections. Be realistic; all products have drawbacks, even yours. If a competitor's product has a feature your product lacks, demonstrate the overriding benefits of your product.

Don't Be Afraid to Pass Up an Objection

Occasionally, you may have a prospect raise an objection or make a statement that requires not addressing it. After introducing yourself, for example, a prospect may say, "I'm really not interested in a service such as yours."

You have two options. First, you can say, "Well, if you ever are, here is my card. Give me a call." Or second, you could take the **pass up** approach used by top salespeople and say something that allows you to move into your presentation, such as immediately using the customer benefit approach or simply asking why.

As you gain selling experience, you will be confident in knowing when to pass up or to stop and respond to the objection. If you pass up an objection and the prospect raises it again, then treat this as an important objection. Use your questioning skills to uncover the prospect's concerns.

Send It Back with the Boomerang Method

Always be ready to turn an objection into a reason to buy. By convincing the prospect that an objection is a benefit, you have turned the buyer immediately in favour of your product. This is the heart of the **boomerang method**. Take, for example, the wholesale drug salesperson who is selling a pharmacist a new container for prescription medicines. Handling the container, the prospect says:

Prospect: They look nice, but I don't like them as well as my others. The tops seem hard to remove.

Salesperson: Yes, they are hard to remove. We designed them so that children can't get into the medicine. Isn't that a great safety measure? [Trial close.]

Another example is the industrial salesperson who responded to the prospect's high price objection by saying, "Well, that's the very reason you should buy it." The prospect was caught off guard and quickly asked, "What do you mean?" "Well," said the salesperson, "for just 10 percent more, you can buy the type of equipment you really want and need. It is dependable, safe, and simple to operate. Your production will increase so that you will pay back the price differential quickly." The prospect said, "Well, I hadn't thought of it quite like that. I guess I'll buy it after all."

Boomeranging an objection requires good timing and quick thinking. Experience in a particular selling field, knowledge of your prospect's needs, a positive attitude, and a willingness to stand up to the objection are necessary attributes for successful use of this technique.

Use Direct Denial Tactfully

You will face objections that are often incomplete or incorrect. Acknowledge the prospect's viewpoint; then answer the question by providing the complete facts:

Prospect: No, I'm not going to buy any of your lawn mowers for my store. The Bigs-Weaver salesperson said they break down after a few months.

Salesperson: Well, I can understand. No one would buy mowers that don't hold up. Is that the only reason you won't buy?

Prospect: Yes, it is, and that's enough!

Salesperson: The BW salesperson was not aware of the facts, I'm afraid. My company produces the finest lawn mowers in the industry. In fact, we are so sure of our quality that we have a new three-year guarantee on all parts and labour. [Pause]

Prospect: I didn't know that. [Positive buying signal]

Salesperson: Do you have more confidence in the quality of our lawn mowers now? [Trial close]

Prospect: Yes, I do. [Appears that you have overcome the objection]

Salesperson: Well, I'd like to sell you 100 lawn mowers. If even one breaks down, call me and I'll come over and have it repaired or replaced. Shall we go ahead? [Close]

As you see by this example, tact is critical in using a direct denial. A sarcastic or arrogant response can alienate a prospect. However, a **direct denial** based on facts, logic, and politeness can effectively overcome the objection.

SELLING TIPS

Be Positive in Discussing Price

All prospects are sensitive to how price is presented. Below is a list of typical negative and positive ways to deal with price issues during the business proposition phase:

Negative Words

- This costs $2,300
- Your down payment . . .
- Your monthly payment . . .
- You can pay the purchase price over a series of small payments
- How much would you like to pay us every month?

- We'll charge you two points above the prime rate.
- We'll take off $6,700 to trade in your used model.

Positive Words

- This is only $2,300.
- Your initial investment . . .
- Your monthly investment . . .
- We would be happy to divide this investment into [number of] monthly shares.
- What monthly investment would you feel comfortable with?

- Your rate will be only prime plus two.
- We are offering you $6,700 to trade in your existing model.

A good salesperson will say, "You know, you're right to be concerned about this. Let me explain," making the buyer right and keeping the buyer's mind open. Another option is to say, "You know, my best customer had those same feelings until I explained that . . ." again making the customer right.

Try an Indirect Denial

An **indirect denial** is different from a direct denial in that it initially appears as agreement with the customer's objection but then moves into a denial of the fundamental issue in the objection. The difference between the direct denial and the indirect denial is that the indirect denial is softer, more tactful, and more courteous. Use the direct denial judiciously, only to disconfirm especially damaging misinformation.

The typical example of indirect denial is the "yes, but" phrase. Here are several examples:

- Yes, but would you agree that it takes information, not time, to make a decision? What kind of information are you really looking for to make a good decision?
- I agree. Our price is a little higher, but so is our quality, which is important since you are interested in saving $1,200 a year on maintenance.
- Sure, it costs a little more. However, you will have the assurance that it will cost much less over its lifetime. Isn't that the way your own products are made?
- Your point is well taken. It does cost more than any other product on the market. But why do you think we sell millions of them at this price?
- I appreciate how you feel. Many of our customers made similar comments before buying from me. However, they all asked themselves: "Can I afford not to have the best? Won't it cost me more in the long run?"

The indirect denial begins with an agreement or an acknowledgment of the prospect's position: "Yes, but"; "I agree"; "Sure"; "Your point is well taken"; and "I appreciate how you feel." These phrases allow the salesperson to tactfully respond to the objection. Done in a natural, conversational way, you will not offend the prospect.

Try this yourself: When a friend says something you disagree with, instead of saying, "I don't agree," say something like, "I see what you mean. However, there's another way to look at it." See if this, as well as the other communication skills you have studied, helps you to better sell yourself—and your product.

Use the Compensation Method

Sometimes a prospect's objection is valid and calls for the **compensation method**. Several reasons for buying must exist to justify or compensate for a negative aspect of making a purchase. For example, a higher product price is justified by benefits such as better service or higher performance. In the following example, it is true that the prospect can make more profit on each unit of a competing product. You must develop a technique to show how your product has benefits that will bring the prospect more profit in the long run.

Prospect: I can make 5 percent more profit with the Stainless line of cookware, and it is quality merchandise.

Salesperson: Yes, you are right. The Stainless cookware is quality merchandise. However, you can have an exclusive distributorship on the Supreme cookware line, and still have high-quality merchandise. You don't have to worry about Supreme being discounted by nearby competitors as you do with Stainless. This will be the only store in town carrying Supreme. What do you think? [Trial close.]

If the advantages presented to counterbalance the objection are important to the buyer, you have an opportunity to make the sale.

Let a Third Party Answer

An effective technique for responding to an objection is to answer it by letting a **third party answer** and using someone else's experience as your proof of testimony. A wide range of evidence statements are used by salespeople today. You might respond to a question in this way: "I'm glad you asked. Here is what our research has shown," or, "CSA tests have shown," or, "You know, my best customer brought that point up before making the purchase . . . but was completely satisfied." These are examples of evidence statement formats. If you use a person or a company's name, be sure to obtain approval first.

Secondary data or experience, especially from a reliable or reputable source, may be successful with the expert or skeptical prospect. If, after hearing secondary testimony, the prospect is still unsure about the product, one successful equipment salesperson asks the buyer to contact a current user directly:

Salesperson: I still haven't answered your entire question, have I?

Buyer: Not really.

Salesperson: Let's do this. Here is a list of several people currently using our product. Why don't you call them up *right now* and ask them that same question? I'll pay for the calls.

A salesperson should use this version of the third-party technique only when certain that the prospect is still unsatisfied with how an objection has been handled, and that positive evidence will probably clinch the sale. This dramatic technique allows the salesperson to impress a prospect. It also shows a flattering willingness to go to great lengths to validate a claim.

DEALING WITH DIFFICULT CUSTOMERS

Most of us have either had or been an angry customer—one thing that most salespeople can live without. On the other hand, taking an angry customer, solving her problem, and converting her to a satisfied customer is a challenge that many salespeople enjoy.

Difficult customers come in many forms. Some are arrogant and their personality rubs you the wrong way. Then there are those who are difficult for everyone: picky people, know-it-alls, condescending egocentrics, fault-finders, and constant whiners. We've all observed these types.

Perhaps the most difficult for everyone is the angry customer. This is someone who feels that he or she has been wronged, and is upset and emotional about it. These customers complain, and they are angry about something you or your company did or—commonly—didn't do.

From a business perspective, it is cheaper to keep customers than it is to find new ones, so companies would prefer not to lose any. Research indicates that as long as they believe they were treated fairly, customers who complain are likely to continue doing business with companies they complain to. It's estimated that as many as 90 percent of customers who perceive themselves as having been wronged never complain; they just take their business elsewhere. So angry, complaining customers care enough to talk to you, and have not yet decided to take their business to the competition. They are customers worth saving.

Some Guidelines for Dealing with Difficult Customers

1. **Respect.** Regardless of her attitude and behaviour, this customer deserves respect. Remember that it is not you (in most cases) who is the target of her anger. You may be just a small part of the situation but yet have the power to solve the problem. Remember, you must stay in control here. *You* are not angry. It is not *your* problem. You are the problem solver, so stay in control. Getting emotionally involved in the issue will not help.

2. **Empathy.** This topic is mentioned several times throughout this text, and it may be here that it is most important. Put yourself in the customer's shoes, and try to see the situation from her perspective. You've likely been there yourself. Your responsibility is to let the customer vent and to listen attentively in order to understand the source of her frustration. When you do this, you are giving a powerful message that you care about her and his situation. Often, as the customer comes to realize that you really *do* care and that you are going to attempt to help her resolve the problem, the customer will calm down on her own and begin to interact with you in a positive way.

SELLING TIPS

A Strategy for Handling Objections

Overcoming objections is critical for success. Here is a strategy top salespeople use to draw out, understand, and overcome objections:.

1. Plan for objections.
2. Anticipate and forestall objections when needed.
3. Acknowledge objections as they arise.
4. Understand objections—ask questions to clarify.

5. Listen to objections—hear them out.
6. Meet the objection by selecting appropriate FABs and evidence to use in responding to the objection
7. Be positive.
8. Confirm that you have met the objection—use a trial close.
9. Where am I? Decide whether you need to keep selling, handle another objection, or close the sale.

The Process

1. **Stop, look, and listen.** Just like crossing the street, you have to be aware of your surroundings and the situation. When an angry customer begins an emotional tirade of how she was wronged, all you can do is *stop* what you were doing, *pay attention* to her, and *listen*. Don't try and cut her off; don't urge her to calm down. Be interested and listen carefully. As you listen, you can begin to piece together her story.

   Once the customer has had the chance to vent a little, there may be a good opportunity to step in. Empathize here. "This is not a good situation, so let's see what we can do to solve it for you." You can apologize and let her know that it's not acceptable to you either. Let her know that she is justified by being upset. Get her to look at you as an ally. Importantly, ask what would be the best outcome for her.

2. **Identify the problem.** In a calm fashion, get all the details as the angry customer sees them. Ask questions to get the customer to think about facts. Once the facts are uncovered, restate them to ensure that both parties have full understanding. Acknowledge again that this problem will be dealt with seriously; you can even offer an apology that it happened in the first place, but avoid placing blame.

3. **No blame.** Even if the customer is to blame here, let it go. Don't place the blame on her. "You see, Ms. Customer, if you had just read the delivery date more carefully on your invoice, you would realize this is your fault—not ours." This approach will get you nowhere. Also, don't blame your suppliers or a delivery service. The customer wants to deal with *you*.

4. **Solve the problem.** This is the satisfying part. If you can solve the problem with a couple of quick calls, do so! If not, you must give the customer the impression that you will do something about the situation. Give a timeline. "I will call you this afternoon to bring you up to date." Now do everything in your power to solve the problem. Keep the customer apprised of everything that is going on. Doing this right will result in a loyal customer who knows that she is being looked out for.

5. **Follow up.** Hopefully, before long the problem has been solved and your customer is happy. This is a great opportunity to follow up with your customer to ensure that things are now running smoothly.

ETHICAL DILEMMA
When All Else Fails

As a salesperson for a large Montreal-based robotics company, you have entered into a very complex negotiation with a major machinery manufacturer. The deal is worth millions to your company. You've been sitting across the desk from a very hard-nosed purchasing manager for days now.

You discover that the purchasing manager is just months away from retirement and this will probably be his last major purchase before retirement. During one of your meetings, the prospect tells you about his impending retirement and without coming out and directly asking, he makes some subtle overtures regarding what it will take to get the deal done.

He strongly hints that if you would make it worth his while personally, that he would arrange to get the deal done. Your guess is that he is looking for a way to supplement his retirement. Perhaps a personal cash payout or a small cottage in the country would suffice. You figure it would cost your company approximately $150,000 to get the deal done.

What do you do?

NEGOTIATING WITH A WIN–WIN OUTCOME

Negotiation skills help you to resolve situations where what you want conflicts with what someone else wants. The aim of negotiation is to explore the situation to find a solution that is acceptable to both parties.

Depending on circumstances, there are many different styles of negotiation. "Playing hardball" and "confrontation" are some of the connotations that spring to mind when thinking about negotiation. These may seem appropriate when you do not expect to ever have to deal with people again and you do not need to cultivate a relationship. People behave this way when they buy or sell a car or a house, which often makes these experiences unpleasant.

The hardball approach to negotiation is usually highly inappropriate when resolving disputes with people you have, or would like to have, an ongoing relationship with. If one person feels disadvantaged and then feels as though she has lost, she will not likely revisit that situation again. This is counterproductive for the salesperson who wishes to establish and cultivate relationships. Similarly, using tricks and manipulation during a negotiation process will have an adverse effect on trust. While a manipulative salesperson may succeed in the short term, it is certainly not conducive to establishing a relationship where salesperson and client will work together frequently. Honesty and openness are the best policies in this case.

Preparing for Win–Win Negotiation

Depending on the size of the deal or the scale of the disagreement, a certain level of preparation may be appropriate for conducting a successful negotiation.

For small negotiations excessive preparation can be counterproductive, because it takes time that is better used elsewhere. Overpreparing can be seen as overkill—beating your opponent into submission.

If a major negotiation needs to be resolved, then it can be worth preparing for thoroughly. Think through the following points before you start negotiating:

Goals: What do you want to get out of the negotiation? What do you expect the prospect will want?

Trades: What do you and the prospect have that you can trade? What do you each have that the other might want? What might you each be prepared to give away?

Alternatives: If you don't reach agreement with the prospect, what alternatives do you have? Are these good or bad? How much does it matter if you do not reach agreement? Does failure to reach an agreement cut you out of future opportunities? What alternatives might the prospect have?

Relationships: What is the history of the relationship? Could or should this history impact the negotiation? What is the future of this relationship? Is it something of value? What's in it for you in the long run? Will there be any hidden issues that may influence the negotiation? How will you handle these?

What do you expect? What outcome will people be expecting from this negotiation? What has the outcome been in the past, and what precedents have been set?

What could happen? What are the consequences if you win or lose this negotiation? What are the consequences for the prospect?

Who has the power? Who controls resources? Who stands to lose the most if agreement isn't reached? What power does the other person have to deliver what you hope for?

What are the answers? Based on all of the considerations, what possible compromises might there be?

For a negotiation to be win–win, both parties should feel positive about the situation when the negotiation is concluded. This helps to maintain a good working relationship

MAKING THE SALE

Negotiation Checklist:

Pre-Negotiation

- Do not begin negotiations until you've fully presented your proposition.
- Adopt and keep a positive attitude.
- Ensure you're dealing with the decision maker so that the negotiation is not fruitless.
- Be prepared to discuss the value your prospect will receive and to quantify it.
- Pay close attention to the interaction during the presentation to determine the prospect's key motivation.
- Be prepared to move toward a **win–win negotiation**.
- Predetermine when you'll have to walk away.

The-Negotiation

- Ensure that you understand the prospect's key needs by using questioning skills.
- Remind the prospect of how he will benefit from your offering.
- Don't be swayed by the non-verbal responses by your prospect (flinching, squirming, etc.).
- Employ all of your listening skills.

- Don't let silence worry you—you don't need to fill in the gaps.
- Try to adjust the value of your offering rather than drop price (faster delivery, preferred service etc.).
- Keep track of small agreements and verbalize them occasionally.
- Be sincere—show your commitment to the success of the negotiation.

Post-Negotiation

If Successful

- Provide a summary of agreement.
- Show an appreciation for the prospect's time.
- Reinforce the purchase decision.
- Watch your attitude—it was a win–win, not an "I WON."
- Learn from the experience—what worked well?

If Unsuccessful

- Show appreciation for the prospect's time.
- Don't burn bridges—leave an opening for future business.
- Learn from the experience—what didn't work well?

afterward, and governs the style of the negotiation—drama and displays of emotion are inappropriate, because they introduce personality to the negotiation instead of logical, objective facts. Drama also introduces a competitive nature to the discussion.

The negotiation itself is a careful exploration of your position and the prospect's position, with the goal of finding a mutually acceptable compromise that gives you both as much of what you want as possible. People's positions are rarely as opposed as they first appear—the other person quite often has very different goals from the ones you expect! In an ideal situation, you will find that the other person wants what you are prepared to trade, and that you are prepared to give what the other person wants.

If this is not the case and one person must give a bit, then it is fair for that person to try to negotiate some form of compensation for doing so—the amount of this compensation will often depend on many of the factors we discussed above. Ultimately, both sides should feel comfortable with the ultimate solution if the agreement is to be considered win–win.

SUMMARY OF MAJOR SELLING ISSUES

People want to buy, but they do not want to be misled, so they often ask questions or raise objections during a sales presentation. Your responsibility is to be prepared to logically and clearly respond to your prospect's objections whenever they arise.

Sales objections indicate a prospect's opposition or resistance to the information or request of the salesperson. The four steps for effectively handling objections are to

(1) acknowledge the buyer's viewpoint, (2) identify the problem and clarify the concern, (3) meet the objection, and (4) trial close.

Before you can successfully meet objections, determine whether the prospect's response to your statement or close is a request for more information, a condition of the sale, or an objection. If it is a real objection, determine whether it is minor or major. Respond to it using a trial close, and if you have answered it successfully, continue your presentation based on where you are in the sales presentation. For example, if you are still in the presentation, then return to your selling sequence. If you have completed the presentation, move to your close. If you are in the close and the prospect voices an objection, then you must decide whether to use another close or return to the presentation and discuss additional benefits.

Be aware of and plan for objections. Objections are classified as stalling, no-need, money, product, and source objections. Remember, the true category of objection could be hidden from you! Develop several techniques to help overcome each type of objection, such as stalling the objection, turning the objection into a benefit, denying the objection if appropriate, illustrating how product benefits outweigh the objection drawbacks, or developing evidence statements that answer the objection.

Welcome your prospect's objections. They help you determine whether you are on the right track to uncover prospects' needs and whether they believe your product will fulfill those needs. Valid objections are beneficial for you and the customer. A true objection reveals the customer's need, which allows a salesperson to demonstrate how a product can meet that need. Objections also show inadequacies in a salesperson's presentation or product knowledge. Finally, objections make selling a skill that a person can improve constantly. Over time, a dedicated salesperson can learn how to handle every conceivable product objection—tactfully, honestly, and to the customer's benefit.

MEETING A SALES CHALLENGE

Before handling an objection, it's important to find out what the *exact* objection is. Is price a stall or bona fide reason for changing suppliers? Is the competitor's cheaper price attractive, or does the problem exist with the salesperson and the possible inability to sell a high-priced line? There could be many problems, so before you answer the objection, do some probing and find out what the real one is. A good question would be, "Would you mind telling me exactly why you're considering this move?" Then continue to probe until you totally understand the buyer's reasoning for wanting to change suppliers.

Listen carefully to what the buyer says. Nonnie Young may be a tough negotiator wanting to see whether you will lower your prices.

PLAYING THE ROLE

At the end of one of your courses you decide that you want to sell one of your textbooks to another student (not your ABC's text because you know it will be a great life-long reference book). Assume that you paid $90 for your text and you decide that you want to sell it for $80 because you kept it in pristine condition. However, anybody you talk to offers you only $25 for the text.

Role A: Textbook owner wanting to sell it. Plan for a negotiating process to maximize the amount you can charge.

Role B: Interested textbook buyer. Plan for a negotiating process that will minimize what you will pay for the text.

Dramatize your negotiation by demonstrating your understanding of win–win negotiation tactics.

KEY TERMS FOR SELLING

boomerang method, 289
compensation method, 291
condition of the sale, 286
direct denial, 289
hidden objection, 277
indirect denial, 290
intelligent questions, 282
money objection, 274
negotiation, 286
no-need objection, 274
objections, 271

pass up, 288
postpone the objection, 280
practical objection, 288
product objection, 277
psychological objection, 288
rephrase the objection, 282
sales objection, 271
source objection, 277
stalling objection, 272
third-party answer, 291
win-win negotiation, 295

SALES APPLICATION QUESTIONS

1. Halfway through your sales presentation, your prospect stops you and says, "That sounds like a great deal and you certainly have a good product, but I'm not interested now; maybe later." What should you do?

2. Assume you are a salesperson for the Japan Computer Corporation. You have finished your computer presentation, and the purchasing agent for Petro-Canada says, "Well, that sounds really good and you do have the lowest price I have ever heard of for a computer system. In fact, it's $200,000 less than the other bids. But we have decided to stay with IBM, mainly because $200,000 on a $1 million computer system is not that much money to us." Let's further assume that you also know that other than price, IBM has significant advantages in all areas over your product. What would you do?

3. When a customer is not receptive to your product, there is some resistance. In each of the following situations, the customer has an objection to a product:
   a. The customer assumes she must buy the whole set of books. However, partial purchases are permitted.
   b. The customer does not like the colour and it's the only colour your product comes in.
   c. The customer doesn't want to invest in a new set of books because she doesn't want to lose money on her old set. You have not told her yet about your trade-in deal.

   In which situations does the objection arise from a misunderstanding or lack of knowledge on the customer's part? In which situation(s) does the product fail to offer a benefit that the customer considers important?

4. Which response is best when you hear the customer reply, "I'd like to think it over"? Why?
   a. Give all the benefits of using the product now.
   b. If there is a penalty for delaying, mention it now.
   c. If there is a special price deal available, mention it now.
   d. None of the above is appropriate.
   e. Depending on the circumstances, the first three choices are appropriate.

5. Cliff Jamison sells business forms and he's regarded as a top-notch salesperson. He works hard, plans ahead, and exhibits self-confidence. One day, he made his first presentation to a prospective new client, the Canadian Steel Company. "Ladies and gentlemen," said Jamison, "our forms are of the highest quality, yet they are priced below our competitors' forms. I know that you are a large user of business forms and that you use a wide variety. Whatever your need for business forms, I assure you that we can supply them. Our forms are noted for their durability. They can run through your machines at 60 per minute and they'll perform

perfectly." "Perfectly, Mr. Jamison?" asked the Canadian Steel executive. "Didn't you have some trouble at Ogden's last year?" "Oh," replied Jamison, "that wasn't the fault of our forms. They had a stupid operator who didn't follow instructions. I assure you that if our instructions are followed precisely you will have no trouble.

"Furthermore, we keep a large inventory of our forms so that you need never worry about delays. A phone call to our office is all that is necessary to ensure prompt delivery of the needed forms to your plant. I hope, therefore, that I can be favoured with your order." Did Jamison handle this situation correctly? Why?

6. One of your customers, Margaret Port, has referred you to a friend who needs your Hercules Shelving for a storage warehouse. Port recently purchased your heavy-duty, 18-gauge steel shelving and is pleased with it. She said, "This will be an easy sale for you. My friend really needs shelving and I told him about yours."

Port's information is correct and your presentation to her friend goes smoothly. The customer has asked numerous questions and seems ready to buy. Just before you ask for the order, the customer says, "Looks like your product is exactly what I need. I'd like to think this over. Could you call me next week?" Which of the following would you do? Why?

a. Follow the suggestion and call next week.

b. Go ahead and ask for the order.

c. Ask questions about the reason for the delay.

SALES WORLD WIDE WEB EXERCISES

Finding People, Organizations, Maps, Areas, Phone Numbers, and Addresses

Opposition or resistance to information or to the salesperson's request is a sales objection. Objections often arise because the salesperson has not researched the individual or organization. Some types of selling require a tremendous amount of research to create a sales presentation. The better your research, the fewer objections, and thus the more likely you are to make the sale. The following URLs can help you in your research:

People Finders

www.canada411.ca

www.switchboard.com

www.bigyellow.com

Organization Finders

www.strategis.ic.gc.ca

www.bigyellow.com

www.bigbook.com

www.companiesonline.com

Maps

www.mapquest.ca

maps.google.com

Geographic Market Areas

www.statcan.ca

E-Mail

www.el.com

Of course, also use your favourite search engines to find out more about people, organizations, markets, and geographical areas.

FURTHER EXPLORING THE SALES WORLD

1. A national sales company is at your school wanting to hire salespeople. What are some objections that such a company might have toward hiring you? How would you overcome them during a job interview?

2. Think of three different types of businesses. (such as a grocery store, a hardware store, and a stereo shop), and think of one product from each business. If you were that store's buyer, think of the major objections you would have or questions you would ask a product salesperson if you were asked to buy a large quantity and promote it. Now, as that salesperson, how would you overcome those objections?

STUDENT APPLICATION LEARNING EXERCISES (SALES)

Part 7

Sales objections are defined as opposition or resistance from the buyer. To complete this part:

1. List three objections a buyer might give you. Use objections that relate to your product. Do not use general objections, such as "I do not like it." The objection should be specific, such as "I do not like the colour."

   Objection 1:

   Objection 2:

   Objection 3:

2. Write the buyer–seller dialogue for each objection. State the buyer's objection and then your response to it. Follow the four-step process, and include the buyer's response to your clarifying probe or rephrasal.

   Buyer's objection 1:

   Your acknowledgment:

   Your probe or rephrase:

   Buyer's response:

   Your FAB:

   Trial close:

   Role-play the buyer giving you the above objections and your response. If possible, use a video or tape recorder to play back the dialogue. Does what you say sound natural and conversational to you? If not, adjust it.

CASE 10–1
Ace Building Supplies

This is your fourth call on Ace Building Supplies to motivate them to sell your home building supplies to local builders. Joe Newland, the buyer, gives every indication that he likes your products.

During the call, Joe reaffirms his liking for your products and attempts to end the interview by saying: "We'll be ready to do business with you in three months—right after this slow season ends. Stop by then and we'll place an order with you."

CASE 10–1

Questions

1. Which one of the following steps would you take? Why?
   a. Call back in three months to get the order as suggested.
   b. Try to get a firm commitment or order now.
   c. Telephone Joe in a month (rather than make a personal visit) and try to get the order.
2. Why did you not choose the other two alternatives?

CASE 10–2
Electric Generator Corporation (B)

George Wynn is a salesperson for EGC whose primary responsibility is to contact engineers in charge of constructing commercial buildings. One such engineer is Don Snyder, who is in charge of building a new School of Business Administration facility. Don's Red Deer–based engineering firm purchased three new EGC portable generators for this project. George learned that Don's company will build four more buildings on the campus, and he felt that Don might buy more machines.

Salesperson: Don, I understand you have three of our new-model electric generators.

Buyer: Yeah, you're not kidding.

Salesperson: I'm sure you'll need additional units on these new jobs.

Buyer: Yeah, we sure will.

Salesperson: I've gone over the building's proposed floor plans and put together the type of products you need.

Buyer: They buy down in Calgary; you need to see them!

Salesperson: I was just in there yesterday and they said it was up to you.

Buyer: Well, I'm busy today.

Salesperson: Can I see you tomorrow?

Buyer: No need; I don't want any more of your lousy generators!

Salesperson: What do you mean? That is our most modern design!

Buyer: Those so-called new fuses of yours are exploding after five minutes' use. The autotransformer starter won't start—Did you see the lights dim? That's another fuse blowing.

Question

George Wynn feels pressured to sell the new EGC. Don Snyder's business represents an important sale both now and in the future. If you were George, what would you do?

a. Have EGC's best engineer contact Don to explain the generator's capabilities.
b. Come back after Don has cooled down.
c. Get Don to talk about problems and then solve them.
d. Do you have any other ideas?

11

CLOSING—THE BEGINNING OF A NEW RELATIONSHIP

MAIN TOPICS

LEARNING OBJECTIVES

If everything has been done to properly develop and give a sales presentation, then closing the sale is the easiest step in the presentation. After studying this chapter, you should be able to:

- Explain when to close.

- Describe what to do if, when you ask for the order, your prospect asks for more information, raises an objection, or says no.

- Explain the difference between aggressiveness and assertiveness.

- Explain why you must prepare to close more than once.

- Discuss the 12 keys to a successful close.

- Present, illustrate, and use several techniques for closing the sale in your presentation.

- Construct a multiple-close sequence.

Jovan made his presentation for in-office coffee service to the office manager. As he neared the end of it, the office manager asked, "What's your price?" Jovan quoted the standard price, and immediately the manager said, "Your competitor's price is $10 cheaper!"

As Sumit, who represented a medical laboratory equipment company, finished her presentation, the pathologist asked her about the cost. She stated the list price and heard, "Your price is too high. I can get the same type of equipment for a lot less."

Ralph, selling a line of office copying machines, was only halfway through his presentation when the director of administration asked for the cost. When Ralph quoted the price on the top-of-the-line model the administrator closed off the interview with the familiar phrase, "Your price is too high."

Jovan, Sumit, and Ralph are facing a real challenge. Their buyers said, "Your price is too high," indirectly saying, "No, I'm not interested." In each situation, what would you do now? (Continued at end of chapter.)

Successful salespeople do not give a presentation and then ask for the order. Successful salespeople cultivate selling techniques that help develop a natural instinct, sensitivity, and timing for when and how to close with each buyer. This chapter wraps up our discussion of the main sales presentation elements. We begin by discussing when to close, showing examples of buying signals, and discussing what makes a good closer. Next we discuss the number of times you should attempt to close a sale, along with some problems associated with closing.

To be a good closer, you must be able to handle objections. Objections frequently arise as the salesperson nears the end of the presentation, as in the case of Jovan, and after the close, as experienced by Sumit. However, as Ralph found out, price objection can pop up anytime. This chapter and the previous chapter on objections will help you solve the "Sales Challenge" above.

ESSENTIALS OF CLOSING

Closing is the process of helping people make a decision that will benefit them. You help people make the decision by asking them to buy. As successful salespeople know, there are no magic phrases and techniques to use in closing a sale. It is the end result of your presentation. If everything has been done to properly develop a sales presentation, closing the sale is the next step in a logical sequence.

Although it seems obvious, some salespeople forget that prospects know that the salesperson is there to sell them something. So, as soon as they meet, the prospect's mind already may have progressed beyond the major portion of the salesperson's presentation. At times, the prospect may be ready to make the buying decision early in the interview. Remember, whatever the nature of a sale, there will always be a point when it's necessary to get a commitment from the buyer.

WHEN SHOULD I POP THE QUESTION?

So when should you attempt to close a sale? Simply, when the prospect is ready! More specifically, when the prospect is in the conviction stage of the mental buying process. A buyer can enter the conviction stage at any time during the sales presentation. As shown in Exhibit 11–1, you might ask someone to buy as early as the approach stage or as late as another day. Much of the time, however, the close comes after the presentation. An ability to read a prospect's buying signals correctly helps a salesperson decide when and how to close a sale.

EXHIBIT 11–1

Close when the prospect is ready.

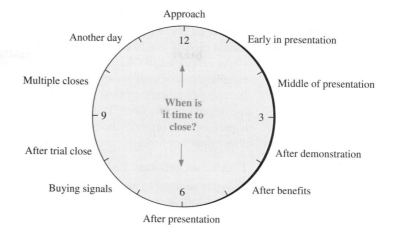

Reading Buying Signals

After prospects negotiate each stage of the mental buying process and are in the conviction stage, they often give you a signal. A **buying signal** refers to anything that prospects say or do to indicate they are ready to buy. Here are several ways a prospective buyer signals readiness to buy:

- **Asks questions**—"How much is it?" "What is the soonest I can receive it?" "What are your service and returned-goods policies?" At times, you may respond to a buying signal question with another question, as shown in Exhibit 11–2, to determine your prospect's thoughts and needs. If your question is answered positively, the prospect is showing a high interest level, and you are nearing the close.

- **Asks another person's opinion**—The executive calls someone on the telephone and says, "Come in here a minute; I have something to ask you." Or the husband turns to his wife and says, "What do you think about it?"

- **Relaxes and becomes friendly**—Once the prospect decides to buy, the pressure of the buying situation is eliminated. A state of visible anxiety changes to relaxation because your new customer believes that you are a friend.

- **Pulls out a purchase order form**—If, as you talk, your prospect pulls out an order form, it is time to move toward the close.

- **Carefully examines merchandise**—When a prospect carefully scrutinizes your product or contemplates the purchase, this may be an indirect request for prompting. Attempt a trial close: "What do you think about . . . ?" If you obtain a positive response to this question, move on to close the sale.

EXHIBIT 11–2

Answering a prospect's buying signal question with a question.

Buyer Says	Salesperson Replies
■ What's your price?	■ In what quantity?
■ What kind of terms do you offer?	■ What kind of terms do you want?
■ When can you make delivery?	■ When do you want delivery?
■ What size copier should I buy?	■ What size do you need?
■ Can I get this special price on orders placed now and next month?	■ Would you like to split your shipment?
■ Do you carry 8-, 12-, 36-, and 54-cm pipe?	■ Are those the sizes you commonly use?
■ How large an order must I place to receive your best price?	■ What size order do you have in mind?
■ Do you have Model 6400 in stock?	■ Is that the one you like best?

**The Trial Close—
A Great Way to
Obtain Buyer
Feedback**

A prospect may send verbal or nonverbal buying signals at any time before or during your sales presentation (remember Exhibit 11–1). Recognizing a buying signal should prompt you to attempt a **trial close**.

As discussed in Chapter 9, during your sales presentation the trial close is an excellent test of your prospect's interest level in buying your proposition. It checks the pulse or attitude of your prospect toward the sales presentation. It helps to elicit the buyer's impressions. You perform a trial close by making a statement or posing a question that prompts the buyer to respond. The trial close should be used at these four important times:

1. After an important FAB.
2. After addressing an objection.
3. Immediately before attempting to close the sale.
4. Whenever the salesperson needs buyer response during the presentation.

The trial close allows you to determine (1) whether the prospect likes your product's FABs (the strong selling point); (2) whether you have successfully answered the objection; (3) whether any objections remain; and (4) whether the prospect is ready for you to close the sale. It is a powerful technique to induce two-way communication (feedback) and participation from the prospect.

If, for example, the prospect says little while you make your presentation, and if you get a no when you come to the close, you may find it difficult to change the prospect's mind. You have not learned the real reasons that the prospect is saying no. To avoid this, salespeople use the trial close to determine the prospect's attitude toward the product throughout the presentation.

**Make Trial Closes
Specific**

The trial close asks for the prospect's reaction to what has just been presented by the salesperson. Most often what has just been presented is verbal—a FAB. Sometimes it may be nonverbal; for example, when the salesperson hands the buyer a testimonial letter and waits while it is read. In either case, a trial close is intended to shed some light on the buyer's black box that you read about in Chapter 3.

An effective trial close, therefore, refers specifically to what occurs just before it is done. After an important FAB, the trial close will request the buyer's response to that specific benefit or advantage or feature. After a testimonial letter, the trial close will ask specifically for the prospect's reaction to the content of the letter. In other words, effective trial closes are specific, not general. "How do you like our colour selection?" is effective because it is specific to colours offered. "How does that sound?" is ineffective because it is too vague to provide the salesperson with valuable feedback.

Trial closes may be open or closed questions. Remember that the intention is to induce two-way communication. Skilled salespeople will use closed trial closes when they want brief responses from the prospect and open trial closes when they want the buyer to expand on his reaction. As they progress through their presentations, effective salespeople alternate between open and closed trial closes as needed to maintain momentum, check on their progress, and keep the buyer involved.

Skilled salespeople also use a variety of trial closes during their presentations to ensure they do not sound robotic. Overuse of phrases such as, "Can you see . . ." or "What do you think . . ." at the beginning of trial closes will sound repetitive and awkward to the buyer. Instead, by using a variety of different words and phrases, the salesperson will make the presentation more natural and conversational.

SELLING GLOBALLY

Doing Business in Korea

Doing business in Korea is still much different than doing business at home, even though the country has adapted well to Western business philosophies.

Relationships: Koreans appreciate an effort on your part to understand their way of life. Koreans will appreciate your effort to express simple phrases in Korean. For example, a simple *gam-sa-ham-di* (thank you) will go a long way in forming a friendship.

They also like to socialize. It is common for Canadian business people visiting Korea to engage in social activities with their Korean host. Joining them for an evening drinking soju (Korean alcohol) and singing karaoke would be a appreciated.

The Business Card: This is an excellent way for your Korean prospect to get to know your name, position, and status. The exchange of cards should be done almost formally, with a high degree of respect. A bilingual card would be ideal.

History: Be sensitive about Korea's historical relationship to Japan. Koreans often don't like things Japanese so avoid comparisons between the two if the topic should arise. If you mention that you like the Japanese Toyota over the Korean Hyundai, you may as well pack your bags.

Business Transactions: Relationships are important. You cannot cold call and it is best to have an introduction or referral. Koreans can be effective negotiators. Often, a Westerner may lose a negotiation due to style, rather than substance. Like the Chinese, Koreans are not big fans of formalized, written contracts. They would rather keep terms flexible so it is important that agreements are understood fully by both parties.

Trial Closes Are Not Needs Analysis or Closing

Trial closes are not needs-analysis questions. They are intended to obtain buyer feedback on the salesperson's offering, not to uncover buyer needs. For example, after presenting a FAB the salesperson should *not* ask, "Is this important to you?" If the buyer replies "No," then time has been wasted and the salesperson appears unprofessional. Equally troublesome is the probe, "Is this something that you are interested in?" The salesperson must know beforehand whether a FAB is of enough importance to present. As mentioned earlier, the salesperson learns this by conducting a needs analysis.

Trial closes are also not closes. They do not ask for the order. While an effective trial close such as "Which covering do you prefer, the vinyl or the leather?" may prompt the buyer to make a decision that could lead to a purchase, it does not request a commitment to buy, nor should it. A statement or question prompting the prospect to commit to buying is a close.

Remember the prospect's positive reactions. Use them later to help overcome objections and in closing the sale. Also, remember the negative comments. You may need to offset the negatives with the positives later in the presentation. Generally, however, you will not discuss the negative again.

If the prospect responds favourably to your trial close, then you are in agreement or you have satisfactorily answered an objection. Thus, the prospect may be ready to buy. However, if you receive a negative response, do not close. Either you have not answered some objection, or the prospect is not interested in the FAB you are discussing. This feedback allows you to better uncover what your prospect thinks about your product's potential for satisfying needs.

SELL SEQUENCE

One way to remember to incorporate a trial close into your presentation is the **SELL sequence**. Exhibit 11–3 shows how each letter of the word sell stands for a sequence of things to do and say to stress benefits important to the customer. By

EXHIBIT 11–3

The SELL sequence: Use it
throughout your presentation.

S	E	L	L
Show	Explain	Lead	Let
feature	advantage	into benefit	customer talk

remembering the word *sell,* you remember to *show the feature, explain the advantage, lead into the benefit, and then let the customer talk by asking a question about the benefit (trial close).*

Example:
Industrial salesperson to industrial purchasing agent: "This equipment is made of stainless steel [feature], which means it won't rust [advantage]. The real benefit is that it reduces your replacement costs, thus saving you money [benefit]! Do you see how choosing stainless steel will save you money [trial close]?"

Example:
Salesperson to consumer goods buyer: "Our company will spend an extra $250,000 in the next two months advertising No Cling fabric softener [feature]. Plus, you can take advantage of this month's $1.20 per dozen price reduction [feature]. This discount means you will sell 15 to 20 percent more No Cling in the next two months [advantage], thus making higher profits and pulling more customers into your store [benefits]. How does our advertising and discount package sound to you [trial close]?"

Once you use a trial close, carefully listen to what the customer says and watch for nonverbal signals to determine whether what you said has had an impact. If you have a positive response to your trial close, you are on the right track.

Remember, the trial close does not ask the customer to buy. It is a statement or question designed to determine the customer's opinion toward the salesperson's proposition (see Exhibit 11–4). It may prompt a signal that the prospect is ready to buy; however, its main purpose is to induce feedback from the buyer.

EXHIBIT 11–4

Examples of features, advantages, benefits, and trial closes that form a SELL sequence.

Features (characteristics)	Advantages (performance characteristics)	Benefits (result from advantage)	Trial Closes (feedback questions)
1. Nationally advertised consumer product	1. Will sell more product	1. Will make you more profit	1. What do you think of our advertising plan?
2. Air conditioner with a high energy-efficiency rating	2. Uses less electricity	2. Saves 10 percent on energy costs	2. How do you like the energy efficiency of our unit?
3. Product made of stainless steel	3. Will not rust	3. Reduces your replacement cost	3. Do you like the fact that it is stainless steel?
4. Supermarket computer system with the IBM 3651 Store Controller	4. Can store more information and retrieve it rapidly by monitoring up to 24 checkout scanners and terminals and looking up prices on up to 22,000 items	4. Provides greater accuracy, register balancing, store ordering, and inventory management	4. Can you see how the increased power of the 3651 will improve your operations?
5. Five percent interest on money in bank when choosing NOW account	5. Earns interest that would not normally be received	5. Gives you one extra bag of groceries each month	5. What is your impression of this interest rate on your account?
6. Aerodynamically designed titanium golf club head	6. Increased clubhead speed, longer drives	6. Lower scores	6. How do you like the design?

WHAT MAKES A GOOD CLOSER?

In every sales force, some individuals are better than others at closing sales. Some persons rationalize this difference of abilities by saying, "It comes naturally to some people," or, "They've just got what it takes." What does it take to be a good closer?

Good closers have a strong desire to close each sale. They have a positive attitude about their product's ability to benefit the prospect. They know their customers and tailor their presentations to meet each person's specific needs.

Good closers prepare for each sales call. They take the time to carefully ascertain the needs of their prospects and customers by observing, by asking intelligent questions, and most of all, by earnestly listening. To be successful, salespeople should keep in mind their ABCs. ABC stands for *Always Be Closing*. Be alert for buying signals and close when the prospect is ready to buy (see Exhibit 11–5).

Do not stop with the prospect's first no. If a customer says no, determine the nature of the objection and then return to the presentation. After discussing information relative to overcoming the objection, use a trial close to determine whether you have overcome the objection, and then determine whether there are other objections. If resistance continues, remain positive and remember that every time you attempt to close, you are closer to the sale.

Ask for the Order and Be Quiet

No matter when or how you close, remember that after you ask for the order, it is important to be silent. Do not say a word. If you say something—anything—you increase the probability of losing the sale.

You must put the prospect in a position of having to make a decision, speak first, and respond to the close. If you say anything after your close, you take the pressure off the prospect to make that decision.

Imagine this situation: The salesperson has finished the presentation and says, "Would you want this delivery in two or four weeks?" The average salesperson cannot wait more than two seconds for the prospect's reply without saying something like, "I can deliver it anytime," or starting to talk again about the product. This destroys the closing moment. The prospect does not have to make the decision. There is time to think of reasons not to buy. By keeping quiet for a few seconds, the salesperson ensures that the prospect must make a decision.

All individuals experience the urge to say no, even when they are not sure of what you are selling or when they want what you propose. To help the prospect make the decision, you must maintain silence after the close.

The professional salesperson can stay quiet all day, if necessary. Rarely will the silence last more than 30 seconds. During that time, do not say anything or make a distracting gesture; merely project positive nonverbal signs. Otherwise, you will lessen your chances of making the sale. This is the time to mentally prepare your responses to the prospect's reaction.

It sounds simple, yet it is not. Your stomach may churn. Your nerves make you want to move. You may display a serious look on your face instead of a positive one. You may look away from the buyer. Most of all, you may want to talk to relieve the uncomfortable feeling that grows as silence continues. Finally, the prospect will say something. Now, you can respond based on the reaction to your close.

Constantly practise asking your closing question, staying silent for 30 seconds, and then responding. This rehearsal will develop your skill and courage to close.

EXHIBIT 11–5

A positive response to the trial close indicates a move toward the close; a negative response means return to your presentation or determine the prospect's objections.

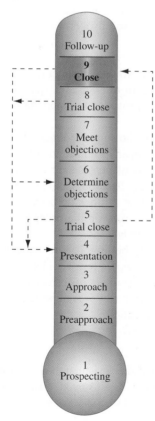

10 Follow-up

9 Close

8 Trial close

7 Meet objections

6 Determine objections

5 Trial close

4 Presentation

3 Approach

2 Preapproach

1 Prospecting

MAKING THE SALE

A Mark Twain Story

Mark Twain attended a meeting where a missionary had been invited to speak. Twain was deeply impressed. Later he said, "The preacher's voice was beautiful. He told us about the sufferings of the natives and pleaded for help with such moving simplicity that I mentally doubled the fifty cents I had intended to put in the plate. He described the pitiful misery of those savages so vividly that the dollar I had in mind gradually rose to five. Then that preacher continued. I felt that all the cash I carried on me would be insufficient. I decided to write a large check. Then he went on," added Twain, "and on and on about the dreadful state of those natives. I abandoned the idea of the check. Again, he went on, and I was back to five dollars. As he continued, I went to four, two, and then one dollar. Still, he persisted to preach. When the plate finally came around, I took ten cents out of it."[1]

How Many Times Should You Close?

Courtesy and common sense imply a reasonable limit to the number of closes attempted by a salesperson at any one sitting. However, salespeople call on customers and prospects to sell their products.

To sell, you must be able to use multiple closes. Keep in mind that three closes is a minimum for successful salespeople. Three to five well-executed closes should not offend a prospect. Attempting several closes in one call challenges a salesperson to employ wit, charm, and personality in a creative manner. So, always take at least three strikes before you count yourself out of the sale.

Closing under Fire

To close more sales effectively, never take the first no from the prospect to mean an absolute refusal to buy. Instead, you must be able to close under fire. See Exhibit 11–6. In other words, you must be able to ask a prospect who may be in a bad mood or even hostile toward you to buy.

Take the experience of a consumer goods salesperson who suggested that a large drug wholesaler should buy a six-month supply of the company's entire line of merchandise. Outraged, the purchasing agent threw the order book across the room. The salesperson explained to the furious buyer that the company had doubled its promotional spending in the buyer's area and that it would be wise to stock up because of an upcoming increase in sales. The salesperson calmly picked up the order book, smiled, and handed it to the buyer saying, "Did you want to buy more?"

The buyer laughed and said, "What do you honestly believe is a reasonable amount to buy?" This was a buying signal that the prospect would buy, but in a lesser quantity. They settled on an increased order of a two-month supply over the amount of merchandise normally purchased. This example illustrates why it is important for the salesperson to react calmly to an occasional hostile situation.

DIFFICULTIES WITH CLOSING

One reason salespeople may fail to close a sale and take an order is that they are not confident of their ability to close. Perhaps some earlier failure to make a sale has caused this mental block. They may give the presentation and stop short of asking for the order. The seller must overcome this fear of closing to become successful.

Second, salespeople often determine that the prospect does not need the quantity or type of merchandise, or that the prospect should not buy. So, they do not ask the prospect to buy. The salesperson should remember that "it is the prospect's decision and responsibility whether to buy." Do not make the decision for the prospect.

EXHIBIT 11–6

Closing under fire.

You can tell this customer is unhappy with your product or you. How do you save the sale and close?

Finally, the salesperson may not have worked hard enough in developing a customer profile and customer benefit plan—resulting in a poor presentation. Many times, a poorly prepared presentation falls apart. Be prepared and develop a well-planned, well-rehearsed presentation.

Remember!   While there are many factors to consider in closing the sale, the following are essential if you want to improve your chances:

- Be sure your prospect understands what you say.
- Always present a complete story to ensure understanding.
- Tailor your close to each prospect. Eighty percent of your customers will respond to a standard close. It is the other 20 percent of customers you need to prepare for. Prepare to give the expert customer all facts requested, to give the egotistical customer praise, to lead the indecisive customer, and to slow down for a slow thinker.
- Everything you do and say should consider the customer's point of view.
- Never stop at the first no.
- Learn to recognize buying signals.
- Before you close, attempt a trial close.
- After asking for the order, be silent.

MAKING THE SALE

Closing Is Not One Giant Step

Too many salespeople regard the close as a separate and distinct part of the sales call. "I've discussed benefits and features, answered some objections, handled price, and now it's time to close."

Chronologically, of course, the close does come at the end. Closing is the natural outgrowth of the sales presentation. If the rest of the sales call has been a success, closing simply means working out terms and signing the order.

What about the salesperson who says, "I always have trouble closing. Everything's fine until it's time to close the sale." Chances are, there's no basis for the sale. "Everything's fine . . ." may merely be a way of saying, "I stated my case and the prospect listened. At least she never told me to pack up and go."

■ Set high goals for yourself, and develop a personal commitment to reach your goals.

■ Develop and maintain a positive, confident, and enthusiastic attitude toward yourself, your products, your prospects, and your close.

Before we discuss specific techniques on how to ask for the order or close the sale, remember that you will increase your sales closings by using 12 simple keys to success, as shown in Exhibit 11–7.

As you see from these 12 keys, a successful close results from a series of actions that you have followed before asking for the order. Closing is not one giant step.

Should you not make the sale, always remember to act as a professional salesperson and be courteous and appreciative of the opportunity to present your product to the prospect. This keeps the door open for another time. Thus, Key 12 cannot be overlooked—always remember to leave the door open!

Often, salespeople believe that there is some mystical art to closing a sale. If they say the right words in the appropriate manner, the prospect will buy. They concentrate on developing tricky closing techniques and are often pushy with prospects in hopes of pressuring them into purchasing. Certainly, salespeople need to learn alternative closing techniques. However, what is most needed is a thorough understanding of the entire selling process and of the critical role that closing plays in that process.

EXHIBIT 11–7

Twelve keys to a successful closing.

1. Think *success!* Be enthusiastic.
2. *Plan* your sales call.
3. Confirm your prospect's *needs*.
4. Give a *great* presentation.
5. Use *trial closes* during and after your presentation.
6. Smoke out a prospect's *real* objections.
7. *Overcome* real objections.
8. Use a *trial close* after overcoming each objection.
9. Summarize *benefits* as related to buyer's needs.
10. Use a *trial close* to confirm Step 9.
11. Ask for the *order* and then *be quiet*.
12. Leave the door *open*. Act as a professional.

EXHIBIT 11–8

Often the seller does not have to close.

In this case, the product sold itself. After examining the business proposition, the prospect bought without the salesperson asking for an order.

A memorized presentation and a hurriedly presented product will not be as successful as the skilful use of the 12 keys to a successful close. A close look at the 12 keys illustrates that a lot of hard work, planning, and skilful execution of your plan occurs before you reach number 11 and ask for the order. The point is that if salespeople understand how each of the 12 applies to them and their customers, and if they perform each successfully, they earn the right to close.

In fact, many times the close occurs automatically because it has become the easiest part of the sales presentation. Often, the prospect will close for the salesperson, saying: "That sounds great! I'd like to buy that." See Exhibit 11–8. All the salesperson has to do is finalize the details and write up the order. Often, though, the prospect is undecided about the product after the presentation, so the skilful salesperson develops a multiple close sequence.

Assertiveness or Aggressiveness?

Understanding the difference between these two terms can make or break a sale. Salespeople should strive for assertiveness. What is the difference between being assertive and being aggressive

Assertiveness is
- Expressing our thoughts, feelings, and beliefs in a direct, honest, and appropriate way
- Respect for ourselves and for others
- Consciously working toward a win–win solution to problems
- Effectively influencing, listening, and negotiating so that others choose to cooperate willingly.

Aggressiveness is
- Expressing our thoughts, feelings, and beliefs in an inappropriate way
- A violation of the rights of others
- Either active or passive; either way, it communicates an impression of disrespect

- Putting our wants, needs, and rights above those of others
- An attempt to get our way by not allowing others a choice
- Striving for a win–lose solution (I'll be the winner; you'll be the loser).

Assertiveness Strategies

Use "I" Messages

An "I" message is a good way to let people know what you are thinking. It is made up of three parts:

Behaviour—"I think that by using our product, your company will experience . . ."

Effect—"By delaying this decision, I think you might run the risk of . . ."

Feelings—"I believe that adopting our solution will lead your company to much greater profits."

By using this kind of message, you are giving another person complete information, leaving no room for second-guessing or doubt. This is much more productive than simply expressing your frustration or resorting to a dubious closing technique.

Choose Assertiveness Words Carefully

Use factual descriptions instead of judgments:

"This product is the only one that can increase your profits." (Aggressive)

"The product has reliably demonstrated that it can cut production costs by up to 20 percent in companies such as yours." (Assertive)

Avoid exaggerations

"We are the best in the world." (Aggressive)

"We have been consistently rated in the top five sellers in our industry by the purchasing association." (Assertive)

Use "I" not "You"

"Your company cannot grow without our product." (Aggressive)

"I would like to show you how our product will help your company grow." (Assertive)

Test Your Assertiveness

These questions will help you to assess your assertiveness;

- When you differ with buyers you respect, are you able to speak up and share your own viewpoint?
- Are you able to refuse unreasonable requests made by buyers?
- Do you readily accept real criticisms and objections?
- Do you seek assistance when you need it?
- Do you have confidence in your own judgment and recommendations?
- If someone else has a better solution, do you accept it easily?
- Do you express your thoughts, feelings, and beliefs in a direct and honest way?
- Do you try to work for a solution that benefits all parties?

A "yes" response indicates an assertive approach.

SELLING TIPS

An Assertiveness Action Plan

Here are some communication techniques that can help you convey a positive, assertive attitude:

■ Use suitable facial expressions, always maintaining good eye contact.

■ Keep your voice firm but pleasant

■ Pay careful attention to your posture and gestures

■ Listen . . . and let people know you have heard what they said.

■ Ask questions for clarification.

■ Look for a win–win approach to problem solving.

SPECIFIC CLOSING TECHNIQUES

Just the fact that "closing techniques" are given a name sometimes implies that they are tricky or manipulative. This need not be the case. In fact, some techniques are simply more useful or effective given different types of buying situations and prospect concerns. To successfully close more sales, you must determine your prospect's situation, understand the prospect's attitude toward your presentation, and be prepared to select instantly a closing technique from several techniques based on your prospect. For example, suppose you profiled the prospect as having a big ego, so you planned to use the compliment closing technique. You find the prospect is eager to buy but undecided about the model or the number of products to buy, so you switch to using your urgency closing technique. By changing to a closing technique that fits the situation, you can speed the sale and keep your customer satisfied.

Successful salespeople adapt a planned presentation to any prospect or situation that may arise. Some salespeople have several closing techniques, each designed for a specific situation. The following are 10 common closing techniques.

■ alternative-choice close
■ assumptive close
■ compliment close
■ summary-of-benefits close
■ minor-points close

■ T-account or balance-sheet close
■ urgency close
■ probability close
■ negotiation close
■ technology close

These closing techniques are used to ask a prospect for the order whether the product sold is an industrial product or consumer product. See Exhibit 11–9.

EXHIBIT 11–9

Techniques for closing the sale: Which close should be used?

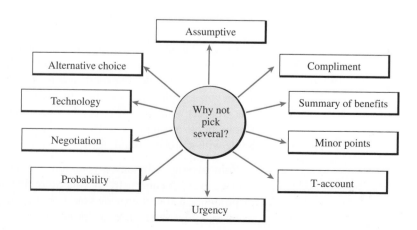

The Alternative-Choice Close Is an Old Favourite

The **alternative-choice close** was popularized in the 1930s as the story spread of the Walgreen Drug Company's purchase of 800 dozen eggs at a special price. A sales trainer named Elmer Wheeler suggested to the Walgreen clerks that when a customer asked for a malted milk at a Walgreen fountain, the clerk should say, "Do you want one egg or two?" Customers had not even thought of eggs in their malteds. Now, they were faced with the choice of *how many eggs*—not whether or not they wanted an egg. Within one week, all 800 dozen of the eggs were sold at a profit. Two examples of the alternative close are

- Which do you prefer—one or two neckties to go with your suit?
- Would you prefer the Xerox 6200 or 6400 copier?

As you see, the alternative choice does not give prospects a choice of buying or not buying but asks which one or how many items they want to buy. It says, "You are going to buy, so let's settle the details on what you will purchase." Buying nothing at all is not an option.

Take, for example, the salesperson who says: "Would you prefer the Xerox 6200 or 6400?" This question (1) assumes the customer has a desire to buy one of the copiers; (2) assumes the customer will buy; and (3) allows the customer a preference. If the customer prefers the Xerox 6400, you know the prospect is ready to buy, so you begin the close. A customer who says, "I'm not sure," is still in the desire stage, so you continue to discuss each product's benefits. However, you see that the customer likes both machines. Should the prospect appear indecisive, you can ask: "Is there something you are unsure of?" This question probes to find out why your prospect is not ready to choose.

If used correctly, the alternative-choice close is an effective closing technique. It provides a choice between items, never between something and nothing. By presenting a choice, you either receive a yes decision or uncover objections, which if successfully met allow you to come closer to making the sale.

The Assumptive Close

With the **assumptive close**, the salesperson assumes the prospect will buy (see Exhibit 11–10). Statements can be made such as, "I'll call in your order tonight," or, "I'll have this shipped to you tomorrow." If the prospect does not say anything, assume the suggested order has been accepted.

Many times the salesperson who has called on a customer for a long time can fill out the order form, hand it to the customer, and say, "This is what I'm going to send you," or, "This is what I believe you need this month." Many salespeople have earned customer trust to such an extent that the salesperson orders for them. Here, the assumptive close is especially effective.

The Compliment Close Inflates the Ego

Everyone likes to receive compliments. The **compliment close** is especially effective when you talk with a prospect who is a self-styled expert, who has a big ego, or who is in a bad mood. Would-be experts and egotistical prospects value their own opinions. When you compliment them, they listen and respond favourably to your presentation. The prospect with low self-esteem or one who finds it difficult to decide also responds favourably to a compliment. Here is an example of a housewares salesperson closing a sale with a grocery retail buyer.

Salesperson: Obviously, you know a great deal about the grocery business. You have every square metre of your store making a good profit. Ms. Stevenson, our products also will provide you with a good profit margin. In fact, our profit will exceed your store's average profit per square metre. And, they sell like hotcakes.

EXHIBIT 11–10

After completing the presentation on a new antibiotic, this pharmaceutical salesperson says, "I appreciate your using Ebiotic for your patients with an ear infection, Dr. Smith." What type of close is he using?

This added benefit of high turnover will further increase your profits—which you have said is important to you. [Pauses, and when there is no response, continues.] Given the number of customers coming into your store, our expected sales of these products due to normal turnover, and our marketing plan, I suggest you buy [he states the products and their quantities]. This will provide you with sufficient quantities to meet your customers' demands for the next two months and provide you with the expected profit from your products. [Waits for the response or again asks for the order using the alternative choice or assumptive close.]

All buyers appreciate your recognition of their better points. Conscientious merchants take pride in how they do business; customers entering the retail clothing store take pride in their appearance; people considering life insurance take pride in looking after their families. So compliment prospects relative to something that will benefit them as you attempt to close the sale. Remember, always give sincere compliments. Nearly anyone can detect insincerity in a compliment. When a compliment is not in order, summarize the benefits of your product for a specific customer.

The Summary-of-Benefits Close Is Most Popular

During the sales presentation, remember the main FABs of interest to the prospect and use them successfully during the close. Summarize these benefits in a positive manner so that the prospect agrees with what you say, then ask for the order.

Here is an example of using the **summary-of-benefits close** on a prospect. Assume that the prospect indicates during your sales presentation that she likes your profit margin, delivery schedule, and credit terms.

Salesperson: Ms. Stevenson, you say you like our profit margin, fast delivery, and credit policy. Is that right? [Summary and trial close.]

Prospect: Yes, I do.

Salesperson: With the number of customers in your store, our expected sales of the products due to normal turnover, and our marketing plan, I suggest you buy [state the products and their quantities]. This will provide you with sufficient quantities to meet customer demand for the next two months and provide you with the profit you expect from your products. I can have the order to you early next week. [Now wait for her response.]

You can easily adapt the FAB statements and SELL sequence for your summary close. The vacuum cleaner salesperson might say, "As we have discussed, this vacuum cleaner's high-speed motor [feature] works twice as fast [advantage] with less effort [advantage], saving you 15 to 30 minutes in cleaning time [benefit] and the aches and pains of pushing a heavy machine [benefit of benefit]. Right? [trial close; if positive response, say] Would you want the Deluxe or the Ambassador model?"

The sporting goods salesperson might say, "As we have said, this ball will give you an extra 10 to 20 yards on your drive [advantage], helping to reduce your score [benefit] because of its new solid core [feature]. That's great—isn't it? [trial close; if positive response, say] Will a dozen be enough?"

The air-conditioning salesperson could say, "This air conditioner has a high efficiency rating [feature] that will save you 10 percent on your energy costs [benefit] because it uses less electricity [advantage]. What do you think of that? [trial close; if positive response, say] Would you want it delivered this week or do you prefer next week?"

The summary close is possibly the most popular method to ask for the order. There are three basic steps to the summary close: (1) determine the key product benefits that interest the prospect during the presentation, (2) summarize these benefits, and (3) make a proposal. The summary-of-benefits technique is useful when you need a simple, straightforward close rather than a close aimed at a specific prospect's personality.

The Minor-Points Close Is Not Threatening

It is sometimes easier for a prospect to concede several minor points about a product than to make a sweeping decision about whether to buy or not to buy. Big decisions are often difficult for some buyers. By having the prospect make decisions on a product's minor points, you can subtly lead into the decision to buy.

The **minor-points close** is similar to the alternative-choice close. Both methods involve giving the buyer a choice between two options. The alternative-choice close asks the prospect to make a choice between *two* products, which represents a high-risk decision to some people that they may prefer not to make. However, the minor-points close asks the prospect to make a low-risk decision on a minor, usually low-cost element of a *single* product such as delivery dates, optimal features, colour, size, payment terms, or order quantity.

Single-or multiple-product element choices may be presented to the prospect. The stereo salesperson says, "Would you prefer the single or multiple disc player for your car stereo system?" The Xerox Business Products salesperson asks, "Are you interested in buying or leasing our equipment?" The automobile salesperson asks, "Would you like to install a satellite radio?"

This close is used widely when prospects have difficulty making a decision or when they are not in the mood to buy. It is also effective as a second close. If, for example, the prospect says no to your first close because of difficulty in deciding whether to buy, you can close on minor points.

The T-Account or Balance-Sheet Close Was Ben Franklin's Favourite

The **T-account close** is based on the process that people use when they make a decision. It should, therefore, be used only when you are faced with a buyer who is indecisive. Some sales trainers refer to it as the Benjamin Franklin close. In his *Poor Richard's Almanac,* Franklin said, "You know, I believe most of my life is going to be made up of making decisions about things. I want to make as many good ones as

I possibly can." So, in deciding on a course of action, his technique was to take pencil and paper and draw a line down the centre of the paper. On one side, he put all the pros, and on the other side he put all the cons. If there were more cons than pros, he would not do something. If the pros outweighed the cons, then he felt it was a good thing to do; this was the correct decision.

This is the process a customer uses in making a buying decision, weighing the cons against the pros. At times, it may be a good idea to use this technique. Pros and cons, debits and credits, or to act and not to act are common column headings. For example, on a sheet of paper, the salesperson draws a large T, placing *to act* (asset) on the left side and *not to act* (liability) on the right side (debit and credit, in accounting terms). The salesperson reviews the presentation with the prospect, listing the positive features, advantages, and benefits the prospect likes on the left side and all negative points on the right. This shows that the product's benefits outweigh its liabilities, and it leads the prospect to conclude that now is the time to buy. If prospects make their own lists, the balance-sheet close is convincing. Here is an example:

Salesperson: Ms. Stevenson, here's a pad of paper and a pencil. Bear with me a minute and let's review what we have just talked about. Could you please draw a large T on the page and write "To Act" at the top on the left and "Not to Act" on the right? Now, you said you liked our fast delivery. Is that right?

To Act	Not to Act
Fast delivery	Narrow assortment
Good profit	
Good credit	

Prospect: Yes.

Salesperson: OK, please write down "fast delivery" in the To Act column. Great! You were impressed with our profit margin and credit terms. Is that right?

Prospect: Yes.

Salesperson: OK, how about writing that down in the left-hand column? Now is there anything that could be improved?

Prospect: Yes, don't you remember? I feel you have a narrow assortment with only one style of broom and one style of mop. [Objection.]

Salesperson: Well, write that down in the right-hand column. Is that everything?

Prospect: Yes.

Salesperson: Ms. Stevenson, what in your opinion outweighs the other—the reasons to act or not to act? [A trial close.]

Prospect: Well, the To Act column does. But it seems I need a better assortment of products. [Same objection again.]

Salesperson: We have found that assortment is not important to most people. A broom and mop are pretty much a broom and mop. They want a good quality product that looks good and that holds up continuously. Customers like our products' looks and quality. Aren't those good-looking products? [Trial close showing broom and mop.]

Prospect: They look OK to me. [Positive response—she didn't bring up assortment so assume you have overcome objection.]

Salesperson: Ms. Stevenson, I can offer you a quality product, fast delivery, excellent profit, and good credit terms. I'd like to suggest this: Buy one dozen mops and one dozen brooms for each of your 210 stores. However, let's consider this first: The XYZ chain found that our mops had excellent drawing power when advertised. Their sales of buckets and floor wax doubled. Each store sold an average of 12 mops. [He pauses, listens, and notices her reaction.] You can do the same thing.

Prospect: I'd have to contact the Johnson Wax salesperson, and I really don't have the time. [A positive buying signal.]

Salesperson: Ms. Stevenson, let me help. I'll call Johnson's and get them to contact you. Also, I'll go see your advertising manager to schedule the ads. OK? [Assumptive close.]

Prospect: OK, go ahead, but this stuff had better sell.

Salesperson: [Smiling] Customers will flock to your stores [he's building a picture in her mind] looking for mops, polish, and buckets. Say, that reminds me, you will need a dozen buckets for each store. [Keep talking.] I'll write up the order. [Assumptive.]

Some salespeople recommend that the columns of the T-account be reversed so that the Not to Act column is on the left and the To Act column is on the right. This allows the salesperson to discuss the reasons not to buy first, followed by the reasons to buy, ending the presentation on the positive side. This decision depends on a salesperson's preference.

Although this close can be used anytime, it is especially useful as a secondary or backup close. For example, if the summary close did not make the sale, use the T-account close. A contrary idea in the prospect's mind is like steam under pressure—explosive. So, when you remove the pressure by openly stating an objection, opposition vaporizes. An objection often becomes minor or disappears. Remember, however, if the customer says, "Well, I'm going to buy it," do not say, "Well, let's first look at the reasons not to buy." Instead, finalize the sale.

Modified T-Account or Balance-Sheet Close

Some salespeople modify the T-account close by listing only reasons to act in one column. They do not want to remind the prospect of any negative reasons not to buy as they attempt to close the sale.

This is a powerful sales tool because the prospects are mentally considering reasons to buy and not to buy anyway. Put the reasons out in the open so that you can participate in the decision-making process.

The Urgency Close Gets Action

What happens if someone tells you that you cannot have something that you would like to have? You instantly want it! When you face an indecisive prospect or if you want to have the prospect purchase a larger quantity, indicate that if she does not act now she may *not* be able to buy in the future. Motivate the prospect to act immediately by using the **urgency close**:

- I'm not sure whether I have your size. Would you want them if I have them in stock?
- My customers have been buying all we can produce. I'm not sure if I have any left to sell you.

SELLING TIPS

Your Prospect's Name Is a Powerful Closing Tool

Dale Carnegie, author of *How to Win Friends and Influence People*, taught his students, "If you remember my name, you pay me a subtle compliment; you indicate that I have made an impression on you." Your prospect's name is one of the most powerful closing tools because most of us are more interested in ourselves than in anyone else.

Repeat your prospect's name several times—but don't overdo it—during your sales call. *Connect your prospect's name with the major benefit statements:*

■ "This automatic dialing feature, Mikkel, will save you a lot of time."

■ "Our warranty is designed to give you peace of mind, Josée."

Your prospect will not know that you are using a powerful psychological strategy referred to as *learned association* or *positive pairing*. If you have connected your prospect's name with three or four prominent product benefits, your customer will expect to hear something positive when you merely mention her name. When you approach the close, remember to use your prospect's name. Chances are that the sound of his name will again evoke positive feelings.

■ Well, I know you are thinking of ordering X amount, but we really need to order (a larger amount) because we now have it in stock and I don't think we will be able to keep up with demand and fill your summer order.

■ The cost of this equipment will increase 10 percent next week. Can I ship it today, or do you want to pay the higher price?

For the right product, person, and situation, this is an excellent close. Both retail and industrial salespeople can use this technique to get prospects so excited that they cannot wait to buy. Prospects realize that factors such as labour strikes, weather, transportation, inflation, and inventory shortages could make it difficult to buy in the future. Do them a favour by encouraging them to buy now using the urgency close but use it honestly.

The Probability Close

When the prospect gives the famous *I want to think it over* objection, or some variation, try saying, "Ms. Prospect, that would be fine. I understand your desire to think it over, but let me ask you this—when I call you back next week, what is the probability, in percentage terms, that you and I will be doing business?" Then pause, and don't say another word until the prospect speaks.

The prospect's response will be from three possible categories:

1. *More than 50 percent but less than 85 percent for buying*. If your prospects respond in this range, ask what the remaining percentage is against buying, then pause and be silent. When you become skilled in this technique, you will see prospects blink as they focus on their real objections.

   Many times, we hear that prospects want to think it over. It is not because they want to delay the decision; it is because they don't fully understand what bothers them. The **probability close** permits your prospects to focus on their real objections. Once you have a real objection, convert that objection with a persuasive sales argument.

2. *Above 85 percent but not 100 percent for buying*. If they're in this range, recognize that there is a minor probability against you. You might want to say, "Since it is almost

certain that we'll do business together, why wait until next week? Let's go ahead now; and if you decide in the next couple of days that you want to change your mind, I'll gladly tear up your order. Let's get a running start on this project together."

When prospects indicate a high percentage of probability, you can use their statements as a lever to push them over the top.

3. *Less than 50 percent for buying.* This is a signal that there is little, if any, chance that you will ever close this particular sale. The only appropriate tactic is returning to square one and starting the reselling process. It is amazing how many professional salespeople in a closing situation expect the prospect to say 80–20 as a probability in their favour, and instead they hear "80–20 against."

The probability close permits prospects to focus on their objections. It allows the true or hidden objections to surface. The more prospects fight you and the less candid they are about the probability of closing, the less likely they will buy anything.

The Negotiation Close

Many sales require some negotiation to complete. Most sales negotiations focus on two major themes: value and price. Customers often demand more value and lower prices. In their quest for more value at a lower cost, prospects often resort to unfair tactics and put heavy pressure on the salesperson. The purpose of a good sales **negotiation close** is not to haggle over who gets the larger slice of pie but to find ways for everyone to have a fair deal. Both the buyer and seller should win. Here are two examples of a salesperson using a negotiation close:

■ If we could find a way in which we would eliminate the need for a backup machine and guarantee availability, would you be happy with this arrangement?

■ Why don't we compromise? You know I can't give you a discount, but I could defer billing until the end of the month. That's the best I can do. How does that sound?

In a negotiation, the attitude that you project determines the attitude you receive. Be positive! Be helpful! Be concerned! Show your interest in helping the prospect.

The Technology Close

You have just completed the discussion of your product, marketing plan, and business proposition. You summarize your product's main benefits to your customer. Now you bring out your laptop computer, placing it on the buyer's desk so she can see the screen, or you prepare to project the computer screen onto the wall. Using graphs and bar charts, you show the buyer past purchases and sales trends. Then you call up your recommended purchase suggestion. If appropriate, you can show payment schedules considering different quantity discounts. This **technology close** is very impressive to some buyers.

The exact use of technology in closing a sale depends on the type of product and customer you're selling. Without a doubt, incorporating technology into your presentation will help you close more prospects and customers.

PREPARE A MULTIPLE-CLOSE SEQUENCE

By keeping several different closes ready in any situation, you are in a better position to close more sales. Also, the use of a multiple-close sequence, combined with methods to overcome objections, enhances your chance of making a sale.

For example, you could begin with a summary close. If the buyer says no, you could rephrase the objection and then use an alternative close. If again the buyer says no and will not give a reason, you could use the four-step sequence method for overcoming objections. See Chapter 10 for procedures on overcoming objections.

Exhibit 11–11 gives an example of a multiple-close sequence developed by Jane Martin, who works for an electrical wholesaler. Notice that she uses both methods to overcome objections and closing techniques. First, she uses the summary-of-benefits close and then waits for a response. Martin does not rush. She realizes it is a big decision and is prepared to handle resistance and ask for the order several times. The buyer is sending out green signals, so Martin does not stop; she continues to respond to the buyer.

EXHIBIT 11–11

Multiple closes incorporating techniques for overcoming objections.

Salesperson: John, we have found that the Octron bulb will reduce your storage space requirements for your replacement stock. It offers a higher colour output for your designers, which reduces their eye fatigue and shadowing. Should I arrange for delivery this week or next week? [Close 1—Summary-of-benefits close.]

Buyer: Well, those are all good points, but I'm still not prepared to buy. It's too costly.

Salesperson: What you're saying is, you want to know what particular benefits my product has that make it worth its slightly higher price. Is that correct? [Rephrase.]

Buyer: Yes, I guess so.

Salesperson: Earlier, we saw that considering the extended life of the lamps and their energy savings, you can save $375 each year by replacing your present lamps with GE Watt-Misers. This shows, John, that you save money using our product. Right? [Trial close.]

Buyer: Yes, I guess you're right.

Salesperson: Great! Do you prefer installation this weekend or after regular business hours next week? [Close 2—Alternative close]

Buyer: Neither; I need to think about it more.

Salesperson: I hear what you are saying. There must be some good reason that you're hesitating to go ahead now. Do you mind if I ask what it is? [Objection handling Steps 1 and 2]

Buyer: I don't think I can afford new lighting all at one time.

Salesperson: In addition to that, is there another reason for not going ahead? [Objection handling Step 2.]

Buyer: No.

Salesperson: Group replacement is not a necessity; however, it does allow you to realize immediate energy savings on all of your fixtures. It saves you much of the labour costs of spot replacement because the lamps are installed with production-line efficiency. See what I mean? [Objection handling Steps 3 and 4]

Buyer: Yes, I do.

Salesperson: Do you feel that installation would be better at night or on the weekend? [Close 3—Minor-points close.]

Buyer: I'd still like to think about it.

Salesperson: There must be another reason why you're hesitating to go ahead now. Do you mind if I ask what it is? [Objection handling Step 2.]

Buyer: Yes. My supervisor will not let me buy anything.

Salesperson: You agree you could save money for your company on this purchase—right?

Buyer: Yes.

Salesperson: Well, John, how about calling your supervisor now and telling her about how much money we can save in addition to reducing your storage space and the eye fatigue of your employees? Maybe both of us could visit your supervisor. [Close 4—Summary-of-benefits close.]

Notice that the buyer finally gave the real reason for not buying when he said, "No. My supervisor will not let me buy anything." By professionally handling John's objections and politely continuing to close, Jane is in a position to talk with the real decision maker—John's boss.

CLOSE BASED ON THE SITUATION

Since different closing techniques work best for certain situations, salespeople often identify the common objections they encounter and develop specific closing approaches designed to overcome these objections. Exhibit 11–12 shows how different closing techniques are used to meet objections.

Assume, for example, that a buyer has a predetermined belief that a competitor's product is needed. The salesperson could use the T-account approach to show how a product's benefits are greater than a competitor's product. In developing the sales presentation, review your customer profile and develop your main closing technique and several alternatives. By being prepared for each sales call, you experience increased confidence and enthusiasm, which results in a more positive selling attitude. You can both help the customer and reach your goals.

RESEARCH REINFORCES THESE SALES SUCCESS STRATEGIES

Although it is difficult to summarize all sales success strategies discussed throughout this book, one research report reinforces several key procedures that improve sales performance. This research sought to examine two key questions all salespeople frequently ask themselves: What makes one sales call a success and another a failure? Do salespeople make common mistakes that prevent success?

To answer questions such as these, Xerox Learning Systems enlisted a team of observers to monitor and analyze more than 500 personal sales calls of 24 different sales organizations. The products and services sold ranged from computers to industrial refuse disposal.

EXHIBIT 11–12

Examples of closing techniques based on situations.

Situation	Alternative-choice	Compliment	Summary	Minor points	Assumptive	T-account	Urgency	Probability	Negotiation	Reason
Customer is indecisive	X		X	X		X	X	X	X	Forces a decision
Customer is expert or egotistical		X				X		X	X	Lets expert make the decision
Customer is hostile		X						X	X	Positive strokes
Customer is a friend					X			X	X	You can take care of the small things
Customer has predetermined beliefs						X		X	X	Benefits outweigh disbeliefs
Customer is greedy, wants a deal							X	X	X	Buy now

Mike Radick, the Xerox senior development specialist overseeing the study, stated that the average successful sales call was 33 minutes long. During that call, the salesperson asked an average of 13.6 questions and described 6.4 product benefits and 7.7 product features. Meanwhile, the customer described an average of 2.2 different needs, raised 1.0 objections, made 2.8 statements of acceptance, and asked 7.7 questions.

The observers noted that it does not seem to matter whether the salesperson is 28 or 48 years old, male or female, or has 2 or 20 years of experience. What matters is the ability to use certain skills and avoid common errors. These six common mistakes have prevented successful sales calls:

- **Tells instead of sells; doesn't ask enough questions**. The salesperson does most of the talking. Instead of asking questions to determine a customer's interest, the salesperson charges ahead and rattles off product benefits. This forces the customer into the passive role of listening to details that may not be of interest. As a result, the customer becomes increasingly irritated.

   For example, a person selling a computerized payroll system may tell a customer how much clerical time could be saved by using this service. However, if clerical time is not a concern, then the customer has no interest in learning how to reduce payroll processing time. On the other hand, the same customer may have a high need for more accurate recordkeeping and be extremely interested in the computerized reports generated by the system.

- **Overcontrols the call; asks too many closed-end questions**. This sales dialogue resembles an interrogation, and the customer has limited opportunities to express needs. The overcontrolling salesperson steers the conversation to subjects the salesperson wants to talk about without regarding the customer. When the customer does talk, the salesperson often fails to listen or respond, or doesn't acknowledge the importance of what the customer says. As a result, the customer is alienated and the sales call fails.

- **Doesn't respond to customer needs with benefits**. Instead, the salesperson lets the customer infer how the features will satisfy his needs. Consider the customer who needs a high-speed machine. The salesperson responds with information about heat tolerance but doesn't link that to how fast the equipment manufactures the customer's product. As a result, the customer becomes confused, loses interest, and the call fails.

   Research shows a direct relationship between the result of a call and the number of different benefits given in response to customer needs; the more need-related benefits cited, the greater the probability of success.

- **Doesn't recognize needs; gives benefits prematurely**. For example, a customer discussing telephone equipment mentions that some clients complain that the line is always busy. The salesperson demonstrates the benefits of his answering service, but the customer responds that busy lines are not important since people will call back. In this case, the customer is not concerned enough to want to solve the problem.

- **Doesn't recognize or handle negative attitudes effectively**. The salesperson fails to recognize customer statements of objection (opposition), indifference (no need), or skepticism (doubts). What isn't dealt with effectively remains on the customer's mind and, left with a negative attitude, the customer will not make a commitment. The research also shows that customer skepticism, indifference, and objection are three different attitudes. Each attitude affects the call differently; each one requires a different strategy for selling success.

■ **Makes weak closing statements; doesn't recognize when or how to close**. In one extreme case, the customer tried to close the sale on a positive note, but the salesperson failed to recognize the cue and continued selling until the customer lost interest. The lesson is that successful salespeople are alert to closing opportunities throughout the call.

The most powerful way to close a sales call involves a summary of benefits that interest the customer. Success was achieved in three out of four calls that included this closing technique in Radick's study.

KEYS TO IMPROVED SELLING

How is the bridge from average to successful salesperson made? Xerox found it involves learning and using each of the following skills:

■ Ask questions to gather information and uncover needs.

■ Recognize when a customer has a real need and how the benefits of the product or service can satisfy it.

■ Establish a balanced dialogue with customers.

■ Recognize and handle negative customer attitudes promptly and directly.

■ Use a benefit summary and an action plan requiring commitment when closing.[2]

Learn and use these five selling skills, use the other skills emphasized throughout the book, and develop your natural ability and a positive mental attitude to become a successful, professional salesperson.

THE BUSINESS PROPOSITION AND THE CLOSE

For some salespeople, the discussion of the business proposition provides an excellent opportunity to close. The business proposition is the discussion of costs, markups, value analysis, or a return-on-investment (ROI) profit forecast. It follows the discussion of a product's FABs and marketing plan. Remember, the marketing plan explains two things:

1. For wholesalers or retailers, how they should resell the product.
2. For end users, how they can use the product.

The product's FABs and marketing plan justify your suggested order. The business proposition is the third step within the presentation and very important to closing the sale. The three steps are discussed in Chapters 6 and 9.

Use a Visual Aid to Close

The use of a visual aid works well in discussing the business proposition and when closing. Immediately after discussing the marketing plan for Cap'n Crunch cereal, the salesperson pulls out the profit forecaster shown in Exhibit 11–13. Notice it is personalized by writing the account's name at the top.

The salesperson discusses each item on the profit forecaster. Then the salesperson says, "Based on your past sales, the profits you will earn, and our marketing plan, I suggest you buy 100 cases for your three stores." The suggested order is written on the profit forecaster.

Now the salesperson remains silent. The buyer will respond with either yes, no, or that is too much to buy. While waiting, the salesperson should mentally go over what to say for each response that can be made by the buyer.

EXHIBIT 11–13

Example of a personalized visual.

Using a visual is an excellent way to close. After discussing the financial information on the visual, close by suggesting what and how much should be ordered.

CLOSING OUT THE SALES INTERVIEW

A group of purchasing agents was asked about their biggest gripes about poor sales procedure. One item on their list was this: "They [salespeople] seem to take it personally if they don't get the business, as though you owe them something because they are constantly calling on you."[3]

Salespeople must learn that they simply cannot close every deal. Failure to close the deal should not jeopardize potential future relationships with this and other potential prospects. Properly handling a no-sale situation can have a big impact on future sales. Attitude is everything here. Some salespeople react with anger, while some may attempt to make the prospect feel guilty or even stupid for making this

EXHIBIT 11–14

Sometimes the salesperson will
not make the sale, but it is
important to leave the door open.

If this software salesperson had not made a sale, he would have left the door open for a
return sales call by being just as friendly leaving as when he came.

decision. These reactions will seldom change the prospect's mind, but what they will
do is make this prospect never want to do business with you in the future. In fact, this
prospect may spread the word that you reacted this way so that others may want to
stay clear of you. See Exhibit 11–14.

After an unsuccessful close:

- Stay professional—Appreciate the prospect's reasons for not buying.
- Stay in touch—Let the prospect know that you're available for other needs.
- Stay cheerful—Don't become despondent or angry.
- Ask for referrals—If you failed to close through no fault of your products.

ETHICAL DILEMMA

You are seated across the table from a serious procrastinator. You have tried several closing techniques to no avail. She just can't seem to make up her mind. Throughout the presentation, you picked up on several cues that suggested that she wants the product and you know in your heart that her company could really use it.

Suddenly, you remember the 'urgency close' technique. You hadn't really thought about it because you knew that you had plenty of merchandise in inventory and there were no price increases planned in the near future. You figure that if you presented this procrastinator with an urgent plea, it may push her over the edge and you could finally get her commitment.

Do you stretch the truth a lot to secure the order and tell her that there is some sort of time limit on the offer?

- Leave your business card.
- Thank the prospect for her time.

  After a successful close:

- Stay professional—Don't become flustered by your own success.
- Stay in touch—Let the customer know you're available for assistance.
- Stay cheerful—Be somebody who is a pleasure to deal with.
- Show appreciation for her time and business. People like to feel appreciated.
- Depending on the situation, it may be a good time to ask for referrals.

Regardless of the outcome of the sales interview, at the end of the day, salespeople should review their successes and failures and use this information to strengthen their ability to present effectively.

Get the Order— Then Move On!

Talking also can stop the sale after the prospect has said yes. An exception would be if you ask the customer for names of other prospects. Once this is done, it is best to take the order and move on.

In continuing to talk, you may give information that changes the buyer's mind. So, ask for the order and remain silent until the buyer responds. If you succeed, finalize the sale and leave.

SUMMARY OF MAJOR SELLING ISSUES

Closing is the process of helping people make decisions that will benefit them. You help people make those decisions by asking them to buy. The close of the sale is the next logical sequence after your presentation. At this time, you finalize details of the sale (earlier, your prospect was convinced to buy). Constantly look and listen for buying signals from your prospect to know when to close. It is time to close the sale any time the prospect is ready, whether at the beginning or end of your presentation.

As you prepare to close the sale, be sure you have presented a complete story on your proposition and that your prospect completely understands your presentation. Tailor your close to each prospect's personality and see the situation from the prospect's viewpoint. Remember that you may make your presentation and close too early, which causes a prospect to say no instead of "I don't understand your proposition, and I don't want to be taken advantage of." This is why you should never take the first no. It is another reason to use a trial close immediately before the close. But, no matter when or how you close, do so in a positive, confident, and enthusiastic manner to better serve your prospect and help you reach your goals. Learn and abide by the 12 keys to successful closing.

Plan and rehearse closing techniques for each prospect. Develop natural closing techniques or consider using closes such as the alternative-choice, assumptive, compliment, summary-of-benefits, minor-points, T-account, urgency, probability, negotiation, or technology close. Consider the situation and switch from your planned close if your prospect's situation is different than anticipated.

A good closer has a strong desire to close each sale. Rarely should you accept the first no as the final answer. If you are professional, you should be able to close a minimum of three to five times.

Do not become upset or unnerved if a problem occurs when you are ready to close. Keep cool, determine any objections, overcome them, and try to close again—you can't make a sale until you ask for the order!

Remember, after either a successful or unsuccessful sales interview, how you close out the sales interview will have a big impact on your future sales ability.

MEETING A SALES CHALLENGE

Sumit had finished her presentation. Jovan and Ralph had not. At least Sumit was able to tell her whole story. Jovan and Ralph should have postponed discussing price. They may have lost all hope of making the sale.

In all three cases, the prospect said, "Your price is too high." Many buyers learn or are trained to say this to see whether the seller will decrease the price.

When the buyer said, "What's your price?" Jovan could have said, "It will depend on the type of service you need and the quantity purchased. Let's discuss that in just a minute." When the buyer said, "Your competitor's price is $10 cheaper!" Jovan could say, "I quoted you our base price. Your actual price will depend on the quantity purchased. We can meet and beat that price [the competitor's price]."

Sumit needs to find out more, such as what specific equipment and from whom. Equipment is different. So are service, terms, and delivery.

When Ralph's buyer says, "Your price is too high," Ralph needs to find out what the buyer is using for comparison. Ralph's buyer may not need the top-of-the-line model. So Ralph must get back to a discussion of the buyer's needs before determining the model and price.

PLAYING THE ROLE

Using a product that you have with you (cell phone, calculator, laptop, pen, pencil, etc.), develop a SELL sequence that would likely form part of a presentation of that product. Follow the sell sequence by demonstrating each of the following closing techniques:

- assumptive close
- minor-point close
- T-account close
- compliment close
- urgency close

Now with a classmate, dramatize the SELL sequence and closing techniques to see how convincing you can be. Have your classmates analyze your close for its delivery, confidence, and conviction.

KEY TERMS FOR SELLING

aggressiveness, 311
alternative-choice close, 314
assertiveness, 311
assumptive close, 314
buying signal, 303
closing, 302
compliment close, 314
minor-points close, 316

negotiation close, 320
probability close, 319
SELL sequence, 305
summary-of-benefits close, 315
T-account close, 316
technology close, 320
trial close, 304
urgency close, 318

SALES APPLICATION QUESTIONS

1. A salesperson must use a closing technique that is simple and straightforward and ask the prospect only to buy rather than something in addition to buying. In which of the following examples, if any, is the salesperson suggesting something to the buyer that is a close, rather than something the buyer must do in addition to buying?

    a. If you have no objection, I'll go out to the warehouse now to see about reserving space for this new item.

    b. To get this promotion off right, we should notify each of your store managers. I've already prepared a bulletin for them. Should I arrange to have a copy sent to each manager, or do you want to do it?

    c. To start this promotion, we should notify each of your store managers. I've already prepared a bulletin for them. On my way out, I can drop it off with the secretary.

    d. We should contact the warehouse manager about reserving a space for this new item. Do you want to do it now or after I've left?

2. Buying signals have numerous forms. When you receive a buying signal, stop the presentation, and move in to close the sale. For each of the following seven situations, choose the appropriate response to your prospect's buying signal that leads most directly to a close.

    a. "Can I get it in blue?" Your best answer is
       (1) "Yes."
       (2) "Do you want it in blue?"
       (3) "It comes in three colours, including blue."

    b. "What's your price?" Your best answer is
       (1) "In what quantity?"
       (2) To quote a specific price.
       (3) "For which grade?"

    c. "What kind of terms do you offer?" Your best answer is
       (1) To provide specific terms.
       (2) "Terms would have to be arranged."
       (3) "What kind of terms do you want?"

    d. "How big an order do I have to place to get your best price?" Your best answer is
       (1) A schedule of quantity prices.
       (2) A specific-size order.
       (3) "What size order do you want to place?"

    e. "When will you have a new model?" Your best answer is
       (1) A specific date.
       (2) "Do you want our newest model?"
       (3) "This is our newest model."

  f. "What is the smallest trial order I can place with you?" Your best answer is
   (1) A specific quantity.
   (2) "How small an order do you want?"
   (3) A variety of order sizes.
  g. "When can you deliver?" Your best answer is
   (1) "That depends on the size of your order. What order size do you have in mind?"
   (2) A specific delivery date.
   (3) "When do you want delivery?"

3. Which of the following is the most frequently committed sin in closing? Why?
 a. Asking for the order too early.
 b. Not structuring the presentation toward a closing.
 c. Not asking for the order.

4. Is a good closing technique to ask the customer at the right time, "Well, how about it? May I have the factory ship you a carload?" Explain your answer.

5. After completing a presentation that has included all of your product's FABs, immediately ask the customer, "How much of the product do you wish to order?" Explain your answer.

6. Each visual aid used during your presentation is designed to allow the customer to say yes to your main selling points. What should your visual aids include that allows you to gauge customer interest and help move to the close? What are several examples?

7. "Now, let's review what we've talked about. We've agreed that the Mohawk's secondary backing and special latex glue make the carpet more durable and contribute to better appearance. In addition, you felt that our direct-to-customer delivery system would save a lot of money and time. Shall I send our wall-sample display or would you be interested in stocking some 9 by 12s?"
 a. The salesperson's closing statement helps ensure customer acceptance by doing which of the following?
  (1) Summarizing benefits that the customer agreed were important.
  (2) Giving an alternative.
  (3) Assuming that agreement has been reached.
 b. The salesperson ends the closing statement by
  (1) Asking whether the customer has any other questions.
  (2) Asking whether the product will meet the customer's requirements.
  (3) Requesting a commitment from the customer.

8. "Assuming agreement has been reached" reflects the kind of attitude you should project when making a closing statement. When you make a close, nothing you say should reflect doubt, hesitation, or uncertainty. Which of the following salesperson's remarks assume agreement?
 a. "If you feel that Munson is really what you want..."
 b. "Let me leave you two today and deliver the rest next week..."
 c. "Well, if you purchase..."
 d. "Well, it looks as if maybe..."
 e. "We've agreed that..."
 f. "When you purchase the X-7100..."
 g. "Why don't you try a couple, if you like..."

9. A good rule is, "Get the order and get out." Do you agree? Explain your answer.

10. The real estate salesperson is showing property to a couple who look at the house and say, "Gee, this is great. They've taken good care of this place and the rugs and drapes are perfect. Do you think they'd be willing to leave the rugs and drapes?" What should the salesperson do or say? Why?

SALES WORLD WIDE WEB EXERCISES

Research Helps You Be a Better Closer!

Pick a good or service of your school to sell to someone or to an organization. Selling advertisements or tickets to events on campus and getting contributions are examples of products to sell. Choose a prospect—someone or some organization that might buy what you are selling. Using the appropriate URLs and your school's library, research the prospect. Begin your research by reviewing the Sales World Wide Web Directory for appropriate URLs.

Write a report to your boss on the sources and URLs you found useful in planning your sales presentation. Be sure to include how you would ask for the order, including what to buy and the quantity.

FURTHER EXPLORING THE SALES WORLD

1. Assume you are interviewing for a sales job and there are only five minutes remaining. You are interested in the job and know that if the company is interested, you will be invited for a visit to the company's local distribution centre and to work with one of their salespeople for a day. What are several closing techniques you could use to ask for the visit?

2. Visit several retail stores or manufacturing plants in your local area and ask their purchasing agents what they like and do not like about the closing when they are contacted by salespeople. See if they have already decided to buy or not to buy before the salesperson closes. Ask how a salesperson should ask for their business.

3. Develop a complete sales presentation that can be given in eight minutes. Include the buyer–seller dialogue. Make sure the appropriate components in Exhibit A are contained in the presentation. Use one of the three approaches shown in Exhibit A depending on your situation. For example, use the SPIN approach if this is the first time you have called this prospect. Use the SPIN or summary-of-benefits approach if this is a repeat sales call on a prospect or customer.

   Your presentation must use several SELL sequences and should contain a minimum of one evidence statement; two similes, metaphors, or analogies; and a demonstration of important benefits. The marketing plan also must incorporate one or more SELL sequences that tie the marketing plan back to the information uncovered in the approach and the first SELL sequence.

   The business proposition is last and contains the appropriate discussion on price and value. Relate the business proposition to the information uncovered earlier in the presentation. Develop visuals for presenting your benefits, marketing plan, and business proposition. Anywhere within the presentation before the close, use a minimum of one objection, and answer one of the buyer's questions with a question.

   Now, ask for the order using a summary-of-benefits close that includes a suggested order if appropriate for your product or service. Use a minimum of three closes. This requires you to develop *a multiple-close sequence* since the buyer has raised an objection or asked for more information after each close. Also, use different methods of handling objections. In the presentation, be sure to (1) have a professional appearance; (2) firmly shake hands and use direct eye contact before and after the presentation; (3) project positive nonverbal signs; and (4) use a natural level of enthusiasm and excitement in conversation.

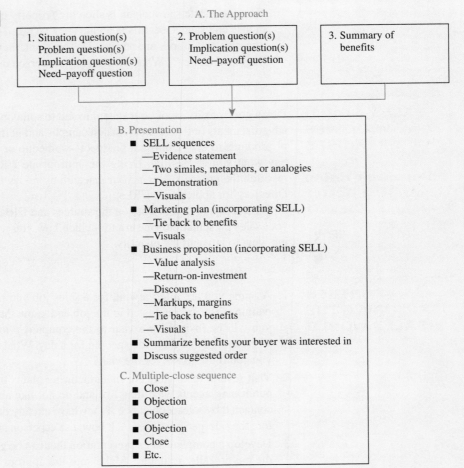

EXHIBIT A

Format of your sales presentation.

A. The Approach

1. Situation question(s)
   Problem question(s)
   Implication question(s)
   Need–payoff question

2. Problem question(s)
   Implication question(s)
   Need–payoff question

3. Summary of benefits

B. Presentation
- SELL sequences
  —Evidence statement
  —Two similes, metaphors, or analogies
  —Demonstration
  —Visuals
- Marketing plan (incorporating SELL)
  —Tie back to benefits
  —Visuals
- Business proposition (incorporating SELL)
  —Value analysis
  —Return-on-investment
  —Discounts
  —Markups, margins
  —Tie back to benefits
  —Visuals
- Summarize benefits your buyer was interested in
- Discuss suggested order

C. Multiple-close sequence
- Close
- Objection
- Close
- Objection
- Close
- Etc.

STUDENT APPLICATION LEARNING EXERCISES (SALES)

Part 8

Now it's time to ask for the order! Frequently, questions and objections arise when you ask someone to buy. Thus, you should anticipate questions and objections and be prepared to use several different closing and objection-handling techniques.

1. List the main benefits discussed in your presentation.
2. Select a closing technique, such as the summary-of-benefits close on page 315. Write out your close and label it with the name of the closing technique in parentheses. Use a trial close after completing the close to verify these are important benefits to the buyer. Write out your trial close and label it using parentheses as shown on page 306 (trial close).
3. Create a visual aid showing your suggested order. See page 324 for an example. This visual aid may be similar to or the same one you developed for discussing your price(s).
4. Now you are ready to construct your multiple-close sequence. First carefully study Exhibit 11–5 on page 307. Now look at the example of a multiple-close sequence on page 320. The multiple-close sequence should be composed of the following:
   a. Your summary-of-benefits close.
   b. Your trial close.
   c. Your suggested order.

    d. Use of the assumptive or alternative close.

    e. Having the buyer ask a question or give an objection.

    f. A response using another objection-handling technique.

    g. A trial close to see whether you successfully handled the objection.

    h. Asking for the order again using an unused closing technique. Don't be pushy. Use a calm, laid-back, friendly conversational style.

    i. Repeating the close–objection–close–objection sequence if appropriate.

5. To complete SALE 8, write up the above *a–i* in a script format. Role-play this dialogue until it sounds natural to you. This may require replacing the used techniques with new ones. Once the manuscript is finalized, input it, and turn it in to your instructor.

CASE 11–1
The Grooming Store

The Grooming Store, a large chain of personal-care retail stores, has mailed you an inquiry on personal-care items. They want to know about your electric shavers, moustache trimmers, and hair grooming kits. On arrival, you make a presentation to the purchasing agent, Christina Mercuri. You state that you have visited several of their stores. You discuss your revolving retail display, which contains an assortment of the three items Mercuri had mentioned in her inquiry, and relate the display's advantages and features to benefits for The Grooming Store.

During your presentation Mercuri has listened but has said little and has not given you any buying signals. However, it appears she is interested. She did not object to your price, nor did she raise any other objections.

You approach the end of the presentation and it is time to close. You have said everything you can think of.

Questions

1. What is the best way to ask Mercuri for the order?

    a. "How do you like our products, Ms. Mercuri?"

    b. "What assortment do you prefer, the A or B assortment?"

    c. "Can we go ahead with the order?"

    d. "If you'll just OK this order form, Ms. Mercuri, we'll have each of your stores receive a display within two weeks."

2. Discuss the remaining alternatives from Question 1, ranking them from good to bad, and state what would happen if a salesperson responded in that manner.

CASE 11–2
Central Hardware Supply

Sam Gillespie, owner of Central Hardware Supply, was referred to you by a mutual friend. Gillespie was thinking of dropping two of his product suppliers of home-building supplies. "The sale should be guaranteed," your friend had stated.

Your friend's information was correct, and your presentation to Gillespie convinces you that he will benefit from buying from you. He comments as you conclude the presentation: "Looks like your product will solve our problem. I'd like to think this over, however. Could you call me tomorrow or the next day?"

CASE 11–2

Questions

1. The best way to handle this is to
   a. Follow his suggestion.
   b. Ignore his request and try a second close.
   c. Probe further. You might ask: "The fact that you have to think this over suggests that I haven't convinced you. Is there something I've omitted or failed to satisfy you with?"
2. What would be your second and third choices? Why?

CASE 11–3

Furmanite Service Company— A Multiple-Close Sequence

Chris Henry sells industrial valves and flanges, tapes, and sealants. He is calling on Gary Maslow, a buyer from Shell Oil, to sell him on using Furmanite to seal all of his plant's valve and flange leaks. Chris has completed the discussion of the product's features, advantages, and benefits, the marketing plan, and the business proposition. Chris feels it is time to close. Chris says:

Salesperson: Let me summarize what we have talked about. You have said that you like the money you will save by doing the repairs. You also like our response time in saving the flanges so that they can be rebuilt when needed. Finally, you like our three-year warranty on service. Is that right?

Buyer: Yes, that is about it.

Salesperson: Gary, I suggest we get a crew in here and start repairing the leaks. What time do you want the crew here Monday?

Buyer: Not so fast—how reliable is the compound?

Salesperson: Gary, it's very reliable. I did the same service for Petro-Canada last year, and we have not been back for warranty work. Does that sound reliable to you?

Buyer: Yeah, I guess so.

Salesperson: I know you always make experienced, professional decisions, and I know that you think this is a sound and profitable service for your plant. Let me schedule a crew to be here next week or maybe in two weeks.

Buyer: Chris, I am still hesitant.

Salesperson: There must be a reason that you are hesitating to go ahead now. Do you mind if I ask what it is?

Buyer: I just don't know if it is a sound decision.

Salesperson: Is that the only thing bothering you?

Buyer: Yes, it is.

Salesperson: Just suppose you could convince yourself that it's a good decision. Would you then want to go ahead with the service?

Buyer: Yes, I would.

CASE 11–3

Salesperson: Gary, let me tell you what we have agreed on so far. You like our online repair because of the cost you would save, you like our response time and the savings you would receive from the timely repair of the leaks, and you like our highly trained personnel and our warranty. Right?

Buyer: Yes, that's true.

Salesperson: When would you like to have the work done?

Buyer: Chris, the proposition looks good, but I don't have the funds this month. Maybe we can do it next month.

Salesperson: No problem at all, Gary; I appreciate your time, and I will return on the fifth of next month to set a time for a crew to start.

Questions

1. Label each of the selling techniques used by Chris.
2. What were the strengths and weaknesses of this multiple-close sequence?
3. Should Chris have closed again? Why?
4. Assume Chris felt he could make one more close. What could he do?

12

FOLLOW-UP—MAINTAIN AND STRENGTHEN THE RELATIONSHIP

MAIN TOPICS

Relationship Marketing and Customer Retention

The Product and Its Service Component

Customer Satisfaction and Retention

Excellent Customer Service and Satisfaction Require Technology

Improving Your Effectiveness

Remember Why You Are Following Up

Turn Follow-up and Service into a Sale

Account Penetration Is a Secret to Success

Increasing Your Customer's Sales

Service Can Keep Your Customers

Cross-Sell Your Way to Increased Sales

If You Lose a Customer—Persevere

Handle Complaints Fairly

Build a Professional Reputation

Dos and Don'ts for Business Salespeople

LEARNING OBJECTIVES

Providing service to the customer is critical in today's competitive marketplace. After studying this chapter, you should be able to:

- State why service and follow-up are important to increasing sales.

- Discuss how follow-up and service result in account penetration and improved sales.

- List the eight steps involved in increasing sales to your customer.

- Explain the importance of properly handling customers' returned-goods requests and complaints in a professional manner.

- Explain how cross-selling as part of your follow-up campaign can contribute to higher sales volumes.

- Understand and explain how and why post-call analysis is done.

FACING A SALES CHALLENGE

As a construction machinery salesperson, you know that equipment malfunctions and breakdowns are costly to customers. Your firm, however, has an excellent warranty that allows you to replace a broken piece of equipment with one of your demonstrators for a few days while the equipment is repaired. King Masonry has called you four times in the past three months because the mixer you sold them has broken down. Each time you have cheerfully handled the problem, and in less than two hours they have been back at work. Your company's mixer has traditionally been one of the most dependable on the market, so after the last breakdown, you let King Masonry keep the new replacement in hopes of solving any future problems.

The owner, Eldon King, has just called to tell you the newest mixer has broken down. He is angry and says he may go to another supplier if you cannot get him a replacement immediately.

How would you handle this situation? (Continued at end of chapter.)

Customer retention, service, and follow-up are essential to the success of a salesperson in today's competitive markets. This chapter, the last in our discussion of the elements of the selling process, discusses the importance of follow-up and service, ways of keeping customers, methods of helping them increase sales, and how to handle customer complaints. It ends by emphasizing the need to act as a professional when servicing accounts.

RELATIONSHIP MARKETING AND CUSTOMER RETENTION

Chapter 1 discussed these three levels of customer relationship marketing:

- *Transaction selling:* a customer is sold and not contacted again.
- *Relationship selling:* after the purchase the seller finds out whether the customer is satisfied and has future needs.
- *Partnering:* the seller works continually to improve the customer's operations, sales, and profits.

Relationship marketing is a creation of customer loyalty and retention. Organizations use combinations of products, prices, distribution, promotions, and service to achieve this goal. Relationship marketing is based on the idea that important customers need continual attention.

An organization using relationship marketing is not seeking simply a sale or a transaction. It has targeted a major customer that it would like to sell to now and in the future. The company would like to demonstrate to the customer that it has the capabilities to serve the account's needs in a superior way, particularly if a *committed relationship* can be formed. Retaining customers is much less expensive and time consuming than finding new ones. Customer relationship marketing provides the key to retaining customers.

THE PRODUCT AND ITS SERVICE COMPONENT

When a customer buys a product, what is being purchased? A **product** (good or service) is a bundle of tangible and intangible attributes, including packaging, colour, and brand, and the services and even the reputation of the seller. People buy more than a set of physical attributes. They buy want-satisfaction, such as what the product does, its quality, and its image.

SELLING GLOBALLY
Customer Service in the Real World

Hartness International is a supplier of case packers and other high-speed packaging equipment. The company has a commitment to be the "best supplier of packaging in the world."

In a large manufacturing company, equipment downtime can be as costly as $150 a minute. If a machine breaks down, how long will it take a technician to get there? Even if you get someone there in 24 hours, the loss in production can be as much as $200,000. To address this problem, Hartness has highly trained customer service personnel who can handle many common problems by telephone. For more difficult problems, Hartness uses videoconferencing. Each Hartness installation comes with a wireless camera and all the equipment needed to transmit images back to Hartness's offices in North Carolina. Technicians there direct in-plant maintenance and repair crews to fix problems. About 80 percent of problems can be fixed this way.

For the serious problems, the other 20 percent, Hartness has a local fleet of four aircraft that will fly technicians to plants without being held hostage to the regularly scheduled airlines.

Even when the customer is paying for the service, this method is a lot less expensive than downtime costs. If you're a sales representative for Hartness International, you can truly commit the highest level of service to your customers!

Note the phrase *and the services*. Buyers usually believe an organization ought to deliver a certain level of service with a product. Here are several expected services:

- Product—the product purchased has no defects
- Price—fair value for the price
- Place—the product is available when and where needed and promised
- Promotion—correct, honest information in advertisements, from salespeople, and on product labels
- Exchange transaction—handled correctly, quickly, and professionally the first time
- After the sale—warranty honoured, repairs or exchanges made cheerfully; written information or company representative available to discuss how to put together, hook up, or use the product.

When buying something, you have certain expectations of what you are receiving for your money. So do organizations. Did the customer receive what was expected? The answer to this question determines the level of service quality perceived by the buyer.

Customer service refers to the activities and programs provided by the seller to make the relationship satisfying for the customer. The activities and programs add value to the customer's relationship with the seller. Warranties, credit, speedy delivery, accurate invoices, financial statements, computer-to-computer ordering, parking, gift wrapping, and not being out of stock are services all designed to satisfy customers.

Expectations Determine Service Quality

The quality of service provided by an organization and its salespeople must be based on its customers' expectations. Customers expect a certain level of service from the seller. Their expectations frequently are based on information provided by the salesperson, past experience, word of mouth, and personal needs.

When buyers perceive service received as what they expected, they are satisfied. Thus, service quality must match the customers' expectations.

EXHIBIT 12–1

Customer retention: when the buyer is satisfied with purchases over time.

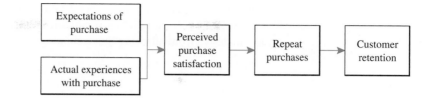

CUSTOMER SATISFACTION AND RETENTION

Customer satisfaction refers to feelings toward the purchase. As illustrated in Exhibit 12–1, perceived purchase satisfaction is the customer's feelings about any differences between what is expected and actual experiences with the purchase. If satisfied, chances of selling the customer in the future increase. If satisfied with repeat purchases, customers tend to continue to buy from the salesperson. Can you afford to lose a customer? Depending on the nature of the business, it can cost up to eight times more to acquire a new customer than it does to retain one. Remember that loyal customers are worth many times the price of a single purchase.

Satisfaction can result in a customer so loyal that it is very difficult for another seller to get his or her business. Thus, customer retention is critical to a salesperson's long-term success.

EXCELLENT CUSTOMER SERVICE AND SATISFACTION REQUIRE TECHNOLOGY

Providing good service to customers in today's competitive marketplace is not enough—service must be excellent. Depending on the size of your customer base, it is often necessary to use technology to manage your relationship with your customers. In Chapter 7, we discussed the usefulness of CRM (customer relationship management) software as it pertains to gathering data for use during the preapproach stage of the selling process.

The importance of this technology is shown by the intense competition among CRM software firms. It has been estimated that the CRM software market will grow by 14.2 percent to $8.9 billion[1] in 2008. This technology is not only useful in preparing for sales presentations, but also often used in the areas of follow-up and relationship management.

With the proliferation of CRM software and the increasing usage of computers, salespeople are able to

1. Develop detailed databases with information about all of their customers and customers' purchases
2. Organize mail-outs, phone calls, and follow-ups
3. Be alerted when it is the best time to call customers after a sale
4. Perform data mining, which involves looking for hidden patterns in a group of data. Data mining can help salespeople find customers with similar interests, needs, and/or purchase patterns.
5. Through email, accept messages or direct messages when absent, then be alerted to the situation when logging on to their system.
6. Sort their customers. Salespeople should know who their best customers are, and sort them by criteria that will allow them to manage their database most effectively.
7. Work independently. By entering all relevant information into their database, salespeople can easily generate reports and electronically share this information with management so that informed decisions can be made relating to customer service.

An Internet search of "customer relationship management" will uncover a vast array of CRM software programs and articles that show the many benefits salespeople can derive from adopting this technology.

IMPROVING YOUR EFFECTIVENESS

In a day rushed with one sales call after another, it is important to discipline yourself to debrief properly after each key customer dialogue. Taking the time to think, plan, and strategize is an effective way to maximize sales. By employing a post-call analysis, you will come across as a true professional at the next face-to-face meeting.

Determine beforehand what it is important for you to accomplish during the sales call and develop your pre-call objectives as discussed in Chapter 7. Then, after each call compare your call results to your call objectives. Develop a post-call analysis form to simplify this process (see below). List only questions that are relevant to your situation. Understand that this analysis will encourage you to look at your prospects and clients in ways you previously may not have considered. Determine what is most important to *you* and what you can use. Then, most importantly, act on the information.

EXHIBIT 12–2

Sales come from present and new customers. Salespeople are constantly involved in follow-up and service and planning their next sales call on the customer; they also spend time prospecting.

10 Follow-up
9 Close
8 Trial close
7 Meet objections
6 Determine objections
5 Trial close
4 Presentation
3 Approach
2 Preapproach
1 Prospecting

Questions for Post-Call Analysis

1. Did you achieve your objective(s) for your meeting?
2. What did you learn about your client's decision-making process?
3. What did you learn about your client's timing of the decision?
4. Who are the key players in the decision-making process?
5. What did you learn about the decision roles within the process?
6. In what ways did you employ your questioning strategy?
7. What are the key solutions that you are considering for this client?
8. Summarize areas of uniqueness and/or competitive advantage.
9. What issues were brought up that could help or hinder you?
10. What is the potential for you and/or your products?
11. What do you need to follow up on?
12. What promises did you make that you need to keep?
13. Summarize your strategy to retain and/or grow this client.
14. Who else within your company should be involved with this client?
15. Who else might need to be involved from the client's organization or business?

Critique your own dialogue with your prospect. Did you

- Explain key FABs?
- Deal adequately with objections?
- Use trial closes in an effective manner?
- Attempt to gain commitment?

How Does Service Increase Your Sales?

Take a look at Exhibit 12–2. By now you are very familiar with it!

You increase sales by obtaining new customers and selling more products to present customers. What is the best method for obtaining new customers? For many types of sales, customer referrals are best. Customers provide referrals when they are satisfied with the salesperson. So how important is it to your success and livelihood to take care of your customers? Even though it is last in the selling process, Step 10 is extremely important to a salesperson's success.

After Step 10 of the selling process, the salesperson moves back to the second step, or preapproach, when it's time to plan the next sales call on a customer. Meanwhile, the salesperson also is prospecting, as discussed in Chapter 6. Thus, the salesperson is involved in the ongoing process of finding new customers and taking care of present customers. With this review in mind, let's discuss service and follow-up techniques.

REMEMBER WHY YOU ARE FOLLOWING UP

Having heard nothing for three months after buying a new car, a customer received a telephone call from the dealer reminding him that it was time for vehicle servicing. Although at first glance this could be viewed as a great service being performed by the dealer for the customer, is it? Is this a follow-up call or is it a prospecting call by the service department for more business? Perhaps it could be considered both.

A **follow-up** services the needs of the customer after the sale in order to ensure customer satisfaction. As a salesperson, the last thing you want is a recent customer experiencing difficulty with a product just purchased. The longer this situation continues, the worse the customer's opinion becomes of the product, you, and your company. Two things can happen. First, the customer will begin talking to anyone who will listen about the terrible experience he is having with your product. This is the beginning of a bad reputation for your business. Second, this customer may feel the need to complain, which leads to an angry call to you. Unfortunately, the timing of this call is likely more convenient for the customer than for you. This may be a very important part of the day for you, perhaps preparing for a major sales presentation to another customer. Having to address calls like this can be time consuming and frustrating.

Fortunately, this whole negative situation can be avoided by salespeople who, with or without the aid of CRM software, develop a regular follow-up campaign. To do this, they must ask three important questions:

1. Who?   Most of the time, the answer to this should be, "everybody who makes a purchase." However, in some instances, salespeople will have to establish some criteria as to which customers warrant a follow-up call and which do not. One must consider factors such as nature of the product, amount of the sale, potential for future sales, etc. Most CRM systems today allow salespeople to sort their customer list by criteria that are useful to their type of business.

2. When?   Although follow-up calls normally are appreciated, some may find them bothersome. "I just bought this product last week, what do you want now?" To prevent problems from developing, salespeople should make their first follow-up call a few days after their customer has taken delivery and had a chance to use the product. Any further delay might provide time to formulate negative attitudes.

Of course, some products may require a call sooner and some later, depending on the nature of the product. A local pizza franchise made it a habit of calling customers about one hour after their pizza had been delivered to ensure customer satisfaction—a call that was often appreciated. A car, or piece of machinery, on the other hand, would require a longer waiting period so that the customer has a chance to experience the product.

3. How?   How salespeople follow up often is determined again by the type of customer and the nature of the product. Some of the options include a telephone call, personal visit, letter or personal note, fax, or e-mail. It is best to personalize the follow-up as much as possible. A telephone call is probably the most time efficient and practical in most situations. Set aside time aside each day or few days to make these calls. This is an excellent use of any downtime that salespeople experience during the day. A personal visit may be appropriate where the sale or product was very large, such as a piece of major machinery, or for a regular customer. Often, it is a nice touch to send a personalized, handwritten note to a customer. Using e-mail or fax machines can be useful, but their impersonal nature makes them less effective methods.

The Call   What do you say? Remember one of the main purposes of making this call—to maintain your relationship with the customer. Show that you care. It's your job to care. Typically, a follow-up call should be short so you're not considered bothersome.

TURN FOLLOW-UP AND SERVICE INTO A SALE

High-performing salespeople can convert follow-up and service situations into sales (see Exhibits 12–3 and 12–4). A large jewellery retailer gives some examples:

> I send customers a thank-you card immediately after the sale, and after two weeks, I call again to thank them and see if they are pleased with their purchase. If the purchase is a gift, I wait before contacting the customer, or I contact the spouse. This has been a key to my success in building a relationship and in farming or prospecting. Very often I get a lead.
>
> Here is how it works. In two weeks they have shown it around to someone who has made a comment. I start with, "Is everything OK?" Then I say, "Well, I know Judy [or Jack] is real proud of it, and I'm sure she's [he's] shown it to someone—parents, family, friends. I was curious whether there is anyone I could help who is interested in

EXHIBIT 12–3

Introduction: Some prospects may need reminding who you are and where you're from.	"Hello Mrs. Marks, this is Gillian Mullet from Star Enterprises. Last week we delivered the photocopier that you ordered three weeks ago."
Identify your purpose for calling.	"The reason I'm calling is to make sure that everything went well with the delivery and that everyone is enjoying the many features of the copier."
Check satisfaction level.	"Do you or any of your employees have any questions about its operation?" "Is it doing the job you wanted it to do?"
Show appreciation. People like to feel appreciated.	"Well, I'd like to thank you once again for your business. I'm sure you and your employees will be very happy with your decision to purchase the LV200."
Inform buyer that you're available for help. Be positive.	"Just so you know, if you have any questions about the copier, you can reach me at (contact information)."
Leave the door open for future opportunities with this buyer or others.	"I'm glad that everything is working out fine. If you or anyone you know needs any of my products, feel free to call any time. I'll check back with you in a few months to see how things are going."

EXHIBIT 12–4

Follow-up calls can be productive.

Here, a sales rep follows up her sale with a fax outlining additional uses for the product before catching a plane to meet another customer.

something. I'd like to talk to them or have you call and see if they'd like me to call them." If I've done a good job, the customer feels good about letting me call this individual and will help me. If I wait too long to call, they say, "Well, someone was asking about it, but I've forgotten who it was."

My biggest sale to a single customer was $120,000. It took about two weeks. A man initially called asking for 12 diamonds to give 2 stones to each of his children. In handling this, I found some other pieces I felt were good for him—a ruby ring, a 4.62-carat sapphire ring, a gold and diamond bracelet, and two other rings. He bought everything. Thus, much of my success comes from follow-ups, suggestion selling [when someone comes in for something and they buy other things], or service situations. Once you realize you can turn routine situations into sales, retail selling becomes exciting and challenging.[2]

Follow-up and service help satisfy the needs of customers. Another way to help customers involves account penetration.

ACCOUNT PENETRATION IS A SECRET TO SUCCESS

Follow-up and service create goodwill between a salesperson and the customer, which increases sales faster than a salesperson who does not provide such service. By contacting the customer after the sale to see that the maximum benefit is derived from the purchase, a salesperson lays the foundation for a positive business relationship. Emmett Reagan of Xerox says

Remember that there is still much work to be done after making the sale. Deliveries must be scheduled, installation planned, and once the system is operational, we must monitor to ensure that our product is doing what is represented. This activity gives us virtually unlimited access to the account, which moves us automatically back to the first phase of the cycle. We now have the opportunity to seek out new needs, develop them, and find new problems that require solutions. Only this time, it's a lot easier because, by now, we have the most competitive edge of all, a satisfied customer.[3]

SELLING TIPS

Can Someone Please Help Me?

Customer: May I speak to Alain, please? I want to reorder.

Supplier: Alain isn't with us anymore. May someone else help you?

Customer: What happened to Alain? He has all my specs; I didn't keep a record.

Supplier: Let me give you Roger; he's taken over Alain's accounts.

Customer: Roger, you don't know me, but maybe Alain filled you in. I want to reorder.

Salesperson: You want to reorder what?

Customer: I want to repeat the last order, but increase your number 067 to 48.

Salesperson: What else was in the order?

Customer: Alain had a record of it. It's got to be in his file.

Salesperson: Alain isn't here anymore, and I don't have his records.

Customer: Who does?

Salesperson: I don't know. I'm new here, so you'll have to fill me in on your requirements. Are you a new customer?

Customer: Does four years make me new?

Salesperson: Well, sir, you are new to me. How long ago did you place your order?

Customer: Last month.

Salesperson: What day last month?

Customer: I don't remember; Alain always kept track of it. Maybe I could speak to the sales manager?

Salesperson: You mean Mort?

Customer: No, I think his name is Enzo.

Salesperson: Enzo left us about the same time as Alain. I can ask Mort to call you, but I'm sure he doesn't have your file either.

Customer: Roger, have you ever heard that your best prospect is your present customer?

Salesperson: Is that true?

Customer: I don't think so.

Multiply this conversation by the millions of times it happens each year, and you have the biggest deterrent to sales in North America.

The ability to work and contact people throughout the account, discussing your products, is referred to as **account penetration**. Successful penetration of an account allows you to properly service that account by uncovering its needs and problems. Achieving successful account penetration is dependent on knowledge of that account's key personnel and their situation. If you do not have a feel for an account's situation, you reduce your chances of maximizing sales in that account.

Tailor the presentation to meet buyers' objectives and provide benefits to them. By knowing your buyers, their firms, and other key personnel, you uncover their needs or problems and develop a presentation that fulfills the needs or solves the problems. Account penetration is determined by

- Your total and major-brand sales growth in an account
- Distribution of the number of products in a product line, including sizes used or merchandised by an account
- Level of cooperation obtained, such as reduced resale prices, shelf space, advertising and display activity, discussion with their salespeople, and freedom to visit with various people in the account
- Your reputation as the authority on your type of merchandise for the buyer.

As a general rule, the greater your account penetration, the greater your chances of maximizing sales within the account. Earning the privilege to move around the account freely, either physically or by phone, allows you to better uncover prospect needs and to discuss your products with people throughout the firm. As people begin to know you and believe that you are there to help, they allow you to take action that ultimately increases sales, such as expanding shelf space or talking with the users of your industrial equipment in the account's manufacturing facilities. A good sign that you have successfully penetrated an account is when a competitor dismally says, "Forget that account; it's already sewn up." You have created true customer loyalty.

| INCREASING YOUR CUSTOMER'S SALES | To maximize your sales to a customer, develop a customer benefit program. This means the account uses in business, or sells to customers, a level of merchandise equal to its maximum sales potential. There are two methods: |

1. Have present customers buy *more* of a product than they currently use.
2. Have present customers buy the same products to use for different purposes. A Johnson & Johnson retail sales representative may encourage accounts to stock the firm's baby shampoo in both the infant care and adult toiletries sections of their establishments.

It is often not difficult to sell repeat orders; however, to maximize sales in an account with a retailer, for example, you must persuade the customer to consistently promote your product through advertisements, displays, and reduced prices. To increase sales with a customer, the following steps can be taken. Each step cannot be used in all situations, but using some can increase sales.

Step 1   Develop an account penetration program. Develop a master plan for each account consisting of specific actions to take toward developing friends within the account and increasing sales.

Step 2   Examine your distribution. Review the merchandise currently used or carried in inventory. If the account is not using or carrying some of your merchandise, concentrate on improving your distribution. For example, if you have four sizes of a product and the account carries only one or two of them, develop a plan to persuade the customer to carry all four sizes. A general goal may be having each account carry all sizes of your products.

Step 3   Keep merchandise in the warehouse and on the shelf. Never allow the account to run out of stock. Stockouts result in lost sales for your firm and account. Routine calls on customers help to avoid stockouts. If the account is critically low on merchandise, telephone in an emergency order. Quick service can maintain, or even increase, your credibility as a sales professional.

Step 4   Fight for shelf space and shelf positioning. If you are selling consumer goods, constantly seek the best shelf space and aisle position. On each sales call, stock the shelf, keep your merchandise clean, and develop merchandising ideas. For example, during a routine visit to a client's store, a consumer-goods salesperson found that one of his products with a list price of $2 was being sold for $1.79. This enterprising salesperson taped a small sign to the shelf showing both prices and later discovered that sales of the product increased. This device is now routine for all of this salesperson's products.

Step 5   Assist the product's users. If you sell business products, help users learn to operate them properly. Make users aware of product accessories that might aid them in performing a function in a safer, better, or more profitable manner. This type of account servicing can increase both account penetration and sales.

Step 6   Assist the reseller's salespeople. To ensure enthusiastic promotion of your firm's products, work closely with your account's sales force. Experience indicates that manufacturers' salespeople who cultivate the friendship of the reseller's salespeople and provide them with product knowledge and selling tips are more successful than salespeople who call only on buyers.

A successful pharmaceutical salesperson suggested to all retail salespeople involved in a certain account that as they hand a customer a prescription for an antibiotic they say, "When taking these antibiotics, you also should double up on taking your vitamins." Well, most customers were not taking vitamins, so when they said, "I don't have any vitamins," the salesperson would hand them a bottle of vitamins, saying, "I take these myself and highly recommend them to you." Of course, this manufacturer's salesperson previously gave the retail salesperson a sample bottle of vitamins. This sales tip accounted for an increase of more than 300 percent in vitamin sales for this reseller.

Step 7   On each sales call, demonstrate your willingness to help the account through your actions. Your actions—not just words—are what build respect or distaste for you. Pull off your coat and dust, mark, stack, and build displays of your merchandise, and return damaged merchandise for credit. Let the buyer know that you are there to help increase retail sales.

Step 8   Obtain customer support. By working hard to help your customers reach their goals through doing the activities just discussed, you will find they help and support you. You help them; they help you. This type of relationship benefits you and the customer.

Again, there is no guarantee that doing everything suggested in this text will always result in a sale. Nevertheless, conscientious use of sound selling principles *will* increase your likelihood of overall success.

Vincent Norris of Scientific Equipment Corporation sent us a copy of his secret to sales success. Although follow-up is at the bottom of his list of secrets shown in Exhibit 12–5, it is extremely important, as you can see.

As mentioned earlier in this chapter, a key characteristic of a sales professional is the ability to accept failure or rejection gracefully and then to quickly move to the next objective.

EXHIBIT 12–5

A super sales success secret.

■ Think positively	. . . and follow up
■ Plan carefully	. . . and follow up
■ Present thoroughly	. . . and follow up
■ And follow up	. . . and follow up
. . . and follow up	. . . and follow up
. . . and follow up	. . . and follow up
. . . and follow up	. . . and follow up

SERVICE CAN KEEP YOUR CUSTOMERS

You work days, weeks, and sometimes months to convert prospects into customers. What can you do to ensure that they buy from you in the future? After landing a major account, consider these six factors:

1. **Concentrate on improving your account penetration**. As discussed earlier, account penetration is critical in uncovering prospect needs or problems and consistently recommending effective solutions through purchasing your products. This allows you to demonstrate that you have a customer's best interests at heart and are there to help.

2. **Contact new accounts frequently on a regular schedule**. In determining the frequency of calls, consider

   ■ Present sales or potential future sales to the account
   ■ Number of orders expected in a year
   ■ Number of product lines sold to the account
   ■ Complexity, servicing, and redesign requirements of the products purchased by the account.

   Since the amount of time spent servicing an account may vary from minutes to days, be flexible in developing a call frequency for each customer. Typically, invest sales time in direct proportion to the actual or potential sales represented by each account. The most productive number of calls is reached at the point where additional calls do not increase sales to the customer. This relationship of sales volume to sales calls is referred to as the *response function* of the customer to the salesperson's calls.

3. **Handle customers' complaints promptly**. This is an excellent opportunity to prove to customers that they and their businesses are important and that you sincerely care about them. The speed with which you handle even the most trivial complaint shows the value you place on that customer.

4. **Always do what you say you will do**. Nothing destroys a relationship with a customer faster than not following through on promises. Promises made and subsequently broken are not tolerated by professional buyers. They have placed their faith (and sometimes reputation) in you by purchasing your products, so you must be faithful to them to ensure future support.

5. **Provide service as you would to royalty**. By providing your client with money-saving products and problem-solving ideas, you can become almost indispensable. You are an adviser to listen to rather than an adversary to haggle with. Provide all possible assistance.

6. **Show your appreciation**. A buyer once said to a salesperson, "I'm responsible for putting the meat and potatoes on your table." Customers contribute to your success, and in return, you must show appreciation. Thank them for their business and do them favours. Here are several suggestions:

   ■ Although you may be hundreds of kilometres away, phone immediately whenever you've thought of something or seen something that may solve one of your customers' problems. See Exhibit 12–6.
   ■ Mail clippings that may interest your customers even if the material has no bearing on what you're selling. They could be items from trade journals, magazines, newspapers, or newsletters.

EXHIBIT 12–6

Three fast and inexpensive tools for customer follow-up and service are the fax machine, the telephone, and e-mail.

- Write congratulatory notes to customers who have been elected to office, promoted to higher positions, given awards, and so on.
- Send newspaper clippings about your customers' families, such as marriages, births, and activities.
- Send holiday or special-occasion cards. If you limit yourself to just one card for the entire year, send a Canada Day card. This makes a big impression on customers.
- Send annual birthday cards. To start this process, subtly discover when your prospects were born.
- Prepare and mail a brief newsletter, perhaps quarterly, that keeps customers informed of important matters.

These are just a few of the many practical ways you can remember customers. The important point is to personalize whatever you send. It doesn't take much thought, energy, or time to send a card, newspaper clipping, or copy of an article. The secret of impressing customers is to personalize the material with a couple of sentences in your own handwriting. Be sure it's legible!

CROSS-SELL YOUR WAY TO INCREASED SALES

Encouraging existing customers to spend more can have a dramatic effect on your sales volumes. However, to successfully cross-sell you have to get your timing right. As we know, it is far more costly to get a new customer than it is to keep an existing one. Therefore, it should become a natural part of every salesperson's follow-up campaign to cross-sell—that is, encourage more business from the customers you already have. This statement is probably true of most businesses, no matter what field they're in. It's a question of knowing what to sell and when to sell it.

Cross-selling should become a natural process—if you are selling photocopiers, selling a maintenance plan would be a natural extension for those requiring frequent maintenance. If you sell machinery, you might try to sell lubricants and an extended warranty. Often all it takes to gain that extra sale is to tell the customer about the product or service.

Some people worry they will irritate customers by cross-selling. Actually, the reverse is usually true—you are demonstrating an interest in them and that you are aware of their requirements, and this is usually appreciated. Cross-selling involves six fundamentals:

1. Know your products.
2. Know your customers and their business.
3. Ask questions and listen for clues.
4. Assess customers' needs and suggest only appropriate products.
5. Treat the sale as a suggestion so that clients will feel comfortable about volunteering the information and it is easy for the customer to accept the offer.
6. Don't make it difficult for the customer to say no. Most customers do not want to be hounded, which will only hurt the relationship.

To get the most from cross-selling, identify the customers who are most appropriate. Using your CRM software, you might identify people who have bought certain products that lend themselves to cross-selling. Your database should flag you on the follow-up to make appropriate cross-selling suggestions.

To make a particular cross-sell more tempting, relate it directly to the customer's needs. For example, if you're selling productivity software to a client, you might also offer them training sessions, or day planners and organizers.

Timing is essential. While you can cross-sell at any time, there are particularly suitable moments.

■ First, many companies have stringent budgeting procedures, so if you push your extra sales at the wrong time you may be up against company policy. To avoid this, try to find out when your client's budgeting takes place. If you time your proposal right, they will have money in hand and maybe even spare budget for extras.

■ The second key moment is when the need is present. For example, when the end of the calendar year is approaching, selling new day planners, organizers, and calendar refills not only will be profitable for you but also will satisfy a legitimate need for your customer.

Another Benefit of Questions

You can increase the chances of making a cross-sale by asking questions. Asking if people want anything else can only gain you business. You won't lose whatever product or service the customer has already purchased, so there is only an upside. Perhaps near the end of a follow-up call you could simply ask, "Is there anything else you might need at this point?" and perhaps even make a suggestion or two. Cross-selling is one of the easiest and least intrusive marketing techniques. If it's well thought out and executed, it can greatly benefit your bottom line.

IF YOU LOSE A CUSTOMER— PERSEVERE

All salespeople suffer losses, either through the loss of a sale or an entire account to a competitor. Four things can win back a customer.

1. **Visit and investigate**. Contact the buyer and your friends within the account to determine why the customer did not buy from you. Find out the real reason.

2. **Be professional**. If you have completely lost the customer to a competitor, let the customer know you have appreciated past business, that you still value the customer's friendship, and that you are still friendly. Remember to assure this lost account that you are ready to earn future business.

MAKING THE SALE

Follow-up: An Often Ignored Step

National Sports Distributors supplied sporting equipment to private schools across Canada through the National Association of Private School Athletics (NAPSA). It operated on five-year-long supply contracts. Kim Sangster, the marketing professional for National, was responsible for handling this contract. Kim thought that this contract had been managed effectively, having had no major complaints over the past several years. Kim made a point of calling on each province's association whenever travelling through the area (approximately once each year). When the contract came up for renewal, NAPSA insisted on two-year contracts from then on and, despite Kim's best efforts, the new contract was lost to a competitor that in fact had higher prices than National. Kim was perplexed and very upset by the decision.

What may have happened? Can you suggest what Kim's next steps should be?

3. **Don't be unfriendly**. Never criticize the competing product that your customer has purchased. If it was a bad decision, let the customer discover it. Sales means never saying, "I told you so!"

4. **Keep calling**. Treat a former customer like a prospect. Continue to make calls normally; present your product's benefits without directly comparing them to the competition.

Like a professional athlete, a professional salesperson takes defeat gracefully, moves on to the next contest, and performs so well that victories overshadow losses. One method of compensating for the loss of an account is to increase sales to existing accounts.

HANDLE COMPLAINTS FAIRLY

Customers may be dissatisfied with products for any number of reasons:

- The product delivered is a different size, colour, or model than the one ordered.
- The quantity delivered is less than the quantity ordered—the balance is back-ordered (to be delivered when available).
- The product does not arrive by the specified date.
- Discounts (trade or promotional payment, see Chapter 5) agreed on are not rendered by the manufacturer.
- The product does not have a feature or perform a function that the customer believed it would.
- The product is not of the specified grade or quality (does not meet agreed-on specifications).

Whenever you determine that the customer's complaint is honest, make a settlement that is fair to the customer. "The customer is always right" is a wise adage to follow. Customers actually may be wrong, but if they honestly believe they are right, no amount of haggling or arguing will convince them otherwise. A valued account can be lost through this way.

Occasionally, a dishonest customer may require you and your company not to honour a request. One of the authors relates the following experience.

ETHICAL DILEMMA
I Appreciate Your Business

People buy from you for many reasons, but primarily because of your excellent products and the service you and your company provide to customers. You follow the Golden Rule: "Do unto others as you would have them do unto you." You feel that customers put the meat and potatoes on your table. They are responsible for the good income you earn. You appreciate that and always try to show how much you thank them for their trust and business.

You occasionally have been taking one of your customers, whom you like personally, out to lunch. Recently, this customer's purchases have increased from $50,000 to $650,000 a year. You want to show your appreciation by buying your customer two season tickets for the local Canadian Football League team. The buyer and his spouse are great football fans.

However, if your other clients and co-workers find out, they may view the gift as unprofessional.

What would be the most ethical action to take?

1. Get a season ticket for yourself and for your client. That way, you can always justify it as a "business meeting" if people ask.

2. Buy your client and his wife the season tickets. You are just trying to show your appreciation for his business.

3. Do not buy the season tickets. It is unprofessional to mix work and social ties. Instead, write your client a nice thank-you letter stating that you appreciate his continued business.

4. Any other suggestions?

Retailer A once purchased some of my firm's merchandise from Retailer B, who had a fire sale and eventually went out of business. Retailer A insisted he purchased it from me and that I return close to $1,000 of damaged goods to my company for full credit. He actually had paid ten cents on the dollar for it at the fire sale. I told Retailer A that I would have to obtain permission from the company to return such a large amount of damaged goods.

That afternoon, a competitive salesperson told me that Retailer A had asked him to do the same thing. I informed my sales manager of the situation. He investigated the matter and found out about Retailer B, who sold most of his merchandise to Retailer A—who happened to be my customer. I went back and confronted Retailer A with this and said it was company policy only to return merchandise that was purchased directly from me. This was a rare situation, yet you must occasionally make similar judgments considering company policy and customer satisfaction.

Customers should get the benefit of the doubt. Always have a plan for problem solving. Some procedures you can use include

- Obtain as much relevant information from your customer as possible.
- Express sincere regret for the problem.
- Display a service attitude (a true desire to help).
- Review your sales records to make sure the customer purchased the merchandise.
- If the customer is right, quickly and cheerfully handle the complaint.
- Follow up to make sure the customer is satisfied.

Take care of your customers—especially large accounts. They are difficult to replace and are critical to success. When you take care of accounts, they take care of you.

BUILD A PROFESSIONAL REPUTATION   This text stresses the concept of sales professionalism. Sales professionalism directly implies that you are a professional person—due the respect and ready for the responsibilities that accompany the title. In speaking before a large class of marketing students, one sales manager for a large university textbook publishing company continually emphasized the concept of sales professionalism. This man stated that a professional sales position is not just an 8-to-5 job. It is a professional and responsible position promising both unlimited opportunity and numerous duties. This veteran emphasized that a sales job is an especially good vocational opportunity because people are looking for "someone we can believe in; someone who will do what she says—a sales professional."

To be viewed as a professional and respected by your customers and competitors, consider these nine important points:

1. Be truthful and follow through on what you tell the customer. Do not dispose of your conscience when you start work each day.
2. Maintain an intimate knowledge of your firm, its products, and your industry. Participate in your company's sales training, and take continuing education courses.
3. Speak well of others, including your company and competitors.
4. Keep customer information confidential; maintain a professional relationship with each account.
5. Never take advantage of a customer by using unfair, high-pressure techniques.
6. Be active in community affairs and help better your community. For example, live in your territory, be active in public schools, and join worthwhile organizations such as the Chamber of Commerce, environmental organizations, and so forth.
7. Think of yourself as a professional and always act like one. Have a professional attitude toward yourself and your customers.
8. Provide service "above and beyond the call of duty." Remember that it is easier to maintain a relationship than to begin one. What was worth attaining is worth preserving. Remember, when you do not pay attention to customers, they find someone who will. The professional salesperson never forgets a customer after the sale.
9. Don't take your best customers for granted. Often, salespeople will unwittingly mistreat their best customers because "they're already customers." They don't offer price breaks and may not even provide their best service. If you continue to do this, you may lose these "best" customers to your competition.

DOS AND DON'TS FOR BUSINESS SALESPEOPLE

What do purchasing agents expect of business salespeople? A survey of purchasing agents showed that they expect results. The following list shows the most important traits that purchasing agents found in their top business salespeople:

- Willingness to go to bat for the buyer within the supplier's firm
- Thoroughness and follow-through after the sale
- Knowledge of the firm's product line
- Market knowledge and willingness to keep the buyer up to date
- Imagination in applying products to the buyer's needs
- Knowledge of the buyer's product line
- Preparation for sales calls
- Regularity of sales calls
- Diplomacy in dealing with operating departments
- Technical education—knowledge of specifications and applications.

EXHIBIT 12–7

The seven deadly sins of business selling.

1. *Lack of product knowledge.* Salespeople must know their product line as well as the buyer's line or nothing productive can occur.

2. *Time wasting.* Unannounced sales visits are a nuisance. When salespeople start droning about golf or grandchildren, more time is wasted.

3. *Poor planning.* A routine sales call must be preceded by some homework—see whether the call is necessary.

4. *Pushiness.* This includes an overwhelming attitude, backdoor selling, and prying to find out a competitor's prices.

5. *Lack of dependability.* Failure to stand behind the product, keep communications clear, and honour promises.

6. *Unprofessional conduct.* Knocking competitors, drinking excessively at a business lunch, sloppy dress, and poor taste aren't professional.

7. *Unlimited optimism.* Honesty is preferred to the hallmark of the good news bearers who promise anything to get an order. Never promise more than you can deliver.

Here are a few comments from purchasing agents:

- "They take it personally if they don't get the business; it's as though you owe them something because they constantly call on you."
- "I don't like it when they blast through the front door like know-it-alls and put on an unsolicited dog-and-pony show that will guarantee cost saving off in limbo somewhere."
- "Many salespeople will give you any delivery you want, book an order, and then let you face the results of their 'short quote.'"
- "They try to sell *you,* rather than the product."
- "After the order is won, the honeymoon is over."
- "Beware the humble pest who is too nice to insult, won't take a hint, won't listen to blunt advice, and is selling a product you neither use nor want to use, yet won't go away."

The survey also asked purchasing agents what they did not like salespeople to do in sales calls. The results, shown in Exhibit 12–7, are "The Seven Deadly Sins of Business Selling."[4] Purchasing agents want salespeople to act professionally, to be well trained, to be prepared for each sales call, and to keep the sales call related to *how the salesperson can help the buyer.*

Professional selling starts in the manufacturer's firm. A professional attitude from the manufacturer reinforces professionalism among the sales force. One such company is B. J. Hughes, a division of the Hughes Tool Company. B. J. Hughes manufactures and sells oil-field equipment and services to companies in the oil and gas industry. Exhibit 12–8 presents Hughes's checklists of *dos* and *don'ts* for its salespeople. By providing these checklists, the company encourages them to act professionally.

SUMMARY OF MAJOR SELLING ISSUES

Salespeople increase sales by obtaining new customers and selling more products to present customers. Customer referrals are the best way to find new prospects. Thus, it's important to provide excellent service and follow-up to customers. By building a relationship and partnership, you can provide a high level of customer service.

Customers expect service. When you deliver service, customers are satisfied and continue to buy; this results in retention and loyalty. Follow-up and service create

EXHIBIT 12–8	**Salesperson's Checklist of Dos**	**Salesperson's Checklist of Don'ts**
B. J. Hughes's checklists of dos and don'ts help it to be a customer-oriented company.	1. Know the current products/services and their applications in your area. Look for the new techniques/services your customers want.	1. Never bluff; if you don't know, find out.
	2. Maintain an up-to-date personal call list.	2. Never compromise your, or anyone else's, morals or principles.
	3. Listen attentively to the customers.	3. Don't be presumptuous—never with friends.
	4. Seek out specific problems and the improvements your customers want.	4. Never criticize a competitor—especially to a customer.
	5. Keep calls under five minutes unless invited to stay.	5. Do not take criticisms or turndowns personally—they're seldom meant that way.
	6. Leave a calling card if the customer is not in.	6. Do not worry or agonize over what you cannot control or influence. Be concerned about what you *can* affect.
	7. Identify the individual who makes or influences decisions, and concentrate on that person.	7. Do not offend others with profanity.
	8. Entertain selectively; your time and your expense account are investments.	8. Do not allow idle conversation to dominate your sales call. Concentrate on your purpose.
	9. Make written notes as reminders.	9. Don't try to match the customer drink-for-drink when entertaining. Drink only if you want to and in moderation.
	10. Plan work by the week, not by the clock. Plan use of available time. Plan sales presentations. Have a purpose.	10. Don't use high-pressure tactics.
	11. Ask for business on every sales call.	11. Never talk your company down—especially to customers. Be proud of it and yourself.
	12. Follow through with appropriate action.	12. If you smoke, never do so in the customer's office unless invited to smoke.[5]

goodwill between salesperson and customer that allows the salesperson to penetrate or work throughout the customer's organization. Account penetration helps the salesperson to better service the account and uncover its needs and problems. A service relationship with an account leads to increases in total and major brand sales, better distribution on all product sizes, and customer cooperation in promoting your products.

To serve customers best, improve account penetration. Contact each customer frequently and regularly; promptly handle all complaints. Always do what you say you will do, and remember to serve customers as if they were royalty. Finally, remember to sincerely thank all customers for their business, no matter how large or small, to show your appreciation.

Should customers begin to buy from a competitor or reduce their level of cooperation, continue to call on them in your normal professional manner. In a friendly way, determine why they did not buy from you, and develop new customer benefit plans to recapture their business.

Always strive to help your customers increase their sales of your product or to get the best use from products that you have sold to them. To persuade a customer to purchase more of your products or use your products in a different manner, develop a sales program to help maximize sales to that customer. This involves

MEETING A SALES CHALLENGE

What a tough situation! You have to keep servicing the equipment if you want to keep King Masonry as a customer. If the customer is misusing the mixer and, causing it to break down, you must train the operators of the mixer and explain to Eldon King what is happening. Before saying anything to King, get his permission to talk with the mixer operators. Find out why the machine is breaking down.

developing an account penetration program; increasing the number and sizes of products purchased by the customer; maintaining proper inventory levels in the customer's warehouse and on the shelf; achieving good shelf space and shelf positioning; communicating clearly with persons who directly sell or use a product; willingly assisting wholesale and retail customers' salespeople in any way possible; willingly helping customers; and developing a positive, friendly business relationship with each customer. By doing these eight things, your ability to help and properly service each customer increases.

Today's professional salesperson is oriented to service. Follow-up and service after the sale maximize your territory's sales and help attain personal goals.

PLAYING THE ROLE

As a newly hired salesperson in a local camera shop, you have just completed your first two major sales of a new top-quality digital camera. The total sale for each amounted to $2,400. Over the next few days, you recalled studying the importance of the follow-up call in your college sales course. You're thinking that you should call the customers about a week after purchase. You've now got to figure out what to say during these calls.

Role A: You, the camera salesperson—Prepare your follow up calls. You don't know what your customer is thinking.

Role B: The customer—You've had the camera for a week and are reasonably happy with it.

Role C: The unhappy customer—You've had the camera for a week and still don't have a clue how it works and are becoming increasingly agitated about the whole purchase to the point that you're considering returning it for a refund.

Dramatize these sales calls in class. Have your classmates analyze the dialogue and make recommendations for improvement.

KEY TERMS FOR SELLING

account penetration, 344
customer satisfaction, 339
customer service, 338

follow-up, 341
product, 337

SALES APPLICATION QUESTIONS

1. What is account penetration? What benefits can a salesperson derive from it?
2. List and briefly explain the factors salespeople must consider to ensure that customers buy from them in the future.
3. What must a salesperson do after losing a customer?
4. A good way for a salesperson to create goodwill is by helping customers increase their sales. What are the steps for the salesperson who attempts to increase customer sales?
5. This chapter discussed several reasons that a salesperson must project a professional image. Why is being a sales professional so important?

6. Return to Exhibit 12–7, "The Seven Deadly Sins of Business Selling." Think of an experience you had with a salesperson who displayed a poor sales image. How did the salesperson's attitude affect your purchase decision?

7. You have just learned that one of your customers, Tom's Discount Store, has received a shipment of faulty goods from your warehouse. The total cost of the merchandise is $2,500. Your company has a returned-goods policy that allows you to return only $500 worth of your product at one time unless a reciprocal order is placed. What would you do?

   a. Call Tom's and tell them you will be out to inspect the shipment in a couple of days.

   b. Ask Tom's to patch up what they can and sell it at a reduced cost in an up-coming clearance sale.

   c. Send the merchandise back to your warehouse and credit Tom's account for the price of the damaged goods.

   d. Go to Tom's as soon as possible that day, check the shipment to see whether there are any undamaged goods that can be put on the shelf, take a replacement order from Tom's manager, and phone in the order immediately.

   e. Call your regional sales manager and ask what to do.

8. Review the section on cross-selling. Imagine yourself as a sales representative in the following scenarios:

   1. You have just sold a water bottling machine to a water bottling company.

   2. You have just sold 25 hot tubs to a chain of fitness centres.

   3. You have just sold 40 high-volume photocopiers to a multi-location insurance company.

   For each situation, try to determine how you could use cross-selling to increase the value of your sale to each customer. Develop a follow-up call with a sample script showing how you would approach each customer. What would you sell? When would you call? Whom would you speak to? Is there anything else you should consider to maximize service and increase your sales to these customers?

FURTHER EXPLORING THE SALES WORLD

1. Contact the person in charge of the health and beauty aids department of a local supermarket. In an interview with this person, ask questions to determine what service activities salespeople perform in the department. For example, do they build product displays, put merchandise on the shelves, straighten products on the shelves, and keep a record of how much product is in the store? Also, determine how the department head believes that salespeople can provide the best service.

2. Contact the person in charge of marketing in a local bank. Report on the role that service plays in attracting and retaining bank customers.

SELLING EXPERIENTIAL EXERCISE

What's Your Attitude toward Customer Service?

Providing excellent customer service often requires a special person—someone who quietly enjoys interacting with people even when they are upset. To help you better understand yourself, respond to each statement by placing the number that best describes your answer on a separate sheet of paper.

1 Never   2 Rarely   3 Sometimes   4 Usually   5 Often

1. I accept people without judging them.
2. I show patience, courtesy, and respect to people regardless of their behaviour toward me.
3. I maintain my composure and refuse to become irritated or frustrated when coping with an angry or irate person.
4. I treat people as I would want them to treat me.
5. I help others maintain their self-esteem, even when the situation requires negative or critical feedback.
6. I do not get defensive when interacting with other persons, even if their comments are directed at me.
7. I realize that my attitude toward myself and others affects the way I respond in any given situation.
8. I realize that each person believes his or her problem is the most important and urgent thing in the world at this time, and I attempt to help each one resolve it immediately.
9. I treat all people in a positive manner, regardless of how they look, dress, or speak.
10. I view every interaction with another person as a golden moment, and I do everything in my power to make it a satisfactory win–win situation for both of us.

Total Score _____

Total your score: If your score is more than 40, you have an excellent service attitude; if it is 30 to 40, you could use improvement; and if you scored less than 30, you need an attitude adjustment.[6]

CASE 12–1
Canada Adhesives Corporation

Marilyn Fowler recently became a sales representative for the Canada Adhesives Corporation and covers Nova Scotia and New Brunswick. After completing a three-week training program, Marilyn was excited about the responsibility of reversing a downward sales trend in her territory, which had been without a salesperson for several months.

The previous salesperson was fired because of poor sales performance and had not left behind any information regarding accounts. After contacting her first 20 or so

CASE 12–1

customers, Marilyn came to a major conclusion: None of these customers had seen a CAC salesperson for six to nine months; they had CAC merchandise that was not selling, and they had damaged merchandise to return. These customers were hostile toward Marilyn because the previous salesperson had used high-pressure tactics to force them to buy, and as one person said, "Your predecessor killed your sales in my business. You said you would provide service and call on me regularly, but I don't care about service. In fact, it's okay with me if I never see anyone from your company again. Your competition's products are much better than yours, and their salespeople have been calling in this area for years trying to get my business." Marilyn was left wondering whether she had gone to work for the right company.

Questions

1. If you were Marilyn, what would you do to improve the sales in your territory?
2. How long would your effort take to improve sales and how would you sell it to your sales manager?

CASE 12–2

Sport Shoe Corporation

You are a salesperson for the Sport Shoe Corporation. At the office, there is a letter marked "Urgent" on your desk. This letter is from the athletic director of Simon Fraser University, and it pertains to the poor quality of football shoes that you sold to him. The director cited several examples of split soles and poor overall quality as his main complaints. In closing, he mentioned that since the season was nearing, he would be forced to contact the ACME Sport Shoe Company if the situation could not be rectified.

Question

What actions would be appropriate for you? Why?

a. Place a call to the athletic director assuring him of your commitment to service. Promise to be at Simon Fraser at his convenience to rectify the problem.

b. Go by the warehouse and take the athletic director a new shipment of shoes and apologize for the delay and poor quality of the merchandise.

c. Write a letter to the athletic director assuring him that SSC sells only high-quality shoes and that this type of problem rarely occurs. Assure him you'll come to his office as soon as possible but if he feels ACME would be a better choice than Sport Shoe, he should contact them.

d. Don't worry about the letter because the athletic director seems to have the attitude that he can put pressure on you by threatening to switch companies. Also, the loss in sales of 20 to 40 pairs of football shoes is a drop in the bucket compared to the valuable sales time you would waste on a small account like Simon Fraser.

PART 4

KEYS TO A SUCCESSFUL SELLING CAREER

Sales personnel are managers of themselves, their time, and their customers. They work in a variety of industries. However, most of the basics of selling remain the same no matter what is being sold. Selling skills frequently need to be adapted to certain situations. Being a professional salesperson involves social, ethical, and legal sales issues. Included in this part are

13

TIME, TERRITORY, AND SELF-MANAGEMENT

MAIN TOPICS

Customers Form Sales Territories

Elements of Time and Territory Management

Using the Telephone for Territory Coverage

LEARNING OBJECTIVES

A salesperson's ability to manage time and territory is important to success. After studying this chapter, you should be able to:

- Discuss the importance of the sales territory.

- Explain the major elements involved in managing the sales territory.

- Discuss the importance of self management and time management to salespeople.

- Discuss the best ways to deal with stress.

- Explain why salespeople need to segment their accounts by size.

FACING A SALES CHALLENGE

How can I manage my time to take better care of my customers? thought Alice Jenson. It seems that each day that I work, I get further and further behind.

Alice had recently taken over the sales territory of Rudy Kavanagh, who retired and moved across the country after 35 years of calling on customers. He kept all records in his head. Alice had to contact the 200 customers in the sales territory with no information other than their past sales. After several weeks, Alice had seen 95 percent of the customers once and 25 percent a second time. Two weeks ago, complaints started coming in that Alice had not followed up on her last calls or that she had not been back to see them.

Alice started telephoning people. That helped some, but customers wanted to see her. She almost stopped prospecting for new customers because she felt it was easier to keep a customer than get a new one. However, as sales started to decline, Alice realized customers were beginning to buy from her competitors.

Alice is in trouble—and it is getting worse. What should Alice do to keep customers, have time to prospect, and increase sales? (Continued at end of chapter.)

Planning your workday and managing your time and customers are key to your success. According to a national survey of thousands of salespeople, managing time and territory is the most important factor in selling. Because of things such as the rapidly increasing cost of direct selling, decreasing time for face-to-face customer contact, continued emphasis on profitable sales, and the fact that time is always limited, it is no wonder that many companies are concentrating on improving how salespeople manage time and territory.[1]

Time is important for salespeople. Yesterday's the past, tomorrow's the future, but today is a *gift*. That's why it's called the *present*.

CUSTOMERS FORM SALES TERRITORIES

A **sales territory** comprises a group of customers or a geographical area assigned to a salesperson. Seven important reasons for establishing sales territories are listed in Exhibit 13–1.

To Obtain Thorough Coverage of the Market

With proper coverage of territories, a company will reach the sales potential of its markets. The salesperson analyzes the territory, identifies customers, and meets customers' needs. Division into territories also allows management to easily realign territories as customers and sales increase or decrease.

To Establish Each Salesperson's Responsibilities

Salespeople act as business managers for their territories, and are responsible for maintaining and generating sales volume. Salespeople's tasks are defined clearly.

EXHIBIT 13–1

Reasons companies develop and use sales territories.

- To obtain thorough coverage of the market.
- To establish each salesperson's responsibilities.
- To evaluate performance.
- To improve customer relations.
- To reduce sales expense.
- To allow better matching of salespeople to customers' needs.
- To benefit both salespeople and the company.

They know where customers are located and how often to call on them. They also know what performance goals are expected. This can raise the salesperson's performance and morale.

To Evaluate Performance

Performance is monitored for each territory. Actual performance data are collected, analyzed, and compared to expected performance goals. Individual territory performance is compared to district performance, district performance compared to regional performance, and regional performance compared to the performance of the entire sales force. With computerized reporting systems, the salesperson and a manager can monitor individual territory and customer sales to determine the success of selling efforts.

To Improve Customer Relations

Customer goodwill and increased sales are expected when customers receive regular calls. From the customer's viewpoint, the salesperson *is,* for example, Procter & Gamble. The customer looks to the salesperson, not to Procter & Gamble's corporate office, when making purchases. Over the years, some salespeople build such goodwill with customers that prospects will delay placing orders because they know the salesperson will be at their business on a certain day or at a specific time of the month. Some salespeople even earn the right to order merchandise for certain customers.

To Reduce Sales Expense

Sales territories are designed to avoid duplicating efforts so that two salespeople do not travel in the same area. This lowers selling costs and increases company profits. Such benefits as fewer travel kilometres and fewer overnight trips, and regular contact with productive customers by the same salesperson, can improve the firm's sales–cost ratio.

To Allow Better Matching of Salespeople to Customers' Needs

Salespeople are hired and trained to meet the requirements of the customers in a territory. Often, the more similar the customer and the salesperson, the more likely the sales effort will succeed.

To Benefit Both Salespeople and the Company

Proper territory design aids in reaching the firm's sales objectives. Thus, the company can maximize its sales effort, while the sales force can work in territories that allow them to satisfy personal needs, such as a good salary.

Why Sales Territories May Not Be Developed

There are disadvantages to developing sales territories for some companies, such as in the real estate or insurance industries. First, salespeople may be more motivated if not restricted by a particular territory; they can develop customers anywhere. In the chemical industry, for example, salespeople may sell to any potential customer. However, after the sale is made, other company salespeople are not allowed to contact that client.

Second, the company may be too small to be concerned with segmenting the market into sales areas. Third, management may not want to take the time, or may not have the know-how, for territory development. Fourth, personal friendships may be

SELLING TIPS

What Makes a Great Sales Environment?

Many argue that the best sales environment is one where you can make enormous amounts of money. This is not always the case. While income is certainly a motivating factor, there are other things that contribute to happiness in the sales environment:

1. A collegial atmosphere with teamwork being part of the relationship.

2. Knowing what is expected of you.

3. Provision of training and materials needed to get the sale made properly.

4. Feeling empowered in your relationship with your customers—rather than simply being an intermediary between them and your company.

5. Recognition for a job well done. This doesn't have to be monetary in nature but people do like to be recognized.

6. Not being made to feel like a number or business unit. People like to be treated like people.

7. Support for personal and professional growth. An environment that supports life-long learning or community involvement is highly motivational.

8. Respect for your knowledge and opinions. Having a meaningful say in company operations is very rewarding.

9. Feeling of security. Knowing that your company's success is related to your personal success allows for a feeling of job security.

10. Social interaction at work. A combination of professional conduct and personal friendship is highly rewarding.

Sales managers can learn from these ideas. It's a tough task building a positive sales environment but incorporating some of these insights will help.

the basis for attracting customers. For example, life insurance salespeople may first sell policies to their families and friends. Nevertheless, most companies establish sales territories such as the one assigned to Alice Jenson in "Facing a Sales Challenge."

ELEMENTS OF TIME AND TERRITORY MANAGEMENT

For the salesperson, time and territory management (TTM) is a continual process of planning, executing, and evaluating. The seven key elements involved in time and territory management are shown in Exhibit 13–2.

Salesperson's Goal Setting

"If you don't know where you want to go, how will you know when you get there?" Without goals, salespeople tend to wander aimlessly through their territory, wasting time and energy. Earlier in the text, we discussed the importance of setting clear objectives for each sales call. It is equally important to look at the bigger picture. Salespeople must establish daily, weekly, monthly, and even yearly goals as well. This **goal setting** helps salespeople manage their jobs better in

EXHIBIT 13–2

Elements of time and territory management for the salesperson.

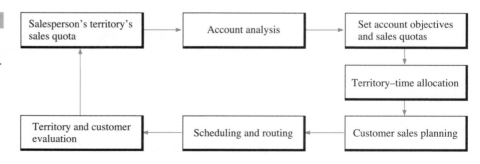

terms of what activities must be performed, whom to see, what to sell, and how to sell it (see Exhibit 13–3).

A salesperson's goals should be

- Specific—You must know exactly when you get there (e.g., "increase sales by 10 percent").
- Measurable—You must be able to quantify your goals (e.g., "develop five new customers per month").
- Reachable—Setting an unrealistic goal simply sets you up for failure and doesn't accomplish anything. (e.g., "open 500 new sales accounts in the next 6 months.")
- Motivating—Setting proper goals, with a time constraint on them, provides a personal challenge and more motivation. (e.g., "Increase sales volume within six months to reach the 'top ten' level, resulting in a summer bonus."

Salespeople should work with their managers to establish a set of goals before the beginning of a particular time period and monitor their performance against their goals. Careful monitoring will determine if salespeople are on track to reach their goal by a specified time period. If obstacles develop, salespeople will have to overcome them or devise strategies to deal with them. in order to stay on track.

Salesperson's Sales Quota

A salesperson is responsible for generating sales in a territory based on its sales potential. The salesperson's manager typically establishes the total sales **quota** that each salesperson is expected to reach.

Once this quota is set, it is the salesperson's responsibility to develop territorial sales plans for reaching the quota. Although there is no best planning sequence to follow, Exhibit 13–2 presents seven factors to consider in properly managing the territory to reach the sales quota.

Account Analysis

Once a sales goal is set, the salesperson must perform an **account analysis** for each prospect and customer to maximize the chances of reaching that goal. First, a salesperson should identify all prospects and present customers. Second, a salesperson should estimate present customers' and prospects' sales potential. This makes it possible to allocate time among customers, to decide what products to emphasize for a specific customer, and to better plan each sales presentation.

Two general approaches to account analysis—identifying accounts and their varying levels of sales potential—are the undifferentiated selling approach and the account segmentation approach.

The Undifferentiated Selling Approach

An organization may see the accounts in its market as similar. When this happens and selling strategies are designed and applied equally to all accounts, the salesperson uses an **undifferentiated selling** approach. Notice in Exhibit 13–4 that the salesperson aims a single selling strategy at all accounts. The basic assumption underlying this approach is that the account needs for a specific product or group of products are similar. Salespeople call on all potential accounts, devoting equal selling time to each. The same sales presentation may be used in selling an entire product line. The salesperson feels she can satisfy most customers with a single selling strategy. For example, many door-to-door salespeople use the same selling strategies with each person they contact (a stimulus–response sales presentation).

EXHIBIT 13-3

In this chart, the salesperson and sales manager set an aggressive 10 percent increase in sales as their goal for 2008. Reaching this goal would result in a hefty bonus for the salesperson. As the year started, the salesperson experienced some obstacles in both February and May. Recognizing that this could prevent the attainment of the yearly goal, the salesperson was able to switch strategies that led to a turnaround in September and October. Ultimately, the goal was reached and the salesperson received her bonus. If the salesperson hadn't carefully monitored her performance, she likely would not have recognized the problem in time and hence may not have been able to change strategies.

	Actual	Sales—2008 Target	Sales—2009 Actual	Variance
JAN	10,000	12,000	13,000	1,000
FEB	12,000	13,200	12,200	(1,000)
MAR	8,000	8,800	7,500	(1,300)
APR	7,000	7,700	7,700	0
MAY	6,000	6,600	6,600	0
JUNE	4,000	4,400	4,400	0
JULY	3,000	3,300	3,300	0
AUG	7,000	7,700	7,700	0
SEP	11,000	12,100	13,100	1,000
OCT	15,000	16,500	17,500	1,000
NOV	17,000	18,700	19,000	300
DEC	18,000	19,800	19,800	0
TOTAL	118,000	130,800	131,800	+1,000

Salespeople whose accounts have homogeneous needs and characteristics may find this approach useful. The undifferentiated selling approach was popular in the past, and some firms still use it. However, many salespeople feel that their accounts have different needs and represent different sales and profit potentials, making an account segmentation approach desirable.

The Account Segmentation Approach

Salespeople using the **account segmentation** approach recognize that their territories contain accounts with differing needs and characteristics requiring different selling strategies. Consequently, they develop sales objectives based on overall sales, and sales of each product for each customer and prospect. Past sales to the account, new accounts, competition, economic conditions, price and promotion offerings, new products, and personal selling are among key elements in the analysis of accounts and territories.

EXHIBIT 13-4

Undifferentiated selling approach.

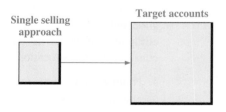

EXHIBIT 13–5

Account segmentation based on yearly sales.

Customer Size	Yearly Sales (Actual or Potential)	Number of Accounts	Percentage
Extra large	over $200,000	100	3.5%
Large	$75,000–200,000	500	16.6
Medium	$25,000–75,000	1,000	33.3
Small	$1,000–25,000	1,400	46.6

Salespeople classify customers to identify profitable ones. This classification determines where the salesperson's time is invested. One method of defining accounts is by using three categories:

1. Key account.
   a. Buys more than $200,000 from us annually.
   b. Loss of this customer would substantially affect the territory's sales and profits.
2. Unprofitable account.
   a. Buys less than $1,000 from us annually.
   b. Little potential to increase purchases to more than $1,000.
3. Regular account.
   a. All other customers.

The unprofitable accounts would not be called on. The **key accounts** and regular accounts become target customers.

Once the accounts are classified broadly, categories or types of accounts are defined in terms such as extra large (key), large, medium, and small, which we refer to as the **ELMS system**. For example, management may divide the 3,000 total accounts in the firm's marketing plan into these four basic sales categories, as shown in Exhibit 13–5.

There are few extra large or large accounts, but they often account for 80 percent of a company's profitable sales even though they represent only 20 percent of total accounts. This is known as the **80/20 principle**. The number of key accounts in an individual territory varies, as does responsibility for them. Even though the key account is in another salesperson's territory, a key account salesperson may call on the extra-large customer. Typically, this is done because of the account's importance or because of an inexperienced local salesperson.

Develop Account Objectives and Sales Quotas

The third element of time and territory management involves developing objectives and sales quotas for individual products and for present and potential accounts. Objectives might include increasing product distribution to prospects in the territory or increasing the product assortment purchased by current customers.

Increasing the number of sales calls each day and the number of new accounts obtained for the year are other examples of objectives developed by the salesperson to help meet sales quotas.

Territory–Time Allocation

The fourth element of time and territory management is how salespeople's time is allocated within territories. Time allocation is the time spent by the salesperson travelling around the territory and calling on accounts. These are seven basic factors to consider in time allocation:

1. Number of accounts in the territory
2. Number of sales calls made on customers

EXHIBIT 13-6

Account time allocation by salesperson.

Customer Size	Calls per Month	Calls per Year	Number of Accounts	=	Number of Calls per Year
Extra large	1	12	2		24
Large	1	12	28		336
Medium	1	12	56		672
Small	1*	4	78		312
--------Total			164		1,344

*every three months

3. Time required for each sales call
4. Frequency of customer sales calls
5. Travel time around the territory
6. Nonselling time
7. Return on time invested.

Analysis of accounts in the territory results in determining the total number of territory accounts and their classification in terms of actual or potential sales. Now the number of yearly sales calls required, the time required for each call, and the intervals between calls can be determined. Usually, the frequency of calls increases as there are increases in (1) sales or potential future sales; (2) number of orders placed in a year; (3) number of product lines sold; and (4) complexity, servicing, and redesign requirements of products.

Since the time spent servicing an account varies from minutes to days, salespeople must be flexible in developing call frequencies. However, they can establish a minimum number of times each year they want to call on the various classes of accounts. For example, the salesperson determines the frequency of calls for each class of account in the territory, as shown in Exhibit 13–6, where all but the small accounts are contacted once a month.

Typically, the salesperson invests sales time in direct proportion to the actual or potential sales that the account represents. The most productive number of calls is reached at the point where additional calls do not increase sales. This relationship of sales volume to sales calls is the **sales response function** of the customer to the salesperson's calls.

The Management of Time

"Time is money" is a popular saying that applies to our discussion because of the costs and revenue generated by the individual salesperson. This is particularly evident with a commission salesperson. See Exhibit 13–7. This salesperson is a territory manager who has the responsibility of managing time wisely to maximize territorial profits. Thus, the effective salesperson consistently uses time well.

Plan by the Month, Week, and Day Many salespeople develop daily, weekly, and monthly call plans or general guidelines of customers and geographical areas to be covered. The salesperson may use them to make appointments with customers in advance, arrange hotel accommodations, and so forth. Weekly plans are more specific, and they include the specific days that customers will be called on. Daily planning may start a few days before, as the salesperson selects the next few day's prospects, determines the time to contact the customer, organizes facts

EXHIBIT 13–7

This salesperson knowing that time is money, works to arrange her next appointment in another province while waiting to board her plane.

and data, and prepares sales presentation materials. Exhibit 13–8 is an illustration of a daily plan, and Exhibit 13–9 shows the location of each account and the sequence of calls.

Qualify the Prospect   Salespeople must be sure that their prospects are qualified to make the purchase decision, and they must determine whether sales to these accounts are large enough to allow for an adequate return on time invested. If not, they do not call on these prospects.

Use Waiting Time   Have you seen salespeople waiting to see buyers? Have you ever noticed their actions? Top salespeople do not read magazines. They work while waiting: studying material about their products, completing call reports, or organizing material for the sales presentation. Also, they quickly determine whether buyers they wait for will be free in a reasonable time. If not, they contact other customers.

EXHIBIT 13–8

Daily customer plan.

| | Sales Calls | | |
Hours	Customers	Prospects	Service Customers
7:00–8:00 A.M.	Stop by office to pick up Jones Hardware order		
8:00–9:00	Travel		
9:00–10:00	Zip Grocery		
10:00–11:00	Ling Television Corp.		
11:00–12:00	Ling Television Corp.		
12:00–1:00 P.M.	Lunch and delivery to Jones Hardware		
1:00–2:00	Ace Computer		
2:00–3:00		Ace Equipment	
3:00–4:00	Travel		
4:00–5:00			Trailor Mfg
4:00–5:00	Plan next day; do paperwork		

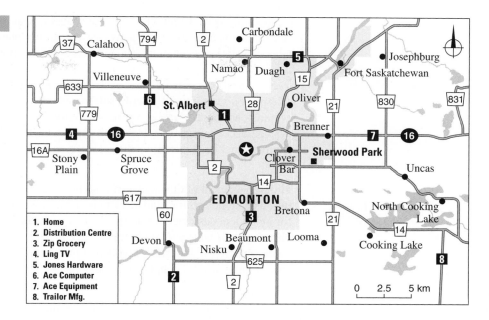

EXHIBIT 13–9

Location of accounts and sequence of calls.

1. Home
2. Distribution Centre
3. Zip Grocery
4. Ling TV
5. Jones Hardware
6. Ace Computer
7. Ace Equipment
8. Trailor Mfg.

Have a Productive Lunchtime Salespeople often take prospects to lunch. However, the results of one study show that the business lunch does not lead directly to a sale but to the buyer and seller knowing each other better, which builds confidence and trust. In turn, this may lead to sales in the long run.

During a business lunch, salespeople must keep an eye on the clock and not monopolize too much of the buyer's time. They should not have a lunchtime cocktail. Although it is customary for some people to have a drink at lunch, the salesperson will be less alert in the afternoon as a result. In fact, in some companies, a luncheon

SELLING TIPS
Managing Your Sales Time Properly

As you will have realized by now, a day in the life of a salesperson can be busy. There are many things that must be done such as prospecting, preparing presentations, presenting, following up, and sales reports to name a few. It is imperative that salespeople manage their time wisely. Consider these tips to help you become a better time manager:

1. Work your numbers. By using sales history, determine how many prospects you'll have to contact to reach your monthly sales target. Follow up with these prospects, then, once you meet your target, you can work on other prospects.

2. Use a set time each day for certain activities. For example, block off one hour each day that you will devote to prospecting. Do nothing else.

3. Keep your goals in sight (by posting a list of them) as a method of keeping focused on what you need to do.

4. Stay focused on your task. Many distractions will keep you from doing your job, such as socializing around the water cooler or taking extended lunch breaks. These distractions will eat away at your selling time.

5. Respect time. Be on time for appointments and meetings, and thank people for their time. They will, in turn respect your time and not waste it.

6. Stay active. Don't become paralyzed with long to-do lists. Stay active and those lists will shrink.

7. Watch your scheduling. Don't schedule things that will cut into your prime productivity time. For example, don't schedule a personal appointment during a time that is often used for prospecting or making sales calls.

cocktail or any use of alcohol (or other drugs) is against company policy. A salesperson's lunch is time to review activities and further plan the afternoon. It is a time to relax and start psyching up for a productive selling afternoon.

Records and Reports   Records and reports are a written history of sales and of the salesperson's activities. Effective salespeople do paperwork during nonselling times; evenings are best. Many companies note these records and reports in performance evaluations of salespeople. However, paperwork should be held to a minimum by the company and kept current by the salesperson.

Customer Sales Planning

The fifth element of time and territorial management is developing a sales-call objective, a customer profile, and a customer benefit program, including selling strategies for individual customers. Refer to Chapter 7 for further discussion of customer sales planning. You have a quota to meet, have made your account analysis, have set account objectives, and have established the time you will devote to each customer; now, develop a sales plan for each customer.

Scheduling and Routing

The sixth element of time and territory management is scheduling sales calls and planning movement around the sales territory.

Scheduling refers to establishing a fixed time (day and hour) for visiting a customer's business. **Routing** is the travel pattern used in working a territory. Some sales organizations prefer to determine the formal path or route that their salespeople travel when covering their territory. In such cases, management must develop plans that are feasible, flexible, and profitable to the company and the individual salesperson, and satisfactory to the customer. In theory, strict formal route designs enable the company to (1) improve territory coverage, (2) minimize wasted time, and (3) establish communication between management and the sales force in terms of the location and activities of individual salespeople.

SELLING TIPS

Dealing with Stress

Salespeople must deal with stress all the time. When stress levels reach dangerous levels, consider the following tips:

1. Determine if there is something you can change about the stressful situation that will make it more manageable.

2. Get away from the stressful situation and revisit it when you feel more able.

3. Prioritize your tasks and knock them off one at a time—the most important ones first.

4. Try meditation and deep breathing exercises—they do work.

5. Set realistic goals. Sometimes, in an effort to motivate themselves, salespeople will set unrealistic goals. This can cause stress.

6. Get enough sleep and eat properly. This will keep your body refreshed and better able to deal with stressful situations.

7. Work off stress with exercise—jogging, gardening, or even a brisk midday walk.

8. Do something for others. This will help you feel appreciated and will take your mind off your stressful situation.

9. Stay positive. As difficult as this may be, keep in mind that you are in control of your own emotions.

10. Learn how to use stress to your advantage. It can be a powerful motivator if used properly. Perhaps your selling energy can act as a "stress buster."

EXHIBIT 13–10

Weekly route report.

Today's Date: November 16		For Week Beginning November 26
Date	**City**	**Location**
November 26 (Monday)	Kingston	Home
November 27 (Tuesday)	Kingston	Home
November 28 (Wednesday)	Cornwall	Holiday Inn/South
November 29 (Thursday)	Peterborough	Home
November 30 (Friday)	Port Hope	Home

In developing route patterns, management needs to know the salesperson's exact day and time of sales calls for each account; approximate waiting time; sales time; miscellaneous time for contacting people such as the promotional manager, checking inventory, or handling returned merchandise; and travel time between accounts. This task is difficult unless territories are small and precisely defined. Most firms allow considerable latitude in routing.

Typically, after finishing a workweek, the salesperson fills out a routing report for the next week and sends it to the manager. The report states where the salesperson will work. See Exhibit 13–10. In the example, on Monday, November 26, she is based in Kingston and plans to call on accounts in Kingston for two days during the week. Then, she plans to work in Cornwall for a day, spend the night, drive to Peterborough early the next morning and make calls, and be home Thursday night. The last day of the week, she plans to work in Port Hope. The weekly route report is sent to her immediate supervisor. In this manner, management knows where she is and, if necessary, can contact her.

Some firms may ask the salesperson to specify the accounts to be called on and at what times. For example, on Monday, November 26, the salesperson may write, "Kingston, 9 A.M., Canada Instruments; Wednesday, Cornwall, 2 P.M., General Motors." Thus, management knows where a salesperson will be and what accounts will be visited during a report period. If no overnight travel is necessary to cover a territory, the company may not require any route reports, because the salesperson can be contacted at home in the evening.

Carefully Plan Your Route

At times, routing is difficult for a salesperson. Customers do not locate themselves geographically for the seller's convenience. Also, there is the increasing difficulty of travelling throughout large cities. Another problem is accounts that will see you only on certain days and at certain hours.

In today's complex selling situation, the absence of a well-thought-out daily and weekly route plan is a recipe for disaster. It's impossible to operate successfully without it. How do you begin?

Start by locating your accounts on a large map. Mount the map on some corkboard or foamboard from an office supply store or picture-framing shop. Use a road map for large territories or a city map for densely populated areas. Also, purchase a supply of map pins with different coloured heads. Place the pins on the map so that you can see where each account is located. For example, use

- Red pins for extra large (**E**) accounts.
- Yellow pins for large (**L**) accounts.

- Blue pins for medium (**M**) accounts.
- Green pins for small (**S**) accounts.
- Black pins for best prospects.

Once all pins are in place, stand back and take a look at the map. Notice first where the E accounts are located. This helps determine your main routes or areas where you must go frequently.

Now, divide the map into sections, keeping the same number of E accounts in each section. Each section should be a natural geographic division; that is, roads should be located in a way that allows you to drive from your home base to each section, as well as to travel easily once you are there. Generally, your L, M, and S accounts will fall into place near your Es, with a few exceptions.

For example, if you work on a monthly or four-week call schedule for Es, then divide your territory into four sections, working one section each week. In this way, you will reach all Es while having the flexibility needed to reach your other accounts regularly.

Section 1	Section 2	Section 3	Section 4
7 **E**	9 **E**	5 **E**	10 **E**
15 **L**	12 **L**	15 **L**	15 **L**
35 **M**	25 **M**	35 **M**	25 **M**
40 **S**	35 **S**	49 **S**	36 **S**

By creating geographical routes this way, you could call on all E accounts every four weeks, half of your L and M accounts (an 8-week call cycle), and 25 percent of your S accounts (a 16-week call cycle) in that period. Allow time for calls on prospective customers, too. Use the same procedure as for regular customers. The only difference is that in most cases, prospects would be contacted less frequently than customers.

SELLING GLOBALLY

Want to Do Business in Russia? Be Prepared!

- Relationships are important so become friends with your prospects. This may involve lots of travel, vodka, and conversation. Small talk is appreciated before talking business. Talk about family and other personal things to break the ice.
- Use local experts to help you navigate the bureaucracy. Laws are different here so be prepared.
- Interpreters (speaking) and translators (written) are critical if you want to avoid miscommunication.
- Be punctual! It is expected of you in Russia—although Russians themselves do not feel uncomfortable about being a little late for an appointment.
- Mail communication may be a little unreliable so faxes and e-mail should be used instead.
- All paperwork should be prepared in order as documents are expected to be signed.

- Authority in companies should be recognized and respected. Know who the bosses and their subordinates are.
- Business cards are good—bilingual cards are better.
- Russians, like many Eastern Europeans, do not often smile openly at the beginning of casual conversation. Don't let this throw you off. Russians prefer to form deep and long-lasting friendships, instead of practising casual friendliness.

If you are invited to your host's home for a meal, be prepared for lots of food. Bring a bottle of good wine or vodka with you. Gifts from home work well too, especially things for the children. If your host spits after you when you leave, don't be offended—this is a form of good luck for a safe journey home.

There is no right number of sections or routes for all salespeople. It depends on the size of your territory, the geographical layout of your area, and the call frequencies you want to establish. Design your travel route so that you can start from home in the morning and return in the evening—or, if you have a larger territory, make it a Monday to Friday route or a two-day (overnight) route. Remember that the critical factor is travel time—not kilometres. In some cases, by using major nonstop highways, your kilometres may increase but your total travel time may decrease.

The actual routes followed each day and within each section are important to maximize your prime selling hours each day. For this reason, make long drives early in the morning and in the late afternoon, if possible. For example, if most accounts are in a straight line from your home, leave early and drive to the far end of your territory before making your first call, then work your way back so that you end up near home at the end of the day, which is called the *straight-line method.* Exhibit 13–11 illustrates three ways to route yourself.

Although pushpins on maps are not an overly sophisticated method of planning sales routes, they can help you visualize an efficient travel pattern. With modern technology, however, salespeople are able to use route planning software to help them manage their sales routes efficiently. There is no more getting lost, travel times can be predicted with more accuracy and salespeople can even shop for and book hotel reservations online. Services such as Map24 (www.ca.map24.com) will help you plan your route and reserve accommodations, all on your laptop. Of course, if you don't want to use your laptop, you can simply plug in one of a variety of route planning technologies that utilize Global Positioning Systems. Some are hand held while others mount in your vehicle and others are contained within some cell phones or PDAs.

EXHIBIT 13–11

Three basic routing patterns.

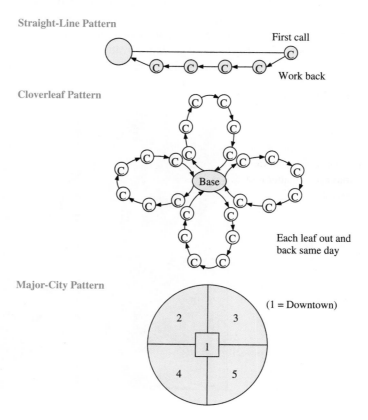

Straight-Line Pattern

First call

Work back

Cloverleaf Pattern

Base

Each leaf out and back same day

Major-City Pattern

(1 = Downtown)

2 3

1

4 5

USING THE TELEPHONE FOR TERRITORY COVERAGE

The telephone can be a great time-waster or time-saver, depending on how it is used. The increasing cost of a personal sales call and the increasing amount of time spent travelling to make personal calls are reasons for the efficient territory manager to look to the telephone as a territory coverage tool.

With field sales costs still rising and no end in sight, more companies are developing telephone sales and marketing campaigns to supplement personal selling efforts. These campaigns utilize trained telephone communicators and well-developed telephone marketing techniques. Usually, they require a companywide effort.

Although each salesperson has to decide the types of calls and accounts that lend themselves to telephone applications, most people benefit from adopting the following practices as minimal territory coverage:

- Satisfy part of the service needs of accounts by telephone.
- Assign smaller accounts that contribute less than 5 percent of business to mostly telephone selling.
- Do prospecting, market data gathering, and call scheduling by telephone.
- Carefully schedule personal calls to distant accounts. If possible, replace some personal visits with telephone calls.

The telephone, PDA, and computer are important selling tools for salespeople. Many sales jobs require extensive travel; however, even in airports, as shown in Exhibit 13–12, travelling salespeople can keep in contact with their offices, access computer files containing customer information, and record customer information.

Territory and Customer Evaluation

Territorial evaluation is the establishment of performance standards for the individual territory in the form of qualitative and quantitative quotas or goals. As with topics discussed earlier in the text, **CRM** software is important in territory and customer evaluation as well. Most CRM packages allow salespeople and sales managers to generate reports that aid in managing each territory. Actual performance is compared to these goals for evaluation purposes. This allows the salesperson to see how well territory plans were executed in meeting performance quotas. If quotas were not met, new plans must be developed.

EXHIBIT 13–12

The telephone is an effective aid that keeps salespeople connected to sales operations no matter where they travel.

EXHIBIT 13–13

Net Sales by Customer and Call Frequency: May 1, 2008.

	Brown (GP)	Peterson (Pediatrics)	Gilley (GP)	Bruce (GP)	Heaton (GP)
Calls					
Month	2	1	1	0	2
Year-to-date	8	4	4	4	9
Last call	4/20	4/18	4/18	3/10	4/19
Net sales in dollars					
Current month	60	0	21	0	500
Year-to-date					
This year	350	200	75	1,000	2,000
Last year	300	275	125	750	1,750
Entire last year	2,000	1,000	300	1,000	5,000

Many companies routinely furnish managers and individual salespeople with reports on how many times during the year salespeople have called on each account and the date of the last sales call. Management can monitor the frequency and time intervals between calls for each salesperson.

As an example, a national pharmaceutical company supplies its sales force with a Net Sales by Customer and Call report, shown in Exhibit 13–13. The report lists each customer's name, address, and medical specialty. The desired number of monthly calls on a given customer and the actual number of calls to date are noted. Net sales are broken down into last year's sales, the current month's sales, and year-to-date sales. Finally, the date the salesperson last called on each customer is reported.

Using the report, you can see that Brown is a physician in a general practice. He should be called on twice a month, and for the past four months, he has been seen

ETHICAL DILEMMA
Technology Helps Win the Day

You have been working for an established mid-sized food processor for the past three months. As a young rookie in the company, you have been assigned to one of the more complex sales territories with extensive travelling. Most of the other sales reps are older, and many have been with the company more than 20 years. The previous salesperson assigned to this territory averaged only about six sales calls per day because of the long travel times. Because of your youth, you have been able to average seven calls per day and hence, have been enjoying a slightly higher income than your predecessor.

On a weekend shopping excursion with friends, you purchased a GPS on a whim and began using it to help you plan your sales routes at work. You found that it cut down on travel time as it helped plan the quickest routes to your destinations regardless of location. It proved so effective that, before long, you could make up to 10 calls per day without any problems. Now you find yourself in a quandary. Should you continue to make your seven calls per day and finish early so you can relax with your friends in the afternoon? Or should you make your 10 calls, which will probably cause your manager to put more pressure on your colleagues to increase their own performance? After all, you had the toughest territory and you were "burning it up."

What would you do?

eight times. He purchased $60 worth of merchandise this month, and his purchases so far are $50 more than last year. He was last called on April 20 of the current year. Using this type of information, which might include 200 to 300 customers for each salesperson, management and salespeople can continually review sales call patterns and customer sales to update call frequency and scheduling.

SUMMARY OF MAJOR SELLING ISSUES

Proper time and territory management is critical for the salesperson to maximize territorial sales and profits.

A sales territory comprises a group of customers or a geographical area assigned to a salesperson. It is a segment of the company's total market. A salesperson within a territory must analyze the various segments, estimate sales potential, and develop a marketing mix based on the needs and desires of the marketplace.

Companies develop and use sales territories for a numerous reasons: to obtain thorough coverage of the market to fully reach sales potential and to establish salespeople's responsibilities.

Territories mean that performance can be monitored and customer relations improved through receive regular calls from the salesperson. This helps to reduce sales expenses by avoiding duplicated effort in travelling and customer contacts. Finally, territories allow better matching of salespeople to customer needs, and benefit salespeople and the company.

However, there are disadvantages to developing sales territories. Some salespeople may not be motivated if they feel restricted by a particular territory. Also, a company may be too small to segment its market, or management may not want to take time to develop territories.

Time and territory management is continual for a salesperson; it involves seven key elements. The first element is establishing the territory sales quota. The second element is account analysis, which involves identifying present and potential customers and estimating their sales potential. In analyzing these accounts, salespeople may use the undifferentiated selling approach if they view accounts as similar or, if accounts have different characteristics, they use the account segmentation approach.

Developing objectives and sales quotas for individual accounts is the third element. How salespeople allocate time in their territories is the fourth element. Salespeople have to manage time, plan schedules, and use spare time effectively.

The fifth element is developing the sales call objective, profile, benefit program, and selling strategies for individual customers. Salespeople have to learn everything

MEETING A SALES CHALLENGE

How Alice Jenson manages her time will determine her productivity. Alice should tell her boss the situation. Then she should analyze her accounts to classify them according to past sales and sales potential. Now she can allocate her time by concentrating on her extra-large and large accounts, contacting each as often as necessary. The medium-sized customers might be seen every one to two months, and the small ones less frequently or contacted by telephone. If needed, Alice's boss could be asked to contact some customers. Alice's situation illustrates why companies require salespeople to do so much record keeping. After each sales call, Alice needs to develop a customer profile, as shown in Chapter 7, to have up-to-date information on all customers.

they can about customers and maintain records on each one. Once this is done, they can create the proper selling strategies to meet customers' needs.

The sixth element is scheduling the sales calls at specific times and places, and routing the salesperson's movement and travel pattern around the territory. The seventh element is using established objectives and quotas to determine how effectively the salesperson performs. Actual performance is compared to these standards for evaluation purposes.

PLAYING THE ROLE

A Tough Situation

You are the sales manager for Acme printing company. You oversee six salespeople, each of whom is responsible for an established territory. Your sales force is considered a good one—highly motivated and professional. However, one of your reps, Howard, has been a cause for concern recently. You've noticed that he has been arriving late for work more frequently and two of his customers have called in recently to discuss the fact that he smelled of alcohol during sales calls. You decide to ask around and you find out that Howard's marriage is in trouble and he's been drinking fairly heavily.

His sales have slipped recently so you decide to call Howard in for an appointment on Friday afternoon. One of your options is to fire him—after all, he's costing you business.

What other options do you have?

Role A: Sales Manager

Role B: Howard

The Task: Having prepared for the appointment, role-play the actual meeting. Once Howard shows up, demonstrate what you would do and how you would handle the situation. Be prepared to defend your actions to the class.

KEY TERMS FOR SELLING

account analysis, 364
account segmentation, 365
CRM, 374
80/20 principle, 366
ELMS system, 366
goal setting, 363
key accounts, 366

quota, 364
routing, 370
sales response function, 367
sales territory, 361
scheduling, 370
time management, 367
undifferentiated selling, 364

SALES APPLICATION QUESTIONS

1. How could you use technology to better manage your customers and your territory? Explain how you could use technologies such as management software, e-mail, and cell phones to manage a sales territory.

2. What is a sales territory? Why do firms establish sales territories? Why might sales territories not be developed?

3. Briefly discuss each of the elements of time and territory management and indicate how these seven elements relate to one another.

4. What is the difference between the undifferentiated selling approach and the account segmentation approach for analyzing accounts? When might each approach be used?

5. Assume a sales manager determines that in a given territory each salesperson sells approximately $500,000 yearly. Also, assume that the firm's cost of

goods sold are estimated to be 65 percent of sales and that a salesperson's direct costs are $35,000 a year. Each salesperson works 48 weeks a year, eight hours a day, and averages five sales calls per day. Using this information, how much merchandise must each salesperson sell to break even?

    a. For the year?

    b. Each day?

    c. Each sales call?

6. What is a key account?

7. What are the factors to consider when a salesperson allocates time?

8. What is the purpose of customer sales planning?

9. Define scheduling. Define routing.

10. Identify five advantages of using the telephone in managing your sales coverage.

SALES WORLD WIDE WEB EXERCISE

Time Is Money, So Make Every Minute Count!

Time wasted trying to find a prospect's address and location can cost a salesperson valuable resources. For this assignment find three potential customers for your organization within a 75 kilometre radius of the city where you currently live. Choose another two potential customers who live in each of two provinces or territories next to the province or territory you live in. Using the following geographic information routing tool, create a travel schedule that would allow you to contact these five potential customers in a two-day period:

www.freetrip.com

Research the standard industrial classifications for each organization and individuals.

Write a memo to your boss showing the addresses of each potential customer, plus the route you'll use on the day you will be at that customer's business.

FURTHER EXPLORING THE SALES WORLD

1. Visit a large retailer in your community and ask a buyer or store manager what salespeople do when they make a sales call. Determine the number of times the retailer wants salespeople to visit each month. Are calls from some salespeople preferable to others? If so, why?

2. Contact a salesperson and sales manager and report on each one's philosophy toward managing time and territory.

SELLING EXPERIENTIAL EXERCISE

Time Management

Make a chart similar to the one below and record the time you spend on various activities for one week. Each day, place codes on your chart to indicate the time spent on each activity. Some codes are suggested here; add any codes you need. At the end of the week, write your total hours in that column. If any activity takes up a great deal of time—such as personal—subdivide it by assigning additional activities such as television, phone, or partying. Now that you have a good idea of how you spend your time, decide whether you want to make some changes.

Name _____ Week beginning _____

(Date)

	Mon	Tue	Wed	Thur	Fri	Sat	Sun
6:30–7:00 A.M.							
7:00–7:30							
7:30–8:00							
8:00–8:30							
8:30–9:00							
9:00–9:30							
9:30–10:00							
10:00–10:30							
10:30–11:00							
11:00–11:30							
11:30–12:00							
12:00–12:30 P.M.							
12:30–1:00							
1:00–1:30							
1:30–2:00							
2:00–2:30							
2:30–3:00							
3:00–3:30							
3:30–4:00							
4:00–4:30							
4:30–5:00							
5:00–5:30							
5:30–6:00							
6:00–6:30							
6:30–7:00							
7:00–7:30							
7:30–8:00							
After 8:00*							

Activity	Code	Total Hours
Class	CL	_____
Sleep	SL	_____
Study	SU	_____
Work	W	_____
Personal	P	_____
_____	_____	_____

*Note: If you need to, make another sheet.

CASE 13–1
Your Selling Day: A Time and Territory Game*

Your sales manager is working with you tomorrow only, and you want to call on customers with the greatest sales potential (see Exhibit A) because you are on a straight commission. The area of your territory that you want to cover contains 16 customers (see Exhibit B). To determine travel time, allow 15 minutes for each side of the square. Each sales call takes 30 minutes. You can leave your house at 8:00 A.M. or later. If you take time for lunch, it must be in 15-minute time blocks (15, 30, 45, or 60 minutes). Your last customer must be contacted by 4:30 P.M. to allow you enough sales time. Your customers do not see salespeople after 5:00 P.M. You travel home after 5:00 P.M.

*Case copyright © 1997 by Charles M. Futrell.

CASE 13–1

EXHIBIT A

Customers' sales potential

Customer	Sales Potential		Customer	Sales Potential
A	$4,000		I	$ 1,000
B	3,000		J	1,000
C	6,000		K	10,000
D	2,000		L	12,000
E	2,000		M	8,000
F	8,000		N	9,000
G	4,000		O	8,000
H	6,000		P	10,000

EXHIBIT B

A partial map of your sales territory

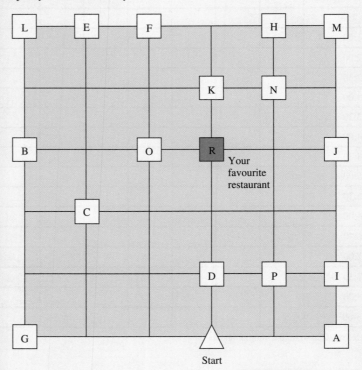

Questions

1. Develop the route that gives the highest sales potential for the day your boss works with you.
2. For the next day, develop the route allowing you to contact the remaining customers in this part of the territory.

<table>
<tr><td>**CASE 13–2**

Naomi Beaupré's District—
Development of an Account
Segmentation Plan</td></tr>
</table>

Naomi Beaupré sat listening to her boss talk about the new time and territory management program being implemented by her company. Her boss was saying, "Since we want to eventually establish priorities for our accounts in order to make time-investment decisions, we must classify the accounts into categories. A simple *A, B, C, D, E* designation of categories is the most commonly used approach, with *A* accounts the most valuable.

"The basis for setting the values or limits for each category is the distribution of sales or concentration patterns in most industries. In general, business in our company is distributed approximately as shown in Exhibit A. Generally, the top 10 percent of the accounts will generate 65 percent of sales, and the top 30 percent will generate 85 percent of the sales in any given territory. Salespeople may use this rule-of-thumb breakdown of accounts in determining the classification system for their accounts." "Once the potential for all their accounts has been calculated, their territory should break down like this:

- *A* accounts = top 10 percent of the accounts
- *B* accounts = next 20 percent of the accounts
- *C* accounts = next 50 percent of the accounts
- *D* accounts = next 10 percent of the accounts
- *E* accounts = last 10 percent of the accounts

"Naomi, I want you to have each of your salespeople take a close look at his or her sales call cycles. As I have explained, a call cycle is a round of calls in which all *A* accounts are called on at least once and some, but not all, *B, C, D,* and *E* accounts are called on. When a salesperson has visited all of his or her *A* accounts, the cycle is completed. Then, a new cycle begins and the series of calls repeats. Since not all *B, C, D,* and *E* accounts are called on in every cycle, the specific accounts to be seen in these classifications differ from cycle to cycle. A call cycle, therefore, is established around the call frequency patterns of *A* accounts."

Suppose that a group of accounts is classified in this way:

Accounts	Expected Value
A	$100,001 and over
B	50,001–100,000
C	30,001–50,000
D	20,001–30,000
E	Under $20,000

Distribution of sales.

Customer Classification	Percentage of Customers	Percentage of Total Sales Volume
A	10	65
B	20	20
C	30	10
D	10	3
E	10	2
	100	100

CASE 13–2

The call frequency patterns, therefore, based on potential and return on time invested, may be as follows:

Accounts	Weeks between Calls	Number of Accounts
A	2	10
B	4	20
C	6	45
D	8	12
E	10	10

Thus, a call cycle in this territory will cover two weeks. This means that in every two-week cycle the salesperson will call on these accounts:

- All of the As.
- Half of the Bs.
- One-third of the Cs.
- One-quarter of the Ds.
- One-fifth of the Es.

Questions

1. Develop a table showing a salesperson's call cycle using the call-frequency patterns.
2. Discuss why this should be done.

14

RETAIL, BUSINESS, SERVICES, AND NONPROFIT SELLING

MAIN TOPICS

LEARNING OBJECTIVES

Retail selling can be challenging and rewarding depending on the particular retailer. Salespeople sell many types of goods and services in business, nonprofit, and consumer markets. After studying this chapter, you should be able to:

- Discuss the importance of personal selling in retailing.

- Describe the retail selling process.

- Discuss the differences between business and consumer products, as well as their markets.

- Describe the characteristics of business markets and products.

- Explain the steps business purchasing agents use in buying decisions.

- Explain what an RFP is and outline how to respond to one.

- Explain the differences between services and nonprofit selling.

**FACING
A SALES
CHALLENGE**

Susan Chung was very surprised to learn at least two people she worked with made more than $4,000 a month selling electronics and computers in a retail store located in a mall. She felt lucky to earn $400 a month. Going to school allowed her to work only 50 hours a month, but the holidays were approaching and her manager said she could work 40 to 50 hours a week after finals.

Being paid the minimum wage and a commission, as well as participating in an occasional sales contest, had not resulted in big bucks for Susan. But if her co-workers were making 10 times her salary, she had room for improvement. In analyzing her procedures, Susan realized that she waited for someone to enter the store and approached quickly asking, "May I help you?" Ten percent of the customers knew what they wanted, so Susan showed it to them, asked questions, and let the prospects make up their own minds. About 15 percent of the people she waited on bought. Most people said no when Susan asked, "May I help you?" Not wanting to seem pushy, she did not disturb shoppers as they looked around the store but waited for them to ask for her help.

Can you suggest to Susan how she might increase her sales and earn more money? (Continued at end of chapter.)

This chapter examines selling careers in four organizational settings—retail, business, services, and nonprofit. Since you are most familiar with retail selling, let's begin there.

**WHAT IS
RETAILING?**

Many of us have worked retail, earning the minimum wage and not being challenged by the job. However, thousands of retail sales jobs are challenging and financially rewarding. Hard work, product knowledge, selling skills, and a good sales commission plan can make it possible to earn $50,000 to more than $1,000,000 a year in retail sales. This chapter introduces you to the selling skills used by retail salespeople making big bucks.

Retailing refers to any individual or organization that sells its goods or services directly to final consumers for their personal, nonbusiness use. The distinguishing characteristic of a retail sale is that a retail transaction involves the final consumer—the retail customer. A retail sale may occur over the telephone, through the mail, on a street corner, on the Internet, in a private residence, or in a traditional retail store.

Goods and services sold to final consumers for their personal, nonbusiness use vary from items such as T-shirts and jogging shoes to stocks and bonds, legal services, cosmetics, cars, real estate, singing telegrams, and wedding cakes. A person selling pantyhose to a department store shopper is engaged in retailing, as is a real estate agent selling a $200,000 house. This section focuses on retail transactions that occur in a retail store.

**CAREER
OPPORTUNITIES**

Retail stores account for more than $400 billion in sales each year.[1] The many salespeople associated with retailing are employed by firms as diverse as huge discount stores, upscale chain department stores, and mom-and-pop operations.

**Financial Rewards
Are Excellent**

As in other forms of professional selling, the financial rewards and promotional opportunities for the retail salesperson are excellent. Earnings as a retail salesperson vary depending on the type of product sold, the compensation plan (straight salary, salary plus commission, or straight commission), and the organization. Salary ranges can be from $7.00 an hour to more than $1,000,000 a year. When you are in a store, ask salespeople whether they are on an hourly salary or commission plan. Those on commissions could be making big bucks if they are (1) order getters, (2) prospectors, and (3) able to obtain referrals.

Nonfinancial Rewards Are Many

Financial compensation is only one part of the reward received as a retail salesperson. Nonfinancial rewards offered by a retail career are numerous. They include excellent training programs, rapid assumption of responsibility, recognition, opportunity for personal growth and development, travel, and satisfaction from work.

RETAILERS SELL LIKE ORGANIZATIONAL SALESPEOPLE

Fundamental sales principles apply to all types of persuasive situations, including retailing. Of course, basic differences exist between retail and organizational sales; the main difference is that many retailers have customers enter their stores to purchase a good or service. However, retailers who sell products such as appliances, real estate, financial services, carpeting, and building supplies frequently send salespeople out to call on customers at home. Whether the retail salesperson is selling in the store, over the telephone, or outside the store, basic selling techniques can be used effectively when adapted to a particular retailing situation.

THE RETAIL SALESPERSON'S ROLE

The role requirements of retail salespeople vary greatly. Some jobs require the salesperson to act only as an order taker. Other jobs require highly skilled people who can successfully identify and arouse customers' needs and persuade them to purchase and satisfy those needs. Generally, a retail salesperson is involved, to some extent, in providing service, working stock or managing inventory, personal selling, and completing transactions. The following sections elaborate on each of these four retail sales functions.

Service

To build clientele—and thus earn top money—retail salespeople need to (1) develop repeat sales from present customers, (2) get new customers through referrals from customers, and (3) sell prospects entering or calling the store. Salespeople do these things by being able to close prospects and provide great service to customers.

Working and Knowing Stock

Maintaining a variety of neatly displayed items for sale to consumers and reordering or replacing stock items when depleted is a tedious, time-consuming, and important function of many retail salespeople. The appearance of a store, or a department within a large store, reflects on the retail salesperson and helps the consumer to develop a good first impression, thereby boosting the retailer's chance of making sales. Working stock also aids a retail salesperson in gaining knowledge of the company's products and their location within the store.

Personal Selling

Of the four functions of the retail salesperson, personal selling is most important. In most cases, the retail salesperson should consider using the same major parts of the sales presentation used by the business salesperson, beginning with the approach. Before continuing, please read "Making the Sale" for an example of creative retail selling.

MAKING THE SALE
Creative Suggestion Selling

A salesperson approached a young customer in a large department store and asked whether she could help her by writing up the sale of a $50 necktie, so she could wait on another customer. She quickly introduced the customer to another salesperson at the counter and walked over to the other customer.

As he began writing up the sale, he looked up and said, "This is a beautiful tie you have selected. What is he going to wear with it?" The woman reached into her purse and pulled out a swatch of fabric. He looked at it a moment and said, "There's an ancient madder pattern that comes in two colour combinations that would go very well with this suit." He pulled out the two ties as he was talking with her. She readily agreed and took both of them—at $50 each.

He asked, "Doesn't he need some new shirts to go with his new suit?" The customer replied, "I'm glad you asked; he does need some, but I haven't been able to find any white ones with French cuffs. Do you have any size 15/33?" He showed her two qualities, pointing out the difference in the cloths. She selected three shirts at $60 each. "Does he ever wear coloured shirts?" he inquired. "Yes; if you have this same shirt in blue, I'll take two."

The sale progressed from there to include gold-filled cuff links, a travel robe to match the ancient madder ties, pajamas, and slippers. The total sale was $1,000, versus the $50 the original salesperson was willing to settle for. Even more importantly, this salesperson made a new customer for the department and himself. That is creative suggestion selling at its very best.

Not once in the course of the sale did he oversell. He related to the customer's desires and wants and knew the content of the stock well enough to fulfill her requirements. Above all, he had the heart of a salesperson who not only thoroughly enjoys the excitement of meeting the expressed request of the customer but also has the imagination to conceive of other things the buyer might find of interest. This type of selling technique can be taught; unfortunately, it doesn't happen very often.[2]

Accurately Completing Transactions

When a customer is ready to make a purchase, the salesperson must complete the transaction before the sale can be completed. A retail transaction should be handled quickly, smoothly, and accurately to avoid frustrating the customer and possibly losing the sale. This is a good checklist to follow when transacting a sale:

- Prepare the sales slip clearly and accurately.
- Accept payment.
- If change is required, count it accurately, and do not place the money received from the customer in the cash drawer until you have made change and the customer has accepted it.
- When accepting a cheque or credit card, make sure all forms are signed by the customer.

Many retailing institutions encourage the use of charge accounts by qualified customers. If that is the case, encourage new customers to participate in your store's charge program by asking them to fill out a credit application. Later that day, you could drop these customers a short thank-you card requesting their regular patronage. This type of retail service builds long-lasting relationships between salespeople and customers.

TECHNOLOGY BUILDS RELATIONSHIPS

Retailers use technology to strengthen customer loyalties and build relationships. Here's an example. A chain of 30 fashion stores in five provinces created its Call Customer Program in which salespeople maintain ongoing relationships with their regular customers. All sales associates maintain personal *call books* that include

SELLING TIPS

The Retail Approach—A Developing Art

Historically, retail selling has been known as transactional selling—once the deal is done, that's it, move on to the next customer. Today, many successful retail salespeople are recognizing the value in practising relationship selling at the retail level. For example, you probably own a cell phone and/or an iPod, and/or a laptop computer. Did you or do you buy all your electronics from the same store or even the same salesperson? With technology changing so quickly, how many home electronics products do you think you'll purchase in your lifetime?

Practising relationship selling can result in a very comfortable living. Retail relationship selling begins with the first time you approach your customer. What makes for an effective approach? The first minute or so is critical for relationship building.

1. The Greeting—Greet customers within 30 seconds of them entering the store or your area. Let them get comfortable in the store and then greet them. Don't be over-bearing like you're trying to make a quick sale. Customers do not like this and may leave quickly. Introduce yourself to personalize the relationship.

2. Your Manner—Be friendly, sincere, and professional. Forget the fake smiles and phony greetings; prospects see right through them. This is your chance to make a good first impression so don't blow it! Appearance is important too. Would you want to do business with you, now and into the future?

3. Rapport—Try to get your prospect to relax. He or she is probably used to being defensive in retail buying situations. You want prospects to feel comfortable dealing with you, so don't rush them.

4. Questioning—Too many retail salespeople are more apt to sell what they want to sell rather than what a prospect wants to buy. Good questioning and listening skills are critical here. Both show empathy and will ensure greater satisfaction.

5. Body Language—This says a lot about you. Fidgeting, slouching, and constantly looking around indicates your impatience and disinterest—hardly things you want to demonstrate if you plan to develop a relationship.

6. Facial Expression—Use eye contact and a friendly smile to show your sincerity and make the prospect comfortable.

Keep in mind that the retail approach is your opportunity to plant the seeds for a long-term relationship with this customer. This is how good incomes are earned in retail selling.

detailed customer information such as size, colour, and style preferences; previous purchases; names of family members; employment; and important dates to remember. (Contact-management software—see Chapter 5—is great for recording customer information.) The associate acts as a purchasing agent for customers, contacting them about special events or when appropriate merchandise arrives, or reminding them of important personal dates (e.g., the birthday of a spouse). Associates often act as personal shoppers, selecting items throughout the store for customers.

Some retailers have salespeople view merchandise at their central warehouse showroom via satellite, make selections for specific customers, and then contact customers.

THE BASIC RETAIL SELLING PROCESS

Why do you shop at a particular retail store? Why do you buy from a particular salesperson? Your reasons will differ depending on the type of product you shop for, such as gasoline, a bank account, a wedding ring, or an automobile.

- **The salesperson**—Is this the right salesperson for me to trust and from whom to buy? Does this salesperson have integrity, judgment, and knowledge concerning my situation?

SELLING GLOBALLY

The Former Soviet Union, Eastern Europe, and the Third World

Despite essential differences between the former Soviet Union, its former satellites in Eastern Europe, and developing countries, all share similar business problems: low productivity, poor-quality products, and, in many cases, a physically run-down manufacturing location with a poor—or nonexistent—infrastructure.

North American retailers wanting to open stores in these countries should expect (1) a bureaucratic tone to the negotiating process, (2) different negotiation methods, and (c) differing expectations on the part of the negotiator. Remember that your partners from these countries may have real security concerns. Their jobs—even their careers—may still depend on the success of the individual negotiation.

Since red tape can be an obstacle, expect to waste a lot of time when dealing with the bureaucracy. Even if there are progressive, liberal laws and regulations, many of these bureaucrats continue to use discretion in approving key parts of foreign investment activities. A significant delay, however, shouldn't necessarily jeopardize the whole transaction.

Settlements are usually written in a highly detailed way; this applies to everything from feasibility studies to multimillion-dollar equipment and construction contracts. Don't expect the negotiation process to move quickly or smoothly. Negotiations are likely to continue right up to (and often through) the drafting of the final contract. Accept the possibility of a slow pace with a lot of attention given to what may seem like insignificant details.[3]

- **Company**—Is this the store for me?
- **Product**—Will this product fulfill my needs?
- **Price**—Should I shop around for price? Will this store lower the price shortly? What about terms and returns?
- **Time to buy**—Should I buy now?
- **Service**—Will the company and salesperson help me if I need further help?
- **Trust**—Can I trust this salesperson, store, and product?

You probably have other reasons to add to the list. However, successful retail salespeople consider these patronage motives when using a selling process similar to these 10 steps:

1. Prospecting
2. The approach
   a. Attitude
   b. Appearance
   c. Manner
3. Presentation
   a. Agreement of need
      (i) Bring sales presentations into focus on product needed
   b. Selling the store
      (i) Your reputation
      (ii) Company reputation
   c. Fill the need
      (i) Stress benefits of features and advantages of products and store using SELL sequence.
4. Use a trial close
5. Respond to objection
6. Use your trial close to determine whether you've handled objection
7. Close the primary sale

8. Suggestion selling
   a. Suggest other items to buy
9. Wrap it up
   a. Remove fears, uncertainties, doubts
   b. Complete the transaction
10. Follow-up and service after the sale.

Carefully orchestrated and executed, these 10 steps can bring you success and satisfied customers.

WHAT'S DIFFERENT ABOUT THE BUSINESS MARKET?

The **business market**, sometimes called the *industrial, producer,* or *organizational market,* consists of all business users. Business users are profit and nonprofit organizations that buy goods and services for one of three purposes:

- **To make other goods and services.** Campbell's buys fresh vegetables to make soup, and Air Canada buys airplanes to transport people.
- **To sell to consumer or other industrial users.** Safeway buys canned tuna to sell to consumers, and Boeing sells its airplanes to organizations such as Air Canada.
- **To conduct the organization's operation.** The British Columbia Institute of Technology buys office supplies and electronic office equipment for the registrar's office, and a dentist buys supplies to use in the office.

In the business market, salespeople can deal with both consumer products and business products. **Business marketing** is the marketing of goods and services to business users, as contrasted to ultimate consumers.

Because the business market is largely unknown, average consumers are apt to underrate its significance. Actually, this market is huge in total sales volume and the number of firms involved in it. About 50 percent of all manufactured products are sold to the business market. In addition, about 80 percent of all farm products and virtually all minerals, forests, and sea products are business goods. These are sold to firms for further processing.

The basic types of goods and services purchased by buyers in the producer market are shown in Exhibit 14–1. In addition to raw materials and components, producers purchase facilities (such as buildings), capital equipment, and a wide array of periodic services such as repairs, legal services, and advertising.

CAREER OPPORTUNITIES

Sales career opportunities in the business, services, and nonprofit areas are excellent. Approximately 1.8 million people are employed in the retail trade in Canada as clerks, sales representatives and sales or store managers.[4] Jobs may increase faster as nonprofit organizations discover the benefits of having a sales force.

SELLING BUSINESS PRODUCT IS DIFFERENT

Selling products to businesses is often different from selling directly to customers. Let's examine the demand, types of purchases, and product characteristics of the business product.

EXHIBIT 14–1

Classification of goods and services in the business market.

- **Entering goods**
  Raw materials:
  - Farm products (wheat, cotton, livestock, fruits, vegetables)
  - Natural products (fish, lumber, crude petroleum, iron ore)
  Manufactured materials and parts:
  - Component materials (steel, cement, wire, textiles)
  - Component parts (small motors, tires, castings)
- **Foundation goods**
  Installations:
  - Buildings and land rights (factories, offices)
  - Fixed equipment (generators, drill presses, computers, elevators)
  Accessory equipment:
  - Portable or light factory equipment and tools (hand tools, lift trucks)
  - Office equipment (calculators, desks)
- **Facilitating goods**
  Supplies:
  - Operating supplies (lubricants, coal, paper, pencils)
  - Maintenance and repair items (paint, nails, brooms)
  Business services:
  - Maintenance and repair services (window cleaning, calculator repair)
  - Business advisory services (legal, management consulting, advertising)

Demand for Business Products

Three important factors distinguish the demand for business products from the demand for consumer goods. When selling in the business market, consider the influences on the demand for your products and services in order to properly plan a sales presentation.

Derived Demand

The demand for many business goods and services is linked to consumer demand for other products—it is a **derived demand**. For example, General Motors purchases tires for its cars. The number of tires purchased is determined by the customer demand for new General Motors cars. We as consumers also buy tires, but as replacements for worn tires on our own cars. This is an example of the same product being defined in a different way. General Motors' demand is based on the eventual consumer demand for its products (derived demand).

Inelastic Demand

The demand for many business products is **inelastic demand**. An increase or decrease in the price of a product usually does not generate a proportionate increase or decrease in sales for the product. The Chevrolet produced by General Motors has many parts. The cost of each part represents a fraction of the total cost. If there is an increase or decrease in the price of a single part, such as the interior cloth, the demand for the car is not significantly influenced. Even if the cost of the cloth doubled (assuming it did not represent a large proportion of production costs), and was passed along to the consumer, the car's sales price would increase by a small amount, having little effect on consumer demand.

Joint Demand

The demand for many business products also is affected by **joint demand**. Joint demand occurs when two or more products are used together to produce a single product. For example, General Motors manufactures automobiles and needs numerous component parts—tires, batteries, steel, glass, and so on. These products are demanded jointly.

The salesperson selling products that are demanded jointly must understand the effect of joint demand on the market. When a customer purchases a product, there is an opportunity to sell companion products. An example is the grocery retailer who purchases computerized cash registers. They require the purchase of associated items such as a small computer, cash registers, product scanners, and other supplies to operate the equipment in the grocery store.

Major Types of Business Purchases

Business purchases are usually one of three general types—new-task purchases, straight-rebuy purchases, or modified-rebuy purchases.

The **new-task purchase** is made when a product is bought in conjunction with a job or task newly performed by the purchaser. A long period is frequently needed for the salesperson to make this type of sale since the buyer is often cautious, especially when confronted with an expensive product or large quantities. This is the most challenging selling situation, since buyers want to consider all alternative suppliers and may need substantial information from each supplier. The salesperson may have to submit a prototype of the product, a price bid, and make several presentations over an extended period before the final purchase decision. New-task purchases include buying capital equipment, construction materials for a new job site, and even an entire plant facility.

The **straight-rebuy purchase** is a routine purchase of products bought regularly. This sale is normally casual order taking. Often, buyers negotiate a blanket purchase order (BPO) agreement, which establishes the price and terms of the sale for a set period. Buyers require little time and information to make a purchase decision.

This type of purchase might include continually used raw materials, office supplies, or MRO (maintenance, repair, and operations items such as spare parts for machinery).

The **modified-rebuy purchase** is somewhat like the straight-rebuy purchase procedure. The buyer seeks a similar product but wants or needs to negotiate different items. The buyer may want a lower price, faster delivery, or better quality. For example, a firm that buys oil field drilling bits from a supplier each month (straight rebuy situation) decides it needs a better-quality drilling bit. The firm goes to the same supplier and others to see whether a better-quality bit is available and at what price (modified rebuy situation). The drilling company still wants drill bits, but looks for a slightly different product to suit its present needs.

Requests for Proposals (RFPs)

If your company becomes involved in a Request for Proposal process (**RFP**), certain issues require careful attention. To maximize your chances of being selected from among other candidates and to avoid getting into a situation that could prove extremely time consuming and costly, consider the following points.

An RFP is a document issued by a company or government agency asking suppliers to send in bids for a contract to supply products or services over a designated period. Included in the RFP may be proposed products or services; proposed budgets; and specific costs, fees, time schedules, and so on.

An RFP can range from being an informal process (a few suppliers are interviewed and a selection is made from among them) to a highly formal process (where

SELLING TIPS

Team Selling

Team selling is the practice of using teams of people from various departments within a company to sell to a large account. Sales teams are formed because large accounts can be quite complex with a variety of purchasing decisions and decision makers.

The selection of the sales team is important. Team members can include different types of salespeople who may have a different skill set to contribute. For example, a lead presenter, skilled presentation designer, and technical expert may form a team to present to an account looking for a technical solution for its problem.

Occasionally, teams can be assembled based on their personalities. Knowing that buying groups can be made up of a variety of personalities, having different salespeople provide input may allow for better communication.

When presenting this textbook to your faculty, the publisher may have used a sales representative, a learning strategist, a technical adviser, and a marketing manager. Between them, they would have all the bases covered in a presentation and would be able to offer their expertise to anyone in the audience requiring detailed information.

---

a larger number of suppliers are requested to make formal presentations to a board). Occasionally, an RFP is a multi-step process, involving several presentations. In this case, a large initial group of suppliers will be narrowed down in stages until a few select suppliers are asked to give final presentations.

More involved selection processes require a greater time commitment from each participant. It is common for total presentation preparation to cost a significant percentage of what a supplier would expect to make during the first year of a contract. For this reason, instructions in RFPs should be followed to make the process as productive and cost-effective as possible.

When you receive an RFP, what is your response supposed to look like? The list below shows steps to take in response to an RFP, although the content will change for each RFP.

1. **Background.** Briefly go over the general requirements. For example, Canadian Petroleum Company would like a local area network installed to connect all of the computers in one office to share disk space and printers and perform automatic backups.

2. **Scope.** Address in detail each item in the RFP and how you intend to manage it. Use diagrams to illustrate your configuration. This will be the longest section of your proposal and will probably have several subsections.

3. **Schedule.** When do you anticipate starting the project? How long will each task take? Make a table of your expected schedule for completing the project.

4. **Staff.** This may be an optional section. Some firms like to see who will be working on the project, along with their credentials and qualifications. This is more important for government projects. Résumés may be necessary here.

5. **Cost.** Break down the cost by equipment and labour time to come up with your expected budget. Include payment terms, discounts for early payment, and other cost or payment information.

6. **Supporting information.** Add any supporting information here (for example, if you're trying to convince a potential client to use a specific type of networking technology, support your reasoning here with third-party quotations, research,

and testimonials). You can also add references to similar projects you have completed for other firms, as well as those results. Include any supporting documentation from clients, clippings from newspapers, and so on.

Product Characteristics

Business products, like business markets, have certain characteristics that a salesperson must consider when selling to buyers of these goods. These product characteristics differ from consumer product characteristics. Business products are (1) technical, (2) in need of specifications and bids, (3) complex in pricing, and (4) standardized.

Technical Products

Compared to consumer goods, business sales are more technical. The business salesperson must have more product knowledge training than a salesperson of consumer goods. Discussing complex production information with knowledgeable customers, which demands considerable expertise, is essential to success. These sales reps are generally referred to as technical sales representatives.

Specifications and Bids

Many business goods are bought based on specifications. These specifications may be determined by the customer, or they may be commonly accepted industry standards. They may be tremendously complex, such as the design of a specialized hydraulic pump, or as simple as requiring a particular colour.

Bids based on stated specifications usually are submitted by several selling firms to the purchasing firm. Each seller bids on a homogeneous, similar product. Depending on the buyer's wishes, bids may range from a similar oral quote given over the phone to a formalized written quotation or a sealed bid held in the buyer's office and opened on a specific closing date along with all other bids. If the purchasing agent does not want to accept any of the bids, suppliers may be asked to submit second bids. Purchasing firms typically use this system to identify the product's true market price.

If all other factors are equal, the company submitting the lowest bid wins the contract. However, other factors frequently affect the buying decision. The product's performance and quality level, for example, may be important considerations in the buying decision. H.J. Heinz of Canada Ltd. may pay a supplier several cents more per bushel for a higher grade of tomatoes so that it can charge a premium price for its products at the retail level.

Complex Pricing

Because of a product's technical nature, its inelastic demand characteristic, the buyer's expertise, and the fact that competitive bidding often is involved in the purchase process, pricing is complex. Final price to the customer can be based on estimates of long-term agreements, present and future labour and material costs, availability of materials, expected salvage value of present equipment, product service agreements, cost-effectiveness of production facilities, and return on investment.

In considering the many factors affecting the price of a business product, a sales manager may give the company's sales force a range of prices to use in negotiations. Avoid trying to use low price alone to make a sale. After all, your selling skills determine success in the long run.

EXHIBIT 14–2

The characteristics of some products make selling them a challenge. How does the product shown on the left differ from the product on the right?

A new office building is unique.

These products are standardized.

Standardization

Many business products tend to be homogeneous. When compared to competing products, they show high similarity. See Exhibit 14–2. When a new product or product feature is introduced to the market, its initial advantage quickly may be lost. It is easy for competitors to improve a product slightly and market it as their own. Most of the time, the salesperson sells products that are similar to a competitor's products.

WHO MAKES THE DECISIONS AROUND HERE?

Business goods have market and product characteristics that differ from consumer goods. Therefore, the buying decision is somewhat different. The eight steps involved in purchasing business products are (1) recognition of the problem or need, (2) determination of the characteristics of the needed product, (3) determination of product specifications, (4) the search for and qualification of potential sources, (5) acquisition and analysis of the proposal, (6) selection of supplier(s), (7) establishment of an order routine, and (8) evaluation of product performance.

Exhibit 14–3 shows the steps in the business buying process, along with the three business buying situations. For the straight rebuy, Steps 2 through 7 can be eliminated. In this situation, a need is recognized, such as a low inventory of a product, and the order is automatically processed. The salesperson supplying a product on a straight rebuy basis contacts the customer periodically to check inventory and to make sure that the order is processed quickly. This procedure strengthens a customer's loyalty to and reliance on a seller, indirectly warding off competition. Salespeople must continually watch for the possibility that present customers may reassess their needs and find some problem with a product, and thus seek another supplier. By routinely contacting the customer, the salesperson becomes aware of changes in the buyer's attitude.

In the new-task and modified-buying situations, several competing suppliers' salespeople may present the prospect with information. The salesperson helps determine the buyer's needs and shows the buyer how the product fulfills the need. The salesperson needs to work closely with everyone who has an influence on the buying decision. When no firm has an initial edge on an industrial order, the salesperson

EXHIBIT 14–3

Business buying process and situations.

	Type of Buying Situations		
Steps in Business Buying Process	New Task	Modified Rebuy	Straight Rebuy
1. Recognition of a problem or need	yes	yes	yes
2. Determination of characteristics of the needed product	yes	yes	no
3. Determination of product specifications	yes	yes	no
4. Search for and qualification of potential sources	yes	yes	no
5. Acquisition and analysis of the proposal	yes	yes	no
6. Selection of supplier(s)	yes	yes	no
7. Establishment of an order routine	yes	yes	no
8. Evaluation of product performance	yes	yes	yes

who spends the *right* amount of time with the *right* people often walks away with the order. This person probably spent some time learning *whom* to talk to. Knowing the right people in an organization is vital to a salesperson's existence. With experience, most good salespeople learn whom they need to contact. But how does the beginning salesperson find these influential people? The next section provides some answers.

WHOM SHOULD I TALK TO?

Many salespeople contact only the buyer or purchasing agent, who often just places the order. The purchasing agent may not actually decide what to buy. It is important to talk to anyone who might influence the purchase decision.

In determining whom to see and how much time to spend with each person, the salesperson should learn who influences the purchase decision and the *strength of each person's influence*. People who may influence the purchase of a product include

- **Initiator**—the person proposing to buy or replace the product.
- **Deciders**—the people involved in making the actual decision—such as the plant engineer, purchasing agent, and someone from top management.
- **Influencers**—plant engineer, plant workers, and research and development personnel who develop specifications needed for the product.
- **Buyer**—the purchasing agent.
- **Gatekeepers**—people who influence where information from salespeople goes and with whom salespeople talk. Receptionists, secretaries, and purchasing agents are gatekeepers.
- **Users**—those people who must work with or use the product; for example, plant workers or secretaries.

It is crucial that the salesperson get by the gatekeepers to talk to the initiators, users, influencers, buyers, and deciders. For example, users of a company's copy machine (initiators) may become dissatisfied with its quality of copies. A secretary (influencer) mentions that Xerox makes an excellent copier that the firm can afford. After a conference with several major users of the current duplicating machine, the office manager (decider) confers with the representatives of several competing copy machine firms and decides to lease the Xerox machine. A purchase order is forwarded to the corporate home office, where a purchasing agent (buyer) approves the machines. Which person should the Xerox salesperson have visited in selling the machine? In this example, each person who participates in the purchase decision should have been contacted—the secretary, major users, and office manager—and the salesperson should have explained the product's benefits to each person.

PURCHASING AGENTS ARE RATIONAL BUYERS

When selling to the producer market, the salesperson deals with well-trained, knowledgeable, and rational buyers. Purchasing agents in large corporations are often specialists, and are experts in dealing with salespeople. See Exhibit 14–4.

Purchasing agents carefully examine information presented to them, and they expect quality sales presentations from salespeople they see. Buying decisions are made based on practical, business reasons, unlike the emotional decisions often made by consumers. As a result, the time required to make a purchase decision is usually longer than in the consumer setting. This is because industrial buyers carefully compare their firm's needs with the features, advantages, and benefits of competing products—a process that takes time.

WHY DO PRODUCERS BUY?

Buyers in the producer market seek to buy for many reasons. Some common reasons usually evolve from an aspect of the product's cost and quality. Specific primary buying needs or motives include

- Increasing profits
- Increasing sales
- Producing a quality product
- Improving the operation's efficiency (resulting in cost reductions)
- Helpfulness of the salesperson

- Service
- Payment terms
- Trade-in allowances
- Delivery service
- Lowest price.

EXHIBIT 14–4

This purchasing agent is an expert on products used in manufacturing. The salesperson must know her product and how it can best be used by the customer.

To be a successful salesperson, determine each buyer's important buying needs. Then develop a sales presentation emphasizing your product's features, advantages, and benefits, and how your products can fulfill the buyer's needs. One of the best and most often used methods of presenting your product's benefits to the buyer is value analysis or showing your prospect how your product provides them with the best value.

SELLING SERVICES IS CHALLENGING

Most people think of selling physical products, such as candy, cars, or copiers. Yet recently we've seen the phenomenal growth of careers in selling services. With its schools, post offices, and social agencies, government is in the service business. With its charities and churches, the nonprofit sector is in the service business. A good part of the business sector, with its airlines, banks, insurance companies, and law firms, is in the service business.

A service is an action or activity done for others for a fee; rock bands and barbers perform services. As you will see, the production of services may or may not be linked to a physical product.

Exhibit 14–5 shows a mix of goods and services on a continuum ranging from relatively pure goods to relatively pure services. There are few pure goods or services, since each usually requires the other. In taking a college course, for example, you may buy a textbook. Similarly, buying salt, soup, and toothpaste requires supporting services, such as totalling up what you owe and bagging the good(s) at the checkout.

Characteristics of Services

The special nature of services creates special selling challenges and opportunities, which are substantially different from those used to sell goods.

Intangibility—Because services are essentially intangible, customers cannot sample—taste, feel, see, hear, or smell—services *before* they buy them. Salespeople must concentrate on the benefits to be derived from the service, rather than emphasizing the service itself. An insurance salesperson thus may stress service *benefits* such as guaranteed payment of a child's post-secondary expenses or a retirement income of so many dollars per month. Telus salespeople discuss how business users can cut selling costs by using the company's long-distance calling system.

Inseparability—Services often cannot be separated from the person of the seller. Moreover, some services must be created and dispensed simultaneously. For example, dentists create and dispense almost all their services at the same time.

From a sales standpoint, inseparability frequently means that direct sale is the only possible channel of distribution, and a seller's services cannot be sold in very many markets. This characteristic also limits the scale of operation in a firm. One person can repair only so many autos in a day or treat only so many patients.

EXHIBIT 14–5

A goods–service continuum.

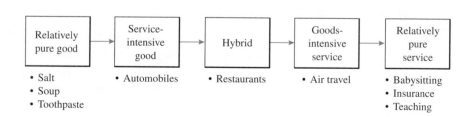

As an exception to the inseparability feature, the service may be sold by a person representing the creator-seller. A travel agent, insurance broker, or rental agent, for instance, may represent and help promote the service that will be sold by the institution producing it.

Heterogeneity—A service industry, or even an individual seller of services, cannot standardize output. Each unit of the service is somewhat different from other units of the same service. For example, an airline does not give the same quality of service on each trip. All repair jobs a mechanic does on automobiles are not of equal quality. An added complication is the difficulty of judging the quality of a service. (Of course, we can say the same for some goods.) It is particularly difficult to forecast quality in advance of buying a service. For example, a person pays to see a ball game without knowing whether it will be an exciting one, well worth the price of admission, or a dull performance.

Perishability and Fluctuating Demand—Services are highly perishable, and they cannot be stored. Haircuts not provided, empty seats in a stadium, and idle mechanics in a garage all represent business lost forever. Furthermore, the market for services fluctuates considerably by season, by day of the week, and by hour of the day. Many ski lifts lie idle all summer, and golf courses go unused in the winter. The use of city buses fluctuates greatly during the day.

There are some notable exceptions to this generalization regarding the perishability and storage of services. In health and life insurance, for example, the service is purchased. Then it is held by the insurance company (the seller) until needed by the buyer or the beneficiary. This holding constitutes a type of storage.

The combination of perishability and fluctuating demand creates product-planning, pricing, and promotion challenges for service company executives. Some organizations have developed new uses for idle plant capacity during off-seasons. Thus, during the summer, several ski resorts operate their ski lifts for hikers and sightseers who want access to higher elevations. Advertising and creative pricing also stimulate demand during slack periods. Hotels offer lower prices and family packages for weekends. Telephone companies offer lower rates during nights and weekends. In some university towns, apartment rates are reduced in the summer.

Selling Services Is the Most Challenging

Selling services is the most challenging sales job you could have because of the characteristics of services. The salesperson, for example, cannot show and physically demonstrate services. Intangibles—including insurance, financial investments, car repairs, and health services—are often difficult for many prospects to understand.

NONPROFIT SELLING—IT'S ABOUT TIME!

A **nonprofit organization** does not have profit as a goal; therefore, it neither intends nor tries to make a profit. Most of the nonprofit organizations sell services rather than tangible products. Here are examples:

- *Cultural*—Museums, zoos, symphony orchestras, opera and theatre groups
- *Religious*—Churches, synagogues, temples, mosques
- *Charitable and philanthropic*—Welfare groups (Salvation Army), research foundations (Canadian Cancer Society, Easter Seals), fundraising groups (United Way)

■ *Social cause*—Organizations dealing with family planning, civil rights, stopping smoking, preventing heart disease, environmental concerns, those for or against abortion, or for or against nuclear energy
■ *Social*—Fraternal organizations, civic groups, clubs
■ *Political*—Political parties, individual politicians.

Business versus Nonprofit Selling

In terms of buyer behaviour, a major difference between business and nonprofit customers involves the groups that the particular organization must deal with. As we know, it is important for salespeople to understand their business buyer and how their customer's business runs. Business executives have traditionally defined their basic markets as comprising their present and potential customers. They have thus directed their selling efforts primarily toward this one group. In contrast, most nonprofits are involved with *two* major markets in their marketing effort. One of these groups consists of the **nonprofit contributors** (of money, labour, services, or materials) to the organization. Here the nonprofit organization's task is that of attracting resources and volunteers.

The other major target market is the organization's **nonprofit clients**—the recipients of the organization's money or services. This recipient market is much like that of the customers of a business company. However, nonprofit organizations—such as churches, Girl Guides groups, or symphony orchestras—are unlikely to refer to their client-recipients as customers. Instead, these organizations use such terms as *parishioners, members,* or *audience*.

This distinction between business and nonprofit selling is significant for this reason: A nonprofit organization must develop two separate sales programs—one looking back at its contributors and the other looking forward at its clients.

Importance of Nonprofit Selling

The attention that is finally being devoted to nonprofit selling is long overdue. Thousands of these organizations handle billions of dollars and affect millions of people. Often the operation of these organizations is inefficient; a large part of the money collected by a nonprofit organization typically goes to cover its administrative expenses rather than to serve the intended customers. This creates a dual social and economic loss—donors' gifts are wasted and clients are not served efficiently.

The importance of selling is clear when nonprofit organizations fail to do an effective sales job. The result may be additional social and economic costs and wastes. If the death rate from smoking rises because the Canadian Cancer Society and other organizations cannot persuade people of the harm of smoking, we all lose. When good museums or good symphony orchestras must cease operating because of lack of contributions or lack of attendance, again there are social and economic losses.

By developing an effective sales program, a nonprofit organization can increase its chances of (1) satisfactorily serving both its contributor and its client markets and (2) improving the overall efficiency of its operations.

Generally speaking, people in most nonprofit organizations do not realize that they are running a business and should employ business management techniques.

How Selling Is Used

Personal selling is frequently used in fundraising efforts. Sometimes a door-to-door campaign is used. During the holiday season, Salvation Army volunteers collect donations in the downtown area or malls of many cities. Potential large donors often are approached by salespeople.

Many nonprofit organizations also use personal selling to reach their public clients. These personal representatives may not be called salespeople, but that is what they are. Personal selling is used to recruit new members for organizations such as

ETHICAL DILEMMA
The Scoop

You work in a large electronics chain store. You and your colleagues work on a commission basis. On a particular busy Saturday morning, you observe one of your colleagues, Anne, spend about an hour with a newlywed couple who are interested in buying his and hers cell phones. Anne spends time going over the different rate plans and the features and benefits of several different styles of phones. The couple seemed hesitant as it was the first time they had bought something with this many choices. After an hour, they told Anne that they would consider all the information and if they decided to buy, they would return on Tuesday with their decision.

The following Monday, business is kind of slow and you recognize the newlyweds as they enter the store. You know this is Anne's day off. You see that they look around for Anne and, not being able to find her, they approach you and ask if you can help. You answer a few questions for them and they decide that they'd like to buy their two phones. You end up spending about 20 minutes with them.

Two thoughts go through your mind:

1. Should I write up the order and keep the commission (scoop her sale)? Anne would probably never find out!

2. If I can start a relationship with this couple, they may buy many things from me over the next few years. Anne would probably never find out!

What would you do here? Justify your reasoning.

the YMCA and Girl Guides. Business executives approach other members of the business community for donations to United Way.

Using salespeople to reach either contributors or clients poses some management problems for a nonprofit organization. In effect, the organization has to manage a sales force—including recruiting, training, compensating, supervising, and evaluating performance. Unfortunately, not many nonprofit organizations think in these terms, nor are they as yet qualified to do this management job.

SELLING IS SELLING　No matter whether you are persuading someone to give you money for a copier, insurance policy, or charity—you are selling. Personal selling refers to the personal communication of information to persuade a prospective customer to buy something—a good, service, idea, or something else—that satisfies the individual's needs. Whenever you are doing this, you are selling.

SUMMARY OF MAJOR SELLING ISSUES　The retailer is extremely important to the Canadian economy, accounting for billions of dollars in sales each year. As a career, retailing offers excellent financial and personal rewards to people who are willing to work hard, have the ability to manage people, and understand the principles of selling.

The retail salesperson's job activities vary from store to store, yet they usually include making transactions, contacting customers, handling complaints, working stock, and personal selling. The fundamentals of selling discussed in earlier chapters and mentioned in this chapter are used by the retail salesperson just as they are used by the business salesperson.

Business products include the raw materials, supplies, equipment, and services used in production, as well as finished goods and services intended for the producer, reseller, and government markets. The producer market contains individuals and organizations that purchase products and services for the production of other goods or services. Characteristics of the producer market include derived demand, inelastic demand, and joint demand. Products are technical in nature and frequently require specifications and bids, complex pricing, and standardization.

The business buying decision may be a complex and lengthy process. It usually involves eight basic steps, depending on whether it is a new-task, a modified-rebuy, or a straight-rebuy situation. It is important for the salesperson to locate individuals who influence the buying decision and to determine the strength of each one's influence in order to allocate the right amount of time and effort needed to solve a customer's problems. Buyers are concerned about costs and product quality, which can result in increased profits and more efficient operations. A value analysis can be used to show the buyer that the salesperson's product is cost-efficient.

A service is an action or activity done for others for a fee. Services can be characterized as intangible, inseparable, heterogeneous, or perishable, and their demand fluctuates compared to physical goods. Nonprofit organizations do sell others on contributing resources, such as money, labour, and materials. They also sell clients on using their services.

MEETING A SALES CHALLENGE

Many retail salespeople earn excellent incomes. It usually depends on what they sell, their store, compensation plan, product knowledge, and selling skills. Assuming Susan Chung knows her products, she needs to develop a selling process to allow her to increase her sales.

Susan needs to prospect, using customers and people who come into the store but do not buy. She can keep a prospect file, take the names of people who are interested in something, and telephone or mail something to them to see whether they are interested in a new product or one that has gone on sale.

Susan should be creative when someone enters the store. She should introduce herself and she should call prospects by name, learn to remember names, and use those names if they return. Ask questions to determine someone's needs, and not be afraid to positively handle objections. Susan needs to use suggestion selling.

If they buy, she should mail a thank-you letter or call to thank them. Maybe she can uncover another prospect and have people ask for her when they need something. Susan must provide service after the sale.

It takes months, even years, to build a clientele. Yet using the 10-step retail selling process will help Susan enjoy her work more and feel she is becoming a sales professional. She should certainly try to use selling skills to work with people buying for the holidays and during the store's January sales.

PLAYING THE ROLE

Read the Ethical Dilemma on page 400.

Assume that you have decided to scoop Anne's sale in this situation. Now it is two weeks later and one evening while you're both working, the newlyweds return with their phones. They see Anne, so approach her with some questions that they have about a couple of the phones' features. A little bewildered, Anne obliges them and spends another half hour explaining how to use the phones.

The next day, Anne discovers that it was you who processed the original order so she approaches you to give her the commission on that sale.

Role A: You (the "scooper")— prepare a defence of your actions.

Role B: Anne—prepare an argument for your request for the commission.

Dramatize this scene to see if you can come to a reasonable resolution. Have your classmates observe and determine if the solution is reasonable or not.

KEY TERMS FOR SELLING

business market, 389
business marketing, 389
buyers, 395
deciders, 395
derived demand, 390
gatekeepers, 395
inelastic demand, 390
influencers, 395
initiator, 395
joint demand, 391

modified-rebuy purchase, 391
new-task purchase, 391
nonprofit clients, 399
nonprofit contributors, 399
nonprofit organization, 398
retailing, 384
RFP, 391
straight-rebuy purchase, 391
users, 395

SALES APPLICATION QUESTIONS

1. Discuss the differences between selling for a retailer and selling for an industrial firm.

2. Suggestion selling is frequently used in retail selling. Explain suggestion selling and give an example of it. Can suggestion selling be used in business-to-business selling as well? Explain.

3. Lynn Madden received four sweaters as holiday gifts. One was too small and she is now on her way to Feldman's Department Store to return it. As usual, the store is full of people with complaints about broken merchandise and wanting to return gifts that they can't use. Lynn spots a clerk in the clothing department and asks where to go for a refund. Annoyed, the busy clerk tells her to go to the window at the back of the store for a refund.

   a. Do you think the clerk did the proper thing?
   b. Analyze the situation and discuss what you believe the clerk could have done differently.
   c. Explain how Lynn Madden, the clerk, and the store may have been hurt in the situation.

4. Ravi Singh has been looking for a new sport coat for weeks. He has finally found one he really likes at Herb's Haberdashery.

   Buyer: I really like this coat.

   Salesperson: It's one of the best we carry. I think you've made an excellent choice.

   Buyer: I've been looking for quite a while, but I'm not sure this is what I really need.

   Salesperson: I don't think you can go wrong with this coat, Mr. Singh. You mentioned that you liked its quality, and it really does show off your good taste.

   Buyer: I am tired of shopping, and it is a good buy . . . OK, I'll take it.

   Salesperson: That's wonderful; I'm sure you'll be extremely happy with your decision. Will that be cash or charge?

   a. What did the salesperson do correctly in this situation?
   b. What opportunities were overlooked?

5. What three types of demand can affect business products? Illustrate each type with an example.

6. Assume you have been offered sales jobs with three different organizations. One sells computers, one sells insurance, and one sells medical equipment to doctors. Describe the differences in the jobs.

7. Assume that the president of your college has put you in charge of selling your college's teaching facilities to a very large organization that is interested in a facility for 22 weekends per year. This would mean a large financial windfall for your college.

   a. Who, from your college, would you want included on your sales team?

   b. Explain what each team member could contribute.

8. Assume you are a representative for Canadian Blood Services. You have been asked by your superior to make a presentation to a local business encouraging people to donate blood. Suggest three FABs you could use in your presentation.

SALES WORLD WIDE WEB EXERCISE

Comparing Places to Live for Your Salespeople

As a newly appointed national sales manager, you often hire salespeople for different locations within Canada. To better help you provide information to new hires and transferees, it pays to have an understanding of the various areas of Canada. Use www.canada-city.ca to research different cities in Canada. Develop a sales plan that accentuates the positive aspects of these cities to potential new hires or when transferring sales representatives.

For specific information on workforce issues, incomes, and so on, go to www.statcan.ca or monster.ca and search for employment outlook for different types of sales jobs in different regions of Canada.

FURTHER EXPLORING THE SALES WORLD

1. Visit three different types of retailers in your community, pose as a customer, and report on the selling techniques used by each salesperson you encounter. Comment on what each person could do to improve the sales presentation.

2. Visit a large retailer in your community that trains its employees in using selling techniques. Report on the company's reasons for sales training, how it trains, and what is included in its sales training program.

3. Select a good, a service, and a product sold by nonprofit organizations and compare their features, advantages, and benefits. How would you demonstrate a main benefit of each?

SELLING EXPERIENTIAL EXERCISE

What Are Your People Skills?

How well do you understand people, observe their behaviour, and address their personal and professional growth? This self-test can help you see your skills. On a separate sheet of paper, write your score for each question.[5]

Strongly Agree			Strongly Disagree
4	3	2	1

1. I think that people often are unaware of their true motivation.

2. Psychological factors often play more of a role in job performance than in the job's required skills.

3. I make a conscious effort to understand the basic needs of others.

4. I am able to empathize with other people, even when I don't share their viewpoints.

5. I consciously try to organize my thinking around others.

6. People often reveal themselves by small details of behaviour.

7. I am usually aware of people's strengths and weaknesses.

8. Most people aren't easy to read.

9. I notice when someone gets a new haircut, eyeglasses, or clothes.

10. After a meeting, I can usually accurately report how others responded to the discussion.

11. People may present themselves in a certain way that doesn't show who they really are.

12. I try not to read my own attitudes into other people's behaviour.

13. I often think about the implications of my past impressions of people on the job.

14. When dealing with others, I try to consider how different they may be from me.

15. I don't judge someone until I have enough information to form a sound judgment.

16. I often think about ways to foster other people's personal and professional growth.

17. I see people for their potential—not how they can be of use to me, but how they can fulfill their life goals.

18. You can't change someone else.

19. When making decisions about people, I deliberately consider a wide range of factors.

20. I consciously try to help people use their strengths and address their weaknesses.

Total Score _____

What are your skills? If your score was

- **75–80**—You're probably strong in solving people problems.
- **61–74**—You have potential strengths in this area.
- **40–60**—You have potential weaknesses in this area.
- **20–39**—You have weaknesses to work on in solving people problems.

Now relate what you've learned to your work experiences by setting goals and intermediate targets. Then adjust!

CASE 14–1

Plimpton's Tire Service

Lauren Yakobosky put on the brakes to stop her car. It was a rainy day and the car seemed to slide a bit too far. When she got home she checked her tires. Sure enough, they were worn almost bare. Have I had these tires this long? Lauren thought to herself. The answer to that question didn't matter. It was obviously time to buy new tires.

Lauren drove her 1966 Mustang to a nearby tire store she had heard advertised many times. She entered the store ready to buy a set of inexpensive, nylon, four-ply tires. She didn't feel she needed more expensive radial tires, because she drove the Mustang only in town, almost exclusively to and from work. While she didn't need a top-of-the-line tire, she did want whitewalls. She thought whitewalls made her car look better. The conversation went like this:

Lauren: Hello, I'm looking for some new tires.

Salesperson: What type of car?

Lauren: A '66 Mustang . . . I think the diameter is 14 inches. Oh, I'm looking for an inexpensive tire.

Salesperson: [*Walking over to a display*] These are our cheapest tires.

Lauren: That's a little more than I wanted to spend. [*She pauses, waiting for a reply; getting none, she continues:*] Well, I guess I'll have to shop around.

Questions

1. Would this salesperson have sold you? Why or why not?
2. What did the salesperson do wrong in this case?
3. If you were the salesperson, what would you have done?

The ad read, "Competition Shoes—We know what it takes to keep you running." Marc Mulletini looked at his running shoes and knew they only had a couple of kilometres left in them.

Marc had only recently taken up running, but he was now addicted and generally ran 25 to 30 kilometres a week. He realized that his running shoes were not high quality, and now that he was a serious runner, he wanted the proper equipment—and that meant better shoes. He decided to see if Competition Shoes had what he needed. That night, he went to the store:

Salesperson: Hello, what can I help you with this evening?

Buyer: I am looking for a new pair of running shoes.

Salesperson: Do you have a particular shoe you would like to try on?

Buyer: To be honest with you, I've been running for only three months, and I don't know very much about running shoes.

Salesperson: How much do you run a week?

Buyer: I'm up to about 30 kilometres.

Salesperson: That's a lot of running for a beginner. Do you plan to compete in the future?

Buyer: Well, I started running for the exercise, like so many people do, but I really enjoy running, and I would like to prove to myself that I can finish a marathon.

Salesperson: So you would like to compete.

Buyer: Come to think of it, I guess I would.

Salesperson: Where do you do most of your running—on a track, grass, or pavement?

Buyer: There is a high-school track a few blocks from my house, but I have to run on the street to get there and back.

Salesperson: Mr. Mulletini, I have two shoes that I believe will work very well for you [*showing Marc two shoes from the display*]. This Nike shoe is very sturdy and generally holds up well for people who put in as many kilometres as you do each week. This Big Paw Olympian [*showing Marc the other shoe*] is just as sturdy and has this wide, vibration-reducing heel. This heel will save your feet and legs a lot of stress. It's especially made for running on hard surfaces.

Buyer: I'll try on the Olympian model. I'll probably need a size 10. [*The salesperson gets the shoes, and Marc tries them on.*]

Salesperson: How do they feel?

CASE 14–2

Buyer: Great [*realizing the difference between these shoes and his old pair*]! I'll take them.

Salesperson: That's wonderful! I know they will suit your needs. Now come over here, I want to show you our new, thick, runners' socks. With your running schedule, I think you will need three pairs of new socks.

Questions

1. What did the salesperson do correctly in this situation? Do you think any errors were made?

2. If you were looking for a new pair of running shoes, would you have bought from this salesperson? Why?

3. How did the salesperson show professionalism in this situation? How did this salesperson differ from the one in Case 14–1?

APPENDIX A

SALES ARITHMETIC AND PRICING

Salespeople want to exchange something for something—usually their products for the customer's money. Organizations and consumers (and even you) want to know, "How much is this going to cost?" Salespeople have to be prepared to discuss all aspects of costs and prices. Consequently, salespeople need some knowledge of the basics of sales arithmetic and pricing.

This appendix discusses sales arithmetic and pricing concepts that are useful in sales to (1) resellers, such as wholesalers and retailers, and (2) end-users, such as businesses and non-profit organizations.

TYPES OF PRICES

Although a firm may engage in many pricing practices, all companies have a list price, net price, and prices based on transportation terms. Five of the most common types of prices are

- **List price**—the standard price charged to customers
- **Net price**—the price after allowance for all discounts
- **Zone price**—the price based on geographical location or zone of customers
- **FOB shipping point**—FOB (free on board) means the buyer pays transportation charges on the goods, and the title to the goods passes to the customer when the goods are loaded on shipping vehicles
- **FOB destination**—the seller pays all shipping costs.

These prices are established by the company, and allow the salesperson to quote prices according to company guidelines.

In Canada, the *Competition Act* prohibits price discrimination and other trade practices that reduce competition. For example, selling the same quantity of similar products at different prices to two different buyers is illegal.

A company can justify different prices if it can prove to the courts that its price differentials do not substantially reduce competition. Often, companies justify price differentials by showing the courts one of two things. First, take the case of one customer buying more of a product than another. For the customer purchasing larger quantities, a firm can manufacture and market the products at a lower cost. These lower costs are passed on to the customer in reduced prices. Second, price differentials can be justified when a company must lower prices to meet competition. Thus, if justified, companies can offer customers different prices. They typically do this through discounts.

DISCOUNTS LOWER THE PRICE

Discounts are a reduction in price from the list price. In developing a program to sell a product line over a specified period, marketing managers consider discounts along with the company's advertising and personal selling efforts. The main types of discounts allowed to buyers are quantity, cash, trade, and consumer discounts.

Quantity Discounts: Buy More, Pay Less

Quantity discounts result from the manufacturer's saving on production costs because it can produce large quantities of the product. As shown in Exhibit A–1, these savings are passed on to customers who buy in large quantities using discounts. Quantity discounts are either non-cumulative or cumulative.

One-time reductions in prices are **non-cumulative quantity discounts**, which are commonly used in the sale of both consumer and industrial goods. A salesperson

EXHIBIT A–1

Various promotional allowances are available to resellers.

GREAT NEW DEAL ON DECONGESTANTS!
Four double-strength sizes to strengthen your profits!

Promotional Allowances					Promotional Support
Free-Goods Allowance*	**Plus Advertising Allowance†**		**Plus Merchandising Allowance**		
	Option A	**Option B‡**	**Reduced Price Feature**	**Display**	
350 mL liquid 8⅓% off invoice	Up to $1.25 per dozen	$1.00 per dozen	$0.75 per dozen reduced-price feature	$0.75 per dozen floor or end cap display	Direct to consumer national TV promotion . . . 1.705 GRPs
150 mL liquid 8⅓% off invoice	Up to $0.75 per dozen	$0.50 per dozen	$0.50 per dozen reduced-price feature	$0.50 per dozen floor or end cap display	88% reach 1.7 billion impressions
60 tablets 8⅓% off invoice	Up to $1.25 per dozen	$1.00 per dozen	$0.75 per dozen reduced-price feature	$0.75 per dozen floor or end cap display	Year-round physician detailing and sampling
24 tablets 8⅓% off invoice	Up to $0.75 per dozen	$0.50 per dozen	$0.50 per dozen reduced-price feature	$0.50 per dozen floor or end cap display	Major trade and medical journal advertising support

Also available—up to 2 percent billback allowance for four-colour roto advertising or consumer coupon programs.
Unlimited purchases allowed for claiming billback allowances.
Retail buy-in period: July 16 through August 31, 2001.
Advertising performance period: July 16 through November 9, 2001.
Claim deadline: 45 days following appearance of ad.
Contact your representative for complete details.

*Through participating wholesaler.
†All ads should feature both liquid and tablets.
‡Provided advertising coverage is in at least 75 percent of the applicant's trading area.

might offer $0.10 per kilogram off potato salad on any truckload-sized order, or one free case of facial tissue with the purchase of 10 cases of facial tissue.

The salesperson is expected to use these discounts as inducements for the retailer to buy in large quantities. The sales goal is to have the prospect display and locally advertise the product at a price lower than normal. Ideally, the retailer's selling price should reflect the price reduction allowed because of the quantity discount.

Cumulative quantity discounts are discounts received for buying a certain amount of a product over a stated period, such as one year. Again, these discounts reflect savings in manufacturing and marketing costs.

To receive a 10 percent discount, a buyer may have to purchase 12,000 units of the product. Under the cumulative discount, the buyer would not be required to purchase the 12,000 units at the same time—say 1,000 units each month, for example. As long as the agreed-on amount is purchased within the specified time, the 10 percent discount on each purchase applies. A cumulative discount allows the buyer to purchase the products as needed rather than in a single order.

Cash Discounts: Entice the Customer to Pay	**Cash discounts on time** are earned by buyers who pay bills within a stated period. For example, if the customer purchases $10,000 worth of goods on June 1 and the cash discount is 2/10, net 30, the customer pays $9,800 instead of $10,000. Thus, 2/10, net 30, translates into a 2 percent discount if the bill is completely paid within 10 days of the sale. If the payment is not made within 10 days, the full $10,000 is due in 30 days.
Trade Discounts Attract Channel Members' Attention	The manufacturer may reduce prices to channel members (intermediaries) to compensate them for the services they perform. These are **trade discounts**. The trade discount is usually stated as a percentage off the list retail price. A wholesaler may be offered a 50 percent discount and the retailer offered a 40 percent discount off list price. The wholesaler's price to its retail customers is 10 percent above its cost or 40 percent off the list price. The wholesaler earns a 10 percent gross margin on sales to retail customers. Channel members are still eligible to earn the quantity and cash discounts.
Consumer Discounts Increase Sales	**Consumer discounts** are one-time price reductions passed from the manufacturer to channel members or directly to the consumer. Cents-off product labels are price reductions passed directly to the consumer. A package marked 15 cents off each product or $1.80 off a dozen uses a consumer discount. See Exhibit A–2.

EXHIBIT A–2	Types of Discounts	Discount Examples
Types and examples of discounts.	Quantity discount	• Buy 11 dozen, get 1 dozen free
	Non-cumulative	• 20 percent off on all purchases
	(one-time)	• $5 off invoice for each floor-stand purchase
	Cumulative	• 5 percent discount with purchase of 8,000 units
	(yearly purchases)	• 8 percent discount with purchase of 10,000 units
		• 10 percent discount with purchase of 12,000 units
	Cash discounts	• 2/10 end-of-month
		• 2/10, net 30
	Trade discounts	• 40 percent off to retailers
		• 50 percent off to wholesalers
	Consumer discounts	• 15 cents off regular price marked on product's package
		• 10-cents-off coupon

The manufacturer expects channel members to reduce the price from their normal price. A mass merchandiser might normally sell a product with a list price of $2.50 for $1.98. The manufacturer might then want salespeople to persuade the retailer to price the product 15 cents lower than the $1.98, or at a price of $1.83.

Cents-off coupons that the consumer brings to the retail store are another example of a temporary price discount. In both the cents-off label and coupon examples, the manufacturer ensures that the price reduction is passed on to the consumer. This occurs because channel members may not have promoted the product or reduced the price, keeping the quantity or off-invoice savings for themselves. An offer of a cents-off product label and coupons is used by the salesperson to sell larger quantities to customers. For a summary of discounts and examples of each, see Exhibit A–2.

RESELLERS: MARKUP, MARGIN, AND PROFIT

The dollar amount between a product's cost and its selling price is sometimes referred to as markup and sometimes as margin. These two terms are frequently used interchangeably; however, this is incorrect and could be a costly mistake for a salesperson to make.

Markup is the dollar amount added to the product cost to determine its selling price. **Margin** is the dollar amount subtracted from the selling price that yields the product cost. The dollar amount of markup or margin will be the same for any given product.

Markup and margin are often expressed as a percentage, however, and this is where confusion can get a salesperson into trouble. It is important to remember that markup is a percentage of the product cost and margin is a percentage of the selling price. The percentage amount of markup or margin will never be the same for a given product!

While markup and margin have different meanings, they both represent gross profit. **Gross profit** is the money available to cover the costs of marketing the product, operating the business, and profit. **Net profit** is the money remaining after the costs of marketing and operating the business are paid.

Exhibit A–3 presents an example of markup and margin for each channel-of-distribution member. Each channel member has a different percentage markup and margin. The product that costs the manufacturer $3 to produce eventually costs the consumer $12. The manufacturer's selling price represents the wholesaler's cost. Price markups enable the wholesaler to pay business operating costs, cover the product's cost, and make a profit. The wholesaler's selling price of $6 becomes the retailer's cost. In turn, the retailer marks up the product to cover its cost and the associated costs of doing business (such as stocking the product and allocation of fixed costs per square metre), and to maintain a desired profit level.

EXHIBIT A–3

Example of markup on selling price in channel of distribution.

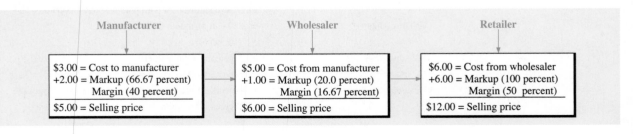

Manufacturer	Wholesaler	Retailer
$3.00 = Cost to manufacturer +2.00 = Markup (66.67 percent) Margin (40 percent) $5.00 = Selling price	$5.00 = Cost from manufacturer +1.00 = Markup (20.0 percent) Margin (16.67 percent) $6.00 = Selling price	$6.00 = Cost from wholesaler +6.00 = Markup (100 percent) Margin (50 percent) $12.00 = Selling price

As mentioned earlier, markup percentage is based on product cost whereas margin percentage is based on product selling price. It is important to know the methods of determining markup and margin percentages. Using a manufacturer's cost of $3, a markup of $2, and a selling price of $5 shown in Exhibit A–3, the methods of determining percentage markup can have different results:

$$\text{Percentage margin on selling price} = \frac{\text{Amount added to cost}}{\text{Selling price}} = \frac{\$2.00}{\$5.00} = 40 \text{ percent}$$

$$\text{Percentage markup on cost} = \frac{\text{Amount added to cost}}{\text{Cost}} = \frac{\$2.00}{\$3.00} = 66.67 \text{ percent}$$

Channel members want to buy goods at low prices and establish selling prices at a competitive level that allows for a reasonable profit. Such objectives result in retailers having different markups and margins on different goods. For example, a retailer may have markups of 10 percent on groceries, 30 percent on cameras, and 50 percent on houseware items. Based on the type of store (discount—high volume; specialty—low volume; department—high service), markups and margins may vary greatly depending on the volume of sales and degree of service rendered.

In preparing the sales presentation for an individual customer, the salesperson should consider all the discounts available to suggest a promotional plan for the retailer. For example, the advertisement shown in Exhibit A–1 illustrates several of the discounts a retailer can receive with the purchase of three decongestants. The salesperson can use these discounts in the sales presentation by suggesting that the retailer advertise the products at a reduced price and place the promotional displays by each of the store's cash registers.

Markup and Unit Price

Sellers, especially consumer-goods salespeople, like to talk in terms of the cost and profits earned from an individual unit. However, wholesalers and retailers do not buy one product at a time. Depending on the customer's size, manufacturers may sell resellers several dozen or thousands of dozens at a time. The cost and profits of an individual unit may not be useful for wholesalers, but they becomes extremely important to retailers since their customers buy the product one at a time.

Here is how it works: Assume you are selling a consumer product to a large chain of grocery stores. As shown in Exhibit A–4, your normal price for each unit is $1.80 and the retailer sells it for $2.19, 10¢ less than the manufacturer's $2.29 suggested selling price. This gives a normal profit of 39¢ or an 18 percent margin [($2.19 − $1.80 = 39¢) then divide by $2.19 (39¢ ÷ $2.19 = 18 percent)]. Subtracting the 53¢ promotional allowance gives the retailer a deal cost of $1.27.

The normal profit, or margin, is 18 percent. If the product is sold at $1.89 for an additional two weeks, the margin reflecting the 53¢ promotional allowance equals 33 percent. If the retailer buys the product and does not reduce the price, the manufacturer is throwing away 53¢ a unit or $6.36 a dozen.

What are the salesperson's objectives? To have the retailer (1) buy a larger quantity than normal; (2) reduce the price for a three-day $1.39 advertised promotion; and (3) run a two-week, in-store promotion at $1.89. The retailer's sale price of $1.39 would provide an 8.6 percent profit and the $1.89 produces a 33 percent profit margin. The manufacturer, retailer, and the retailer's customers all win in this deal.

EXHIBIT A–4

Example of using unit cost.

Consumer-goods salespeople often break down costs and talk of unit costs and profits. Here is the arithmetic one salesperson used in her presentation:

$1.80 = Regular price of each unit
$–0.53 = Special promotional allowance
$1.27 = Deal cost
$2.29 = Manufacturer's suggested selling price
$2.19 = Normal retail selling price
 18%   = Retailers' normal profit ($2.19 − $1.80 = 39¢ margin) (39¢ ÷ $2.19 = 18% margin)
$1.39 = 3-day special price suggested for retailer to advertise product
 8.6% = 3-day sale profit margin ($1.39 − $1.27 = 12¢) (12¢ ÷ $1.39 = 8.6% margin)
$1.89 = 2-week special price suggested for in-store promotion.
 33%   = After-sale profit margin ($1.89 − $1.27 = 62¢) (62¢ ÷ $1.89 = 33% margin)
 18%   = Normal profit ($2.19 − 1.80 = 39¢) (39¢ ÷ $2.19 = 18%)

The above information (except for the arithmetic in parentheses) was on a sheet of paper with the buyer's company name at the top. The seller showed how the buyer could purchase a large quantity and make 8.6 percent profit by selling each item for $1.39 instead of the normal $2.19. The retailer's customers save 80¢ ($2.19 – $1.39 = 80¢). After the three-day sale, the retailer increases the price to $1.89 for two weeks and makes 33 percent instead of the 18 percent margin.

Markup and Return on Investment

Consumer-goods salespeople also can use return on investment (ROI) in their presentations. **Return on investment (ROI)** refers to a sum of money expected from an investment over and above the original investment. ROI often is expressed as a percentage; however, a dollar return on investment also can be used by salespeople. The information shown in Exhibit A–5 illustrates the actual ROI used by a salesperson. Continuing the previous example, the salesperson wants the customer to have a three-day advertised special and a two-week in-store price reduction, and to buy a large quantity for normal stock. The purchasing agent buys for a chain of 100 grocery stores.

EXHIBIT A–5

Profit forecaster for granola bars shown to buyer.

	Three-Day Special	One-Month Special	Normal
Total stores	100	100	100
Deal dates		June 1 through June 30	
Regular cost per dozen	$21.60	$21.60	$21.60
Less allowance ($.53)	−6.36	−6.36	
Deal cost per dozen	$15.24	$15.24	$21.60
Feature price	1.39	1.89	2.19
Cases purchased	500[a]	1000	1,500
Total investment	$7,620[b]	$15,240	$32,400
Total gross sales	$8,340[c]	$22,680	$39,420
Total gross profit	$ 720[d]	$ 7,440	$7,020
Return on investment (ROI)	9.5%[e]	48.8%	21.7%

[a] 5 cases per store
[b] 500 @ 15.24 = $7,620
[c] 500 @ 12 = 6,000; 6,000 × $1.39 = $8,340
[d] $8,340 − $7,620 = $720
[e] $720 ÷ $7,620 = 9.5%

Normally, the chain sells on average 1,500 dozen in six weeks. The salesperson believes that the promotion and price reduction will increase sales to 3,000 dozen. As seen in Exhibit A–5, the salesperson asks the retailer to invest $55,260 ($7,620 + $15,240 + $32,400). Sales are projected to be $70,440 ($8340 + $22,680 + $39,420) with profits of $15,180 ($720 + $7,440 + $7,020). The retailer's return on investment is 27.5 percent, as shown here:

$70,440 = total gross sales
$\underline{-55,260}$ = total investment
$15,180 = total gross profit
27.5% = ROI ($15,180 ÷ $55,260)

Discounts, payment plans, markups, margins, unit prices, and return on investment are important for salespeople to understand thoroughly. Customers are extremely interested in listening to this information during the salesperson's presentation.

ORGANIZATIONS: VALUE AND ROI

Business salespeople often include a value analysis in the sales presentation. A **value analysis** determines the best product for the money. It recognizes that a high-priced product may sometimes be a better value than a lower-priced product. Many firms routinely review a value analysis before deciding to purchase a product.

The value analysis evaluates how well the product meets the buying company's specific needs. It addresses such questions as

- How do your product's features, advantages, and benefits compare to the product currently used?
- Can your product do the same job as your buyer's present product at a lower price?
- Does the buyer's current equipment perform better than required? (Is the equipment too good for present needs?)
- On the other hand, will a higher-priced, better-performing product be more economical in the long run?

As you can see from the examples in this chapter, frequently you must analyze the buyer's present operation carefully before suggesting how your product might improve efficiency, enhance the quality or quantity of the product produced, or save money.

In discussing how to present a value analysis to a buyer, Patrick Kamlowsky, who sells drilling bits for oil and gas wells, said:

> It's not as simple as it may appear to make a recommendation and have the oil company adhere to it. You must be thorough in the presentation and present the facts in an objective manner. After all, their money is at stake. The presentation must be logical and based on facts that are known; it must be made with as little speculation as possible.
>
> What is difficult is presenting a recommendation to one who has spent 30 or more years in the oil field and has drilled all over the world. I am confronted with the challenge of explaining to this man that the methods he has employed for years may not be the best application where he is currently drilling. The presentation of the recommendation must therefore be thorough and to the point. When talking to him, I do not imply that his method is outdated or wrong, but that I believe I can help him improve his method. To be successful, I must establish two things very quickly—his respect and my credibility. Showing him my proposal and supporting evidence, and permitting him the time to evaluate it, are vital. I don't wish to come on too strong, just show him that I genuinely want to help.

A salesperson can develop numerous types of value analyses for a prospective buyer. Three types frequently used are (1) product cost versus true value, (2) unit cost, and (3) return on investment.

Compare Product Costs to True Value

All buyers want to know about costs. The value analysis developed for a customer should present cost in a simple, straightforward manner. A product's costs are always relative to something else; thus, cost must be judged in value and results. The base cost of your product should never be the determining factor of the sale. Buying a product solely on cost could cause a customer to lose money.

Never discuss costs until you have compared them to the *value* of a product. In this manner, the customer intelligently compares the true worth of the proposed investment in your product to its true monetary cost. In effect, a good purchase involves more than initial cost; it represents an investment and you must demonstrate that what you sell is a good investment.

Exhibit A–6 provides an example of how a salesperson might compare the cost of a copier (Product X) with a competitive copier (Product C). It illustrates how you can demonstrate to a buyer that your product is a better value than one would think from looking only at purchase price. Another value analysis technique is to further break down a product's price to its unit cost.

Unit Costs Break Down Price

One method of presenting a product's true value to a buyer is to break the product's total costs into several smaller units or the **unit cost**. Assume you sell a computer system that costs $1,000 per month and processes 50,000 transactions each month. The cost per transaction is only 2 cents.

Return on Investment Is Respected

Return on investment refers to a sum of money expected from an investment over and above the original investment. Buyers are interested in knowing the percentage return on their initial investment. Since the purchase of many business products is an investment in that it produces measurable results, salespeople can talk about the percentage return that can be earned by purchasing their products.

Again, assume you sell computer equipment requiring a $10,000 per month investment. Benefits to the buyer are measured in hours of work saved by employees, plus the resulting salary saving. First, have the buyer agree on an hourly rate, which includes fringe benefit cost; let's say salaries average $5 an hour for employees. The

---

EXHIBIT A–6

Cost versus value of a small copier.

	Product C	Product X
Initial cost	$2695	$3000
Type of paper	Treated paper	Plain paper
Copy speed	12 copies per minute	15 copies per minute
Warm-up time	Instant	Instant
Cost of each copy	3¢ a copy	1¢ a copy
Monthly cost (assuming 10,000 copies)	$300	$100

Conclusion: The difference in the purchase price of the two copiers is $305 ($3000 – $2695). Product X saves $200 on monthly copy costs. The savings on monthly copy costs pay for the higher-priced Product X in one and one-half months. In 15 months, savings on the monthly copy equal the purchase price of Product X. Therefore, Product X is less expensive in the long run.

hours saved are then multiplied by this hourly rate to obtain the return on investment. If hours saved amounted to 2,800 per month, it is a savings of $14,000 per month (2,800 hours × $5 hourly rate). You could develop a table to show the potential return on investment:

Value of hours saved	$14,000 per month
Cost of equipment	−10,000 per month
Profit	$ 4,000 per month
Return on investment ($14,000 − $10,000	140 percent

Subtracting the $10,000 cost per month from the return of $14,000 per month provides a $4,000 a month profit or a 140 percent return on investment. This is taken one step further by considering return on investment after taxes—calculated like this:

$$\frac{\$14,000\ (1 - \text{Tax rate})}{\$10,000}$$

This return on investment presents the buyer with a logical reason to buy. Remember to let the customer make the cost estimates. The buyer must agree with the figures used for this to be effective in demonstrating the real value of buying your product.

KEY TERMS FOR SELLING

cash discounts on time, 409
consumer discount, 409
cumulative quantity discounts, 409
FOB destination, 407
FOB shipping point, 407
gross profit, 410
list price, 407
margin, 410
markup, 410

net price, 407
net profit, 410
non-cumulative quantity discount, 408
return on investment (ROI), 412
trade discounts, 409
unit cost, 414
value analysis, 413
zone price, 407

SALES APPLICATION QUESTIONS

1. Many companies offer customers various discounts from their normal or list price to entice them to buy. Discuss the main types of discounts offered.
2. Should the salesperson mention a discount at the beginning, middle, or end of a sales presentation? Why?
3. It cost a company $6 to manufacture a product that it sold for $10 to a wholesaler who sold it to a retailer for $12. A customer of the retailer bought it for $24. What was the markup on selling price for each member of this product's channel of distribution?
4. Determine the markup of a product that costs your customer $1 with the following potential suggested resell prices: $1.25, $1.50, $2. How much profit would the wholesaler or retailer make selling your product at each of the three suggested resell prices?
5. Assume you sell hardware supplies to grocery, drug, and hardware retailers. Tomorrow, you plan to call on the Real Hardware chain—your largest customer. To reach your sales quota for this year, you must get a large order. You know the purchaser will buy something; however, you want him to purchase an extra amount. Furthermore, you know the company is 120 days overdue on paying for

what you shipped months ago, and your company's credit manager will not ship more merchandise until the company pays the bill. How would you handle the sales call? Include in your answer where you would discuss the overdue-bill problem in your sales presentation. Also include what you would do if the buyer said, "I haven't paid for my last order yet! How can I buy from you today?"

6. List and define five commonly quoted types of prices.

7. The following examples are several types of discounts. In each situation (a) explain what type of discount is used, (b) determine by what percentage the *cost* of the product has been reduced, as well as savings per unit, and (c) answer other questions asked for each situation.

   a. Bustwell Inc., a regional business computer firm, is attempting to sell a new computer-operated gasoline pump meter to a convenience store chain, Gas 'N' Go. The device will help reduce gasoline theft, give an accurate record of each sale, and aid in determining when Gas 'N' Go should order more gasoline. Gus Gas, of the convenience chain, seems interested in your initial proposal but believes the price may be too high. The cost of each computer is $1,000, but you could sell Gas 50 computers for $45,000. The Gas 'N' Go chain owns 43 stores and is building eight more that will open in about one month.

   b. The Storage Bin Warehouse in your territory has reported a number of break-ins in the past three months. As a salesperson for No-Doubt Security Products, you believe your extensive line of alarm systems and locks could benefit the warehouse greatly. You make an appointment with the manager at the Storage Bin for early next week. During your preparation for the sales call, you discover that the warehouse currently uses poor-quality locks and has no security system. You plan to offer the manager a security package consisting of 150 Sure-Bolt deadbolt locks (for the company's 150 private storage rooms) at a price of $10 each, and a new alarm system costing $5,000. The terms of the sale are 2/10, net 30. How would the total cost change if the terms of the alarm system alone were changed to 5/10, net 30 (and the locks remained 2/10, net 30)? What is the cost of the security package if the Storage Bin takes 25 days to pay for the purchase?

   c. You are a salesperson for Madcap Arcade Games, selling video games and pinball machines. A local business wants to open an arcade and would like to buy a new game about every two weeks. A new game costs $3,000. You can offer a 5 percent discount (an end-of-year rebate) if at least 25 games are purchased from you during the next year. What will the discount be in dollars?

   d. The XYZ company is having its year-end sales push. As a salesperson for XYZ, a manufacturer of consumer goods such as toothpaste, shampoo, and razor blades, you have been instructed to give a "buy 11 get 1 free" discount to half of your accounts. The remainder of your accounts, because of their small volume, are offered 10 percent off all purchases. Compare the two situations. Which is the better deal?

8. As a salesperson for the Electric Generator Corporation, you have decided to attempt to sell your EG 600 generator to the Universal Construction Corporation. The EG 600 costs about $70,000. You estimate that operating and maintenance costs will average $3,000 a year and that the machine will operate satisfactorily for 10 years. You can offer a $65,000 price to Universal, if it purchases 10 to 20 machines. Should Universal purchase more than 21 machines, its cost would be $58,000 per generator. The generators currently used originally cost $65,000, have

a life of seven years, and cost $5,000 each year to operate. As far as you know, Universal's present supplier cannot offer them a quantity discount.

    a. Develop a value analysis table comparing the two generators.

    b. In your presentation, what are the selling points you would stress?

9. Value analysis is an effective sales tool. Define value analysis and describe its use in a selling situation.

CASE A–1
Claire Cosmetics

June Sathi was hired recently by a national cosmetics manufacturer. She just graduated from college. Having no previous work experience, she always feels nervous about making sales presentations. Her large customers make her especially nervous. However, for the first month she was in her territory, June only took orders, which relieved much of the pressure, and the salesperson whom June replaced did an excellent job; customers seemed to accept June because of this.

In today's mail, June receives information on products the company wants the sales force to emphasize next month. She is instructed to review the material and come to next week's sales meeting prepared to discuss the information. Of the four products to concentrate on, one product will receive special emphasis. Claire Super Hold hair spray will have the following sales promotion aids and price allowances:

- Floor stand containing twelve 230 mL and thirty-six 350 mL sizes
- Counter display containing six 230 mL and six 350 mL sizes
- $1 floor stand and counter display off-invoice allowance
- 10 percent co-op advertising allowance requiring proof of advertising
- 10 percent off-invoice discount for each dozen of each size purchased

The 230 mL size has a suggested retail price of $1.39 and has a normal invoice cost of 83 cents or $9.96 a dozen. The more popular 350 mL size retails for $1.99 and costs $1.19 each or $14.28 a dozen. June knows that she, like each salesperson, will be called on at the meeting to give her ideas on how to sell this product in front of the 10 salespeople in her district. Her boss will be there and, it is rumoured, the national sales manager will be in the area and may attend. This makes June really nervous.

Questions

1. What can June do to prepare herself for the meeting to reduce her nervousness?
2. If you were attending the meeting, what ideas would you present?

CASE A–2
McBath Women's Apparel

Getting a new, improved product into a chain of stores that has never carried her line of women's apparel is a new experience for Lynn Morris. Lynn has been promoted to key account sales representative for McBath Women's Apparel in the past month.

She has worked for McBath since graduating from college three years earlier. As a novice salesperson in a large metropolitan market, she inherited a sales territory in which all the major department stores carried the popular McBath line. By displaying a service attitude, Lynn kept all her original accounts and managed to help several outlets increase sales of McBath products, but she was never given the opportunity to sell to new accounts.

Now, she has accepted the key account (a key account is one that generates a large volume of sales for the company) sales position in another region of the country. Also, she has the responsibility of selling to a large chain of department stores (Federale) that has never carried McBath products. Maurice Leverett, vice president of marketing at McBath, is counting heavily on adding the Federale chain because the company's president is intent on continuing McBath's rapid sales growth.

Lynn firmly believes that her products are the best on the market. She is concerned, however, about the sales interview she has scheduled with the chief purchasing agent at Federale, Mary Bruce. Despite McBath's high-quality image and its reputation for having a dependable, hard-working sales force, Mary Bruce has turned down other McBath salespeople several times over the past six years, saying, "We already stock four manufacturers' lingerie. We are quite happy with the lines we now carry and with the service their salespeople provide us. Besides, we only have so much floor space to devote to lingerie and we don't want to confuse our customers with another line."

Lynn has decided to make her company's new display system her major selling point for several reasons:

- Several high-ranking McBath executives (including Leverett) are strong backers of the new display and want it in all retail outlets.
- The stores currently using the display for test-marketing purposes have shown an increase in sales for McBath products of 50 percent.
- Federale will not have to set aside much space for the new system, and it can be installed, stocked, and ready for use in less than one hour.
- The display will increase shopping convenience by allowing shoppers easy access to the well-known, trusted line of McBath products with the aid of clear, soft-shell plastic packaging and easy-to-understand sizing.
- A new advertising campaign will start in a few weeks and will emphasize the revolutionary display. Other promotions, such as coupons and special introductory sales, will also be tried.

Questions

1. Lynn believes a good presentation will be critical for her to sell Bruce the new display. How should she structure her presentation? What are the key selling points to discuss?

2. Assume you are Maurice Leverett. Give an example of each of the four major types of discounts discussed in this chapter that your salespeople could use to help put the new display into retail stores. What type of discount will be most effective and least effective? Explain your reasoning.

3. How can Lynn use quantity (cumulative and non-cumulative), cash, trade, and consumer discounts to her advantage?

The Electric Generator Corporation was founded in the early 1970s to develop and market electrical products for industrial and commercial markets. Recently, the company has developed a new electric generator, the EGI, with a revolutionary design. While its initial cost is $2,000 higher than any competing generator, reduced maintenance costs will offset the higher purchase price in 18 months. The Electric Generator

CASE A–3

sales force has been instructed to concentrate all effort on selling this new generator as the company believes it has a sales potential of $500 million.

Ontario salesperson Sandy Hart has as her main customer the E. H. Zachary Construction Company of Toronto, which is the largest non-union construction firm in the world. Because of the importance of potential Zachary purchases of the EGI (estimated at $1 million), Sandy's boss asks her to spend two days developing a plan for contacting and selling to Zachary. Monday morning, she is expected at the regional sales office to present this plan to her boss, the regional sales manager, and the divisional sales manager. These two people will critique the presentation, and then the four of them will finalize a sales plan that Sandy will present to Zachary's buying committee.

Questions

1. If you were Sandy, what would be your suggested sales plan?
2. How would a value analysis enter into your presentation?

CASE A–4
Frank's Drilling Service

Frank's Drilling Service specializes in drilling oil and gas wells. Salesperson Dushan Bednarsky was preparing to contact the drilling engineer at Oilteck, an independent oil company. Dushan has learned that Oilteck plans to drill approximately 12 new wells in the next six months.

Dushan estimates that each oil well will require a drilling depth of approximately 3,000 metres. The drilling service the company uses charges $2.70 a metre, plus $1,200 per hour for personnel to operate the equipment. They take about 16 days to drill each well.

Frank's charges $1,200 per hour for personnel and their costs are $3 a metre. Dushan believes his drilling crews save customers time and money because they can drill a 3,000 metre well in 12 days.

Questions

1. Using the above information, develop a value analysis that Dushan could use to sell to his customer.
2. What are several features, advantages, and benefits Dushan should discuss with Oilteck's drilling engineer?

NOTES

Chapter 1

1. Excerpts from Xerox Corporation sales literature.

Chapter 2

1. Weld F. Royal, "It's Not Easy Being Green," *Sales & Marketing Management*, July 1995, pp. 84–90.
2. Larry G. Mayewski, Michael L. Albanese, and Cynthia J. Crosson, "Market Conduct Emerges as Rating Issue," *Best Review*, November 1995, p. 30.
3. Amanda Richards, "Does Charity Pay?" *Marketing*, September 21, 1995, pp. 24–25.
4. Steven R. Covey, *Seven Habits of Highly Effective People: Restoring the Character Ethic* (New York: Simon & Shuster, 1990).
5. Also see Thomas R. Wotruba, "A Comprehensive Framework for the Analysis of Ethical Behavior, with a Focus on Sales Organizations," *Journal of Personal Selling & Sales Management*, Spring 1990, pp. 29–42; and Michael A. Mayo and Lawrence J. Marks, "An Empirical Investigation of a General Theory of Marketing Ethics," *Journal of the Academy of Marketing Science*, Spring 1990, pp. 163–172.
6. *Canadian Charter of Rights,* http://canada.justice.gc.ca/Loireg/charte/const_en.html.
7. Ibid.
8. Ibid.
9. Also see Leslie M. Fine and Janice R. Franke, "Legal Aspects of Salesperson Commission Payments: Implications for the Implementation of Commission Sales Programs," *Journal of Personal Selling & Sales Management*, Winter 1995, pp. 53–68.
10. Direct Sellers Association of Canada, www.dsa.ca.
11. Ibid.
12. Courtesy of the Competition Bureau.
13. Courtesy of the Competition Bureau.
14. Les Andrews, "Watch What You Say," *Distribution*, April 1997, p. 23.
15. Charles H. Schwepker, Jr., O. C. Ferrell, and Thomas N. Ingram, "The Influence of Ethical Climate and Ethical Conflict on Role Stress in the Sales Force," *Journal of the Academy of Marketing Science*, Spring 1997, pp. 99–108. See also wwwlia.org/~wwlia/ca-comp1.htm.
16. Based on Bart Victor and John B. Cullen, "The Organizational Bases of Ethical Work Climates," *Administrative Science Quarterly,* 33 (1988), pp. 101–125.

Chapter 3

1. Carl Jung, *Psychological Types* (London, England: Routledge and Kegan Paul, 1923).
2. Ibid.

Chapter 4

1. Gerhard Gschwandtner, *Nonverbal Selling Power* (Englewood Cliffs, N.J.: Prentice Hall, 1995), p. 3.
2. Adapted from Ethel C. Glenn and Elliot A. Pood, "Listening Self-Inventory." Reprinted by permission of the publisher from *Supervisory Management*, January 1996, pp. 12–15.

Chapter 5

1. Based on Charles Futrell's conversation with Jack Smith of the Colgate Company about his first month's selling.
2. Wikipedia, "PDA" accessed October 2008.
3. Wikipedia. "CDMA" accessed October 2008.
4. Wikipedia, "Instant Messaging" accessed October 2008.
5. Ibid.
6. Adapted from Elwood N. Chapman, *Sales Training Basics* (Menlo Park, Calif.: Crisp Publications, 1992), p. 11.

Chapter 6

1. Also see Malcolm Fleschner, *Selling Power*, January/February 1997, p. 60.
2. Donald L. Brady, "Determining the Value of an Industrial Prospect: A Prospect Preference Index Model," *Journal of Personal Selling & Sales Management*, August 1987, pp. 27–32; and Roger Pell, "It's a Fact . . . Qualified Referrals Bring More Sales in Your Company," *Personal Selling Power*, March 1990, p. 30.
3. "Trade Shows: Creating Sales Leads," *Marketing Communications*, November 1993, pp. 36–40.
4. Also see Herbert E. Brown and Roger W. Brucker, "Telephone Qualifications of Sales Leads," *Industrial Marketing Management*, August 1987, pp. 187–190; and Sandler, "Prospecting for Profit."
5. Portions of this section are adapted from Scott Krammick, *Expecting Referrals: The Resurrection of a Lost Art* (Fredericksburg, VA: Associate Publishing, 1994).

Chapter 7

1. George W. Dudley and Shannon L. Goodson, *Earning What You're Worth? The Psychology of Sales Call Reluctance* (New York: Behavioral Sciences Research Press, 1992).
2. Ibid.
3. Ibid.
4. Example provided by Professor Richard D. Nordstrom, California State University—Fresno.
5. Adapted from G. M. Grikscheit, H. C. Cash, and W. J. E. Crissy, *Handbook of Selling: Psychological, Managerial, and Marketing Bases* (New York: John Wiley & Sons, 1981).
6. Also see Tony Alessandra, Phil Wexler, and Rich Barrera, *Nonmanipulative Selling* (Englewood Cliffs, N.J.: Prentice Hall, 1997).
7. From Crisp: *Successful Negotiation*, Third Edition, *Effective "Win–Win" Strategies and Tactics*, 3rd edition by MADDUX. © 1995. Reprinted with permission of Course Technology, a division of Thomson Learning: www.thomsonrights.com. Fax 800-730-2215.
8. For 18 concession strategies useful during sales negotiations, see Homer B. Smith, "How to Concede—Strategically," *Sales & Marketing Management,* May 1998, pp. 79–80.
9. Adapted from Joseph P. Smith, *Dress for Business* (Menlo Park, Calif.: Crisp Publications, 1997), p. 23.
10. Adapted from John A. Firestone, *Sales Fundamentals* (Menlo Park, Calif.: Crisp Publications, 1993), p. 12.

Chapter 8

1. For a complete discussion, see Neil Rackham, *SPIN Selling* (New York: McGraw-Hill, May 1988).

Chapter 9

1. Rosemary P. Ramsey and Ravipreet S. Sohi, "Listening to Your Customers: The Impact of Perceived Salesperson Listening Behavior on Relationship Outcomes," *Journal of the Academy of Marketing Science*, Spring 1997, pp. 127–137.
2. Patricia M. Doney and Joseph P. Cannon, "An Examination of the Nature of Trust in Buyer–Seller Relationships," *Journal of Marketing*, April 1997, pp. 35–51.
3. Jacklyn Boice, "Story Selling Happily Ever After," *Selling Power*, June 2001, p. 21.
4. Sam Lovejoy, "Technology Improves Communications," *Sales & Marketing Management*, September 4, 1997, pp. 34–37.
5. Alice Graham, "Put Some Zip in Your Presentations," *Sales & Marketing Management*, August 14, 1997, pp. 26–29.

Chapter 10

1. Adapted from Tom Hopkins, *How to Master the Art of Selling* (New York: Warner Brooks, 1994), p. 191.

Chapter 11

1. Adapted from John L. Johnston, *Works of Mark Twain* (New York: Harper & Row, 1989), p. 133.
2. Mike Radick, "Training Salespeople to Get Success on Their Side," *Sales & Marketing Management*, August 15, 1993. Also see Neil Rackham, *SPIN Selling* (New York: McGraw-Hill, 1988).
3. John C. Young, "When You Strike Out," *Journal of Purchasing*, December 1991, pp. 3–8.

Chapter 12

1. "Gartner: CRM Market to Grow 14 Percent in 2008," *PC World*, at http://www.pcworld.com/businesscenter/article/145016/gartner_crm_market_to_grow_14_percent_in_2008.html (accessed October 8, 2008).
2. Charles M. Futrell, *ABC's of Relationship Selling* (Burr Ridge, Ill.: Richard D. Irwin, Inc., 1997), p. 373.
3. Ibid.
4. James Lewis, "These Sins Will Kill a Sale," *Selling*, October 1997, p. 6.
5. Reprinted with permission of B. J. Hughes, Inc.
6. Adapted from Richard F. Gerson, *Beyond Customer Service: Keeping Customers for Life* (Menlo Park, Calif.: Crisp Publications, 1992), p. 79.

Chapter 13

1. Charles M. Futrell, "Survey of America's Top Sales Forces," private research project, 1998.

Chapter 14

1. Statistics Canada, "Retail Trade by History," at http://www40.statcan.ca/l01/cst01/trad15a.htm (accessed October 8, 2008).
2. Adapted from Stanley Marcus, "Fire a Buyer and Hire a Seller," *International Trends in Retailing*, Fall 1986, pp. 49–55.
3. Adapted from Wayne Rodgers, *People Management* (Menlo Park, Calif.: Crisp Publications, 1994), p. 25.
4. Statistics Canada, "Employment, Payroll Employment, by Industry," at http://www40.statcan.ca/l01/cst01/labr71a.htm?sdi=retail%20employment (accessed October 8, 2008).
5. Adapted from Wayne Rodgers, *People Management* (Menlo Park, Calif.: Crisp Publications, 1994), p. 25.

A

acceptance signals   signs that your buyer is favourably inclined toward you and your presentation, p. 100

account analysis   the process of analyzing each prospect and customer to maximize the chances of reaching a sales goal, p. 364

account penetration   the ability to work and contact people throughout the account, discussing your products, p. 344

account segmentation   the process of applying different selling strategies to different territories, p. 365

action   the last of the prospect's mental steps—when the prospect buys your product, p. 189

add-on selling   the process of generating additional revenues after you've closed a sale by selling additional complementary products or by increasing the value of the sale by simply selling more product, p. 257

advantage   the performance characteristic of a product that describes how it can be used or how it will help the buyer, p. 125

alternative-choice close   a type of close that does not give the prospect a choice of buying or not buying but instead asks which one or how many items he or she wishes to buy, p. 319

analogy   a comparison between two different situations that have something in common, p. 247

aggressiveness   expressing oneself in an inappropriate way; being forceful and demanding, p. 311

assumptive close   a type of close that assumes the prospect will buy, p. 314

assertiveness   expressing oneself in a direct and honest way; seeking a win–win outcome, p. 311

attention   the first mental step in the buying process, p. 187

attitudes   a person's learned predispositions toward something, p. 68

autosuggestion   a kind of suggestion that attempts to have prospects imagine themselves using the product, p. 243

B

belief   a state of mind in which trust or confidence is placed in something or someone, p. 68

benefit   a favourable result the buyer receives from the product because of a particular advantage that has the ability to satisfy a buyer's need, p. 125

benefit selling   a method of selling whereby a salesperson relates a product's benefits to the customer's needs using the product's features and advantages as support, p. 125

black box   the unobservable, internal process taking place within the mind of the prospect as he or she reaches a decision whether or not to buy, p. 61

blog   a frequently updated personal journal using the Internet; intended for people to read, p. 123

body language   nonverbal communication that includes facial expression, appearance, handshake, and body movement, p. 246

boomerang method   the process of turning an objection into a reason to buy, p. 289

breach of warranty   a situation in which a product does not perform as promised by the company's representatives, p. 46

bribe   the process of giving something to somebody to get them to do something, p. 44

bundling   offering several products as one combined product, p. 48

business market   the market where all profit and nonprofit organizations buy goods and services for a specific purpose, p. 389

business marketing   the marketing of goods and services to business users, p. 389

buyer   the purchasing agent, p. 395

buying signal   anything that prospects say or do that indicates they are ready to buy, p. 303

C

calendar management   forms a part of the electronic sales automation, which makes time management easier and less prone to errors or oversights, p. 134

call reluctance   a feeling of not wanting to contact a prospect or customer, p. 182

career path   the upward sequence of job movements during a sales career, p. 9

cash discounts   discounts earned by buyers who pay bills within a stated period, p. 409

caution signals   signs that a buyer is neutral or skeptical toward what the salesperson says, p. 101

CCC GOMES   a stakeholder acronym: customers, creditors, community, government, owners, managers, employees, and suppliers, p. 30

cell yell   yelling into a cell phone thinking that it is necessary to be heard, p. 139

centre of influence method   a method whereby the salesperson finds and cultivates people in a community or territory who are willing to cooperate in helping to find prospects, p. 159

closed-ended questions   questions that can usually be answered with yes or no or by a very short response, p. 222

closing   the process of helping people make a decision that will benefit them, p. 302

code of ethics   a formal statement of the company's values concerning ethics and social issues, p. 51

cognitive dissonance   tension on the part of a buyer regarding whether the right decision was made in purchasing a product, p. 79

cold-calling prospecting method   a method whereby the salesperson contacts as many leads as possible with no prior knowledge of the business or individual called upon, p. 156

collect information   the process by which buyers visit retail stores, contact potential suppliers, or talk with salespeople about a product's price, size, advantage, and warranty before making a decision regarding buying, p. 77

communication   the act of transmitting verbal and nonverbal information and understanding between seller and buyer, p. 92

compensation method   the method of offsetting negative product aspects with better benefit aspects, p. 291

compliment close   a close wherein the salesperson ends with a compliment to the prospect, p. 314

complimentary approach   an approach that opens with a compliment that is sincere and therefore effective, p. 217

competitive advantage   an advantage held over the competition, p. 197

computer-based presentations   dramatic and interactive presentations created at relatively low cost with the help of sales force automation using a computer, p. 135

condition of the sale   a situation wherein an objection becomes a condition of the sale, such that if the condition is met the prospect will buy, p. 286

consultative selling   the process of professionally providing information to help customers make intelligent actions to achieve short- and long-term objectives, p. 240

consumer discount   a one-time price reduction passed on from the manufacturer to channel members or directly to the customer, p. 409

consumer sales promotion   a promotion that includes free samples, coupons, contests, and demonstrations to consumers, p. 129

contact management   a listing of all the customer contacts that a salesperson makes in the course of conducting business, p. 133

conventional moral development level   an individual conforms to the expectations of others, such as family, employer, boss, and society; upholds moral and legal laws, p. 33

conviction   the fifth mental step in the buying process, p. 189

cooling-off period   a period during which the buyer may cancel the contract, return any merchandise, and obtain a full refund, p. 49

CPSA   Canadian Professional Sales Association, p. 14

countersuggestion   a suggestion that evokes an opposite response from the prospect, p. 244

creative imagery   a relaxation and concentration technique that aids in stress management in which a salesperson envisions successful coping in various sales situations, p. 212

creative problem solvers   individuals who have the ability to develop and combine nontraditional alternatives to meet the specific needs of the customer, p. 173

credibility   a salesperson's believability, established through empathy, willingness to listen to specific needs, and continual enthusiasm toward his or her work and the customer's business, p. 111

CRM   Customer Relationship Management; the process of organizing, tracking, and communicating with a group of customers, p. 374

cross-selling   occurs when a salesperson encourages a customer to purchase goods or services from other areas that may satisfy some of their needs. For example, selling a maintenance and supply agreement on a photocopier would serve as cross-selling, p. 257

cumulative quantity discounts   discounts received for buying a certain amount of a product over a stated period, p. 409

curiosity approach   an approach whereby the salesperson asks a question or does something to make the prospect curious about the product or service, p. 219

customer benefit approach   an approach whereby the salesperson asks a question that implies that the product will benefit the prospect, p. 218

customer benefit plan   a plan that contains the nucleus of information used in the sales presentation, p. 184

customer profile   an outline that gives relevant information regarding the firm, the buyer, and individuals who influence the buying decision, p. 183

customer satisfaction   the feelings about any differences between what is expected and actual experiences with the purchase, p. 339

customer service   the activities and programs provided by the seller to make the relationship a satisfying one for the customer, pp. 165, 338

D

deciders   those persons actually involved in making the decision to buy, p. 395

decoding process   receipt and translation of information by the receiver, p. 93

demonstration   the process of showing a product to a prospect and letting him or her use it, if possible, p. 252

derived demand   demand linked to consumer demand for other products, p. 390

desire   the third mental step in the buying process, p. 187

direct denial   the method of overcoming objections through the use of facts, logic, and tact, p. 289

direct-mail prospecting   the process of mailing advertisements to a large number of people over an extended geographical area, p. 159

direct question   a question that usually can be answered with yes or no or by a very short response, p. 222

direct suggestion   an approach that suggests prospects buy rather than telling them to buy, p. 243

disagreement signals   signs that the prospect does not agree with the presentation or does not think the product is beneficial, p. 101

discretionary responsibility   behaviours that are purely voluntary and guided by the desire to make social contributions not mandated by economics, law, or ethics, p. 32

dramatization   the theatrical presentation of products, p. 251

E

economic need   the buyer's need to purchase the most satisfying product for the money, p. 64

80/20 principle   eighty percent of sales often come from 20 percent of a company's customers, p. 22

electronic mail (e-mail)   sending messages electronically through a computer system that delivers them immediately to any number of recipients, p. 132

ELMS system   the process of dividing broad accounts into varying sized accounts, p. 366

empathy   the ability to identify and understand another person's feelings, ideas, and circumstances, pp. 15, 105

employee rights   rights desired by employees regarding their job security and the treatment administered by their employer while on the job, p. 38

encoding process   conversion of ideas and concepts into information, p. 93

endless-chain referral method   a method whereby a salesperson asks each buyer for a list of friends who might also be interested in buying the product, p. 156

enthusiasm   a state of mind wherein a person is filled with excitement toward something, p. 111

ethical committee   a group of executives appointed to oversee company ethics and provide rulings on questionable ethical issues, p. 51

ethical ombudsman   an official given the responsibility of corporate conscience who hears and investigates ethical complaints and informs top management of potential ethical issues, p. 52

ethics   the code of moral principles and values that governs the behaviours of a person or a group with respect to what is right or wrong, p. 34

evidence statements   statements that substantiate claims made by the salesperson, pp. 112, 247

exclusive dealing   prohibiting a channel member from carrying competitive products, p. 48

exhibitions and demonstrations   a situation in which a firm operates a booth at a trade show or other special-interest gathering staffed by salespeople, p. 158

extensive decision making   decision-making characteristic of buyers who are unfamiliar with a specific product and who must therefore become highly involved in the decision-making process, p. 81

FAB selling technique   a technique stressing features, advantages, and benefits of a product, p. 125

feature   any tangible or intangible characteristic of a product, p. 125

feedback   verbal or nonverbal reaction to communication as transmitted to the sender, p. 93

ferris-wheel concept   an analogy that compares prospecting to the management of a ferris wheel. As riders (customers) exit the ferris wheel, the attendant (salesperson) must replace them in order to keep the ride profitable, p. 150

financial rewards   rewards given or compensation given by a company, p. 10

flash drive   a small portable device used for storage of data; allows for transfer of data from one computer to another, p. 135

FOB destination   the point at which the seller pays all shipping costs, p. 407

FOB shipping point   the shipping process in which the buyer pays transportation charges for goods, the title for which passes to the customer when the goods are loaded onto the shipping vehicle, p. 407

follow-up   one of the last steps in the selling process, involving servicing the needs of the customer after the sale in order to build a long-term relationship, p. 341

formula sales presentation   a presentation by which the salesperson follows a general outline that allows more flexibility and tries to determine prospect needs, p. 192

G

gatekeepers   people who influence where information from salespeople goes and with whom salespeople will be allowed to talk, p. 179

geographic information system   allows salespeople to view and manipulate customer or prospect information on an electronic map, p. 135

goal setting   establishing what one wants to accomplish and what activities need to be performed in order to reach desired career or performance goals, p. 363

GPS   Global Positioning System; a device that uses satellite navigation to pinpoint the user's location, p. 137

hearing   the ability to detect sounds, p. 107

hidden objection   an objection that disguises the actual objection either with silence or triviality, p. 277

I

ideal self   the person one would like to be, p. 69

incentive   a reward that serves to motivate someone, p. 11

indirect denial   an apparent agreement with the prospect used by the salesperson to deny the fundamental issue of the objection, p. 290

indirect suggestion   a statement by the salesperson recommending that the prospect undertake some action while making it seem that the idea to do so is the prospect's, p. 244

inelastic demand   demand that does not change in direct proportion to a change in price, p. 390

influencers   people who influence the decision to buy a product, p. 395

information evaluation   a process that determines what will be purchased as the buyer matches this information with needs, attitudes, and beliefs in making a decision, p. 77

initiator   the person proposing to buy or replace a product, p. 395

instant messaging   real-time communication over the Internet, p. 139

intelligent questions   questions relating to a prospect's business that show the salesperson's concern for the prospect's needs, p. 282

interactive need-satisfaction presentation   a flexible, free flowing, and interactive sales presentation, p. 194

interest   the second mental step in the buying process, p. 187

Internet   a global network of computers connected to one another; also referred to as the Net, p. 132

intimate space   a spatial zone up to 0.5 metres, about an arm's length from a person's body, that is reserved for close friends and loved ones, p. 94

introductory approach   the most common but least powerful approach; it does little to capture the prospect's attention, p. 216

J

joint demand   demand that occurs when two or more products are used together to produce a single product, p. 391

K

key accounts   your largest customers, the loss of which would greatly affect a territory's sales and profits, p. 366

KISS principle   a memory device standing for keep it simple, salesperson, p. 105

L

lead   a person or organization that might be a prospect, p. 150

learning   acquiring knowledge or behaviour based on past experiences, p. 65

limited decision making   characteristic of a buyer who invests a moderate level of energy in making the decision to buy because, although the buyer is not familiar with each brand's features, advantages, and benefits, the general quality of the good is known to him or her, p. 80

links   connection points to other Web sites, p. 140

list price   a standard price charged to all customers, p. 407

listening   ability to derive meaning from sounds that are heard, p. 107

logical reasoning   persuasive techniques that appeal to the prospect's common sense by applying logic through reason, p. 243

looking-glass self   the self that people think other people see them as, p. 69

M

MAD   an acronym for the three questions that determine whether a prospect is a qualified one; a qualified prospect needs the money, authority, and desire to buy, p. 151

markup   the dollar amount added to the product cost to determine its selling price, p. 130

medium   the form of communication used in the sales presentation and discussion; most frequently words, visual materials, and body language, p. 93

memorized presentation   a type of presentation in which the salesperson does 80 to 90 percent of the talking, focusing on the product and its benefits rather than attempting to determine the prospect's needs, p. 190

message   information conveyed in the sales presentation, p. 93

metaphor   an implied comparison that uses a contrasting word or phrase to evoke a vivid image, p. 247

minor-points close   a close where the salesperson asks the prospect to make a low-risk decision on a minor element of a product, p. 316

misrepresentation   statements made by salespeople that exaggerate the capabilities of their products or services and false statements made to close a sale, p. 46

mobile offices   small offices installed or located in vehicles such as minivans, p. 138

modified rebuy purchase   a type of purchase made when regular purchasing patterns are slightly changed to suit customers' present needs, p. 391

money objection   a price-oriented objection, p. 274

N

need arousal   a situation in which a salesperson triggers a psychological, social, or economic need in the buyer, p. 77

needs   the desire for something a person feels is worthwhile, p. 62

needs analysis   the process of uncovering a prospect's needs, p. 194

negotiation   the act of reaching an agreement mutually satisfactory to both buyer and seller, p. 286

negotiation close   a close in which buyer and seller find ways for everyone to have a fair deal, p. 320

netiquette   proper rules and manners for communicating over the Internet, p. 106

net price   the price after allowance for all discounts, p. 407

net profit   money remaining after costs of marketing and operating the business are paid, p. 410

networking   the continuous prospecting method of making and utilizing contacts, p. 161

new-task purchase   a type of purchase made when a product is bought in conjunction with a job or task newly performed by the purchaser, p. 391

noise   factors that distort communication between buyer and seller, including barriers to communication, pp. 93, 101

non-cumulative quantity discount   a one-time price reduction, p. 408

no-need objection   an objection in which the prospect declares he or she does not need the product and implies the end of the selling effort but that may actually be either a hidden or a stalling objection, p. 274

nonfinancial rewards   rewards that are generated by the individual, not given by the company; also called psychological income or intrinsic rewards, p. 10

nonprofit clients   the recipients of nonprofit organizations' money and services, p. 399

nonprofit contributors   the providers of a nonprofit organization's resources, p. 399

nonprofit organization   in this type of organization, profit is not a goal; most sell services rather than tangible products, p. 398

nonverbal communication   unspoken communication such as physical space, appearance, handshake, and body movement, p. 94

O

objection   a statement by your buyer indicating resistance to your proposal, p. 271

observation method   the process of finding prospects by a salesperson constantly watching what is happening in the sales area, p. 161

open-ended question   a question that opens up two-way communication by beginning the question with who, what, where, when, how, and why, p. 222

opinion approach   an approach whereby a salesperson shows that the buyer's opinion is valued, p. 220

order getter   an individual who gets new and repeat business using a creative sales strategy and a well-executed sales presentation, p. 8

order taker   an individual who asks what the customer wants or waits for the customer to order, p. 8

orphaned customers   customers who are abandoned as a result of a salesperson leaving the company, p. 157

P

parallel referral sale   a method of selling that makes the sale and gains referrals, p. 164

partnering   the third level of selling where the seller works continually to improve the customer's operations, sales, and profits, p. 22

pass up   the option of a salesperson not to pursue a presentation or sale or not to respond to an objection, p. 288

perception   the process by which a person selects, organizes, and interprets information, p. 68

PDA   personal digital assistant; small handheld devices used for communication and many other computer applications, p. 138

personal productivity   improvement of an individual's performance through more efficient data storage and retrieval, better time management, and enhanced presentations, p. 133

personal selling   the personal communication of information to persuade a prospective customer to buy something that satisfies that individual's needs, p. 3

personal space   an area 0.5 to 1.5 metres from a person; it is the closest zone a stranger or business acquaintance is normally allowed to enter, p. 94

personality   a person's distinguishing character traits, attitudes, or habits, p. 69

personality typing   classifying people into different personality types, p. 70

persuasion   ability to change a person's belief, position, or course of action, p. 104

postpone the objection   the option of a salesperson to respond to an objection later during the sale presentation, p. 280

practical objection   an overt objection based on real or concrete causes, p. 288

preapproach   planning the sales call on a customer or prospect, p. 172

preconventional moral development level   an individual acts in his or her own best interest and thus follows rules to avoid punishment or receive rewards; will break moral and legal laws, p. 33

premium   an article of merchandise offered as an incentive to the user to take some action, p. 130

premium approach   an approach in which the salesperson offers a prospect something as an inducement to buy, p. 217

prestige suggestions   a technique in which the salesperson has the prospect visualize using products that people whom the prospect trusts use, p. 243

price discrimination   the act of selling the same quantity of the same product to different buyers at different prices, p. 48

principled moral development level   an individual lives by an internal set of morals, values, and ethics; these are upheld regardless of punishments or majority opinion, p. 34

probability close   a close that permits the prospect to focus on his or her real objections that a salesperson attempts to reverse with a persuasive sales argument, p. 319

probes   questions that help salespeople obtain information from the prospect, develop two-way communication, and increase prospect participation, p. 222

probing   the act of gathering information and uncovering customer needs using one or more questions, p. 104

problem-solution presentation   a flexible, customized approach involving an in-depth study of a prospect's needs, requiring a well-planned presentation, p. 196

product   bundle of tangible and intangible attributes, including packaging, colour, and brand, as well as the services and even the reputation of the seller, p. 337

product approach   an approach in which the salesperson places the product on the counter or hands it to the customer, saying nothing, p. 218

product objection   an objection relating directly to the product, p. 277

proof statements   evidence statements that have been accepted by the prospect as true, p. 112

proposal   a formal suggestion put forth by an individual, p. 197

prospect   a qualified person or organization that has the potential to buy a salesperson's product or service, p. 151

prospecting   the process of identifying potential customers, p. 150

prospect's mental steps   the five steps or phases that salespeople believe constitute a purchase decision, p. 186

psychological objection   a hidden objection based on the prospect's attitudes, p. 288

public space   distances greater than 3.5 metres from a person, p. 94

purchase   the fifth and last step in the buying process, p. 189

purchase decision   a buyer's decision to purchase something, p. 77

purchase satisfaction   gratification based upon a product that supplies expected, or greater than expected, benefits, p. 79

Q

qualified prospect   a prospect who has the financial resources to pay, the authority to make the buying decision, and a desire for the product, p. 151

quota   an expected level of performance often established by sales managers for their sales force, p. 364

R

real self   people as they actually are, p. 69

receiver   the person a communication is intended for, p. 93

reciprocity   an agreement whereby a person or organization buys a product if the person or organization selling the product also buys a product from the first party, p. 49

redirect question   a question that guides the prospect back to selling points that both parties agree on, p. 223

referral   a person or organization recommended to you by someone who feels that this person could benefit from you or your product, p. 157

referral approach   an approach that uses a third person's name as a reference to approach the buyer, p. 217

referral cycle   the process that provides guidelines for a salesperson to ask for referrals, p. 163

relationship marketing   the combination of products, prices, distributions, promotions, and service that organizations use to create customer loyalty, p. 20

relationship selling   the second level of selling where customers are contacted after a purchase to determine future needs, p. 16

request for proposal (RFP)   purchasing process often used for large purchases when large organizations invite bids on a project, p. 391

rephrase the objection   a method of identifying a prospect's concerns and clarifying and confirming your understanding of objections, p. 282

rephrasing question   a question whereby the salesperson rephrases what the prospect has said in order to clarify meaning and determine the prospect's needs, p. 223

retailing   any individual or organization that sells goods or services directly to final consumers for their personal, non-business use, p. 384

return on investment (ROI)   the additional sum of money expected from an investment over and above the original investment, p. 412

routine decision making   the process of being in the habit of buying a particular product, so attitudes and beliefs toward the product are already formed and are usually positive, p. 80

routing   the travel pattern used in working a sales territory, p. 370

S

sales call objective   the main purpose of a salesperson's call to a prospect, p. 175

sales objection   the prospect's opposition or resistance to the salesperson's information or request, p. 271

sales planning   the process of preparing to approach a prospect and attempting to make a sale, p. 175

sales presentation   the actual presentation of the sales pitch to the prospect, p. 186

sales presentation mix   the elements the salesperson assembles to sell to prospects, p. 241

sales process   a sequence of actions by the salesperson that leads toward the prospect taking a desired action and ends with a follow-up to ensure purchase satisfaction, p. 22

sales response function   the relationship between sales volume and sales calls, p. 367

sales territory a group of customers or a geographical area assigned to a salesperson, p. 361

sales training the effort put forth by an employer to provide the opportunity for the salesperson to acquire job-related attitudes, concepts, rules, and skills that result in improved performance in the selling environment, p. 120

scheduling the establishment of a fixed time for visiting a customer's business, p. 370

selective distortion the altering of information when it is inconsistent with a person's beliefs or attitudes, p. 67

selective exposure the process of allowing only a portion of the information revealed to be organized, interpreted, and permitted into awareness, p. 66

selective retention the act of remembering only the information that supports one's attitudes and beliefs, p. 67

self-concept a person's view of himself or herself, p. 69

self-image how a person sees himself or herself, p. 69

SELL sequence a sequence of things to do and say to stress benefits important to the customer: show the feature, explain the advantage, lead into the benefit, and let the customer talk by asking a question about the benefit, p. 305

shelf facings the number of individual products placed beside each other on the shelf, p. 129

shelf positioning the physical placement of the product within the retailer's store, p. 129

shock approach an approach that uses a question designed to make the prospect think seriously about a subject related to the salesperson's product, p. 220

simile a direct comparison statement using the words *like* or *as,* p. 246

SMART objectives that are specific, **m**easureable, **a**chievable, **r**elevant, and **t**ime bounded, p. 176

social networking meeting and communicating with different people; often done using the Internet, p. 123

social responsibility the responsibility to profitably serve employees and customers in an ethical and lawful manner, p. 30

social space a zone that is 1.5 to 3.5 metres from a person and is the area normally used for sales presentations, p. 94

source the origin of a communication, p. 93

source objection a loyalty-related objection by which the prospect states a preference for another company or salesperson, and may specify a dislike for the salesperson's company or the salesperson, p. 277

space invasion a situation in which one person enters another person's personal or intimate space, p. 95

space threats situations in which a person threatens to invade another's spatial territory, p. 95

SPIN an acronym describing a sequential questioning approach used by salespeople; **s**ituation, **p**roblem, **i**mplication, **n**eeds **p**ayoff, p. 225

stakeholder any group within or outside the organization that has a stake in the organization's performance, p. 30

stalling objection an objection that delays the presentation or the sale, p. 272

stimulus–response model a model of behaviour that describes the process of applying a stimulus (sales presentation) that results in a response (purchase decision), p. 61

straight rebuy purchase a routine purchase of products bought regularly, p. 391

strategic programs, goals, and problems of great importance to customers, p. 172

strategic customer relationship formal relationship with the customer, the purpose of which is joint pursuit of mutual goals, p. 172

suggestive propositions a proposition that implies that the prospect should act now, p. 243

summary-of-benefits close a close wherein the salesperson summarizes the benefits of the product in a positive manner so that the prospect agrees with what the salesperson says, p. 315

surfing the Internet exploring the different Web sites found within the web of links, p. 138

T

T-account close a close that is based on the process that people use when they make a decision by weighing the pros against the cons, p. 316

technology close a close in which the buyer is shown past purchases, sales trends, purchase suggestions, and payment schedules by graphs and bar charts, p. 320

telemarketing a marketing communication system using telecommunication technology and trained personnel to conduct planned, measurable marketing activities directed at targeted groups of consumers, p. 160

telephone prospecting the process of reaching potential customers over the phone, p. 160

territorial space the area around oneself that a person will not allow another person to enter without consent, p. 94

territory manager a person who plans, organizes, and executes activities that increase sales and profits in a given territory, p. 18

testimonial using a third-party statement as proof to substantiate a claim, p. 249

third-party answer the technique of responding to an objection with testimony from authoritative sources, p. 291

three realms the three aspects involved in selling; salespeople must have the ability to sell the company, the company's products, and themselves, p. 128

tied selling selling in which a buyer is required to buy additional products not wanted when purchasing particular items, p. 48

time management the process of utilizing a given period of time for maximum effectiveness, p. 367

trade discounts discounts on the list retail price offered to channel members, p. 409

trade sales promotion a promotion that encourages resellers to purchase and aggressively sell a manufacturer's products by offering incentives such as sales contests, displays, special purchase prices, and free merchandise, p. 129

transactional selling   the first level of selling where customers are sold a product or service and not contacted again, p. 21

trial close   a technique that checks the attitude of your prospect toward the sales presentation, p. 304

U

undifferentiated selling   the process of applying and designing selling strategies equally to all accounts, p. 364

unit cost   total cost of one unit of the product, p. 414

urgency close   a close whereby a salesperson suggests that if a prospect does not act now, he or she may not be able to buy in the future, thus motivating the prospect to act immediately, p. 318

users   people who must work with or use the product, p. 395

V

value analysis   an investigation that determines the best product for the money, p. 413

video calling   using a cell phone or computer to communicate while being able to see the other party on the device, p. 139

visuals (visual aids)   illustrative material that aids a prospect in increasing memory retention of a presentation, p. 250

W

wants   needs that are learned by a person, p. 62

Web page   a site on the World Wide Web that contains information and usually a number of pointers or links to other pages of information, p. 140

whistle blowing   employee disclosure of illegal, immoral, or illegitimate practices on the employer's part, p. 52

win–win negotiation   a negotiation result where both parties have gained and neither party perceives that he or she gave up too much, p. 295

word processing   production of typewritten documents (such as business letters) with automated and usually computerized typing and text-editing equipment, p. 136

World Wide Web   part of the Internet that houses the Web sites that provide text, graphics, video, and audio information on millions of topics, p. 139

Z

zone price   the price based on geographical location or zone of customers, p. 407

Chapter 1

Exhibit 1–3 Comstock Images/ PictureQuest

Exhibit 1–5 Big Cheese Photo/Jupiter Images/DAL

Exhibit 1–6 Data reprinted with the permission of the Canadian Professional Sales Association, 2008.

Exhibit 1–7 Rob Melhychuk/Getty Images

Exhibit 1–9
(top left) Javier Pierini/Getty Images
(top right) RF/CORBIS
(bottom left) Ryan McVay/Getty Images
(bottom right) RF/CORBIS

Chapter 2

Exhibit 2–3 © Marcus Clackson/ iStockphoto

Exhibit 2–4 Keith Brofsky/Getty Images

Exhibit 2–5 Stewart Cohen/Digital Vision/Getty Images

Exhibit 2–6 © Jacob Wackerhausen/ iStockphoto

Exhibit 2–7 © Ryan McVay/Photo Disc

Chapter 3

Exhibit 3–2 iStockphoto

Exhibit 3–3 Ryan McVay/Getty Images

Exhibit 3–4
(left) Jeff Greenberg/PhotoEdit
(right) Thinkstock/Jupiter Images/ DAL

Exhibit 3–6
(left) Amy Etra/PhotoEdit
(right) RF/CORBIS

Exhibit 3–8
(left) Bob Krist/CORBIS
(right) Janeart Inc./The Image Bank/Getty Images

Exhibit 3–10
(left) Jeff Greenberg/PhotoEdit
(right) Thinkstock/Jupiter Images/ DAL

Exhibit 3–12 Royalty-Free/CORBIS

Exhibit B Adapted from I. Myers, *The Myers–Briggs Type Indicator* (Princeton, NJ: Educational Testing Services, 1962).

Chapter 4

Exhibit 4–3
(top left) Getty/Royalty-Free
(top right) Getty/Royalty-Free
(bottom left) Jupiter Images/DAL
(bottom right) Stockbyte/Punch Stock Images/DAL

Exhibit 4–4 Steve Mason/Getty Images

Exhibit 4–6
(left) David Lees/Taxi/Getty Images
(right) Jeff Zaruba/CORBIS

Exhibit 4–7
(left) Courtesy of Lucille Pointer/Charles Futrell
(centre) Courtesy of Jeffrey S. Conant/Charles Futrell
(right) Courtesy of Larry Gersham/ Charles Futrell

Exhibit 4–8 Keith Brofsky/Getty Images
Exhibit 4–9 Miao Wang/CORBIS/DAL
Exhibit 4–10 John A. Rizzo/Getty Images

Chapter 5

Exhibit 5–1
(left) Mark Richards/PhotoEdit
(right) Getty/Royalty-Free

Exhibit 5–2
(left) Royalty-Free/CORBIS
(right) McGraw-Hill Companies, Inc./Gary He, photographer

Exhibit 5–4 Roberts Publishing Services
Exhibit 5–5 Claro Cortes, IV/Reuters/ CORBIS

Exhibit 5–7 Stockbyte/Getty Images/ DAL

Exhibit 5–8 S. Pearce/PhotoLink/ Getty Images

Exhibit 5–9
(left) Jose Luis Pelaez, Inc./ CORBIS
(right) Royalty-Free/CORBIS/DAL

Exhibit 5–10 David Young-Wolff/ PhotoEdit

Chapter 6

Exhibit 6–4 Geostock/Photo Disc Green/Getty Images

Chapter 7

Exhibit 7–3 Ryan McVay/Getty Images/DAL

Exhibit 7–15 Adapted from G.M. Grikscheit, H.C. Cash, and W.J.E. Crissy, *Handbook of Selling: Psychological, Managerial, and Marketing Bases* (New York: John Wiley & Sons, 1981).

Chapter 8

Exhibit 8–8 RF/CORBIS

Chapter 9

Exhibit 9–7 (all photos) Courtesy of Charles Futrell
Exhibit 9–8 © Kim Kulish/ CORBIS
Exhibit 9–10 RF/CORBIS

Chapter 10

Exhibit 10–3 Keith Brofsky/Getty Images

Exhibit 10–4 Stockbyte/Punch Stock Images/DAL

Exhibit 10–5 Keith Brofsky/Getty Images

Exhibit 10–7 RF/Comstock Images

Chapter 11

Exhibit 11–6 Stockbyte/Punch Stock Images/DAL

Exhibit 11–8 Digital Vision/DAL
Exhibit 11–10 Digital Vision/DAL
Exhibit 11–14 Digital Vision/DAL

Chapter 12

Exhibit 12–4 RF/CORBIS

Exhibit 12–6
(left) Frank Herholdt/Stone/ Getty Images
(right) Tom & Dee Ann McCarthy/CORBIS

Chapter 13

Exhibit 13–7 Ryan McVay/Getty Images
Exhibit 13–12 Will & Demi McIntyre/ Stone/Getty Images

Chapter 14

Exhibit 14–2
(left) Doug Menuez/Getty Images
(right) C. Borland/PhotoLink/ Getty Images
Exhibit 14–4 Comstock Images/ PictureQuest

Sales Success Stories

Part I, *page 1* Louis Gagnon; photo provided courtesy of Louis Gagnon.

Part II, *page 59* Todd Cullum; photo provided courtesy of Todd Cullum.

Part III, *page 147* Kim McDonald; photo provided courtesy of Kim McDonald.

Part IV, *page 359* Karin Zandbergen; photo provided courtesy of Karin Zandbergen.

Online Mike Cassar; photo provided courtesy of Mike Cassar.

St. Clair College logo provided courtesy of St. Clair College.

BCIT logo provided courtesy of British Columbia Institute of Technology.

Conestoga College logo provided courtesy of Conestoga College.

George Brown College logo provided courtesy of George Brown College.

430

Index